RECORDS

OF

EFFINGHAM COUNTY, GEORGIA

CONTAINING

ANNALS OF GEORGIA
VOLUME II

AND

EFFINGHAM COUNTY LEGAL RECORDS
FROM
THE GEORGIA GENEALOGICAL MAGAZINE

SOUTHERN HISTORICAL PRESS INC.

Please direct all correspondence and orders to:

www.southernhistoricalpress.com
or
**SOUTHERN HISTORICAL PRESS, Inc.
PO BOX 1267
375 West Broad Street
Greenville, SC   29601
southernhistoricalpress@gmail.com**

Originally published: Easley, SC. 1976
Reprinted with New material by:
Southern Historical Press, Inc.
Greenville, SC 2017
New Material Copyright 1976 by:
Southern Historical Press, Inc.
ISBN #0-89308-019-5
All rights Reserved.
Printed in the United States of America

Introduction By Publisher

This volume called by me"Records of Effingham County,Georgia"
is actually a joining together of two separate works,viz. Mrs. Caroline
Price Wilson's Vol. 2, Annals of Georgia,Records of Effingham County, which
was reprinted in 1969 under my Georgia Genealogical Reprints imprint; and
various legal records that have appeared in the Georgia Genealogical
Magazine between 1961 and 1975, together with some newly Effingham County
records that heretofore have not appeared in print.

Since there has been a growing interest in the Georgia
Salzburger Society over the past years and since members of this group all
have their roots in Effingham County, it was my personal feeling that
a companion book needed to be done to "Georgia Salzburgers and Allied
Families" by Mrs. Gnann and Mrs. LeBey. Mrs. Gnann's book is primarily a
genealogy of the Salzburger families with names, dates etc., but does not
contain legal records such as Wills, Deeds, Court Minutes, Marriage Bonds
etc. to document descent of these various families. Hence,since there is
a growing interest in genealogy and people wanting copies of old legal
records concerning their families, I felt obliged to provide for the
Salzburger's and others with roots in Effingham County, a book of source
material for their home use.

This book is not to be used as a substitute for copies of
such legal records, because most readers will probably want to obtain full
copies of the various document from the Court House. Hopefully, it will
provide persons so interested a form of relaxation as they peruse Mrs.
Gnann's book and then look for the records of their ancestors in this
volume.

At the beginning of the second volume in this two volume work,
there will be found a Table of Contents of the records found in that work
together with a newly compiled Index of all persons listed in this second
Volume.

A final word to Salzburgers. Mrs. LeBey is continually trying
to up-date her mother's work in the Salzburgers, so if any of the readers
of this book have not done so, please get Mrs. LeBey posted with new
information on your Salzburger families so that it can be included in a
possible new revision to that work in the future.

ANNALS OF GEORGIA

IMPORTANT EARLY RECORDS
OF THE STATE

ABSTRACTED AND COMPILED BY

CAROLINE PRICE WILSON

*Member National League of American Pen Women; Georgia Historical
Society; State Consulting Registrar, Georgia D. A. R.;
French Huguenot Society of South Carolina, etc.*

VOLUME II

EFFINGHAM COUNTY RECORDS,

AND

CONNECTING LINKS IN OTHER COUNTIES.

DEDICATED

IN LOVING APPRECIATION TO

MY DAUGHTERS

PAULINE MARTIN NOYES

KATHARINE WANSLEY OTTO

CAROLINE PRICE GREGORIE

WHOSE UNFAILING SYMPATHY AND ENCOURAGEMENT

HAVE MADE THIS WORK POSSIBLE.

CONTENTS

FOREWORD

"Both justice and decency require that we should bestow on our forefathers an honorable remembrance." (Thucydides.)

All over our land there is a growing interest in the study of genealogy, which is of far more fundamental value than is accorded it by the casual thinker. We are still a melting pot, and within us are the contending spirits of Huguenot and Bourbon, Saxon and Norman, baron and thrall; so, royalist or puritan, aristocrat or peasant, we of the many nations may be enabled through the study of genealogy, to get a deeper insight into the material of our lineage, and thereby gain some answers to the many "Whys" of our diverse natures.

Many vicissitudes have limited the records which would be so valuable to us now, so it behooves each one of us to glean all that are available, and to put such data into permanent form.

Honorable ancestry begets the responsibility of Noblesse Oblige upon every one of its descendants. To be willing to rest upon the shields of our fathers, and to wear their laurels, is a blot upon our escutcheons. "He who boasts of his descent, praises the deeds of another," and as Daniel Webster has so forcibly expressed it, "There often is a regard for ancestry which nourishes only a weak pride . . . but there is, also, a moral and philosophical respect for our ancestors which elevates the character and improves the heart." The Bishop of Warburton presents a worthy thought along this line: "High birth is a thing which I never knew any one to disparage except those who had it not, nor any one make a boast of it who had any thing else to be proud of."

Painstaking care has been bestowed upon these records in order to establish their accuracy, but if errors should be found they may be traced, possibly, to one of several causes: That marriages were not (always) recorded until long after the actual date; To illegibility of handwriting; To the European custom of recording married women under their maiden names. Another source of difficulty has been the repetition of names in generations after generations—intermarriages and cross intermarriages, making entanglements that cannot be straightened without further resources of information. It has also been evident that such names as Sarah and Salome are used interchangeably, as are Joannah and Hannah—Catherine and Christiana—Ann and Nancy.

However, in the main, these are very well established, and will be a source, it is hoped, of much satisfaction, to all whose ancestry is connected with the founding of St. Mathew's Parish and its neighbors.

7

Ebenezer Church is, of course, the Mecca of Effingham County, and the history of its Register is of special interest.

In the winter of 1909 the writer located this manuscript of Births, Marriages and Deaths in the home of the pastor at Rincon. Its existence had apparently been unobserved for over a hundred years, and as it was written for the most part in old German script, it seemed of little interest or value. With the consent of the pastor she brought it to Savannah and had it bound and made efforts towards its translation. Mr. J. H. Moellering began this work but gave it up when he was called to his "colors" for the World War, and no other person was available at that time who could complete it. During a visit to Washington she outlined this situation to the Librarian of the Congressional Library, who showed such interest, that permission was granted by the Ebenezer Church to place the manuscript in the vaults of the Library for safe keeping. By the courtesy of the Librarian two photostat copies were made of the manuscript, one of which was sent to the Church, and the other presented to the writer who placed it in the archives of the Georgia D. A. R. From this copy Rev. A. G. Voight made, by his translation, a most valuable contribution to the history of our state.

While this manuscript survived the vandalism of the British troops (who used the church for a stable), and the celebrated destructive "March to the Sea", it could not altogether withstand the delicate finger of Time which had gleaned from its frail leaves four hundred of its first entries.

It can readily be seen that its translation involved more than usual difficulties, for, aside from the changes in language and the condition of the paper, there have been also changes in the spelling of the names of the people who still bear these patronymics. Because of many years intimacy with these names, and from access to other sources, the writer has taken this opportunity to make some additions and corrections to Mr. Voight's translation, for there will not probably be another edition at an early date.

The Register does not consist entirely of German names, for the Swiss of Purysburg, just across the Savannah River, and a number of English pioneers availed themselves of the priestly offices of Jerusalem Church. One incident is almost pathetic where it is recorded that an infant was brought from Purysburg and baptized at Ebenezer, in January, on the day it was born.

Among the Swiss-French names was that of DeRoche, to which the Register gives a German twist in "Rosch;" the name "Taescher" is now known as "Dasher"; Tussing or Toosing was originally "Dussiegn", so found on original documents in S. C. In the Court House of Richmond County, Ga. is an interesting example of phonetic spelling in the will of "Louis Voicle", who signs his name thus, but the amanuensis who wrote the body of the will enscribes it as "Louis Weakly."

Other examples are easily cleared: Molet should read Mallett; Scraggs is Scruggs, and Unterword is of course Underwood. The name Paulitsch is now interchangeable with Powledge.

There has been no effort made in these chronicles to complete any family chart—the aim is to give data which will serve as connecting links, or furnish clues for further research.

It is the desire of the compiler to express here her appreciation of the valuable help which has been so freely given by Mrs. S. Branch LaFar and Mrs. W. G. Gnann; this work could not have been as accurate and copious without the efficient assistance of these dear friends.

Caroline Price Wilson.

ADDENDA TO EBENEZER CHURCH RECORDS

1768 Oct. —, —David, son of Peter Heidler and wife was born.

1775 Aug. 31—Elizabeth, daughter of Valentine and Elizabeth Grumbling (born).

1775 Dec. 15—Jacob, son of Peer and Elizabeth Kettle (born).

1776 Nov. 14—Sarah, daughter of John and Mary Rose (born).

1778 Jan. 2—Sarah E., daughter of George and Francis Guin. This birth is incorrectly transcribed under "Quin". See Ebenezer index, p. 65.

1778 April 16—Sarah Ann, daughter of Richard and Ann Stephens (born).

1779 Jan. 16—Salome, daughter of John Casper Hirsch and wife Sophia (born).

1775 Oct. —, —Sarah, an English child, daughter of John and Mary Davis was born, and baptized in Jerusalem Church, July 23, 1756.

1781 Oct. 16—Sarah, daughter of Adam and Elizabeth Radlift (born).

1837 ——, —James Munro, son of David A. and Ann Morgan (born).

TYPOGRAPHICAL ERRORS, CLARIFIED
(EBENEZER RECORD)

Page   6—No. 446—Daniel Reinshardt should be Remshart.

"   16—No. 540, etc. Larrimoz should be Larrimore.

"   19—No. 567 should read "Neidlinger."

"   21—No. 587—"Heintz" is probably "Buntz," as that accords with court records.

"   47—No. 870, and pages 32, 73 and 82, the name Royall should read Ryall.

"   54—No. 999, should read "Benjamin and Esther Lanier."

"   61—Martin Shiedman should read Martin Shewman.

"   79—"Maner" instead of "Mane."

"   82—Robert Beirl is "Bevill."

"   84—The blank in marriage of Daniel Weitman refers to Miss Salome Lemcke.

"   84—The marriage of William Kennedy to Elizabeth Quillen is an error; the correct marriage is recorded on same page.

"   5—No. 431—"Kiefer" has been also translated "Reiser" from this entry: compare p. 12, No. 504 and p. 95, No. 510.

"   84—The bride of Christopher Bailey was "Grace." (He died in 1828.)

In Index the name "Margon" should appear "Morgan.")

In Index, page I read "Bailey" instead of Baile and Baill.

"   "   "   " Ann Bexle instead of Ursula.

"   " VI—insert Hannah Elizabeth Gronau on p. 72.

"   " X—insert Timothy Lemcke, p. 109.

"   " XIII—read Elijah Radclift instead of Eliza.

"   " XV—read Radlift instead of Sadlift.

"   " XVIII—"Wilson," not "Wissin."

"   " XIX—Add to "Zeigler," the name of "Luke," p. 75.

Correction in Georgia Historical Mag., Dec., 1929, p. 377: "Daniel Remshart" should be "Daniel Weitman."

EFFINGHAM COURT RECORDS, MARRIAGES, DEEDS, ETC.

Ambrose. The will of David Ambrose was probated in October, 1825. He mentions wife Elizabeth and son David—"All my children." The executors were William King and John Goldwire. The witnesses were Christian Treutlen and Benj. Kennedy, both of whom were dead in 1826.

In 1832 the "heirs of David Ambrose" are named as, Elizabeth, the widow, Hezekiah and Maria Ambrose; James Dickerson in right of his wife Dorothy, late Ambrose, and William, Sarah and Sidney Ambrose.

David Ambrose married Grace Morgan, Feb. 1, 1825.

Hezekiah Ambrose married Kesiah Lee of Screven Co., March 7, 1829.

William Ambrose married Mrs. Kesiah Ambrose, March 28, 1844.

Dorothy Ambrose married James M. Dickenson, Dec. 5, 1828.

Audiburt, John, and wife Judith of Lincoln Co., S. C., Parish of St. Peter's, Beaufort, S. C., to Thomas Campbell. Wit.: John Hutchison and Martha Jaudon, 1792.

John Audiburt had a dau. Rachel who married Leroy Stafford. She is spoken of as his dau. & heir, March 31, 1785. Feb. 20, 1808 Leroy Stafford & wife Rachel make deed. Wit.: Thomas Polhill, Samuel Brock.

Alexander, Benjamin, to Eleanor Crawford, Feb. 8, 1808.

Anderson, James, to Hannah Glaner, March 22, 1809.

Abbott, Edwin, to Jane Elizabeth Ann Wolf, Nov. 4, 1849.

Arnsdorf, Peter, and wife Barbara, had:
Dorothea, born Oct. 8, 1757.
John George, born Feb. 26, 1759.
Jonathan, born April 6, 1761—married Christiana Elizabeth, widow of Solomon Schrimph (died Nov. 1, 1780) and daughter of John Cronberger and wife Lucia.
Ebenezer Records (Voight) give:
Hannah Elizabeth Arnsdorf died May 16, 1759.
John Peter Arnsdorf died Oct. 13, 1770—age 1 year.

Arnsdorf marriages in Effingham Co.:
Solomon Arnsdorf to Sarah Weitman, April 1, 1815.
John Arnsdorf to Sarah Morgan, Jan. 25, 1819.
George Arnsdorf to Phebe Wheeler, Sept. 23, 1819.

Israel Arnsdorf to Kratzy Gnann, Nov. 16, 1822.

Solomon Arnsdorf to Elizabeth Staley, July 17, 1823.

Godlip Arnsdorf to Ann Margaret Freyermouth, Jan. 29, 1829.

Solomon Arnsdorf to Ann Eve Weitman, March 24, 1831.

William H. Arnsdorf to Mrs. Sarah Metzger (nee Snider) widow of David Metzger, Sept. 12, 1849.

Lydia C. Arnsdorf to Ephraim Seckinger, Dec. 9, 1841.

Esther Caroline Arnsdorf to Jonathan Snyder, Nov. 12, 1838.

Ash (Ashbocker). Mathias Ashbocker (more recently referred to as Mathias Ash) married Hannah Gugel, daughter of John and Anna Maria Gugel. It is indicated that Hannah Gugel had previously married Christian Dasher who was dead in 1793; Mathias Ash died 1801, and she died in Savannah, Ga., Jan. 26, 1806. Hannah Gugel was a legatee of Mrs. J. C. Wertsch, and in 1793, receipts for this legacy as the widow of Christian Dasher.

In Effingham Court, 1801, William and Susannah Burnside entered caveat against Mrs. Hannah Ash and Daniel Gugel "in behalf of John Ash or Ashbocker, child of George Adam Ash, a nephew of Mathias Ash, or Ashbocker," Savannah Record Room: Book "T," 1798; Susannah Ash, adm. est. of Geo. Ash.

Susannah Burnside Ash, born Jan. 4, 1824; died May 13, 1907; married Charles B. Patterson, born July 19, 1809; died April 10, 1858.

1792—Mathias Ash makes deeds of gift to children of John G. Neidlinger and wife Hnanah (Dasher): Joh Neidlinger; Anna (married Godlip D. Neiss, and Emilia, who married John George Mingledorf, Nov. 26, 1807.

From the dates of the baptism of two of Mathias Ashbacher's negroes, 1762, sponsored by himself and "wife," it is evident that he had been married prior to his marriage to Hannah Gugel.

1808—The adms. of est. of Mathias Ash were defendants against Ann Christiana Dasher, who was also p'ff. against Mrs. Mary Gromet, widow of John Gromet in 1805. (Stray paper in basement of Sav. Record Room. In Book K, p. 330 in that office, reference is made to "Mrs. Christiana Dasher, widow, of Goshen."

Baas. Will of Samuel Baas, June 29, 1814. Wife Rebecca. Daughter Ann, (married John Knight Sept. 1, 1817; he was probably the son of John Knight and wife Rachel, 1799.) Rosannah Baas, Selina, Sarah (daughters), and son Daniel Alexr. Baas. Exrs.: Zara Powers and John Delburge of Savannah.

1833—"Heirs of Samuel Baas: Alexander Elkins, Rosannah Baas and Celina Smith."

1788—Jan. 21—"Capt. John Bass married widow of Dr. Smith of Holland, at Goose Creek." (S. C. Mag. of Hist., Vol. 5, P. 119.)

1806—Deed in Savannah Record Room: from Sarah Gibson to grand-daughters Rosannah and Serena Sarah, daughters of Samuel and Rebecca Baas. In trust to Dr. Henry Bourquin. See Book K, p. 244.

Bevan. Will of Joseph Bevan, "All to son, Joseph N. Bevan." Dec. 11, 1818.

Basinger, John, and wife Barbara, of Ogeechee, had son David, born March 24, 1773.

1820—Elizabeth Basinger was an heir of Elisha Elon.

Bechtle, John George, and wife, Eva Barbara, had:

Mary Magdaline, born May 3, 1757.

Mary Catherine, born June 8, 1759.

George Bechtle and wife had son David, born Jan. 11, 1770.

Feb. 21, 1795, Jonathan Bechtly, "son of George," married Mary Reiser. (His first wife was Nancy Porter.) Mary Reiser was the daughter of Benjamin Reiser, and wife Catherine; the daughter of John Michaeler, and formerly the widow of (John) Michael Exley. He was dead in 1821 and left minor orphans—Sukey **Backley**, Harty, Frederick, Sarah, and a widow, Mary.

Oct. 16, 1799—Christian Bechtly married Elizabeth Reiser. In division of his estate 1806, his heirs were: widow Elizabeth, Jonathan George Backley, Paul Toosing, Jacob Beeler, and heirs of Christian Backley. (See Rhinelander).

Eliza Bachley married Thomas Wilson, Dec. 29, 1831.

1801—Mathias Bechtly left widow Hannah.

1802—March 2, Barbara Backley makes deed of gift to her grand-children: Josiah and Hannah, children of her son, Christian Backley. Wit.: Josiah and Hannah Margaret Backley.

Baxley, Thomas, (was dead 1763) and wife Feribe (an English family) had:

Salome, born "about 1754."

Johannah, born 1757.

Ann, born March 8, 1759; died June 4, 1768.

Berry. Will of John Berry, Aug. 8, 1817. Wife Mary (Maria); sons, Benajah and Obadiah are "two youngest children." Daughter Salome (married Emanuel Rahn, Nov. 26, 1811.)

Daughter Salome, the deceased wife of John Metzger, whose children are: Maria, Louise, and John Benajah Berry Metzger.

The will of Mrs. Mary Berry was probated March, 1820, and shows the marriage of Salome, but mentions only Louise and John B. Metzger, grand-children.

John Benajah Berry appears to have married 3 times:

(1) Rhody Tiner, Dec. 18, 1815.

(2) Mary A. Metzger, April 27, 1826.

(3) Ann C. Kennedy, Jan. 26, 1859.

His children:

Washington, married Minnie Jaudon.

John, married Margaret Mingledorf.

Reuben.

Mary, married William Mingledorf.

Martha, married James Bird.

Margaret, married Nesbit Morgan (son of James Morgan).

Susie, married Benjamin Porter.

Amelia, married Peter Porter.

Brothers—sons of

Alexander Porter.

Frank, married Amelia Wilson, dau. of Henry M. & Hannah (Mingledorf) Wilson.

Jane, married (1) Edward Rahn; (2) John Simmons.

Sarah (only child of last marriage), married Wesley Morgan, son of Lewis M.

1801—"John O'Berry, wife Ellender." (McIntosh Co.)

Biddenback. There was a Christian Biddenback who was born 1710 and died May 5, 1770. His wife was living in 1756 and they had a daughter Catherine, who was sponsor at a baptism in 1767. She may have been the Catherine Biddenback who married John Justus Grabenstein, Feb. 22, 1763.

(A) Wm. Biddenback married Margaret, dau. of Dr. William Howell Wilson.

(A) Sophia Biddenback is sponsor at baptism in 1760.

(A) Christian Biddenback married Mrs. Mary E. Foy, April 25, 1798.

John Biddenback married Naomie Seckinger, Dec. 2, 1809.

Mathew Biddenback married Anna Margaret (?), had:

John Adam, born 1755; died April, 1758.

Christian, born Sept. 21, 1757.

Nathaniel, born Nov. 6, 1760; died July 13, 1776.

Anna Catherine, born Feb. 23, 1763; died Jan. 11, 1767.

Anna Margaret, born Sept. 27, 1764; died Sept. 17, 1777.

Mathew Biddenback married 2nd Anna Paulus, Nov. 7, 1770, had: Catherine, born Sept. 6, 1773.

Mary, born Oct. 10, 1775.

Mathew, born Dec. 28, 1777. (Will in 1821 leaves "all to brother John Biddenback."

Anna Paulus Biddenback died April 27, 1778, age 37, and Mathew Biddenback married (3) Apolinia Kiefer, July 28, 1778. He died 1793 and his exrs. were Trustees of Ebenezer Congregation: Mathew Rahn, President; Jonathan Rahn, John G. Neidlinger, John Kogler, Michael Exley, Godhilf Smith, John Haugleiter, Jonathan Seckinger, John Michler.

1791-1793—The estates of Andrew Biddenback and Miss Mary Biddenback were adm. by Christian Biddenback.

Bird Cemetery in Effingham Co.:

John Bird, born Sept. 27, 1827; died Aug. 28, 1860.

John Wilson Bird, born Feb. 5, 1838; died July 7, 1890.

James Bird, born April 27, 1833; died Dec. 21, 1911; wife, Martha H. Bird, born Jan. 16, 1840; died July 18, 1909. Their daughter, Hattie Talulah, born June 1, 1861; died Oct. 28, 1863.

Maria Bird, born Jan. 28, 1804; died Feb. 10, 1880.

William Edwards Bird, born Feb. 14, 1856; died July 17, 1890.

Effingham Co. marriages:

Silvanus Bird to Dinah Stafford, March 4, 1768.

Israel Bird to Anna Stafford, Sept. ——, 1767.

William Bird to Elizabeth Steiner, April 7, 1798.

Ann Bird to Christian Dasher, Jan. 31, 1801.

Lewis Bird to Hannah Neisler, Dec. 15, 1802.

Samuel Bird to Ann Elliott, 1798—Liberty Co.

1808—Sept. 14—Will of James Bird: "Brother William give Joseph to Dorcas if I should not see you again at my death."

Andrew Bird and wife Elizabeth, had:

Margarethe, born Aug. 1, 1776.

Andrew Hamil Bird, died Jan. 13, 1847. His wife, born 1815, was Eleanor Giles from New England to S. C. Their children, as far as known, were:

Andrew 2nd, married 1842 to Mrs. Frances (Wilson) Fox.

James married Sarah, daughter of Gotlip Smith.

Andrew Bird and wife Frances, had:

Irene Bird, born March 14, 1844.

Andrew 3rd, born April, 1846; died Jan. 18, 1863.

1784—Grant to John Bird in Franklin Co., Ga., for Revolutionary service.

1820—Wm. Bird appoints his son, William, "exr. of his estate according to laws of United States and Commonwealth of America." Wit.: David Wood, John Harmes, Lewis Bird.

Bishop—1792—Elizabeth Bishop mentions her children Mary, Margaret, Elizabeth, John, William and Rachel.

1798—William Bishop makes division of his property between his wife Judith, (daughter of James Cook), and his son Stephen and daughter Rebecca. (See will of James Cook).

1788—Jan. 1—Peter Augustus Bishop married Mrs. Jane Hill. In 1791 he was dead, and in that year she married James Mulryne.

1777—May 9—Martha Bishop was sponsor for Martha, the daughter of John Wilson and wife Susannah. Martha Wilson married Gideon Zettler April 16, 1797, and her sister Susannah Wilson married Chrisian Zipperer, Feb. 22, 1801.

1836—Nov. 25—William H. Bishop married Mary Ann Nettles.

Bulloch—1809—James Bulloch left widow Dinah. Their daughter, Abigail, married Silas Hilliard, and daughter Ann married Mathew Albrighton.

Bergsteiner—1774—The wife of Daniel Bergsteiner was Mary, the daughter of J. M. Dasher. They had a daughter Salome born 1774. Mathew Bergsteiner came from Lendau to Georgia in 1738.

Burksteiner, Samuel, married Mrs. Ann Catherine Seckinger, Feb. 12, 1822. She was the widow of William Shrimpf, whom she married July 27, 1805.

Sept. 13, 1826—Jas. Alexander Bucksteiner married Eliz. Cath. Kebler.

Sept. 28, 1843—Jeremiah Berksteiner married Ann M. Weitman. (Samuel Bucksteiner was dead in 1838.)

Buntz, Bunce. The following four men were collaterals, and possibly brothers:

Urban Buntz—wife Margaret.

John George Buntz—wife Barbara.

Henry Louis Buntz—wife Barbara, in 1759.

John Christopher Buntz—died Jan. 17, 1756.

Urban Buntz (who died Nov. 18, 1774) and wife Margaret (Mrs. Margaret Buntz was paid Rev. Service. "Annals," Vol. I), had:

John Christopher, born Jan. 11, 1758—married Hannah Elizabeth Hangleiter, March 13, 1778. She died Feb. 3, 1779. Their son, John Chris., born Jan. 25, 1779.

Anna Barbara, born Dec. 3, 1760.

Christina, born Aug. 31, 1773; died April 18, 1844—married Jonathan Rahn.

Henry Lewis, born Sept. 23, 1766.

Anna Margaret.

John George Buntz was a glazier. His wife was Barbara; children:

John George, born July 19, 1756; died Nov. 13, 1757.

Christian, born April 30, 1759; died May 4, 1759.

John George, born Sept. 13, 1761; died June 7, 1778.

Mary, born April 13, 1764; died June 2, 1766.

Christina, born Oct. 4, 1766.

Ann Mary, born Sept. 2, 1769.

It appears from court records that Henry Louis Buntz left a widow Judith, who married (2) Martin Busche, June 9, 1796; (3) Henry Lewis Grabenstein, Oct. 19, 1797, who subsequently married Hannah, daughter of Benjamin and Elizabeth Dasher.

In 1815 Simon Bunce and wife Lucretia sign deeds. (He was son of Henry Lewis Buntz and wife Judith.)

Bostwick—Richard Bostwick's wife appears as Hannah and Mary Hannah on deeds.

1799—Samuel Bostwick (who had married Mary Ann Maner, July 9, 1771, makes deeds of gift to sons: John Graves Bostwick, William Bostwick, and Littleberry Bostwick of Richland, S. C. Also to daughter Sarah Porter.

Birch—1802—April 12—Estate of John Birch adm. by John Gray. Mrs. Elizabeth Ann Birch declining.

Bryan—1833—Catherine Bryan adm. estate of James Bryan.

Barber—1790—John Barber deed of gift to son John Barber, and to grandchildren James Barber and Alexander Stewart Barber. John Barber married Miss Jane Stewart, Oct. 31, 1814.

Brownson—1790—John Brownson deeds "all to daughter Elizabeth Brownson."

Blackman—1790—The wife of William Blackman was Ann.

Beal—1804—The wife of William Beal was Gracy.

Belcher—1804—The wife of James Belcher was Ann.

Britton—1809—The wife of Stephen Britton was Sarah.

Broxson—1810—The wife of George Broxson was Elizabeth.

Beagle—1806—July 21—Valentine Beagle, an orphan, was bound to Joshua Dasher.

Beville—1828—Feb. 8—Deed of Paul Beville, Sr., to daugher, Sarah Ford Mathers, the wife of John G. Mathers, to land called Ford Tract, mill, dwelling, etc.—other tracts which were original grants to Daniel Harris, Wm. Dampier, Jeremiah Gill. Also one negro woman, six children, three fellows, three horses, gig, harness, twenty-five cows, silver time piece with initials P. B.

1829—Jan. 6—(Same to same)—land on which he now resides which is to be known as "Bevilton." Also a tract in Screven Co., orig. grant of Benjamin Goldwire; twenty head of sheep, etc. Wit.: Paul B. Colson, Chas. M. Hill, Henry White.

Burton, Benjamin, married Eleanor Rowell, Feb. 9, 1808. She was a widow in 1824, and reference is made to her step son, Robert Burton, and to her neice and nephew, Eleanor, and Henry Rowell.

Mrs. Benjamin Burton married 2nd William Black of Bulloch Co., Nov. 5, 1825.

Robert Burton married Elizabeth Denmark, Oct. 11, 1811, but had previously been married as he makes deed to his son Henry Burton in 1811, who, on Oct. 1, 1825 was married to Sarah Evans.

"1788—Joseph Burton, native of District of 96, S. C."

1827—Robert Burton adm. estate of Benjamin Burton.

1830—Henry A. Burton estate adm. by Sarah and Robert Burton.

Robert Burton is buried in St. Mary's, Camden Co. (See Vol. 3rd.)

Black. (a) William Black "of Screven Co.," had a daughter Ann who married John Warnock. Savh. Rec. Room, Book "K," p. 378.

(a) Wm. A. Black married Miss Eliza Jane Rawls, March 25, 1831.

Bolzius, Gronau, Lemcke. Any data bearing on the above names, can be but intriguing to those interested in the early history of the Salzburger settlement. They represent the fine scholarship and spirituality upon which that settlement was founded, and to trace their descendants has been an undertaking most delightful, but very difficult.

The first two pastors to come with the Salzburgers were Rev. John Martin Bolzius and Rev. Israel Christian Gronau. We do not know

that they came from Salzburg, but they were appointed by the
"Fathers" as ministers and teachers to accompany that immigration.
They married sisters, the daughters of a widowed lady who came with
them, but her name is not now known. The wife of Rev. Mr. Bolzius was
Gertraut, who died Nov. 7, 1766, in the 48th year of her age, leaving
a daughter Catherine Margaret, who died unmarried March 9, 1778,
age 36—the last of her line in this country.

Rev. Israel Christian Gronau's wife was Hannah Catherine (born
Nov. 1716; died Feb. 21, 1776), and they had two daughters: Hannah Elizabeth, who married John Casper Wertsch, March 14, 1758;
and Frederica Mary who married Rev. Chrisopher Frederick Triebner, April 18, 1769.

The children of John Casper Wertsch and Hannah Elizabeth
(Gronau) were:

Christian Israel, born Nov. 22, 1759; died Dec. 2, 1759.

Benajah, born Nov. 29, 1761; died June 25, 1762.

Catherine, born Aug. 13, 1763; died Aug. 16, 1763.

Hannah Elizabeth (Gronau) Wertsch died June 17, 1769, age
30 & 10 months, and John Casper Wertsch married 2nd Elizabeth
Kogler, Oct. 10, 1769, who had one child, a daughter Hannah, or as
some times written Joannah, born Aug. 21, 1770. She married 1st
an Ernst, and had one son Gotlieb Ernst, and 2nd to Herman Hersen,
who left no child. Thus is closed one of the lines from Rev. Mr. Gronau and the line of John Casper Wrtsech is extinct in the male line,
and his descendants are entirely through the name of Gotlieb Ernst,
who married Catherine Fields, Dec. 18, 1798. (John Casper Wertsch
died June 24, 1779.)

Rev. Mr. Gronau died Jan. 11, 1745, and his widow Hannah Catherine married in 1747, Rev. Henry Herman Lemcke, who came over
on the "Judith" as successor to Rev. Mr. Gronau.

Rev. Henry Herman Lemcke (died April 4, 1768, age 48), and wife
Hannah Catherine (born 1717; died Feb. 9, 1776), had:

Timothus, born circa 1752—wife Joannah.

Salome, born about 1750—married Daniel Weitman.

Hannah, born about 1754, married:

(1) Jacob Wisenbaker;

(2) Joseph Tribble, who was dead in 1798;

(3) William Dupuis, June 20, 1805. This last marriage settlement appears on the court records of Liberty, Effingham, and Chatham counties. Securities: Chr. Treutlen & Wm. Kennedy.

Rev. Herman Lemcke died April 4, 1768, age 48, greatly mourned
and honored. His wife Hannah Catherine died Feb. 9, 1776, age 59.

Jacob Wisenbaker and Hannah (Lemcke), had:

Ann Mary Wisenbaker, and Margaret Wisenbaker (married J. A. Snoden)—no children of her other marriages are recorded. Ann Mary Wisenbaker married: (1) C. F. Triebner, 2nd (born July 12, 1775) (the son of her mother's half sister, Mary Frederica (Gronau) Triebner); and, (2) Garrard Mason (marriage settlement Feb. 14, 1817; (3) to Benjamin Kennedy, grandson of Gov. John Adam Treutlen, in 1824, March 17. The heirs at law of Rev. Herman Lemcke in 1793, were Herman Hersen, wife Joannah, and Daniel Weitman and (2nd wife) Mary Frederica.

Rev. C. F. Triebner and wife Frederica Mary (Grounau), had:

Christopher August, born August 8, 1770; died Aug. 16, 1770.

Christopher Frederick, 2nd, born July 12, 1775, m. cousin Ann Mary Wisenbaker.

Timothy Traugott, born Dec. 29, 1777.

Christopher Frederick Triebner, 2nd, is the only one of Pastor Triebner's children of whom we have any record. He became "planter and shopkeeper," and was also Justice of Inferior Court of Effingham Co. in 1814. Rev. Mr. Triebner came to Ebenezer as co-pastor with Rev. Mr. Rabenhorst, and the unhappy difficulties which arose during this time are matters of history. Gov. John Adam Treutlen was a bitter foe of Rev. Mr. Triebner, and it seems the very irony of fate that the very name of Triebner is extinct, and that his only descendants are merged with the name of Treutlen.

Christopher F. Triebner, 2nd (was dead 1819; adm. Gottlieb Ernst), and Ann Mary (Wisenbaker), had:

Ann Mary Triebner who married Christian E. Treutlen, Jan. 8, 1819, grandson of Gov. Treutlen, and

Hannah, who died Sept. 5, 1807, age 13 months. (City Hall, Savannah, Ga.)

The will of Ann Mary (Wisenbaker) (Triebner, Mason, Kennedy), was probated Jan. 22, 1827 in Effingham Co., in which she refers to son Richard Alexander Thadeus Mason of N. C., and to her mother Hannah (Dupuis).

Mrs. Hannah Dupuis was Mrs. Joseph Tribble at the time of her marriage to William Dupuis (the son of James. (James Dupuis was dead in 1768. In 1804 "John Dupuis & wife Mary" on deeds) and Fannie (Stafford) Dupuis of Beaufort, S. C.). Mrs. Dupuis' home is described as "Being on road leading from Savannah to Augusta, adjoining lands of William Kennedy, James Porter, etc." Effingham Co., Book E-F, p. 176.

Boston family settled in Acomac Co., Va., prior to 1649. They came from Scotland.

Maj. John Boston, born N. C., 1737, died in Effingham Co,. May 8th, 1810. His wife was Rebecca Randal, born 1740, married about 1760—probably in Onslow Co., N. C. They only child living to maturity was James, born Dec. 14, 1767; died 1837; married Nov. 19, 1794 to Elizabeth Briggs. She died April 3, 1812. Their children:

James Beville Boston, born 1795, died (unmarried) Oct. 13, 1816 or 1818.

Ira Boston, born June 26, 1797; died 1863.

Nancy Dell & Franklin (twins) born June 21, 1799. He died in Fla., Feb. 7, 1818.

John Boston, born Sept. 3, 1801; married June 9, 1830 to Mary A. Roberts (Screven Co.)

William Fletcher Boston, born July 20, 1803.

Rebecca Randal Boston, born Aug. 24, 1805.

Faris Boston (government surveyor).

Eliza Dorothy Boston, born Dec. 3, 1807; 2nd wife of Col. Maxey Dell.

Mary Matilda Boston, born May 24, 1810, married Philip, son of Col. Dell.

George Whitfield Boston, born March 23, 1812; married Elizabeth Tison who was born in 1818.

James Boston married (2) Nov. 14, 1814 to Mrs. Sarah Kettles (widow of Peter) and had:

Thomas Boston, married Rebecca Goldwire, and moved to Thomas Co.

Stray notes:

N. C. Records, Vol. 22, p. 966: "Maj. John Boston, 1st Onslow Militia, Feb., 1780."

N. C. Records, Vol. 10, p. 546: "James Boston, ensign in the Co. between New River and Deep Creek."

Rev. Thomas Boston had a daugher, Christina, who married Tucker Harris. Dalcho's Church Hist. (S. C.), p. 213.

Briggs, James (?), married Agnes Dell about 1747, and had:
Elizabeth, married James Boston.
Sarah Briggs, married —— Pierce.
Delia Briggs, married —— Beville.
Nancy Briggs, married —— Colding.
(From family records.)

Marriages in Effingham Co.:

Buker, John Colthal, to Catherine Amber (Ambrose ?), March 10, 1769.

Braddock, John, to Lucy, daughter of James Cook, July 16, 1769.

Blair, William, to Sibilla Earl, Oct. 16, 1771.

Boykin, John, to Sarah Tanner, April 26, 1772. (He was living in 1794.)

Boykin, Hardy, to Susannah Young, Nov. 7, 1772.

Burnett, John, to Winifred Wilson, Jan., 1773.

Bilbo, John "Capt. of Horse," to Jane Hudson, Feb. 12, 1778.

Busby, Jesse, to Molly Pierce, of S. C., Jan. 26, 1774.

Beville, Robert, to Sarah Hudson, Dec. 27, 1774.

Blitch, Spear, to Zilpah Hurst, Oct. 17, 1803.
Blitch, Benjamin, to Mrs. Sarah Spears, Sept. 24, 1803.
Blitch, Willis, to Amy Fryer, March 1, 1819.
Blitch, Thomas, to Lydia Wilson, Feb. 2, 1827.
Blitch, James, to Mahala Tyson, July 23, 1830.
Blitch, William, to Elizabeth Tullis, Dec. 15, 1831.
Blitch, James, to Martha Ann Willis, Oct. 14, 1835.
Blitch, Benjamin, to Harriet Wilson, June 12, 1832.
Blitch, Keland S., to Martha A. Hurst, March 18, 1844.
Blitch, Thomas, to Mary Ann Jane Brogdon, Dec. 19, 1838.
Blitch, Simeon, to Henrietta Warren, May 31, 1848.

Bedford, Gunning, to Mrs. Ann Elizabeth Busch, March 15, 1805.

Bell, Eleazer, Esqr., mariner, to Mary Causey, Jan. 27, 1805.

Brewer, George W., to Penelope Elkins, Dec. 2, 1809.
Brewer, Burris, to Lydia Mobley, Nov. 25, 1819.
Brewer, Thomas H., to Ann Tullos, Feb. 7, 1833.

Bridges, George J., to Sarah O. Bowman, May 11, 1835.

Berkstein, John R., to Mary Elizabeth Helmly, July 18, 1836.

Box, Allen, of S. C., to Maria Newton, Feb. 15, 1813 .

Brogden, William, to Mary Cochran, Nov. 20, 1821.

Bryan, Solomon, to Mary Ann Keiffer, April 20, 1822.

Blake, William, to Mrs. Amy Kettles, Aug. 1, 1822.

Brogden, William, to Mary E., daughter of Israel Shuptrine and wife Mary, daughter of George Heidt and Salome (Remshart), June 9, 1848.

Boutwell, William, to Rebecca Dugger, April 14, 1838.

Boutwell, William, to Sabina Davis, no date.

Bowman, Henry G., to Isoline Heidt, Feb. 11, 1837.

Beebee, Willis G., to Mary Seckinger, Nov. 29, 1842.

Beebee, Gordon, to Hannah M. Weitman, May 3, 1845.

Barnwell, Edward W., to Sarah Ann Lee, Aug. 3, 1840.

Barrett, Joel, to Georgianna Elkins, April 17, 1846.

Blount, Samuel A., to Ann D. Colson, Dec. 29, 1847.

Bealls, ——, of Screven Co., to Ann Wilder, Dec. 2, 1809.

Barber, John, to Miss Jane Stewart, Oct. 31, 1814.

Bergman, Rev. C. F., to Mary C. Floerl, Oct. 26, 1826.

Boutwell, William, to Mary Ann Jane Brogdon, Aug. 3, 1840.

Blitch, Simeon, to Henrietta Warren, May 31, 1848.

Clark. The relationship of the Clarks to several families in adjoining or nearby counties is not very clear in some instances, but the compiler has tried to synchronize the avialable data, hoping that a future genealogist may be enabled to establish more clearly any doubtful inferences, or make needful corrections.

Donald Clark, of McIntosh Co.

Some family tradition is that his wife was Mrs. Gindrat, the widow of Abraham Gindrat, the elder. As far as now known his children were:

Hugh, who married a daughter of Capt. James Mackey.

William, who was his brother Hugh's executor in 1793.

Catherine, married Alexander Fyffe. Catherine Fyffe died before her husband, leaving two daughters, Catherine and Elizabeth Fyffe. (Who was the Catherine Clark who had married Joachim Hartsfne before 1772?)

Angus.

Will of Hugh Clark, dated Oct. 15, 1775—proved by Roderick McIntosh and Robert Mackay June 16, 1793, is in the State Archives in Atlanta. The will was entrusted to the care of Mrs. Ann Mackay, the wife of Capt. John Mackay, and was not witnessed. His executors were Capt. James Mackay, William McIntosh, William and Angus Clark. "Planter of St. Andrew Parish." Body to be buried in Sunbury with deceased wife and children. Brothers William and Angus. Sister-in-law Sarah Stevens a tract on St. Mary's River. Niece Mourning, daughter of brother Angus. Remainder to daughter Barbre Clark in management of brother William Clark.

John Clark married Elizabeth Jones, 1839.

(Judge) Richard H. Clark married Harriet G. Charlton, Aug. 7, 1845. Effingham C. Records.

Clarke. Barbara Clarke married William Clarke, and Court Records in Savannah show that he squandered Barbara's property. Record Room, Book "A," p. 53, gives a full account of compensation by the State of Georgia for this property, 1778. The marriage settlement of Barbara Clarke, spinster, daughter of Hugh Clarke, is recorded in Book "A," p. 79. Savannah Record Room, Feb. 16, 1785.

In the same book, p. 53, Nov. 6, 1778, Barbara Clarke petitions for all of William Clarke's estate in compensation for her property taken by him. Refers to Feb. 11, 1757 when Wm. Clarke had grant on Sapelo Island. William Clarke was a British subject. Ibid, p. 76, Feb. 15, 1785, William Clarke of "Whitehall" transfers all his rights to James Mackay.

Scattering "Clarke" notes. (See Gindrat and Mackay).

Bryan Co., 1779. Deed of William Clarke to beloved niece Elizabeth Fyffe. Savannah Record Room, Book "R," p. 18, and Book "T," p. 331: 1799—Barbara, wife of William Clarke of Bryan Co., a lot on Broughton St.

Richmond Co., Book "I-G," folio 43: William Clarke and wife Barbara of Chatham Co., in re land granted said Barbara in 1775. In 1792 William Clarke, planter of Great Ogeechee in Chatham Co., lot in Augusta, No. 37, Greene St.

1792—William Clarke adm. estate of Miss Sarah Ross, vs. Andrew Johnson.

1797—William Clarke, Tax Coll., with James Jones, Exrs. of Robert Holmes, sell land on Ogeechee Neck, usually called Baldwin's, original grant to Sam'l Miller, and by him sold to Thomas Goldsmith, as whose property it was confiscated and sold to John Harvey.

Clark. Book "Y," p. 186—John Clark of Beech Island, S. C., to daughters Helena Howell and Margaret Clark, lot in Savannah, now occupied by Mrs. Ernst, widow, 1803.

Book "E," p. 327—William Clarke, guardian of James Maxwell, in behalf of John Maxwell, "now at Princeton College." Signed: Simon, Mary and John Butler Maxwell, Jan. 18, 1788.

Cook. Effingham Co. Will of James Cook, 1786. Wife Sarah Cook, children:

Judea Bishop.

Lucia (married John Braddock, July 16, 1769.)

Tabby Johnston.

Polly Bennett.

James Cook (now deceased.)

John Cook (was dead in 1793.)

Benjamin Cook.

Lewis Cook.

Rev. Henry Cook (wife Lydia.)

Aug. 15, 1825. Will of (Rev.) Henry Cook. Wife Lydia. Brother Lewis Cook. Nephew George Cook. Wife's grandson Jesse L. Pitts. (She also had a niece Lydia Mercer.) Cherokee Land Grants: "Lydia Cook, widow of Rev. soldier."

1811. John Cook makes deeds to a son in law Edmund Tison, who had married his daughter Nancy Cook, Dec. 25, 1804; and to his grandchildren Sabrina and Selina Grooms.

Rev. Joseph Cook married Anne Boullineau, May 11, 1778. "Both of S. C."

1782. Liberty Co. Nathaniel Hawthorne deeds to his grandchildren, Mary, Samuel, Elizabeth and Nancy, the children of James Cook and his wife Peggy.

1808—James Cook and wife Margaret (Peggy), signs deeds.

1783—James Cook was paid for provisions and forage for Wayne's troops.

1830—Est. of Margaret Cook, widow, adm. by Amos Cook.

1803—Edward Cook of Bulloch Co., married Sarah Bird.

Colson (see Mott). 1750—Charleston, S. C. Inventory of effects of Abraham Colson.

1793—Dec. 13—Abraham Colson married Elizabeth Mott.

1773—Feb. 16—Mathew Colson married Chloe Woods.

William Colson married Martha, daughter of Paul Beville and wife Sarah, (Scruggs), and had:

Martha Colson, born 1769; bap. Oct. 27, 1772.

Sarah Colson, born 1771; bap. Oct. 27, 1772.

Paul Beville Colson.

William Colson—the last two are mentioned in their gr. father's will.

In 1829 the wife of Paul Bevill Colson is recorded on deeds as Elizabeth.

The revolutionary service of Capt. Jacob Colson is recorded in McCrady' Hist. of S. C., page 91; and, McCall's Hist. of Georgia, pp. 95, 293, 294.

Service of James Colson in War of 1812, see "Officers of U. S., Vol.," p. 318.

Grants in Georgia:

Mathew Colson, 1778-1796.

William Colson, 1761.

Hon. Jacob Colson, 1783-1785.

Smith's Story of Georgia Peoples, pp. 67-566.

Dennis Colson of English extraction, lived in Md. and had son James born 1824 who married Eva, daughter of Andrew Inaboinet, a planter of Barnwell Dist., S. C., where she was born in 1828. Their son, M. J. Colson, settled in Brunswick, Ga.

Marriage Records in Gainesville, Fla. (Alachua County):

Colson, Paul Beville, to Clarissa Keit, Dec. 29, 1852.

Colson, William H., to Louisa Cole Wilson, Feb. 17, 1859.

Colson, William G., to Mrs. Adeline A. Mott, Aug. 2, 1869.

Colson, James W., to Frances Hagin, Dec. 19, 1858.

Colson, Georgianna, daughter of Elijah Colson, to Wm. W. Pope, March 31, 1959.

Colson,Margaret, to Charles Younge, Sept. 23, 1866.

Marriage Records in Savannah, Ga.:

1888—Aug. 27—James Colson to Sarah Brown.

1901—April 30—James H. Colson to Eloise Weeks.

Crews. The will of Isham Crews (1802) is found in Vol. 1 of Annals of Georgia, and his wife Sarah was the widow of James Clyatt. This is established by the administration of the latter's estate (1790) in Savannah.

Cruse—1812—The names of James and Asa Cruse appear on deeds in Effingham Co.

Effingham Co. marriages:

1803—June 1—James Cruse to Mary Wilson.

1809—June 12—James Cruse to Anna Cruse.

1818—"Hannah, widow of James Cruise."

1835—May 25—James Cruse married Mrs. Kesiah Taylor.

Jan. 14, 1818—The will of Christopher Imhoff: "All to Eliza Crew of Burke Co." Wit.: John Lyneberger, William Shrimph, John Neidlinger.

Cronberger, Kronberger. 1757—John Cronberger had a grant in Ebenezer. He died Nov. 12, 1770. His wife was Lucia. They were from Augsburg. In 1738, they had two children. (Candler.)

Jacob Cronberger and wife Elizabeth, had:

Hannah Frederica, who died Feb. 9, 1768.

Jacob Cronberger was Ast. Q. M. 1782, and he and his wife gave "service" in the Rev. War. (Annals of Ga., Vol. 1.)

Nicholas Cronberger was granted land in Purysburg, S. C., 1768-1772. He died Jan. 8, 1776, age 59. His wife was Margaret Elizabeth, and they had a son, John Christopher, born Dec. 15, 1757. In 1757 they had three children. (Candler.)

Johannah Cronberger married Frederick Roesburg of Savannah, Oct. 30, 1769, had:

Naomi, born Sept. 13, 1770. (1st wife of Col. Thos. Wyly.)

1807—John Cronberger to daughter Christian, wife of Jonathan Arnsdorf. She was first married to Solomon Shrimph.

1813—Herman Crum deed to Sarah King. He was dead in 1818, leaving a widow Ann, and his estate was adm. by Benj. Morel, James Wilson and James Porter, Oct. 16, 1818.

1793 (circa), John Christopher Cramer left a widow Ann Catherine and minor orphans. Guardians appoined were Daniel Weidman, Andrew Gnann, John Kogler. Ann Catherine was the wife of Ephraim Keiffer in 1818.

1784—May 16—Power of attorney by William Coker to Henry Allison to "receive my warrants that I am entitled to for serving in the Second Georgia Regiment of the Continental Army," etc. (Edgefield, S. C.)

1802—March 21—Will of Martin Cruger: wife Catherine and her son Samuel Fitzpatrick. Wit.: John Wisenbaker and William Townsend.

June 11, 1820—Buyers at the sale of David Cannady (Kennedy?), dec'd.: Joseph Seckinger, William, David and John Dugger, Sr., Thomas and Hannah Elkins, Isaac, David and Darius Garrison, Isaac Cannon, Paul Marlow, I. Ihly, John Murphey, John Dugger, Jr., Samuel Parish, Tullos Daley, Christ. Dasher.

1820—Feb.—Estate of John Creel adm. by Levy Stephens.

1829—Christian Cope left minor heirs, John, Jr., and Maria Cope. Joseph Helvenstine was appointed guardian. John Cope, Jr., married Selina Crews, May 30, 1827.

Cubbedge, Fyffe. (Principally from private records.)

John Cubbedge, who owned the vessel, "Mary," which was captured and paroled, married Jean Donovan from Bermuda, had:

John Cubbedge, 2nd, who settled in Bryan Co., and whose wife was Alsie McNeverin, and had:

John Cubbedge, 3rd, married Sarah Frances Fyffe.

Mary Cubbedge.

Margaret Cubbedge.

"Other children."

John Cubbedge, 3rd, and wife Sarah Frances (Fyffe), had:

Mary A. Cubbedge.

Margaret C. Cubbedge.

George S. Cubbedge.

Stephen J. M. Cubbedge, married Caroline Rebecca Tubbs, Dec. 1837. (Sav. Ga.)

Barbara C. Cubbedge. (One of these daughters married Mr. Austin.)

All of the above children are mentioned in a suit in re a plantation in Lincoln Co., Ga., deeded to George M. Waters in trust for wife and children of John and Sarah Cubbedge. The defendant was Alexander W. Stephens. Dec. 20, 1827.

Cox. 1797—The estate of Jasper Cox was adm. by Spencer Cox and William Dupuis. The latter declined and Henry Rowell was put in his place. Spencer Cox married Mary Ryal, Feb. 25, 1795. He was dead in 1806, and his widow, "now Hickman," adm. his estate.

Craft—1792—Est. of David Craft adm. by John Waldhauer.

Copeland—1791—"Mary, widow of James Copeland."

Cope—1792—"John Jacob Cope, wife Elizabeth."

Calfrey—1811—"Lewis Calfrey, wife Frances, of Augusta."

Cox—1815—"Orphans of Joseph Cox: Martha and Delilah. Walter Leigh, Guardian. (From Richmond Co. Records, Davidson.)

Effingham Co. marriages:

Carlton, William, of the up country U. S. Troops, to Sarah McRory, June 27, 1814.

Curry, John, to Rhoda Tyner, Dec. 18, 1815.

Chamblis, Henry, to Milly Parish, Feb. 24, 1820.

Champion, Henry, to Isabella Gilden of Savannah, Nov. 14, 1824.
Champion, Francis, to Eliza Ann Driscombe, Dec. 9, 1828.

Conner, James, to Eleanor Marlow, Dec. 27, 1836.

Connor, James, to Frances Elinor Jane Wood, May 14, 1840.

Conoway, Charles, to Sarah Hester, May 19, 1837.

Coursey, Wherry, to Anne Pitts, June 20, 1844.

Cooksey, John, to Sarah Ann McRory, July 27, 1846.

Cooper, Rev. William, to Valeria Powers, Jan. 27, 1848.

Cunningham, Archibald, to Rachel Robert, April 27, 1769.

Cole, Jonathan, to Nancy Radliff, Nov. 19, 1770.

Clifton, Daniel, to Lucy (or Liny) Warren, March 26, 1792.

Cantey, Mathew, to Mrs. Lydia Ford, Dec. 11, 1793.

Conrad, John, to Lydia Rollison, Jan. 3, 1800.

Campbell, Thomas, to Sarah Cox, Nov. 19, 1770.

Crawford, John, to Grace Beall, July 10, 1821; William Beall, trustee.

Crawford, James T., to Ann Wheeler, Aug. 20, 1823.

Crane, James, to Mrs. Keziah Taylor, May 26, 1835.

Crosby, Josiah, to Catherine Hinely, July 27, 1835; adm. est. of Joseph Taylor, 1835.

Crosby, Josiah, to Catherine Hinely, July 27, 1835.

Crawford, Emanuel, to Julian Eliz. Heidt, Dec. 26, 1836.

Clark, John M., to Elizabeth Jones, 1839.

Cope, John, to Selina Crews, May 30, 1837.

Clark, Richard H., to Hariet G. Charlton, Aug. 7, 1845.

Courvoisie, Jas. Armstron, to Mary Ann Olcott of Chatham Co., Nov. 12, 1840.

Crawford, William, to Patsy Bailey, July 4, 1793.

Davant. James and John Davant were Huguenots who settled on James Island and Johns Island "about 1690."

(a)   James Davant was a Rev. soldier, and his service is referred to in "Columbia State," 1904.

In the Diary of Revolution (Frank Moore): "Capt. Davant who conspicuously distinguished himself in leading the forlorn hope at Ninety-six, was killed at Eutaw. (Letter from Gen. Greene to President of Congress.)"

The will of John Davant, dated Dec. 5, 1776, is in Charleston, S. C., —"Of St. Helena's Parish, Granville Co." Wife Ann, brother James, daughter Sarah. "Wife Ann one-half of estate if she die without issue." Wit.: Joseph Steel, Wm. Parton, Richard Adams. (See S. C. Hist. Mag., Vol. 28.)

Stephen Blount. who died in Savannah in 1804, had a sister Elizabeth Davant, who died in Savannah 1821. He was from Beaufort, S. C. Her will in Savannah, mentions daughter Elizabeth, wife of John Mingledorf; Rachel, wife of Samuel Sturgis; grandson Fred'k. Robinson Schubert, son of deceased daughter Jane.

Will of James Davant, 1801 mentions daughter Elizabeth Ficklin.

Savh. Rec. Room, Book R., p. 139, 1797—Marriage settlement of James Davant of St. Luke's Par., S. C., and Mrs. Elizabeth, relict of Samuel White of Burke Co., Ga.

Depp—1798—Estate of Samuel Depp was adm. by John Kogler.

Dykes—1793—Estate of Levi Dykes adm. by Jesse Dykes.

1799—Estate of Noah Dykes adm. by James Garrison, who divides a portion between Noah, Rebecca, and Martha Dykes, and William Neely.

Dininger—1806—Deed of Ann Barbara Dininger (et al) to Elizabeth Exley, widow, John Eppinger and wife Hannah, Adam Cope and wife Mary of Savnanah, George Neiss and wife Rebecca, their shares in certain tracts.

Dampier—1810—Daniel Dampier to John Dampier and wife Alcey. Wit.: Jordan Williams and Stephen Dampier.

Densler—1811, March 20—Will of Philip Densler. Wife Ann. Children: Frederick, Henry Joseph, and John Washington Densler. Exrs. Wife, John H. Wisenbaker, Christian H. Dasher. Wit.: John More, William Hines, David Hines, J. P.

Dugger—1812—John Dugger, planter, deed to John Goldwire.

Dailey—1829, March 23. Will of John Dailey; to five youngest children, Frances (called Fanny), Susan, Matilda, James and Mary, son and daughters of my wife Priscilla, who is appointed Exr. and guardian. Brother William Dailey and deceased brother Josiah Dailey. Wit.: Edith Hester, Clem Powers.

Denny—1829—Estate of John Denny adm. by Thomas Elkins.

Douglas—1791, Sept. 10—Estate of Jos. or Jas. Douglas appraised by Francis Jones, John Mizell, Samuel Williams.

Densler—1790—Will of Henry Densler—wife Catherine. Youngest child Susannah. Sons in law John Venago (?), Christian Dasher. My four sons, Michael the eldest. In 1810 the name of Michael's wife was Polly. (Savannah Record Room, Book DD.)

1807—The wife of Henry Densler of Savannah, was Priscilla. (Deeds in Effingham Co.) See will of John Dailey.

In 1807 Ann was the widow of (a) Michael Densler).

Daniel—Edgefield, S. C., March 11, 1807—Will of William Daniel, wife Lucretia. Sons: John, Jesse, James, Stephen, William. Daughters: Mary, Catherine, Martha, Marsh and Elizabeth Raiford. Exrs.: Son Jesse and Philip Raiford.

Daniel. (Ibid), April 3, 1816—Will of James Daniel: Wife. Children: Lucretia, Mary Catherine, William Washington, Martha Sarah, Susan Caroline, James Lodowick.

Tyrell Co., N. C., 1752. Will of Elizabeth Daniel. Sons: Robert, Thomas, John Wm., Aaron, Josiah. Daughter Sarah Wilson.

Effingham County Marriages:

Daniel, Josiah, to Elizabeth Dixon, April 23, 1772. Both of S. C.

Daniel, Josiah, to Sarah, widow of Thos. Campbell, Feb. 18, 1795.

Daniel, Elizabeth, to Peter Kettles, May 11, 1773.

Daniel, John, to Hannah Dammons, Feb. 16, 1775.

Daniel, Seth, to Mary Kennedy, dau. of Wm. and Eliz. (Treutlin), March 12, 1807.

DeRoche (see "Mallette"). In Hirsch's "Huguenots of Colonial S. C.," the name "DeRoche" is listed. Henry DeRoche, (1735), and John H. DeRoche (1741), received Land Grants in Purysburg.

Mesne Office, Charleston, S. C., Book G. G., p. 708: Abraham Frederick DeRoche planter of Ebenezer, to Adrian Mayer of Purysburg, 150 acres bounded by land of Benjamin Heurion, Walter Culliat, land which was granted to Ann Jeaneret and Abraham Mouzon. Wit.: David Girond and Daniel Marette (Mallette). Aug. 10, 1767

(Adrian Mayer buys bench in St. Peter's Parish Church.)

Mesne Office, Charleston, S. C.: Book G 3, p. 86—Margaret DeRoche, widow of John Henry DeRoche of Purysburg, with her father John Jacob Metzger, sell lot No. 10 in Purysburg to David Girond. March 19, 1742.

Effingham Co. land transfer from Daniel DeRoche to Hannah Elizabeth Mallet.

Abraham DeRoche was a member of Jerusalem Church in 1775.

Marriages:

Dascher, Christian, to Anna Christiana Meyer, Feb. 10. 1754.

Dindal, Nehemiah, to Elizabeth Miller, Jan. 3, 1757.

Ducker, James, to Alice Heaton, April 1, 1758.

Davis, Thomas, to (?) Sutherland, Aug. 2, 1758.

Dunn, John, to Mary Palmer, Nov. 28, 1679.

Dixon, Robert, to Lucy Jones, Jan., 1770.

Daley, Benjamin, to Susannah Garnet, Jan. 6, 1774.

Dasher, John Martin, Jr., to Hannah, widow of Christopher Hudson, July 31, 1800. He was dead in 1804.

Dampier, John, to Esenure Hodges, Oct. 5, 1801.

Dasher, Joshua, to Dolly Moore, March 10, 1804. (Will.book 1798-1840, Richmond Co., Ga., page 14, Mary Moore, widow, of Augusta. Chil. Sarah (wife of Math. Henderson), Mary Dolly, Susannah Betsy, and James, a minor—Jan. 28, 1802—Probated April 12, 1802. Dolly, one of the daus. "now Dolly Dasher," "Expenses to Edgefield, Riceboro and Orangeburg." Wit.: Robt. and Jane McCrary.)

Dasher, Christian H., to Elizabeth Waldhauer (Savh. Records), March 30, 1809.

Dampier, Stephen, to Ann Graham, Oct. 31, 1811.

Dasher, Solomon, to Maria Wylly, Feb. 9, 1813.
Dasher, Martin, to Lydia Weitman, Oct. 13, 1813.

Dowdy, Benjamin, to Elzabeth Brock, Sept. 12, 1814.

Davis, Levi, to Susannah Bragg of Bulloch Co., Dec. 9, 1819.
Davis, Richard, to Elizabeth Porter, March 10, 1820.

Dasher, Thomas, Rebecca Zitterauer, Sept. 25, 1820.
Dasher, Samuel, to Jane Maria Zitterauer, Jan. 6, 1821.

Dudley, Guilford, to Susan Gilleland, Dec. 3, 1823.

Dasher, Gotlieb, to Susan Waldhauer, Feb. 15, 1823, Savh. Records.
Dasher, Benjamin, to Elizabeth Leimberger, dau. of David, Dec. 15, 1825. (She had a nephew Joshua Leimberger.)
Dasher, Gideon, to Ann Rebecca Zitterauer, April 17, 1828.

Davis, Jesse, to Margaret Metzger, Jan. 28, 1829.

Dasher, John, to Mary Miller, Feb. 25, 1829.

Dykes, Geo. D., to Mary Rosannah Hurst, Dec. 22, 1829.
Dykes, Jesse D., to Fanny Ann Blitch, Dec. 23, 1830.

Dasher, Edwin, to Susannah C. Wisenbaker, Feb. 6, 1833 (p. 77 Minute Book 3, 1827-1850.)
Dasher, Jas. A., to Mary A. Wisenbaker, Oct. 19, 1833.
Dasher, Joshua Martin, to Hannah Grovenstein, March 21, 1838.

Daniels, Irby, to Lydia Ann Bowman, Feb. 2, 1843.

Dugger, Wm., to Sarah Ann Shearouse, March 11, 1844.

Douglas, Stephen, to Keziah E. Ambrose, Dec. 11, 1844.

Dasher, Wm. B., to Ann Eliza Gnann, June 12, 1846.
Dasher, Benjamin, to Mary Sophia Gnann, Oct. 15, 1849.

Dawson, Dr. Richard S., to Martha M. Morgan, Dec. 18, 1849.

Dasher, Israel, to Mary M. Williams, Savh., March 3, 1842.
Dasher, Wm. B., to Ann Eliza Gnann, June 12, 1846.
Dasher, Benj. J., to Mary Sophia Gnann, Nov. 21, 1849.

Tondee. In Record Room, Savannah, Ga., Book "H," pp. 61-62-63, is recorded a deed which establishes the "heirs at law" of Peter Tondee: Son Charles Tondee, daughters: Mary, wife of Benjamin Jones; Elizabeth, wife of Nicholas Champagne (or Champius); Ann, wife of Elisha Elon; Lucy, wife of John Hero; Frederick Shick and Peter Oates. Dated Nov. 7, 1789.

Elon. 1820. "Heirs of Elisha Elon, late of Savannah." Widow Ann Elon. Son Felix Elon. Deceased son William Elon.

Daughter Rebecca L. McKay, (widow).

Daughter Elizabeth Bassinger. Widow. John Bassinger and wife Barbara, of Ogeechee, had son David, born March 24, 1773. (Ebenezer Record.)

Daughter Mary, wife of Morris Doty.

Daughter Sarah, wife of Charles Gregory.

(Family records state that Mary Elon married (1) Peter Wyley in 1805; married (2) Mr. Hewlet; married (3) —— Doty, March 27, 1818.

Sav. Record Room, Book "2 K," pp. 165-180.

1820. Deed of gift to Mrs. Ann Picket, wife of Daniel Pickett, daughter of Mrs. Ann Elon, and to her children: Ann Brown (by marriage Ann Crane), Mary Pickett, Charles S. Pickett.

Ernst (see Herman Hersen.) (A) Gotlieb Ernst married Catherine Fields, Dec. 18, 1798.

(A) Gotlieb Ernst married Margaret, daughter of Jonathan Rahn.

(A) Gotlieb Ernst married Catherine Kieffer, Jan. 27, 1812.

James H. Ernst married Mary Gnann, Feb. 26, 1846.

Gotlieb Ernst died Feb. 16, 1828.

Gotlieb Ernst died Oct. 5, 1836, age 46.

Lewis Ernst and wife Christine, had:

Salome, born Sept. 8, 1777.

David, born Jan., 1780.

Charleston, S. C., 1788—Christian Gotlieb Belzer was attorney for the heirs of John Ernst, and gives deed of release to Jacob Sass, et al.

Charleston, S. C., Ordinary's Office—Will of John Ernst, April, 1777; "Brothers Michael, Joseph, James, George and Paul, who when last heard from, were living in village of Eringen, 12 miles from Emendengen, dominion of Marquis of Baden Dullach.

Eirick—1769—Adam Eirick had 500 acres in Effingham Co., Book "G," p. 298.

Easter—1804, Sept. 29—Will of Augustus Easter: Wife Mary, Sons: William, George, Giles, David, Isaac. Daughters: Mary and Elizabeth. An equal share to son John if he returns. Exrs.: John Strawhorn, Darius Garrison. Wit.: Stephen Wolf, John Elkins, Camel Tison.

1804—appears the name "Augusta Mary Easter."

Elkins. Thomas Elkins is listed in Georgia Roster (Rev.) as private in Col. John Stewart's Regt. It is believed that he was the father of Thomas and Alexander Elkins of Effingham Co.

Thomas Elkins, 2nd, was born Oct. 25, 1783, and married:

(1) Oct., 1808 to Ann Simson. Only child Simson, born July 1809,

(2) Aug. 22, 1811 to Sarah Powers, born May 3, 1793.

(3) Oct. 14, 1830 to Mrs. Maria (Tondee), widow of Wm. Patterson; children:

Mozelle (also written Rozelle Martha), born Jan. 10, 1814. Married to Robt. Hamilton Bourquin, Oct. 13, 1831. Son of Maj. David Bourquin.

Charles N., born April 1, 1815; married Ann Carle, Nov. 11, 1857.

Julia, born Oct. 6, 1816; married Ebenezer Jencks, July 21, 1836.

Wyley, born June 12, 1818.

Lydia Ann, born Jan. 26, 1821; married Mr. E. Allen.

Thomas, born Jan. 10, 1822; married Lavinia Blackman, Sept. 12, 1849.

Sarah E., born May 7, 1829; married H. Kallach Harrison, Oct. 13, 1849.

Caroline M., born Dec. 12, 1831; married James G. Watts, May 31, 1855.

Selna V., born Feb. 27, 1833; married Morgan Rawls, Oct. 22, 1851.

Charles E., born May 20, 1835, and Leander L., born June 10, 1837.

Thomas Elkins was sheriff of Effingham Co. in 1825, and perhaps earlier. In 1847 he adm. estate of Phares Elkins in regard to deed to Mozelle Elkins, who, after the death of her husband Robert Bourquin, married Mr. Zettler.

Will of Thomas Elkins in Effingham Co., Jan. 20, 1854. Daughters: Mozelle Zettler, Julia Jencks, Lydia Elkins, Sarah Harrison, Caroline Elkins, Selina Rawls. As guardian of daughter Sarah Harrison, "I hold $300 given her by her grandmother." Sons: Thomas P., Charles and Leander L. Grant of land in Dooley Co. to Thomas Elkins. Lands in Houston, Pike and Baker Counties. Stepdaughter Harriet Patterson, (who had bro. Joseph,) 500 acres in Effingham Co. known as Tondee Place.

Alexander Elkins married (1) Elizabeth Tondee, sister of Mrs. William Patterson who married Thomas Elkins. They were daughters of Charles Tondee. Alexander Elkins married (2) Mrs. Ann, widow of John Knight, and daughter of Samuel Baas.

Effingham Co. marriages:

Smith, Hugh, to Catherine Elkins, May 30, 1805.

Elkins, Herman, to Selina Tondee, June 19, 1824. She was dead in 1830.

Elkins, Samuel, to Harriet Patterson, June 18, 1836.

Elkins, Florence, to Hosie Clark, June 25, 1905. (Savannah C. H.)

1852—June 23—Will of John Elkins. All to wife Mary and her children. (She appears on deeds with him Sept. 3, 1811.)

Alexander Elkins was born 1775; died 1837. He had a son Lawrence Tondee Elkins born 1819; died 1878, who married Margaret Frances, the daughter of James Wilson and wife Ann Eliza Bourquin, 1831-1912.

Lawrence T. Elkins and wife Ann Eliza, had:

Georgiana Bartow Elkins, married David Ignatius DeFoor.

Franklin Elkins.

1697. S. C. Land Warrant to William Elking.

S. C. Mag. Vol. 5, pp. 117 and 149: Rev. Service for William & Johnson Elkins 1794, Franklin Co., Ga., William Elkins, Sr. and Jr. were tax payers. At same time and place was James DeFoor.

Eilkens—1640—Jacob Eilkens, put in command of a fort, now Albany, N. Y. (Fiske's Dutch and Quaker Colony.)

Elkins—1809, Nov. 19—Ann, wife of Mr. Elkins of N. C. died. (Savannah City Hall.)

Exley. John Exley married Mary Wooten, May 27, 1790 (Georgia Gazette.) Had:

John W. Exley, born Oct. 10, 1794; died Sept. 22, 1855; married Elizabeth Margaret Mallette Jan. 17, 1822. She died Jan. 23, 1880.

Children (from family Bible):

Elizabeth Ann, born Jan. 30, 1823.

James Barnard, born March 28, 1825.

John Jeremiah, born Nov. 16, 1826; married Susannah C., dau. of Rev. J. C. Edwards.

Margaret Josephine, born Jan. 28, 1829.

William Lewis, born July 26, 1831; died April 9, 1909. Married Caroline H. Miller.

Gibeon Henry, born July 17, 1833.

Caroline Eliza, born Oct. 4, 1835.

Francis Abiah, born Jan. 20, 1838; married Berta Crum (cousin).

Adelaide Victoria, born June 8, 1840; married Emanuel Reiser.

Fletcher Asbury, born May 3, 1842; married Josephine Morgan.

Marquis Lafayette, born June 19, 1845; married Emma Grovenstein.

William Lewis Exley and Caroline Harriet Miller were married Jan. 1873; she died March 22, 1896; had:

Lilla Eliza, born Nov. 4, 1874; married John S. Sims, July 5, 1900.

John Samuel Sims (born Oct. 11, 1872) and Lilla E. (Exley), had:

Lilla Exley Sims, born March 6, 1903.

1799—April 12—Will of John Michaeler: dau. Catherine, former wife of Michael Exley, and her son John Exley. (She married (2) Benj. Reiser and had dau. Mary who became 2nd wife of Jonathan Backley.) Dau. Susannah wife of John Ernst Bergman. Exrs.: friends Jonathan Rahn and John Kogler.

It is said that there were two "Exley" families in Effingham Co. —one of English and the other of German extraction. The origin of the latter, (Oxley, Oschle, and other spellings) is one of the interesting illustrations of a man becoming named from his occupation. In this instance the progenitor was an inn keeper, and according to the customs of the time made necessary when many of our forebears could not read, the name of the hostelry was an illustrated one, oftener than otherwise that of some animal, and this name was adopted from the sign of "The Little Ox.'

Will of John Michael Exley. (Name in marriage license to Elizabeth Groover, appears as John Michael Oxley). Will probated Jan. 22, 1814. Wife Elizabeth, sons Solomon and John, the latter being Exr. Wit.: Jonathan Backley, Thomas Mock, Emanuel Rahn. (See will of John Michaeler, 1799.

1814—Will of Ebenezer Exley: To Lutheran Church at Ebenezer; to Rev. John Ernst Bergman; to Elizabeth, daughter of John Eppinger; to Ann, wife of John Gnann, to Susannah and Salome, daughters of Jonathan Rahn; Christina wife of Jacob Gnann; to Ann Barbara Reiser and Christina Mock. Exrs.: Jonathan and Emanuel Rahn. Wit.: Jonathan Rahn, John Freckinger, Jacob Gnann, Jr.

Solomon Exley married Sarah Backley, Jan. 25, 1818. See "Backley.''

John Exley married Mrs. Sarah (Berry) Rahn, 2nd wife.

Zacharius Exley married Susannah Grovenstein, April 10, 1834.

Solomon Exley married Maria Christina Rahn, Nov. 22, 1832, 2nd wife.

Luke Exley, married Lydia Grovenstein, Oct. 2, 1834.

Solomon Exley married Hannah Elizabeth Reiser, Nov. 11, 1843. 3rd wife.

(a) John Exley is buried in Colonial Cemetery, and is said to have married Mary Trevor, who married 2nd James Johnston.

(a) John **Wooten** married Priscilla Mosely.

Eppinger. Savannah Record Room, Book "R," p. 58: "Barbara Eppinger, widow of John Eppinger, and John Eppinger, Jr., George Eppinger, Mathias Eppinger and Balthazar Shaffer in right of his deceased wife Margaret, daughter of John Eppinger deceased; and Joseph Roberts in right of his wife Winifred, daughter of deceased John Eppinger; John Jones in right of his wife Sarah, daughter of deceased John Eppinger. June 1, 1797."

"James Eppinger and wife Elizabeth, 1803." (Deeds in Savannah.)

Johan (John) Eppinger and wife Barbara, had a daughter Anna Magdalena, born July 15, 1759. (Ebenezer Ch. Records.)

English, James, to Mary May of St. Philips Parish, S. C., June 6, 1771.

Marriages in Effingham Co.:

Ewing, David, to Mary Conway, Dec. 3, 1794.

Evans, James, to Louisa Cook, Nov. 1, 1808.

Edwards, John, to Hannah Shearous, Dec. 19, 1819.

Edwards, James, to Nancy Pitts, Nov. 25, 1822.

Edwards, Daniel, to Maria Tyner, Oct. 6, 1823.

Edwards, Charles G., to Mehitable Hilton, Dec. 22, 1826.

Edwards, William, to Eleanor Southwell, Oct. 21, 1831.

Edwards, Joseph Chapman, to Frances Cone of Bulloch Co., Feb. 11, 1832.

Edwards, Obadiah, Jr., to Mrs. Lydia Womack, Nov. 2, 1838.

Everett, Joseph A., to Grace Ann Blitch, Nov. 29, 1838.

Edwards, John W., to Susannah E. Dasher, Sept. 3, 1849.

Eigle—1838—John Eigle wasc dead and left a widow Hannah.

Floerl. Hans (John), and Charles Floerl came from Memminger, Germany. (Candler).

In 1758-68 John Floerl was Collector and Assessor, also Surveyor for Ebenezer. He was one of the commissioners for erecting forts.

Charles Floerl died May 2, 1764. His wife was Mary. The records do not show that there were children. (She was form. wid. of Peter Gruber & left son Peter Gruber.)

John Floerl died Oct. 19, 1770, age 60. It appears that his mother was Anna Floerl who died Jan. 18, 1774, age 81.

John Floerl, 2nd, married Jan. 15, 1765 to Elizabeth Hannah Brander, who died Dec. 12, 1773, age 30.

Children:

Judith, born Dec. 25, 1765; died Oct. 10, 1766.

Mary, born Sept. 19, 1767; married J. C. Waldhauer.

John, born Sept. 3, 1769; died Nov. 15, 1773.

Israel, born 1771; married Sarah Salome Waldhauer, Nov. 5, 1800. He was dead in 1813, and his widow married Lewis Weitman. She was the dau. of Jacob C. Waldhauer and Mary V. Floerl.

John Floerl married 2nd Dorothea Keiffer, Feb. 23, 1774. He died the latter par of 1776, naming in his will Mathias Brander as "father in law," (father of his first wife). His Exrs. were John Wertsch, Jacob C. Waldhauer and John Adam Treutlen. Sept. 27, 1776—probated Jan. 16, 1777. Wit.: Nathaniel Reisser, Mathew Zettler, Andrew Seckinger.

The wills of Charles and Mary Floerl mention as "relatives": Mary Floerl, John Wertsche, Philip Parlz, George Heckel, John Gruber, Peter Imber, Johan Martin Paulitz, Andrew Seckinger.

Hannah and Judith Floerl appear to have been sisters of John Floerl. Hannah married Thomas Schweighoffer in 1758, and died April 1, 1769, age 29 & 9 mos., and Judith Floerl married Samuel Kraus, Jan. 24, 1764.

Thomas Schweighoffer and Hannah (Floerl), had:

Abiel, born Dec. 15, 1758.

Benaiah, born Feb. 27, 1760.

Thomas, born July 8, 1761.

Salome, born Dec. 24, 1762.

Elisha, born April 8, 1764.

Obadiah, born Feb. 4, 1766.

Elizabeth, born March 25, 1769.

Brandner. Mathaias Brandner and wife Mary (who died Dec. 11, 1768, age 65), had:

Hannah Elizabeth, married "young" John Floerl, Jan. 15, 1765.

Mary, married Joseph Schubtrein; their dau. Mary married J. Chris. Gugel.

Effingham Co. marriages:

Fitzpatrick, Samuel, to Vinia Bugg, June 24, 1809.

Fell, Frederick S., to Harriet Neisler, Nov. 18, 1820.

Foy, George, to Rebecca Dasher, Feb. 10, 1825.

Fawcett, Wm. H. C., to Martha O. Farmer, May 1, 1847.

Flood, Thomas, to Martha Smith, Nov. 3, 1849.

Floerl. Division of estate of Isranel Floerl, Effingham Co., Book A, p. 275. By John Waldhauer, Christian H. Dasher, David Gugel, Sept. 26, 1824. Israel Floerl died in 1813, and in 1818 his widow had married Lewis Weitman.

Estate divided into five shares: Lewis Weitman, in right of wife; to John Helvenstine in right of his deceased wife Esther (married Jan. 2, 1822), to son Thomas Floerl, to daughters Catherine and Sarah Israline Floerl. Mary Catherine Floerl married Rev. C. F. Bergman in 1826, and Sarah married Rev. P. A. Strobel Jan. 31, 1846. (See will of Fred. Herb, in Savh.) which speaks of daughter, the wife of Rev. C. F. Bergman.)

Oct. 11, 1788—Samuel Kraus (whose wife was Judith Floerl), made deed of gift to "Niece Salome, wife of Abiel Schweighoffer." (Samuel Kraus was son of Leonard Kraus.)

Jan. 29, 1814—Will of Samuel Kraus: To Martin Dasher and his heirs. To Mrs. Salome Sarah Waldhauer, and heirs of her former husband Israel Floerl. To Mary, wife of John Waldhauer, Sr., and Elizabeth, wife of Benjamin Dasher. Exrs.: Benjamin Dasher and John Waldhauer, Sr. Wit.: John Neidlinger, William Schrimph and Gotlieb Ernst.

Bibliography for "Floerl":

White's Hist. Coll., pp. 60-65.

Georgia Hist. Coll., Vol. 5, p. 60.

Journal of Council of Safety, p. 137.

Strobel's "Salzburgers," pp. 195, 196, 286, 287.

Jones' Hist. of Georgia, Vol. 2, p. 184.

Chatham Co. Deed Book "Y," p. 177.

Georgia Colonial Records: Vol. 1, pp. 20, 229, 230; Vol. 6, pp. 234, 374; Vol. 10, p. 864; Vol. 11, pp. 28, 29.

Freyermouth. From "Peter Freyermouth's Bible."

John Adam Freyermouth, deceased March 1, 1825; born Jan. 11, 1821.

Esther Carline Freyermouth, born Oct. 10, 1818; deceased April 19, 1836.

Peter Freyermouth was born March 27, 1787; departed this life Sept. the 26th, 1867, being 80 years old, 6 months and 2 days. (He married Lydia Gnann, Nov. 25, 1817.)

Salome Freyermouth was born Jan. 15, 1832, departed this life April 27th, 1888. (Married —— Rahn.)

Lydia Freyermouh was born Oct. 15, 1793, departed this life Oct. the 4th, 1869, being 73 years old, eleven month 21 days.

Levinia Freyermouth was born March 20, 1821; departed this life Dec. 25, 1901. (Married Ephraim Seckinger.)

Christina Elizabeth Freyermouth was born July 25, 1826.

Jacob Lot Freyermouth was born May 18, 1830. (Married Amanda Weitman).

Stray notes:

1749-67. There were grants in Saxe Gotha, S. C., on the Saluda River, to John Freyermouth and John Adam Freyermouth.

John Peter Freyermouh (a Rev. soldier), married May 23, 1769 Anna Catherine Groll, daughter of Mathias Groll.

Children, as far as known:

Daniel Freyermouh, born Oct .10, 1770.

Tobias Freyermouth, born Dec. 8, 1773; died April 30, 1777.

Joshua Peter Freyermouth, born Oct. 18, 1775.

Solomon Freyermouth, born Feb. 25, 1780.

John Adam Freyermouth married Mary Elizabeth Buehler Oct. 7, 1766; she died March 31, 1781, age 33. Children, as far known:

Frederick Freyermouth, born Jan. 25, 1768; died Feb. 11, 1768.

John Adam Freyermouth, born Nov. 23, 1769; died Feb. 5, 1772.

Israel Freyermouth, born Aug. 17, 1774.

Marriages in Effingham Co.:

Freyermouth, John, to Susannah Thomas, Jan. 29, 1800.

Freyermouth, John, to Hannah Elizabeth, widow of Jedediah Weitman.

Deed, 1811—John Freyermouth and wife Salome.

Fresh. Nov. 9, 1804. Will of Jacob Fresh. To John B., Timothy, Hannah, Mary and Elizabeth, the children of Timothy Staley. Exr.: brother Timothy Staley. Wit.: Henry M. Williams.

Frazer. Dyer (Barrer) Frazer was dead in 1791, and his widow Elizabeth was Exr. His estate was appraised by William and John Fletcher and Joshua Hedges.

Fetzger. John Gotlieb Fetzger married Elizabeth Erhardt, March 21, 1807. He was the son of Jonathan Gotlieb Fetzger, whose will,

Dec. 20, 1818 mentions wife Ann Magdalen; son Gotlieb, and daughter Lydia Spann. Wit.: Israel Weitman, George Foy, Gotlieb Ernst.

John F. Fetzger married Christian Biddenback, Feb. 25, 1837.

Richard J. Fetzger married Salome C. Keiffer, Oct. 1, 1838.

Fabian. 1806—Martha, wife of James Fabian, gentleman, was the daughter of Mrs. Jane Winn.

S. C. Mag., Vol. 11, p. 258: Lydia Ford in 1790 adm. the estate of her husband, Anthony Ford of Effingham Co., Ga. Before May 23, 1794 she was the wife of a Mr. Canty.

1786—Isaac Ford of Effingham Co. makes deed to Wm. Dupuis of S. C.

Farrar. S. C. Grant to Benjamin Farrer of Saxe Gotha, 1774.

Fyffe. Alexander Fyffe, whose home appears to have been at Beach Island, near Augusta, married (according to the authority of Judge Richard Clark), Miss Clark, and their children were, as far as known:

Elizabeth married (1) Stephen Maxwell; (2) Alexander Netherclift.

Catherine married Maj. George Waters.

A daughter who married Mr. Harden.

In Book "C," Bryan Co., July 18, 1815, George M. Waters deeds to White Eberson Harden, 440 acres of Indian Mound Tract. Wit.: John Cubbedge.

Alexander Fyffe married (2) Margaret Gindrat, had:

Sarah Frances, who married Stephen J. M. Cubbedge.

(An affidavit in posssesion of the family shows that Alex. Fyffe left a widow "Margaret," who married a "Shaffer." See "Gindrat."

Elizabeth and Catherine Fyffe were married the same day at "Whitehall" the residence of their uncle William Clark, in Bryan Co.

"Fyffe" notes:

Charleston, S. C. Will of William Fyffe of Craven Co. Wife and wife's daughters. Brothers John and Charles. Sisters Elizabeth and Magdalen Oct. 17, 1771. (Book 1771-1774.)

Mesne Office, Chas., S. C., 1768—Dr. Charles Fyffe and wife Ann of Craven Co., and Dr. William Fyffe of Pr. George Parish.

Prince Frederick Parish Register:

John Fyffe married Sarah Dott, July 2, 1775.

Mrs. Sarah Fyffe married Andrew Quelch, April 2, 1779.

St. Helena's Parish Register: "Dr. Fyffe and wife Ann, had son Joseph bap. May 9, 1744, and daughter Margaret born June 11, 1744."

S. C. Mag., Vol. 27: Dr. Charles Fyffe married Ann Rowe, "about 1751." She was probably a second wife.

Ibid, Vol. 28—Charles Fyffe was Church warden, 1775.

Ibid, Vol. 26—Charles Fyffe adm. estate of George Skinner of Peedee.

Ibid Vol. 23—Dr. Charles Fyffe with James Gordon of Pr. George Parish were securities.

Jan. 2, 1770—Charles Fyffe of Georgetown was passenger on "Beaufain," from London.

Alexander Fyffe had grant of 500 acres in St. Patrick's Parish 1765.

John Fyffe had 50 acres in St. Paul's Parish 1764. (Candler).

Marriages:

Fletcher, James, to Margaret Figg, Feb. 7, 1758.

Ford, John, to Mary Moore, March 7, 1768. They were of "Norfolk, Collenage of Vardeny" (Va.)

Folk, John, to Mary Shealy, May 5, 1795.

Fell, Frederick S., to Harriet Neisler, Nov. 18, 1820.

Frazer, Thomas, to Mrs. Martha Lancaster, June 28, 1828.

Fetzger, John F., to Christian Biddenback, Feb. 25, 1837.

Fetzger, Richard J., to Salome C. Keiffer, Oct. 1, 1838.

Gindrat. The first known of this name was Abraham Gindrat the elder, who settled in Purysburg, S. C., and said to be of Burgundy, France, thence Berne, Switzerland, at the Revocation. He married Mary Margaret, the daughter of Benjamin "Tallet" in 1739. All temporary records of Purysburg and its vicinity indicate that this name was "Mallet," as several grants were made to Abraham Mallet, and only once has the name occurred as "Tallet."

1738-39 there were grants to Abraham Gindrat, also occurring as "Gendraw" and Jindrat, were in Purysburg, S. C., Granville Dist., St. Peter's Parish.

Abraham Gindrat the elder left a widow, Margaret, and three children:

Henry, who married (1) Mary May; (2) Mrs. Dorcas (Williams), widow of Capt. Sam'l Stafford.

Abraham, II.

Margaret, who married Alexander Fyffe.

Mary May, the first wife of Henry Gindrat, was one of seven daughters of John May and his wife Mary—the daughter of Col. William Stafford, of N. C. Mrs. May had first been married to a Mr. Patterson, and after the death of John May she married Mr. James Mallet of S. C. and died at the age of 106, "about 1820." She is buried in the Bostwick Cemetery, near Garnett, S. C.

Henry Gindrat, 1740-1801, and Mary (May), had:

Abraham 3rd, married Barbara, daughter of Hugh Clarke.

John.

Mary-May, married Dr. Benjamin St. Mark.

Rhoda, married William Gilliland—had a daughter Susan who married Guilford Dudley, Dec. 3, 1823.

Susannah, married Benjamin Morel, Dec. 28, 1798, had a dau. who was 2nd wife of Lewis Grovenstine.

Henry Gindrat married (2) Mrs. Dorcas (Williams), the widow of his first wife's uncle, Capt. Samuel Stafford. and had:

Dorcas, married —— Washburn.

Henrietta, married (June 11, 1823), Josiah Clark (parents of Judge Richard Clark).

Henry Gindrat was a commissioned officer under Gen. Greene. Wounded at Battle of Eutaw; removed from Beech Island, near Augusta, Ga., to Beaufort, S. C., where he died Jan. or Feb., 1801 & is buried at Sisters' Ferry. He was Mem. House of Rep. from Effingham Co., 1787-1794.

Will of Henry Gindrat, Effingham Co., Probate Jan. 10, 1801. Wife Dorcas, formerly widow of Capt. Samuel Stafford. Daughters: Henrietta, Dorcas, Rhoda, Susannah, Mary. Sons: Abraham and John.

In Re the children of Henry Gindrat:

Susannah, who married Benjamin Morel, had a daughter Mary Morel, whose marriage settlement with Francis Haygood is dated Feb. 25, 1828. In this is stated that he is a grandson of Susannah Yonge, and heir of Gideon and Harriet P. Haygood. That Mary Morel has a legacy from her uncle Abraham Gindrat. (Effingham Court Records.)

May 21, 1790—Dr. Benjamin St. Mark and his wife Mary May St. Mark, buy the house of John Neidlinger. Wit.: Thomas Wylly, H. Abraham Gindrat. (H. Abraham Gindrat was the son of Abraham

Gindrat, 2nd, and nephew of Henry, and he had a grant in Oglethorpe Co. in 1806.)

Effingham C. H., 1815. A very puzzling situation is apparent in the following record: "John Gindrat, Exr. of Henry Gindrat, in right of his wife Susan, daughter of Henry Gindrat. Henrietta Gindrat gives receipt."

Richmond Co. C. H., Dec. 7, 1818—John Gindrat adm. estate of Rhoda Gilliland. On back of papers: "See Susan R. Gilliland's receipt to Adms., Book H, Clerk Superior Court's Office."

Family Chart: "John Gindrat married S. S. Stallings in 1811."

Southern Recorder, Oct. 2, 1826: "Died at Milledgeville, Ga., Miss Amanda Gindrat."

Abraham and Henry Gindrat are on the Revolutionary Pay Rolls of S. C.

1772—Grant to Henry Gindrat of 100 acres in St. Peter's Parish, Granville, by lands of William Stafford. (Richard Stafford had grant on Boggy Gut, 1773.)

Henry Gindrat had a grant on Black Swamp.

1764 both Henry and Abraham "Ginderal" and "Ginderau" have grants in Purysburg.

1805—from loose papers in Basement of Record Room: William Lewden and wife Mary, late Mary Glass, suit against John and Abraham Gindrat. Stephen J. Maxwell, S. B. C. states that "John Gindrat does not reside in my county."

Mrs. Dorcas Gindrat makes a will Sept. 9, 1797, and appoints her husband Henry Gindrat her Exrc. However this will was not probated, as she outlived him, and married 3rd William Dupuis, July 3, 1802, and died 1804. The children of Capt. Samuel Stafford and Dorcas, were Seth, William, Elizabeth (who married John Tison, Sr.) and Mary, who married Reuben Grant Taylor, Dec. 18, 1800. (There is a Mary Stafford who married Elijah Radclift, Nov. 23, 1773.)

June 22, 1802, Dorcas Gindrat makes deed of gift to her children, and mentions her granddaughter Virginia Taylor, the daughter of her daughter Mary. "Stepson John Gindrat."

Abraham Gindrat, 2nd. (Brother of Henry.)

Will Feb. 19, 1785, Effingham Co. Son Henry Abraham. Brother Henry's two sons. Capt. Cook's son Nathan. To Jane Forgason. Nothing further is now known).

The marriage settlement of Abraham Gindrat (son of Henry) and Mrs. Barbara Clarke is dated March 17, 1803. "Whitehall," the late residence of William Clarke and fifty-seven negroes are to descend to any children who may be living, or their survivors. Trustee Joseph

Clay, Jr. Wit.: John Maxwell, Mary Maxwell. Bryan Co., C. H., Book "B."

"Book B" is marked "Abraham Gindrat's Book, Anno Domini 1779." He was Clerk of Superior and Inferior Courts of Bryan Co., Dec. 12, 1798-Dec. 9, 1799.

Also Mem. House of Rep. from Bryan Co., 1801-1807.

Commissioner of Bryan Co. Academy, Dec. 3, 1812.

Deed in Bryan Co.: From Abraham Gindrat for love and affection to Martha Harn, a lot near Court House on road to Hardwick, leading to Darien, being a part of Mulberry Hill tract. Wit.: James Bird. Jan. 31, 1804. Book "B," p. 152.

Savannah Record Room, Book A.A., p. 3, 1806—Abraham Gindrat and wife Barbara of Bryan Co. in re estate of William Clarke.

1784—Wm. LeConte deed to Wm. Clarke, tract of Ogeechee, Mulberry Hill, now the property of John McQueen, and Sedgefield, property of Sam'l. Stirk, adjoining Joseph Butler. Book G, p. 536.

Graber, George—wife Mary Magdalen, 1772.

Gill, Jeremiah—wife Lucy, 1812.

Guinn, Richard—widow Eliazbeth, 1793.

Gromet, John—widow Mary Magdalen, 1806.

Gaffney, James—Salome (Sarah), 1812.

Gruber, David, estate of, 1806.

Dupuis, James, and wife Fannie (Stafford) of Beaufort, S. C., to Effingham Co., had:

Fannie, born S. C., March 30, 1768.

William Dupuis, married Dorcas (widow of Henry Gindrat and (2) Hannah Lemcke), widow of Joseph Tribble.

Gugel. Will of John (Johannes) Gugel, dated Jan. 25, 1786, and probated in Savannah, May 27, 1788. Wife Anna Maria. Children:

David, born Jan. 21, 1754; died April 24, 1842. (Wife Margaret, dau. of Jacob Waldhauer. She was born 1759; died Sept. 21, 1841. Married Jan. 10, 1789.)

John Christopher, born March 5, 1757; married Mary Schubtrein.

Samuel, born Sept. 3, 1758. (Had daughter Sarah who married James Lavinder.)

Salome, married Peter Millen.

Daniel—"wife Mary Ann, born Oct. 10, 1772; died July 22, 1847."

Johannes, born Aprnl 1, 1761. (Ebeneezr Ch. Records. Voght.)

Christian, died 1815. His wife was Frances, daughter of John Hubbard.

*Joshua, born Sept. 28, 1768. Will probated March 7, 1801. Widow "Sophia."

Hannah, married (1) Christian Dasher; (2) Mathias Ash. (See "Ash-Ashbocker.)

Charlotte Dorothea, married —— Reiser.

*Joshua left son Charles who died Sept. 21, 1806, age 9. In Savannah Record Room, Book DD, p. 354: "Sophia, widow of Joshua Gugel, married Israel Meserve."

Dec. 25, 1841-May 2, 1842. Will of David Gugel. Daughter Eliza, wife of John Charlton. Grand daughter Ann E. McDonell house in Savannah now occupied by the Rev. John B. Davis. To grand daughter Margaret G. Saussy house in Savannah (wife of Dr. J. R. Saussy). Grand daughter Georgiana A., wife of Daniel Remshart, house, etc., in Savannah, also half of a certan tract in Effingham Co. Grand son James S. Olcott, son of my late daughter, Mary Ann Olcott, a lot in Savannah, and land in Thomas County (to revert to his brothers and sisters now living with his step mother in Savannah.) My silver watch to my g. son, David Charlton.

(1849.) The will of John Charlton mentions wife Elizabeth; son Wm. O. Charlton; son in law George R. Wright. Does not mention son David as in David Gugel's will.

Rev. George R. Wright married Margaret Eliz. Charlton, Dec. 27, 1831. William O. Charlton married Teresa Fulton, March 29, 1848.

James Olcott married Mary Ann Gugel, Dec. 20, 1816. They had daughter, Mary Ann, who married James Armstrong Courvoisie, Nov. 12, 1840. In Effingham Co., 1824, James Olcott and wife Esther of N. J., and Frederick Millen and wife of Bulloch Co. deed two fifths of a tract to Thomas and William Morgan.

*Will of Frederick Fahm (Savannah) mentions his daughter, Mrs. Sophia Gugel.

Savannah C. H. Will of Daniel Gugel, March 16, 1832-May 7, 1832. (Daniel Gugel had no children—an adopted daughter, Elizabeth Jane married Thomas Purse, Nov. 13, 1824.)

It will be seen that most, if not all, legatees were his nieces. "To Esther, wife of James S. Olcott (daughter of Salome (Gugel) and Peter Millen.)

To Mary, wife of Solomon Creamer. (He was born July 8, 1878; died Feb. 18, 1839.)

To Lydia, widow of Ephraim Cooper.

To Esther Stewart.

To Salome, wife of William Groover.

To Eliza, wife of John Charlton.

To Sophia, wife of Israel Weitman.

To Margaret, wife of Gottlieb Zitterauer.

To Mary, and her children, wife of John Zipperer.

To Mary A. M. Anderson, house and let in trust.

To Frances (Hubbard) Gugel and her two children, William and Daniel, a house and lot. To revert to children if she remarries.

Remainder to wife—after her death to Eliza Jane, wife of Thomas Purse.

Exrs. David Gugel, Thomas Purse, Hanford Knapp.

Wit.: Fred. Herb, John Murchison, Jacob Chadburn.

John Christopher Gugel, born March 5, 1757; died Dec. 2, 1819; married Mary Schubtrein, who was born March 26, 1760; died Nov 2, 1827, had:

Mary, born Sept. 6, 1783; married Solomon Creamer.

Salome, born Oct. 17, 1875; died Sept. 8, 1862; married (1) Lewis Cooper; (2) William Groover.

Lydia, born May 2, 1789; married Ephraim, brother of Lewis Cooper.

*Sophia, born Jan. 9, 1793; married Israel Weitman in 1820, and died Jan. 30, 1864.

Naomi, born Jna. 9, 1793; died Dec. 16, 1794.

Naomi (2nd), born Oct. 27, 1795; married (1) Patrick Stanton; (2) Math. Weitman.

Christian, born and died Feb. 25, 1788.

John, born Feb. 2, 1792; died May 2, 1792.

Catherine, born Sept. 7, 1798; died Nov. 11, 1798.

Susannah, born March 5, 1800; died Oct. 12, 1800.

Rosannah, born July 11, 1801; died Oct. 12, 1801.

*Israel Weitman and wife Sophia, and John Ihly and wife Mary Ann were "joint heirs" in 1823.

The will of Mary (Schubtrein) Gugel is on file Savannah C. H., Sept. 25, 1825; mentions grand daughter Rosannah Creamer.

In 1791 the wife of John Millen was "Rosannah."

(a) Hannah Elizabeth Gugel married Nicholas Michel, Jan. 28, 1772.

Harriet Gugel married John J. Dews, April 29. 1828.

Christian, son of Johannes (John) Gugel, married Frances Hubbard. They had William H., and Benjamin who died in 1812. There was also a son Daniel, who is mentioned in will of Daniel Gugel.

Frances Hubbard was the only child of John and Catherine Hubbard. Frances married (2) Henry Hope, June 6, 1815; she married a William Boyd also.

Mrs. Catherine Hubbard's marriage settlement with Benjamin Webly is of date Sept. 13, 1800. In 1809, Dec. 9th, she married James Clark. Savannah Record Room, Book "X," p. 305, and Book CC, p. 355.

Benjamin Webly, gentleman, had married Mary, the widow of Edmund Wiggins, Feb. 11, 1791. (Book "A," p. 528.)

Book "M," p. 228; Feb. 13, 1794. Benjamin Webly in trust to James Bowen, for his daughter, Elizabeth Mary Webly.

Patrick Stanton, born March 14, 1788; died July 16, 1820; married (1) Naomi Gugel, March 13, 1817; she died Jan. 25, 1879, had:

John Harvey Stanton, born and died Oct. 5, 1817.

Patrick Stanton, Jr., born Sept. 13, 1820; married April 23, 1850 to Jane Eliza Gnann, born March 29, 1827; died Oct. 26, 1835.

Naomi (Gugel) Stanton married (2) Mathew Weitman Nov. 19, 1829, had:

John Lewis Weitman, born Oct. 4, 1830; died Dec. 8, 1859.

Patrick H. Stanton and wife Jane Eliza Gnann, had:

Naomi Stanton, born June 22, 1851; married Thomas L. Wyly, Oct. 17, 1883.

†Charles Everett Stanton, born Jan 2, 1853; married Susie May St. John, born Jan. 20, 1860.

Mary Ella Stanton, born Oct. 22, 1855; died Oct. 26, 1860.

Walter Curran Stanton, born Dec. 8, 1857; died July 8, 1859.

Henry Kolloch Stanton, born Dec. 30, 1860; died May 12, 1877.

George Haltiwonger Stanton, born Aug 5, 1862; died April 2, 1868.

Sophia Gugel married Nov. 30, 1820 to Israel Weitman, born April 1, 1792 and died Dec. 23, 1848. She died Jan. 30, 1864, had:

Elbert Weitman, born Sept. 7, 1821; married (1) C. J. Arnstoph; (2) Hannah Reiser.

Lavinia Weitman, born May 5, 1823; died Feb. 28, 1825.

Joseph Marion Weitman, born Nov. 14, 1825; died March 4, 1857.

Amanda Louise Weitman, born Oct. 25, 1827; married Jacob L. Freyermouth, Oct. 10, 1853.

Mary Gugel Weitman, born June 5, 1830; married Cletus Rahn, July 29, 1852.

Ann Salome Weitman, born June 5, 1830; died Sept. 2, 1835.

(a) Mathew Weitman, born Nov. 39, 1763 (son of Lewis Weitman and wife Eva) was dead in 1806, leaving a widow Mary, son Nathaniel and daughter Margaret.

†Susie May St. John was the daughter of George A. St. John (of New York), and his wife Laura Eugenia Wyly, who died Dec. 26, 1862.

Salome Gugel married (1) Lewis Cooper, had:

Sarah Lewis Cooper married Frederick Roesburg Wyly, Dec. 31, 1834. He died June 16, 1872, age 62.

Frederick R. Wyly and Sarah Lewis (Cooper), had:

Harriette Wyly, born Spet. 7, 1835; married Joseph A. Rahn, Jan. 3, 1861.

Laura Eugenia Wyly, born July 20, 1837; marred George A. St. John, April 15, 1859.

William Bainbridge Wyly, born June 1, 1839; died Jan. 25, 1881.

Sarah Naomi Wyly, born July 22, 1841; married Patrick H. Mallette, April 30, 1868, who died July 25, 1871.

Mary M. Wyly, born Jan. 5, 1844; married George B. Clark, June 7, 1866.

Thomas Leonidas Wyly, born Oct. 18, 1846; married Naomi Stanton, Oct. 17, 1883.

Catherine Ann Wyly, born Aug. 3, 1849; married Henry W. Butler, Nov. 5, 1873.

(For other Wyly records see "King.")

These valuable records are from the Stanton Family Bible, the property of Mrs. Thomas L. Wyly, through whose courtesy they were obtained.

Goldwire. The following marriage records on file in Effingham Co., with some court records, form the basis of the Goldwire data, supplemented by a memorandum furnished by Mrs. Agnes Obedience Boyd, a daughter of John Wire Goldwire and wife, Frances Offutt.

There are records in other branches of this family which do not co-ordinate in every detail with these records, but such discrepancies may arise from the many repetitions of names, intermarriages, and mistakes in copying.

From Colonial Records of Georgia (Candler), we find these entries:

Vol. 25, pp. 320-1: That in 1748 John Goldwire and his youngest brother Benjamin were residents of Augusta, having formerly lived in Savannah, etc.

In 1756—"John had wife and four children; Benjamin had wife and five children."

From the same authority it is found that John married a widow (her two former husbands being Mr. Polhill and Mr. Betford.)

Her name "Sarah" is found in an old book in which she has recorded the dates of some of her children.

The will of John Goldwire is on file in Atlanta, which was proved March 8, 1775. In his will he refers to "Ann Goldwire, widow of Savannah, and her children: Ann, Benjamin, Mary Morel, Amey McGilvary, Joseph and John." (Bro. Benj. had died in 1769.)

John Goldwire and wife Sarah, had:

Sarah Goldwire, born Savannah, Ga., Feb. 6, 1741; married William King. (See King.")

(Rev.) John Goldwire, born Dalocholas, S. C., Oct. 7, 1774; married Elizabeth Motte.

James Goldwire, born Augusta, Ga., April 15,1747; married Sarah Stuart.

Rev. John Goldwire married Elizabeth Moote (or Moore), Nov. 8, 1769. There were no children, but adopted Ann Abigal Scruggs. She married (1) James Greenhow, a British merchant, and had two children, James Goldwire Greenhow and Jackson Mason Greenhow. She married (2) William Wilson of Savannah, also an English merchant; and (3) Mr. Brigges, an Englishman. The marriage of Abigail Scruggs to James Greenhow was March 12, 1794.

Rev. Mr. Goldwire died 1792, and his estate was left to James King, youngest child of his sister Sarah King. John Wire Goldwire was Exrc.

James Goldwire married Sarah Stuart, Aug. 18, 1772, had:

Sarah Goldwire, born May 19, 1773. Married John Tison. (See "Our Family Circle" by Mrs. A. E. Miller.)

James Little Goldwire, born May 25, 1775; married Sarah Grace King (cousin) ; died 1851.

John (Wire) Goldwire, born Sept. 1779; married Mar. 9, 1809 Frances Offutt, born 1787. (See Offutt.)

The will of James Goldwire (in Augusta) dated March 10, 1780— proved by Charles Stuart, March 16, 1781, mentions James Little Goldwire as "oldest son," and "youngest son John." He was killed at Beach Island, 1780. See McCall's Hist. of Ga., p. 488.

James Little Goldwire and wife Sarah Grace (King), had:
Sarah.

Mariah, married James Offutt Goldwire, March 6, 1833. (Had Sarah, John, Maria).

Caroline, married George King, son of John and Jane King, Feb. 15, 1821. No chil.

John Wire Goldwire married Frances Offutt, March 9, 1809. Had:
Henrietta O., born Jan. 20, 1810; married James M. Anthony, Nov. 25, 1851.

James Offutt Goldwire, born Nov. 19, 1811; married Mariah Goldwire (cousin).

Edwin Baker Goldwire, born June 12, 1813.

John Wise Goldwire, born Nov. 29, 1814.

Frances Victoria and Amanda Viola, born Feb. 12, 1816.

Rebecca Jane, born March 7, 1820; married Thomas Boston.

Obedience Agnes, born Nov. 21, 1821; married (1) Middeton Saxon; (2) Jefferson Boyd.

William Henry Goldwire, born Aug. 1, 1825; married Mary Ann Saxon, born Nov. 20.

Mary Ann Goldwire, born Nov. 20, 1826.

Joseph John, and Mary Ann.

John Wire Goldwire died 1830, and his wife Frances died 1833.

James O. Goldwire who married Mariah Glodwire, had: Sarah. John and Mariah.

Offutt. Dr. William Offutt married Letitia Harris; (children now known):

Anne, married Hampton Lillibridge (had daughter Henrietta).

Cassandra, married James McIntosh.

Ezekiel, married Jamima Wilkins.

Jesse, married Obedience Jones.

Henrietta Lillibridge's marriage settlement with James, son of John and Jane (Hudson) Bilbo, dated March 14, 1812, in which she refers to her "beloved uncle, Jesse Offutt of Columbia Co." Wit.: Joseph Grant, Sarah King, Ann Courtney. (Savannah Record Room).

From C. H. in Columbia Co., records are found of the marriage of William Pearre to Aggy (Agnes) Offutt, and of his brother Nathaniel Pearre to Rebecca Offutt. No dates. In 1793 there is a deed of a Nathaniel Pearre and wife Anner.

The Offutts were originally from Maryland, and intermarried with the Harris Family of that state.

Marriages:

Groves, Allen, to Mary Lanier, June 27, 1769.

Garnet, Thomas, to Rachel Wilson, "By license from His Honor the Commander," Jan. 8, 1772.

Goldwire, James, to Sarah Stewart, Aug 18, 1772.

Grumbler, Valentine, to Elizabeth Tulpher (?), March 8, 1773.

Gruver, Solomon, to Hannah Elizabeth Powledge, Oct. 7, 1791.

Grovenstein, John, to Sarah Ziegler, April 30, 1793.

Greenhow, James, to Abigail Scruggs, March 12, 1794; (a) James Greenhow married Hannah, dau. of John Stirk, and Hannah, the widow of John Stirk married James Holton.

Garrison, James, to Martha Dykes, July 4, 1794.

Garnet, John, to Mary Bostwick, July 30, 1794.

Gachet, Charles, to Mary Robert, Feb. 9, 1795.

Griffien, Walden, to Esther Rawlinson, June 20, 1795. He was dead in 1803.

Grabenstein, John, to Mrs. Ann Catherine Hangleiter, Nov. 8, 1796. (Benj. Grovenstein's first wife was Thursa Morel.)

Grabenstein, Henry Lewis, to Mrs. Judith Busche, Oct. 19, 1797. (See Bushe.) (He married Hannah, dau. of Benj. and Elizabeth Dasher.)

Gruver, David, to Hannah Sherouse, Oct. 13, 1798. He was dead in 1803.

Guttery, James, to Elizabeth (Liddy) Jenkins, July 26, 1799.

Gnann, Timothy, to Catherine Limberger, Nov. 6, 1799.

Grabenstein, John, to Mary, dau. of Israel Reiser and Hannah Margaret Shuptrine, April 25, 1800. Hannah Margaret, dau. of Joseph Shuptrine and Mary Brandner, dau. of Mathews.

Gibson, James, to Mrs. Sarah Parker of Chatham Co., Aug. 9, 1802.

Gooldsbie, Charles, to Mrs. Abigail Gooldsbie, March 9, 1804.

Gibson, James, to Elizabeth Denny, Nov. 7, 1806.

Greiner, Andrew, to Ann Gnann, Oct. 1, 1807.

Geyer, William Ernst, to Elizabeth Helmly, June 10, 1808.

Gnann, Solomon, to Sarah Mary Heidt, Dec. 15, 1812.
Gnann, Jacob, to Mrs. Christine Metzger, nee Rahn, Dec. 15, 1812.

Godley, Nathan, to Mary Martha Ryall, Sept. 13, 1821.

Greene, William Henry, to Elizabeth King, Nov. 16, 1821.

Garrison, David, to Mary Gilbert, Oct. 21, 1822.

Griffin, John C., to Frances Ann Ball or Bell, Oct. 31, 1823.

Gnobly, John, to Julia Hinely, by Rev. Abiel Carter, rector of Christ Church, July 28, 1824.

Gnann, Joshua, to Mary Zeigler, Dec. 2, 1824.

Glaner, George, to Mrs. Margaret D. Spencer, Feb. 2, 1826.

Gnann, Solomon, Jr., to Margaret Fetzger, Feb. 1, 1827.
Gnann, Benjamin, to Salome Rahn, Nov. 27, 1827.

Grouver, Joshua, to Sarah Snider, March 7, 1829.
Grouver, Elias, to Susannah Reiser, May 22, 1829.

Gnann, Jonathan, to Maria Metzger, May 11, 1830.

Griner, Caleb, to Sarah Shuptrine, dau. of Israel Shuptrine and Mary Eula Heidt, Feb. 16, 1832.

Gnann, Benj., to Mrs. Hannah Christie, Jan. 14, 1833.
Gnann, John W., to Ann Brewer, Jan. 25, 1835.

Griffin, Franklin, to Prudence Willis, July 4, 1836.

Grovenstein, Lewis, to Kesiah Ellen, dau. of James and Elizabeth Wilson, June 14, 1838. Married second Miss Morel, dau of Benj. and Susannah (Gindrat) Morel.

Gnann, Joshua, to Susannah Hinely, Nov. 26, 1847.
Gnann, Geo. B., to Rebecca Dasher, Dec. 16, 1847.

Grover, John D., to Elvra C. Davis, Dec. 20, 1848.

Grovenstein, Geo W., to Cornelie Metzger, March 1, 1849.

Gnann, Christopher, to Elizabeth Fetzger, Sept. 23, 1835. (He was bro. of Lewis Gnann.)
Gnann, John Benj., to Elizabeth Morgan, Feb. 1, 1840.

Griner, Joshua, to Eleanor Wilson, Feb. 13, 1841.

Grouver, Elias, to Susannah Snider (2nd wife), Oct .17. 1846.
Grouver, John D., to Elvira C. Davis, Dec. 20, 1848.

Graham, Jesse, to Margaret A. Walker, July 22, 1848.

Grovenstein, Geo. W., to Cornelia M. Metzger, Feb. 6, 1850 (date of license.)

Guyer (or Gier.) 1812—Nov. 29—Will of Elizabeth Guyer (or Gier). Son William Ernst Geyer, deceased daughter Dorothy, wife of John Winter. Grandchild Anna Winter.

1821—Elizabeth Guyer takes child's part in estate of her husband, Frederick Guyer. His will in 1818-1821 is signed George Frederick Guyer, "at present of Savannah." (No date of probate.)

1812—Nov. 20—Milledgeville, Ga. Edwin Baker testifies that in this year he was at the house of Jacob Darden in Warren Co., and assisted in laying out a Mr. Solomon Griner, a tailor.

Geiger. 1789—Land surveyed for Felix and Abraham Geiger.

177_—The grant of Christian Geiger was made over to his wife Sibilla and only heir. In March, 1789, she was the wife of Jacob Mohr.

Gaskins. 1799—Nov. 14—Will of Rosannah (or Susannah) Gaskins of Parish of St. Peter in Beaufort Dist., S. C. Son Amos. Son William to be guardian to my grandchildren: John Harril Gaskins, Waight Harril Gaskins. Daughter Rosannah (or Susannah). Daughter Elizabeth Williams. Exrs.: son William. Michael Mixon, and Howard Wall. Wit.: Grimball Robert, Thos. S. Chesher.

Griner. 1811—Dec.—Will of Hannah Griner. Sons: Solomon, Andrew and John Godliph. Grand daughter Sophia Griner. Exrs. David Nowlan and George Nowlan.

Gruber. Chas., S. C., Jan. 3, 1779-Aug. 30, 1780—Will of Christian Gruber, wife Mary. Children: Christian, John Samuel, Daniel. Exrs.: Wife, John Wagner (?), Chas. Gruber.

Hines. 1791—David Hines to grand daughter Susannah Grant: a negro slave named Harbred.

1796—James and Drusilla Hines to son-in-law Peter Grant: 231 acres, part of a grant to James Hines. (April 2).

1801—Sharrod Hines of Pitt Co., N. C. appoints Edmund Dupree of Pitt Co., as his atty. in re estate of David Hines of Effingham Co., Ga., to recover from Hannah Hines, a negro "Mingo," deeded him by Richard Proctor. Attested by Gov. Benjamin Williams of N. C. (Sharrod Hines "eldest son of David Hines").

1820—Aug. 7. Will of Hannah Hines. Sons: Sherrod, Howell and his son Thomas R.

Dau. Tempe Wolfe and her son David Wolfe.

Dau. Cynthia Garrison and her son Richard Garrison.

Dau. Winny Tison and her oldest daughter Antoinette Tison.

Daus. Nancy Womack and Mary Lemler.

1812—Howell Hines and wife Margaret (Mrs. West) deed to Philip Jones, David Hines, J. P.

1813—Elijah Lewis and wife Sally (Hines) to David Hines, Sr. Wit: Jesse Hines.

1814—Deed from Charlton Hines, James E. Hines, William Lewis Hines and Allen Hines, to Abner Ross (wife Elizabeth) and Oliver Martin Littlebridge, in re est. of Drusilla Hines.

1828, Nov. 7—Solomon Shad of S. C. Deed to Howell Hines.

1799, April 28—Will of James Hines, wife Drusilla. Sons: Charlton, James, William Lewis, Allen, David.

Daughters: Sarah, wife of Elijah Lewis, and Susannah Hines. Estate appraised by Darius Garrison, Howell Hines, John Moore.

(Drusilla was *apparently* the dau. of Samuel Lewis of Va.)

(Howell Hines' first wife was "Martha". In 1817 he married Mrs. Margaret West, who *appears* to have been the sister of Capt. James Wilson. Eliza Hines, dau. of first wife, married 1829 to Dr. Josiah Wilson of Liberty Co., Ga.

1793—Estate of David Hines adm. by James Hines.

1814, June 26—William Hines to Elizabeth Williams (or Wilson).

1811—Nancy, widow of David Hines.

Howell. 1785—Daniel Howell had grant of 287½ acres; and a second grant the same day on Little Ogeechee.

His daughter America, born 1814; married Robert Peacock (born 1792 in Wayne Co., N. C.) son of Simon Peacock, who came to Georgia 1817.

1792—Caleb Howell, Sr., dec'd. Caleb, Jr., receipts for his share and transfers some property to Wm. Pearce. Wit: Daniel Howell.

Hall. Rev. Wm. Foote says that Hall Co., Ga., was named for Rev. James Hall of Iredell Co., N. C,, a chaplain in the Revolutionary War. White's Statistic's claim that the name was given in honor of Gov. Lyman Hall.

Although Gov. Lyman Hall left no descendants, his only son, John, dying early, yet there are records of the collateral branches which are of interest. The will of Mrs. Mary Hall, his widow, Oct. 10, 1790, (Savannah, Ga.) says she was of "Bourke Co.", her heirs being her brother Daniel Osburn, and sister Abigail Wyncoop, heirs of Thadeeus Osburn, late of Fairfield, Conn.

Lyman Hall had a brother Street Hall, and a sister Hannah Hall. Elnathan Street, of Wallingford, Conn., claims interest in estate of Mrs. Hall in right of his late wife Susannah Hall, and he is appointed atty. for the heirs, with Wm. Stephens, Charles Odingsells and Joseph Watts, Esq. Wit.: Joseph Noyes, Lewis Bun Sturges, Eliakim Hall, Russel Barker, James Wyncoop. (Book AA, Savannah Record Room.)

As early as 1770 there was a Nathaniel Hall in Effingham Co., where he receives deeds from John Ford and wife Mary.

1786—Deed of John Hall and wife Sarah, a grant from King George 1765, to John Hall. Wit: Nathaniel Hall.

1799—"Nathaniel Hall of East Florida, formerly of Effingham Co."

The will of Nathaniel Hall is recorded in Savannah C. H. under dates of 1805-1807. "Nassau, New Providence, Bahama Islands: Nathaniel Hall, formerly of East Florida." Wife Ann; sister Sarah Powell; brother Joseph Hall; nephews George Webb Hall and Samuel Hall of Bristol.

Savannah C. H. Will of Ann Hall, widow of Nathaniel Hall, Esqr. 1817. Friends Alexander Martin Edwards, William Martin and William Webb of Bahama. John McQueen and George Jones of the state of Georgia. Sister Hannah McAllister, mother of Mathew Hall McAllister and Harriett A. McAllister. To Rebecca Holmes, an orphan in my care.

Fayetteville, N. C.: 1793—Silvey Hall, adm. estate of John Hall. Am. Archives: Cath. Hall, heir of John Floyd who d. 1821, and lived 20 miles from St. Augustine since 1799 (alias Jose Juaneda).

Scattering "Hall" Notes:

1812—Mary, wife of Thomas Hall of Savannah, was the widow of Jacob Florsheim.

———Capt. William Hall married Miss Poyas.

———Dr. Charles Hall married Miss Sarah Kenan of Sapelo Island.

1778—Durham Hall married Frances Hicks in Brunswick Co., Va. D. Wake Co., N. C.

1773, July 6—Charles Hall married Ally Dupuis. (Effingham Co.)

1806, May 30—Nathaniel Hall married Mary Pace. (Effingham Co.)

———"Samuel Hall, son of Rev. James Hall of N. C. married Martha McCreary".

1843, Nov. 3—Geo. Hall married Grace Crawford.
1803, July 29—Will of William Lister Hall. All to George Galpin Nowlan. Excr.: William J. Spencer, of Savannah, Ga. Will recorded in Suffolk Co., N. Y., Nicol Floyd, surrogate. Wit: Moses Clark, William J. Bryson, John N. Fordham. (Sagg Harbor).

Effingham Co.—1786—John Hall, wife Sarah (on deeds)

Jackson Co., Ga.: John Williams had dau. *Sarah* who m (1) Nathan Hall, one son; (2) Benj. Stockton, daus: Eliz., Adeline, Patsy, Thirsa, etc.

Nath. Hall's exr. was wife Sarah, & Robert Williams was to be brought up on the estate. He married (an) Ann Hall.

1821 Sarah and Robert give 12 acres to Daniel Lester and Shephard Williams was witness. A negro "Charlotte" was sold to Samuel Williams & Robert rec'd $125.00 as "his part."

1778—Nath. Hall of Christ Ch. Par., Ga. & John Stafford of Greenville Co., S. C., planter, & wife Susannah, a tract bounded by lands of John Peter Pury, now called Oglethorpe's land. Fireproof Building, Chas. S. C. Book W, p 445.

Heidt. Book O, p. 9—Abel Heidt's (son of George), first wife was Lydia Shearouse, daughter of John Shearouse and wife Mary, who was a daughter of Jacob Maurer, whose son Gotlieb Maurer had a daughter Hannah who married John Edwards. Abel married Mrs. Agnes Allen, May 7, 1816.

Heist. 1775—Dec. 18—Will of Math. (or Nath.) Heist. Wife Mary Magdalene. Daughter Christina and "other daughters." Exr.: Rev. Christian Rabenhorst. Wit.: Henry Treutlen, John Keebler, Christian Griner.

Hodges. 1779—Aug. 19—Will of Elias Hodges of Granville Co,. S. C. To cousin Drury Hodges. Wife Mary. Brother Robert Hodges. Wit.: Elizabeth Hudson, Thomas Daniel, John Daniel.

Hardeman. 1791—Estate of Thomas Hardeman adm. by John Woolf, John Lowe, John Wright.

Hunold. 1796—Estate of John Hunold ——.

Helmly. 1802—Oct. 29—Will of Nicholas Helmly. Wife Maria Magdalena. Children: David, Joshua and Elizabeth. Wit.: John Kogler, Ernst Zitteraurer.

Heidt. 1806—March 20—Will of Mary Elizabeth Heidt of St. Peter's Parish, S. C. Daughter Elizabeth Christian Myerhoff and Jacob Holbrook "and such other children as I might have." Exr.: Uncle Godlip Smith of Georgia. Wit.: Hezekiah Winkler, John Burgomaster, Nicholas Winkler.

Hester. 1856—Will of Edith Hester, widow of Stephen Hester. To sister Ann Williams, to Tempe Davis, to Frederick Womack, ward of former husband Stephen Hester.

Marriage Record in Effingham County:

Hester, Stephen, to Mrs. Hannah E. Heidt, April 3, 1850.

Hodges, Israel, to Flora Graham, Dec. 11, 1840.

Hodges. 1790—Wife of John Hodges was Tabby.

Hodges, Samuel, to Margaret Ann Graham, Aug. 20, 1840.

Hodges. 1798—Wife of Benj. Hodges was Letitia.

Hodges, William, to Martha Colson, April 5, 1833.

Helvenstine. Effingham Co. Will of Jacob Helvenstine. "All to honored father." 1773-02.

1774-1802—Will of John Helvenstine. To honored father, brothers Jacob and Daniel, sister Hannah.

1793, April 5—Will of Frederick Helvenstine, wife Blandina; sons, Jacob Daniel, Joshua, Joseph; daughters, Hannah, Mary Magdalen, Mary Christina. Wit: Vield Lochner, Christoph. Cramer, John Gnann.

1804, Aug. 29—Will of Blandina Magdalena Helvenstine; son Joseph; daughter Mary Magdalen Gromet; grand-daughter Mary Susannah Fosby. Mentions grants from George 1st, and George 2nd to Balthazer Reiser, Jacob Helvenstine in 1772, and to Daniel Bergsteiner in 1757.

Marriages in Effingham County:

Joseph Helvenstine to Sarah Fresh, June 6, 1792.

Joseph Helvenstine to Sarah Read, Jan. 23, 1804.

J. J. Helvenstine to Margaret Tiner, Jan. 3, 1814.

John Helvenstine to Esther, daughter of Israel Floerl, Jan. 2, 1822.

Joseph Helvenstine to Mrs. Rosannah Cope, Nov. 8, 1828.

Mary Helvenstine to John Palmer, Nov. 9, 1830.

Effingham Co.: It is ordered that the Clerk appropriate the sum of one hundred dollars, not exceeding that, for the entertainment of General LaFayette in passing through the county of Effingham.

> HOWELL HINES,
> C. DASHER,
> JOHN WALDHAUER,
> JOHN C. HELVENSTINE.

Herb. Frederick Herb was born Feb. 4, 1728, and died Oct. 26, 1790. The adm. of his estate is recorded in Book D. D., Record Room, Savannah, Ga. His son Frederick Herb was adm. and the widow was Ursula, "of the sea island." Son John Herb was then deceased (in 1810), and his widow was Catherine. Daughter Catherine was the wife of Rev. John Ernest Bergman; daughter *Mary was the wife of Moses Cleland, and daughter Rebecca was the wife of Slaughter Cowling. Wit: C. Gugel and George Harral.

In the above administration no mention is made of the son George Herb, whose will is in the C. H. in Savannah, probated in 1823. His wife was Ann Mary, and reference is made to his brothers John and Frederick Herb, and to his sisters Mary Cleland, Rebecca Cowling and Catherine Bergman

In 1785 the heirs of Christopher Peters of Savannah, were:

Frederick Herb and wife Ursula;

Walter Coleman and wife Elizabeth;

Miss Ann Peters.

Ursula (Peters) Herb was born Oct. 28, 1741, and died Nov. 9, 1814.

*Moses Cleland died Aug. 18, 1834. His wife Mary (Herb) who was born 1774; died July 24, 1846.

Herson. It is difficult, often, to establish certain facts in genealogy, even by documentary evidence, for family names vary in their usage, or spelling, in different branches. This difficulty is met in regard to the name of the wife of Herman Herson. In his will she is called "Joannah Christina", scarcely recognizable as "Hannah", the daughterf of John Casper Wertch, but this conclusion seems justified in a deed by Herman Hersen, in which he says, "my wife Joannah, daughter and only heir ofJohn Casper Wertch." Hannah was born in 1770, and her father died in 1779, and as Pastor C. F. Triebner had married a sister of Wertch's first wife (Miss Gronau), this may explain why "Nana Wertch" was with the Tory minister when he fled to St. Augustine. However she returned to Effingham Co., and (it seems) married, quite young, a Mr. Ernst, and had a son Gotlip Ernst, to whom Herman Herson refers to as his "loving step-son".

Herman Herson left no children, but he was an outstanding man of this time, and by some authority, was said to have been a nephew of Rev. Herman Lemcke. He had grants in 1769 in St. Philips Parish on the Ogeechee. In 1785 he bids in the confiscated estates of Josiah Tatnall.

1793—Herman Herson and wife Joannah, with Daniel Weitman and wife Mary Frederica (former wife was Salome Lemcky), sell land which was granted to John Grover in 1756, and transferred to Rev. Herman Lemcke in 1764.

In 1791, Herman Herson pays to Hannah Gugel a legacy of 25 guineas, left to her by Mrs. Casper Wertch, who was Eliz. Koegler, whose will was adm. by Rev. C. F. Triebner, who had left Ebenezer, and Herman Herson had been appointed adm. in his place.

Hannah Gugel was the daughter of John Gugel, and the relationship, if any, does not now appear. (She receipts for this legacy as "the widow of Christian Dasher."

The will of Herman Herson, ship carpenter, was probated in Chatham Co., 1793, and various administrations up to 1815 by: John Wisenbaker, Charles Ulmer, Jeremiah Cuyler, C F. Triebner, John Herb.

"Wife Joannah Christiana, exr., with John Wisenbaker and John Herb. Wit: John Y. White, Christ. F. Triebner, Joseph Welscher.

Legatees: children of John Wisenbaker; Mathias Wisenbaker, and Jacob Wisenbaker; children of brother Henry Herson in Oldenburg, Germany; half brother Claus Jacobs, and sister Margaretta Dershon.

(Much more in re this will may be found in Book Y, p 509, dealing with the heirs in Germany. Savannah Record Room.)

The children of John, Mathias and Jacob Wisenbaker were:

John and Christian, children of John who died 1803; guardian Chris Dasher.

Jacob left two daughters, Ann Mary and Margaret. Their mother was Hannah Lemcke.

The chlidren of Mathias Wisenbaker were: Mathias, Jr., Mary, Sophia, Elizabeth, John Herman, Lucy, George Herman, Catherine. Savannah Record Room, Book Q. pp 248-301.

1804, Aug. 15—Mathias Wisenbaker, formerly of Savannah, now of New London, Conn., appoints Christopher F. Triebner his atty. for children's part of Herman Herson's estate. April, 1819, Lucy Wisenbaker of New London appoints atty. to secure her part.

Gotlib Ernst is not mentioned in will of Herman Herson, but his deed of gift to "loving step-son Gotlib Ernst," establishes his relationship, which is again in evidence in 1798, when he and his wife Catherine Fields, with Daniel Weitman, who had married Salome, the daughter of Rev. Mr. Lemcke, are "heirs of Mr. Lemcke."

Harvey. Prior to 1787, John Harvey had bequeathed to his daughter (John (sic) and daughter Ann, and their husbands Col. Huston and William Ashmead.

Hollinger. 1805—Martha Hollinger of Screven Co., widow of Titus Hollnger of Richmond Co.

Holloman. 1790—Ann Holloman to son in law John Peterson (or Paterson). Wit.: Nancy Holloman.

Horrocks. 1825—Aug. 3—Will of Catherine Horrocks. To sister Sophia Densler of Savannah, a tenement in Washington Ward on lot belonging to estate of late Mr. John Roberts. To sister Susannah, wife of James Watson. "If I should draw a lot in contemplated Lottery." Exr.: John Charlton. Wit.: David Gugel, Joshua Keebler, Elizabeth Charlton. (John Haupt appraised goods and chattels in above estate in 1825.)

Hoffman. 1791—Jacob Hoffman and wife Mary to daughter Hannah E. Dolwich. (Jacob was a son of Daniel Hoffman.)

Horton. 1789—Moses Horton wit. to deed.

Haberer. 1771—Feb. 8—Michael Haberer for "natural love & affection to Eva Weitman, widow."

Hughes. 1806—Robert H. Hughes deed to children: Bob, Michael, Richardson, Robert Henry Utz, Mary Richardson Hughes, Carter. Land in Hanover Co., Va., about seventeen miles from Richmond; also 4,444 acres in South Carolina in Lawrence (Laurens ?) and Union Counties, on Enoree and Dinkins Creek, adjoining lands of Dru Ross, Esqr., Montgomery and James Dileet and the widow Jones. (The wife of Robert H Hughes was Chloe.) (John D. Hughes married Kesiah Wilson, Feb. 12, 1838..

Hensler. 1802—Jacob Hensler to daughter Hannah. (His wife was Hannah also.)

Holzendorf. Charleston, S. C. Will of Dr. Frederick Holzendorf, Jan. 9, 1754-May 1, 1764. Wife, Rosina (daughter of Christian L. Dasher). Sons: Charles Frederick Holzendorf, Earnest Frederick Holzendorf, Albrough Frederick Holzendorf, Charles William Frederick Holzendorf, John Frederick Holzendorf. Daughters: Rosina, Louisa, Elizabeth. Wit.: Chas. Foucherand, Francis Postell, John Toulee.

Grants in S. C.: To Capt. John Frederick and Frederick Holzendorf in Purysburg. (1737).

Frederick Holzendorf married Mary Ann Miller, July 26, 1758. (Prince Frederick Parish Register.)

June 6, 1768—James Charles Frederick Holzendorf and wife Ann Mary, land lease to Clemens Keller, tract in Amelia Township.

1774—Joseph Strable (Strobel ?) and wife Mary Ann, deed tract in Amelia Township to Clement Keller.

1774—William Holzendorf and wife Mary to John Frederick Holzendorf tavern keeper of Purysburg, ½ of 200 acres, grant to late Capt. John F. Holzendorf. Wit.: John Lewis Bourquin, Esqr., J. P., of Beaufort Dist. (Book P, p. 416. Mesne Office, Chas., S. C.)

Lancaster, S. C.: John Holzendorf of Camden, planter, wife Elizabeth, deed lot in the village of Camden to Henry Rugsley. May 1, 1789.

1774—April 1—John Holzendorf married Elizabeth Erhardt. (Effingham Co.)

Frederick Holzendorf had a daughter Mary Rose, born 1763. (Family Rec.)

1793— —— Holzendorf, wife Sarah and daughter Sarah. (In deed.)

1804—Deed of William Holzendorf of Darien, McIntosh Co., to Richard M. Williams of Savannah. Wit.: John L. K. Holzendorf, Gardner Tufts.

Marriages:

Heckel, Christian, to Mrs. Ann Thornsbie, April 30, 1801.

Hurst, William, to Rosannah Blackington, Aug. 17, 1801.
Hurst, Jesse, to Mary Hodges, Sept. 20, 1802.

Hawthorne, William, to Elizabeth Canada (Kennedy ?), June 2, 1805.

Holliday, Joseph, to Cynthia Hines, Sept. 2, 1805.

Heidt, Christian, to Elizabeth Pepper, July 22, 1806.

Hester, Edmund, to Idy Lanier, Sept. 9, 1806.

Hartshorn, Peter, to Margaret Cook, Oct. 6, 1806.

Hinely, Israel, to Hannah Heisler, Nov. 23, 1807.

Hurst, John, of Burke Co., to Elizabeth Blitch, Jan. 22, 1808.

Haines, William, to Elizabeth Wilson, June 26, 1811.

Helmly, Joshua, to Salome Seckinger, April 23, 1811.

Hinely, Solomon, to Elizabeth Bruckenback, Jan. 17, 1812.

Heidt, Israel, to Catherine Nettles, Nov. 13, 1815.
Heidt, Mathew, to Hannah Weitman, Nov. 17, 1815.

Hitchcock, Joseph, to Martha Crawford, Jan. 29, 1817.

Harmes, John, to Margaret Bird, Dec. 28, 1819. Wm. Bird Security.

Heidt, Christian Israel, to Elizabeth Martin, March 30, 1820.

Hinely, John, to Dorothy Weitman, Dec. 3, 1821.

Hurst, William, to Mary Blitch, June 2, 1821.

Heidt, John G., son of George, to Ann Cath., dau. of **John Chris.** Miller, Dec. 3, 1821.

Hinely, Solomon, to Hannah Elizabeth Arnsdorf, April 7, 1825.

Horning, Philip, to Gracey Weitman, June 3, 1825.

Helmly, David, to Mary Ann Hinely, Feb. 19, 1826.

Heidt, Samuel (son of George), to Elizabeth Ann Elkins, April 16, 1827; (2) Mary Dugger, Oct. 18, 1844; (3) Parmelia Futrell, Sept. 9, 1856.

Hurst, James, to Ann Wilson, Dec. 31, 1827.
Hurst, Jesse, and wife Madlen, 1796.

Harriott, James, and wife Mary of Savannah, 1780.

Harrison, Joseph, and wife Sarah (Pearce), 1788.

Hangleiter, and wife Catherine (Weidman), 1796.

Howell, John, Master of revenue cutter Eagle, wife **Catherine,** 1794.

Holliday, Joseph, left a widow Ferny, 1800.
Holliday, Joseph, and wife Mary, 1806.
Holliday, Milner, and wife Elizabeth, 1806.

Henderson, Zachariah, and wife Elizabeth, 1802.

Hinely, Jacob, and wife Elizabeth, 1805.

Hendly, George, of Savannah, and wife Mary, 1803.

Holliday, Christian Israel, and wife Elizabeth, 1804.

Hill, Charles, and wife Area, 1811.
Hill, Benjamin, and wife Jean, 1816.

Hunter, William, left widow Margaret (Hurst), 1818.

Haid, Johan George, to Eleanora Kurtz, March 3, 1754.

Holliday, James, to Catherine Gaskins, March 7, 1768.

Harper, Shadrack, to Sarah Farmer, March 7, 1773. She was bap-
March 5, age 16.

Heidt, George, to Sally Remshart, July 2, 1795. (10 chil., all married.)

Heck, John, to Agnes Powledge, Aug. 29, 1795.

Hudson, Christopher, to Hannah ——, March 6, 1798.

Holton, James, to Mrs. Hannah (Greenhow) Stirk, March 21, 1798.

Hinely, Jacob, to Elizabeth Mick, Jan. 16, 1799.

Helmly, David, to Dorothy, dau. of John Shearouse, Oct. 29, 1800.

Hill, Green, to Cherry Bridges, Oct. 11, 1799.

Howard, Samuel, of Chatham Co., to Esther S. Maxwell of Bryan
Co., April 6, 1827.

Hinely, Joshua, to Eliza Ann Berksteiner, May 28, 1827.

Hagood, Dr. Francis F., to Mary G. Morel, Feb. 25, 1828.

Hinely, John, to Elizabeth Helmly, Jan. 14, 1828.

Hurst, Jesse, to Mary Ann Lee, Dec. 12, 1831.
Hurst, Thomas, to Elizabeth Lee, Nov. 24, 1832.

Hinely, David, to Salome Arnsdorf, Dec. 9, 1833.

Hurst, Felix, to Mrs. Orfy Cole, Dec. 9, 1833.

Heidt, Daniel, to Mary Biddenback, March 27, 1834.

Hinely, Jacob, to Mary Magdalene Guyer, Oct. 29, 1832.
Hinely, John J., to Sarah Dugger, Feb. 8, 1836.

Hester, William, to Jane Zipperer, Dec. 27, 1836.

Hannah, Thomas, to Martha Graham, Aug. 25, 1838.

Hinely, Israel N., to Ann Abigail Scruggs, April 15, 1839.

Hinely, John J., to Salome Griner, Nov. 15, 1838.

Hinely, John J., to Hannah Guyer, Feb. 8, 1841.

Heindly, William Charles, to Tabitha Heidt, July 8, 1849.

Hurst, Henry, to Nancy Caque, Apr. 10, 1844.

Heidt, Samuel, to Mary Dugger, Oct. 12, 1844.

Hinely, Frederick, to Elizabeth A. Wisenbaker, Jan. 18, 1845.

Hays, James, to Esther Griffin, Jan. 20, 1845.

Hinely, John J., to Dorothy Guyer, April 22, 1845.

Harms, William B., to Unity E. Woolf, Feb. 7, 1846.

Hawley, Henry S., to Ellen Kellog, Sept. 25, 1847.

Hinely, Israel, to Ellen Conway, Nov. 13, 1848.

Helmly, Charles E., to Sophia L. Horning, Sept. 20, 1848.

Hinely, Israel, to Mary Ann Morgan, April 27, 1850.

Hendricks, Thomas B., to Elizabeth Dixon, April 28, 1850.

Heidt, Christopher, wife Catherine, 1829.

Ihly. 1830—The minor orphans of John Jacob Ihly: Robert, who chose John C. Rahn his guardian; James Pace was appointed guardian for Jane Maria, James Wallace, Ann Lavinia, and Ann Caroline.

Jenkins. 1803—Sept. 27—Will of William Jenkins: children—Thomas, Gills and Sally. Six youngest children—Liddy, James, Jiney, Silus, William, Ann. Exrc.: William Cook. Wit.: John Crawford and John Martin.

Jackson. 1784—Mary Jackson of Colonel's Island was formerly wife of John Jones.

Jones. 1834—Jan. 18—James Jones married Elizabeth Hubbard. (Ch. of Ascension.)

Imhoff. For will of Christopher Imhoff see "Crew-Cruse."

Jones. 1793—Will of Mary Jones (widow). Son James Jones, daughter Civility Jones; (a) James Jones had daughter Pheribe who married John Williams of Sav'h.

S. C. Land Grants: Susannah Jones was granted 800 acres on Santee River by lands of Martha Howels. (See Jones-Strobhar-Howell "Marriages.")

Benjamin Jones married Mary, daughter of Peter Tondee. Savannah Record Room, Book H, p. 61.

Tattnall Co. (Ga.) marriages:

Jones, Gabriel, to Mary Knight, April 19, 1813.

Jones, John, to Clarissa Stradley, Nov. 10, 1822.

Jones, Rev. John, to Mrs. Harriet Clifton, April 6, 1844.

Jones. In 1815 the wife of Daniel E. Jones was "Susannah."

Ihly. 1785—The wife of John Ihly was Catarina Margaret.

Ihle. Jacob and Hannah Ihle had Mary, born Oct., 1781.
Jacob and Eva, had:
John Jacob, born Jan. 16, 1757.
John, born Aug. 16, 1758.
Jonathan, born Sept. 30, 1759; died June 20, 1760.
Samuel, born Nov. 7, 1760.

Jones. 1784—James Jones left widow Mary Jones who is now Mrs. Jackson.

1806—John Jones' wife (of St. Mathew's Parish, S. C.,) Jane: the daughter of Thomas Curtis of Orangeburg, S. C. (St. Mathew's Par.) His daughter Catherine Curtis married John Baylord. Isabelle Curtis appears to have been a second wife, and not the mother of these daughters.

Jackson. 1806—Ebenezer Jackson of Savannah married Mrs. Charlotte Pierce.

Effingham Co. marriages:

Jones, Thomas, to Mary Howell, June 11, 1770.

Jones, John, to Mary Powell, alias Brown, Sept. 15, 1769.

Jones, John, to Susannah Strobhar, April 1, 1769.

Jackson, Jarvis, to Catherine Hodges, March 14, 1792.

Jones, Benjamin, to Rebecca Bishop, Nov. 24, 1804. He was of Bryan Co.

Jennings, James, to Angelina Ryall, March 1, 1823.

Jones, Mintor (?), to Sarah Hinely, June 10, 1833.

Jennings, Benjamin, to Mrs. Rebecca Kettles, Jan. 1, 1838.

Jenkins, William A., to Eliza T. Williams, Nov. 9, 1839.

Johnson, William G., to Parmela Rooks or Parks, no date.

Ihle, Jacob, to Mrs. Jane Border, March 10, 1778.

Isaacks, Samuel, to Sarah E. Guin of S. C., July 14, 1825.

Ivy, John, to Naomi Woodliff, Aug. 4, 1795.

Ironmonger, Joseph, to Sarah Johnson, May 27, 1770.

Kennedy. Hugh and William Kennedy were brothers, "late of Pennsylvania", who took up grants in Georgia on the Savannah and Ogeechee Rivers in 1753. William must have returned to Penn., for the following notice appears in S. C. Mag., vol. 21, p 25; "William Kennedy, brother of Hugh Kennedy of Georgia and of James Kennedy of S. C., died in Chester Co., Pa., May 30, 1787.

From Hist. of Upper Octorara, Chester Co., Pa. (Futhey):

"William Kennedy died 1821, age 79.

"Martha Kennedy died 1825, age 83.

"Robert Kennedy supplied the pulpit for a few months."

In Columbia, Tyrrell Co., N. C. is recorded the will of a William Kennedy, Jr., April 13, 1761. Exrs. wife Cathron and John Kennedy. Son Benjamin. Daughter Sarah's property was never any part of my estate"

Records of Old Swede's Church, Philadelphia, Nov. 22, 1795: Married—Patrick, son of Hugh Kennedy and wife Catherine of Ireland, to Mrs. Mary Smith, daughter of George Allen and wife Mary of England.

If the above Hugh Kennedy is the one who came to Georgia, his wife Catherine was dead, as he married Mrs. Ottilie Schremps, Sept. 22, 1756. Their son William was born at Mt. Pleasant, Aug. 12, 1757, and married April 8, 1778 to Elizabeth the daughter of Gov. John Adam Treutlen.

(A) Hugh Kennedy died in Savannah in 1804, recorded as having been born in N. Britian in 1789. An elder Hugh Kennedy was an ensign in Capt. Conrad Rahn's Co. 1760. (Hist. Com. Atlanta).

William Kennedy, 1757-1808-10, is the only child recorded of this marriage. In Effingham Co., Book E-F, p 187 is deed of acknowledgment from William Kennedy to John Adam Treutlen, Jr., for legacy to his wife Elizabeth, daughter of John Adam Treutlen, Sr

William Kennedy and wife Elizabeth (Treutlen) had:

Reuben—1779-1804. Died in Savannah, unmarried.

Benjamin—1781-1826, married Ann, dau. of Thomas & Sarah (Cox) Campbell.

Mary—married Seth Daniels of Beaufort, S. C., March 12, 1807.

Daughter—Name not now known.

Benjamin & Ann (Campbell) Kennedy had:

Reuben.

Benjamin.

Thomas.

William Hardwick, b 1815; married Leonora Metzger (see Metzger). 3rd wife.

Sarah, married Benjamin Porter, March 22, 1827. Had: Benj., Alex. & Edward.

Dorothy, married John, son of David & Mary Metzger, Dec. 9, 1829.

Ann Campbell, married Benajah Berry (whose first wife was Mary Metzger.)

Ruth Campbell

Elizabeth, married (1) Edw. Dudley, cousin; (2) John G. Morel. Had: Annie, Thursa, Joe, Jack, Georgia.

In 1829 ''Dorothy, William and Ann were minor heirs of Benjamin Kennedy.''

Benjamin Kennedy married (2) Mrs. Ann Mary Mason, March 17, 1824. No children.

Mrs. Mason was the daughter of Jacob Wisenbaker and Hannah (Lemecke). She married: (1) Christopher F. Triebner, Jr., her cousin; (2) Gerrard Alexander Mason, Feb. 14, 1817; (3) Benjamin Kennedy, March 17, 1824.

Benjamin Kennedy died in 1826, and his wife's will was probated in 1828, in which she mentions her son Thadeus Mason as being the grandson of Hannah Dupuis. (See Effingham Court Book G. H. p 356.)

1804—David Kennedy, wife Ruth. (on deeds).

William Hardwick Kennedy married:

(1) Emily Whetstone, one son D. J. Kennedy.

(2) Catherine Cook, son John, married Mary Agnes Henson.

(3) Leonora, daughter of John Jacob & Lydia (Dasher) Metzger.

William Hardwick Kennedy and wife Leonora (Metzger—see DeRoche), had:

Henry E.

Hattie E.

Lewis A.

Julia F.

Benjamin F.

Walter A.

Willie, (daughter), b April 1867; d Feb. 1894; married Lemuel Wilson Colson, Nov., 1891. (see Colson).

Note: Ann Campbell, the first wife of Benjamin Kennedy was the daughter of Thomas Campbell and Sarah Cox, married in Effingham Co., Dec. 29, 1770. Thomas Campbell was dead in 1794 and his widow married Josiah Daniels of S. C., Feb. 18, 1795. Josiah Daniels first wife was Elizabeth Dixon, married 1772.

The following heirs of Thomas Campbell appear in the adm. of his estate by James Boston: Wife Sarah; daughter Ann Kennedy; Samuel Ryal, William Dupuis, and "only son Thomas Campbell."

From office of Judge of Probate, Charleston, S. C.:

Will of William Kennedy, Prince William Parish. July 30, 1754. Wife Sarah; son William; daughter Mary.

Will of Dr. Mathew Kennedy, St. Bartholomew Parish. Jan. 3, 1784-March 13, 1784. Exrs: Wife Ann Kennedy, Edward Rutledge, William Skirving, Thomas Osborn, John van Marjenhoff.

Will of Mathew Kennedy—Son Roger; sister Mary Kennedy, "otherwise McKnamara;" brother Brian Kennedy of the Kingdom of Ireland, atty. at law; cousin O'Brien Swint of Charleston. gentleman, exr. of will, and late of Tennahalla, Ireland, Dec. 17, 1784-May 12, 1786.

Will of James Kennedy. Wife Ann Bensley, (who renounces dower, May 12, 1796. (He was sheriff 1786.)

Book "F"—Peter Kennedy mentions wife Margaret. Sister Molly Shaw (or Shan). To Edward Welch and Ann McBride. Aug. 3, 1821. (Wife Margaret was Margaret Wall of St. Helena's Parish).

1810—Will of James Kennedy, "son of Andrew and Mary Kennedy" of Parish Morne near Newry in Ireland. Sister Margaret; sister Elizabeth, wife of Samuel Barber of Parish of Ruthfryland; and sister Frances, wife of James Malcolm of Hill Hall near Lisburn in Ireland.

1801—Will of John Kennedy; wife Susannah; daughters Mary Hunter and Elizabeth Kennedy.

Will of Andrew Kennedy; wife Bulah Elliott Fitch Kennedy; brother William Kennedy's daughter Isabella, and his son Andrew; brother John's son John and brother Alexander's son Alexander.

In Index in Charleston is note: "Hugh Kennedy's will proved March 29, 1775", but so far the will cannot be located.

Other Kennedy references in Charleston:

Bryan Kennedy, Book 5 E, p 8;

William Kennedy, Book 5 W, p 48, merchant in Charleston 1788;

Margaret Kennedy, Book 7 O, p 13;

Thomas Kennedy, Book 8 W, p 48;

Hugh Kennedy, Book 9 V, p 40.

King. William King of Virginia, married Sarah Goldwire, Sept. 14, 1769 (see Goldwire). Had:

John King, born July 25, 1770; married Jane Jones.

Sarah Grace King, born May 19, 1773; died 1851; married (1) James Little Goldwire, (2) Col. Thos. Wyly, in 1812 or 1817. He died June, 1846, age 86 & 7 months.

William King, 2nd, born May 19, 1775, married Margaret Marie Ravot. (see Ravot.)

James King, born Dec. 8, 1777. (His mother died Dec. 9, 1777).

("William King alone obeyed orders". Ga. Col. Records, Vol. 1, p. 95).

William King, Sr., married (2) Mary, daughter of ~~Jacob~~ *Joachim* Hartsine, Had: *Harstene*

Mary King, born July 3, 1781.

Thomas King, born Jan. 2, 1783.

Benjamin King, born Sept. 21, 1788.

Joseph King, born Oct. 5, 1790.

Elizabeth King, born Oct. 9, 1797; married Wm. Henry Greene. No children. Estate left to James Offutt Goldwire and his wife Mariah.

John King and wife Jane (Jones). Had:

John Goldwire King. (Did he marry Mrs. Julia Harper, Oct. 12, 1844?)

Sarah Naomi King, married Dr. DeGraffenried.

Mary Ann King, married Maner Lawton, Dec. 13, 1819.

Agnes King.

Eveline King.

George King, married Caroline, daughter of James Little Goldwire, Feb. 15, 1821.

(The last four were minors in 1819, and were wards of John Goldwire).

Jane Jones, wife of John King, is believed to have been the daughter of John Jones and wife Susannah (Strobhar), who married March 9, 1769. It is known that the wife of John King was a sister of Obedience Jones who married Jesse Offutt (the parents of Frances who married John Goldwire March 9, 1809), and the children of John and Susannah Jones, were:

Jane Jones;

Obedience Jones, born Aug. 13, 1773;

William Jones, born June 14, 1777;

and these were also of Effingham Co. It has been assumed (without proof) that they were the sisters referred to. (A) Jacob Strobhar married Judith Godin, Nov. 29, 1777 of S. C., but married in Effingham Co.

In re Sarah Grace (King) Goldwire, and (2) Col. Thomas Wyly, the following is of interest. Col. Wyly who died in 1841 left the following heirs: Sons, Leonidas, and William (who married Naomi, daughter of John Martin Dasher, Jan. 4, 1802), Frederick Thomas (who died 1851). Daughters, Naomi Cely, Elizabeth Williams, Sarah K. Meeks; and grandchildren, the children of daughter Maria (who married Solomon Dasher, Feb. 9, 1813).

Other heirs mentioned were James and Henry Tison; the children of James Goldwire and George Boston.

"Widow Sarah Grace." (She died 1851.)

Savannah Record Room, Book "Y", p. 157: Aug. 15, 1800—a letter from James Jones to John King in re Effingham Co. Academy: "Mr. Morel is about to leave his place in Burke Co.———I am just going on board the Ceres to sail—adieu."

City Hall, Savannah: "Sarah, wife of Mr. King, merchant, was born Baltimore, died July 19, 1812, age 27."

William King, Jr., born April 10, 1775, died Oct. 3, 1834; married Margaret Marie, daughter of Abraham Ravot (Rev. soldier). She was born 1785, married July 12, 1810, and died May 25, 1837. Had:

Margaret E. King, born Sept. 1815; died Aug. 6, 1841

Sarah G. King, born May 2, 1819; died Sept. 24, 1840.

James G. King, born ——, 1816; died Aug. 24, 1839.

Mariah King, born Dec. 14, 1820; married Dr. Sidney Smith.

John King, born May 22, 1822; died Sept. 3, 1844.

Mary Ravot King, born April 29, 1824; died Sept. 27, 1840.

Caroline G. King, born April 6, 1826; died ——, 1846.

Elizabeth G. King, born Dec. 24, 1827; died Oct. 20, 1855. Married Wm. Frank Maner.

William King died intestate and his estate was adm. by John Goldwire, Benjamin King and James Boston.

In Colonial Cemetery, Savannah: "Jane, wife of John R. King, died Oct. 4, 1817." She was Jane Achord whom he married May 14, 1816. He married (2) Sarah Cannon in 1818.

Notes from C. H. in Wilkes Co., Ga.:

1785—John King of Gloucester Co., Va., buys tract from Robert Middleton, on the Ogeechee River.

1796—John King and wife Jane, make deeds with William King, "all of Camden Co."

1794—"William King, tax payer," in Camden Co.

"Sarah, relict of Col. John King," died in Effingham Co., 1808.

1799—To John King from the State of Georgia, the right to erect a toll bridge over Ebenezer Creek. "He allowed all persons from John Martin Dasher's to Henry Gindrat's to pass free."

1702—James King's lands were confiscated in Ireland. and he, with Barnwells, Talbots and Twiggs came to America. (O'Hart's Irish Pedigrees).

1774—(A) William King was at Battle of Maiden Springs in Dunmore's War.

Strobhar excursus:

George Strobher's will 1771, names heirs: Catherine, Mary, Susannah Jones. Sister Mary; bro. Nicholas Strobhar; wife Jane (Jenny).

Kirkland. 1792—Estate of Richard Kirkland was adm. by Isaac and Samuel Kirkland.

Keiffer. 1790—Emanuel Keiffer, gentleman, deeds to Christina, David, Salome, and Solomon, the children of Godhilf Smith. (Barbara was wife of Emanuel Keiffer. See Record Room, Savannah, Book "S," p. 44.)

1801—Heirs of Jacob Keiffer, dec'd: Jedediah Weitman and wife Hannah; Naomi and Lydia Keiffer relinquish their claims to their brother Joel Keiffer, adm. of estate. (Naomi also spelt Naemah.)

1795—Estate of Christiana Keiffer, spinster, adm. by Joshua Zant and Godliph Smith. Joint heirs were Israel Keiffer, Fred'k. Nesler, Joshua Zant.

Kogler. 1818—Will of John Kogler: legatees—Valentine Kessler, Margaret Bechtly, Gratiosa Weitman, daughter of Jedediah Weitman; John Hinely's children; Eliza, wife of Gotlieb Fetzger. Exrs.: Gotlieb Ernst, Israel Weitman, John Neidlinger. Wit.: David Helmly, Gottlieb Zitterauer, Benj. Dasher. Codicil: Lewis, youngest son of Cate John Hinely, and John Gottlieb, son of Valentine Kesler. Wit.: David and Joshua Helmly, David Zeigler. (The wife of John Kogler Christina Elizabeth.)

Keiffer. 1806—the wife of David Keiffer of Savannah, was Mary, daughter of Michael Gasper Switzer.

1786—"Emnauel Keiffer and wife Anna Barbara."

1818—The wife of Ephraim Keiffer was Catherine, widow of Chris. Cramer.

Knight, John, and wife Rachel, 1799.

Keebler, Joshua, and wife Elizabeth, 1815.

Marriages:

King, William, to Sarah Goldwire, Sept. 14, 1769.

Kettles, Peter, to Elizabeth Daniels, May 11, 1773.

Kettles, John, to Mary Shuman of S. C., Nov. 7, 1773. Bap. just before her marriage.

Kettles, John, to Amy Garnett, March 11, 1795.

Keebler, John, to Rosina, widow of John Stockman, May 9, 1797.

Kahlden, Fred W., to Rosina, widow of John Keebler, June 2, 1800.

Keiffer, Emanuel, to Martha, widow of Gideon Zettler, and dau. of John Wilson, Sept. 26, 1803.

Keiffer, Joel, to Mrs. Catherine Zant, nee Schweighoffer or Steiner, Feb. 23, 1804.

King, William (Jr.), to Margaret Mary Ravot, July 12, 1810.

Keebler, James, to Elizabeth Ihly, Nov. 22, 1827 or 1847.

Knight, John, to Ann M. Baas, Sept. 1, 1817.

Keebler, Thos., to Louisa A. Ward, Sept. 29, 1834.

King, George W., to Caroline Goldwire, Feb. 15, 1821.

Kesler, Valentine, to Catherine Seckinger, Feb. 18, 1828.

Kettles, Peter, to Rebecca Wilson, Jan. 26, 1832.

Kesler, Wm. B., to Catherine Zipperer, June 7, 1844.

King, John, to Mrs. Julia Harper, Oct 12, 1844.

Kean, Simeon, to Caroline McRory, June 27, 1846.

Keebler, Thomas, to Louisa A. Morel, Nov. 22, 1827.

Kesler, Joshua, to Louisa E., only daughter of Solomon Gnann, March 9, 1847.

Nail. This family appears to have gone from Effingham Co. to Edgefield, S. C., where the following wills are of record.

Barbara Nail, Sept. 1, 1775. Sons Casper and Daniel. Daughters Ann Howell and Elizabeth Savage. Wit.: William Tabler, Roger Tuflett. (In the will of Daniel Nail the name also appears as "Neal."

Will of Casper Nail, Sr., Oct. 25, 1793. "Trusty and beloved friend Casper Nail, Jr., Executor." Son Daniel and his son Casper Nail, Jr., David Nail, son of Mance Nail, John Nail, son of Casper Nail, Jr. Sister Ann Zubly, and her children Polly and Charlotte Zubly.

The will of John Nail on file 1825. (See also Ebenezer Ch. Records. Voight.)

1774—Nov.—David, son of John Conrad Nail and wife Sofie Marie, was born.

Nelson. 1792—Estate of Malcolm Nelson adm. by John Boykin.

Neiss. 1792—Feb. 1—Will of Johannes Georg Neiss. Wife Sibilla, son George, daughters Elizabeth. Exr.: Joseph Schubtrein. Wit.: Christopher Cramer, George Zeigler. Proved 1792, May 1, before Abraham Ravot.

Noble. 1802—Will of Hannah Noble. To Mrs. Mary Hodges. To grandson Joshua, son of Simon Howard. Granddaughter Hannah Zitterauer. Exr.: grand son-in-law Godlieb Zitterauer. (Joshua Howard chose Godlieb Zitterauer as guardian.)

Nowlan. 1816—Will of George Galpin Nowlan, Dec. 16, at Milledgeville, Ga. Wife Hannah (Gugel). Children: Anna Elizabeth, Margaret Glorianna, Amanda Georgianna, and an infant born since I left home. Exrs.: John McPherson Berrien, and David Gugel, Esqrs. Wit.: John Wisenbaker, E. Emanuel, Joel Crawford.

Neidlinger. 1819—Samuel Neidlinger adm. estate of John Neidlinger.

Newton. 1860—Est. of Barnet Newton adm. by Jane A. Newton & J. D. Lee.

Nevill. 1790—John Nevill to son Jacob 200 acres on Great Ogeechee, granted to said John, Aug., 1786. Other chil. Sarah, Mary Winslow, Francis Neville, Eliz. Neville. Wit.: Jeremiah Jones, Philip Howell, Caleb Howell, J. P.

Netherclift. Thomas Netherclif married Ann McQueen (S. C.), had:

Henrietta, born 1767; died 1808; married (1) John Morel in 1789; (2) Louis Trezevant; (3) William O'Bryan.

Oatt. 1794—Jan. 25—Will of Nathaniel Oatt. Wife Christina Elizabeth. Exr.: Brother Godlip. Wit.: Solomon Gnann.

Oates. (Savannah C. H.) Heirs of Jacob Oates: John Peter Oates, Lucy Ayrough (signed Lucy Hearo), and Elizabeth Manning. These connect with family of Peter Tondee.

Nevill—Effingham Co., 1790— John Nevill, who married Frances Mixon, Oct. 13, 1768, deeds all his property to his children, who were: Jacob, born 1772, married Amanda Hudson; Sara; Mary (Mrs. Winslow); Frances; Elizabeth. Property consisted of an original grant to Samuel Carney, dated Nov. 20, 1769, wo tracts granted John Nevill, Aug. 8, 1787, of 600 acres. Exrs.: Friends Joseph Pearce, Sr., Joseph Pearce, Jr. Wit.: Jeremiah Jones, Phillip Howell, Caleb Howell, J. P.

A John Nevill of Bulloch Co., Ga. (wife Ann), had a daughter Delilah who married Samuel Williams, who was dead in 1818.

Samuel Williams and wife Delilah (Nevill). Had:

John Williams.

William Williams.

Garrett Williams.

Delilah (Dilly).

There is a record of a Jacob Nevill, who married in 1778, Nancy, the daughter of Capt. Michael William Henderson. (Lane)

Jacob Nevill and Amanda (Hudson) had:

Thomas Nevill, born March 12, 1808; died Oct. 21, 1870; married Nov. 8, 1835 to Rachel Parker, born Oct. 30, 1818; died Jan. 12, 1859.

Thomas Nevill and wife Rachel (Parker), had:

John Nevill.

Jacob Nevill, born July 27, 1838; died May 23, 1861; married July 8, 1858, Moselle Parish, born May 24, 1836; died June 3, 1922, daughter of Ancel & Mary (Holloway) Parish.

Joe Nevill.

Simon Nevill.

Peter Nevill.

William Nevill.

Charlie Nevill.

Dock Nevill.

Tom Nevill.

Daughters:

Janie.

Bess.

Mary.

Sallie.

Dicie.

Marriages:

Neidlinger, John, of Savh., to Catherine Dasher, April 2, 1812.

Neidlinger, John, to Ann Catherine, dau. of Rev. Mr. Bergman, Sept. 18, 1814.

Napper, Drury, to Nicey Jones, Oct. 4, 1819.

Nostrand, George, to Jane Jenkins, Oct. 4, 1821.

Neisler, Thomas, to Elvira Neiss, Oct. 20, 1823.

Neidlinger, Samuel, to Salome Gnann, widow of Solomon Gnann, Jr. (nee Heidt, dau. of Geo. G. and Sallie Remshart Heidt), March 10, 1825.

Niess, George, Jr., to Christina Elizabeth Schrimp, Feb. 14, 1828.

Nease, John R., to Mary E. Shearouse, Dec. 8, 1835.

Nease, Wm. F., to Rosinna Neise, Sept. 4, 1839.

Newton, David B., to Mary Ann Tullis, Feb. 12, 1837.

Nease, James J., to Susan E. Dasher, born Jan. 1, 1795; died Jan. 31, 1819; married Nov.21, 1849.

O'Brien, William, to Mary Charnock, Dec. 15, 1768.

O'Neal, Daniel, to Ann Clyatt, March 31, 1793.

Oglesby, Benjamin, to Mrs. Mary Wisenbaker, Dec. 13, 1793.

Oglesby, Anthony, to Salome, widow of Jacob Metzger, June 28, 1800.

Orvis, Waitstill C., to Susannah J. Gromet, Jan. 17, 1812.

Olcott, James, to Mary Ann Gugel, Dec. 20, 1816.

Olcott, James Sands, to Esther Millen, both of Chatham Co., Oct. 18, 1822.

Ott (or Oatt) Jonathan, to Sarah (Salome) Gnann, Dec. 23, 1824.

Nichols, Henry, wife Nelly, 1811.

Norment, Wm., wife Elizabeth, 1799.

Neidlinger, Jno. Gotlieb, wife Hannah, 1792. (Wdiow of **Daniel** Zettler & dau. of John Martin Dasher.

Overstreet, James, wife Elizabeth, 1800.

Paulitsch. While the name Paulitsch is still borne under this spelling, it has undergone the change into Pauledge and Powledge.

It appears that the first two of this name to settle at **Ebenezer,** were Johan Martin Paulitsch and Johan Philip Paulitsch, who were probably brothers.

Johan Martin Paulitsch married Ursula Schweighoffer, April 22, 1754. Children:

Sulamith, born Oct. 3, 1757.

Hannah Elizabeth, born July 15, 1759.

Gratiosa, born May 7, 1761.

Daughter (died at birth, March 25, 1762).

Jonathan, born July 21, 1763.

Gideon, born Feb. 4, 1766; died Aug. 12, 1827.

Johan Philip Paulitsch and wife Anna Magdalen, had:

Anna Magdalen, born Dec. 16, 1758.

John George, born April 12, 1764.

Gideon Paulitsch's will recorded Aug. 12, 1828, wife Hannah; children, Gideon, Jr., appointed attorney for the heirs; John Martin, Philip, Christian. Some of these heirs moved to Macon, and on the court administration papers, the name is spelt variously.

John Martin, the son of Gideon Powledge was born Feb. 1796, and died Oct. 8, 1881. He married Miss Frances Foy and were the parents of eleven children, one of whom was Robert, born Sept. 25, 1835, and married Miss Nancy Caroline White, who was born Jan. 2, 1835; their son; John Martin Powledge, born April 25, 1878, married Miss Lizzie Lou Reid, born Aug. 27, 1881.

A grant of land in the Lottery of 1821 is recorded in Thomaston, Ga., to Ezekiel Pouledge of Effingham Co.

Price. 1775—Deed of John Price, planter, to Lewis Perry.

Polhill. 1787—The heirs of Nahaniel Polhill, Sr., were: Nathaniel, Jr., Mary, Thomas, and Hannah, the deceased wife of Alexander Scott of Beaufort.

Potet (or Patet.) 1791—Estate of Joseph Potet (or Patet), adm. by Thomas Garnet, Enoch Daniel and Philip Dell.

Pleiger. 1796—Estate of John Pleiger adm. by Emanuel Zeigler (son of George.)

Prison. 1789—June 3—Deed of Elizabeth Prison to children: Elizabeth Prison and Mary Nix. In trust to John Gnann, godfather of Mary, and guardian to both children.

Prosser. 1829—Minor heirs of Joab H. Prosser were: Ann Matilda and Caroline. Solomon Zipperer was made guardian.

Powers. 1832—July 21—Will of John Powers. Wife Lydia. Sons Zara (who married Eliza Elkins, Nov. 17, 1839), and Clem. Eight slaves and land in Bulloch Co., to son-in-law Thomas Elkins, husband of my late daughter Sarah, who left several small children. Land in Bryan Co. to son-in-law, Henry W. Crum, husband of my late daughter Abigail, who left no children.

1837—Sept. 4—Will of Lydia Powers is testified to by Robert Bourquin (Minute Book No. 3, p. 136.)

Parish. 1839—March 13—Lydia Parish adm. estate of Edwin Parish.

Powers. 1848—Sept. 22-Nov. 6, 1848—Will of Clem Powers: wife Ann Elizabeth; sons: Milton H., Virgil, William Cooper, Horace; daughters: Indianna and Virginia. (Powers from Connecticut.)

1853—Estate of Zara Powers was adm. by Archibald Guyton.

1855—Estate of Milton H. Powers adm. by L. T. Elkins and A. Guyton.

Crum. 1839—James S. Crum wills to brother Henry W. Crum, and to the children of his sister, Ann E. Powers.

*Mrs. Mary Prosser married Theopilus Zipperer, March 3, 1829.

Porter, Wm., wife Rachel (Wilson) widow Thomas Garnett, 1800.

Pitts, Anthony, wife Nancy, 1807.

Pauledge, George, wife Salome, 1801.

Porter, James, wife Elizabeth, 1808.

Porter, Thomas, wife Susannah, 1808.

Patterson, Wm., widow Maria (Tondee), 1822; married (2) Thos. Elkins.

Polhill, Thomas, wife Rebekah, 1810.

Pendleton, Nathaniel (of Sav.) & wife Susan, 1805.

Pritchard, Jos. P., of Chas., S. C., wife Claudia (Kelsall), 1811.

Palmer. Charleston, S. C.—Will of John Palmer, Sr., of St. Stephen's Parish. Sons: John & Joseph; daughter: Mariam Gendron Porcher; grand daughters: Ann Palmer Stevens and Laura Stevens.

Chas., S. C.—Will of Evans Palmer, Jan. 11, 1753. Father John Palmer, dec'd. Nephews: John, William, Peter, James & Charles Palmer; sister: Hannah Deveaux, and her daughter Margaret; sister: Lucia Cussings; Exrs.: Hugh Bryan and bro.-in-law Andrew Deveaux. Wit.: James Girardeau, Andrew Postell. (Silver chalice and cups to Stony Creek Church, Prince William Parish.)

(Bro. William Palmer was father of "five nephews," and had also daughters Elzabeth and Mary.

Marriages:

Pugh, Francis, to Martha Raines, Feb. 12, 1759.

Perthero, Solomon, to Elizabeth Miles, Oct. 25, 1768.

Perry, Abiel, to Sarah Asque, July 22, 1772.

Pace, Samuel, to Mary Glasher, Dec. 18, 1774.

Porter, John, to Henrietta Ravot, dau. of Abraham, Jan. 16, 1795.

Powledge, to Sarah Steiner, Sept. 7, 1795.

Porter, David, to Sally Bostwick, July 9, 1797.

Pace, Tryon, to Mary Dykes, Aug. 16, 1798.

Palmer, John, to Elizabeth Mikell (step dau. of Abraham Ravot), Aug. 3, 1799.

Pitts, Anthony, to Ann Rawlinson, May 24, 1794 (date may be incorrect. His wife was Nancy, (a form of Ann,) in 1808.)

Peterson, Jacob, to Mary Holliday, Nov. 15, 1802.

Pugh, Whitson, of Burke Co., to Mrs. Hannah Grant, June 12, 1806.

Pitts, Hardy, to Patsy Neal, in Warren Co., Ga., April 6, 1808.

Pearce, John F., to Rosannah Calder, April 6, 1808.

Porter, Thomsa, to Salome Gruber, Oct. 17, 1808. (Susannah was wife of a Thomas Porter, Aug., 1808.)

Pelham, Richard, to Mrs. Sarah Wilson, April 1, 1815.

Pearson, William, to Hannah Gilchrist, Dec. 5, 1821.

Purse, Thomas, to Elizabeth Gugel, Nov. 13, 1824. Adopted dau. of Daniel Gugel.

Pace, Noah, to Sarah Zitterauer, Nov. 23, 1826.

Phillips, William, to Susannah Thrower, Jan. 15, 1827.

Pace, James, to Mrs. Mary Ann Ihly, Sept. 16, 1830.

Palmer, John, to Mary Helvenstine, Nov. 9, 1830.

Pitts, John G. W., to Jane Schroder, Oct. 11, 1831.
Pitts, Hardy G., to Mrs. Elizabeth Hudson, July 21, 1832.

Parish, Wm., to Evelyn Freymouth, April 4, 1833.
Parish, Edward, to Elizabeth Bryan, Dec. 7, 1833.

Pace, Geo. C., to Johannah Gnann, Oct. 7, 1833.

Platt, Chas. C., to Lucretia G. Davis, Nov. 27, 1833.

Porter, John, to Hannah C. Grovenstein, Sept. 17, 1836.

Pace, Tryon, to Mrs. Sarah Stevens, Sept. 18, 1838.

Powers, Zora, to Eliza Elkins, Nov. 17, 1838.

Porter, Albert, to Mrs. Evaline (Reisser) Humbert, Jan. 4, 1838.

Ryall, Samuel, ot Esther William, March 8, 1759.

Robbins, Thomas, to Sarah Harnage, Jan. —, 1770.

Rogers, William, to Celia Benson, Nov. 4, 1771.

Radcliff, William, to Dianna Moon, Nov. 11, 1771.
Radcliff, Elijah, to Mary Stafford, Nov. 23, 1773.

Reiser, Daniel, to Mary Grovenstein, April 16, 1792.

Rahn, Joseph, to Naomi Zettler, April 25, 1794.

Robarts, Thomas, to Elizabeth Penninger, Sept. 8, 1795.

Reiser, Israel, 1st wife Hannah Margaret Shuptrine, dau. of ~~Christian~~ (2) married Anna Barbara, widow of Emanuel Keiffer.

Roper, William, to Sarah Metzger, Dec. 2, 1800.

Rahn, Mathew, to Hannah Elizabeth Dolwich, Feb. 2, 1802. Mar. sett., Jan. 25.

Rhinelander, John Christopher, to Elizabeth, widow of Christian Bechtly, dau. of Israel Reiser and Hannah Shuptrine, Nov. 2, 1807.

Ridgeland, John, to Mary Wheeler, July 9, 1813.

Rahn, Emanuel, to Sarah (Salome) Berry, Nov. 26, 1811.

Reid, Murry, to Lydia Reiser, dau. of Israel Reiser and Hannah Margaret Shuptrine, Jan. 12, 1814.

Reiser. James, to Dysie Dykes, April 29, 1816.

Rahn, John, to Margaret Zipperer, April 27, 1820.

Roberts, Reuben, to Amy Wylly, July 26, 1811. Sol Dasher, Sec.

Rhinehour, Benjamin, to Hannah Powledge, Dec. 9, 1827.

Rahn, James, to Jane Elizabeth Neace, Nov. 20, 1828.

Rooks, Seaborn, to Sophia Holliday, March 26, 1831.

Rahn, Cletus, to Elizabeth H. Rahn, Dec. 29, 1832.

Remshart, Daniel, to Amanda G. Nowlan, Oct. 5, 1836.

Reiser, C. F., to Charlotte C. Rahn, Feb. 12, 1838.

Rahn, Alex. Hamilton, to Jane Caroline Dasher, Sept. 15, 1838.
Rahn, William, to Henrietta Myers, Aug. 5, 1842. His first wife was Mary Borum of Boston, Mass.

Rogers, Peter, to Gracey Wheeler, April 8, 1841.

Rahn, William O., to Hannah (Mingledorf), widow of Henry Wilson), Dec. 18, 1849.

Reiser, John J., to Emily Dasher, Oct. 22, 1844.

Rahn, William O., to Amanda Exley, Jan. 4, 1857.

Rahn. George and Conrad Rahn settled in Penn. in 1737. Conrad came to Georgia about 1750.

Conrad and Barbara Rahn had:

George, born 1753; died March 26, 1756.

Mathew, born Oct. 2, 1754; died Nov. 4, 1822.

John Martin, born April 8, 1756; died April 16, 1756.

Obadiah, born Sept. 1, 1758; died April 28, 1769.

Lydia, born June 15, 1760.

Jonathan, born March 21, 1762; died July 18, 1840; married Christina Buntz, Nov. 18, 1783.

Mary, born Dec. 2, 1764; died Nov. 14, 1769.

Anna Margaret, born Feb. 19, 1767.

Joseph, born Aug. 9, 1769; married Naomi Zettler, April 25, 1794.

Jacob, born Nov. 1772.

Mathew Rahn's first wife is unknown, but she had two children:

Samuel, born 1786; died Jan. 3, 1823.

Agneta Rahn, who married John C. Seckinger, Nov. 23, 1807

Mathew Rahn married (2) Feb. 4, 1802, Mrs. Hannah E. Dolwich, born Aug. 30, 1782; died June 25, 1837, the daughter of Jacob Hoffman and his wife Mary (Reiser).

Mathew Rahn and Hannah E. had:

Josias, born Nov. 15, 1802; died Nov. 24, 1802.

Mary Florinthia, born Oct. 16, 1803; died Sept. 13, 1854.

James, born Nov. 14, 1804; died Oct. 29, 1822.

Irwin, born Sept. 14, 1806.

Frederick, born Dec. 11, 1807; died July 19, 1831.

Alexander Hamilton, born Dec. 23, 1809; died April 1, 1866; married Jane Caroline Dasher, Sept., 1838.

Eliza Hannah, born April 28, 1811; married Cletus Rahn.

Archibald, born July 11, 1812; died May 7, 1824.

Joshua, born July 5, 1814; died Jan. 8, 1849.

Israel Herito, born Feb. 10, 1816; died June 19, 1864. Unmarried.

Appolina Margaret, born Aug. 28, 1817.

Richard, born March 10, 1819; died Dec. 8, 1819.

The will of Mathew Rahn was probated 1834. Mentions wife and son John, and son-in-law Christopher Seckinger.

John Rahn married Margaret Zipperer, April 27, 1820.

Jonathan Rahn married Christina Buntz, Nov. 18, 1783; born Aug. 31, 1783. Children:

Anna Margret, born Sept. 10, 1784; married Gotlieb Ernst.

Christina, born Feb. 22, 1787; married (1) Adam Metzger, (2) Jacob Gnann.

Emanuel, born Oct. 9, 1789; died Sept. 19, 1822; married Sarah Berry, Nov. 26, 1811.

Hannah, born Oct. 3, 1791; died Sept. 19, 1846; married (1) Robt. Christie, (2) Benj. Gnann.

Jonathan, born Dec. 6, 1793; died Sept. 19, 1816.

William, born April 15, 1796; married (1) Mary Gorham of Boston, Mass., (2) Henrietta Myers, Aug. 5, 1842.

Susannah, born Oct. 8, 1798; married John W. Wilson, Aug. 7, 1820.

Cletus, born March 5, 1801; died Jan. 15, 1856; married Hannah Elizabeth Rahn, Dec. 29, 1832.

Salome, born April 6, 1804, died Oct. 27, 1830; married Benjamin Gnann.

(Christina Buntz was the daughter of Urban and Margarethe Buntz).

William O. Rahn to (1) Mary Pengree, Jan. 14, 1843; (2) Mrs. Hannah (Mingledorf), wid of Henry Wilson, Dec. 18, 1849; (3) Amanda Exley, Jan. 4, 1859.

Ravot. The earliest record of this name is that of Francis Gabriel Ravot, who in 1733, June 10, was granted 50 acres in Purysburg, adjoining lands of Rodolph Netman and Abram LeRoys.

In 1767, March 2, Francis Gabriel Ravot deeds tract in Purysburg, adjoining lands of John Rodolph Netman and Abram LeRoy, to Adrian Mayer, Parish of St. Peter's. Wit: Daniel Mallet and Melchior Fulcher.

1764—Gabriel Ravot was granted 500 acres in Purysburg, adjoining lands of John Peter Pury, Jacob Strobhar and David Gerond, on Savannah River.

The will of Gabriel Francis Ravot is recorded in Charleston, S. C., Book 1761-7, dated July 23, 1769—probated Nov. 23, 1769. Wit: David Saussy, Jr., who in the event of the death of the testator's wife becomes Excr. Wife Louise Catherine; son Abraham; daughters Ann Henrietta and Jane Mary.

In the will of Daniel Mallette it is shown that Louise Catherine Ravot was his eldest sister, and that she married (2) Peter Francois Greniere.

The name of the first wife of Abraham Ravot is not now known, but his will is of record in Effingham Co., dated July 16, 1795. His second wife was Mrs. Mary Mikell who had 2 daughters, Mary and Elizabeth Mikell. Elizabeth Mikell married John Palmer, Aug. 3, 1799. No record of Mary's marriage has been found. (A John Palmer married Mary Helvenstein, Nov. 9, 1830.) David Hugenin of S. C. was appointed Exr. of Abraham Ravot's will, and the Witnesses were Charles Ryal, David Morgan and John Frickenger.

The children of Abraham Ravot, as far as known, were:

Abraham, born 1773.

Henrietta, born about 1775; married John Porter, Jan. 16, 1795.

Margaret Marie, born 1786; died 1837; married Wm. King, Jr., July 1, 1810. (see King).

(From the dates it seems that Margaret Marie was daughter of 2nd wife).

There is of record in City Hall, Savannah, the death of Lt. Vivian Ravot, of French corvette, L'Amitie, "born in France", died Sept. 14, 1804; age 27.

Mrs. Abraham (Mary) Ravot died 1811.

Abraham Ravot served in Revolution. (Knight's Roster).

Reiser. Balthazer Reiser and wife Mary came from Augsberg. Brother of Michael I. (He had royal grant in 1770). Children:

John Gotliph, born Jan. 29, 1758.

Michael, born Sept. 6, 1760.

Catherine, born April 3, 1764; died Sept. 24, 1764.

Michael, died Feb. 21, 1775; married Appolinia, had:

David, born July 8, 1765.

Hannah Elizabeth, born Oct. 9, 1758.

Catherine, born Feb. 1, 1760.

Mary, born Sept. 25, 1762; married Jacob Hoffman.

(A) Daniel Reiser married Mary Grovenstein, April 16, 1792.

(See Ebenezer Records, p. 12, No. 504; should read Daniel Reiser— not Kiefer. Compare No. 510, p. 95.)

Mrs. Mary Reiser married John George Winkler, Sept. 30, 1777.

Benjamin Reiser and wife Catherine had Mary, born Jan. 13, 1779.

George Reiser married Mrs. Anna Dorothea Mayer, April 22, 1754. She married George Fisher, June 24, 1760, and died Oct. 3, 1763, age 42.

Israel Reiser married Hannah Margaret (or Maria) Shuptrine, Had:

Lydia, married Murry Reid, Jan. 1, 1814.

Elizabeth, born July 23, 1778. (see Bechtly and Rylander).

Israel Reiser married June 2, 1800, (2) Mrs. Anna Barbara, widow of Emanuel Keiffer.

His will was made in 1801, in which he speaks of (wife **Barbara,** and son Mathew.'' "Equal parts to all children.''

Nathaniel Reiser and wife Dorothea had daughter Christine, born July 7, 1779. He died in 1800 and his estate was adm. by David Reiser.

Dorothy Reiser married Solomon Zant, Jan. 31, 1775; was a widow in 1778.

John George Reiser and wife Sybilla Regina had Elizabeth, born July 19, 1763.

Christian Lebrecht Reiser died April 23, 1766, age 11; and Christine Reiser died April 14, 1775, age 8. (Parents not known.)

Marriages:

James Reiser to Dysie Dykes, April 29, 1816.

John J. Reiser to Emily Dasher (2nd wife), Oct. 22, 1844.

C. F. Reiser to Charlotte C. Rahn, Feb. 12, 1838.

Ryall. Arthur Ryall came to Georgia from N. C., about 1764, and had a wife and 5 children. He died July, 1798, leaving wife Ann, the date of whose death is not known.

Children:

Moses.

Samuel, married Esther Williams, March 8, 1759.

(A) Samuel Ryall married Virginia Godbee, March 27, 1774.

Mary, married Spencer Cox, Feb. 25, 1795.

Charles David, born July 25, 1770; died June 30, 1836.

Charles David Ryall married (1) Elizabeth and had:

Martha Mary, Born Feb. 23, 1791; died Feb. 6, 1823; married Nathan Godley, Sept. 10, 1821.

Charles David Ryall married (2) Mary Boston, April 2, 1802.

Charles David Ryall married (3) Christina, daughter of Gotlieb Smith, May 5, 1808.

Children of Chas. D. Ryall and Christina (Smith):

William Arthur, born Feb. 8, 1809; died Oct. 10, 1839; married Sarah Ann Best, Jan. 1, 1839.

Isaiah Benjamin, born April 1, 1810; died Oct. 22, 1860; married Rachel A. Folsom, Oct. 6, 1842.

Ann Elizabeth, born Oct. 6, 1812; died June 15, 1875; married John R. Morgan.

Sarah Dorothea, born Nov. 9, 1814; died Sept. 2, 1893; married James Morgan.

Edna Preventia, born, May 2, 1817; died Oct. 1, 1842; married David Snooks.

Rebecca T., born July 20, 1819; died Dec. 23, 1873; married David Snooks.

Mary Massey, born July 10, 1826, died July 11, 1870; married John W. Wilson.

Mrs. Christina (Smith) Ryall died Jan. 1, 1843; born about 1785.

"Skip", a slave of Arthur Ryall, was, at his master's death set free, and Charles and Samuel Ryall asked that he be "permitted to be unmolested," etc. This old negro is remembered by residents of Effingham Co., and the white people of the neighborhood saw that he was provided with all comforts until his death in the 1890's.

1822—Est. of Arthur Ryall adm. by Emanuel R. & Benj. Cox. Caveat by Wm. Stafford.

Montgomery Co., Ga., 1828—Will of William Ryals: Wife Edith; children, Joseph Ryals, William K. Ryals, Elizabeth Womack, Matilda Winifred Colquhoun, John B. Ryals, Mary Hall, Penelope Connor; grandchildren, Thos. B., Mary Ann Edith Calquhoun); son-in-law, Angus Colquhoun. Wit: Geo. Wyche, Needham R. Bryan, Benj. F. Harris.

Grant in McIntosh Co. to Henry Ryals, "soldier".

Rylander (various spellings). John Martin Rheinlander married Frederica Catherine Bruckner, May 31, 1763, their children:

John Martin, born Aug. 31, 1764; died Aug. 28, 1769.

Daniel, born March 16, 1769; died Feb. 2, 1774.

Christian, born June 17, 1772.

John Christopher, born July 15, 1767; died July 10, 1769.

*John Christopher, born Oct. 3, 1773.

Johanna Frederica, born Nov. 11, 1774, died Oct. 15, 1775.

John Martin Rheinlander's first wife was Mary Kalcher, whom he married Dec. 1, 1758. She died in Savannah March 15, 1760, age 21. He died Jan. 16, 1776 in 40th year of his age.

*John Christopher Rhinelander married Nov. 2, 1807 to Elizabeth, the widow of Christian Bechtly, and the daughter of Israel Reiser and wife Hannah (Shuptrine). They had a son Mathew E. Rylander whose daughter, S. E. Rylander married George W. Sirrine, who at the age of 80 (1927) gave this data.)

Mathew Rylander had 5 daughters who attended Wesleyan College at Macon where he lived. He moved to Sumter Co., Ga., in 1855. His sons John Emory Rylander and Joseph Rylander were killed in Civil War.

"Charles Ulmer Zitterauer married Ann C. Rylander, Nov. 3, 1828." (Effingham Co. Records).

1823—Estate of Elizabeth Rylander was adm. by Murry Reid.

Roberson. Silvanus and Ann make deed to Israel Bird, 1791. Wit.: Arb. Bird.

Robert, Elias, lays off land on the Bluff, 1789.

Remshart. "Daniel and wife Elizabeth," 1811.

Rantz. "John, and wife Barbara," 1768.

Richards. "John, and wife Barbara," 1785.

Rawls. "John, and wife Franky," 1792.

Russell. "Mathew, and wife Sarah, of Charleston," 1805.

Ross. "Abner, and wife Elizabeth," 1814.

Ricker. "Shapleigh, and wife Esther," 1819. (Now a widow.)

Schaeffer (Shaffer.) Copied from a German Bible of Balthasa Schaeffer, who was born at Seckback, near Frankfort-on-the-Mayn, April 1, 1742, came to Savannah, Ga., in 1770, and married Margaret Eppinger (born at Wilmington, N. C., Jan. 14, 1755) at Savannah, May 30, 1772.

Balthasa died in Savannah, May 1, 1811. In the mortuary records in City Hall in Savannah is found the following entry: "Balthazer Shaffer, gentleman, came to America in 1772, was born in Hanan, Germany, 1742.

His first wife was Margaret Eppinger, daughter of John and Barbara Eppinger, who died in Savannah, Oct., 1793.

Children of Balthazer Shaffer and wife Margaret Eppinger:

John William, born Dec. 15, 1773; died April 10, 1809; married Mary Lawrence.

George, born Sept. 8, 1775; died N. Y.; married Mary Morgan of N. Y.

James, born Oct. 25, 1777; died April 10, 1807; married Susannah, dau. of J. M. Dasher (see "Dasher").

Frederick, born June 15, 1779; died Nov. 14, 1820; married Mary, dau. of John Cole, Sr.

Margaret, born March 21, 1781; died 1801; married Mr. Gugel. One son, John.

Jacob, born July 1, 1783; died March 26, 1859; married widow of his bro. John William.

Sarah, born April 9, 1785; died June 21, 1809.

Hannah Eppinger, born Oct. 25, 1789; died July 3, 1827; never married; will on file.

Elizabeth, born Aug. 23, 1787; died June 2, 1809.

Simon Peter, born Feb. 8, 1792; killed on Harlem R. R. 1849. Left no children.

John William Shaffer and wife Mary Lawrence of S. C., had:

Joseph Lawrence, died 1850; married Henrietta Banna of Sparta, Ga, and had:

Lucy Green, married Mr. Danly. One son Lawrence Danly.

Sarah Margaret, married Mr. Thomas Baker of Liberty Co., Ga. Several children, among them Mary Elizabeth, who married John Baker of Liberty Co.

(After the death of Thomas Baker, his widow, Sarah Margaret married Rev. Robert Quarterman of Liberty Co.)

George Shaffer and wife Mary Morgan, had:

George Washington.

Mary Elizabeth, married George W. Savage of N. J. (died 1859), leaving 3 sons.

Helen Margaret, married Cornelius Williamson, of N. Y. Son Edward left 4 sons.

John William.

Edward.

James Shaffer and wife Susannah Dasher, had:

Elizabeth Margaret, born 1798; married Joseph Robert Thompson in 1824.

Harriet Susan, never married.

Joseph Robert Thompson and wife Elizabeth Margaret Shaffer, had:

James Couper Thompson.

Susan Rosamond Thompson.

Virginia Ann Thompson, married John G. Green of Burke Co., Ga.

Joseph Robert Thompson, Jr.

Georgia Elizabeth Thompson.

Harriet Schaeffer Thompson, married James Eppinger Cope of Savannah.

Augusta Louisa Thompson.

John G. Green and wife Virginia Ann Thompson, had:

Henry Thompson Green, married Miss Sue (?) of Burke Co.

Lucius Clifford Green, married Mrs. Lillian (Goldwire) Harrell.

Anne Maria Thompson, married —— Burdell, of Bath, Ga.

Arthur, lives in Atlanta, Ga.

James Eppinger Cope and Harriett Schaeffer Thompson, had:

Eliza (Lila) Thompson Cope, married Dr. Frank Holland. Two children Joe Thom. & Hattie May.

Harriett Susan Schaeffer Cope; never married.

Frederick Shaffer, and wife Mary Cole (of Beaufort, S. C.), had:

Ann Margaret.

William Jackson.

John Balthazer.

Rebecca Caroline.

James Madison.

Mary Elizabeth.

Jacob Shaffer and wife Mary (widow of brother John William), had:

Elizabeth Amanda, married John Edward Davis of Savannah, and died 1854, leaving 5 children.

Mary, married John D. Cox of Griffin, to Phoenix, Alabama. Daughter Mary.

John Edward, died 1861-65.

Henry Lawrence.

Jacob George.

Joseph.

Margaret, married Thos. S. Mann of Oxford, N. H. Left son William.

Mary Margaret.

George Washington; died 1895; unmarried.

Jacob Shaffer's will probated Aug. 18, 1807. (Savannah, Ga.)

To Margaret Lawrence, sister of deceased wife. Dau. Elizabeth Amanda, wife of John E. Davis; daughter Mary Margaret. Son George Washington Shaffer.

Balthazer Shaffer married (2) Ann Mary Gertrude ——?. Below is an abstract of his will in Savannah, C. H. June 14, 1810-June 11, 1811. Wife Ann Mary Gertrude; sons: Frederick, George, Simon Peter, Jacob; daughter: Hannah; grandchildren: Joseph Lawrence Shaffer and Sarah, children of my eldest son, John William Shaffer, decd; Elizabeth Margaret and Harriet, children of my son, James Shaffer, decd; grandson; John Martin Gugel. Exrs: sons George and Jacob, with Ulrich Tobler and Jeremiah Cuyler. Wit: Jos. S. Pelot, Caleb Harrison, Phllip Jones. Codicil appoints son Frederick as co-exr. Wit.: George Meyers, Random Stone and George Penny.

(A) Diedrick Schaffer married Mrs. Mary Ann Colson, March 28, 1844.

Mortuary Records in City Hall, Savannah, Ga.:

1809, April 10—John W. Shaffer, died age 35.

1809, June 21—Eliza, daughter of Balthazer Shaffer, age 21.

1809, Oct. 29—Ann Mary Shaffer, age 67; wife of John Vaivres.

1810, Jan. 17—(torn off) husband of Ann Mary Shaffer, born in Landau, exiled to Cuba.

Savannah Record Room, Book "R", p. 58:

Barbara Eppinger, widow of John Eppinger, decd., John Eppinger, Jr., Mathias Eppinger, and Balthazer Shaffer in right of his late wife Margaret, daughter of deceased John Eppinger, John Jones in right of his wife Sarah, dau. of John Eppinger, deceased. June 1, 1797.

The wife of James Eppinger was Elizabeth, on deeds in 1803.

Schuman. 1793—Oct. 4—Will of Martin Schuman, Sr. Wife: Tabitha; sons: John, Martin, Henry; daughter: Elizabeth Womack. To sons James, William and Jonathan my estate in Germany, from my father Henry Schuman. Wit.: William Ray, Ann Robertson, James Kirk. (Elizabeth had a son Wiley Womack.)

Schweighoffer. 1803—Dec. 8—Will of Abiel Schweighoffer, wife Margaret; son Abiel, Exr. My four minor children. Wit.: Thomas Polhill, John Waldhauer, Lucy Maner. Abiel Schweighoffer is mentioned in will of Samuel Kraus as "nephew."

Spear. 1802—Will of Moore Spear: wife: Milly; child in esse; sons: James, Willis, William, Nuett Pittman; daughters: Sarah and Patience. Exr. brother Capt. Willis Spear.

1817—March 3—Will of Willis Spear—wife: ——. legatees: Henry Strickland, William Spear, John Morris Spear, Patience Tullis, daughter of Moore Spear. Newett and Willis Spear. Exrs.: Robert Burton, James Spear. Wit.: Benjamin Hill, William Hurst.

Schubtrein. 1803—''Nicholas Schubtrein of Wilkes Co., planter.'' Nicholas Schubtrein of Effingham Co., carpenter.''

Strahan. 1813—Moses Strahan atty. for John Strahan and wife Naomi.

Steiner. 1806—Estates of Christian and David Steiner adm. by Samuel Kraus.

Shuman. 1822—Will of James Shuman—wife Martha; five children: John, Wm. Henry, Rebecca, James, Doctor Henry. Exr.: brother Geo. Henry Shuman. Wit.: C. Loper, Benjamin Harvey, Mary Harvey. Adm. by Clem Powers.

Shultz. 1819—William B. Shultz adm. estate of David Shultz of Charleston, S. C.

Snyder. 1821—Daniel Snyder adm. estate of Catherine Limberger.

1848—Gotlieb Snyder, a Revolutionary soldier of Effingham Co. died age about 90. (Srtobel, p. 273.)

Scruggs. In D. A. R. Lineage Book, Vol. 37, No. 36122, is found the record of Mrs. Mary McNeely, born 1797, and living in 1901, age 103. She is recorded as the daughter of Richard Schruggs, 1758-1832, and wife Sarah Jones, who were married, 1790.

''He was born in Va. and died in Greenville, S. C.''

From Records in Screven County:
Richard Scruggs, 1757-1832 and wife Ann (Sissom) (?), had:
Cassandria, born June 3, 1781.
Thomas, born Sept. 18, 1788.
Sarah, born June 7, 1792.
Richard, born Sept. 8, 1795.
John Greene, born Aug. 12, 1798 (wife was ''Araminta'').
William H., born Nov. 22, 1801.
Ann Abigail, born June 15, 1805; ward of Rev. John Goldwire; she married (1) James Greenhow; (2) William Wilson of Savannah; (3) Mr. Bridges (?).

1801—Richard and Ann Scruggs deed to Jackson Mason Greenhow and James Goldwire Greenhow.

John Green Scruggs and wife Araminta, had:

Richard, born 1820; died Morven, Ga., 1897; married (1) Mary Ann Goldwire; (2) Margaret Horn.

William and Eliza; both died in epidemic.

John Greene Scruggs was a lumber merchant on Bay St., Savannah. His will is in Screven Co., Ga.

Ebenezer Church Record: Drury Scruggs, born Sept., 1768. Sponsors: Drury Scruggs, Thomas and Elizabeth Howell.

"The wife of Drury Scruggs, an English woman, died Aug. 1, 1769; age 30." (Ebenezer Records.)

1783—Land surveyed for Richard Scruggs, Sr. and Jr. (Effingham Co.)

1784—Richard Scruggs deed to Gross Scruggs. Wit: Paul Bevil & Thos. Lane.

1807—Gross Scruggs from Claiborn Bevill. Wit: Moses Oglesby. (Screven Co.)

1819, May 17—Will of James Hamilton Scruggs. Uncle Joseph Perry and cousin Gross Scruggs. Wit.: Wm. Lowry, Sarah and Henry White.

1798—Gross Scruggs of Screven Co., formerly of Effingham Co., with wife Margaret, signs deeds.

1809—Gross Scruggs and wife Ann deed tract to Miss Ann Marks. Gross Scruggs married Ann Lundy, July 24, 1799.

Effingham Co., Nov. 28, 1822. Will of Gross Scruggs. Sons; Gross Scruggs and Josiah F. Scruggs. To children of Elizabeth Hudson: Louisa Hudson, Fanny Hudson, Abigail Hudson and child in esse.

Hardy Griffin Pitts married (a) Mrs. Elizabeth Hudson, July 21, 1832. (Book No. 3, p. 68. Effingham Co.)

Book O, Clerk's office: April 9, 1839. H. G. Pitts grants and bequeaths to stepdaughters Caroline Clinton and Elizabeth Fredonia Hudson, some slaves. John F. Scruggs is appointed guardian to the two girls. Wit: Robert N. Williamson, John F. Scruggs.

1783-92—Bonds of Sale, Deeds, etc. (Effingham Co.): Mary Scruggs, late Mary Butts, sells negroes.

Sarah Scruggs married Abraham Mott, Feb. 16, 1769. (Ebenezer Church Record).

1828—Paul Beville, Sr., to daughter Sarah Ford Mathews, wife of John G. Mathews, property in trust for Wm. H. Scruggs.

Robert Scruggs' name appears in Roll & Legend of Georgia Huzzars, p. 49.

The will of Jesse Scruggs was probated in 1819. His wife was Alethia, the sister of William Sisson. Sons: John Frederick Scruggs,

William Sisson Scruggs, James H. P. Scruggs. Wit.: Chris. G. White, Hugh Graham, Groce Scruggs.

The division of the estate in 1822, shows that there were minor children, John Frederick and Richard Scruggs—that daughter Elizabeth Scruggs had married Charles M. Hill; that the widow Alethia was sister of William Sisson who was sergeant in Capt. Montgomery's Co., U. S. Inf., "She having produced satisfactory papers to that effect."

1827—McLin Lundy, adm. est. of Gross Scruggs.

June 6, 1827—Upson Co., Ga., Gross and Mary Scruggs of Clark Co., Ala. make deeds to Thomas Harley. At the same time & place Wm. G. Scruggs of Warren Co., Ga., deed of lot in Monroe Co., Ga. to Arthur Mathews.

Stafford. (See "Gindrat.") 1799—The estate of William Stafford was adm. by his mother, Mrs. Dorcas Gindrat. Reuben Kennedy and Richard Davis attest that said Stafford declared that he wanted his estate to go to his sister Elizabeth, wife of John Tison "as she was always willing to do for him."

1791—Nov.—Bill of sale from Henry Gindrat to William, Mary, and Seth Stafford, heirs of Samuel Stafford.

Mary Stafford married Reuben Grant Taylor, Dec. 8, 1800.

Smith, John, and wife Julianna, had:

Jacob.

John Godhilp Israel, born 1755; died June 4, 1820. (Rev. soldier). He married Mrs. Christina (Kieffer) Mingledorf, born 1755; died March 10, 1841, children:

Christina, married Charles Ryall.

Hannah Elizabeth, married Mathew Carter.*

David.

Sarah, married James Bird of Bryan Co.

Solomon.

Joshua.

Susannah.

*In Bulloch Co. a Mathew Carter married Miss Barber, and her sister Kesiah Barber married Capt. Wm. Cone. These came from N. C.

1792-1802—John Frederick Schmidt and William Bradnt Schmidt are referred to as sons of John Frederick Schmidt and wife Elizabeth.

Strobhart. (Other Spellings.) Were of Purysburg, S. C., where they received grants (see S. C. Land Grnats). George, Nicholas and Jacob were brothers. George died in 1771, leaving wife Jane (Jenny), and daughters: Catherine, Mary and Susannah Margaret—the last named married John Jones, April 1, 1769 in St. Mathew's Par. Ga. George's sister Mary married Mr. McKensie.

Jacob Strobhar's first wife was named Mary Catherine, and their son Henry was born in Purysburg, July 19, 1765. A marriage of Jacob is recorded to Judith Jourdine (also spelt Gourdin), April 29, 1777.

Nicholas married Eva Mary Mengersdorf, April 16, 1765. In another record gives his wife as Mary Ann, their son Abraham born April 5, 1777.

John and Ann Strobhar had Ann, born Feb. 12, 1777.

Stafford, Joshua, to Margaret Fremonger, March 4, 1768.

Stafford, John, to Susannah Evans, of province of S. C., May 26, 1768.

Stephens, to Nancy Brady, Aug. 24, 1770.

Stafford, William, to Ann Maria Guyer, May 18, 1773. She was a widow in 1778, and deeds to her "mother Ann Mary Magdalene Geiger."

Samson, William (captain of vessel), to Mary Ann Kirk, April 14, 1776.

Shearouse, John, "wife Anna Margaret," 1777.

Strohaker, Rudolph, "wife Elizabeth," of Savannah, 1786.

Schweighoffer, Abiel, "wife Margaret," 1788.

Scheuber, Justus Hartman, "wife Priscilla," 1792.

Slaton, Solomon, "wife Sarah," 1793.

Snooks, David, to Elizabeth Porter, Jan. 4, 1794.

Shuptrine, Christian, to Ann C. Duncan, June 27, 1794. He died Sept., 1800. Was the "only son and heir of Daniel Shuptrine."

Stafford, Joshua, to Mrs. Mary Lane, widow of Thomas Lane, Aug. 2, 1794.

Stanton, John, to Penelope Sellers, Aug. 4, 1794. (Recorded 1796.)

Snyder, Jonathan, to Elizabeth Gnann, Aug. 18, 1794.

Stringer, William ,of Screven Co., and "wife Susannah," 1796.

Schweighoffer, Thomas, to Sarah Salome Zant, June 10, 1797. She married (2) Seth George Threadcraft of Chatham Co.

Stockman, John, had left widow Rosannah, "now Keebler," 1797.

Scarborough, James, to Mrs. Mary Lewis, July 20, 1797.

Seagraves, James, and "wife Ann," 1798.

Snyder, Samuel, to Catherine Zeigler, June 20, 1798.

Stewart, John, to Mrs. Mary Hunter, Oct. 14, 1798.

Sweat, Rev. James, to Susannah (or Hannah) Anderson, March 7, 1799.

Scruggs, Gross, to Ann Lundy, July 24, 1799. (His wife was "Margaret" in 1794.

Snyder, John Taylor of Chatham Co., to Salome Gnann, Nov. 27, 1800. In same marriage and date he is written "John Gotlieb Snyder."

Shewman, William, to Mary Bridges, June 5, 1801.
Shewman, James, to Martha Key, Sept. 19, 1801.

Spear, Blitch, to Zilpah Hurst, Oct. 17, 1803.

Seckinger, Andrew, left widow Catherine, 1803.

Smith, Hugh, to Catherine Elkins, May 30, 1805.

Shrimph, William, to Ann Catherine Seckinger, July 27, 1805.

Seckinger, John Christian, to Agueta Rahn, Nov. 23, 1807.

Stafford, Abraham, "wife Elizabeth," 1808.

Slazer, John, to Gratiosa Zitterauer, July 29, 1808.

Stephens, William, to Mary Causey, March 23, 1809.

Seckinger, Gotlieb, to Mary, widow of Mathew Weidman, March 13, 1810.
Seckinger, Benjamin, to Salome Zitterauer, May 10, 1810.

Stewart, Thomas, to Hannah, widow of John M. Dasher, June 27, 1810.

Staley, John Barnett, to Mrs. Elizabeth Ann Bedford, Aug. 2, 1810.

Shearouse, Emanuel, to Lydia Heidt, Jan. 7, 1813.

Snoden, John Alexander, to Ann Margaret Wisenbaker, May 20, 1813. (She was prob. the daughter of Jacob Wisenbaker and Hannah (Lemcke).

Seckinger, Joshua, to Salome Neiss (Neace), Sept. 2, 1814.

Sheraus, Godhilf, to Salome Freyermouth, Jan. 29, 1818.

Spencer, William J., to Margaret DeGreet Blackley, Nov. 23. 1820. (See Spencer wills in Savannah, Ga.)

Strickland, Henry, to Sarah Lanier, Nov. 23, 1820. (This date may be 1827.)

Spier, William, to Henrietta Willis, April 12, 1821.

Strobhar, John W., to Rachel W. Kettles, Nov. 15, 1821.

Strickland, James, to Sarah Mills, Dec. 16, 1823.

Shuman, Samuel, to Sarah Jones, Jan. 24, 1824.

Spier, William, to Elizabeth Futrell, July 11, 1825.

Strickland, James, to Seneth Evers, June 23, 1825.

Spencer, George J., to Caroline Esther, dau. of Seth G. Threadcraft, March 21, 1825.

Schweighoffer, Thomas, to Sarah Ann Todd, Feb. 22, 1826.

Shearous, Emanuel, to Elizabeth Miller, July 10, 1826.

Strickland, Henry, to Sarah Lanier, of Screven Co., Nov. 23, 1827.

Saussy, Dr. Joachim, to Margaret G. Nowlan, Nov. 19, 1829.

Smith, Middleton, to Sarah G., daughter of Moses Newton, Feb. 8, 1836.

Stafford, Wm. G., to Mary Ann Garnett, Dec. 3, 1834. (Ch. of Ascension, Sav.)

Southwell, Rev. John L., of S. C., to Mrs. Mary Archer, April 5, 1836.

Shuptrine, John C, to Christina (or Catherine) Gnann, Nov. 17, 1838.

Seckinger, John L., to Mary Grovenstein, Feb. 5, 1838.

Snyder, Jonathan, to Esther Caroline Arnstoph, Nov. 12, 1838.

Shearouse, John Richard, to Eveline Naese, Feb. 3, 1839.

Sherouse, William H., to Rosannah H. Neice, Feb. 16, 1839.

Shellman, Joseph M., to Martha Marion Charlton, Sept. 12, 1839.

Snooks, David, to Edna P. Ryals, Sept. 20, 1841.

Seckinger, Ephraim, to Lydia C. Arnsdorf, Dec. 9, 1841.

Smith, Daniel A., to Elizabeth, daughter of Obadiah Edwards, Feb. 7, 1843.

Strobhar, Henry J., to Henrietta E. Bevill, Nov. 18, 1843.

Snooks, David, to Rebecca S. Ryals (sister of 1st wife), Jan. 31, 1844.

Smith, George W., to Maria A. Wolf, March 8, 1845.

Strobart, W. D., to Jane Elizabeth Gnann, Aug. 9, 1844.

Strobel, Rev. Philip A., to Sarah Floerl, Jan. 31, 1846.

Shuptrine, Daniel C., son of Israel and ~~Margaret~~ *Mary*, to Caroline, daughter of Moses and Mary Ann Newton, Nov. 18, 1846.

—?—, Christian Edward, to Salome Seckinger, April 17, 1846.

Seckinger, William, to Lydia H. Shearouse, Feb. 8, 1847.

Seckinger, Frederick, to Christina M. Zipperer, his second wife, March 4, 1850. His first wife was Eliza Zipperer; third, Mrs. Eoline Bingham.

Seckinger, Joshua, to Lavinia Cochran, Feb. 14, 1848.

Spencer. Dec. 19, 1850—Will of John Spencer (Savannah), bequeaths sword, "which was my companion in the Revolution," to nephew Wm. Joseph Spencer.

Stirk. 1776—John Stirk left a widow, Hannah (Greenhow), March 21, 1798, who married James Holton.

Shearouse. 1792—The estate of Joseph Shearouse was adm. by Mathew Rahn and Godlip Smith & Geo. Zitterauer.

Shealy. 1793—Estate of John Shealy; widow Mary. Andrew Gnann is greatest creditor. Wit.: John Gnann, Jonathan Fetzger, J. Strickland.

——, Rosetta, orphan of Jacob Schroeder, was bound to C. F. & Ann Mary Triebner.

Sellers. 1794—Aug. 29—Will of Samuel Sellers—"wife, sons John and Samuel, dau. Penelope.

Schermerhorn. 1795—Cornelius Schermerhorn of N. Y. and wife Rebecca, deed to Peter Schermerhorn, a tract of 1000 acres in Effingham.

Seckinger. 1798, June 30—Jonathan Seckinger was appointed guardian to Gotlieb and Hannah, orphans of Christian Shuptrine.

Strickland. 1799—Inventory of estate of Jacob Strickland; widow Elizabeth. Wit.: Anderson Williams, Samuel Parish.

Shearous. 1812—Joannah, widow of John Shearous and dau. of And. Gnann, had a sister Catherine.

Slater. 1812—William Slater left widow Martha.

Steiner. Mrs. Anna Margaret Steiner (widow of Christian), puts in trust to Mr. Israel Keiffer, a negro for each of her daughters: Lydia, wife of Israel Keiffer; Salome, Catherine, Elizabeth and Sarah Steiner.

Catherine married Joshua Zant, May 9, 1796. He was dead in 1801. She died Aug. 31, 1831.

Elizabeth married Wm. Bird, April 7, 1798.

Sarah married —— Powledge, Sept. 7, 1795.

Sumersall. 1792-3—Estate of Jesse Sumersall appraised by Mathew Rahn, Gothilp Smith, George Zitterauer, Joseph Shearaus, Luke Pridgen, John Fletcher.

Spencer. John Spencer, who had married Mrs. Rosina Postell in 1790 (James Greenhow being trustee of their marriage settlement), enters caveat against Wm. Holzendorf, Esqr., for letters on estate of Rosina Spencer, formerly Postell.

Savannah C. H., May, 1788—John Spencer of Effingham Co. is appointed guardian of Samuel, James and Mary Dinah, children of Samuel and Jane Bowen. Adms. of Bowen estate were Samuel Beecroft and Joseph William Spencer.

1786—Joseph William Spencer empowers his wife Dorothy to make her will. She was daughter of Clement Martin, Jr., and former wife of Henry Cuyler. (Richard Leake married Jean, daughter of Clement Martin, Sr.)

Shearouse. 1832—Will of Godhilp Shearouse—wife Mary; children: Hannah Edwards, Agatha Freyermouth, Mary (who married Dr. Wm. Watkins Wilson) and son, Emanuel and Godhilp.

Tondee (see Elon.) Charles Tondee (son of Peter), according to family tradiion married (1) Harriet Parmeter. In Savannah court records appears the marriage of (a) Charles Tondee to Mrs. Elizabeth Nelson, Dec. 6, 1810. He died about 1842-5 "aged 82."

In Effingham court records are found the following items: Charles Tondee, Jr., born Savannah, June 8, 1803; died 1888. He married (1) Cenia Gaddy, born 1807; (2) Valeria Womack, born 1814; died 1850; (3) Mary Bivins, said to have "had eight sons. (Valeria Womack was a niece of Cenia Gaddy.)

In 1827 Thomas S. Tondee—(wife Julia, who was daughter of William H. Womack,) and William H. Prevatt, who had married Sarah, the widow of Womack, were heirs of said Womack, who left also minor heirs, Valeria, Alfred, Jackson and William G.

In Effingham County marriages is found:

Amelia Maria Tondee, married (1) William Patterson; (2) Thos. Elkins, Oct. 16, 1830.

Serena Tondee, born 1801; died 1856; married (1) Herman Elkins, June 19, 1824; (2) A. Guyton.

In Savannah Record Room, Book "W," p. 125. 1779—The marriage settlement of Mrs. Mary Patterson and John Dews. Security, Charles Tondee.

Savannah Record Room: Baptized, Marie Josephine and Maria Amelia, daughters of Charles Vincent Tarseille and his wife Marie Joannah Amelia Tondee.

Toosing-Dusseign. This name occurs often as Toosing or Tussing, but on a deed in S. C. it is found spelt interchangeably with "Dusseign," which was probably the original form.

In 1759 Jacob Toosing had grant on Blue Bluff on the Savannah River, and had "been in the province eight years. Had wife and one child." (Candler.)

Jacob Toosing married Mrs. Mary Kaemmel, Sept. 14, 1756; children:

John Jacob Toosing, born Sept. 17, 1757; died Nov. 25, 1757.

Anna Margaret Toosing, born April 10, 1759.

John Paul Toosing, born April 16, 1761.

Joseph Toosing, born April 22, 1763.

"Paul Toosing, a Revolutionary soldier, died in Effingham Co., Dec. 26, 1826."

1802—In Effingham Co. is recorded deeds of "Joseph and Paul Toosing of S. C."

1805—Joseph Toosing and wife Susannah, of Beaufort, S. C., sign deeds in Effingham Co.

1828—Esate of John P. Toosing was adm. by Henry L. Grovenstein

Tuttle. 1836—May 16—Estate of Caroline Amanda Tuttle adm. by James Tuttle.

Tison. Feb. 2, 1808—Estate of William Tison adm. by Edmund Tison.

Treutlen. Little is known of the family of Gov. John Adam Treutlen, who has given to this name one of the most honored places in the history of Georgia. Nor indeed do records reveal many of the events in his own life, and the manner of his cruel death remains to this day an unwritten story.

Rev. Mr. Strobel gives a few details concerning Gov. Treutlen, and in "Lutheran Land Marks" Rev. W. J. Finck has added some interesting facts. From these two authorities we glean that Mrs. Treutlen, Sr., was a widow when she came to this country, bringing with her two sons, Frederick and John Adam, but what year is not stated. Mr. Finck refers to the drowning of an older son at Gosport, England, and this statement is also of record in family history, to which is added the tradition that the father was a naval officer stationed in England, where he also was drowned.

Mrs. Treutlen, Sr. married again, and our historians have stated that it was on account of the unfortunate influence of the stepfather, that John Adam was transferred from his home at Vernonsburg, near Savannah, to Ebenezer, "where he was confirmed in 1747 at the age of fourteen". Upon this record is based the year of his birth as 1733, although a family record states that "he was born in Berckbesgaden, Austria in 1726", to which is added that his death was brought about by being tied to a horse which was made to dash off at random at great speed. This horrible deed of the tories was perpetrated near Orangeburg, S. C., but if his body received burial, the spot is unknown.

The wife of John Adam Treutlen was Margarethe, but her surname is unknown. She was of the Purysburg colony, just across the Savannah River from Ebenezer, and this was the home of the Mallettes, Schads, Ravots, Gindrats and other French-Swiss families. Margarethe was confirmed at Ebenezer in 1754 as Ann Margaret, and was married there in 1756.

Children of John Adam Treutlen and wife Margarethe:

Elizabeth, born Feb. 13, 1757; died Dec. 9, 1759. One of her sponsors was Katherine Schad.

Jonathan, born Aug. 22, 1758; died Aug. 29, 1758.

Elizabeth, born April 8, 1760; married William Kennedy, April 8, 1778.

Dorothea, born Feb. 21, 1762.

Mary, born Nov. 16, 1764.

Hannah, born Feb. 26, 1766.

Christian, date of birth not known; died about 1820. Wife Mary ?.

John Adam, 2nd, born Aug. 29, 1770; married 1793 to Ann M. Miller.

Among some papers in Ordinary's Office in Effingham Co., is a marriage license dated Jan. 14, 1778 to John Adam Treutlen—the name of the bride not appearing, but the "Ebenezer Record Book", (Voight), completes the register, supplying the name of Mrs. Anne Unselt. (Widow of David Unselt).

(Mrs. Margarethe Treutlen died June 25, 1777. Finck).

Christian Treutlen and wife Mary; born 1775, died Sept. 26, 1825, had:

Joseph C., adm. of father's estate. J. was dead in 1828; John Charlton, adm.

Mary Ann, born Dec. 24, 1792; married Wm. G. Porter, April 6, 1813; born 1782; died 1825 (son of James and Elizabeth Porter.)

Christian E.; married Ann Mary Triebner, Jan. 8, 1819. (See Gronau-Triebner).

Maria S., married Wm. J. Dudley.

Savannah Record Room, Book "K", page 139. Deed of gift of Christian Treutlen to daughter Maria S. Dudley, 1820. In 1830 she makes deed as Mrs. Maria S. Dudley, wife of Wm. J. Dudley.

John Adam Treutlen, 2nd, married Ann M. Miller in 1793, had:

Gabriel, married Ann M. Conner.

Catherine, married Daniel Wade.

Gabriel Treutlen and Ann (Conner), had:

Carrie, married Thomas Berry.

Oct. 20, 1792—John Adam Treutlen, 2nd, conveyed all his property to his brother Christian, to protect himself from a law suit. This property was transferred back in 1801, and he is referred to as being "now of Orange Co., S. C."

Effingham C. H., Book G. H., p. 157: James Dupuis and wife Elizabeth of Beaufort, S. C. deeds to Christopher Frederick Triebner, planter and shopkeeper, the land what had formerly belonged to Christian R. Treutlen. (1813).

The wife of Frederick Treutlen (brother of Gov. Treutlen) was also named Margaret, and in her death record in City Hall Savannah, it is stated that she was born in Switzerland. She died July 23, 1807, age 79.

Family records state that she was Margaret Schad, daughter of Solomon Schad.

In Ebenezer Records: "Elizabeth, daughter of Frederick Treutlen and wife, was born Feb. 24, 1758, baptised March 4, sponsors were: Mathias and Magdalena Wurst and Katherine Schad."

Will of Frederick Treutlen, Probate Court, Savannah, Ga. Feb. 17 1798. Probated Nov. 15, 1798. "Of Wilmington Island, aged and infirm." Wife Margaret. Daughters Ann Prevost and Catherine Tebeau. Wit: John Dillon, Henry Addington, Ann Mary Dillon. Exrs: John Tebeau and William Lewden. "Estate not to be subject to Peter Prevost."

In "Swiss Emigration to America in the 18th Century," p. 19:
"Marc Prevost, of Geneva, distinguished in the Indian War."

John Tebeau was dead in 1822 and Catherine and F. E. Tebeau
were joint Adms.

1786, Dec. 24—Deed of gift from Frederick Treutlen to loving
grandson William Prevost (of a negro woman and child). Wit: Bannister Winn, Jasper Reddick. Savannah Record Room, Book Q, p. 216.

(The wife of Bannister Winn was Jane, in 1798).

Porter. William Porter, Sr., was dead in May, 1791, and his
estate was adm. by David Porter. Inventory by Christian Treutlen,
Samuel Bostwick, John Boykin. He left children:

Susannah, who married William Cox of Barnwell, S. C.

James, married Elizabeth——?

William, Jr., married Mrs. Rachel (Wilson), widow of Thomas
Garnett, Jon. 14, 1795.

Benjamin, whose wife was Elizabeth.

David, married Sally Bostwick, July 9, 1797.

James Porter (who died 1806), and wife Elizabeth, had:

William G. (dead in 1825), married in 1813 to Mary Ann, daugh-
terof Christian Treutlen. Their dau. Mary, married Jeremiah
Mallet, May 15, 1847. She was born March 24, 1822.

James, Jr., was dead 1822; estate adm. by William G. Porter.

Elizabeth, married David Snooks, Jan. 4, 1794.

Ann Harriet.

Thomas, married Salome Gruber, 1808.

(There was a Thomas Porter whose wife was Susannah in 1808.)

Benjamin Porter was dead in 1807. Estate adm. by Jas. Porter.
His heirs were: Wife, Elizabeth; children, Henry, Elizabeth, Benja-
min (who married Sarah Kennedy, March 22, 1827). "Payments to
Sally Stewart."

1797, Oct. 10—Deed of gift from William Porter to Mrs. Amy Kettles, wife of friend Jacob Kettles. Wit: James and Elizabeth Porter.

1818—James Porter, deed of gift to granddaughter Luesener Ann
Rieser.

1808—Hardy Pitts receipts to James Porter and Herman Crum
for his part of estate of Benjamin Porter.

18——The orphans of Thomas D. Porter were Ann, and Elvira
Ann, who chose Benjamin C. Porter as guardian. Elvira Ann married
William P. Dopson, Dec. 30, 1830; died in 1831.

There was a John Porter who married Henrietta Ravot, Jan. 16,
1795.

Winnsboro, Fairfield Co., S. C. Will of James Porter, April 5, 1775. Of St. Marks Parish, Craven Co., Jackson Creek. Wife Margaret; sons, James Porter and John Porter; daughters, Mary Porter and Janet Robinson. Exrs: Wife, David McCreight, Sr. and Jr., and Robert Martin.

S. C. Land Grants: 1730—To William Porter 700 acres and a lot in Kingston Township.

William G. Porter and Mary Ann (Treutlen), had:

George W., born 1814.

Albert G., born March 21, 1815; married (2) Mrs. Evelyn Humbert; daughter Amanda.

Evaline M., born Nov. 20, 1816.

Amanda, born June 11, 1818.

(July 20, year not given—Miss Isabelle E. Treutlen died at the residence of Jeremiah Mallette, age 61.)

Thilo (or Thylo.) Oct., 1737—Mr. Thilo (or Thylo) went to Salzburgers at Ebenezer as surgeon. Col. Records of Ga., Vol. 3, p. 170.

In 1740 his term having expired he was petitioned to remain; and in 1757 "he had a wife and child." Ebenezer Records state that his daughter Ann Mary Frederica died Dec. 24, 1757.

However "Hannah Elizabeth Thilo, only heir of Dr. Chirstian Ernst Thilo married John Jacob Heinle, Jan. 5, 1773."

In 1778 the property of Dr. Thilo was in possession of Anna Barbara Buntz, from her husband Henry Ludwig Buntz, and sold to Ebenezer Church.

Townsend. 1797—William Townsend, mariner, died intestate, leaving minor children, Thomas and William. Martin and Catherine Cruger were "next of kin."

1828—Is recorded marriage settlement of William Townsend with Margaret, widow of John Hinely.

Threadcraft. 1813—Seth G. Threadcraft and wife Sarah (Zant), widow of Schweighoffer, make deed to Samuel Wilson, for 200 acres on N. E. side of Snales Creek.

At same time he puts 66 acres in trust to William J. Spencer and George J. Spencer, for the use of his wife Sarah, and the children of his present marriage.

William J. Spencer died Dec. 17, 1823.

March 19, 1825, is recorded the marriage settlement of George J. Spencer with Caroline Esther, the daughter of Seth G. Threadcraft.

1822—Seth G. Threadcraft, with Margaret, Mary and Abiel Schweighhoffer make deeds to Benjamin Dasher.

Tison. 1810—Camel Tison applies for letters on the estate of George Dykes, who died in Richmond Co., Ga. Caveat by Noah Dykes.

Taylor, Nathan, to Susannah Glazer, Dec. 8, 1768.

Teffer, John, to Judith Dixon, Feb. 6, 1769.

Tyner, Elijah, to Selina Rogers, Feb. 15, 1774. (His wife was Frances in 1813.)

Touchstone, Richard, to Mrs. Martha Penrose, Jan. 5, 1813.

Thonica, James, to Ann Hynes, Aug. 3, 1802.

Townsend, William, to Mary Ernst, Sept. 22, 1803.

Tison, Edmund, to Nancy Cook, Dec. 25, 1804. (Son of Wm. Tison) was dead in 1808.

Tison, Eliakim, to Ann Hearn or Harn, Nov. 20, 1805.

Tullis, Rev. Stephen, to Sinai London, Feb. 23, 1807.

Threadcraft, Seth George, to Sarah Salome (Zant), widow of Thomas Schweighoffer, Sept. 19, 1807.

Tullis, Temple, to Patience, dau. of Willis Spier, Nov. 13, 1809.

Touchstone, Richard ,to Mrs. Martha Penrose, Jan. 5, 1813.

Teleton, Thomas, to Mrs. Elcy Coleman, March 31, 1813.

Toomer, David, to Martha Hodges, Dec. 6, 1813.

Tison, Luther, to Winifred Hines, Sept. 3, 1814.

Tyner, John G., to Mary Curry, Dec. 18, 1815.

Tyner, Jonathan, to Ann Harris, Nov. 5, 1819.

Tyner, Jurdon, to Mary Stokes, Sept. 16, 1820.

Thomas, C. Basil, to Lydia Rahn, Dec. 19, 1821.

Tyson, Clavin, to Mary Johnson, Feb. 11, 1822.

Tyner, Simeon, to Anna Highsmith, Feb. 11, 1824.

Tyner, Simeon, to Esther Ann Southwell, April 20, 1827.

Townsend, William, to Mrs. Ann Margaret Hinely, "heir of Emanuel Zeigler," Sept. 17, 1828.

Tyner, Jackson, to Sarah Pace, Dec. 10, 1832.

Tullis, Henry J., to Rebecca Futrell, Oct. 13, 1843.

Thiot, Charlton H., Anna Charlton, Feb. 21, 1850.

Tumblin, Thomas, wife Amelia, 1808.

Thompson, James, wife Margaret, 1801.

Thorn, William, wife Rebecca, 1789.

Ulmer, Charles, wife Kesiah, 1816.

Ulmer, John Philip, to Sarah Eliza Fox of Chatham Co., Dec. 30, 1828.

Ulmer, Thomas, to Letitia Ann Parish, Sept. 28, 1836.

Venieur, John, of Purysburg, S. C., to Elizabeth Winkler, Aug., 1777.

Ulmer. 1806—Sav. Rec. Room, Book AA, p. 162. Wm. Ulmer's dece'd father, Philip Ulmer & wife Ann. Charles & Philip Ulmer Exrs. with *Christoph F. Triebner.*

Wilson. 1788—James Wilson, Sr., "To son John." 1794—"To loving brother, Dr. Jesse Wilson." Wit.: E. Tiner.

Wheeler. 1816—Nov. 4—Phoebe Wheeler chose her mother Sabria (Edwards) Wheeler as guardian.

Wilson. 1786—April 8—William Wilson of Georgetown, S. C., deeds to daughter-in-law Elizabeth, wife of Stephen Ford. Wit.: Anthony Ford, Edmund Martin, J. P.

1830—Elizabeth, widow of Jesse Wilson, to grandson, Wlliam Wilson.

Walter (or Waller.) 1808—Samuel Walter (or Waller), deed of gift to nephew William Watkins Wilson, son of William Wilson and wife Olive (Day). At same time Philip Jones, "at present of Effingham," deed of gift to William Watkins Wilson.

1793—Estate of William Wilson adm. by J. G Neidlinger.

(1807. See will of William Wilson in Chatham Co. Wife Ann Abigail, who was a Miss Scruggs of Effingham Co.) (Different men.)

1799—Estate of John Wilson adm. by Gideon Zettler (son-in-law).

Abbott. 1787—Benjamin Warren to John Abbott of Burke Co. Wit.: Sanai Warren, Richard Rogers.

Williams. 1791—"Lands of Chaplin and Pride Williams."

Warren. Margaret, to John M. Dasher, 1791.

Woolf. 1807—Stephen Woolf to children: David, Halacannah, Ann, Vashti, Isaiah.

Womack. 1827—Heirs of Wm. H. Womack (was dead 1819): widow Sarah (now the wife of Wm. Prevatt), Thomas S. Tondee and his wife Julian. William Gaddy, guardian, of Valeria, Alfred, Jackson and Wm. W. Womack, minors. John Womack of Sav. one of adms.

1835—March 2—Will of Frederick Womack—"all to wife Lydia."
Wit.: Edith & Stephen Hester.

1826—Deed of William Womack to son Frederick.

Weidman. 1804—Estate of Daniel Weidman (June 26). Wife
Catherine. Major son Solomon. Heirs: Andrew Gnann and Daniel
Weidman. Speaks of grant to J. C. Creamer, 1759.

Williams. 1803—Jan. 31—Will of John Williams (of Savannah).
Wife Pheribe, the daughter of James Jones. To James Hudson, tract
bordering lands of Samuel and Robert Hudson and Richard Scruggs.

Weist. 1791—Oct. 13—Will of Mathias Weist of Goshen, St.
Mathew's Parish. Wife Mary Magdalena. "To daughter Christian
over and above the other daughters," not named. Exr.: Rev. Christian Rabenhorst. Wit.: Frederick Treutlen, John Keebler, Christopher Steiner. Signature to will is *"West."*

Wellman. 1817—Francis H. Wellman of firm of Brooks & Wellman, mortgage on James Crum.

Webber. No date. "Michael Webber died about May 17, 17—;
left daughter Dorothy who married Jesse Sanderlin. She died Aug.
28, 1786, and her heirs were: Nathaniel Ott and his wife Christina
Elizabeth, and Solomon Gnann."

Webb. 1793—Sept. 25—Will of Wentworth Webb. Exr.: Robert
Kelly. Jesse Mixon enters caveat aganist Robert Kelly, who is also
made adm. of the estates of Henry Webb, Rachel Shorter and Co.
Caveators reason that Robert Kelly was co-equal heir of Wentworth
Webb. Signed by William and Benjamin Cook and Rachel Philips.
Wit.: Christian Treutlen, J. P., and Abraham Ravot, J. P. "Mr.
Robert Kelly not being pleased with the Openian, prays for an
appeal." Appraised by Robert Scott McKeen and William Cone.

1797—May 8—Will of James Webb. To half brother Jesse Webb,
and half sisters Lydia, Elizabeth, Sarah, Martha, Jane. Wit.: Asa
Loper, Abel Loper, Josua Loper.

Walsingham. 1825—Orphans of John G. Walsingham: to Herman
Elkins guardian of Charles, and John W. Exley guardian to Clarissa
Maria. His widow was Catherine, & he was dead Dec. 1819.

Whiteman. 1819—Feb. 7—Israel Whiteman adm. est. Daniel
Whiteman. (Weitman.)

Wilson. 1829—Elihu Wilson made guardian of Gabriel Wilson's
(died 1819) orphans.

West. 1819—Estate of Wm. West adm. by Levy Parker.

Wertsch. 1792—Estate of Jahn Casper Wertsch in acct. with **John** Wisenbaker. Adm. by Hergen Hersen.

Wilson. 1791—John Wilson for "love & affection" to **Ephriam,** son of Elijah Tiner.

Woolfe. 1827—John Woolfe adm. est. Geo. Woolfe who left **minor** son, Irvin W.

Marriages:

Walker, Thomas, to Rebecca Emanuel, Jan. 7, 1757.

Wilson, John, "a foreigner," to Maria, widow of Christian Rudel-sperger, Nov. 19, 1760.

Williams, Chaplin, to Susannah Green, Jan. 20, 1772.

Williams, John, to Rhetta London, March 24, 1794.

Williams, Henry W., to Sarah, dau. of Thomas McCall, April 22, 1794. (McCall d. before 1791.)

Weightman, Daniel (died March 3, 1819), to Miss Ann C. Cramer, July 8, 1794. (Dau. of John Chris Cramer. Had sister Agatha, w. of Andrew Gnann.) (First wife Salome Lemcke; second wife Frederica Maria ?).

White, Henry, to Sarah Butts, March 25, 1795.

Winkler, Elias, to Mary Penninger, July 1, 1796.

Wilson, Jesse, to Eliza Cook, Aug. 10, 1796.

Waugh, Thomas, to Mary Lewis, May 14, 1801.

Westcoat, Joel, to Cynthia Miller, Feb. 1, 1802.

Wylly, William, to Naomi Dasher, Jan. 14, 1802.

Wright, John, to Sarah Jenkins, Oct. 3, 1802.

Wisenbaker, John, to Mary Densler, May 23, 1803.

Wilson, William, to Olive Day, Oct. 12, 1804.

Walker, Ansel, of Glynn Co., to Ally Tison, Jan. 21, 1805.

Wilson, Luke, to Patience Crawford, March 6, 1806. Her mother Grace married second Christ. Bailey.

Wilson, David, of Bulloch Co., to Polly Temple, Sept. 30, 1806.

Waldhauer, John, Jr., to Margaret, dau. of Mathew and **Mary** Weidman, Feb. 23, 1807.

Wilson, Gabriel, to Sarah Oglesby, Dec. 26, 1807.

Winter, John, of Savannah, to Dorothy Guyer, May 21, 1811.

Wilson, Elihu, to Catherine, Nov. 6, 1815. Dau. of John and Elizabeth Tullis. Married second Mrs. Jane (Achord) Warren.

Walsingham, Elijah, to Mary Sheffield, July 1, 1816.

Weitman, Lewis, to Sarah, widow of Israel Floerl, July 1, 1818.

Wilson, John, to Susannah Rahn, Aug. 7, 1820.

Weitman, Israel, to Sophia Gugel, Nov. 30, 1820.

Williams, William, to Mrs. Elizabeth Wood, June 23, 1821.

Wilson, Allen, to Mary Hurst, Nov 29, 1821.

Wall, Alexander, of Chatham Co., to Hannah Ann Hines, Oct. 23, 1825.

Weitman, Solomon, to Margaret Rahn, April 26, 1826.

Wilson, Elias, to Amelia Ann Hurst, March 18, 1827.

Wisenbaker, James, to Sarah A. Dasher, Oct. 16, 1827.

Wilson, William W. (son of Dr. Wm. Wilson and wife Sarah (Hines), to Mary Shearouse, Sept. 26, 1827..

Whebell, Robt. D., to Elizabeth Ambrose, Dec. 2, 1828.

Weitman, Mathew, to Mrs. Salome Stanton, Nov. 16, 1829 .

Wilson, Josiah, of Liberty Co., to Eliza Mary, dau. of Howell and Martha Hines), 1829.

Wisenbaker, John, to Margaret Waldhauer, Dec. 15, 1831.

Wilson, Thomas, to Elizabeth Backley, Dec. 27, 1831.

Wright, Rev. Geo. R., to Margaret Elizabeth Charlton, Dec. 27, 1831.

Wilson, Dr. William Watkins, to Mrs. Henrietta (Gindrat) Clark, April 18, 1835.

Wilkins, Archibald, to Amanda M. Porter,

Wilson, Jeremiah, to Lavitha Kettler, Sept. 5, 1836. He also married a Miss Reed. (To Brooks Co.)

Wilson, Henry M., to Hannah Mingledorf, Dec. 18, 1832.

Waldhauer, John, to Christine Gnann (2nd wife), Jan. 28, 1839.

Wilson, Elbert, to Lavinia Graham, April 8, 1833.

Wilson, Allen, to Amy Griner (also written Annah), March 30, 1839.

White, Samuel B., to Mrs. Mary B. Harrison, May 21, 1839.

Wilson, John B., to Jane A. Edwards, June 6, 1841. She married 2nd Barnett Newton in 1845.

Williams, Harmon E., to Susan E. Hodge, Dec. 6, 1838.

Wilson, Henry M., to Hannah Mingledorf, Dec. 29, 1832.

Willis, Joseph J., to Martha Pengree, June 6, 1841.

Wilson, Luke C., to Ann Catherine Greiner, Aug. 10, 1841.

Willis, Turner, to Elizabeth Spier, March 31, 1848.

Wilson, Eli Wesley, to Sarah J. Davis, Oct. 21, 1854.

Wilson, Stephen A., to Jane L. Dasher, Jan. 30, 1852. She.died Sept. 22, 1852, age 25.

Wilson, Stephen A., to Laura Davis, Jan. 24, 1854.

Wilson, Stephen A., to Tabitha Ann Edwards, May 27, 1857.

Young, Cuyler W., to Sarah McDonell, Aug. 31, 1841.

Zipperer, Christian Jonathan, to Gratiosa Zitterauer, March 10, 1778.

Zant, Joshua, to Catherine Steiner, May 9, 1796. (See **Purysburg** burial records.) Joshua Zant was dead in 1801. "Ann Catherine Zant, w. of Joshua Zant, was born June 8, 1806; died Aug. 31, 1831."

Zitterauer, Solomon, to Elizabeth Oglesby, Nov. 21, 1799; born Sept. 23, 1779; died June 5, 1829.

Zipperer, Christian, to Susannah Wilson, Feb. 22, 1801.

Zitterauer, Gotliph, to Margaret Gugel, April 6, 1811.

Zettler, Nathaniel, to Mary Jones, Dec. 27, 1820.

Zipperer, Gideon, to Sarah Pauledge, Jan. 28, 1823.

Zitterauer, David, to Theresa Fitzpatrick (or Thursa), June 27, 1825.

Ziegler, David, Jr., to Evaline Creamer, Jan. 10, 1828.

Zitterauer, John Robert, to Eliza Remshardt, March 13, 1828.

Walsingham, John G., wife Catherine, 1801.

Ward, John, wife Ann, 1810.

Wilder, William, wife Mary (Newton), 1811.

Williams, John, of Savannah, Widow "Feriby" (dau. of Jas. Jones), 1800.

Weitman, Daniel, wife Mary Frederica, 1792.

Wade, Samuel, wife Hannah, 1804.

Wood, Henry, of Liberty County, wife Rebecca, 1790.

Waldhauer, Jacob, wife Hannah, 1797.

Weitman, Mathew, Widow "Mary," 1805.

Wheeler, James, Widow Sabria (Edwards), dau. Phoebe, 1811.
Wheeler, Shadrack, wife Christian, 1813.

Wilcox, Eli, wife Ann, 1815.

Wilson, Henry, Widow Hannah, 1833.

Wisenbaker, Jacob, Widow Hannah (dau. of Rev. Mr. Lemcke), 1797.

Wilkins, Paul H., of Liberty Co., wife Ann M., 1803.

Weidman. 1804—Estate of Daniel Weidman, June 26, wife Catherine. Son Solomon. Heirs Andrew Gnann & Daniel Weidman.

Zittrouer, Robert, to Eliza Remshart, March 1, 1828.

Zitterour, Chas. Ulmer, to Ann C Rylander, Nov. 3, 1828.

Zipperer, Theophilus, to Mrs. Mary Prosser, March 3, 1829.

Zitterauer, Edward, to Johannah Zeigler, Feb. 19, 1833.
Zitterauer, Simeon, to Ann Hinely, April 6, 1836.

Zipperer, Jeremiah, to Mrs. Lavitha Kell, Sept. 5, 1836.

Ziegler, Joshua, to Susannah Dasher, Oct. 31, 1838.

Zipperer, Christian Edward, to Salomi Seckinger, April 22, 1845.

The Zitterauers, Zants and Zettlers came from Meminger in 1738. Balthazer Zant is the first of the name appearing, and was one of the founders of Ebenezer. Solomon and Joshua Zant were probably sons of Balthazer, and they settled in Purysburg, S. C.

Zant. Solomon Zant married Elizabeth Keiffer, March 24, 1767. She died Jan. 1, 1773, age 26. She had Beneaiah, born Oct. 1, 1769, who died Nov. 11, 1772, and Joshua, born Sept. 1, 1772. She may have been the mother of Salome, who died Aug. 3, 1770, age 2.

Solomon Zant married Dorothea Reiser (by Rev. Mr. Muhlenberg), Jan. 31, 1775. She was left a widow in 1778.

An interesting connection may here be noted: Sept. 19, 1807, Mrs. Sarah Salome (Zant), the widow of Thomas Schweighoffer 2nd married Seth George Threadcraft only child of George Threadcraft, who was a brother of Sarah Threadcraft, the wife of Gen. Lachlan McIntosh.

Joshua Zant married Catherine Steiner, May 9, 1796. (This was probably the son of Solomon, not the brother.) See Annals, Vol. 3, for Purysburg burials.

Thomas Schweighoffer was the son of Thos. and Hannah (Floerl) Schweighoffer, and was born July 8, 1761.

Effingham Co. Marriages:

Zettler, Gideon, to Martha, daughter of John Wilson, April 16, 1797. (Gideon was dead 1803), and his widow married Immanuel Zipperer (son of Jonathan), Sept. 26, 1803.

Joshua and Solomon Zant of Purysburg, S. C., deed tract in Effingham Co. to Joshua and Catherine Glover—part of a grant to Solomon Zant.

Zipperer. Christian Zipperer and wife Anna Mary, had:

Christian Jonathan, born Jan. 30, 1757.

Samuel, born Oct. 2, 1759.

In 1829 Jonathan Zipperer deeds to son Emanuel, who had married the widow of Gideon Zettler.

Gideon Zipperer married Sarah Pauledge, Jan. 28, 1823. He was dead in 1829, and his minor heirs were: Sophia, Jacob, and Salomi. George Pauledge was appointed guardian, and Samuel and Solomon Zipperer adm. the estate.

Zipperer, Gideon, married Ann Hester, Dec. 21, 1832.

Zipperer, Christian, married Susannah Wilson, Feb. 22, 1801.

Zipperer, Jefferson, married Caroline, daughter of Elihu Wilson, Feb. 22, 1836. She married 2nd Benjamin Davis.

Zipperer, Gideon Emanuel, married Ann Hester, Dec. 21, 1832.

Zipperer, Christian Edward, married Salome Seckinger, April 17, 1846.

Zitterauer, John Robert, married Eliza Remshart, March 13, 1828.

Ziegler, David, Jr., married Evaline Creamer, Jan. 10, 1828.

Zettler, Nathanel, married Mary Jones, Dec. 27, 1820.

Zipperer, Theopilus, married Mrs Mary Prosser, March 3, 1829.
Zipperer, John, married Louisa M. Kesler, Jan. 9, 1843.

Zitterauer. John George Zitterauer married Catherine Brandwein May 19, 1761, and had:

Timothy, born Dec. 7, 1762.

John Gotlieb, born July 8, 1766.

Mary Margaret, born Dec. 2, 1768; died Aug. 31, 1771.

Mary Margaret, born May 6, 1774.

John George Zitterauer is recorded with wife Mary, as having son Solomon, born Nov. 14, 1777.

The will of John George Zitterauer is recorded Sept. 3, 1812. Wife Anna (who is apparently his third wife). Sons, John Gotlieb and Solomon; daughter, Hannah, the wife of John Christopher Miller (Mueller). To Rev. John Ernst Bergman and Hannah Schubtrein. Exrs: son John and J. Kobler and J. Neidlinger. Wit: Joshua Helmly, Israel & John Hinely.

1821, Nov. 12—Will of Anna Zitterauer. Stepson Solomon. Brother Jonathan Seckinger. In the division Starling Parker receives "his part" in the estate. Will proved by Joshua Seckinger. Exr: son John Christopher Miller.

Solomon Zitterauer married Elizabeth Oglesby, Nov. 2, 1799. She was born Sept. 23, 1779, and died June 5, 1829.

George Zitterauer married Anna Louisa Neace, Sept. 17, 1829.

There are indications that Anna Zitterauer had been the wife of Christian Schubtrein, and the mother of Hannah Schubtrein. She was the daughter of Mathias and Anna Catherine Seckinger, and married John Paul Mueller (Miller), July 18, 1769. He died Feb. 21, 1772, leaving son John Christopher Mueller. The widow married John Maurer July 1, 1777. (See Maurer).

John Gotlieb Zitterauer and wife Hannah deed to Solomon Zitterauer and wife Elizabeth, and to Anna, widow of George Zitterauer, and to John C. Miller. 1821.

Dec. 17, 1822—Solomon Zitterauer makes deed to son-in-law Samuel Dasher.

June 3, 1830—Solomon Zitterauer married Esther Gnann.

John Gotlieb Zitterauer married Margaret Gugel, April 6, 1811. His will is recorded in 1845. Wife Margaret; children: Charles J., Hannah M. Candal (?), Richard C., William J., Sarah Ann, and Louise Amanda Barnwell.

Paul Zitterauer and wife Margaret had Gratiosa, born Dec. 12, 1757, who married Christian Jonathan Zipperer, whose son Jonathan Christian Zipperer was born Jan. 25, 1779. Paul Zitterauer died Feb. 1, 1758, and his widow Margaret married George Schweigher May 19, 1761.

Ernst Christian Zitterauer married Johannah (Hannah) Reiter (Reuter), Oct. 2, 1770. She was probably the daughter of Simon Reuter.

David Zitterauer married June 24, 1797 to Elizabeth Ihly. His son David Zitterauer married Theresa Fitzpatrick June 27, 1825.

In 1823—William Zitterauer claims share in estate of his grandfather Ernst Zitterauer, from Catherine Zitterauer, the widow. (Probably a second wife).

1827—David Zitterauer applies for adm. on estate of Mary Catherine Zitterauer.

Ann Zitterauer, nee Seckinger, married (1) Christian Schubtrein, and became the second wife of John George Zitterauer. But she married John Paul Mueller (Miller) July 18, 1769. (Ezenezer Record).

1795, March 21—Will of John George Zeigler. Wife Anna Catherine; sons Emanuel and David. Wit: John C. Neidlinger, Hannah Neidlinger.

1817, Aug. 8-Sept. 21, 1820—Will of Ernst Zitterauer. Wife Anna Catherine; son Gotliph and daughter Salome Seckinger; grand children William and David, sons of decd. son David. Exrs: son Gotliph, J. Zitterauer, John Kogler, John Neidlinger. Wit: Joshua Helmly, Israel Hinely, John Hinely.

1827—David Zitterauer applies for adm. on Mary Catherine Zitterauer, a widow.

1829—Jonathan Zipperer to son Emanuel.

1829—Minor heirs of Gideon Zipperer were Sophia, Jacob and

Ziegler. Lucas Ziegler married Salome Zettler, June 25, 1765, and had Lydia, born April 20th, 1766; and Agnesia, born Sept. 27, 1768—In Ebenezer Ch. Records, p. 66, is recorded the birth of Anna, "daughter of Lucas Ziegler and wife Anna", born June 26, 1779.

John George Ziegler married Anna Catherine Rau, June 1, 1755, and their children:

Hannah Elizabeth, born April 17, 1757; died Oct. 21, 1757.

Hannah Elizabeth, born Sept. 20, 1760.

Mary, born Jan. 3, 1763; died Sept. 7, 1771.

Immanuel, born Jan. 21, 1765.

Catherine, born Aug. 25, 1767.

Lydia, born May 18, 1779.

David, born Nov. 27, 1769.

Mrs. Agnes Ziegler married Andrew Seckinger, May 17, 1756.

Agnesia Ziegler married J. Casper Waldhauer, June 27, 1758.

Eva Maria Ziegler married John Casper Beth, "Tuesday after Whitsunday, 1754."

Zettler. Mathias Zettler, who died Feb. 3, 1769, and his wife Elizabeth, who died June 9, 1768, had:

Nathaniel, born June 7, 1761.

Rosina, born Aug. 9, 1763.

Daniel Zettler and wife Hannah (Dasher), had:

Christian, born 1772.

David Zettler, an infant died Jan. 26, 1760.

Esther Zettler, an infant died July 9, 1760.

1800—(Chatham Co.) Will of Nathaniel Zettler. Children under age Mary, Catherine and Nathaniel; nephew Gideon Zettler. (Nathaniel, the elder, was a Revolutionary soldier), and he, with Daniel and Mathias Zettler had royal grants in 1770.

MARKS AND BRANDS

1790

Thomas Tumblin,
Gideon Zettler,
Stephen Denmark,
Alexander Stuart,
John Kolger,
William Denmark,
Godlieb I. Smith,
John King,

Philip Dell,
Ellender Garners,
Theophilus Lunday,
Richard Bennet,
John Gotlieb Neidlinger,
Thomas Lane,
John Wilson, Jr.
John Barber, Jr.

Seaborn Denmark,
Frederick Buntz,
John Mongerstorphus,
Robert Hudson, Sr.
Ernest Zittrouer,
Nathaniel Lunday,
Asa Tanner,

William Wilkins.
John Chris. Cramer,
John Barrie,
Hannah Ziegler,
Jonathan Seckinger,
Andrew Seckinger,

1791

Jacob Gnann,
Josiah Loper,
Justus H. Scheuber,
Isaac Carters,
Solomon Gnann,
Samuel Kraus,

Simeon Kraus (1792),
Thomas Schweighoffer,
John Freyermouth,
David Reiser,
Sarah McCall,
Daniel Remshart.

1793
Amos Richardson.

1794
John Moore.

1795

James Porter.

Benjamin Porter,

William Dupoise (?).

1798

Charles Ryall,

Henry Cook,

Joseph Davis.

1799

Josiah Loper,
John Neidlinger,
Benjamin Gnann,
Timothy Gnann,

Daniel Toomer,
John Michael Mock,
Sarah McCall,
Andrew Gnann,

Samuel Neidlinger,
William Shrimph,
John Christopher Miller,
John Christopher Gnann.

1800

Israel Lemburger,

John Grovenstein,

Willis Spier.

1801

David Ziegler,
Israel Flerl,
William Morgan,
Benjamin Dasher,

John Limburger,
Rosana Dankalden,
Walden Griffin,

Thomas Morgan,
Emanuel Zitterouer,
John Godlieb Zitterouer.

1802

William Hawthorn,
Tryon Pace,

David Metzger,
John Cowards,

Anthony Oglesby.

1803

John McCall, Sr.,
John McCall, Jr.,
James McCall,
  (Son of John),

Thomas McCall,
John Forsyth,

Sarah Edwards Forsyth,
Emanuel Glover,

1804

Mariah Gaddy,
Sally Gaddy,
Jesse Dykes,

William Beall,
William Edwards,

Peter Hawthorne,
Martha Hollinger.

1805-1806

Solomon Hinely,
Joshua Dasher,

Jonathan Loper,
Solomon Zitterouer,

John Waldhauer,
William Gaddy.

1807

Asa Loper,

William Wilder,

Christian Dasher.

Lewis. Alachua Co., Fla. In "1831 the wife of John H. Lewis was the daughter of Samuel Bell."

Lane. 1793—March 11—"That the late Thomas Lane, Esqr. had given certain gifts to his wife Mary, and sons Thomas and Samuel, and daughters Jancey and Elizabeth." This was attested by Philip Dell, Mary Hurst, and Mary Crawford. In 1784 Thomas Lane was "Acting Provost Marshall for Province of Georgia." (At this time there was also a Mary Lane, the widow of William Lane.)

Langley. 1797—Heirs of Nathaniel Langley: wife Catherine, daughter Elizabeth, and son Benjamin.

Leimburger. 1791—Inventory of the estate of Israel Leimberger by Thomas Wylly, John Kogler, Andrew Seckinger. Attested by Appolinia Seckinger.

Lane. 1793—Estate of Thomas Lane by John McCall, William Hurst, David Thorn.

Lyon. 1792—Estate of Thomas Lyon adm. by Robert Greer.

Langley. 1796—Estate of Samuel Langley adm. by James Bryan and Benjamin Langley

London. 1800—Estate of John London adm. by widow Mary Elizabeth. Caveat by John Willams and Mary Howard.

Lewis. 1800—Sept. 22—Will of Joseph Lewis. Wife Mary. Uncle Elijah Lewis. "Beloved children." Wit.: Isaac Lewis, Caleb Touchstone, Thomas Waugh. (In Savannah C. H. is deed of Mary Ann Lewis to daughter Mary Ann Independent Lusinia Lydia, age about seven years, gives negro boy and lots in Savannah and Georgetown, S. C. Refers to son Nicholas Lewis. 1805.)

Loper. 1806—March 13—Will of Joshua Loper of Bryan Co., Ga., Wife Mary. Sons Curtis, Asa, Abel G., and Ara. Daughters, Abigail Goolsbie and Lydia Loper. Wit: John Forganson, Winnsford Forganson, Joshua Loper, Jr. (Last named does not seem to be son.)

MARRIAGES

Little, John, of Chas., S. C., to Mary Newman, who was bap. just before marriage, Nov. 7, 1775.

Lanier, Bird, to Elizabeth Dixon, Dec. 22, 1793.

Lucas, John, to Clarissa Denmark, Aug. 20, 1794.

Lichner, John F., to Hannah Heisler, May 2, 1799.

Leimberger, Israel, to Mary C. Sneider, May 2, 1799. (This Leimberger was dead in 1811. There was an Israel Christian Leimberger who died 1791, leaving widow Appolinia.)

Lamly, Minis, to Polly Hines (Mary, on deeds), May 28, 1799.

Leimberger, David, to Naomi Keiffer, Dec. 27, 1800.

Loper, Asa, to Esther Lanier, Feb. 17, 1802.

Loper, William, of S. C., to Hannah Bergsteiner, Oct. 17, 1804.

Lee, Joshua, of S. C. to Sarah Elkins, Nov. 8, 1806.

Lovett, James, to Catherine Zitterauer, Nov. 13, 1809.

Loper, Abel C., Esqr., to Phoebe O'Neal, Jan. 23, 1811.

Lovett, David, Jr., to Mary Sheffield, Dec. 6, 1813.

Lessler, John, to Mary, daughter of Camel Tison, Jan. 22, 1814.

Lovett, Aaron, to Esther Rahn, Sept. 22, 1809.

Leimberger, John C., to Ann Blitch, March 25, 1824.
Leimberger, Joshua, to Salome Schrimp, Jan. 10, 1830.

Limberger, Benjamn, to Salome Geyer, July 12, 1831.

Lovett, Joshua, to Mrs. Ann Elizabeth Keebler, Dec. 13, 1831.

Lee, James, to Cynthia Richardson, Jan. 12, 1833.

Lanier, Isaac, to Sarah Hurst, March 4, 1833

Lee, James A, to Ann Edwards, Jan. 6, 1845.

Lovett. The children of David Lovett, Sr., were:
James, born March 2, 1787.
David, born Jan. 19, 1785.
Moses, born Feb. 12, 1791.
Aaron, born April 20, 1793.
Joshua, born May 6, 1795.

Loper. There was a Curtis Loper whose wife in 1796 was named Lydia.

Grant in S. C. to David Loper for fifty acres in Granville Co., June 21, 1775.

Love. The wife of Dr. John Love of Chatham Co. was "Louise" in 1798.

McCall. Charles McCall, born in Va, 1735; died in Bulloch Co., Ga., 1816, formerly residing in St. David's Parish, S. C., married Nancy Ann Williams, niece and adopted daughter of Gov. Williams. (Society Hill), had:

Robert McCall, married Mary Lanier.
William McCall, married Ann Fletcher.

Francis McCall, married Sally Pearce.

Eleanor McCall, married James Green.

Nancy McCall, married Stephen McCoy.

Sarah McCall, married James Groover.

Charles McCall, married Elizabeth Stith.

Mary McCall, married William Wright.

Elizabeth McCall, married Eli Kennedy.

George McCall, married Elizabeth Burnett, and returned to S. C.

Henry McCall.

David McCall.

Celeta McCall.

Savannah Record Room, Book 2 A, p. 534: Sharrod McCall and wife Margaret, heirs of Thomas McCall, receipts to Lemuel Lanier. 1805.

"Jesse McCall and wife Mary" of Liberty Co., 1810. (Savannah Rec. Room.)

Effingham Co.: 1791—Estate of Thomas McCall was adm. Widow Sarah. Wit.: Thomas Lane, Joseph Mikell, James Moore.

Feb. 5, 1823—March 3, 1823. Will of John McCall. Sons: James B., Thomas, George E. Daughters: Elizabeth and Hannah. Wit.: William and John Hurst, Lewis Lanier.

1791—Richmond Co.: "Thomas McCall and wife Henrietta."

Mobley. 1820—The minor children of Edward Mobley were made wards of Lewis Lanier.

Morel. 1834—John G. Morel adm. the estate of Benjamin Morel, who left minor children, Georgianna, Homer S., and Edwin P.

McGee. 1786—Deed of Shadrack McGee to his daughter Ann Dukes. (She was the wife of Green Dukes of Savannah, who died 1821, leaving widow Ann, and daughter Martha the wife of George Sharp, and a son Thomas Dukes.)

Milledge. 1787—April 3—Deed of John Milledge to Fanny Dupuis, spinster.

Moss. 1787—Grant to John Moss of 200 acres.

Mills. 1792—Estate of William Mills adm. by Mrs. Mary Mills and Stephen Pearce. (Stephen Pearce had married a daughter of William Mills.)

1812—Hugh C. Mills deeds negroes to John Exley. (Mills was of Rockingham Co., N. C.)

Muter. 1807—James Muter deed to son Robert Muter.

McCrory. 1800—Oct. 7—Will of John McCrory. Wife Rachel; son John (who married Jane Pitts in 1815). Wit.: Walden Griffin, Senate Powers, Henry Cook.

McCoy. 1811—Heirs of deceased Charles McCoy: James McCoy and wife Sophia of Pendleton, S. C.; Samuel McCoy and wife Polly; Elizabeth, wife of Austin Mayfield. Samuel McCoy is appointed atty. for property in Effingham Co.

McCall. 1798—"David McCall and wife Fanny." (Deeds).

Moore. 1793—Estate of John Moore by Wm. Moore. Appraised by John King, David Thorn, Philip Dell.

1819—Estate of John Moore, by widow Marcy. John McCall, security.

Mingledorf. 1796—Christina E. Mingledorf appoints her brother Godhilp Smith her atty. in re estate of her husband George Mingledorf.

Martin. 1798—Estate of Clement Martin, adm. by relict Mrs. Elizabeth Nowlan and George Nowlan. Reference is made to William Martin, son of Clement Martin. In 1829 William Wallace Martin is called "grandson of Joseph Helvenstine."

1808-1813—Lewis and Richard Martin sign deeds.

Mallette (and various spellings.) The earliest record of this name (now known), was Gideon Mallette, Sr., whose will was probated in 1771—witnessed by Henry Gindrat. His wife was Mary Lombard. He left a son Daniel, died Nov. 5, 1775, whose will was probated Nov. 1775, in Charleston, S. C., mentioning wife Mary Ann, decd; eldest son Gideon, son Abraham; daughter Mary Ann; eldest sister Luisanne Catherine Greniere, wife of Peter Francois Greniere, and her two daughters Mary and Nancy Ravot. (See "Ravot").

Son Gideon was born June 14, 1759 at Purysburg; died Effingham Co., Sept. 3, 1822. (Revolutionary soldier).

Abraham, born Jan. 13, 1761; died Nov. 26, 1790.

Mary Ann, born Nov. 24, 1764; died May 2, 1807.

Bartholomew, born Oct. 20, 1766.

Mrs. Mary Mallette died Oct. 20, 1766.

Gideon Mallette, Sr. had various grants in Purysburg 1736-1739, and Daniel Mullett grant in 1764 by lands of Gedion Mulletts and Abraham Ginderaus (Gindrat); Peter Melat in 1773, and Daniel Meret in 1738 (Purysburg).

Gideon Mallette, 2nd married Nov. 6, 1783 to Hannah Elizabeth DeRoche, who was born Nov. 22, 1767, and died Jan. 16, 1848. She was the daughter of —— DeRoche and his wife Hannah, who also had a son Gideon DeRoche, born Feb. 18, 1770.

Children of Gideon and Hannah Mallette:

Gideon.

Mary Ann, born March 19, 1788; died May 2. 1807.

Abraham, born Nov. 5, 1790; died 1867; married Katherine Kennedy, Dec. 24, 1812. (Bulloch Co.). J. P. of Effingham Co., 1817.

Daniel, born Oct. 20, 1792; died 1830; married Susannah Ziegler, Oct. 21, 1821 (or Nov. 9, both records).

Lewis, born March 21, 1800.

John Henry, born Oct. 1, 1795; died May 15, 1818 at sea.

Margaret, born April 1, 1798.

Jeremiah, born Aug. 25, 1802; married (1) Eliza Metzger; (2) Mary Porter.

Daniel Mallette and Susannah (Zeigler), had:

Elbert Lewis, born.Jan. 31, 1825; married Grace Eliza, dau. of Gabriel Wilson.

Patrick Hardy, born July 31, 1828; married Miss Wyly—no children.

(1830—Jeremiah Mulett applies for adm. of estate of Daniel Mulett. March 6.)

Jeremiah Mallette (died Oct. 30, 1865) and (1) Eliza, dau. of David Metzger, had:

Robert Taylor, born June 15, 1833; died Nov. 15, 1858.

Francis M., born Jan. 24, 1835; died Sept. 19, 1870; married Louisa J. Morgan, March 5, 1851.

Julia Emeline, born March 15, 1837; died June 5, 1859; married Augustus Mallory.

Elvira Leonora, born April 9, 1839.

Laura Anna, born Sept. 22, 1843.

Mrs. Eliza (Metzger) Mallette was born June 26, 1812; died Oct. 19, 1845.

Jeremiah Mallette married (2) Mary Porter (born March 24, 1822); married May 13, 1847; dau. of Wm. G. Porter; (see Treutlen-Porter), had:

Lawrence Elliott, born July 15, 1859.

Lily, born ——; married —— Grady: sons F. M. & Thomas Edward Grady.

Amanda Porter, born 1848; died Oct. 26, 1853.

Isabelle Evaline, born 1851; died Oct. 27, 1853.

Mary Elizabeth, born July, 1850; died Oct. 29, 1853.

Alice Jeannette, born Nov. 25, 1854.

Leila Corinne, born March 21, 1857.

Lillian Venta, born Oct. 10, 1861.

Jeremiah Alberti, born July 28, 1853.

Eliza Margaret Mallette married John W. Exley Jan. 17, 1822. (See Exley.)

Elbert Lewis, son of Daniel and Susannah (Ziegler) Mallette, married Eliza Gracy Ann Wilson, May 9, 1831. She was the daughter of Gabriel Wilson and wife Sarah (Oglesby), who were married Dec. 26, 1807.

Children of Lewis Mallette and wife Eliza Gracy Ann:

Julia, married Benjamin Arnsdorf.

Albert Bachman, married Ella Weekly.

John Lewis, married Lily, daughter of Wesley Edwards.

George, married Emily Zitterauer.

Claud, married Hattie, daughter of Martin Gnann.

Ossie.

Ollie, married Bessie, daughter of Joseph Hodges.

Allen, married Amelia Hinely.

William, married Lucretia Hinely.

Jerry, married Alberta Usher; (2) Emma Stevens.

Josephine, married Elton Hodges.

Stray Notes:

David Mallette of France died in England, 1691.

Peter Mallet, born March 31, 1712; died 1760 in Conn. His wife Mary Booth; son Peter born Nov. 14, 1744, resided in N. C. and died in Fayetteville, N. C., Feb. 2, 1805. His first wife was Eunice Curtis; 2nd wife Sarah Mumford. He had a son Daniel who married Mary Lillington—no children.

In Moore's N. C., Vol. 2, p. 189: "Col. Peter Mallette was from Stockholm."

Round's Peerage: "The forfeited fief of Robert Malet 'The Honor of Eye,' " was founder of Benedictine Nunnery of Wix, Sussex. Fief was bestowed on Stephen Malet.

Record Room, Savannah C. H. 1808—Maria Louise Mallet was the name of the wife of Mathias de Monet of Matanza, Cuba, who sells Bonabella, near Thunderbolt. Wit.: by Louis Mallet. Many deeds of Monets on file.

From Hist. Comm., Atlanta, Ga.:

"Gideon Asbury Mallette, son of Abraham and Sarah Mallette born June 6, 1817; died Feb. 20, 1891.

Married (1) 1849, Mrs. Sarah Chevalier, born Sept. 1, 1821; died Feb. 21, 1852; (2) Susan Lang, July 5, 1853; died Aug. 11, 1864;

(3) Dec. 8, 1867, Georgia Jane Sheffield, born May 6, 1834; died March 22, 1923.

Gideon A. Mallette was J. I. C. of Camden Co., Ga., 1858-1862. Mem. House Rep. Ga. Legislature from Camden Co., 1877.

Pr. Fred'k Par., S. C.: James Mallet and wife Mary, had

Mary Elizabeth, born Dec. 30, 1724; baptized Feb. 7, 1725.

1819—March—Estate of Daniel Malett adm. by John Malett.

1786 (Chas., S. C.)—Will of Wm. Baker: "Sister Rachel Mallet."

1772 (Chas., S. C.)—Peter Malett as "nearest of kin," adm. estate of William Williams of St. Bartholomew's Parish.

Metzger. (Principally from Family Bible of Mrs. Rebecca (Metzger) Wolf.)

Jacob Metzger, one of the original members of Jerusalem Church, and who died Feb. 10, 1781, had wife Margaret, their children:

John, born 1754; died 1814. Wife Mary Magdalene.

Jacob.

Samuel.

Sarah, born June 4, 1758.

Catherine, born Sept. 10, 1760.

Lucia, born April 15, 1762.

David, born Jan. 15, 1765; married (1) Mrs. Waters, nee Reiser; (2) Mrs. Sarah (Snyder) Groover.

John Metzger and wife Mary Magdelene, had:

John Adam, born 1782; died April 30, 1808; married Oct. 17, 1807 to Christina Rahn, born Feb. 22, 1787; died Oct. 23, 1849. No children.

John Jacob, born 1790; died April 12, 1846; married (1) Naomi Berry, Nov. 11, 1811; (2) Lydia Dasher, Oct. 30, 1817.

David Metzger married (1) Mrs. Mary (Waters) Reiser, and had:

Solomon, born June 19, 1800; married Mary Timmons.

John, born May 11, 1802; married Dorothy Kennedy, born Nov. 8, 1812; died Oct. 14, 1881; married Dec. 9, 1829.

Moses, born June 20, 1804; married Jane Mingledorf. (He died Aug. 27, 1878.)

Benjamin, born Feb. 11, 1806.

Mary A., born May 8, 1808; married John Berry, April 27, 1826.

Margaret, born April 17, 1810; married Jesse Davis, Jan. 28, 1829.

Elizabeth, born June 26. 1812; married Jeremiah Mallette, Dec. 22, 1831. (See Mallette.)

Samuel, born July 26, 1814.

David Metzger married (2) Mrs. Sarah (Snyder) Groover, and had:

Philitia, born Aug. 9, 1839.

John Jacob Metzger and (1st wife) Naomi Berry, had:

Maria Elizabeth, born July 2, 1812; died Jan. 31, 1866; married Jonathan Gnann, May 11, 1830.

Louisa B., born Oct. 1, 1813; died Oct. 28, 1853; married (1) Fred. Backley; (2) —— ?.

John, born Jan. 18, 1816; died June 25, 1851.

John Jacob Metzger and (2nd wife) Lydia Dasher, had:

Rebecca, born 1818; died Sept. 8, 1851.

Rosannah, born 1820; died Dec. 25, 1820.

George, born 1825; died March 4, 1862.

Amelia.

Rebecca Elizabeth, born Oct. 24, 1827; married Irwin L. Wolf, April 28, 1850.

May Caroline Leonora, born July 14, 1821; married W. H. Kennedy. (See "Kennedy.")

David, born 1822—Killed at Battle of Chicamauga, Sept. 20, 1863.

Reuben ——, died June 26, 1825.

William.

(Mrs. Lydia (Dasher) Metzger, was born Sept. 5, 1793; died Oct. 2, 1851).

Solomon Metzger and wife Mary Timmons (died Aug. 16, 1879), had:

James T., born Aug. 11, 1829.

William W., born April 25, 1831.

Caroline S., born April 12, 1833; married William Carruthers.

John Metzger and wife Dorothy Kennedy, had:

Cornelia Naomi, born April 6, 1831; died April 5, 1879; married Geo. Grovenstein, Feb. 6, 1850.

Julia Francis, born Dec. 13, 1832; died Aug. 12, 1835.

Emma Jerusha, born Feb. 12, 1835; died Sept. 16, 1876; married Benj. Grovenstein, Feb. 28, 1855.

Augustus William, born Nov. 28, 1837; died Oct. 27. 1857.

Sophronia Kennedy, born Nov. 6, 1839; died Oct. 15, 1876; married Augustus Mallory, Oct. 1, 1861.

Raymond Howard, born Oct. 3, 1846; died Nov. 18, 1846.

Moses Metzger married Jane Mingledorf, Sept. 10, 1835. She was born July 5, 1819; died June 15, 1887; children:

Isadore Bartow, born Nov. 2, 1836.

Benjamin Jefferson, born Nov. 21, 1838; married Mary Felicia Reiser, born Sept. 19, 1846, and died Jan. 15, 1873.

Oscar Evans, born March 10, 1841; married (1) Miss Puder; (2) Susie Kelley, born May 3, 1853, and died Sept. 30, 1884.

William Backman, born March 18, 1844; married Anna Grovenstein.

Emmet Bloise, born May 25, 1846.

Moses Backster, born June 28, 1849.

Frank Howard, born April 17, 1852; married Mary Agnes Dawson, born Aug. 2, 1856.

Margaret Victoria, born Sept. 7, 1856; married Marion Maner.

Savh. Rec. Room, Book 2-A, p. 393. 1807—"John Metzger, planter of Effingham, and his wife Mary Magdalene." Wit.: Mathew Rahn, Thomas Wyly.

Effingham Co., Feb. 12, 1822: John J. Metzger prays to be appointed guardian to his three children: Maria Eliza Frances, Louisa Naomi Kalista, John Benajah Washington.

Notes:

1800-1804—The estate of John Metzger was adm. by John Jacob Metzger.

1781—"Jacob Metzger and wife Salome," sponsors. (Ebenezer Records, p. 68.)

"Hannah Metzger married Jacob Gnann, April 6, 1773."

1734—Jacob Metzger had a grant of 350 acres in Purysburg, and a town lot No. 75.

In Pike Co., Ga., is a deed from Luke Exley of Pike Co., to John F. Metzger, of a lot in Monroe Co., drawn by Exley in 1821. Wit.: Ephraim Kieffer. Jacob Gnann, Jr.. Henry L. Grovenstein. (Dated 1823.)

Georgia Rev. & Colonial Records (Candler), Vol. 3, pp. 147-203-213: (Jacob and John Metzger)—among others—"Should not be compelled to serve as continental soldiers in the Georgia Battalion, for the space of two years or during the continuance of the present war, the committee having fully investigated their several characters and have found them to be friends to the American Cause." July 27, 1782.

Mott. (See Colson.) In 1706 John Abraham Mott was a member of Assembly convenes in Charles, S. C., for the Church of England. (Rivers' Hist. of S. C., p. 227.)

About 1716 John A. Mott was one of nine commissioners appointed to look after the trade with the Indians. (Logan's Hist. of S. C.)

Effingham Co., Ga.—Abraham Mott married Sarah Scruggs, Feb. 16, 1769. (Ebenezer Ch. Records.)

"Mathew Mott and wife Catherine," on deeds in Savannah C. H., 1794.

Gainesville, Fla. C. H.: Abraham Mott married Eliza Skipper, Jan. 11, 1846.

Effingham Co. marriages:

Mathew, Aaron, to Mary Davey, Jan. 6, 1772.

Milliner (?) William, to Mary Goodall, Sept. 4, 1773.

Moore, John, to Maxey McCall, Jan. 16, 1792.

Morgan, William, to Sarah Bailey, May 4, 1795.
Morgan, Thos., to Creasy Crawford, Sept. 5, 1803.

Mingledorf, John George, to Emilia Nightlinger, Nov. 26, 1807.

McLimner, John, to Chloe Day, March 8, 1808.

Morton, Silas, to Mary Hunter, May 19, 1813.

McRory, John, to Jane Pitts, April 17. 1815.

Maner, ——, to Mary Ann King, Dec. 13, 1819.

Martin, Stephen H., to Maria C. Helvenstein, Nov. 25, 1820.

McCardle, William, to Margaret McGahagin, dau. of Wm., June 7, 1821.

McCool, John J., to Lucy Highsmith, Nov. 9, 1821.

Morgan, William J., to Christiana Elizabeth Heidt, Feb. 7, 1822.

Miller, Samuel Peter, to Elizabeth Hannah Zipperer, Dec. 25, 1822.

Morgan, Christopher Lewis, to Christina Heidt, Dec. 13, 1823.

McKensie, Daniel James, to Elizabeth Gnann, Nov. 12, 1825.

Miller, Joshua, to Louisa Holliday, Dec. 5, 1825.
Miller, John F., to Angelina Holliday, Nov. 1, 1827.

McDonell, Alexander H., to Ann Elizabeth Nowland, dau. of George N. and Hannah Guge, Nov. 24, 1830.

Mingledorf, Robert J., to Levinia Zitterauer, Jan. 12, 1832.

McDonell, William, to Agnes Melrose, March 18, 1833.

Morgan, Math. M., to Mary C. Carter of Bryan Co., Feb. 7, 1837.
Morgan, Mathew, to Mary M. Carter, Feb. 7, 1838.

McRory, Edum, to Martha J. Edwards, Nov. 15, 1841. Mar. sett. Nov. 4, 1830.

Morgan, John L., to Ann Dorothy Gnann, Oct. 21, 1839.

Morgan, David A., to Ann C. Christie, Feb. 10, 1834.

Mingledorf, Edmund A., to Juliana A. Dasher, April 29, 1839.

Morgan, James W., to Sarah Dorothy Wall, Jan. 19, 1839.

Murray, Edward, to Mrs. Selina Watts, Nov. 1, 1841.

Morgan, Wm. C., to Abigail Gnann, Feb. 19, 1845.

Miller, Wm. Jacob, to Mary Ann Hinely, July 27, 1846.

Mingledorf, John C., to Eliza S. Dasher, Feb. 6, 1844.

Molder, George, to Mary Ann Weitman, Nov. 19, 1845.

Mingledorf, William B., to Mary M. Berry, Jan. 1, 1850.

Morton, Henry O., to Belinda Caroline Morgan, Jan. 2, 1848.

Nevil, John, to Frances Mixon, Oct. 13, 1768.

Neiss, Gothilf Israel, to Anna Neidlinger, March 24, 1804. (He married 2nd Mary Shuptrine, widow of Israel Shuptrine, 1840.)

Nowlan, George, to Hannah Gugel, Dec. 28, 1807. A "Geo. Nowlan, wife Elizabeth, Nov. 14, 1797. Book C. D., 434.

McCrory, John, Widow "Rachel", 1800.

McCall, Thomas, Widow "Sarah", 1791.

Mohr, Jacob, wife Sibilla, 1789. (Widow & only heir of Christian Geiger, 1777.)

Moodie, Benj., wife Carolina (of Charleston, S. C.), 1803.

McLane, Lewis (of Wilkes County), wife Rhoda, 1788.

Mulryne, John, wife Claudia (Tatnall), 1764.

Meyers, James, of Savannah, wife Mary, 1790.

McGarver, Daniel, wife Dorcas, 1790.

McCall, David, wife Fannie, 1798.

McKinnon, John, wife Ann, 1795.

Mountford, Robert, Widow Elizabeth H., 1795.

Miller, Jno. Christopher, wife Hannah, 1799.

Morel, James, wife Mary, 1812.

Maurer—Mueller (Miller). Many difficulties are met in the endeavor to synchronize the data gleaned on the name of Maurer, gathered principally from Court records and the Register of Ebenezer Church.

The earliest of the name is Hans (John) Maurer who died Aug. 31, 1766. It may be presumed that his widow was Hannah Margaret, who died Nov. 30, 1775. The next record of the name is that of John Paul Maurer who married Mary Magdalene Zant, Feb. 24, 1767, and had:

Catherine, born Feb. 1, 1769.

Solomon, born Oct., 1770; died Dec. 24, 1777.

Mrs. Maurer died Oct. 11. 1775, and her husband married July 1, 1777 Mrs. Ann (Seckinger), widow of John Paul Mueller, Jr., had:

Solomon, born April 11, 1778.

Mueller, John Paul, married Ann Seckinger, July 18, 1769, had:

John Christopher, born Sept. 1, 1772; married Hannah Zitterauer. John Paul Mueller died Feb. 21, 1772, age 27.

Apparently John Paul Mueller, Sr., married (2) Elizabeth Maurer, Nov. 2, 1768, had:

Frederick William, born Oct. 1, 1769.

John Paul, born Sept. 1, 1772. (John Paul Mueller, Sr., died April 11, 1775.)

John Remshardt, married Mary Margaret Mueller, 1764.

George Schleigh, married Mary Magdalen Maurer, 1763.

John George Maurer, married Sybilla Saecht, ——, 1775.

Gabriel Maurer and wife Anna had daughter Catherine Margaret, 1762.

George Meuller and wife Rosina had daughter Anna Mary, 1757. Rosina had been the widow Schubtrein, whom he married May 31, 1756.

The name Mueller was changed to Miller, and is frequently found interchanged.

WILLS IN ALACHUA COUNTY, FLORIDA. (GEORGIA AND S. C. NAMES), BOOK A

Coker, Joseph B., died Aug. 12, 1856—leaving wife Amanda M., and children.

Conyers, Daniel—daus. Mary A. Richmond, Asenath Conyers. Exr. Andrew Bates. Wit.: Samuel Kenerly, James Tompkins, James M. Kingsley. Sept. 17, 1856.

Child, James, dec'd father Alexander Child. Sister Emma C. Child and Brother Robert A. Child. Rufus T. A. Humphreys and Margaret Jane Humphreys, children of my dec'd sister. Nov. 20, 1850.

Cason, Ransom, Sr., wife Phoebe, dau. Martha Hallbrook, son John Cason, dau. Phoeba, wife of John R. Cason, son Moses, son James, son

William, dau. Clemintine Douglas. Wit.: John C. Hatley, Walter
Batton, Elisha Carter. Probated Nov. 12, 1853.

Chestnut, Ellen, Kershaw Dist., S. C., widow of John Chestnut.
Dec'd brother William Whitaker. Chil.: Serena, wife of Thomas E.
Haile, Mary Whitaker Chestnut, James, John and Ellen. Niece Ellen
Chestnut Reynolds. Gr. son, John Chestnut Haile. Father James
Chestnut, Sr., brother Thomas Whitaker, bro-in-law James Chestnut,
Jr., sister Sarah Chestnut. Wit.: Ed. M. Boykin, J. D. Murray, B. H.
Matheson. Probated April 15, 1851.

Dell, William—nuncupative will, Brothers Philip and Amos, and
sister Mary S. Duer, Oct. 15, 1854.

Dell, Bennett Maxey—present wife Eliza Dorothy, dau. Sarah
Angeline, son Charles who died in Texas. Dau. Mary, wife of Christian
F. Duer, now in Texas. Sons Philip and John—the latter not of age.
Feb. 21, 1855. George W. Boston, Probate Judge.

Davis, Jesse—wife Margaret, dau. Catherine E., wife of Joseph
Whitman. Daus. Caroline and Louisa. Son Henry. Exrs.: W. H.
Kennedy, George Boston and Samuel R. Pyles. Wit.: P. W. Cato,
Samuel R. Pyles, George A. Clotfetter. March 1, 1858.

Devlin, Isaac (Fort Walker), private in Capt. James Fitzgerald's
mounted Militia. To Alfred Mooney. Aug. 5, 1840.

Dewees, Mary, widow. Son Henry W. Maxey, dau. Louisa, wife of
Lewis A. Mattair of Columbia Co. Brothers Simeon and Bennett Max-
ey Dell; nephew Philip J. Dell, son of Col. James Dell. Wit.: James B.
Colding, Cotton Rawls, Abraham Colson. E. K. White, Probate Judge.
Dec. 26, 1840.

Daskin, Michael of Stewart Co., Georgia. Wife Elizabeth. Daus.
Mary Gordon Miller, Elizabeth Jane Bartlett. Son John L. B. Daskin.
Wit.: M. Gresham, Young H. Gresham, Richard Kidd. Jan., 1848.

Dell, James of Duvall Co. Children: William Thomas, Ann Louisa,
James Gadsen, Martha Mary, Delia. Exrs.: Bro. Bennett Maxey
Dell and Samuel K. Piles. Wit.: John Parsons, J. W. Pearson, Samuel
Russell, J. P.. Nov., 1848.

Gibbons, Charles—all to Sylvester Bryant, Jr., son of Sylvester
and Elizabeth Bryant. May, 1844. Probated Jan. 28, 1845. Wit.:
Jacob Summerlin, D. I. Bryant, Jacob Summerlin, Jr.

Hague, John, wife Maria. Chil.: James, John R., Gideon, Mary
Kelly, Rusina, Archibald, Vicy, Amelia and John Caspar Hague.
Archalus Lipsey and Dr. James Kelly to have no part in my estate.
Aug. 4, 1836. Wit.: M. Garrison, E. Bird, John Miller.

Harville, Samuel, of Liberty Co., Georgia. Sons: Warren, John Elliott and Edward McVean. Wife Rebecca. Daus.: Rebecca Lowther, Celia Zoucks, Elizabeth Cash, Susan Mitchell Harville, Sarah Smylie Harvill. To Richard F. Baker. "Lands in Houston Co." Gr. sons Berrien Harvill and Samuel Rivers Harvill. To Stephen Fuller Baker and Mary Harvill Baker. Wit.: Willam Hope, Jr., Henry Hope, John Elliott Harvill. Jas. McNeill, Clk. Aug. 5, 1840.

Hall, Dorothy, widow—late of Duvall Co. Ex. Dr. Edward S. Aldrich. Plantation "The Grange" in Duvall Co. to Nephew George S. Brown in trust for my neices Corinna E. Aldrich, wife of Dr. Edward S. Aldrich, and Ellen M., wife of James W. Anderson, now residing in Buffalo, N. Y. To Ellen S. Wood, dau. of Oliver Wood of Duvall and gr. dau. of my deceased husband, Dr. James Hall. Corinna, dau. of James W. Anderson. Wit.: Susan A. Watson, George Watson, Louis Aldrich. Proved Jan. 28, 1845.

Geiger, Washington W., wife Sarah G. "all my children." 1855.

Jones, William of Fairfield, S. C. Wife Sarah, dau. Cynthia Kennedy. Son Osmand S. Jones and his son William Harrison; chil. of Elisha Jones and friend Osmond Woodward. Daus.: Lucretia Wylie, Nancy Kennedy, Mahaloth Davis, son Elisha H. Jones. Codicil—Gr. chil. Polly Mickle Kennedy and Sarah Kennedy. Wit.: M. A. M. Leggo, C. H. & J. F. Durham. Sept. 28, 1854.

Knight, George—nephew Jeptha Knight and his six children: David Levy, George Montgomery, Thomas Jasper, Margaret Frances, Eliza, Lemuel LaFayette. Wit: Samuel Geiger, Jonathan Turner, Andrew Robb. June 23, 1855.

Payne, Catherine, wife of Geo. B. Payne. Chil.: Ida Marion, Sarah Penn, Virginia, Virginia Morton, Rosa. July 18, 1859.

Standley, Jesse. Wife Dicey. Sons: Sebron J., William S., Thomas C. Daus.: Eliza Harvil, and Mariah Floyd. Property in Marion Co. Wit.: George S. Brown, Richard Ryan, Thomas J. Prevatt. George Watson, Probate Judge. Nov. 14, 1844.

COLUMBIA COUNTY (GEORGIA) MARRIAGES

1 8 0 6

Slaughter, Henry, to Betsy T. Blackwell, Aug. 13.

Brooks, Jonathan, to Nancy Monk, Sept. 15.

Blady (?), Israel, to Elizabeth McDonald, Sept. 11.

Cobbs, Nathaniel, to Flora Fee (?), Nov. 5.

Wooley, Joel, to Patsy Leath, Oct. 21.

Ward, Solomon, to Jane Danielly, Dec. 15.

Bacon, John Parks, to Mary Lanier, Dec. 31.

Dent, George W., to Nancy Hutchinson, Aug. 18.

Williams, James, to Nancy Hill, Oct. 21.

Romic (?), Maurice, to Nancy Flyn, Dec. 26.

McDonald, Daniel, to Jane Fuller, March 7.

1 8 0 7

Hannon, John, to Elizabeth Wright, Jan. 7.

Cobb, Joseph, to Nancy Reynolds, Jan. 10.

McCord, James, to Nancy Neal, Feb. 9.

Harris, Juriah, to Elizabeth D'Antignac, Feb. 12.

Williams, Gabriel, to Sarah Williams, Feb. 20.

Castles, Absolom, to Rebecca Jones, Jan. 5.

Jelks, Richard, to Mrs. Hannah Germany, June 9.

Gammon, Willis, to Rebecca Willis, May 13.

Sutherland, John, to Hannah Martin, Aug. 10. (See Effingham Church Records.)

Murray, John, to Elizabeth Watson, Nov. 16.

1 8 0 8

Smith, John, to Levincy Payne, Jan. 20.

Wilson, David, to Anney Drane, Jan. 20.

Roberts, George, to Catherine Shields, Dec. 5.

1 8 0 9

Hoge, Solomon, to Nancy Sutherland, Oct. 8.

Yarbrough, Thomas, to Jane Warren, Dec. 21.

Burton, Thomas, to Charity Wright, Sept. 16.

McDonald, John, to Susan Jones, Sept. 24.

Morris, Jesse, to Jane McCorkle, Sept. 8.

Mitchell, John, to Rebeckah Crabb, Sept. 28.

Culbreath, Thomas, to Catherine Hagins, Sept. 22

1 8 1 0

Richardson, Laurence, to Nancy Glover, Jan. 6.

McKinsey, George, to Mary Lacey, Feb. 21.

Crabb, Benjamin, to Rachel Wade, Feb. 24.

Rousan, James, to Levina Frew, Feb. 1.

Turner, Thomas, to Eliza Worshing (?), March 1.

Roberts, Herod, to Linder Beall, March 6.

Mitchell, Amos, to Jane Taylor, April 17.

McClary, James, to Catey Edmondson, April 17.

Richards, Burrell, to Ann Linn, April 28.

Russell, Isaac, to Ann Youngblood, April 28.

Lovelace, William, to Jane Hunt, May 28.

Boswell, Hendley, to Polly Collins, April 30.

Grey, Walter, to Nancy Carr, Sept. 5.

Sutton, Booker, to Nancy Stapler, Sept. 5.

Watson, John, Jr., to Casandra Hoge, Sept. 11.

Wiley, Taylor, to Verlinda Finney, Sept. 4.

Dooley, Thomas, to Palatier Jones, Dec. 5.

Powell, Lewis, to Elizabeth Chenault, Dec. 12.

Dunn, John, to Patsey Simmons, Dec. 5.

Reynolds, William, to Serena Fuller, Dec. 18.

Parker, Zenus, to Elizabeth Burnsides, Dec. 15.

Eubanks, Reuben, to Polly Sturgess, Dec. 18.

Cash, Dawson, to Rebeckah Miles, Dec. 22.

1 8 1 1

Collins, Peter H., to Jane Stewart, Jan. 1.

Johnson, Benjamin, to Ann Allen, Jan. 4.
Johnson, Thomas, to Elizabeth Jones, Jan. 7.

Templeton, Greenberry, to Betsy Mathews, Dec. 17.

Sullivan, William, to Betsy Burnsides, Feb. 25.

Day, Joseph, Jr., to Jincey Dunn, March 16.

Johnson, Mordecai, to Frances Cosby, June 29.

Wooding, John, to Elizabeth Drane, July 3.

Walker, David, Jr., to Polly Crawford, Aug. 28.

Wiley, William, to Pricey Youngblood, Sept. 4.

Watson, Peter, to Elizabeth McCormick, Oct. 15.

Wright, James, to Casandra Drane, Nov. 5.

Burnsides, Thomas, to Elizabeth Pierce, Nov. 6.

Banks, David, to Camilla Wade, Nov. 12.

Johnson, Nehemiah, to Elizabeth Wright, Nov. 14.

Wheat, Henry, to Nancy Darry (?), Nov. 14.

Hunt, Thomas, to Sarah Miles, Nov. 18.

Copeland, Henry, to Sarah McIntire, Dec. 2.

1 8 1 2

Reese, Jeremiah, to Ann Hollyman, Feb. 28.

Day, William, to Nancey McDonald, May 2.

SCREVEN COUNTY (GEORGIA) WILLS

Anderson. 1826—Feb. 10—Will of Hezekiah Anderson—wife Alley and small children. Exr.: wife and son William. Wit.: Moses N. McCall, Charles H. McCall, James P. Thompson, John L. Dowdy.

Beard. 1832—April 26—Will of John Beard—wife Susan and son William. Exrs.; Wm. Wilder, Alex. T. Dopson.

Best. 1821—Dec. 17—Will of Tarlton B. Best—To John H. Smith, John B. Best, John Mears, John H. Mitchener, Orasmus H. Best, William D.Campbell. Exrs.: Wm. B. Mitchener and John B. Best. Wit.: Thomas Scarborough, Paul Williamson, Joseph Y. Garlington.

Bonnell. 1808—July 25—Will of John Bonnell—wife Winneford. Grandsons, Thomas Cuyler Lovett and Robert Watkins Lovett; granddaughters, Eliza Maria Hues and Rowsamon Hues. Daus.: Elizabeth Lovett and Martha Hues. Exrs.: Owing Hues and John Forbes Lovett. Wit.: N. Paramore, Robert Dixon, David Curtis.

1804—Nov. 19—Will of Anthony Bonnell—Son William original grant. Dau. Elizabeth Bonnell; gr son John Bonnell. Wife Mary. Archibald Mills, Henry Bryant, Anthony Bonnell, Jr., Thomas F.

Lovett. Exrs.: Archibald Mills and William Bonnell. Wit.: John F. Lovett, John Salter, Abraham Lewis.

Bevill. 1809—James Bevill, wife Delia, adopted son Paul Bevill Garnett. Exrs.: Wife and brother Paul B. Bevill. Wit.: William Howell, A. Colson, John Beard. Probated June 6, 1814. (Wife Delia was daughter of Philip and Nancy Dell.)

Boykin. 1818—Jan. 5—Will of John Boykin, Sr. Wife Sarah, Exr. Dau. Kodiah. Sons John and Luedowick. Wit.: Henry Crosby, Stephen Blackburn.

Bryan. 1816—Sept. 7—Will of John Bryan—wife Mary. Heirs: Solomon, Samuel, Isaac, Jacob, Alexander, William, and James Bryan. Also Rachel McQueen, Elizabeth Strawhaker and Margaret Smith. Gr. daus. Eliza and Mary Roberts. Gr. son John Henry Bryan. Exrs. Wife and sons. Wit.: Reuben Wilkinson, Robert M. Wilkinson, Stephen S. Perkins.

Buford. 1831—Nov. 4—Will of John Buford, Sr. Son Henry, son-in-law Anthony Mills; other children—John Buford, Elizabeth Vasser, Wm. G. Buford, Ann Overstreet, William Mills, Jamerson V. Buford, Archibald V. Mills, Benj. F. Chew, Abram Buford, Greenberry Buford, Simeon and Perthane Buford. Exrs.: John Buford, Jr. and Elizabeth Vassar. Wit.: Benjamin Green and Elijah Roberts, J. P.

Basemore. 1840—Sept. 8—Will of Humphrey Basemore—wife Elizabeth, sons Perry, James, and Thomas. Dau. Eliza Scott, wife of Drewey R. Scott. Daus. Penelope and Mary. Exrs.: Wife and son James A. Basemore. Wit.: Starkey Basemore, G. H. Maner, William Shepherd.

Black. 1848—Nov. 5—Will of Edward S. Black; sons George Robinson and William Raymond. Children: Elizabeth Hanson, Edward James, Thomsa Jefferson, Charles Augustus. Exr.: Wife Augusta Georgianna Black. Wit.: Robert Williamson, John Miller, Lucretia Miller.

Burke. 1843—May 3—Will of David Burke, Sr. Wife Martha. Sons William, Abraham, David, Simeon, James. Daus. Smithey Brinson, Martha Daughtry, Mary Belcher; the children of Sarah Forehand, my dau.; Wm. R. Berryman, David and Martha Forehand. Exrs.: David and Simeon Burke. Wit.: Thomas U. Lewis, Alex. Kemp.

Conyers. 1835—July 15—Will of John Conyers; sons Isaac and Daniel. Dau. Elizabeth Atkins. Children of deceased son James. Grandsons, John and Jesse Freeman. Exr.: dau. Polly Conyers. Wit.: Rachel and Seaborn Goodall.

Congrow. 1814—Feb. 10—Will of Joseph Congrow. Sons Mathew and James. Dau. Hannah. Gr. son John Congrow, son of my dau. Isabel Hannah. Gr. son Antonio Ivey, son of my dau. Mary Ivey. Gr. chil.: William Usher, Thomas, Martha and Isabel Usher, chil. of my dau. Sarah, wife of Abel Usher. Margaret, Catherine and James, chil. of my son Robert. Wife Marthew. Exrs.: Mund Gross and James Archer. Wit.: Hugh Congrow, Hardy Everitt, William Donaldson, Hugh Donaldson.

Conyers. 1822—July 3—Will of Sarah Conyers. Dau. Cynthia. Son Richard W. Miller. Gr. son John Milo Miller. Dau. Sarah Knight. Gr. son Byrd Ferrill. Gr. son Cullen Williamson, agent for deceased dau. Lucy Williamson, and brother of Washington Williamson. Exrs.: Richard W. Miller, Reuben Wilkinson. Wit.: James Boston, Thomas Pengree, J. R. Kittles, Joshua Bealls.

Cooper. 1838—May 18—Will of William Cooper. Brothers and sisters children: Jane and William Carter, children of sister Rachel Carter, deceased. Wilson, Mary, Penelope, Ellen, Luvannah (or Susannah), George William Thomas, Rachel and Randolph Cooper, chil. of my brother George. Exrs.: brother George and Theophilus Williams. Wit.: Robert Lundy, Henry A. Dodge, Michael Henderson, Sarah Evans.

Connor. 1839—May 2—Will of James Connor. Son John. Wife Ann. Dau. Elizabeth Bevill. Exrs.: Wife and son Simeon D. Connor. Wit.: Sarah A. Faligant, William G. Falligant, John M. Lucas.

1847—Oct. 23—Will of Lewis Connor. Wife Lucretia. Dau. Sarah, wife of Archibald Bryan. Susan, wife of John H. Mercier. Gr. son James T., son of my dau. Mary Burnes, dec. Heirs of sons David and John Connor. Sons Charles Marion, Anthony Lafayette and Wilson Connor. Exr.: Wife Lucretia. Wit.: H. S. Lawton, M. E. Jaudon, C. Y. I. Singleton, W. I. Lawton.

Dunnington. 1814—May 4—Will of William Dunnington. To James Scott, Dr. John Connolly, John Arnett, Dr. Houseal, and Richard Boyd. Heirs of Norton and heirs of Moore. Wit.: William Scott, William Gross.

Dopson. 1835—May 4— Will of William Dopson. Wife Catherine. Sons Benjamin and William. Exr.: Wife. Wit.: Rebecca Dopson, Alexander Dopson.

Daughtry. 1841—May 8—Joseph Daughtry, deed of gift to Mary Ann Murry, and gr. son Francis, son of Lemuel Daughtry. Wit.: Simeon Burke, James Dixon, John F. Davis.

Freeman. 1814—Sept. 11—Will of Noah Freeman. Wife Lucy. Chil.: Elizabeth, Sarah, Rachel, Garnett, Noah, John David, and unborn ch. Exrs.: Bro. Jacob Freeman, Elijah Lipsey, Rger McKenny. Wit.: Joseph Button (?), Stephen Allen.

1809—Aug. 13—Will of Jacob Freeman. Wife Jane. Son Britton. Dau. Lueza—unborn child. Sons John, Jacob, James and Thomas. Daus.: Nancy Mills, Chaney and Mahaley. Exrs.: Roger McKinney, Jordan Floyd. Wit.: Theophilus Thomas, Stephen P. Floyd, John McGowen.

1815—Will of John Freeman. Wife Elizabeth. Gr. sons John F. and Jesse Freeman and Solomon Kemp. Wit.: William Blair, James C. Humphreys, Joseph Hitchcock.

1830—May 30—Will of Mary Ann E. Freeman. Brother John Freeman of Wilkinson County. Niece Mary Elizabeth Freeman. Aunt Levicy Lipsey. Exrs.: Willis Young and John Torrence. Wit.: Roger L. Gamble, Charles M. Hill.

Ferrill. 1833—July 1—Will of Benjamin Ferrill, Sr. Daus. Martha Lovett, Mary Miriam, J. E., and Julia Ferrill, land in Lumpkin County. Exrs.: John C. Ferrell, my oldest son. Wit.: Joseph G. Lawton, Virgil Bobe, H. Buford.

Butts County, Georgia. Henry Hatchey, Francis Hatchey, Elizabeth Simmons and John Simmons attest before Justices that about the 10th of Sept. (no year stated) at the house of Rev. John Simmons, they were called upon by Byrd Ferrell, late of Screven Co., and witnessed the following deposition:—gave and bequeathed all property to brother John Cuthbert Ferrell.

Foxwell. 1818—Oct. 2—Will of William Foxwell. Brother Edward, sister Kesiah. Exr.: John McWade. Wit.: Wm. P. Oliver, George R. D. Patterson, George Pollock.

Hurst. 1808—May 1—Will of Major Hurst. Sons Major, Jacob and Swicord. Daus. Pinkey and Rebecca. Excrs.: Bates Barley and brother Jesse Hurst. Wit.: James Oliver, Patience Mobley, William Graves.

Howell. 1809—Oct. 5—Will of Daniel Howell—my nine children: Caleb, Mary Ann, Daniel, Frances, William M., Samuel W. Aceneth, Civility and Juleann. Exrs.: Caleb Howell, Jr., Daniel Howell, Jr., James Bevill and Caleb Howell, Sr. Wit.: Stephen Tilley and William Howell.

Howard. 1812—Sept. 8—Will of Hezekiah Howard. Wife Sarah. Dau. Dorcas. Sons Levi and Moses. Children Rachel Strawhorn, Axa Howard, Nathan Howard. Wit.: John Best, Jacob Best, Daniel Blackburn.

Hogg. 1820—March 21—Will of John Hogg—to Chas. I. McQueen in trust for dau. Elizabeth Hogg or son-in-law. Wit.: James H. Wade, Eliza Stone, Jet Wade.

Herrington. 1830—Oct. 19—Will of Richard Herrington, Sr. Wife Martha. Children Alexander, John, Nelson, Benjamin and Joseph Tarpley. Sons Jeremiah and Martin. Dau. Myra McConson Simeon (?). Gr. son John Connell and son Stephen I. Exrs.: Wife and George Pollock. Wit.: Roger L. Gamble, Thomas Glascock, Alex. Kemp.

Jones. 1817—Dec. 3—Will of Mathew Jones of Tattnall Co. Wife Polly. Nephew and nieces Henry P., son of my dec. bro. Philip; Frances Lavinia, young wife of James Young; Mathew Berrien, Thomas Mitchell Lyman, Elizabeth, wife of William Evers; Betsy and Harriet, chil. of my bro. James Jones. John Jones, Frances Jones, Susannah, wife of William A. Courcy, Barbara Ann Humphrey, wife and children of dec. brothers Francis and JKohn Jones. Wit.: James Blackman, Michael Young, John Moore.

Kettles. 1808—March 12—Will of Peter Kettles. Wife Sarah. Children James W., John P. and Luisah Kettles. Exrs.: Wife and Jacob Kettles. Wit.: Geo. Williamson, Richard W. Miller, Thomas Brannen. (Wife Sarah married James Boston, Nov. 14, 1814.)

Lunday. 1811—Nov. 6—Will of Frances Lunday. Son-in-law Gross Scruggs. Dau. Frances Andoy (?), dau. Elizabeth Hudson. Son-in-law Richard Wiggins. Louisa and child or children of dau. Elizabeth Hudson. Gr. son Richard Wiggins. Sons Mechlin, Robert and William. Dau. Mary. Exrs.: Paul Bevill, Sr., and son Mechlin. Wit.: Joseph Ball, Sarah White, Lewis Lanier.

Lee. 1835—May 5—Will of John Lee, Sr. Wife Rachel and son David legatees and exrs. Wit.: William Wilder, Paul B. Garnett, James A. Mock.

Lanier. 1817—April 21—Will of Benjamin Lanier. Wife Ann. Dau. Mary and her children: Sally, Lucy, Betsy, Hannah. Gr. son Benjamin Warnock. Son Clement and his children; Benj. S., Bird I., Elizabeth W., Sally M. and Susannah. Gr. son John I. Lanier. Daus. Lucy and Nancy. Dau.-in-law Hannah Lanier and children—Clement, Elizabeth, James, Augustus, Anna, Solitan and Lucy. Gr. son Bird Newton and son-in-law Philip Newton and Robert Dickson. Exrs. Sons-in-law Thomas Mills and John Wolf. Wit.: John Mills, John Hendricks, Joshua Daughtry.

1838—April 18—Will of Lewis Lanier. Wife Esther. Sons Noel, Isaac, Thomas B. and James. Sarah Strickland, wife of Henry. Dau. Polly, wife of Robert McCall, Betsy B. McCall, Ann Kelly, William Jackson, husband of my dau. Clarissa. Exrs.: Wife Esther and Noel Lanier. Wit.: Isaac Hodges, Thomas H. Brewer, Hardy Hodges.

Lipsey. 1838—March 22—Will of Levicy Lipsey—to David Freeman. Niece Levicy Charlton. Sister Lucy Charlton, property in Pike

Co. Exrs.: George Pollock and Henry Best. Wit.: R. D. Black, Sarah Evans, Francis Marlow.

Long. 1846—Aug. 7—Will of Zacheus Long. Wife Elizabeth. Daus. Sarah (of Burke Co.), Mary W. Long. Exr.: Son-in-law William Cox of Burke Co. Wit.: John Robert Kittles, R. H. Saxon, John M. Miller.

Lovett. 1850—Nov. 30—Will of John F. Lovett. Wife Mary Ann, 3 minor chil. Exrs.: Anthony B. Lovett, John R. Kettle. Son Crawford Lovett. Wit.: Edward Lambert, Robert Watkins Lovett, Seaborn Jones.

Mock. 1810—July 4—Will of Andrew Mock. Dau. Charlotte. Eldest son Benjamin, exr. Other children. Wit.: Benjamin Morell, Richard Scruggs, Daniel Blackburn.

McBride. 1837—May 7—Will of James McBride. Daus. Mary Jane and Sarah Rebecca. Exr.: John Robert Kittles. Wit.: Augustus Seaborn Jones, Patrick McGowen, Alexander McBride.

Megee. 1820—April 1—Will of Henry Megee (?). Wife Ellender. Son Eli and other heirs. Exrs.: Wife and James Ponder. Wit.: Rennel Evans, Littleton Smith, Alex. Hendry.

Murray. 1826—Sept. 30—Will of William Murray. Wife Mary Ann, child in esse. Mother Mary Murray, Dunduffs Fort, Roye Co., Ireland. Exrs.: George Newton and Hardy Scarborough. Wit.: William Daughtry, John Mills, Moses Howard.

Mizell. 1827—Sept. 29—Will of Luke Mizell, wife Patience. Gr. son Guilford Peavy. Daus. Nancy Peavy and Jincey Douglas. Exrs.: Wife, Daniel B. Douglas, John Moore. Wit.: Peter Rogers, George Newton, James L. Dickson.

Mitchener. 1809—Oct. 6—Will of John Mitchener. Wife Luvisa— Exr. with John Best. Wit.: James Nesmith, Joseph Butler, John McWade.

Marlow. 1867—Will of Stephen M. Marlow. Wife Elenor. Gr. son Israel Connor. Gr. dau. Moselle Connor. Daus. Ann Blitch, Susan, wife of Hardy Hodges. Son Robert.

Newton. 1832—Oct. 9—Will of Moses Newton. Wife Mary Ann. "Small children." Wife exr. Wit.: David B. Newton, Isaac Newton, William H. Wade, J. P.

1841—May 9—Will of George Newton. Wife Mary. Daus. Elizabeth, Margaret, Mary, Susannah, Sarah Tabitha, Emily, Priscilla.

Nicholson. 1817—March. 12—Will of John Nicholson. Wife Elizabeth. Dau-in-law Margaret Streigle and her dau. Mary. To Sarah

Streigle, dau. to Martha Herrington. Gr. son John Sowell. Wit.:
Nicholas Streigle, Toby Herrington.

Kent. 1837—Sept. 4—Will of James R. Kent. Wife Penelope
(dau. of Robert Williams). Son Jesse. Exrs.: James Williams and
Theophilus Williams. Wit.: D. B. Brower, James Young, Theophilus
Williams.

Oliver. 1807—Nov. 13—Will of John Oliver, Sr. Sons Thomas,
Risden and Elijah. Dau. Sarah. Sons Jacob, William and Moses.
William Shroud and son John. Exrs.: Brother James and son John.
Wit.: Wm. A. Pickren, John Smith, William Graves.

Pearce. 1807—Sept. 10—Will of Joshua Pearce, Sr. Wife Hannah. Sons William, Stephen and Joshua. Dau. Sarah McKay. Exrs.:
three sons. Wit.: Gideon Reynolds, Joshua Bealls.

Poythress. 1828—May 18—Will of Cleton Poythress. Father Mere-
dith Poythress. Sister Elizabeth Brannen. Niece Sarah Elizabeth
Poythress. Exr.: Hope Brannen. Wit.: Cullen Williamson, William
Brannen, Jane Brannen.

Philips. 1843—Nov. 7—Will of Richard Philips. Wife Ann. Daus.
Naomi Morton and Orphy Hunt. Son Burrel. Gr. dau. Nancy Coge.
Exrs.: Edward Jones and Noel Lanier. Wit.: Shepard Williams,
John F. Helmly, Robert F. Jackson.

Parker. 1848—Jan. 4—Deed of gift from Elizabeth Parker to chil-
dren Henry and Betty. Daus. Clarissa Waters, Eliza Key, Jemina
Newton, Tabitha Griner, Mary Ann Lee and Jane Griner. Wit.: Alex.
Kemp, James Griner, Lewis Lewis.

Pearce. 1827—Nov. 10—Will of Stephen Pearce. Wife Mary.
Sons Green, Joshua, William F., youngest son Stephen C. Pearce.
Daus. Sarah M. Pearce and Jane E. Pearce. Gr. sons Stephen Green
Bray, Stephen Green Pearce, Stephen P. Bevill, John G. Bevill. Exrs.:
Wife and son Stephen C. Pearce. Wit.: M. N. McCall, J. W. P. Mc-
Call, John G. McCall.

Phillips. 1846—May 8—Will of Benjamin Phillips. Wife Lucy.
To Sarah Daughtry, wife of Lemuel, and Lucinda Burk, dau. of Sarah
Daughtry. Nephew David T. Phillips, son of my brother David.
Exrs.: Wife Lucy, David Burk, Jr., and Adam Brinson. Wit.: E.
H. Scarborough, Peter Arnett, Alexander Kemp.

Roberts. 1840—July 8—Will of Roland B. Roberts. Wife Sarah.
Son Bolan. Gr. son Hiram Roberts of West Florida, son of John B.
Exrs.: Bolan Roberts, Benjamin Phillips, Jason Brinson. Wit.:
Adam Brinson, Sr., Enos Scarborough, Patrick O'Haire, James Bel-
cher.

Rieves. 1841—Sept. 6—Will of John S. Rieves. Wife Jane Elizabeth, Exr. "Children," but not named. Wit.: Sarah M. Warren, John S. Warren, Daniel C. Howell.

Rushing. 1836—March 17—Will of Ely Rushing. Sisters Mahala and Caroline. Brother Michael J. Rushing. Brother-in-law Sion L. Boykin, Exr. Wit.: J. W. P. McCall, J. G. McCall.

Rieves. 1808—Jan. 1—Will of Rebecca Reives. Sister Elizabeth Scott. Exrs.: Brothers John and Thomas Reives. Wit.: William Dunnington, Thomas Brannen.

Attestation that Simeon Reives left property to Richard, infant son of William Scott, and other property to sons John and Thomas. Test.: Willaim Blair, Thomas Colding, Richard Herrington, Solomon Kemp, John Connelly, John Walters (doctor).

The Reives are kin to Williamson and Mickleberry families. (Ed.)

Scruggs. 1832—July 17—Will of Richard Scruggs. Wife Ann. Son William H. Scruggs. Gr. children Richard, William and Eliza R. Scruggs. Daus. Cassandra Lucas and Ann Abigail Chase, and gr. dau. Rebecca Pearce. Exrs.: Wm. H. Scruggs and John G. Mathews. Wit.: Stephen P. Bevill, John G. Bevill, David Stewart.

Simmons. 1834—July 11—Will of Samuel Simmons. Wife Mary. Sons Samuel, Jr., James, George and Elijah property in Cherokee Co. To John, Elizabeth, Samuel, and James Simmons and Miriam Wilson. To son Moses. Exr.: John Simmons. Wit.: William Wade, George Newton, William L. Dodd.

Sheppard. 1825—Aug. 20—William Sheppard—to daus. Sophie Boykin, Martha J. White, Elizabeth Sheppard. Sons David B. M. Sheppard, Lorenzo Dew, Lymon, William T., John B., Harvey, James. Gr. son James Russell. Wife Martha. Wit.: Rachel Blackburn, Stephen Blackburn. Exrs.: John B. Sheppard, Harvey Sheppard.

Scott. 1828—May 3—Will of James Scott. Wife Temperance. Children Benjamin Franklin, George Washington, and Sarah Ann. William Thomas Scott and children of my first wife. Codicil names James Scott, Sr., and Elizabeth, the wife of Joseph McGowen. Wit.: Richard R. Scott, Jacob Wells, Meredith Poythress.

Scruggs. 1826—Oct. 26—Will of John G. Scruggs. Wife Arimenta. Son Richard. Daus. Julia Ann and Harriet Ann. Exrs.: Bro. William Scruggs and William King. Wit.: B. D. Colson, John Stephens.

Stewart. 1838—July 6—Will of Tabitha Stewart. Gr. dau. Mary Ann, dau. of Susan Stewart. Gr. daus. Sarah Ann and Elizabeth

Stewart, chil. of Charles Stewart. Exr.: William Kemp. Wit.: W. G. Taylor, Thomas Robbins, Elizabeth Kemp.

Scarborough. 1842—Sept. 2—Will of Hardy Scarborough. Wife Jemima. Son Enos. Wit.: James Parker, Jesse Lee, Samuel Simmons.

Stephens. 1837—Oct. 9—John Stephens. Wife Eliza. Sons William, Benj. Franklin, James. Daus. Ann Elizabeth, Mahaly, Jane, Mary and ch. in esse. Exr.: Barnet Newton. Wit.: Wm. Stephens, Asa F. Mock.

Walker. 1823—Nov. 9—Thomas G. Walker. Wife Elizabeth, lots in Greenville, S. C. Wit.: Joseph Eve, George Twiggs, Thomas Green.

Williamson. 1825—Oct. 25—Robert Mickleberry Williamson, Jr., brothers Richard M. and Paul Williamson. Exr.: John R. Kittles. Wit.: James Boston, Ira Boston.

1807—Oct. 28—Robert Williamson, the elder. Sons Robert Micklebery, John and Benjamin. Daus. Sarah, Abigail, Lucy and Casandra. Wife Sarah. Exrs.: Robert Micklebery Williamson, Peter Kittles, Richard Miller. Wit.: George Williamson, Seaborn Jones, Maner Tenbrook.

Wilkinson. 1826—May 25—Reuben Wilkinson. Wife Ann D., Exr. Wit.: Thomas G. Little, Byrd Ferrell, Jas. R. Kent.

Williams. 1827—Oct. 28—Robert Williams. Sons Robert and Theophilus. Daus. Nancy, Penelope (mar. Jas. Kent), and Sarah. Sons Exrs. Wit.: Patience Mizell, Jinsey Gordon, Jane Mills, John J. Twiggs.

SCREVEN COUNTY MARRIAGES

1 8 3 5

Usher, William H., to Harriet Graham, Feb. 7.

Barton, Joseph L., to Mary Oglesby, Dec. 12.

1 8 3 7

Taylor, James, to Susannah Coger, June 29.

Herring, Benjamin, to Lucitta Jacobs, Aug. 19.

Joyner, William, to Clara Bragg, Sept. 23.

Taylor, John, to Margaret Bolton, Nov. 4.

Hollingsworth, Isaac, to Phoebe Lee, Nov. 7.

Dell, Benentt M., to Eliza D. Boston, Nov. 26.

Mitter, William P., to Ann James, Dec. 30.

1 8 3 8

Waters, Henry, to Clary C. Parker, Feb. 26.

Campeau, William P., to Mary Ann Herring, June 22.

Woodward, George R., to Ann M. Dell, Sept. 4.

Redding, Alexander, to Zene Kelly, Nov. 7.

Moorhouse, Joseph M., to Mary McQueen, Nov. 24.

Gardner, Morgan, to Mary Roberts, Nov. 30.

Blackburn, Allen, to Harriet Evans, Dec. 19.

Royals, William A., to Sarah Ann Best, Dec. 24.

Thornton, Daniel, to Mary Burns, Dec. 27.

Simmons, Samuel, to Martha Cale, Dec. 13.

1 8 3 9

Newton, Robinson, to Anna Daughtry, Jan. 14.

Hurst, Willis, to Sarah Bolton, Jan. 25.

Loper, Reuben, to Mary Clary, Jan. 31.

Parker, Mathew, to Martha Waters, Feb. 2.

Hines, Henry H., to Rebecca C. Beard, Feb. 3.

Buckston, Benjamin, to Elizabeth Oliver, Feb. 17.

Herrington, Richard M., to Julia Ann Pollock, Feb. 27.

Lawton, Winburn, to Harriet Jaudon, April 1.

Hodges, Ambrose, to Penny Newton, July 6.

Cox, William, to Sarah S. Long, Sept. 18.

Ziegler, Solomon, to Victoria J. Thompson, Sept. 30.

Burk, James, to Salina Evelyn Barfield, Nov. 16.

Lanier, Neel, to Martha Tullis, Nov. 21.

Dickey, Joseph W., to Mary Thompson, Aug. 5.

Coulson, Sheppard Williams, to Martha Usher, April 28.

Jackson, Andrew, to Martha P. Coulson, June 26.

Bevill, Robert, to Janes Barnes (or Burnes), Oct. 8.

Newton, Reuben, to Lucy Ann Braswell, Dec. 25.

Burnes (or Barnes), Thomas H., to Mary Ann Rieves, Dec. 26.

1 8 4 0

Gross, Edmund B., to Susan Mercer, Jan. 1.

Parker, Samuel, to Eliza Griner, Jan. 7.

Bert, Levi H., to Elizabeth Cole, Jan. 7.

Baymen, John, to Harriet Willis, Jan. 21.

Alesby, James, to Ruth Reddick, Jan. 9.

Scott, Richard P., to Mary Ann Wells, March 4.

Robert, Elias, to Louisa Stone (?), April 11.

Bragg, Thomas, to Susan Ann Burke, May 8.

Smith, John A., to Elisabeth Scott, May 8.

Chisholm, Robert, to Charity Styles, Oct. 7.

Bevill, Garnett B., to Francis Bevill, Oct. 17.

Thorn, William, to Luchebe Bileorn (?), Oct. 21.

Lovett, William H., to Jane C. Wade, Dec. 17.

Hampton, John, to Charlotte Mitchell (or Mizell), Dec. 20.

Wells, Frederick, to Sarah Streigle, Dec. 24.

1 8 4 1

Church, Charles, to Elizabeth Robins, Jan. 6.

Harrington, Robert M., to Nancy Lewis, Jan. 9.

Call, Edmund, to Jane Bort, Jan. 29.

Favins, William H., to Amelia A. Wilson, Jan. 21.

Waters, G. D., to Penelope Thiot, Feb. 2.

Cake, John, to Therba Lanier, Feb. 16.

Levin, Saulla K., to Rebecca Herrington, March 3.

Mathews, William, to Mary E. Overstreet, March 18.

Bennett, William A., to Sealia Brannen, Feb. 19.

Herrin, Samuel S., to S. Lewis, March 26.

Scott, B. T., to Catherine Miller, June 9.

Lee, William W., to Ann Anderson, June 24.

Burnes, James T., to Frances Andrews, Aug. 2.

Emmants, Joseph, to Ann Loper, Aug. 2.

Mimms, Thomas S., to Mary E. Lines, Aug. 22.

Oliver, Mack C., to Sarah Ann Freeman, Sept. 1.

Marshall, Mallard, to Mary Mizell, Sept. 14.

Williams, David, to Margaret Ann Archer, Oct. 7.

Spell, Howard, to Sarah Kelley, Oct. 27.

Thompson, William, to Martha Ann Hurst, Nov. 22.

Kittles, John R., to Clara McBride, Nov. 29.

Freeman, Noah, to Elizabeth Ann Andrews, Dec. 23.

1 8 4 2

Potter, Young, to Easler Oliver, Feb. 20.

Perry, Joseph C., to Julia Ann Bolton, Feb. 24.

Everett, Hardy, to Sarah Stewart, Jan. 26.

Black, John I., to Caroline Stewart, March 26.

Brinson, Benjamin, to Sarah L. Schiff, Jan. 2.

Griner, William, to Tabitha Parker, April 13.

Wells, John, to Elizabeth Hamilton, April 16.

Roberts, Robin, to Virginia Young, April 26.

Lee, Josiah, to Charity Ann Bert, May 19.

Connor, Lewis, to Lucretia Daniels, June 30.

Scott, George W., to Kesiah Cowdy, Sept. 11.

Rahns, C. S., to Ann Maria Tuttle, Dec. 18.

Mercer, John H., to Susan Connor, Dec. 20.

1 8 4 3

Basemore, Robert, to Sarah Williams, Jan. 5.

Barber, Wade, to Rebecca Green, Jan. 9.

Oglesby, Elisha, to Percy Jenkins, Jan. 29.

McBride, Alexander, to Mary M. Lovett, Feb. 21.

Clifton, Levin, to Morning Bert, Feb. 23.

Bolton, John L., to Vicy Herrington, Jan. 16.

Evans, Charles, to Levicy Charlton, March 9.

Coulson, T., to Frances Bevill, March 24.

Cale, Bud, to Jane Howard, May 18.

McGrady, Thomas, to Ellen Woods, May 21.

Cooper, George W., to Sarah M. S. Evans, May 25.

Reynolds, William B., to Lucretia Gross, May 24.

Odom, James, to Caroline E. Herrington, July 20.

Lee, Benjamin, to Ellen Jeffers, July 26.

Hughes, Patrick, to Ellender Stile, Sept. 7.

Waters, William G., to Miriam Evans, Sept. 21.

Meeds, James, to Sarah Ann Cox, Oct. 9.

Lovett, James C., to Parmelia Oliver, Oct. 11.

Basemore, Thomas, to Elizabeth J. Taylor, Oct. 26.

Blackburn, William, to Jane Waters, Nov. 7.

Robins, Stephens M., to Rodey E. Mock, Nov. 7.

Wells, Jacob H., to Caroline Tuttle, Nov. 1.

Ziegler, Israel, to Margaret Waters, Nov. 2.

Rooks, Isaac, to Sarah Fisher, Dec. 3.

Banks, Simeon C., to Martha Streigle, Dec. 6.

Mineas, John T., to Ann Coney, Dec. 27.

Jenkins, Charles, to Lavinia James, Dec. 31.

1 8 4 4

Sausy, William, to Mary Ann Potter, Jan. 4.

Gross, Thomas, to Clary Ziegler, Jan. 4.

Mock, John B., to Penelope Basemore, Jan. 17.

McLendon, Benjamin F., to Mary Shealy, Jan. 21.

Wilson, James, to M. Lee, Jan. 27.

Williams, William, to Abigail Pye, Feb. 8.

Young, James, Jr., to Margaret Oliver, Feb. 1.

Basemore, James, to M. E. Beard, Feb. 14.

Freeman, Alfred, to Sarah Bryan, Feb. 15.

Newton, William, to Jemima Parker, Feb. 22.

Banks, Aylor, to Catherine Stregles, Feb. 28.

Hillis, Jacob, to Martha Oglesby, Jan. 22.

Griner, Jonathan, to Jane Parker, March 14.

Bealls, Benjamin, to Sarah Lambert, March 15.

Brigham, William, to Caroline M. T. White, April 10.

Poythress, John W., to Mary Ann Wilder, Feb. 15.

Sharpe, Robert C., to Rachel Lewis, April 11.

Arnett, William, to Elizabeth Ziegler, May 1.

Oliver, Thomas W., to Eliza Mimms, March 17.

Barber, Thomas, to Dicey Beasley, June 18.

Wells, Alexander, to Elizabeth Hunter, Sept. 4.

Cale (or Cole), Edmund, to Sidney Freeman, Sept. 8.

Basemore, Perry, to Adaline Mock, Sept. 30.

Scarborough, James, to Sarah Ann Clifton, Oct. 3.

Boyd, Edward, to Priscilla Parker, Oct. 13.

Morgan, John, to Elizabeth Simmons, Oct. 19.

Long, Zacheus, to Elizabeth McLendon, Nov. 12.

Clifton, John, to Martha Lewis, Nov. 30.

Evans, John R., to Elizabeth Lucas, Dec. 22.

Key, William S., to Eliza Parker, Dec. 31.

Beard, Jesse, to Louisa Perger, Dec. 12.

1 8 4 5

Humphrey, John W., to Mary Roath, Jan. 1.

Connor, William L., to Sabina A. Hodges, Jan. 2.

Herrington, Simeon, to Abigail Roath, Jan. 10.

Freeman, John F., to Elizabeth Meades, March 4.

Pye, Edward, to Elizabeth Blackburn, March 9.

Cubbedge, John A. W., to Mary Ann Janis (sic), March 14.

Mock, Lodiwick, to Margaret Lee, March 17.

Thompson, John G., to Kitsey Wells, March 25.

Humphrey, Joseph C., to Julia Rogers, April 22.

Littlefield, Samuel H., to Martha Lovett, May 8.

Blackburn, Stephen, to Rachel Connor, May 13.

Newton, Barnet, to Mrs. Jane Wilson, June 12. (Wid. of John and dau. of Obadiah Edwards.)

Oglesby, Anthony, to Kesiah Roberts, Sept. 3.

Carter, Samuel, to Jane Nealin, Sept. 17.

Lee, Jesse, to Mary Ann Parker, Dec. 3.

Cale (or Cole), John, to Francis Redding, Dec. 4.

Griner, Mathew M., to Jane Moore, Dec. 10.

Roberts, Robert W., to Jane V. Mills, Dec. 24.

Moore, William F., to Ann Priest, Dec. 26.

Wallace, Simeon, to Janie Key, Dec. 29.

1 8 4 6

Meades, John F., to Mary A. Beard, Jan. 1.

Owens, William A., to Elizabeth Nason, Jan. 1.

Hurst, John, to Martha A. Bragg, Jan. 3.

Sharp, Green D., to Ann Ziegler, Jan. 8.

Dickey. Samuel, to Nancy Ann Burk, Jan. 25.

Hurst, William, to Margaret Mobley, Feb. 1.

Freeman, Jacob, to Caroline Sheppard, March 18.

Reddick, Jacob G., to Mary I. Jackson, March 25.

Dixon, William W., to Susannah Dixon, March 26.

Humphrey, Sam'l C., to Sarah A. Meades, Aug. 6.

McDaniel, Oliver, to Lucy Ann E. Bolton, Aug. 29.

Liver, John, to Mahala Ann Ennis, Sept. 18.

Flake, William H., to Alice Ann E. Wilson, Oct. 16.

Boykin, John B., to Mary Archer, Oct. 28.

Olmstead, Francis, to Susan C. Maner, Dec. 23.

Perry, George S., to Jane Pollock, Dec. 23.

Thompson, Robert F., to Susan C. Gross, Dec. 31.

1 8 4 7

Heinly, Israel, to Ann Eliza Wilson, Jan. 18.

Lee, Hamilton, to Martha Mattox, Feb. 3.

Wheldon, William, to Elizabeth Bragg, Feb. 10.

Mills, Henry F., to Candace Lovett, Feb. 10.

Creach, H. S., Georgia Ann Jackson, Feb. 16.

Lowell, Josiah, to Margaret Meades, Feb. 25.

Farniss, William H., to Sarah Jane Morgan, March 2.

Archer, James E., to Mary Ann Best, March 11.

Jenkins, John, to Jane Williams, March —.

Lee, John, to Mary Basemore, April 6.

Bragg, David, to Sarah Ann Taylor, June 27.

Frawley, Jeremiah, to Mary Ann Lewis, Aug. 20.

Park, Hardy C., to Sarah Scarborough, Sept. 29.

Scott, Lorenzo, to Jane Griner, Oct. 5.

Hutchinson, Richard P., to Ezenah Archer, Oct. 26.

Bragg, Seaborn, to Elizabeth Sumner, Nov. 21.

Humphrey, A. W., to Barbara Stowell, Nov. 24.

Jarmon, James T., to Sarah M. Saxon, Dec. 5.

Blackburn, Paynes R., to Sarah Moore, Dec. 6.

Bevill, Robert, to Jane Thomas, Dec. 9.

Evans, Hezekiah, to Evelina W. Thorne, Dec. 9.

Blackburn, James R., to Sarah Moore, Dec. 12.

Hunter, William E., to Frances Hunter, Sept. 20.

1 8 4 8

Archer, David I., to Sarah E. Lee, Jan. 20.

Morton, Simeon L., to Hannah F. Dasher, Jan. 30.

Johnson, Nathan M., to Susan Lewis, Feb. 24.

Jeffers, Elbert, to Sophia McGowen, March 2.

Mimms, Britton, to Mary A. Pollock, March 24.

Brown, George, to Ann Austin, May 13.

Archer, Avon N., to Charity A. Robins, May 28.

Jones, Edward, to Eliza Brown, June 29.

Griffin, Israel S., to Elizabeth Stewart, Aug. 23.

Wilson, William I., to Martha Ann Lee, Aug. 27.

Griner, James, to Julia Waters, Sept. 1.

Reddick, John I., to Sarah Oglesby, Sept. 28.

Thompson, John T., to Mary K. Thompson, Oct. 16.

Wildes, Macklen, to Lavinia Hodges, Oct. 21.

Hurst, Napoleon B., to Plortha Ann Gumbert, Nov. 7.

Freeman, Jesse, to Susan Ann Brannen, Nov. 16.

Woods, William, to Ann Archer, Dec. 28.

1 8 4 9

Bennett, Joseph A. R., to Mary A. Green, Feb. 26.

McLaughlin, F. H., to Emily Stile, Feb. 29.

Evans, Francis, to Mary Ann Connor, March 15.

Sasser, Thomas, to Mary O'Connor, March 18.

Newton, James, to Margaret Barbara——, April 24.

Joyner, William, to Mary Bragg, April 26.

Best, John W., to Rebecca Hunter, May 24.

Blackburn, Ephraim, to Louisa Best, Aug. 2.

Guest, Seaborn, to Sophia White, Aug. 21.

Waters, William F., to Ann Hunter, Nov. 16.

Hunter, Abraham, to Amanda Boykin, Nov. 21.

Moore, John, to Margaret Coulson, Nov. 22.

Hislop, Robert, to Mary Hines, Nov. 28.

Evans, John C., to Mary Ann Waters, Dec. 16.

Bragg, William, to Charity Jenkins, Dec. 16.

Stowell, Edward W., to Letitia A. C. Graham, Dec. 18.

Cone, William W., to Maria H. B., Dec. 20.

Griffin, Lemuel, to Jane Mobley, Dec. 30.

Burnes, Thomas H., to Mary Jane McBride, Dec. 30.

1 8 5 0

Canty, Thomas H., to Celia E. Dell, Jan. 17.

Jackson, John W., to Ann G. Norment, Feb. 7.

Hollingsworth, Isaac, to Mary Ann Simmons, Feb. 26.

Lee, Robert P. E., to Sarah Ann Wilson, March 2.

Wells, Alexander I., to Mary Basemore, March 7.

Poythress, Isaac, to Mary Ann Thompson, April 7.

Herrington, Robert M., to Nancy Pollock, April 17.

Williams, William K., to Sarah Martha Vest, June 9.

Thompson, John S., to Caroline E. Lowden, June 9.

Williamson, Robert C., to Eugenia Bryan, June 10.

Burke, Sampson, to Nancy A. Dixon, June 20.

McCarter, Marvin, to Julia A. Burns, June 23.

Thompson, John, to Nancy Jackson, Aug. 6.

West, Thomas, to Mary Spell, Sept. 9.

Howard, William H., to Jane E. Newton, Sept. 17.

Williamson, Samuel, to Elizabeth Andrews, Oct. 16.

Lowder, James S., to Jane Howell, Nov. 26.

Gille (?), John, to Mary Ann Stewart, Dec. 7.

1 8 5 1

Roberts, James M., to Elizabeth Prescott, Feb. 14.

Connor, James, to Mary E. Roberts, Feb. 25.

Fuller, Thomas J., to Mary C. E. Kittles, Feb. 26.

Blackburn, Mayberry, to Juliana Jeffers, March 6.

Oglesby, John M., to Natalie Bolton, March 27.

Dauhtry, Augustus, to Betty Parker, Aug. 8.

Williams, James E., to Sarah McCall, Aug. 21.

Dixon, James A., to Mary Frawley, Sept. 25.

Connor, Isaac B., to Sarah Ann Jackson, Sept. 25.

Bowie, William C., to Lucy Humphrey, Oct. 6.

Blackburn, Stephen, to Elizabeth Jeffers, Dec. 20.

Walker, John M., to Mary B. Campbell, Dec. 30.

1 8 5 2

Taylor, William, to Margaret Bragg, Jan. 14.

Green, Benjamin P., to Mrs. Mary A. Prescott, Aug. 13.

Hurst, Joseph W., to Amelia Ellis, Sept. 11.

Farr, W. B. C., to Mrs. A. Reddin, Sept. 19.

Phillips, Enos, to Patience Peavy, Sept. 26.

Walker, Samuel L., to Susannah White, Oct. 28.

Owens, Hansford R., to Zipporah Brannen, Dec. 1.

Brinson, William E., to Mary Buford, Dec. 20.

Lewis, Stephen, to Martha E. Howard, Sept. 9.

1 8 5 3

Wilson, Francis, to Lucreda Waters, Jan. 4.

Andrews, Amos, to Drucilla Oliver, Jan. 6.

Jacobson, David, to Elizabeth Wells, Feb. 16.

Boykin, Ludowick, to Caroline Southwell, Jan. 26.

Williams, Robert, to Nancy Larissay, March 24.

Odum, Nicholas, to Caroline Freeman, May 1.

Moore, John, to Mary Ann Lee, June 5.

Simmons, Williams, to Elender Dickey, June 12.

Stewart, James A., to Lucinda J. Flake, June 13.

Evans, James W., to Seleba Ann Thorne, Aug. 7.

Freeman, Bryant, to Louisiana Mendes, Sept. 19.

Jackson, Robert F., to Rebecca Y. Connor, Sept. 26.

Reddick, Peter, to Adaline Reddick, Oct. 6.

Mock, George E., to Caroline Ziegler, Nov. 10.

Wilson, Moses P., to Laura Hotchkiss, Nov. 28.

Rushing, Miles, to Mary Mock, Nov. 30.

Kelly, Robert, to Mrs. Julia Ann Williams, Dec. 15.

Wade, J. D., to Sarah Bowse, Dec. 20.

Roberts, Augustus, to Susan Poythress, Dec. 30.

Herrington, Simeon, to Mary A. Mills, Dec. 22.

1 8 5 4

McGee, James, to Emily J. Walker, Jan. 1.

Overstreet, S., to A. T. Brown, Jan. 1.

Brown, Daniel W., to Susan Mincey, Jan. 12.

Parker, Henry, to Margaret Ziegler, Feb. 2.

Parker, Lemuel, to Clary Mincey, Feb. 9.

Poythress, John M., to Rhody Gross, April 5.

Gardner, John F., to Martha Smith, June 11.

Lucas, Robert E., to Sarah R. Strickland, July 5.

Mock, Robert A., to Nancy Robins, Sept. 21.

Lanier, Augustus B., to Margaret Meldrim, Oct. 8.

Parker, Moses, to Mary Brinson, Oct. 8.

Wolf, Robert T., to Caroline M. Furness, Oct. 1.

Muller, John A., to Jane L. George, Oct. 19.

Stewart, W. S., to Mary A. Stephens, Oct. 19.

Humphrey, Samuel, to Margaret Sowell, Oct. 21.

Andrews, Paul B., to Sarah L. Morgan, Nov. 18.

Connor, Edward T., to Sarah V. Marsh, Dec. 5.

Arnett, George, to Elizabeth Scott, Dec. 6.

Glisson, Henry H., to Sarah Ann Haynes, Dec. 14.

Oaton, William, to Martha Williams, Dec. 20.

Arnett, Joseph, to Sarah A. Robbins, Dec. 21.

Schley, Richard W., to Marietta McLelland, Dec. 21.

1 8 5 5

Burke, Lawson D. S., to Frances Oglesby, Jan. 7.

Herrington, Martin, to Sarah A. Prescott, Jan. 24.

Brown, Joseph F., to Mrs. Ann E. Henderson, Jan. 25.

Singleton, William A., to Caroline A. E. Bryan, Jan. 31.

Johnson, William, to Virginia Powers (of Floyd Co.), Jan. 6.

Parker, James, Jr., to Clarissa Parker, Feb. 28.

Jeffers, John S., to Ann Elizabeth Basemore, April 4.

Rosser, James A., to Temperance Ziegler, April 8.

Sasser, Howell, Jr., to Mary Ann Daughtry, April 12.

Sowell, Franklin, to Emily Daniel, April 26.

Averitt, Alexander, to Mary Ann Lively, May 19.

Anderson. Hezekiah, to Jane B. Sheppard, May 15.

Jeffers, Allen D., to Sarah Hollands (of Bulloch Co.), Aug. 27.

Darlington, Richard H., to Louisiana Lovett, Aug. 30.

Fox, William, to Mary A. Rushing, Oct. 8.

Herrington, Benjamin R., to Sarah A. Prescott, Oct. 17.

Mock, Josiah M., to Elizabeth Wilson, Nov. 18.

Smith, Joseph, to Martha Jenkins, Dec. 30.

1 8 5 6

Farr, William J., to Sarah M. Moore, Jan. 1.

Evans, George W. R., to Mary Ann A. Hughes, Jan. 13.

Lee, Nathan W., to Sarah M. Mock, Jan. 27.

Lee, Ransom, to Rebecca J. Wilson, Jan. 24.

Connor, James G. W., to Martha Jane Stephens, Feb. 26.

Williams, Robert, to Louisiana Jane Carr, March 13.

Overstreet, Causey, to Rebecca D. Bryan, March 15.

Ambers, William, to Susan Waters, April 10.

Wade, Archibald, to Amanda L. Bowie, April 20.

Hobby, Wensley, to Gertrude Livingston, June 25.

Johnson, John Wesley, to Margaret A. Ziegler, July 15.

Lee, Joseph B., to Sarah Waters, July 16.

Smith, John H., to Mary Smith, July 24.

Roberts, Augustus, to Jane Waters, July 30.

Ennis, Johnson A., to Emily Sharp, Aug. 1.

Roberts, Henry, to Elizabeth Parker, Aug. 27.

Hale, Elbert, to Mamie Roberts, Sept. 9.

Hurst, James, to Candicy Burke, Sept. 20.

Brinson, John E., to Sarah Ann Parker, Sept. 25.

Burke, Joseph, to Sarah M. Lewis, Oct. 6.

Newton, William R., to Liza A. Best, Oct. 14.

Reckley, Seaborn F., to Amanda W. Lovett, Oct. 20.

Waters, Green B., to Susan Willis, Oct. 30.

Morgan, David E., to Mary M. Lucas, Nov. 27.

Andrews, George, to Barbara Roberts, Oct. 23.

Jarrell, William J., to Hannah Brannen, Dec. 3.

Cone, Lawrence P., to Sarah Colding, Dec. 8.

Hancock, William, to Mary Ann Evans, Dec. 21.

Sharp, Robert D., to Martha A. Sowell, Dec. 31.

Boyd, John Jefferson, to Mrs. Agnes O. Saxon (nee Goldwire), Aug. 25.

1 8 5 7

Williams, Williams L., to Sarah Ann Newton, Feb. 4.

Murray, Dempsey, to Mary A. Lovett, Feb. 21.

Larisey, John R., to Sarah Ann Lewis, March 8.

Moore, Charles H., to Julia R. Douglas, March 12.

Thompson, George W., to Elizabeth W. Scott, March 8.

Gross, David C., to Mary E. Thompson, April 2.

Rushing, Silas E., to Mary Ann E. Poythress, April 4.

Graham, William F., to Elizabeth Julia Brannan, April 29.

Sowell, William, to Rebecca Jane Prescott, May 10.

Davis, Charles, to Julia Oglesby, May 11.

Roberts, Benjamin C., to Mary E. Roberts, May 27.

Waters, George W., to Susan Willis, May 27.

Williamson, Benj. M., to Mary White, May 31.

Howell, Daniel J., to Julia Powell, June 3.

Caile, Thomas, to Rochanna Parker, June 28.

Wallace, Mathew, to Ann Mary Clifton, July 14.

McMillan, W. J., co Martha Taylor, Aug. 5.

Pearce, John R., to Nancy Bolton, Aug. 11.

Lovett, John F., to Elizabeth Bates, Aug. 20.

Mock, George H., to Frances A. Lee, Sept. 15.

Mixon, James, to Delia Joyner, Sept. 21.

Bragg, Howell, to Eliza Jenkins, Sept. 23.

Marsh, William M., to Elizabeth A. Walker, Oct. 21.

Connor, John H., to Dorcas Howard, Nov. 4.

Scott, John M., to Frances Thompson, Nov. 18.

Andrews, Thomas, to Sarah M. Williams, Nov. 22.

Jeffers, George M., to Matilda Waters, Nov. 25.

Roberts, William J., to Cynthia L. Howard, Dec. 17.

Bragg, Henry, to Mary Taylor, Dec. 20.

Lee, Benjamin R., to Lucretia Waters, Dec. 29.

1 8 5 8

Newsome, Joel, to Maria Wilson, Jan. 21.

Singleton, C. T. J., to Rebecca Rogers, Feb. 3.

Wilson, Robert D., to Matilda L. Thompson, Feb. 25.

Sasser, Henry, to Mary Waters, Feb. 26.

Connor, Isaac B., to Jane A. Burns, March 3.

Lee, William W., to Sarah Ann Lowther, March 30.

Stephens, James, to Susan Connor, Aug. 28.

Williams, Willis T., to A. E. Lafitte, Sept. 27.

Lafitte, Charles A., to Martha J. Boston, Oct. 7.

Stewart, Daniel J., to Martha Holman, Nov. 4.

Davis, E. C., to Susan Brinson, Dec. 12.

Skinner, William R., to Sarah H. McLelland, Dec. 19.

1 8 5 9

McGee, David A., to Martha J. Wilson, Jan. 12

Bragg, Littleton, to Margaret Sasser, Jan. 30.

Sasser, Littleton, to Mary A. Parker, Jan. 20.

Ellison, James H., to Nancy Ann Brinson, March 13.

Miller, Thomas G., to Sarah L. Dixon, March 15.

Ivey, John M., to Catherine Martin (Liberty Co.), April 2.

Stewart, Charles J., to Emily E. Gross, May 6.

Middleton, James, to Laura Wilson, May 31.

Hurst, Emanuel, to Martha McGee, May 31.

Heiman, A., to Elizabeth Dickey, June 12.

Hamilton, William D., to Alice L. Young, July 18.

Waters, James W., to A. L. Usher, Aug. 11.

McCall, P. J., to A. A. Colding, Sept. 27.

Parker, Henry, to Martha Ann Lee, Oct. 25.

Kemp, William W., to Julia A. H. Mills, Oct. 30.

Monk, John P., to Mary Ann Basemore. Nov. 27.

Sugg, Jesse E., to Malinda Burke, Dec. 4.

Roberts, Daniel E., to Mary A. E. Boston, Dec. 14.

Mock, Ludowic, to Cynthia E. Basemore, Dec. 22.

Pye, James H., to Nancy Ann Howard, Dec. 27.

Parker, Hardy, to Sophia Parker, Dec. 28.

1 8 6 0

Lowther, James H., to Mary Ann Joiner, Jan. 5.

Waters, James, to Susan Sasser, Jan. 8.

Flake, Richard S., to Margaret A. Williams, Jan. 11.

Thompson, Robert F., to Lavinia Mock, Jan. 19.

Connor, John R., to Susan Ann Mercer, Feb. 9.

Johnson, Sterling M., to Rebecca M. Robbins, Feb. 12.

Hills, George W., to Patience A. Mobley, Feb. 12.

McCoy, Samuel, to Nancy Sapp, March 1.

Lanier, Lewis L., to Molissa L. Newton, March 3.

Mixon, Benjamin F., to Mary Taylor, March 10.

Burke, James D., to Elmira Sharpe, March 15.

Kimbrel, Green B., to Jane Smith, March 17.

Tuttle, James S., to Sophia Boykin, March 22.

Ward, James, to Mary A. Hodges, April 25.

Screven, Samuel G., to Catherine E. Videlo, **May 6.**

Jackson, George W., to Victoria A. Sheppard, **May 19.**

Lightfoot, Thomas A., to Georgia Ann Wallace, June 10.

Ennis, Alexander A., to Caroline M. Thompson, June 24.

Jenkins, Crawford C., to Jane Dickey, July 25.

Bevill, Paul, to Jane Caile, Aug. 13.

Bryan, Joseph C., to Sophia Brannen, Aug. 14.

Pottle, Mathew, to Sarah Ann McKinley, Aug. 18.

Oglesby, Allen, to Mary Ann Vickery, Oct. 4.

Boykin, Edwin, to Jane Brinson, Oct. 18.

Brinson, William J., to Frances Ziegler, Oct. 19.

Parker, David, to Charity Ann Ziegler, Oct. 19.

Meares, John B., to Mary Glisson, Oct. 24.

Jenkins, Triggs, to Caroline E. Taylor, Oct. 11.

Bolton, John W., to Sarah Ann Ziegler, Nov. 6.

Colson, Sheppard, to Harriet J. Dugger, Nov. 24.

Payne, Lewis B., to Sarah M. Currell (Washington Co.), Dec. 15.

Millford, James M., to Laura Roberts, Dec. 19.

Strickland, John W., to Julia A. Burns, Dec. 26.

Stead, E. A., to Juliana Powers, Dec. 27.

SIGNATURES TO WILLS, DEEDS, ETC., IN BULLOCH CO. GIVING NAME OF WIFE.

1 7 9 7

Pridgen, Luke—Amelia.

Denmark, Stephen—Elizabeth.

Braswell, Kindred—Ricey (probably dau. of Isham Roberts of Montgomery Co.)

McCall, Wm., Esq. & wife to David McCall & wife Frances

Audibert, John—Judith of Beaufort, S. C.

Etheridge, John A.—Elizabeth of Beaufort. S. C.

Butler, Elizabeth, Sr., of Jefferson Co.

1 7 9 8

Ewing, William, of Savannah—Mary.

Mizell, Joseph David—Sarah.

Gruver, John—Hannah.

Williams, Seth (bro. Amon)—Betsy.

Mizell, James—Eleanor.

Hodges, Joshua—Rebecca (dau. Wm. Fletcher).

Fletcher, Joseph—Elizabeth.

1 7 9 9

Daughtry, Joseph—Mary Ann.

Jones, Drewry—Sallie.

Wise, William—Margaret.

Fletcher, John—Susannah.

McCall, Charles—Betsy Butler McCall.

1 8 0 0

Mikell, James—Margaret (Liberty Co.)

Brunson, Wm.—Jane (Burke Co. Heirs of Ebenezer Brunson).

DeLoach, Hardy—Mary.

Lanier, Clement—Sallie (Screven Co.)

Lanier, John—Sallie (also Bryan Co.)

Bulloch, Archibald S.—Sarah.

Mizell, Luke—Suckey.

Hoffman, Jacob—Ann Mary (in German).

Johnson, David—Martha.

Hagin, John—Mary.

Jackson, Jarvis—Katherine (Hodges).

Williams, James—Elizabeth (Screven Co.)

Hagin, John—Mary.

Williams, James—Elizabeth (Screven Co.)

1 8 0 1

Deveaux, Peter (son of James Deveaux of Chatham Co.)—Mary Eleanor.

Shivers, James—Judith.

Stafford, Thos. Peter—Maria.

Rogers, Joseph—Mary (Montgomery Co.)

1 8 0 2

Cook, John—Elizabeth.

Daniel, Elias—Elizabeth.

Dowell, Peter—Sarah.

Winbourne, Andrew—Casandra (Barnwell, S. C.)

Newman, James—Mourning.

Dowell, Thos.—Elizabeth.

Smith, Godhilp—Christina (Bryan Co.)

1 8 0 5

Webb, Jas.—Mary (Savannah.)

Tennille, Francis—Mary B. (Washington Co.)

Partin, Peter—Mary.

Lowther, John—Mary.

Foreacres, John—Edy.

Jernagen, Moses—Charity.

Lanier, Lewis—Hester.

Williams, James, Sr.—Penelope.

Lott, Mark—Delilah.

Craddock, Samuel—Unity.

Roberts, Isham—Pattie.

Jernagen, Jas.—Polly.

McCall, Sharrod—Margaret.

Singleton, David—Mary.

1 8 0 6

Stafford, Abraham—Elizabeth.

Rester, Frederick—Louisa.

Richardson, John—Nancy.

Rawls, John—Frankie.

Thornton, Samuel—Naomi.

Wills, Francis—Senath.

Dasher, Benj.—Elizabeth.

Gay, Lewis—Mary.

Knight, Robt.—Mary.

Moore, Lewis—Charity.

Albritton, Richard, Jr.—Sallie.

Cook, Wm.—Susannah.

Phillips, William—Rachal (mar. 2nd Johnson).

1 8 0 8

Heisler, George—Mary.

Plummer, Joseph—Mary (Burke Co.)

Lastinger, Dav. (mother's name Barbara)—Sarah.

Rester, Gideon—Sarah.

1 8 0 9

Kirby, Arthur—Sarah.

Armstrong, Thos.—Rachel.

Driggers, Wm.—Millie.

Coward, Nat.—Sallie (to daughter Elizabeth Roberts).

1 8 1 0

Everett, John (of Glynn Co.)

Amoons, Wm.—Elizabeth.

Williams, Arthur—Peggy Ann (dau. Mary Patterson of Randolph Co.)

Burkwalter, Peter—Sallie.

Geiger, Felix—Mary.

Mizell, Griffin—Susannah.

Lanier, John—Sarah.

Bragg, Eljah—Sophia.

Bridges, Wm.—Levina.

Driggers, Simeon—Mary.

Hobbs, Abraham—Celia.

Bennett, Jas.—Mary Ann.

Dowdy, Richard—Penelope.

1 8 1 3

Wisenbaker, John—Mary.

Stewart, Alexander—Hannah.

Futch, Thos.—Elizabeth.

1 8 1 6

Hodges, Benj.—Dorathy.

Dell, John—Mary.

Jackson. In 1809 Katherine Jackson, dau. of Joshua Hodges, Sr. The land obtained in N. C. for military services of Hardy Hodges, bro. of Joshua.

Price. 1810—Jean Price of S. C. deed of gift from Jacob Nevill.

West. 1810—Redding West of N. C. lands in Bulloch Co. Wit.: Robt. Williams.

Ryals. 1809—Elizabeth Ryals adm. on the estate of Samuel Ryals, who died March 6. Heirs: Ann C., Sarah, Massie, Rebecca, Susannah. Cattle in Wayne Co. Exrs.: John Boston & Chas. Ryals. Will made March 3. 1807 recorded April 29. 1809. He had a son Zacheus living in 1819. In 1807, Wright Ryals was in Telfair Co. (White's Col.), Elizabeth was probably not his first wife.

Hudson. In 1812 Sarah & Robt. Hudson, deed to Paul Beville and wife Martha. Wit.: Nath. Lunday, Owen & Frederick Williams "kin to David Williams."

Hardy. In 1812 Robert & Thos. Hardy heirs of Isaac Hardy (wife Casandra Jones) deed of gift to Sheppard Williams.

Bush. In 1813 William Bush for Jordan Bush of Jefferson Co. to James Bush of Richmond Co.

Barber. In 1813 John Barber, "related" to Alexander Gordon & David Stewart.

Parish. In 1809 Henry Parish had lands on "Conethee."

Price. In 1814 Isaac Price of Richland Dis., S. C.

Williams. In 1815 David Williams adm. on estate of Elizabeth Ryals.

Dell. 1841—John Dell of Emanuel Co. (wife Mary), died. Phillip Dell, adm.

O'Neall. 1829—Zilpah O'Neall to sisters Mary Dugger wife of Wm. Dugger of Thomas Co., Ga. and Rachel Ward of Columbia Co., N. C. (Wm. Dugger removed to Leon Co., Fla.)

Lanier. 1844—Will of Frederick Lanier, wife Catharine. Heirs: Gazan Hendricks, Hester Bird, Lucy Lee, Anny Holloway, Martha Waters, Roxie Ann Hodges, Augustus Lanier, Leviny Hodges, Samuel, Benjamin, James Madison, Sarah Allen, Perry Lanier. (Admrs.: Augustus Lanier & Berrien Lanier.)

Partin. 1806—Peter Partin's will—probated July 28, wife Mary, exr. Children: Martha, Robert, Ann. Orig. grant 1788.

1 8 2 5

Gray, Wm.—Jane.

1 8 2 9

Nesmith, John H.—Ellender.

STRAY NOTES ON ABOVE NAMES

Jernigan. In 1800 James Jernigan died, leaving wife Janet and children: Sarah, wife of James Thompson. Edith who married John Foreacres. James, Jesse, Moses, Aaron, Elias, Joseph and Isaac.

Martin. In 1795 John Martin of Bryan Co., was a minister. His wife was Elizabeth and he deeds land in Baldwin Co. to James Martin of Bryan Co.

McNeely. Prior to 1797 Andrew McNeely had married the widow of Thos. Hearn.

Smith. In 1822 Godhilp Smith's will was probated; his wife was Christina nee Rahn. Heirs: Sarah Bird, Solomon, Elizabeth, Joshua, Susannah.

Dell. In 1804 Jospeh Dell suit versus Theophilis Williams.

Jernigan. In 1805 Aaron, Elias, Joseph and Isaac Jernigan deed to Jesse Jernigan, Ezekiel and Amy Self, Tattnall Co.

Stafford. Thos. Peter Stafford was the son of John Stafford who had land grant from King George in 1760 in Bryan Co.

Rester. 1806—Frederick Rester, wife Louisa, children Stephen, Elizabeth (Denmark), Frederick, Louise.

Carr. 1807—William and Susannah Carr administered on the estate of Archibald Carr. During the same year Oliver Bowen, Gent. of Providence, R. I. deed to Jabez Brown.

Dean. 1809—Allen I. Dean to bro. Richmond Darley Dean, Elizabeth Ford Dean, John and Patience Dean, bro. Gidean. Wit.: Cornelius Mays.

Richardson. 1800—John, William and Hardy Richardson, William and Penelope Williams and Frances Patterson were heirs of Benj. and Amos Richardson.

Williams. 1801—William Williams of Montgomery Co. sold his estate in Bulloch Co. to his brother John Williams.

Patterson. 1801—Mary Patterson administered on the estate of John Kennedy.

Williams. 1825.—William Williams deed to dau. Ann Kennedy.

1844—James B. Williams & Roxy (widow of Washington Williams) adm. on estate of Washington Williams. Land in Houston Co.

1845—Robert Williams—Sarah Dell adm. on estate of Nath. Dell.

1819—Garrett Williams guardian of David and John G., orphans of Garrett Williams, Sr.

1827—Garrett Williams & William Williams on the will of Seth Williams.

1818—Sheppard Williams and John Dell adm. estate of Drury Jones.

1818—Samuel Williams, son of Samuel Williams, guardian for Rowland, Deborah, Robert, Sarah Williams, instead of Dilly Williams. John Williams is relieved of Dilly's securityship. Dilly (Delilah) Williams was the widow of Samuel Williams, Sr., and was the daughter of John & Ann Nevill. She is listed as widow of Rev. soldier in Land Lottery 1827.

Sheppard. 1804—Martin Gardner Sheppard of Richland, S. C., deeds negroes to John E. Sheppard in Georgia, who deeds them to Sheppard Williams. At the same time Samuel & Robert Hudson relinquished claims to negroes, Charity and Billy, to Sheppard Williams.

Williams. 1805—John Williams, Sr., and wife Penelope deed of gift to Fannyriah, Harold, dau. of Elisha & Jane Harold (nee Richardson).

Hudson. 1846—Robert Hudson, Sr., gift to grand-daughter, Mary Hudson, wife of Sheppard Williams (Screven Co.)

Williams. 1824—Sheppard Williams guardian of Ann, orphan of Robert Hardy. Had land in Habersham Co.

EARLY BULLOCH CO. MARRIAGES

1 7 9 5

Driggers, Mathews, to Mary Crawford, June 18.

1 7 9 6

McCoy, Stephen, to Nancy McCall, Jan. 27.

Driggers, Henry to Elizabeth Willis, Sept. 18.

Scarborough, Samuel, to Elizabeth Bennett, Oct. 5.

1 7 9 7

Perkins, Zachens, to Sarah Bailey, May 16.

Mizell, Griffin, to Susannah Carter, May 29.

Everett, Joshua, to Jane Carter, Oct. 7.

Coulton, John, to Lydia Sharp, Nov. 2.

Price, John, to Penelope Lane, Dec. 25.

1 7 9 8

Waldron, Richard, to Elizabeth Moore, Feb. 6.

Wolf, Charles, to Elizabeth Mizelle, March 27.

Hendley, John, to Elizabeth Coward, July 16.

Sellers, John, to Jane Carter, July 28.

Nevil, Jacob, to Nicy Henderson, Nov. 26.

Gruver, Solomon, to Elizabeth Wise, Nov. 29.

1 7 9 9

Bowing, John, to Margaret Molden, Jan. 1.

Bowing, Elijah, to Elizabeth Davis, Feb. 9.

Holloway, Jeremiah, to Mary Molden, Feb. 9.

Driggers, Dennis, to Elizabeth Nevill, March 9.

Jones, Thomas, to Martha Denmark, April 17.

Gruver, David, to Martha Shuffield, May 17.

Pinson, Isaac, to Elizabeth Frazier, May 18.

Hodges, Benj., to Dorathy Carr, Oct. 15.

Livingston, Peter L., to Nancy Lebey, Oct. 31.

Lowk, Henry, to Mercy Knight, Dec. 4.

Kirkland, John, to Elizabeth Lane, Dec. 14.

McCall, Charles, to Betsy Butler Stith, Dec. 15.

Williams, David, to Sabra Lanier, Dec. 31.

1 8 0 0

Simmons, Henry, to Mary Tilman, March 4. (Prob. dau. of Capt. John Tilman of Dobbs Co., N. C.)

Lastinger, George, to Selfier Sapp, March 25.

Mixon, Jesse, to Sarah Fletcher, March 15.

Williams, John, to Fannie Richardson, May 10.

Rogers, Frederick, to Patsy Griffin, July 28.

Hagin, David, to Elizabeth Lowther, July 28.

Fletcher, Joseph, to Elizabeth Lanier, Sept. 25.

Spivey, Joshua, to Cressey Tomberlin, Dec. 23.

1 8 0 1

Collins, Josiah, to Susannah Summerlin, Feb. 9.

Daniel, Aaron, to Mary Standland, Feb. 23.

McCall, Robert, to Polly Lanier, Feb. 25.

Hagin, John, to Nancy Cone, March 9.

Rushing, William, to Elizabeth Tilman, March 13.

Williams, Samuel, to Sarah Banks, April 24.

Lane, John, to Elizabeth Gwynn, April 24.

Wise, Henry, to Elizabeth Gruver, May 20.

Irwin, Samuel, to Hester Ball, July 27.

Reeves, William, to Mary Lott, Dec. 23.

Mixon, Jesse, to Sarah Bowen, Aug. 3.

1 8 0 2

McCall, Francis, to Sallie Pearce, Jan. 24.

Denmark, Redding, to Winny Wise, Aug. 17. (Dau. of Wm. Wise and wife Margaret).

Lawrence, John, to Chloe Deal, Oct. 4.

Williams, Rowland, to Jean Banks, Oct. 19.

Williams, William, to Winnie Mizell, Oct. 25.

Richardson, Benj., to Nancy Hendricks, June 25.

Chambliss, Ephraim, to Elizabeth Driggers, Nov. 2.

1 8 0 3

Lanier, Lewis, to Hester Thorn, Aug. 26.

Sheppard, Absolom, to Tabitha Sheppard.

1 8 0 4

Kirkland, Richard, to Levicy Williams, Sept. 24. (Son of Richard who died 1804 and wife Hester.)

Deloach, Abraham, to Elizabeth Row, Nov. 26.

Caswell, Martin, to Elizabeth Tilman, July 18.

Harrell, Elisha, to Jane Richardson, Nov. 27.

House, William, to Susannah Monk, Aug. 4.

Hagin, Solomon, to Margaret Sheppard.

1 8 0 5

Lanier, Benjamin, to Sarah Pridgen, Sept. 24.

Lanier, Frederick, to Elizabeth Studstill, Oct. 7.

Harris, Sirus, to Nancy Bennett, Nov. 19.

1 8 0 6

Mills, Shadrack, to Sarah Lanier, March 8.

Miller, Benjamin, to Polly Williams, July 8.

1 8 0 7

Williams, Owen, to Mary Donaldson, Jan. 7.

Buie, Archibald, to Polly Patterson, Nov. 18.

Johnson, James, to Amy Lanier, Jan. 30.

Carter, Mathew, to Mary Rester.

McAully, John, to Katherine McCall, Aug. 8.

1 8 0 8

Jordon, Jos., to Mary Cox.

1 8 0 9

Denmark, William, to Elizabeth Taylor, Jan. 21

Newton, Phillip, to Ann Lane, June 5.

Hagin, Malachi, to Elizabeth Sheppard, Nov. 27.

1 8 1 0

Stewart, Alexander, to Elizabeth Waters, July 10.

Dell, John, to Mary Jones, Nov. 5.

1 8 1 1

Williams, Willoughby, to Susannah Denmark, May 29.

Williams, Garrett, to Charlotty Jones, Aug. 3.

Gruver, Benj., to Jane Townsend, Sept. 11.

Williams, Samuel, to Nancy Jones, Dec. 22.

1 8 1 2

Southwell, John, to Mrs. Mary Hilton, Sept. 10.

Williams, James, to Anne Elkins, Dec. 24.

Mallett, Abraham, to Katharine Kennedy, Dec. 24.

1 8 1 3

Williams, William, to Sarah Harvey, Feb. 24.

Richardson, Abraham, to Rebecca Bulloch, March 1.

King, Willis, to Nancy Williams, Dec. 30.

1 8 1 5

Groover, John, to Mary Mariah Redding, Nov. 27.

1 8 1 6

Stafford, William, to Marcia Ryalls, Aug. 20.

1 8 1 7

Rawls, Thos., to Sarah Ryals, May 1.

1 8 1 8

Cone, William, to Sabrina O'Neill, Oct. 19.

1 8 2 0

Davis, Richard, to Elizabeth Chambliss, Feb. 19.

1 8 2 2

Robert, Elias, to Nancy Nevill, Jan. 2.

1 8 2 3

Jones, Allen, to Ann Cone, Jan. 13.

Allen, William, to Deborah Williams, Oct. 25.

1 8 2 4

Cone, Robert, to Mary Hylton, Jan. 22.

Williams, Robert, to Ann Hall, Jan. 26.

Williams, Rowland to Susannah Lewis, April 29.

1 8 2 6

Wilson, Andrew, to Sarah Rawls, Dec. 14.

1 8 2 7

Cone, James, to Mary Ann Smith, Jan. 4.

Williams, Thos., to Mary Ann Lockhart.

1 8 2 8

Bird, Parker, to Hester Lanier, June 16.

Fletcher, John, to Sarah Dell, Sept. 18.

1 8 3 1

Denmark, Thos. J., to Amanda Gruver, Dec. 31.

1 8 4 1

Williams, David, to Margaret Ann Archer, Oct. 7.

1 8 4 2

Williams, Washington, to Roxy Ann Johnson.

EARLY MARRIAGES IN DUVAL CO., FLORIDA
JACKSONVILLE

Stafford, James, to *Sarah* Green, April 27, 1825.

Stafford, Joshua, to Elizabeth Branning (?), Feb. 22, 1825.

Stafford, John W., to Susan Branning, June 30, 1829.

Harrison, Ephriam, to Mary C. O'Neil, Aug. 18, 1832. **By Rev.** Hanson Benedict.

Dell, James, to Martha Colson, Oct. 4, 1832.

Parker, William, to Mrs. *Sarah* Stafford, Feb. 10, 1833. (See **James** Stafford.)

Blitch, Moore, to Nancy Hagin, May 7, 1833.

Tison, James, to Elizabeth Youngblood, Jan. 23, 1834.

Hampton, Robert C., to Eliza Ann Phelps, July 2, 1836.

Blitch, Elijah, to Mrs. Sarah Pace, April 12, 1837.

Williams, William H., to Michaul Harvey, July 19, 1837.

Price, William, to Prudence McPhadden, July 14, 1838. Both of Mandarin Co.

Akin, James, to Ellenor Ryals, June 1, 1838.

Allen, A. Y., to Rosannah Tyner, April 3, 1839.

West, Cornelius, to Winifred Tison, Aug. 24, 1839.

Higginbotham, John G., to Mary Ann Wilson, Feb. 27, 1841.

Price, John, to Mrs. Lucretia Carter, Sept. 15, 1841.

Varns, Samuel, to Martha Tyner, Oct. 11, 1841.

McDonald, James, to Teatesee (?) A. Pendarvis, May 10, 1842.

Tison, William C., to Mary A. Tison, Jan. 7, 1843.

Clark, John, to Mrs. Elizabeth Miller, Dec. 5, 1843.

Wilson, William, to Sarah Conway, July 2, 1844.

Roche, William, Esqr., to Mary Prevatt, April 13, 1846.

Clinch, Gen. Duncan L., to Mrs. Sophia A. Cooper, Jan. 13, 1846.

Price, John, Jr., to Adeline Roberts, Sept. 18, 1849.

Harrison, Ephraim L., to Julia Ann Cooper, Oct. 17, 1850.

Price, John W., to Sabina Dupont, Dec. 23, 1852.

Mills, James T., to Lucinda Fitzgerald, March 1, 1853.

Floyd, James, to Rosalie Andrews, April 20, 1857.

Wilson, John, to Rebecca Woods, April 25, 1857.

Price, John, to Catherine Jones, April 13, 1859.

EARLIEST MARRIAGES IN CAMDEN CO., GEORGIA

Beall, Henry, to Nancy Reddy, March 8, 1819.

Perkins, Samuel, to Hannah Cone, May 9, 1820.

Boutham, James, to Harriet Blount Miller, Dec. 20, 1820.

Lang, Wm., to Ann (sister of Alexander & Burwell Atkinson), Feb. 12, 1821.

Sheffield, Bryant, to Elizabeth Ogden, March 18, 1821.

Jones, Jesse, to Kesiah Pearce, Dec. 27, 1821.

Pearce, James, to Fanny Mizell, Dec. 6, 1821.

Williams, Wm.·H., to Ann Church, Jan. 30, 1822.

King, B., to C. Nephew, 1822.

Jones, C. G., to M. A. McIntosh, 1822.

Stafford, John, to Hannah Cone, March 20, 1822.

Hall, H. T., to S. H. Gignilliat, 1823.

Snow, L. (or S.), to Sarah Harrison, 1823.

Rogers, G. S., to E. L. Pelot, 1824.

Bell, John G., to Eugenia Brilsford, 1825.

Sheffield, John, to Sarah Ann Cook, Oct. 20, 1825.

Thomas, Joseph, to Jane Tison, March 2, 1826.

Cone, William, to Sarah Peeples, Jan. 1, 1826.

Walker, James, to Kesiah Cone, Feb. 8, 1827.

Stiles, Rev. Joseph C., to C. C. Nephew, 1827.

Mizell, David, to Mary Pearce, Dec. 22, 1829.

Silva, Silvester, to Elizabeth J. Hannay, March 19, 1830.

Tompkins, James, to Ann Pearce, July 29, 1830.

Winston, Rev. Dennis M., to Mary McIntosh, 1830.

Pratt, N. A., to C. B. King, 1830.

Rogers, Wm. B., to Jane M. Holmes, 1830.

Wylly, W. C., to Elizabeth Spalding, 1830.

Brannen, Wm., to Abagail Barber, Nov. 19, 1831.

Peck, Mr., to Mary Pilcher, 1832.

Homer, Charles, to Nancy Barber, June 25, 1835.

Mitchell, A., to Mary McCoy, 1835.

Gignilliat, Norman, to Barbar Gignilliat, 1835.

Peeples, John, to Jemina Barber, Dec. 31, 1836.

Vorhees, Cornelius, to Elizabeth Barber, Sept. 4, 1842.

PREFACE TO INDEX AND ADDENDA TO VOLUME I

To avoid repetitions the surname only is indicated in the index.

Note carefully that several references to the same name may appear on the same page.

ADDENDA TO VOLUME I
(See That Index)

Martha, daughter of William Dunham, was born Nov. 11, 1759, and married James Carter, Feb. 20, 1775. (He was son of Thomas, whose will in S. C.)

The date of Sir Simon Munro's marriage was Mar. 7, 1768.

Ann Shumate was baptized Feb. 13, 1813.

May 20, 1780—Marriage settlement of Philip Lowe, planter of "Ricehope" Liberty Co. and Mrs. Mary Jones of Chatham Co. (Sav. C. H.)

Mathew Smallwood married Rebecca Summer, Jan. 15, 1760; their daughter Martha married William, the son of Benj. Baker and wife Elizabeth (Lax).

Will of Richard Baker "the elder" (son of Thomas Baker, Sr.) on file in Charleston, S. C. "Only son Richard, to Georgia." Brothers Joseph and Samuel.

Daughter Elizabeth (first wife of John Quarterman).

Daughter Rebecca (married Richard Quarterman).

Daughter Mary (married John Summer).

Daughter Abiah (married Joseph Stevens). Will proved June 20, 1737.

Savannah Record Room, Book H, page 377: Affidavit of Eunice Hogg (widow) and Martha Stephens, that the marriage certificate of John Stephens to Mary Borland, Sept. 3, 1752 in Georgia, Chatham Co. was that of their father, who was a minister of the dissenting church, and died March, 1776. Sworn to Oct. 18, 1790.

Jan. 23, 1778—Marriage settlement of Mrs. Elizabeth Bosomworth, sister of Mr. John Maxwell and widow of Adam Bosomworth, to Thomas Young. Bondsmen: John Maxwell, John Graham, John Sandiford.

Mrs. Hannah Godfrey, who married Rev. John Alexander March 27, 1764, was the daughter of John Andrew and the widow of George Godfrey.

1772. Nathaniel Saxton was a "mariner," also Thos. Sterling in 1786.

Mr. Richard Curd, Revolutionary soldier, died Henry Co., Ga., May 16, 1827, born in Va. Juror in trial of Aaron Burr. Member of Presbyterian Church. Age 65. (Milledgeville Recorder.)

Charleston, S. C. Will of Shem Butler, "wife and children." Daughter Elizabeth, wife of John Bellinger. Son Thomas. Brother Richard Butler. Brother-in-law, Samuel West. May 13, 1723.

Nov. 6, 1804—Jordon Ryals married Elizabeth Howell. Security John Hill.

Maj. John Winn, born Black River, S. C., 1779, died at Midway, Ga., Aug., 1820.

Rebecca, who was the wife of William Graves in 1774, was the daughter of Richard Quarterman.

The wife of William Girardeau was Patience Harris, who died 1799.

The name "Mutier" on page 49 should read "Matteair".

The widow of John Kelsall was Amelia (Coddington).

Levi Horton left orphans and wife Sarah in Washington Co., Ga. (Milledgeville paper) 1827.

Savannah Record Room, Book "K," page 256. Mrs. Hannah, widow of Capt. Wm. Peacock of Liberty Co., files complaint (1778) in re the desecrations of the British at Fort Morris on Colonels Island.

South Carolina Grants, 1752: Esther Sullivan and her daughters, Margaret and Esther, 400 acres N. side Santee, called Taw Caw Swamp.

INDEX

ANNALS OF GEORGIA

Volume II

Revised Additions and Corrections for Reprint Edition

Page 13: Additions

1. Ambrose - see North Carolina records

Page 15: Corrections

1. Bevan. "All to son, Joseph V. Bevan."

Page 22: Corrections

1. The will of Ann Mary (Wisenbaker).....................son Richard Alex-
    ander Thadeus Macon of Prine, William Co., Va.

Page 25: Corrections

1. Clark.........Catherine, married Alexander Fyffe.............who had
    married Joachim Hartsene......

Page 31: Corrections

1. Crane should be Cruse, James.....see p. 28

Page 35: Corrections

1. Tondee. .....wife of Nicholas Champagne.

Page 36: Additions

1. Elon. (1) Peter Wyley on Jan 4, 1805; married (2) Mr. William Hewlet;
    married (3) Morris Doty, March 27, 1818.

Page 38: Corrections and Additions

1. Elkins, Harman
2. Lawrence Tondee Elkins (Ann Eliza (Tondee) was his mother) and wife
    Margaret Frances (Wilson)
3. Alexander Elkins..........He had a grandson Lawrence Tondee Elkins....

Page 51: Corrections

1. Patrick Stanton, born March 14, 1788.......omit (1) before Naomi Gugel.

Page 53: Additions

1. James Offutt Goldwire, born Nov. 19, 1811; married Mariah Goldwire
    (cousin) 5/8/1833. Chh. records.

Page 56: Corrections

1. Griner, Caleb....omit Eula from the name of Mary Heidt.

Page 66: Corrections

1. Haid, Johan George should be Heidt, Johan George.

1

Page 68: Additions

    1. Jackson. 1806 - Ebenezer Jackson of Savannah married Mrs. Charlotte Pierce, widow of Maj. William L. Pierce; nee Fenwick.

Page 72: Corrections

    1. William King, Sr., married (2) Mary, daughter of Joachim Harstene....

Page 83: Corrections

    1. Reiser, Israel, 1st wife Hannah Margaret Shuptrine, dau of Joseph....

Page 96: Corrections

    1. Shuptrine, Christian, to Ann C. Duckins

Page 98: Corrections

    1. Shuptrine, John E. to Christina (omit Catherine).

Page 99: Corrections and Additions

    1. Shuptrine, Daniel C.,.......and Mary....
    2. The American Patriot, Tuesday, April 21, 1812. Mar. on Thurs eve. last by the Rev. Mr. Polhill, Mr. John Charlton to Miss Eliza Gugel of Eff. Co.

Page 100: Corrections

    1. Steiner. Mrs. Anna Margaret Steiner (widow of Christian 'David'(?))
    2. Tondee (see Elon.) Charles Tondee (son of Peter)................to Mrs. Elizabeth Colson.....

Page 107: Corrections

    1. Ulmer, John Philip, to Mary Sarah Fox.......

Page 111: Additions

    1. Wilder, William, wife Mary (Newton), 1811, widow of Moses Newton.

Page 114: Additions and Corrections

    1. Re. Anna Zitterauer. Lucy Seckinger was undoubtedly the first wife of Christian Shuptrine and the mother of Hannah and Gotlieb.

Page 115: Additions and Corrections

    1. Re. Ann Zitterauer - see note of page 114 additions.

Page 120: Corrections

    1. Eleanor McCall, married McKeen Green

Page 122: Additions

    1. Elbert Lewis, born Jan. 31, 1825; married Grace Eliza Ann........

Page 130: Corrections

    1. Chestnut - should be Chesnut

Page 139: Additions

    1. Mitchener. 1809............John McWade, married Ann Holcombe 6/3/1796, in Screven Co. Sister of Rev. H. Holcombe of Beaufort, S. C. Ga. Gaz.

Page 145: Corrections

    1. Mimms, Thomas S., should be Mims

Page 147: Corrections

    1. Banks, Aylor, should be Cuylor
    2. Oliver, Thomas W., to Eliza Mimms should be Mims

Page 155: Corrections

    1. Hurst, James, to Candicy should be Candacy

Page 172: Corrections

    1. Boutham should be Bentham

Page 182: Additions

    1. Shick, Fredk, 36
    2. Strobhar (Strobart), 68, 72, 74, 95, 98, 99

Page 183: Corrections

    1. Wiggins, 51, 138
Williams, 42(?)

Page 184: Additions

    1. Gugel, Hannah (3) 14, 49, 62
           John, 14, 48
           Anna Maria, 14
           Daniel, 14, 48, 49, (2) 50
           J. Chris, 41, 48, 50
           David, 48, 49
           Samuel, 48
           Salome, 48, 49, 52
           Johannes, 48, 50
           Christian, 49, 50
           Joshua, 49
           Sophia, 49, 51
           Charlotte Dorothea, 49
           Mary Ann, 49
           Frances Hubbard, 50
           William, 50
           Mary Shuptrine, 50
           Hannah Elizabeth, 50
           Naomi (2) 51
    2. Bourquin, Dr. Henry, 15
           Robert Hamilton, 37
           Mozelle, 37
           Maj. David, 37
           Ann Eliza, 38

3. Ulmer, Charles, 62, 107
         William (1806) 107
         Philip, 107
         Ann, 107
         Kesiah, 107
         John Philip, 107

Page 185: Additions

1. Heidt family Bible record: James Evans Heidt b. 12/14/1838, Macon, Ga.,
    Catherine Lawson Clinton b. 2/21/1839, Burke Co. Ga., m. by Rev. E. Heidt
    in Burke Co., Ga. 11/15/1860. Children: Frances Isalella Heidt b. 8/16/1861
    Savh., Ga., d. 7/14/1862, Burke Co., Ga.; Sarah Clinton Heidtb., 6/7/1863
    Burke Co., Ga., d. 8/4/1867 Burke Co., Ga.; James Evans Heidt d. 9/5/1864
    in the city of Macon, Ga., aged 24 yrs. 9 mos. 21 days. He was wounded by
    a fragment of shell in the trenches around Atlanta eleven days after entering
    service.

2. Mrs. Catherine Tebeau, daughter of Lawson Clinton, departed this life on the
    13th July, 1871.

3. DeWitt Clinton d. 2/13/1872 Burke Co., Ga.

4. Mrs. Sarah Douse Corker d. 1/4/1869

5. Ernest Drury (?) Corker b. 1/27/1856

Page 186: Additions

1. Roster of the Va. Daus of the American Rev. 1892 - 1936.
    J. P. Bell Co., Inc., Lynchburg, Va., 1938; p. 513
    Thomas Wylly: b. West Indies 2/10/1762, d. Savh, Ga., June 1846. Ass't
    Quartermaster.

    P. 285: Mary V. Rahm (Mrs. Dwyce Van Wagener) resigned

Page 187: Early Effingham County marriages taken from an unknown newspaper clipping.

    1795, Aug. 4: John Ivy to Naomi Woodliff
    1792, March 14: Jarvis Jackson to Cath. Hodges
    1800, June 21: Fred W. Kahlden to Rosina, relict of John Keibler
    1786: Emanuel Keifer's wife was Anna Barbara
    1797, May 9: John Keebler m. Rosannah, wid of John Stockman (see above)
    1795, March 11: John Kettles to Amy Garnett
    1795: Anne Catherine was wid. of Christopher Kreemer (or Creamer)
    1794, Aug. 20: John Lucas to Clarissa Denmark
    1799, March 30: John F. Lichner to Hannah Heisler
    1799, May 2: Israel Leimberger to Mary C. Snider (was wid. in 1811)
    1799, May 28: Minis Lamly to Polly Hines
    1800, Dec. 27: David Lemberger to Naomi Keiffer
    1799: Christian Israel Limberger left a widow, Appolonia
    1792, June 16: John Moore to Maxey McCall
    1793, Dec. 7: Isaac Mott to Polly Colson
    1794, Nov. 1: David Metzger to Mrs. Mary Reiser
    1795, May 4: Wm. Morgan to Sarah Bailey
    1798, Augl 28: Benjamin Morel to Susannah Gindrat

WILLS:

Adams Metzger, May 16, 1806, Wife, Christiana, late Rahn; father, John Metzger; ex. Bro. Jacob. Wit., Chris Gnann, Gottlieb Ernst, Mary Madelina Metzger.

4

On estate Daniel Weidman, June 26, 1804, Wife, Catherine. Major son Solomon;
   heirs, Andrew Gnann and Daniel Weidman. Part of this estate was granted J. C.
   Creamer 1759.
John McRory, Sept. 15, 1800. Wife, Rachel, minor son John.
Susannah Gaskins, Beaufort, S. C., 1799: Widow. Sons Amos and William; daughters,
   Rosannah and Elizabeth Williams. Gr. sons, John Harrell Gaskins and Weight
   Gaskins.
Estate Samuel Hudson, 1769. Son, Robert.
John Geo. Zeigler, 1795. W., Anna Catherine; sons, Edward and David.

MARRIAGES:

1797: Hannah, widow of Jacob Wisenbaker
1793: Hannah, widow of Daniel Zettlers
1796: Ann C., widow of George Zeigler
1796, May 9: Joshua Zant, married Catherine Steiner; was widow 1807
1797, June 24: David Zitteraner married Elizabeth Ihly
1797, April 16: Gideon Zettler married Martha Wilson dau. of John. (She was a
   widow in 1803.)
1799, August 10: Jesse Wilson married Eliza Cook
1796, July 11: Elias Winkler married Mary Penninger
1795, March 25: Henry White married Sarah Butts
1794, July 8: Daniel Weitman married Mrs. Ann C. Cramer
1794, April 22: Henry W. Williams married Sarah McCall
1794, March 24: John Williams married Rhetta London
1791: Jenkin Davis married Anna Catharine (?)
1800, July 31: John Martin Dasher married Hannah, the widow of Christopher
   Hudson, and was dead October 12, 1804.
1801, Oct. 5: John Dampier to Esnure Hodge
1794, Dec. 3: David Ewing to Mary Conway
1798, Sept. 18: Gottlieb Ernest to Catherine Fields
1802, July 5: Gottlieb Ernst to Margaret, daughter of Jonathan Rahn
1812, Jan. 27: Gotlieb Ernst to Catherine Keiffer
1808, June 10: Wm. Geyer Ernst to Elizabeth Helmly

From old Ebenezer record: 1768, Oct. 13: John Nevil to E(?) Nicson

WILLS:

1792: Will of Johannes, George Neiss, wife Sybilla, son George, daughter Elizabeth
1792: John and Christian Trentlew were brothers
1792: James Hines administered on the estate of David Hines, Sr.
1792: Sarah Friarwood: deed to daughters, Mary Thornton and Elizabeth, wife of
   Aaron Crosby, Jr., son Henry Crosby
1807, Oct. 10: Will of John G. Heidlinger: wife Hannah, sons Samuel and John,
   daughter Anna, wife of Gatthilp J. Neiss, and daughter Emilia
   Ex: Hannah and Golliph Neiss
   Wit: Daniel Bergsteiner, Mathew Bernsteiner, Jonathan Fetzger and George John
   Mingledorff. (Emilia Neidlinger married John George Mingledorf, Nov. 26, 1807)

Part 2
Effingham County Legal Records
from
The Georgia Genealogical Magazine

Table of Contents

GEORGIA COURT-HOUSE RECORDS

EFFINGHAM COUNTY

FOREWORD: Effingham County is one of the original seven counties of Georgia made out of the Colonial parishes that existed under the Colonial government; and was made out of St. Matthews Parish. By reference to Hall's Map of Georgia reproduced in this issue, the reader can easily tell its original lines and size. Although the new counties were set up out of parishes in 1777, for the first few years (which was during the progress of the Revolution) the people still had their wills probated and estates administered and deeds recorded at the seat of government as had been done under Colonial government. As a result, county government as we know it to-day did not begin to function in hardly any of the new counties until a few years after the War was over and independence was secured. Wilkes County which was an original county created in 1777, was made out of newly-ceded Indian territory which had just been ceded when the Revolution began, therefore was not made out of any of the old parishes; and probably due to its frontier condition and remoteness from the older settled sections, its county government seems to have begun started functioning immediately after the Constitution of 1777 was adopted, since no previously functioning local government existed. But that situation did not seem to prevail in the other seven original counties. In Effingham the deed records begin early in 1786, and those in the Ordinary's office date only from 1791. That there was some kind of record kept in that office prior to 1791 is indicated by the fact that the first book is designated as Book "B". Book "A" is supposed to have been lost. None of the records have ever been burned. Book "A" probably covered the period from 1786 to 1791.

For many years after 1791 all the various records of the Ordinary's office, instead of being kept in separate books as was supposed to have been, were kept in one book, and thus the first two records (Book "B" and Book "C") are called Miscellaneous Records. They contain all records, those of administrations, wills, guardianships, marriage-licenses and other proceedings. For the first few years it seems that deeds of gift and gifts of personal property were also recorded in it, though they should have been recorded in the office of Clerk of Court.

The first county to be made out of Effingham was Screven in 1793; Bulloch was made in 1796 out of Screven and Effingham. A small portion of Bryan was taken from Effingham when it was made in 1793. And in 1812 when Emanuel was formed a considerable portion of that county was taken from Effingham.

In abstracting Miscellaneous Book "B" we omit the marriage licenses and will group them together and publish later. We have not listed Inventories of estates, they having no genealogical significance. (See exception on next page).

****

BOOK "B", MISCELLANEOUS RECORDS
Ordinary's office

(p.1) Letters of Administration to THOMAS WYLLY, Esq., as Admr. of estate of JOHANNAH ROSSBERGER, deceased, dated Sept. 17, 1791.

(p.1) Letters of Administration to CHRISTIAN BIDDENBACH as Admr. of estate of ANDREW B. DINBOCH?(not plain), dec'd., dated Sept.17, 1791.

(p.1) Letters of Administration to MRS. SARAH McCALL, relict of THOMAS McCALL, as Admx. on his estate, dated Oct. 3, 1791.

(p.1) Inventory of estate of JAMES DOUGLASS, dated Sept. 9, 1791. No other record of estate.

(p.2) Gift of slave from JANE LUNDAY of Effingham Co., to her son, THEOPHILUS LUNDAY and her daughter MARY E. LUNDAY of same county, dated March 7, 1791.

(p.3) Deed of Gift dated July 3, 1790, from JOHN NEVELL, carpenter, of

Effingham County, to his children as follows: To his son, JACOB NEVILL of Great Ogeechee, said county, 200 acres on Nevill's Creek granted Samuel Carney Nov. 20, 1769; also two 200-acre tracts adjoining, and granted grantor Aug. 2, 1786; to his five children, JACOB NEVILL, SARAH NEVELL, MARY WINSLOW, FRANCES NEVELL and ELIZABETH NEVELL, all the remainder of his estate consisting of 40 cattle, 3 horses, hogs, household goods. Joshua Pearce "the elder" and Joshua Pearce "the younger", are named as Trustees for said children. Wit: Jeremiah Jones,Phillip Howell.

(p.7) Deed of Gift dated Oct. 3, 1791, from JOHN WILSON, Jr., of Effingham Co., shoemaker, to EPHRIAM TINER, son of ELIJAH TINER of same county, for 30 acres where said Elijah Tiner now lives, adjoining donor's home-place lands. Witnesses: James Wilson Sr., James Wilson Jr., Thomas Wylly J.P.

(p.10) Inventory of estate of THOMAS HARDAMAN, deceased, dated Aug.27, 1791. Note: No other mention of this estate appears in the book.

(p.10) MRS. ELIZABETH FRAZIER, relict of DYER FRAZIER, dec'd., applies for administration on his estate Nov.29, 1791. She was appointed Jan. 5, 1792.

(p.11) MRS. MARY MILLS and STEPHEN BRINSON apply for administration on estate of WILLIAM MILLS,dec'd.,Nov.29, 1791. No record of appointment.

(p.12) Account of Sales of estate of RICHARD KIRKLAND made Mar.15,1789 by Isaac and Samuel Kirkland, Admrs. No other mention of estate in the book.

(p.6) Inventory of estate of CHRISTIAN ISRAEL LIEMBERGER, dec'd.,dated July 18, 1791. On p.13 is record of Account of Sales of estate made Sept.2, 1791, by Apolona Liemberger, Admx.

(Editor's Note! For the first two or three years it appears that a lot of the proceedings were not recorded as to some estates; for example, the Inventory of the Hardaman estate and the Sales-Account of the Kirkland estate shows there were such estates being administered but yet no proceedings appear of record. Hence the Editor will list all Inventories and Sales-Accounts for the first year or two. Later on, the Editor will check the files of original papers in the Ordinary's office to see if any other papers relating to the estates are to be found; the Ordinary says that original papers are not there for many of the estates.)

(p.6) Inventory of WILLIAM PORTER,Sr.,estate, dated May 23, 1791.

(p.12) Inventory of JOSEPH PATCH estate, dated Dec. 25, 1791.

(p.14) Inventory of BARRER FRAZE estate, dated April, 1792.

(p.15) Return showing receipts and disbursements of JOHN GASPER WERTCH estate for the period of Feb.17, 1789 to 1792, John Wisenbaker, Admr.

(p.17) JOHN WALDHAEUR applies for admn.on est.of DAVID CROFT,Aug.6,1792.

(p.17) NATHANIEL LUNDAY and CHRISTOPHER HUDSON apply for administration on estate of CHRISTOPHER HUDSON, Sr., Aug. 6, 1792. No record of appointment.

(p.17) HERGEN HERSON was appointed Admr.of JOHN GASPER WERTCH estate March 2, 1792.

(p.17) ROBERT GRIER of Chatham Co. applies Sept.22, 1792, for administration on estate of JOSEPH LYON, dec'd. No record of appointment.

(p.17) JOHN BOYKIN applies for administration on estate of MALCOLM NELSON, dec'd., Oct. 27, 1792. No record of appointment.

(p.17) JOHN GOLDWIRE, Admr. of estate of JOHN GOLDWIRE, Sr., applies for dismission, Sept.22, 1792. No record of final order dismissing him.

(p.18) Last Will and Testament of GEORGE NIESS of Ebenezer, dated Feb. 21, 1772, probated May 1, 1792. Bequeaths to son GEORGE NIESS the testator's home-place plantation;;to daughter, ELIZABETH NIESS, one calf. Residue of estate to wife SIBELLA NIESS, she to have the whole estate if the son George should die without issue. Joseph Schubtrine of Ebenezer appointed executor, also guardian for testator's children. Witnesses: Jacob Cronberger, Christopher Cramer and George Zeigler.

(p.19) JAMES HINES applies for administration of estate of DAVID HINES,

Sr., Feb. 4, 1793. No record of appointment.

(p.19) WILLIAM MOOR applies for administration on estate of JOHN MOOR, Sr., Feb.16, 1793. No record of appointment. ("Moor" is probably same as "Moore").

(p.20) Deed of Gift from JOHN ADAM TRUETLIN, planter, of Effingham Co., to his brother, CHRISTIAN TRUETLIN of same county,planter, dated Oct.20, 1792, conveying his whole estate consisting of lands,negroes,&c. (not described).

(p.21) Deed of Gift dated June, 1789, from ROBERT HUDSON of Effingham Co., planter, to his grandson, MAXWELL HUDSON, minor son of ROBERT HUDSON the younger,deceased; conveying a negro boy now in possession of Rhoda Hudson, widow of said Robert, deceased. Witnesses: John R. Cleary, Isaac Hudson.

(p.22) Same grantor or donor to his grandson ROBERT HUDSON, minor son of donor's deceased son ROBERT HUDSON the younger, dated June 20, 1789, conveying slave now in possession of Rhoda Hudson, relict of dec'd. Same witnesses.

(p.23) Deed of Gift dated Oct. 10, 1792, from SARAH FRIARMOOD (sic) of Effingham Co., to her daughter MARY THORNTON, conveying horse, bridle, saddle, household goods; and portion of her homeplace; also to daughter, ELIZABETH, wife of AARON CROSBY, part of said homeplace; also to HENRY CROSBY, son of said Aaron and Elizabeth; a cow and calf. Witnesses: Thomas and Elizabeth Readin and Abraham Ravot, J.P.

(p.24) Deed of Gift dated July 1, 1792, from RHODA HUDSON, relict of ROBERT HUDSON Jr., late of Effingham Co.,dec'd., to her children born by her said husband, viz: Samuel, Robert, Mary, Maxfield Hudson, conveying three slaves, household goods, horse, carriage and chair; life estate reserved. Witnesses: William Colson, Enoch and Sarah Daniel. Probated by Enoch Daniel before Abraham Ravot J.P., Nov.22, 1792. (Note: The son Maxfield,as named in this instrument, is named Maxwell in the above deed of gift from his grandfather.)

(p.27) MRS. MARY LANE, relict of THOMAS LANE, applies for administration on his estate, March 22, 1793. Appointed as Admx.,May 9, 1793.

(p.27) Affidavit of MARY HURST and MARY CRAWFORD dated March 16,1793, before John Moore J.P., to the effect that they were at the home of THOMAS LANE Esq., on March 11, 1793, he being then and there indisposed, and he at that time told them he had given his wife Mary a certain slave named Rachel, and had given his son THOMAS LANE a negro boy named Will and a negro girl Hannah; and had given his daughter Jancey (sic) a negro girl Silvia, and his daughter Elizabeth a negro girl named Celia, and his son Samuel two slaves named George and Henrietta.

(p.28) Affidavit before same officer and on same date by WILLIAM STEWART and MARY HURST who testified that they were at the house of THOMAS LANE in said county on March 11, 1793, and saw him give and deliver to his son, SAMUEL LANE, two slaves named George and Henrietta.

(p.28) WILLIAM MOORE of Chatham Co., was appointed administrator of estate of JOHN MOORE, dec'd., April 2, 1793. (This is evidently same proceeding already referred to above on this page,where the name is spelled "Moor").

(p.29) Inventory of JESSE SUMMERALL estate, dated June 22, 1792. No further record of the estate.

(The reader is referred to Issue #2 of GGM,Oct.1961, to the citations for appointment of administrators,etc.,published in "The Georgia Gazette" in Savannah, and in subsequent issues, which show where and who applied for administration on these estates like the Summerall estate where there is no mention made in the Ordinary's records of any one ever applying for or being appointed as administrator.)

(p.29) Inventory of JAMES SHEROUSE estate,dated Oct. 1, 1792. No further record of estate.

(p.30) Will of JOHN FREDERICK HELVENSTINE, planter, of Effingham Co., dated July 8, 1775, probated April 5, 1793. Gives and bequeaths to his wife, Blandina Magdelina, all his estate, except he gives to his eldest son, JACOB,

4

two shillings; to his son, DANIEL, one shilling; son HOSHUA, one shilling; daughter MARY MAGDALENA one shilling; daughter, MARY CHRISTINA, one shilling. Names his wife as sole executrix. Witnesses: Vield? Lockner, Christopher Cramer, John Gnann. Receipts recorded with the will for one shilling each paid in Savannah March 15, 1793, to Joseph and Maria Christinah Helvenstine and Maria Magdalene Gromet. Witness: John Gromet.

(p.34) MRS. SARAH THORNTON applies for administration on estate of HENRY ROGERS, deceased, June 10, 1793.

(p.34) MRS. ELIZABETH GUIN, relict of RICHARD GUIN, applies for administration on his estate June 11, 1793. She was appointed July 27, 1793.

(p.34) JESSE DIKES applies for administration on estate of LEVI DIKES dec'd., June 25, 1793. Appointed Aug. 24, 1793.

(p.34) Bastardy bond dated June 29, 1793, by FRANCES LUNDAY, principal, and ROBERT BEVILLE and NATHANIEL LUNDAY sureties, given for support of McLIN BEVILL, bastard son of said Frances.

(p.35) MRS. ANN CATHERINA CRAMER applies for administration of estate of CHRISTOPHER CRAMER, dec'd, July 30, 1793. Appointed Sept. 10, 1793.

(p.36) Sales Account, estate of WILLIAM WILSON, JOHN G. NEIDLINGER, Executor of the deceased Wilson; dated June 1, 1793.

(p.38) The Trustees of the Ebenezer Congregation apply for administration on estate of MATHIAS BIDDENBACH, Sept.21,1793,and were appointed Nov.9,1793.

(p.39) ROBERT KELLY of Effingham Co.,applies for administration on estate of WENTWORTH WEBB, dec'd.,Sept.25, 1793. Caveat (objections) filed by JESSE MIXON, Oct. 9, 1793. (see leter, p.40).

(p.39) CHRISTIAN BIDDENBACH applies for administration on estate of MISS MARY BIDDENBACH, Oct.15,1793, and was appointed Nov.14, 1793.

(p.39) JESSE MIXON applies for administration on estate of HENRY WEBB and Estate of RACHEL SHORTER & CO. (sic), all of Effingham Co.,Nov.11, 1793. He was appointed Dec. 27, 1793. (Note: It is not clear who "Rachel Shorter & Co." was.)

(p.40) Abraham Ravot, Register of Probate, and Christian Truetlin,J.P., heard and passed on the caveat of Jesse Mixon against Robert Kelly who seeks appointment as Admr. of Wentworth Webb. Trial had Oct.26, 1793. Mixon objected on grounds that under the will of deceased there had been a division of the estate through arbitration proceedings whereby each of the five co-equal heirs bound himself or herself to abide the terms thereof. Copy of bond attached to caveat, whereby said five heirs agreed to abide the terms of the arbitration award, signed by JESSE MIXON, WILLIAM COOK, BENJAMIN COOK, ROBERT KELLY and RACHEL PHILLIPS. The Court ruled against the caveat and dismissed it, whereupon Mixon appealed the case to the Superior Court.

(p.41) ANDREW GUANEN? (probably meant for "Gnann") applies as greatest creditor for administration on estate of JOHN SHEILEY, dec'd., Nov. 20, 1793. No further record, probably because that on Nov. 25, 1793, the will of JOHN SHEALEY was probated (p.42); it was dated Sept.30, 1793, and bequeathed his estate consisting of 50 acres where he lived and 200 acres on the Three-Runs and town lot in Ebenezer, to his wife Mary whom he named as executrix. He also gave her his household goods and cattle. Witnesses: John Gnann, Jonathan Fetzger, John C. Stockman. On p.50, is the record of Letters Testamentary issued to her as executrix on said will, dated Feb. 4, 1794.

(p.41) MRS. MARY CRAWFORD applies for administration on estate of ALEXANDER CRAWFORD, dec'd., Nov.23, 1793; and was appointed Feb. 15, 1794.

(p.41) JOHN McDONALD applies for administration on estate of his father ALEXANDER McDONALD, dec'd., Nov. 23, 1793; and was appointed April 10, 1798.

(43) CHRISTOPHER HUDSON was appointed administrator of estate of his deceased father CHRISTOPHER HUDSON Sr., Dec.5, 1793, in place of himself and Nathaniel Lunday.

(p.44) Annual Return dated Dec.14, 1793, of JOHN G. NEIDLINGER as Admr. on estate of JENKIN DAVIS. No further record.

(p.44) WILLIAM and JOSEPH DAVIS apply for probate of the will of JOHN DAVIS, Dec. 5, 1793. (p.47) They were appointed as Administrators with the Will Annexed, Jan. 27, 1794. (p.47) The will of JOHN DAVIS written out but un-signed, was recorded, was dated May 30, 1793; and was probated as a non-cupative will Jan.27, 1794. It bequeathed to his wife Elizabeth, three slaves; to his sons Joseph, John, James, William and Samuel L10 each, and to sons George and Walter L20 each; to daughter, Nancy 20L, to William O'Steen, 10L. The will directs that testator's lands at Buckhead be disposed of according to his contract with his sons William and Samuel, to be theirs by them paying what he owes for same. To his son Walter he gives his home plantation; to son George, the adjoining lands. Witnesses: Joseph, George and Agnes Davis, Elizabeth O'Steen. In an attached statement, Joseph,John, Samuel, George, Nancy and William Davis and William O'Steen join in signing the statement to the effect that they believe the fore-going to be will and desire of their deceased father JOHN DAVIS, and do agree that the same be carried out as though signed by him; dated Sept.9, 1793. Joseph Davis in his affidavit made in court Jan. 27, 1794, says that at the request of his father JOHN DAVIS he wrote out the above will and that it was read over to him and he assnted to it in his (affiant's) presence and in presence of George and Agnes Davis and Elizabeth O'Steen, but never did sign it, dying soon after.

(p.46) Annual Return of HANNAH ZETTLER ("now Mrs. Neidlinger") as Admx. of DANIEL ZETTLER's estate, dated Dec. 14, 1793. Among the disbursements were payments as follows: "Paid for making coffin, April 4, 1784"; "for making the grave" and "for laying out the corpse". This shows dec'd died in Apr. 1784.

(p.47) JOSHUA LOPER and JOSEPH DAVIS were appointed Jan. 27, 1794, as Administrators with the will annexed on estate of MRS. ELIZABETH DAVIS. On p.49: Will of MRS. ELIZABETH DAVIS, dated June 2, 1793, probated Jan. 27, 1794, gives "what my deceased husband left me" to her four children, Elizabeth, George, Ann and Walter Davis. Executors: Joseph Davis,her son, and Joshua Loper. Wit-nesses: Joseph Davis, Miss Elizabeth Lanier, Joshua Loper. In an annexed paper recorded with will John, Samuel,George and Nancy Davis and William O'Steen join in assenting to the probate of the will, paper signed Sept. 9, 1793; it refers to the testatrix as their mother.

(p.50) MRS. SARAH CAMPBELL and JAMES BOSTON apply for administration on estate of THOMAS CAMPBELL, dec'd.,March1, 1794,and were appointed May 7, 1794.

(p.51) Will of NATHANIEL OATT, of Effingham Co., dated Jan.25, 1794, probated Feb. 15, 1794; gives and bequeaths to his brother GODLIP OATTS one cow and two hogs; to hestator's wife CHRISTIANAH ELIZABETH OATTS, 50 acres where he lives together with the residue of his estate; sheto be the executrix. Witness-es: Solomon Gnann and Godlip Oatt.

(p.64) MRS. ELIZABETH GUIN, Admx. of RICHARD GUIN estate, applies for dismission June 29, 1794. On page 66: Johnson and Robertson (otherwise un-named) caveat to her being dismissed, July22, 1794.

(p.67) SAMUEL KRAUS and MRS. MARGARET STINER, relict of DAVID STIN-ER, apply for Administration on estates of DAVID and CHRISTIAN STINER, Sept. 19, 1794, and were appointed Sept. 25, 1794.

(p.70) JESSE MIXON, Admr. of estates of HENRY WEBB and RACHEL SHOR-TER, applies for dismission, Dec. 23, 1794.

(p.71) WILLIAM KING applies for admr. of HENRY KING, Jan.22,1795.

(p.72) WILLIAM MOORE, Admr.of JOHN MOORE,applies for dis.Mar.25,1795.

(P.73) Deed of Gift dated April 2, 1786, from WILLIAM WILSON of Geor-getown, S.C., to his daughter-in-law, ELIZABETH FORD and STEPHEN FORD her husband, also of Georgetown, conveying 8 slaves. Witness: Anthony Ford. Record shows in-strument recorded in Book "A" page 4, April 12, 1786, in Georgetown, S.C., by J. Shackleford, Register of Mesne Conveyances there.

(p.74) Annual Return of HARMON CRUM, Guardian of SUSANNAH PORTER for her estate received from her father,WILLIAM PORTER. Dated June 30, 1795.

(p.82) On this page it is stated that it is the end of the records kept by ABRAHAM RAVOT, REGISTER OF PROBATE. Last Entry made by him,Sept.18,1795.

He was succeeded by William Kennedy as Register of Probate. Judge Ravot had sevred several years by legislative appointment as one of the Commissioners for Confiscated Estates to dispose of estates that had been confiscated and owned by the Tories and other disloyalists in the Revolutionary War. Judge Ravot served as Representative from Effingham County, 1781-2;member of the Executive Council, 1781-2, Magistrate of his county, 1781, and was first appointed one of the Commissioners of Confiscated Estates in 1781. (From "Revolutionary War Records of Ga.".)

(p.83) Will of ABRAHAM RAVOT, dated July 16, 1795; probated May 25, 1796. He directs that his one-acre lot in Purysburgh, S.C., and all his personal property be sold, and after all accounts owing him are collected, the proceeds be paid one-third to his wife Mary; one-third to his daughter, Henrietta Ravot "now by marriage, Henrietta Porter"; and one-third to his daughter, Marguerite Mary Ravot, and 20 shillings each be paid to his two daughters-in-law, Mary Mikell and Elizabeth Mikell. Executors: Wife Mary, and David Hugienin of S.C. Witnesses: David Morgan, Charles Ryall, John Frickinger. Letters Testamentary issued May 28, 1796, to Mrs. Mary Ravot as Executrix of the will.

(p.85) MRS. JUDITH BUNTZ applies for administration on estate of HENRY LEWIS BUNTZ, dec'd., June 6, 1796.

(p.88) Will of JOHN GEORGE ZEIGLER, dated March 21, 1792, probated July 18, 1796. Bequeaths to his son EMANUEL ZEIGLER fifty acres where said Emanuel lives; to son, DAVID ZEIGLER, 200 acres; to wife, ANNA CATHERINA, the residue of his estate, she to be executrix. Wit: J.G. Neidlinger, Mrs. Hannah Neidlinger.

(p.90) EMANUEL and DAVID ZEIGLER apply for administration on estate of JOHN HUNOLT, dec'd., Aug. 1, 1796; appointed Aug. 27, 1796.   (p.90) Same applicants apply for admn. on estate of JOHN PFLIEGER, Aug.1,1796; appointed 8/27/1796.

(p.91) MRS. ANNA CATHERINA ZEIGLER qualified as Executrix of the will of John George Zeigler, Aug. 6, 1796.

(p.91) JOHN GRABENSTINE and MRS. CATHERINE HANGLEITER apply for admn. on estate of JOHN HANGLEITER, dec'd., Sept.3, 1796; appointed Oct. 1, 1796.

(p.99) JAMES BRYAN and BENJAMIN LANGLEY apply for admn. of estate of SAMUEL LANGLEY, dec'd., Oct.25, 1796; and were appointed Nov.21, 1796.

(Due to new page numbers in book not extending further than page 99, the old page numbers begin there with #65)

(p.65) MRS. ROSANNA STOCKMAN and MR. CHRISTIAN SHUBTRINE apply for admn. on estate of JOHN STOCKMAN, Dec. 17, 1796, and were appointed Jan.7, 1797.

(p.66) MRS. HANNAH WISENBAKER applies for admn. on estate of JACOB WISENBAKER Jan.15, 1797, and was appointed Feb. 15, 1797.

(p.66) On this page it is stated that certain papers relative to the estate of JOHN BILBO had been deposited in office by Nathaniel Lunday, Admr. of the estate, together with his account against the estate and his account against the estate of his father, ABRAHAM LUNDAY,dec'd. The papers referred to were two accounts against the John Bilbo estate, one owing Robert Hudson and the other to David Thom; also another account of John R. Cleary for schooling John Bilbo's son (unnamed). (Note: John Bilbo was the ancestor of the late Senator Bilbo of Miss.)

(p.67) MRS. JUDITH BUSH applies for administration on estate of MARTIN BUSH, dec'd., Feb. 15, 1797.

(p.67) MRS. HANNAH HERSON applies for admn. of estate of HERGAN HEERSON, Feb.27, 1797, and was appointed June 5, 1797. At the same time she applied for admn. on estate of JOHN CASPER WERTSCH, late of Ebenezer, merchant, that is, administrator de bonis non with the will annexed; and was appointed May 3, 1797.

(p.68) GODHELF SMITH, Guardian of JACOB and GEORGE MINGLEDORFF,minors, makes his return March 24, 1797. (First mention of this case).

(p.69) Letters Testamentary issued May 29, 1797, to JOHN POWERS and CURTIS LOPER on the will and estate of JAMES WEBB, dec'd. On p.72: Will of JAMES WEBB,dated May 8, 1797, probated May 29,1797. Gives half of his estate to his brother JESSE WEBB when 21, residue to his five half-sisters Lydia, Elizabeth,Sarah, Martha,Jane. Executors: John Powers,Curtis Loper. Wit: Asa,Abel,Joshua Loper.

(p.71) Annual Return of Nathaniel Lunday, Admr. of JOHN BILBO estate for the period 1782-1795. First entry under disbursements dated May 4, 1782, showing costs paid to William Harden, Ordinary, for fees in connection with appointment of the administrator; also shows paid 1789, 8 months tuition for JAMES BILBO, son of deceased, paid to John R. Cleary.

(p.73) WILLIAM MOORE of Chatham Co., Admr. of JOHN MOOREestate, applies for dismission June 25, 1797.

(p.73) Return of JAMES WEBB estate shows that most of the estate was paid over to Joshua Loper for taking care of him 105 days in his last sickness and burial, $375.00. The estate inventoried $447.00.

(p.74) JOSHUA ZANT and GODHELF SMITH as next of kin apply for administration on estate of CHRISTINA KIEFFER, spinster, July 26, 1797. Later,Smith declined to serve and Zant alone was appointed Oct. 24, 1797.

(p.78) Will of BORCAS GINDRAT, dated Sept. 9, 1797,with an assent in writing by her husband HENRY GINDRAT; probated Sept. 1997. She gives a certain slave to her husband for his lifetime then to go to her daughter MARY STAFFORD. She bequeaths a slave to her daughter DORCAS and to daughter HENRIETTA, minors, and the increase of said slaves to become the property of her other children ELIZABETH TISON, WILLIAM STAFFORD, SETH STAFFORD. Husband to be executor.

(p.78) SPENCE COX and WILLIAM DuPREE apply for administration on estate of JASPER COX, Sept.14, 1797. Later, DuPree declined serving and HENRY ROWELL was substituted in his place.   (p.80) Spence Cox and Henry Rowell were appointed Oct. 16, 1797.

(p.79) Deed of Gift dated Sept.22, 1797, from WILLIAM THORNTON to his son JOHN THORNTON, a minor, both of Effingham Co., conveying his plantation where he lives consisting of about 50 acres, also all his cattle and hogs. Witnesses: William Kennedy, Tryon Pace.

(p.79) Deed of Gift dated Oct. 10, 1797, from DAVID PORTER, planter, to his friend's wife AMY, wife of JACOB KITTLES; gift of slaves. Witnesses: James Porter and Elizabeth Porter.

(p.80) JAMES BRYAN, Admr. of SAMUEL LANGLEY estate, applies for dismission, Nov. 22, 1797.

(p.85) JOHN WISENBAKER appointed Admr. of estate of JACOB WISENBAKER, deceased, in place of Mr. CHRISTIAN TRUETLIN, who declined to serve any longer; April 27, 1798.

(p.85) SAMUEL PARRISH and wife ELIZABETH apply for administration of estate of JACOB STRICKLAND, May 12, 1798, and were appointed June 11, 1798.

(p.86) JOHN KOGLER as principal creditor applies for administration on estate of SAMUEL DEPP, dec'd., Aug.1, 1798, and was appointed Sept.1, 1798.

(p.86) JOSHUA ZANT, Admr. of CHRISTINA KIEFFER, spinster, applies for dismission Aug. 1, 1798, and was dismissed Sept. 1, 1798.

(p.86) SAMUEL RYAL applies for administration on estate of ARTHUR RYALL, dec'd., Aug.4, 1798, and was appointed Aug.30, 1798.

(p.90) JACOB KITTLES gives receipt at Savannah Jan. 28, 1797, fo WILLIAM PORTER for his part of the THOMAS GARNETT estate. Witnesses: James Porter, David Porter, Charles Cope.

(p.91) MRS. ELIZABETH NOWLAN, widow, applies for administration on estate of CLEMENT MARTIN, Jr., March 5, 1799. At the same time she also applied for admn.on estate of GEORGE NOWLAN, and was appointed April 5, 1799.

(p.91) JACOB KITTLES as nearest of kin, applies for admn. on estate of JOHN KITTLES,late of Chatham Co.,dec'd.,Mar.12,1799,and was appointed 4/13/1799.

(p.91) Deed of Gift dated March 7, 1799, from SAMUEL BOSTICK to his daughter SARAH PORTER of Effingham Co., conveying fifty acres on Big Tuckaseeking (Creek?).

(p.92) Will of JOHN MICHALER, planter,of said county,dated April 12,1799, probated Apr. 22, 1799. Devises to MICHAEL EXLEY, husband of testator's daughter CATHERINE, 50 acres granted Henry L.Buntz Sr.. Aug.7, 1759: to JOHN

FRICKINGER, 50 acres granted John Happacher, July 1, 1760; to SUSANNA CATHERINA, wife of JOHN ERNST BERGMAN $60.00; to friends JONATHAN RAHN and JOHN HOGLER the sum of $100.00 in cash; to grandson, JOHN EXLEY (son of Michael and Catherine) three slaves; to grand-daughter, MARY, wife of BENJAMIN BECHTLY, daughter of BENJAMIN REISSER and CATHERINA his wife (who is testator's daughter), 6 slaves. Remainder of testator's lands in Effingham Co., amounting to 900 acres, he gives to his said two grandchildren. Executors: Jonathan Rahn and John Kogler who are also named trustees for said John Exley, a minor. Witnesses: Nathaniel Reisser, Gottlieb Ernest, Christian Biddenbach. (p.94) The said Executors and trustees qualified April 22, 1799, and received their Letters Testamentary as such.

(p.95) MRS. APPOLONIA LEIMBERGER, Admx. of ISRAEL LEIMBERGER estate, applies for dismission April 24, 1799; and was dismissed May 25, 1799.

(p.95) MRS. DORCAS GINDRAT and her husband HENRY GINDRAT apply for admn. on estate of her dec'd son, WILLIAM STAFFORD, May 3, 1799. App'td June 3, 1799.

(p.95) GIDEON ZETTLER applies for administration on estate of JOHN WILSON, Sr., May 11, 1799, and was appointed June 11, 1799.

(p.95) Will of SAMUEL SELLERS of Effingham Co., dated Aug.29, 1794, probated May 11, 1799. Bequeaths to his son JOHN SELLERS, one-half of all his lands and to his son SAMUEL SELLERS the other half, together with certain personalty. To daughter, PENELOPE, he gives certain items of personalty. Executor: Son, John Sellers. Witnesses: John Strahan, Howell Hines, John Moore J.P. (Editor's Note: This family moved to Effingham Co., from Sampson Co. N.C., c1790, and the three children all later moved around 1805-1808 to Tattnall Co., then about ten years later to Appling County when it was first opened up to settlers. Samuel Sellers, the testator, married his cousin, Zilpha Sellers, May 11, 1767, in Duplin Co.N.C. She was deceased when the will was made.)

(p.97) JAMES BRYAN and BENJAMIN LANGLEY, Admrs. of SAMUEL LANGLEY estate, were dismissed May 8, 1799.

(p.97) Affidavit of JOHN TISON, Jr., made in court June 25, 1799, to the effect that he heard WILLIAM STAFFORD state a short time before he died, at a time when he was very sick, that when he died he meant to leave his property only to his sister MRS. ELIZABETH TISON because she was always willing to do anything for him and the rest of his people were not willing. Affidavit of REUBIN KENNEDY made at the same time, states that he heard WILLIAM STAFFORD say a few days before he died, that he wished his brother-in-law JOHN TISON to have his property at his death. Affidavit dated July 3, 1799, by RICHARD DAVIS of South Carolina, in which he testifies that in March previously the said WILLIAM STAFFORD came up from Savannah with him by water, and enroute told him that he would like for affiant Davis to carry him in his boat to John Tison's and that he wished to go to Mr. Gindrat's and get his clothing, and that he didn't think he would live long and wished his sister MRS. ELIZABETH TISON to have his property at his death. Note: The inventory of the estate of said William Stafford shows that his estate consisted of one slave and six head of cattle.

(p.102) Deed of Gift dated July 30, 1799, from JOHN PALMER to MISS ELIZABETH MIKELL, conveying a slave and household goods. Witnesses: Mary Ravot and Christian Truetlin J.P.

(p.102) Deed of Gift dated Aug. 14, 1799, for three slaves, from SAMUEL BOSTICK, planter, to his sons JOHN GRAVES BOSTICK, WILLIAM BOSTICK and LITTLEBERRY BOSTICK of Richland Co. S.C.

(p.103) Indemnity Bond dated Aug. 19, 1799, of JAMES PORTER of Effingham Co., whereby he binds himself in sum of $10,000 to stand by and abide an agreement made with his wife, ELIZABETH PORTER, whereby the property owned by them was divided between them, she receiving certain slaves, all the cattle he owned except five heifers which he states he "had given the children", also household goods; she agreeing that at her death she is to leave it to her five children, William, Thomas, James, Elizabeth and Ann Harriott. (Note: The sur-names of the children are not given, but presumably they were Porter children born by said James).

On p.104, is record of a similar bond she gives to her said husband, agreeing that all other property than the above that he owns or may hereafter acquire she shall not have any claim or demand against it on her part "forever".

(p.104) MRS. ROSANNA KEEBLER applies for administration on estate of JOHN KEEBLER, dec'd., Oct. 29, 1799.

(p.106) EMANUEL and DAVID ZEIGLER, Admrs. of JOHN HUNOLD estate, apply for dismission, Jan. 6, 1800. At the same time the Emanuel and David as Admrs. of the JOHN G. ZEIGLER estate, apply for dismission.

(p.107) GEORGE HENRY SHUMAN applies for administration on estate of his dec'd father, MARTIN SHUMAN, Jan.21, 1800, and was appointed July 21,1800.

(p.167) DAVID REISER applies for administration on estate of his dec'd brother, NATHANIEL REISER, Feb.10, 1800, and was appointed July 21, 1800.

(p.108) On the application of JOHN WILSON, Jr., minor son of JOHN WILSON, dec'd., JOHN WILSON Sr., was appointed guardian for the minor,Feb.18,1800.

(p.108) WILLIAM LISTER was appointed Guardian of ANN NOWLAN and GEORGE GALPHIN NOWLAN, minor children of GEORGE NOWLAN, dec'd., Feb. 18, 1800.

(p.108) JONATHAN SECKINGER was appointed Guardian of GODLIEB and HANNAH SHUBTREIN, minors, Feb. 18, 1800.

(p.108) GOTLIEB ZITTERAUER was appointed Guardian of JOSHUA HOWARD, a minor, at the latter's request, Feb. 18, 1800. (Note: This indicates the minor was over 14 years of age, the age at which, then as now, minors can select their guardians.)

(p.109) JOHN TISON applies for will of WILLIAM STAFFORD to be established, Feb. 18, 1800.

(p.109) WILLIAM HOLZENDORF, Esq., applies for administration on estate of ROSINA SPENCER, "formerly ROSINA POSTELL", dec'd., June14, 1800. On p.110: JOHN SPENCER, Esq., caveats to the appointment, June 23, 1800, at the same time offering her will for probate, and it was duly probated July 2, 1800.

(p.111) On the testimony contained in the affidavits above abstracted in re: WILLIAM STAFFORD (p.97) the non cupative will of said William Stafford was probated July 21, 1800, and letters of administration with the will annexed were ordered issued to John Tison,the applicant.

(p.116) Will of ROSINAH SPENCER, dated Aug. 19, 1791, probated July 19, 1800, bequeathed her whole estate to her husband (unnamed) and named him as sole executor.

(p.118).JOHN METZGER applies for admn. on estate of JACOB METZGER, dec'd., Aug.15, 1800, and was appointed Oct. 7, 1800.

(p.118) WILLIAM BIRD and MRS. MARGARET BIRD applies for admn. on estate of ABRAHAM BIRD, Aug. 11, 1800, and wereappointed Oct. 7, 1800.

(p.120) Will of JOHN McCRORY, dated Sept.15, 1800, probated Oct. 6, 1800, bequeathed his estate to his wife RACHEL and son JOHN, a minor. Witnesses: Walden Griffin, S---- Powers, Henry Cook.

(p.121) Will of ROSANNAH GASKINS, widow, of St. Peters Parish, Beaufort Dist.S.C., dated Nov. 14, 1799, probated in Effingham Co., Oct.31, 1800. She devised to her son AMOS GASKINS, daughter ROSANNAH GASKINS, grandson JOHN HARRIL GASKINS and grandson WRIGHT HARRIL GASKINS; son WILLIAM GASKINS to have charge of said grandsons who are minors. Says she had already given her son the said William and her daughter ELIZABETH WILLIAMS their shares of her estate. Executors: Son, William Gaskins, and friends and neighbors MICHAEL MIXON and HOWELL WALL, Executors. Witnesses: Grimball Roberts and Thos. S. Chesher.

(p.123) Three receipts: (1) ROBERT HUDSON to CHRISTOPHER HUDSON, Admr. of SAMUEL HUDSON estate, dated Sept.27, 1769, for said Robert's share of the estate of said father Samuel Hudson, dec'd. (2) From WILLIAM THOMSON to ROBERT HUDSON dated March 27, 1769, for 1650₤ owing him by said Robert's father, Samuel Hudson. (3) SAMUEL HUDSON, CHARLES HUDSON, JOHN BRADY, to CHRISTOPHER HUDSON, Admr.as aforesaid, dated Feb.29, 1769, for 5 shillings "in full for all demands".

(p.124) Will of MARTIN SHUMAN, of Effingham Co., dated Oct.4, 1793, probated Dec. 1, 1800. He devised all his estate to his wife TOBITHA for her lifetime or widowhood; and after her death or re-marriage he directed that his son JOHN SHUMAN take charge of the estate and also takecharge "of the young children until the youngest of them is 16. He gives to his sons JOHN and MARTIN SHUMAN the cattle he has already given them; to his son, GEORGE HENRY SHUMAN the cattle he has already given him; to his daughter ELIZABETH WOMACK, certain cattle, and if she leaves no issue at her death, such cattle and their increase to return to his estate; to son, JAMES SHUMAN, certain cattle when he is of age, and also the upper half of 400-acre tract on the OgeecheeRiver inEffingham County, and sons John and Martin Shuman to be trustees for said James during his minority, and if he dies without issue then the property bequeathed him to return to his estate. To son JONATHAN SHUMAN certain cattle when he is 21, and the lower half of said 400-acre tract of land being the place where testator lives, sons John and Martin to be trustees for said Jonathan during his minority. In his will testator requests his son John to take care of and support his mother, &c. Says he has an estate in Germany left him by his father HENRY SHUMAN there, and he directs that it be equally divided among his children . Executors: Sons John and Martin Shuman. Witnesses: William Ray, Ann Robertson, James Kirk.

(p.127) Will of ELIAS HODGES of Granville Co. S.C., dated Aug. 19, 1779, probated Oct. 25, 1800. He gives to his cousin DRURY HODGES when 16 years old, certain cattle. Residue of his estate to his wife MARY. Executors: Wife Mary and brother, ROBERT HODGES. Witnesses: Thomas Daniels, Elizabeth Hudson. The will was probated on the testimony of Capt. THOMAS DANIELS of Beaufort Dist. S.C., whose affidavit made there was recorded with the will; in it he states the signature of his father, THOMAS DANIELS, now dec'd., was genuine, etc. Affidavit signed in Beaufort Dist.S.C., before Robert Tanner, J.P.

(p.133) WILLIAM LISTER HALL applies for administration de bonis non on estate of CLEMENT MARTIN, Jr., late of Effingham Co., dec'd., Jan.8,1801; and he was appointed Feb. 17, 1801.

(p.133) WILLIAM LIMBERT, merchant, of Savannah, applies for administration of estate of FREDERICK WILLIAM KAHLDEN, late of Effingham Co. dec'd., Nov. 10, 1801; and he was appointed and qualified Feb. 17, 1801.

(p.133) WILLIAM SHEPPARD, Admr. of estate of JOHN BAPTIST SHEPPARD dec'd., applies for dismission, Jan. 10,1801.

(p.134) CHRISTIAN TRUETLIN of Effingham Co., planter, by Deed of Gift, conveys back to his brother JOHN TRUETLIN now of Orangeburg Dist.S.C., all the property (undescribed) given him by said John in October, 1792, and which he says was given him to protect him the said John against a suit at law then about to be filed against him. Instrument dated Feb. 23, 1801.

(p.135) Will of HENRY GINDRAT, planter, of Effingham Co., dated Jan.10,1801, probated Feb.23, 1801, bequeathing to his wife DORCAS six negroes in fee simple, and three other slaves for her lifetime, also all his live stock,tools, household goods and the plantation where he lives, all for her lifetime, then to return to his estate. After her death the home and plantation then to go to his youngest daughter HENRIETTA. He directs that his daughters Dorcas and Henrietta be decently reared and educated. He givesho his daughter RHODA GILLELAND two slaves; to daughter MARY H. MARK (or MARY ST.MARK,not plain) one slave; to son ABRAHAM GINDRAT one slave; to daughter SUSANNAH MORRELL one slave; to daughters Dorcas and Henrietta eight "little slaves". He gives to his sons ABRAHAM and JOHN GINDRAT all his real estate except that given said Henrietta and which she is not to possess until after her mother's death. Executors: Wife Dorcas, and sons JOHN and ABRAHAM GINDRAT. Witnesses: Wm. Kennedy, William Porter, Benjamin Kennedy. (p.137) Mrs. Dorcas Gindrat and John Gindrat qualify as Executors Feb.23, 1801. Inventory of estate (p.138) totals $7983.25. (NOTE: It is not clear how the will of his wife Dorcas was probated Sept. 1797 if she was still in life when she and her husband applied for admn.on son Wm.Stafford's estate in May 1799, and

if she was still alive when the above will was made and probated,in 1801. The
Editor knows of another similar situation that existed in the 1860s in Coffee
Co. Ga., where the man was shown by the census to be still alive after his
will had been probated about nine years before. Assuredly it has never been
legally possible to probate a will until after the DEATH of the maker of the will.
Too, it has always been the law that it takes the death of the testator to bring
his will into force after it has been probated.

(p.139) JOSEPH RAHN and GIDEON ZETTLER were appointed Guardians
of MARY and CATHERINE and NATHANIEL ZETTLER to take cnarge of the legacy left
them by their deceased grandfather, MARTIN SISSON; guardians' bond fixed at
$7000.00. Dated July 29,1801.

(p.140) JOHN VALENTINE BEGEL, age about 11 years, was bound out
to DAVID REISSER until said minor is 21, to learn the shoemaker's trade, and to
be educated &c. Dated July 29,1801.

(p.140) MRS. HANNAH ASH, relict of MATTHIAS ASH, applies for
dministration on his estate July 20, 1801.

(p.140) MRS. ELIZABETH BECKTLY, relict of CHRISTIAN BECKTLY,
applies for admn. on his estate July 20, 1801, and was appointed Feb.15, 1802.

(p.141) JONATHAN BECHTLY applied for admn. on estate of BENJAMIN
RIESSER, dec'd., July 20, 1801, and was appointed Feb. 15, 1802.

(p.141) GODHELF SHEAROUS, Admr. of JOHN SHERRAUS, Sr., estate,
applied for dismission July 20, 1801, and was dismissed Feb. 15, 1802.

(p.141) Will of ANDREW GNANN, df Effingham Co., dated Dec. 24,
1800, probated Aug. 17, 1801. He devised to his son CHRISTOPHER GNANN the home-
place of 50 acres; to his son BENJAMIN an adjoining tract of 50 acres; to sons
CHRISTOPHER and BENJAMIN the 100-acre tract of river swamp he owns. To his sons
TIMOTHY and ANDREW GNANN the 300 acres above Turkey branch which he owns. To his
three daughters HANNAH, SALOME and CATHERINA, 100 acres of land lying between
John Metzger's and Hollingsworth's; to his son CHRISTOPHER, certain live-stock.
Residue of his estate to all of the said children. Executors: Brother, Solomon
Gnann and son Christopher Gnann. Witnesses: Gottlieb Ernest, David Gruber.
The said designated executors qualified Aug.17, 1801.

(p.146) MRS. SALOME SCHWEIGHOFFER applies for administration of
THOMAS SCHWEIGHOFFER's estate Oct.10,1801, and was appointed Feb.15, 1802.

(p.146) MRS. BLANDINA MAGDALENA HELVESTEIN applies for administration with the will annexed on JOHN and JACOB HELVENSTEIN estates, Oct. 10, 1801
and was appointed Feb. 15, 1802.

(p.150) Will of JOSEPH LEWIS, dated Sept. 22, 1800, probated Oct.
22, 1801. He gives to his wife MARY his whole estate, she to rear and educate the
children (unnamed). Executors: Wife Mary and his uncle, ELIJAH LEWIS. Witnesses:
Isaac Lewis J.P., Caleb Touchston, Thomas Waugh.

(p.151) Caveat filed Oct. 22, 1801, by WILLIAM BURNSIDE and SU-
SANNAH his wife, on behalf of JOHN ASH (otherwise Ashbocker) and GEORGE ASH (otherwise Ashbocker) minor children of GEORGE ADAM ASH (otherwise Ashbocker) who was
nephew of MATTHIAS ASH (or Ashbocker), objecting to appointment of HANNAH ASH and
David Gugel as Admrs. of said Matthias Ash estate on the grounds that Gugel is
neither a relation or creditor of deceased, and because caveators are the natural
guardians of said John and George Adam Ash who it is alleged are nearest of kin.

(p.152) MRS. FRANCES LUNDAY, relict and admx. of THEOPHILUS LUNDAY
applies for dismission Nov. 27, 1801.

(p.152) MRS. CATHERINA ZANT, relict of JOSHUA ZANT applies for
administration on his estate Nov.20, 1801. Was appointed Feb.15, 1802.

(p.152) MRS. ELIZABETH ANN BIRCH, relict of JOHN BIRCH, of Eff.
Co.,and JAMES I. GRAY of Chatham Co.,apply for administration on the estate of
said John Birch, Dec.31, 1801. She afterwards declined serving and Gray was
appointed alone as Admr. April 12, 1802.

12

(p.152) JAMES BOSTON applies for administration on estate of
THOMAS CAMPBELL, Jan. 2, 1802. He was appointed April 12,1802.
(p.153) Will of ISRAEL RIESSER, dated Dec. 15, 1801, probated
Jan. 2, 1802. He directs that his wife(unnamed) shall have the use of his whole
estate to be finally divided equally between her and their children (unnamed).
Executors: William Kennedy, Christopher Gugel and son MATTHEW RIESSER. Witnesses:
David Riesser, Jesse Bell. The nominated executors duly qualified Jan. 5, 1802.
(p.154) Will of ABIEL SCHWEIGHOFFER, dec'd., dated Dec.8, 1801;
probated Jan. 2, 1802. Gives to his son ABIAL the home plantation consisting of
200 acres; residue of estate to be kept together until youngest child is of age,
then to be divided between his saidwife and the four children (unnamed). Executors: Wife Margaret and son ABIAL SCHWEIGHOFFER. Witnesses: Thomas Polhill, John
Waldhauer, Lucy Mannan. The widow qualified as Executrix Jan. 5, 1802.
(p.155) MRS. RACHEL PORTER, relict of WILLIAM PORTER, applies
for admn. on his estate Jan.22, 1802, and was appointed Apr. 12, 1802.
(p.155) Marriage Contract made in anticipation of marriage, dated Jan. 23, 1802, between MATTHEW RAHN and MISS HANNAH ELIZABETH DOLIVICH, both
of Effingham Co.He conveys to her a slave wench and agrees that said wench and all
the property she already has, shall be and remain hers free from his control and
from his liabilities after their marriage.
(p.156) The caveat filed by WILLIAM BURNSIDE and wife to the
appointment of MRS. HANNAH ASH as Admx. on estate of her dec'd husband MATTHIAS
ASH, was heard and considered by the Court, and was overruled, and said widow was
appointed admx. as prayed, Feb. 15, 1802.
(p.157) THOMAS POLHILL Esq.,applies for administration de bonis
non on estate of JOHN STIRK, Feb.16, 1802, and was appointed Apr. 12, 1802.
(p.157) Will of JOHN HELVENSTINE dated Dec. 4, 1774, probated
Oct. 16, 1801. Gives to his father (unnamed) the 100 acres he bought from George
Burkholder, together with all his personal property, except one pair breeches and
a hat which he gives to his brother JACOB; his said father to pay testator's sister HANNAH £2, and she to have certain items of personal property. To his brother
DANIEL HELVENSTINE he gives the 100 acres that had been granted him (testator).
Witnesses: John Lowreman, Lionel S-----?, Jacob Hensler. Will was probated on the
testimony of the said Jacob Hensler.

    NOTE: All parties in these abstracts were shown by the record to be
    residents of Effingham County,unless otherwise shown. The term "of
    Effingham County" is omitted from the abstracts to save space. If
    no county is shown it is so stated.

(p.157) Will of JACOB HELVENSTINE of St. Matthews Parish, dated
Dec.20, 1775; probated Feb.16, 1802. To his father (unnamed) 100 acres of land in
said parish, adjoining Jacob Waldhauer, Esq., and John Stirk Esq. Witnesses:
John Lowrman, Lionel Snyder, John Moxham. Will probated on testimony of last-named.
(p.158) Will of MARTIN CRUGER, undated; probated Mar. 22, 1802.
Bequeaths to his wife CATHERINA for her lifetime and then the residue of his estate to go to her son SAMUEL FITZPATRICK. Witnesses: John Wisenbaker, Wm.Townsend.
(p.158) Deed of Gift dated March 22, 1802, from BARBARA BACKLEY
to her two grandchildren JOSIAH and HANNAH MARGARET BACKLEY, children of her son
CHRISTIAN BACKLEY, the sum of $80.00 owing her by said Christian in his lifetime,
same to be collected by Jonathan Backley and to be kept out at interest until said
two children are 21. Witnesses: Basil Foosing and Thomas Trowell.
(p.160) Will of JOHANNAH CHRISTIANA HERRSON of near Ebenezer,
widow, dated Feb.12, 1802, probated Apr. 15, 1802. To son GOTTLIEB ERNST and his
lawful heirs all her household goods, debts and other moveable effects. To said
son three slaves,he to be executor. Witnesses: Matthew Weitman, Solomon Whitman
and Christian Biddenbach

(p.161) Last Will and Testament of HANNAH NOBLES, widow, dated Nov.21, 1801, probated May 3, 1802. Devises to Mrs. Mary Hodges all of her household goods and certain live-stock; to her grandson, JOSHUA HOWARD, son of Simon Howard, 200 acres lying on Belcher's Mill Creek in former Effingham County, and live-stock; to grand-daughter, HANNAH wife of Godlieb Zitteraeur, a certain bed and bedding; testatrix's wearing apparrel to be equally divided between said Joshua Howard, Mary Hodges and Hannah Zitterauer. Executor: Gottlieb Zitterauer. Witnesses: Jonathan Seckinger, John G. Neidlinger, Clerk Court of Ordinary.

(p.164) MRS. MARY GNANN, relict of DAVID GNANN, applies for administration on his estate June 16, 1802. She was appointed July 26, 1802.

(p.164) MRS. CATHERINE CRUGER, relict of MARTIN CRUGER, was appointed Administratrix of his estate with the will annexed, July 26, 1802.

(p.164) MRS. HANNAH TRIBLE applies for administration on estate of JACOB WISENBAKER, deceased, July 26, 1802.

(p.166) Last Will and Testament of MOORE SPEAR (SPIER?), dated Feb. 16, 1802, probated July 26, 1802. Bequeathed to his wife Miley 200 acres and after her death same to son JAMES on his paying $200 to WILLIS SPIER (son of testator) when of age. Devises to son WILLIAM, 250 acres adjoining O'Berry and McCall, he to pay to Nueit Pittman Spear when of age $200.00; and to daughter, Sarah, two cows and calves; to daughter Patience, two cows and calves; and to his unborn child four cows and calves. Executors: Son, James Spear, and Willis Spear, testator's brother. Witnesses: John Yarbrough and John McCall. Capt. Willis Spear qualified as Executor of the will, July 28, 1802.

(p.169) Last Will and Testament of JOHN WISENBAKER, dated (blank), probated Aug.23, 1802. He says he has given property to his children by his first wife, viz,, Mary,John and Christian Godlip Wisenbaker; and has also given deed of gift to his wife Mary for a lot on Broughton Street inSavannah. The remainder of his estate, being 350 acres in Effingham Co., and 50 acres where he lives, and 100 acres in Bulloch County, he gives to his wife Mary;after her death to be divided between the children by her and by hisfirst wife. She and Jeremiah Cuyler named Executors. Wife's son, Joseph Traylor, to have $60.00 when of age. Witnesses: Christian Dasher and Samuel Zipperer.

(p.172) JONATHAN BECHTLY applies for administration on estate of his deceased father, GEORGE BECHTLY, Jan. 13, 1803.

(p.172) Deed of Gift dated Sept.27, 1802, from JOHN GEORGE ZITTERAUER to his son, SOLOMON ZITTERAEUR, conveying 100 acres being the E½ of 200-acre tract granted grantor Feb. 7, 1788.

(p.172) MRS. MARTHA ZETTLER, relict of GIDEON ZETTLER; applies for administration on his estate Jan. 1, 1803, and was appointed June2, 1803.

(p.172) MRS. HANNAH EIGLE, relict of JOHN EIGLE, applied for administration on his estate Jan. 30, 1803, and was appointed May 2, 1803. She did not qualify as Admx. until Feb. 25, 1804.

(p.174) Last Will and Testament of NICHOLAS HELMLY, dated Oct.29,1802, probated June 18, 1803. Devises to his wife Maria Magdalena his whole estate for her lifetime, and at her death the residue to his three children,provided however that his oldest son David shall have over half to include the homeplace and all cleared lands; the remainder of estate to the other two children, Joshua and Elizabeth. Executors: Friends John Kogler and Ernst Zitterauer, they to also be trustees for his son Joshua until he is 21. Witnesses: Jacob Godhelp Zitterauer and Jacob Hensler.

(p.175) MRS. CATHERINE SECKINGER applies for administration on estate of ANDREW SECKINGER, dec'd., Aug.6, 1803. She was appointed temporary Admx. Sept.5, 1803, and permanent Admx. Feb. 25, 1804.

(p.175) JONATHAN BECHTLY was appointed temporary Admr. of estate of his father, JOHN GEORGE BECHTLY, Sept.5,1803, and permanent Admr.,Feb.25, 1804.

(p.177) Last Will and Testament of WILLIAM JENKINS, deceased, dated Feb. 1, 1803, no date of probate shown. Bequeaths 300 acres where he lives to hic children William, Liddy, James, Jincy Jenkins and Ann Silas, they being the hix youngest children; he gives his stock of cattle except two heifers, to Thomas Gill's daughter Sally, and William son of James. Other personal property to be sold. Executor: Henry Cook. Witnesses: John Martin, John Crawford.

(p.179) GEORGE PAULITSCH applies for Administration on estate of MRS. MARGARET SEEINER, widow, dec'd., Nov.28, 1803,and was appointed Dec. 30,1803.

(p.179) JOHN VALENTINE BEGAL not having been bound out as previously ordered by the Court, was bound out to Matthew Reiser, Feb. 25, 1804.

(p.179) JAMES CRUSE (CREWS) was appointed Guardian of WILLIAM STANDLEY, a minor, Feb. 25, 1804.

(p.179) MRS. MARY WISENBAKER, Admr. of JOHN WISENBAKER estate, having married BENJAMIN OGLESBIE and he having made much waste of the estate to the injury of the orphans of the deceased, CHRISTIAN DASHER was appointed Guardian for saidorphans, viz., John, Christian G. and Hannah Wisenbaker, children of said John Wisenbaker, Sr.,deceased, said Guardian to take charge of estate of said deceased for the benefit and use of said children; so ordered, Feb. 25, 1804.

(p.180) DANIEL WEIDMAN, ANDREW GNANN and JOHN KOGLER were appointed Guardians of JOHN CHRISTOPHER CRAMER and CATHERINE CRAMER, orphans of John Cramer, deceased, Feb. 25, 1804.

(p.180) SETH STAFFORD and REUBIN G. TAYLOR apply for administration on estate of DAVID DUPIUS, lately deceased, May 24, 1804; and were appointed Admrs. Feb. 18, 1805.

(p.180) MRS. HANNAH WEIDMAN applies for administration on the estate of her late husband SOLOMON WEIDMAN, dec'd., June 20, 1804; and was appointed as Admx. of same, Feb. 18, 1805.

(p.181) Bill of Sale for slave, dated Feb.16, 1804, from JOHN KOGLER to JOHN GEORGE ZITTERAUER; consideration $425.00.

(p.181) Daniel and Ann Catherine Wiedman, Admrs. of the J. C. Cramer estate, on June 21, 1804, divide the lands of the estate by lot by consent of all the heirs, as follows: Lot #1 drawn by Kogler as Guardian of Christopher and Catherine Cramer, minors, same being or consisting of 150 acres granted J.C. Cramer, Sr., in 1759, together with town lots; Lot #2 drawn by Solomon Cramer, consisting of 150 acres on the Old Ebenezer Creek granted April 5, 1757, and town lot; Lot #3 consisting of 100 acres on old Ebenezer Creek, drawn by Andrew Gnann as an heir; Lot #4 consisting of 150 acres granted David Stiener Feb.2, 1768, and 100 acres granted John Martin Bolzius June 7, 1757, drawn by Christopher Cramer by his Guardian John Kolger; Lot #5 consisting of 50 acres granted Frederick Buckner May 5, 1757, and 100 acres given by John Hanglieter to his two daughters Agatha Hangleiter and Catherine Hanglieter (now Weidman), late Ann Catherine Cramer, lying on Turkey branch, also 50 acres known as Blue Bluff,all drawn by Daniel Wiedman as an heir.

(p.182) Last Will and Testament of JAMES HINES, dated Apr. 28, 1799, probated July 12, 1804, devises to his wife Drusilla, all the estate for her lifetime or widowhood, then to descend to sons Charlton, James, William, Lewis and Allen Hines, they to have all the real estate and a slave, and son Charlton to be allowed a reasonable sum for rearing and educating his said brothers. Residue of testator's estate to all his children viz:Susannah, David, Sarah, Drusilla, Jesse, Allen, James, Charlton, William and Lewis, share and share alike. Executors: Wife Drusilla and son Charlton and son-in-law Elijah Lewis. Witnesses: John Moore, William Wilson, Susannah Lewis.

(p.183) Last Will and Testament of BLANDINA MAGDALENA HELVESTINE, dated Aug.29, 1804, probated Oct. 10, 1804. Gives to her son Joseph, 200 acres where she lives, same having been granted Feb.7, 1758, to John Frederick Helvenstine, Sr.; together with the mill &c., and two slaves and certain personalty; to daughter, Mary Magdalena Grummet, 300 acre pineland tract granted Sept.4,1770, to said John F. Helvestine Sr.; together with lot #7 in Ebenezer granted Dec. 4, 1759, to Balthazer Rieser and deeded by him to said John F.Helvestine Sr., Apr. 20, 1777; also a slave; to testatrix's grand-daughter Mary Susanna Fofly? (not plain) 100 acres of pine land granted Jacob Helvestine May 3, 1772, and town lot #3 in Ebenezer granted Daniel Burgstiener April 5, 1757 and by him deeded Veit? Lechner Feb.2, 1775, and by him deeded said John F. Helvenstine Sr., Sept.6,1780, also a slave. Residue of her estate to be the property of the three said legatees jointly. Executors: Son, Joseph Helvenstine, and friend John Kogler. Witnesses: Ernst Zitterauer, John Heinley, Jacob Hensler. The nominated executors qualified as such Oct. 12, 1804.

(p.184) MRS. HANNAH DASHER applied for administration of estate of JOHN M. DASHER, Jr., her dec'd husband, Oct. 12, 1804; and was appointed as Admx. of the estate, Feb. 18, 1805.

(p.184) Last Will and Testament of AUGUSTUS EASTER, dated Sept. 29, 1804, probated Jan. 21, 1805. Bequeaths to wife Mary Easter his whole estate for her lifetime, then to pass to sons William, George, Giles Easters and daughter Mary and sons David and Isaac and daughter Elizabeth. Testator directs that if his son John, now absent, returns then he is to receive an equal share with his brothers and sisters. Executors: Friends, John Strawhorn and Darius Garrison. Witnesses: John Elkins and Cammel Tison.

(p.185) GEORGE W. NICHOLS of Savannah applies Dec.22, 1804, for administration de bonis non on estate of Clement Martin, Jr. On Jan. 31, 1805, George G. Nowland caveated to the appointment asked for, claiming he is next of kin. The caveat was sustained and Nowland and Thomas Polhill Jr., were appointed administrators with will annexed, Feb. 18, 1805.

(p.186) SAMUEL ROYALL, Admr. of estate of ARTHUR RYALL, dec'd., applied for dismission, Feb.20, 1805, having fully administered the estate; and he was ordered dismissed July 22, 1805.

(p.186) John G. Neidlinger applies for administration of CHARLES McCoy, deceased, Feb. 20, 1805.

(p.186) HARMON CRUM applies for administration on estate of THEOPHILUS WARD, schoolmaster, dec'd., Apr.27,1805, and was appointed July 22, 1805.

(pp. 186-7) Last Will and Testament of JACOB FRESH, dated Nov. 9, 1804, probated Dec.29, 1804. He directs that the money due him by John Spencer be collected and distributed after payment of debts, among the children of Timothy Staley, viz., John B., Timothy, Hannah, Mary and Elizabeth, they to have all his other assets. Executor: Brother, Timothy Staley. Witness: Henry W. Williams.

(p.188) Warranty deed dated Aug.21, 1805, from JACOB HINELEY and wife Elizabeth, of Effingham Co., to CLARK TINKHAM, mariner, ofCharleston, S.C. Conveys 100 acres in said county granted Matthew Mick and at his death the same passed to his daughter, the said Elizabeth Hinely. Witnesses: Joseph Helvenstine and John Waldhauer, J.P.

(p.189) MAJ. JOHN KING of Effingham Co., applies for administration on estate of JOHN LINDER, Jr., late of East Florida, deceased, Oct. 7, 1805. He was duly appointed Admr. Feb. 17, 1805.

(p.189) BENJAMIN MORRELL of South Carolina applies for administration on estate of JOHN MINCEY, late of Effingham Co., dec'd., Oct.7, 1805; and was appointed Admr. Feb. 17, 1806.

(p.190) MRS. HANNAH GRUBER, relict of DAVID GRUBER, together with MICHAEL EXLEY apply for administration on estate of her said husband, Dec.17,1805; and were appointed Admrs., Feb. 17, 1806.

16

(p.190) Trust deed of Gift, dated Dec.23, 1805, from JOSEPH
TOOSING of St. Peters Parish, Beaufort Dist. S.C., and his wife Susannah, to
PAUL TOOSING of Ga., as Trustee for grantors; conveying six slaves, horse, all
their household goods, riding chair and harness, to be held by said Trustee for
and applied to their use and benefit. Executed in Beaufort Dist. S.C. Witnesses:
William C. Wylly and Eliza Ann Henderson. Shows to have been recorded in Beaufort
Dist. S.C., in Deed Book #5, page 58, Jan. 4, 1806.

(p.191) MRS. MARY WEIDMAN, relict of MATTHEW WEIDMAN, dec'd.,
applies for administration on his estate Feb. 17, 1806.

(p.192) CHSITOPHER GUGEL and CHRISTIAN GUGEL of Savannah ap-
ply for administration de bonis non on estate of MATHIAS ASH, dec'd.,and on the
estate of MRS. HANNAH ASH, dec'd., Feb.22, 1806. On April 2, 1806, WILLIAM BURN-
SIDE and wife on behalf of George and John Ash, caveated. The caveat on being heard
was overruled, and applicants were appointed Admrs. July 11, 1806.

(p.192) MRS. MARY HOWARD and DAVID B. MITCHELL, nominated executors, filed the will of JOHN LONDON for probate, April 14, 1806. JOHN WILLIAMS
having already applied March 31st, for administration, caveated to the probate of
the will same date, April 14, 1806.

(p.192) HON. DAVID B. MITCHELL applied for administration on
estate of WILLIAM L. HALL, dec'd., Apr. 14, 1806. Caveat was filedsame day by
George G. Nowlan, objecting to the applicant being appointed Admr.

(p.193) Last Will and Testament ofJOSHUA LOPER, Esq., dated
March 13, 1806, probated June 10, 1806. Bequeaths to his wife Mary his personal
property; to son Curtis Loper, 250 acres; and to sons Asa, Abel G. and Ara Loper
the remainder of his lands together with all his tools, livestock and slaves;
and to son Ara, a town lot in Savannah, being lot 28 in Yamacraw. He gives to
Sarah Hudson $10.00; to daughter Abegail Goolsby $10.00. Residue of his estate to
be divided equally between his five children Lydia, Curtis, Asa, Abel G. and Ara
Loper. The said four sons to be executors. Witnesses: John Ferguson, Winnifred
Ferguson, Joshua Loper, Jr. The said four sons qualified as executors June 17,1806.

(p.195) The Court considered the claim of MATTHEW WEIDMAN,
youngest son of late MATTHEW WEIDMAN, Sr., for a certain mare and colt supposedly
the property of the estate, and his mother Mrs. Mary Weidman, the Admx.,consenting,
the mare and colt ware ordered delivered to him. The Court also allowedthe claim
of Margaret Weidman, a daughter of dec'd., for a certain cow.

(p.195) JOHN VALENTINE BEAGLEm an orphan child, was bound
out to Joshua Dasher, June, 1806.

(p.195) Last Will and Testament of WILLIAM LISTER HALL of
Effingham Co., dated Aug.29, 1803, probated in Suffolk Co. N.Y., July 21,1806.
Bequeaths all his estate to George Galphin Nowlan. Executor: William Joseph
Spencer of Savannah. Will signed and executed in New York City.

(p.196) MARY HICKMAN, relict of SPENCE COX, applies for administration on estate of said Cox, Aug.29, 1806; and was appointed Oct.6, 1806.

(p.196) MRS. MARY MAGDALENA GROMET, relict of JOHN GROMET,
applied for admn. on estate of her said husband Aug.29,1806,and was appointed as
Admx., Oct. 6, 1806.

(p.197) Last will and Testament of MARY ELIZABETH HEIDT, spin-
ster, of St. Peters Parish, Beaufort Dist. S.C., dated Mar.20, 1806; probated July
15, 1806 in Effingham Co. Gives all her estate to her daughter Eleanor Eliza Christina Meyerhoff and son Jacob Hollbrook and such other children as she may have
living at her death. Executors,Her uncle, Godlip Smith and John Kogler of Ga.
Witnesses: Hezekiah Winkler, John Burgamaster, Nicholas Winkler.

(p.198) MRS. ELIZABETH PORTER, relict of BENJAMIN PORTER, applies for admn. on his estate Nov.13, 1806,and was appointed Admx.,Feb.16,1807.

(p.200) James and Mary Shuman apply for administration on
estate of WILLIAM SHUMAN, deceased, April 10, 1807.

(p.200) Receipt by PAUL TASSING to Jonathan Backley, Admr. of estate of JOHN GEORGE BECKLY, Sr., for his share as an heir, dated Feb.17, 1807.

(p.201) Solomon Gruber applies for administration on estate of GEORGE GRUBER, dec'd., Aug.31, 1807. Granted July 25, 1808.

(p.201) William Morgan applies for administration on estate of LEWIS MORGAN, dec'd., Sept.2, 1807. Granted July 25, 1808.

(p.201) Emanuel Zeigler applies for administration on estate of JACOB LANG, deceased, Nov. 2, 1807.

(p.202) Benjamin Kennedy applies for administration of the estate of WILLIAM KENNEDY, his dec'd father, Feb.9, 1808. Granted July 25, 1808.

(p.203) Sarah and John Goldwire Jr., andJames King apply for administration on estate of James L. Goldwire, Feb.15, 1808. Granted July 25, 1808.

(p.205) Mrs. Sarah King, relict of COL. JOHN KING, dec'd., applies for administration on his estate May 23, 1808. Granted June 23, 1808.

(p.205) Last Will and Testament of JOHN ADAM METZGER, dec'd., dated April 28, 1808, probated May 16, 1808. Gives all his estate to hiswife Christina "late Christina Rahn". Executors: His father, John Metzger, brother Jacob Metzger. Witnesses: Christopher Gnann, Gottlieb Ernst, Mary Magdalena Metzger.

(p.209) Edmond Tyson applies for administration on estate of WILLIAM TYSON, dec'd., July 27, 1808. Granted Aug.29, 1808.

(p.209) Letters of Administration, granted Aug. 1, 1808, to Herman Crum and JamesPorter on estate of BENJAMIN PORTER, dec'd.

(p.210) Inventory of estate of JOHN KNIGHT, dec'd. (Editor's note: The estate being rather large,some extracts from same are given; inventories not usually abstracted). Total inventoried value of estate, $18,165.56. Includes 100 head of sheep $200; 52 slaves. No land listed. In a certificate attached, The widow as Admx., certifies that the inventory includes allthe personal property of the dec'd., and includes five certain slaves who should not have been listed they not being estate property but were part of a number of slaves conveyed Oct.23,1803 in trust to Thomas Gibbons and John Y. Noel by deed from John King and Sarah Weed recorded in Chatham Co., Sept.4, 1794. Under the Act of Dec.10,1807, she elects to take a child's part of the estate with the minor children.

(p.213) Sarah Goldwire, widow of JAMES L. GOLDWIRE, elects to take child's part of estate and notifies the other Admrs., John Goldwire Jr., and James

King, "they being the only other persons concerned", Oct. Term, 1808.

(p.214) Receipts dated Jan. 1, 1809, to Willis Spear, Executor of will of Moore Spear, dec'd., for their shares of estate in full, signed by JAMES SPEAR and BENJAMIN BLITCH.(Editor's note: The family name SPIER, an old Effingham County family, appears spelled in many places in these records as SPEER and SPEAR, but is one and the same family).

(p.214) CHRISTIAN G. WISENBAKER petitions the Court to appoint JOHN WISENBAKER as his Guardian, and he was appointed Jan. 2, 1809.

(p.217) Receipt dated Sept.12, 1799, by James Garrison to Noah Dyke for his part of a slave left to Noah Dykes, Rebecca Dykes, and Martha Dykes (now Garrison) by their deceased father (unnamed). On page 217, is a similar receipt of same date, signed by William Kelly for his part.

(p.217) The will of CHRISTIAN L. DASHER was probated Apr.3,1809 (This is not a record of the will but a statement in the court minutes).

(p.218) Solomon Gnann applies for administration of estate of MRS. CHRISTINA ELIZABETH MEYER, dec'd.,June 13, 1809. Granted Aug. 7, 1809.

(p.218) Bond of the heirs, viz., Matthew Riesser, John Grovenstein Elizabeth Rylander and Liddy Riesser, undated, binding themselves "to stand by" the division of estate of ISRAEL RIESER. Recorded July 18, 1809. On same page: Receipt dated Apr. 18, 1809, by or from Ann Barbara Rieser in full for her full share of estate of her dec'd husband ISRAEL RIESER.

(p.220) Jonathan Seckinger, Guardian of Gottlieb and Hannah Shub- treen, Receipt in full, undated, said Gottlieb and Hannah being minor children of Christian Shubtreen, dec'd) to John George Zitterauer and Christian Heidt, Trus- tees appointed by the dec'd for said children under his deed of gift June 30,1798

(p.222) Last Will and Testament of MATTHEW WEST of Goshen, St. Matthews Parish,Ga., planter, dated Dec. 18, 1775, probated Oct. 13, 1791, in Chatham County. Certified copy from that county recorded in Effingham Co. Gives to his wife Mary Magdalene West his whole estate for her lifetime, and at her death to go to his children (unnamed), except to his youngest daughter Christiana whenever she marries,"she to have two cows and calves over her portion with the others of my daughters." Executors: Wife and Rev. Christian Rabenhorst of Ebenez- er. Witnesses: Frederick Truetlin, John Keebler. Probated on the testimony of said Frederick Truetlin.

(p.223) Mary Hickman, Admr. of SPENCE COX estate, made her annual return Jan. 1, 1810. The Court on examining same, finds the estate has been wast- ed to an amount of or more than her portion. (From the Minutes).

(p.223) JOHN G. NEIDLINGER was appointed Receiver of Tax Returns, Jan. 1, 1810.

(p.225) William King Jr., applies for administration on estate of WILLIAM KING, Sr., March 16, 1810. Granted May 7, 1810.   (Editor's note: Statements like this one relative to applications for administration, are from the Court's minutes of the date shown. After an application was granted, it was then as now, necessary for the appointee to take the usual oath of office and give bond for the performance of his,her or their duties,and receive Letters of Administration before beginning to function. With few exceptions the oath and bond and Letters do not appear in these "Miscellaneous Records" books; and the Editor as a rule does not make any mention of same in these abstracts,they not having any genealogical significance.)

(p.225) John C. Cramer and John Waldhaeur Jr., apply for adminis- tration de bonis non on estate of MATTHEW WEIDMAN, dec'd., May 7, 1810.

(p.225) Cammel Tyson applies for administration on estate of GEOR DYKES,dec'd., May 7, 1810. Whereupon, caveat to his appointment was filed by Noa Dykes. "It appearing to the Court that the deceased died in Richmond County, the caveat was sustained" and the application dismissed.

(p.226) John C. Crowder was appointed Guardian of MATTHEW WEIDMAN Jr., orphan of MATTHEW WEIDMAN Sr., at said minor's request, May 7, 1810.

(p.226) Benjamin Kennedy was appointed Guardian of SARAH RYALL at her request, May 7, 1810.

(p.227) Gottlieb Ernst applies for administration on estate of MARY WEIDMAN (relict of Matthew Weidman Sr.), Sept.17,1810. Granted Jan. 7, 1811.

(p.227) Ann Sibley applies for administration on estate of her deceased husband, - - (blank) - Sibbly, Dec. 17, 1810.

(p.227) Receipt dated Sept.5, 1808, from Hardy Pitts to James Porter and Harmon Crum, Admrs. estate of BENJAMIN PORTER estate, for his share.

(p.227) Christian Truetlin applies for administration on estate of MARY RAVOT, dec'd., Jan. 7, 1811.

(p.230) Cynthia Holliday, relict of JOSEPH HOLLIDAY, applies for administration on his estate, Apr. 30, 1811.

(p.231) Sarah Goldwire, William King for himself and minor sister, Joseph King and James King, apply for leave to sell negroes belonging to the estate of WILLIAM KING, Sr., May 6, 1811.

(p.231) Sabra Wheeler, relict of JAMES WHEELER, applies for administration on his estate, July 10, 1811. Granted Aug. 10, 1811.

(p.231) Johanna Sherraus, relict of JOHN SHERRAUS, applies for administration on his estate, July 15, 1811.

(p.232) Mary Liemberger, relict of ISRAEL LEINBERGER, applies for administration on his estate Sept.27, 1811. Granted Oct. 27, 1811.

(p.234) Last Will and Testament of ANN CHRISTIANA DASHER of Effingham Co., dated Jan. 1, 1802; probated June 8, 1811. Bequeaths to grand-daughter, Mary Ulmer $500.00; to grandson, John Wisenbaker $500.00; to grandson, Christian Wisenbaker $500.00; to said grandchildren, $300.00, jointly; to Christian L.Dasher certain negroes and 200 acre tract of land and 100-acre tract. Residue of estate to her seven grandchildren, viz., Elizabeth, Christian, John, Rosina, Samuel, Catherine and Gottlieb Dasher. She directs that if her grandchildren (the children of John Wisenbaker) or any of them calls for a settlement or any portion of the estate of her late husband CHRISTIAN DASHER, then the part of such grandchild or grandchildren doing same shall descend to her other grandchildfen (children of her son Christian L.Dasher). Executors: Son, Christian L. Dasher, and grandson Christian H. Dasher. Witnesses: John Spencer J.I.C., Samuel Spencer, John Russell. Christian H. Dasher qualified as executor, Sept.20, 1811.

(p.236) Salome Gaffney applies for administration of JAMES GAFFNEY estate, Feb. 17, 1812. Granted March 21, 1812.

(p.236) Susannah Zipperer applies for administration of estate of CHRISTIAN J. ZIPPERER, dec'd., Apr.27, 1812. Granted June 3, 1812.

(p.236) Martha Slater applies for administration on estate of WILLIAM J. SLATER, dec'd., June 3, 1812. Granted July 27, 1812.

(p.238) Heirs of ISRAEL REISSER dec'd., receipt John Christopher Gugel and Benjamin Kennedy, Executors, for their full shares of estate December 16, 1811; signed by John Grovenstine, Matthew Reisser, Elizabeth Rylander, Lydia Reis-

(p.242) Order for division of estate of MATTHEW WHITEMAN, (ser. granted on the application of John Waldhauer, Jr., Jan.4, 1813. (From Minutes).

(p.242) Solomon and Benjamin Dasher qualify as Executors of will of JOHN MARTIN DASHER, dec'd., Jan.4, 1813 (from the Minutes).

(p.242) John Gotlieb Fetzer applies for administration on estate of JONATHAN FETZER, dec'd., Jan.7, 1813. Granted March 1, 1813.

(p.242) John Wisenbaker and C.H. Dasher apply for administration on estate of PHILLIP DENSLER, dec'd., Jan.7, 1813.

(p.242) Mrs. Mary Grovenstein applies for administration on estate of JOHN GROVENSTEIN, dec'd., Jan.7, 1813. Granted March 1, 1813.

(p.243) Last Will and Testament of JOHN MARTIN DASHER, of Effingha Co., dated Nov. 9, 1812; probated Jan. 4, 1813. Gives to his son Joshua Dasher, 197 acres in said county, known as the 15-mile House purchased lately from James England and sold to said Joshua conditionally, now devised in fee simple; also 200 acres known as Dasher's Old Cowpens and 300 acres adjoining, and 900 acres of pine land adjoining; also 1000 acres adjoining the pine land, six slaves and 10 shares of stock in The Planters Bank of Georgia, which also had been given said Joshua conditionally but now given unconditionally. To son, Solomon Dasher, testator's homeplace together with adjoining tracts, and 12 slaves. To grandson, Thomas Dasher 8 slaves when he becomes 17 years of age, and 10 shares of the 50 shares he owns in said Planters Bank; and to testator's daughter, Naomi Wylly (wife of William C. Wylly) 9 slaves. To grandchildren (the children of his daughter, Susannah late Susannah Franklin, 8 slaves when 16 years of age, and 10 shares said stock. Also, he gives ten shares of said stock to his grandchildren Elizabeth and Henrietta Shaffer and John Robert Franklin, jointly. He gives to said John R. Franklin the testator's houses and two town lots he owns in Savannah. To grandchildren, Thomas Dasher, Elizabeth and Henrietta Shaffer, J.R. Franklin and Sarah Ann Wyllgy 150 acres of land, together with 400 acres adjoining, also 700 acres on Cross Swamp in said Effingham County. To his son-in-law, Wm. C. Wylly, 25¢ also same amount to his son-in-law Selby Franklin, and same amounts to each of his daughters in-law, Hannah Stewart and Dolly Dasher. Residue of estate to be sold and proceeds divided between said Solomon Dasher, Naomi Wylly, Thomas Dasher, Elizabeth Shaffer, Henrietta Shaffer, John R. Franklin and Joshua Dasher. Executors: Son, Solomon Dasher, and brother, Benjamin Dasher. Witnesses: George Powledge, Joel Kieffer and David Leimberger.

(p.248) Last Will and Testament of HANNAH GRINER, of said county, dated Dec. 9, 1811, probated Feb.5, 1813. Gives to grand-daughter Sophia Griner (daughter of Andrew Griner) a feather-bed. Balance of estate is given to testatrix's three sons Solomon, Andrew and John Godlip Griner. She directs that if said John G. does not claim his legacy in seven years after her decease then same is to go to the said Sophia. Executors: David Gugle, George Galphin Nowland. Witnesses: William J. Spencer, John Wisenbaker and John Waldhauer, J.P.

(p.249) The following administrators and Executors qualified as such March 1st, 1813, and received Letters of Administration or Letters Testamentary: Mrs. Sarah Flerl as Admx. on estate of Israel Flerl; John Neidlinger as Executor of John G. Neidlinger; David Gugel as Executor of Hannah Griner; Nancy Crawford as Executor of Mary Crawford, dec'd.

(p.251) George Powledge was appointed Guardian of Hannah Steiner; and Thomas Mock was appointed Guardian of Henry L. Grovenstein at the latter's request, both appointments made March 7, 1813. And on same date, John G. Zitterau and John Kogler qualified as Executors of will of JOHN GEORGE ZITTERAUER, dec'd.

(p.252) Division of estate of MATTHEW WEITMAN, dec'd., made Jan. 19, 1813, by partitioners, to-wit: Property divided into shares and drawn for, and Share #1, consisting of 500 acres pineland, drawn by Sarah Weidman; #2, consisting of part of homeplace, 50 acres, drawn by Lewis Bird; #3, 60 acres oak land, drawn by John Waldhauer; Matthew Weidman drew #4, being 202½ acres lot of land in Baldwin County; Lewis Weidman, #5, consisting of 39 acres of the homeplace. Said Sarah and Matthew being minors, were represented by their guardians.

(p.263) Last Will and Testament of JOHN GEORGE ZITTERAUER of Effingham Co., dated Sept.5, 1812; probated March 1, 1813. Gives cow and calf to Rev. John Ernst Bergman; to Hannah Shuptrine, one heifer. Residue of estate to wife Anna and sons John Godlieb and Solomon Zitterauer, and daughter Hannah wife of John Christopher Miller. Executors: Son, John G. Zitterauer, and friend John Kogler. Witnesses: David Gugle, John Waldhauer, Wm. J. Spencer.

(p.254) Last Will and Testament of JOHN G. NEIDLINGER of said county, dated Oct. 17, 1807, probated March 1, 1813. Gives to his wife Hannah all his estate for her lifetime except a silver watch given to his younger son, Samuel Neidlinger, and shotgun to his oldest son John. At the wife's death the estate on hand to be divided between sons, John and Samuel (not now of age), and the residue to divided between his children John, Samuel, Anna wife of Godhelf I. Niese, and Emelia Neidlinger. Executors: Wife, Hannah, son John, son-in-law Niess. Witnesses: Matthew and Daniel Burksteiner, Jonathan G. Fetzer, John George Mingledorff.

(p.256) Last Will and Testament of MARSY CRAWFORD of Effingham
County, dated May 11, 1812, probated March 1st, 1813. Gives to her grandchildren
John, Nellie and Pollie, the heirs of her son David Jones alias David Crawford,
12 head of cattle. Residue of estate to her sister Nancy and her children, Martha,
Frances and Thomas. Executor: Sister, Nancy Crawford. Witnesses: Thomas Hurst
and Joseph Brewer.
          (p.259) William McGaghagan applies for administration of estate
of JOSEPH BREWER, dec'd., April 16, 1813. Granted July 26, 1813.
          (p.261) Leave to sell a slave was granted July 5, 1813, to Jon-
athan Gotlieb Fetzer, Admr. of Jonathan Fetzer estate.
          (p.272) Henry L. Grovenstein, Admr. "by marriage" of estate of
HENRY LEWIS BUNTZ, dec'd., certifies that on Nov.22, 1813, he delivered to SIMON
BUNTZ, son and heir of dec'd., certain slaves and notes of the estate in full for
said son's share of estate, in presence of Jonathan Rahn. Receipt attached for
same signed on said date by said Simon Buntz.
          (p.273) The Last Will and Testament of JOHN MIKELL EXLEY was duly
probated and Mrs. Elizabeth Exley qualified as Executrix of same, Jan. 3, 1814.
          (p.276) Last Will and Testament of JOHN M. EXLEY of Effingham Co.,
planter, dated Oct. 9, 1813, probated Jan. 3, 1814. Appoints his wife Elizabeth and
to his son Solomon Exley as executors, and directs that his estate be divided between his said wife and children (unnamed), except that his son John is to have
only 25¢. Witnesses: Jonathan Backly, Thomas Mock, Emanuel Rahn J.P.
          (p.278) Last Will and Testament of JOHN METZGER of Effingham Co.,
dated Jan. 6, 1814, probated Jan. 10, 1814. Gives to Mrs. Christiana Gnann, 200
acres in Wilkinson County and two cows and stock of hogs. Residue of estate to his
son Jacob Metzger. Witnesses: Christian Biddenbach and Christopher Frederick Bergman. The will not designating an executor, J. J. Metzger was appointed administrator with the will annexed, March 7, 1814.
          (p.280) John G. Fetzer was appointed administrator of estate of
JOHN COOK, dec'd., March 7, 1814 (Minutes); and on same date Gottlieb Seckinger
was appointed Guardian of Catherine and Christiana Seckinger, minors.
          (p.280) John Wisenbaker and C. H. Dasher applies for administra-
tion on estate, with will annexed, of PHILLIP DENSLER, March 7,1814. Granted,May 2,
          (p.282) Receipt dated June 21, 1814, from Solomon Dasher (1814.
to Benjamin Dasher, Executor, in full for his share of estate of his dec'd father
JOHN MARTIN DASHER. Also, Receipt same date, by William C. Wylly for his 1/5th
part of proceeds of sales of land devised by the will to his (testator's) grandchildren "one of whom was Sarah Ann Wylly and to whom I am an heir"; receipt given
to Solomon and Benjamin Dasher, Executors.
          (p.283) Certificate of settlement dated Sept.3, 1814, signed by
David and Mary Metzger,Admrs. of MICHAEL REISSER estate, certifying that they have
duly settled with James Riesser, son and only heir of dec'd., by giving him 200
acres of land lying on the Three Runs and Deep branch which had been granted dec'd.
Receipt attached signed by said James Reisser.
          (p.285) Series of Receipts in re: JOSHUA LOPER estate, viz:
(1st) Receipt, undated, by James Hudson given to Asa and Abel G. Loper, Executors,
for $10.00 in full for his share. (2nd) Abel G. Loper of Effingham Co., to Asa Lo-
per of Effingham Co., by bill of sale dated Feb.27, 1811, transfers all his interest in two slaves belonging to the estate; (3rd) Asa Loper to A. G. Loper, Executor,
dated May 23, 1811, for his full share of the estate, consisting of 600 acres in
Effingham Co., granted dec'd Sept.21, 1796 for 1000 acres,lying on Big Reedy branch.
(4th) On page 287, Receipt from Asa Loper to Asa and A.G. Loper, Executors, dated
May 23, 1811, for his full share, being 300 acres in Effingham Co., granted the
deceased, Oct. 10, 1798. (5th) On same page, Receipt by A.G. Loper to Asa Loper,
Executor, same date, for 400 acres being the s.e. part of 1000 acres in said county, on Big Reedy Creek, granted dec'd Sept.21, 1796. (6th) Same page, Receipt dated Dec.25, 1810, from Abby Goolsby to said Executors for her share in full of the
estate of her father Joshua Loper, Sr. (7th) Same page, Receipt dated May 23,1811,

from C. Loper to the said Executors in full for his share of the real estate of deceased, his share being 1000 acres in Effingham County granted dec'd Sept. 21, 1796, located on Little Ogeechee River. (8th) Receipt dated May 23, 1811, from John Powers to the said Executors in full for his share of the lands of the dec'd his share being 475 acres granted dec'd Sept. 21, 1796, located then in Effingham but now in Bulloch County on Ogeechee River and Caney branch.

(p.285) Noel Tison applies for administration on estate of GEORGE TISON, dec'd., Nov. 7, 1814. At the same time, John McLogan was appointed Admr. on estate of DR. JACOB SCHRODER, deceased.

(p.286) ROSETTA SCHROEDER, orphan child of JACOB SHROEDER and wife was ordered bound out to E. F. and Ann Mary Triebner, Nov. 7, 1814.

(p.288) CHARLES RYALL manumits (frees) a certain slave called Skip which his late dec'd father had desired should be freed, directing the said Chas. and Samuel (also a son) to protect him , etc., Oct. 2, 1806.

(p.290) James Anderson having applied for administration on estate of B. Gloner, dec'd., MRS. HANNAH M. GLONER objected, whereupon the Court appointed her as Admx., May 1st, 1815.

(pp. 293-4) The following matters attended to by the Court at its regular meeting held Nov. 6, 1815: (1) John Wisenbaker and Christian H. Dasher were appointed Admrs. with will annexed on estate of Phillip Densler, dec'd. (2) Benjamin Kennedy, Admr. of William Kennedy, applied for dismission; (3) Christian Dasher and Lewis Bird were appointed Admrs. estate of JAMES BIRD, dec'd; (4) Geo. F. Gyer as greatest creditor applies for administration on estate of JOHN D. MOOR, dec'd, and was later on Jan. 1, 1816, duly appointed. (5) Joel Tyson, Admr. of George Tyson estate, applied for dismission; (6) James applies for Admn. on estate of GABRIEL WILSON, dec.d; (7) John Wisenbaker, Guardian of Christian Wisenbaker, applies for dismission. (8) Christian Zipperer was appointed Admr. of Benjamin Gloner estate. (9) Ann Mary Triebner and Godlip Ernest were appointed Admrs. of estate of CHRISTOPHER FREDERICK TRIEBNER, dec'd.

(p.295) Receipt dated Nov. 1, 1815, from Sathey? Parker to Jonathan Seckinger, Guardian of the heirs of CHRISTIAN SHUPTRINE dec'd., in full "for my part of the estate".

(p.295) Last Will and Testament of PHILLIP DENSLER of Effingham Co. dated March 20, 1811; probated Nov. 25, 1815. Gives to wife Ann "in case she does not marry during the minority of my children", all of his estate; "and if she then marries after the children are grown shall shall have a child's part". To his children Frederick, Henry, Joseph and John Washington Densler to have the whole estate subject to wife's part as aforesaid, same to be divided to each as he becomes of age.Executors: Wife, Anne, and friends John H. Wisenbaker,Christian H. Densler. Witnesses: John Moore, William Hines, David Hines J.P.

(p.300) Last Will and Testament of CHRISTIAN L. DASHER of Eff.Co.; dated Oct. 18, 1808, probated April 3, 1809. Gives to sons Christian Herman Dasher and Godlip Dasher his homeplace consisting of 400 acres, subject to life estate given his wife Elizabeth. Gives to daughters Elizabeth, Rosannah and Catherine, 500 acres, also 200 acres pine land, and the lot of land he had drawn in the late state land lottery. Devises a certain slave to his daughter Elizabeth. Residue to be used by wife as long as remains a widow, and then or after her death (as the case may be) to be divided between said five children; and in the meantime, son Christian H. Dasher shall manage the property left for wife's use. Executors: Son, Christian H.Dasher, and John Waldhauer, Sr. Witnesses: Wm. J. Spencer, Samuel Fitzpatrick, James Anderson. Executors qualified April 3, 1809. Will and probate not recorded until Dec. 17, 1815, the recording having been overlooked.

(p.304) Christian Dasher and Lewis Bird apply for Admn. with will annexed on estate of JAMES BIRD, dec'd, Jan.1, 1816. Granted March 4, 1816. The instrument called a will reads as follows: "Bro.William: Give Joseph to Dorcas if I should not see you at my death. Sept. 1814. (signed) J.Bird."

(p.308) MATTHEW COLSON in his affidavit dated Jan. 9, 1816, says that in a conversation he had with the late JOHN D. MOORE, the latter told him that the cattle he bought at the sale of the Mrs. Jennette Clement property was for his father; and that he, affiant, then asked him who was his father and he replied that his father was George F. Geyer.

(p.309) Thomas Wylly petitions the Court for an order directing Mrs. Hannah Glover, Admx. of SOLOMON GROVER estate, to make him titles to lot 91 in 9th district of Wilkinson Sounty and lot 23 in the 18th dist. of Baldwin County which he had purchased of deceased in his lifetime, taking the latter's bond for title to make deeds to said lots to him. Citation was ordered to issue, March 4, 1816; and at the next term of court July 1, 1818, the petition was granted and the Admx. directed to make titles as prayed.

(p.313) John Kogler and Israel Weitman apply for administration on estate of JAMES GAFFNEY,dec'd, May 7, 1816. Granted July 1st, 1816.

(p.314) Receipts for legacy to William J.Spencer, Executor of will of CAPT. JOHN SPENCER, dec'd, viz: (1) Dated Jan.17,1814,at Savannah, signed by Susannah Rogers, for her legacy in full. (2) Dated, Effingham Co., May 17,1816, signed by Mary and Archibald Wilkins in full for her legacy. (3) Dated Apr.19,1816, Effingham Co., signed by Anne Spencer for her legacy in full.

(p.316) The will of SAMUEL KRONDE? was duly probated and Letters Testamentary order to issue, Sept. 2, 1816.

(p.317) Statement signed by Edwin Baker, dated at Milledgeville, Nov.29, 1816, stating that he happened at the house of Jacob Darden in Warren County sometime in 1812 where "he assisted in laying out a Mr. SOLOMON GRINER, a tailor by trade, who died there supposedly of consumption". Witness: George G. Nowlan. On the basis of this statement, David Gugel and George G. Nowlán, Executors of will of MRS. HANNAH GRINER, were granted leave to divide the property (or inheritance) of Said Solomon Griner between his heirs, Nov. 4, 1816.

(p.317) WILLIAM BLAND of the 4th District, Wilkinson County, in his petition of record, applies to the Court praying that Sabrina Wheeler,the widow of JAMES WHEELER and executrix of his will, be directed to make him a deed for land lot 180, 4th dist. of Wilkinson Co., in terms of a Bond for Title given him the deceased, then in life, on Feb. 26, 1816.   Filed Nov.4, 1816. At the same she applies for dismission.   Granted May 5, 1817, and she was accordingly authorized and directed to make deed as prayed.

(p.319) PHOEBE WHEELER asks that he mother, MRS. SABRINA WHEELER, be appointed her Guardian. Signature witnessed by Wm. Bland. Granted Nov.4,181(

(p.321) Last Will and Testament of SAMUEL KRAUS of Effingham Co., dated Jan. 29, 1814; probated Sept.2, 1816. He gives to Martin Dasher ¼ of his household goods, and the remainder of same to MRS. S. Flerk and her heirs by her former husband Israel Flerl, Mary Waldhauer wife of John Waldhauer Sr., and Elizabeth wife of Benjamin Dasher. Executors: John Waldhauer and Benj. Dasher. Witnesses: John Neidlinger, William Shrimpt, Samuel Dasher, Gottlieb Ernet, J.P.

(p.326) Rebecca Baas applies for administration on estate of SAMUEL BAAS (sic) of said county,dec'd.,Jan.1,1817. Granted May 5, 1817.

(p.328) Last Will and Testament of GEORGE G. NOWLAN of Effingham Co., dated at Milledgeville, Ga., Dec.16,1816; probated Feb. 3, 1817. Directs his estate be divided between his wife Hannah and his four children Anna Elizabeth, Margaret Glonvina, Amanda Georgiana and "the infant son born since I left home and so far as I know,is not yet named". Executors: Friends, John MacPherson Berrien and David Gugel, they also to be Testamentary Guardians for said children,minors. Witnesses: E. Emanuel, Joel Crawford, John Wisenbaker J.P.

(p.329) Last Will and Testament of WILLIS SPEIR of said county, dated Sept.16, 1811; probated March 3, 1817. "Lends" unto his wife Millie for her lifetime or widowhood the entire estate including 305 acres adjoining Wm. Hurst, three negroes, live-stock, etc. After her death, 155 acres of the plantation to go to Henry Strickland together with one slave, and to James Strickland one feath(

bed and furniture. Residue after wife's death to go to James Speir, Patience Tillis, Newet Speir, Willis Speir. He gives to Elizabeth Parrish $1.00. Executors: Robert Burton and James Speir. Witnesses: William Hurst, Benjamin Hill.

(p.333) Leave to sell lot 227, 23rd dist. of Wilkinson County was granted to the Admrs. of the C. F. Triebner estate, May 5, 1817.

(p.335) Rebecca Baas was appointed Guardian for Rosannah and Celina S. Baas, minors over age of 14, Aug. 30, 1817.

(p.336) Last Will and Testament of JOHN BERRY of Eff. Co., dated Aug.18, 1817; probated Sept. 1, 1817. Devises to his wife Mary his whole estate for her lifetime as a support for her and their two youngest children Benajah and Obediah. After her death he directs the personal property except the negroes, be sold and proceeds divided between said sons and their daughter Salome and his grandchildren Maria and Louisa Metzger (children of daughter Naomi, late wife of John Metzger). After wife's death, slaves to be hired out until the children arrive of age and then be divided between them including the said Salome, wife of Emanuel Rahn. All real estate to go to the said two sons. Executors: Emanuel Rahn, Benajah Berry, Gottlieb Ernst. Witnesses: Ephriam Kieffer, John Exley.

(p.341) The will of ERNST ZITTERAUER was probated Nov. 3, 1817.

(p.342) The will of ELIZABETH EXLEY was probated May 4, 1818, and Jonathan Rahn qualified as executor.

(p.342) The will of JAMES KING was probated May 4, 1818.

(p.342) The will of CHRISTOPHER EMHOFF was probated May 4, 1818.

(p.343) Benjamin Canady, Admr. of WILLIAM KENNEDY estate was dismissed, May 4, 1818.

(p.342) The estate of JAMES GOLDWIRE was ordered divided on the petition of John Goldwire, Sarah the wife of John Tyson, and Thomas Wylly and Sarah his wife, May 4, 1818.

(p.344) Last Will and Testament of CHRISTOPHER EMHOFF of Effingham Co., dated Nan.14, 1818, probated March 2, 1818. Bequeaths to Eliza Crew of Burke County all his estate. Witnesses: John Leimberger and William Schrimp.

(p.346) Last Will and Testament of MRS. ELIZABETH EXLEY of Eff.Co., dated Sept.30, 1815; probated May 4, 1818. Gives $10 to the Lutheran Church at Ebenezer; to Rev. John Ernst Bergman, $7.00; to Ann,the wife of John Gnann,$5.00; to Elizabeth Eppinger, daughter of John Eppinger, $5.00; to Susannah and Salome Rahn, daughters of Jonathan Rahn, all of her bedding; to Mrs. Rahn, all her wearing apparrel and feather-pillows; to Christina, wife of Jacob Gnann, two pewter basins and a Dutch oven; to Mrs. Ann Barbara Reisser, one pewter basin; to Christina Mock, one pewter bason; to Emanuel Rahn,a cow. Residue of estate to Jonathan Rahn. Executors: Jonathan Rahn and Emanuel Rahn. Witnesses: Jonathan Rahn, John Frickenger, Jacob Gnann, Jr.

(p.351) JOHN CHARLTON waselected Clerk of the Court of Ordinary,and qualified June 6, 1818, and assumed office.

(p.351) James Herman Crum applies for administration on estate of HERMAN CRUM, late of Effingham Co.,July 20, 1818. Granted Sept. 7, 1818.

(p.355) Re: Estate and will of JOHN BERRY: Affidavit of Gottlieb Ernst of Effingham County, made in court Oct. 29, 1817, says that he was sent for by the late JOHN BERRY to write his will, and that in writing same he named"only two children of the daughter of Mr. Berry, late wife of Jacob Metzger, but that he (affiant) was told by Mr. Berry'the children of Naomi,wife of Jacob Metzger', and I seeing no more than two in the room" he wrote their names, not realizing there was another, viz: John Benajah Metzger, then at David Metzger's. Affiant certifies that said John Benajah was inteded to be included in the will along with the other two children of his parents. Affidavit ordered recorded.

(p.359) Bill of Sale, gift, dated July 4, 1818, from JAMES PORTER of Eff.Co., to his grand-daughter Lupina Ann Reisser, conveying a slave. Witnesses: Lewis S. and Hannah Grovenstine.

(p.360) George Foy applied for administration on estateof CHRISTIAN BETESBACK, dec'd., Sept.7, 1818. Granted Nov. 2, 1818.

(pp.360-1) LastWill and Testament of SAMUEL BAAS of Effingham County, dated Sept. 22, 1814; probated Feb.2, 1818, in Chatham Co. Certified copy from Chatham County recorded here. Gives to wife Rebecca, his homeplace on the Louisville Road for her lifetime and then to be sold and proceeds divided between his three daughters, Ann, Rosanna and Serena Sarah. The slaves, live-stock &c., to be disposed of the same way, and proceeds to be divided between his son Daniel Alexander Baas and said three daughters, except his land in Bryan County which shall be the property of his said son. Directs his Executor to see after the house and lot in Charleston, S.C., left him by his late uncle, Thomas Buckle in the latter's will, and the executor to sell same and divide proceeds between said children. Executor: Zara Powers, Esq., he also to be Testamentary Trustee for the said wife and children. No witnesses.

(p.367) Marsey (Marcia?) Moore applies for administration on the estate of JOHN MOORE, dec'd., Nov.2, 1818. Granted Jan. 4, 1819.

(p.368) Bond dated May 4, 1818, of John Goldwire, Guardian of Maria and Caroline, minor heirs of JAMES GOLDWIRE, dec'd.

(p.368) Thomas Wylly and his wife Sarah, John Tison and Sarah his wife, John Goldwire as Guardian of Maria and Caroline Goldwire,minors, apply for division of the personal property of JAMES GOLDWIRE, dec'd., May 4, 1816. Granted Nov.28, 1816, and partitioners appointed.

(p.374) Richard Richardson of Savannah applies for administration on estate of JOSEPH BEVAN, dec'd., Jan. 29, 1819. Granted April 3, 1819. And on same date the Court attended to the following other business (Minutes): Timothy Gnann applied for admn. on JOHN BECK estate; John Duggar applied for administration on estate of DAVID CANNADY, and same was granted May 3, 1819.

(p.374) Jonathan Seckinger and Ann Catherine Shrimp apply for admn. on estate of WILLIAM SHRIMP, dec'd., Feb.15, 1819. Granted May 8, 1819.

(p.374) Inventory of Estate of COL. GEORGE G. NOWLIN dated March 10, 1819, shows he owned at his death 22 slaves. Total estate valued at $13760.00.

(p.376) Joseph Beck filed his caveat to the appointment of Timothy Gnann as Admr. of the JOHN BECK estate, Feb. 26, 1819.

(p.380) The will of JOSEPH BEVAN was probated May 3, 1819.

(p.380) The will of JONATHAN GOTLIEB FETRE? was probated May 3,1819

(p.381) Mrs. Alisthea Scruggs as nearest of kin applies for admn. on estate of WILLIAM CAPAM?, late in the U.S.Army, May 3, 1819. Granted July 5,1819.

(p.381) The will of JESSE SCRUGGS was probated May 8, 1819.

(p.381) Sarah King was appointed Guardian of GEORGE KING,MORGAN KING and EVELINE KING; minor children of JOHN KING, dec'd., at their request (they being over 15), May 3, 1819.

(p.387) Last Will and Testament of JOSEPH BEVAN, dated Dec.17, 1818; probated May 3, 1819. He designates his son Joseph N. Bevan as executor and directs that Richard Richardson of Savannah be the temporary administrator on his estate until said son arrives. He directs that all his debts be paid. Makes no bequests or devises to any one. Will executed in Savannah. Witnesses: F. D. Petit DeVillers N.P., and N. A. Adams.

(p.383) Timothy Gnann was appointed Admr. of John Beck estate, and John Mallett was appointed temporary Admr. on Daniel Mallett estate; and Solomon Hinely was appointed temporary Admr. on John Bittenback estate, May 3, 1819.

(p.388) Last Will and Testament of JESSE SCRUGGS of Eff. Co., dated Oct.28, 1818, probated May 3, 1819. Gives to wife Alethea and hisfour children Elizabeth Henrietta, MaryAnn, John Frederick and Richard Sisson Scruggs, all his estate in Effingham Co. To said two sons, the land lot in 8th dist. Wilkinson County drawn by Joseph Pannell, also his lands in Screven Co. To his eldest son, James H.P.Scruggs, 6 slaves and 300 acres on Ogeechee River granted Stephen Sasser, and a land lot in 23rd dist. of Wilkinson Co.,drawn by Wm.Wright. Executors: Wife and Richard Scruggs,John Goldwire. Witnesses: Gross Scruggs Sr.,Hugh Graham, Christopher G. White.

(p.391) Last Will and Testament of JOHN KOGLER, late a member or Justice of this (the Inferior) Court, was probated, June 2, 1819, and on the same date the Executors Gottlieb Ernst and Israel Weidman qualified.

(p.393) Last Will and Testament of JONATHAN GOTLIEB FETZER of Effingham Co., dated Dec. 20, 1818; probated May 3, 1819. Devises to his wife Anna Magdalena the fifty acres on Blue Bluff he received from her father (unnamed) also the household goods and a life-estate in his homeplace. To son, John Gottlieb Fetzer, 200 acres being testator's homeplace subject to wife's life estate. To his daughter, Lydia Spates, wife of (blank) Spates, a confectioner of Savannah, 200 acres located at the head of Whitehead branch in Effingham Co., also a town lot in Ebenezer. Executor: John G. Fetzer. Witnesses: Israel Weitman, George Foy and Gottlieb Ernst.

(p.405) From the Minutes of the Court's regular term held July 5, 1819: (1) Letters Testamentary were issued to the executors on the will of JOHN KOGLER. (2) The will of J. G. Fetzer was duly probated and the executor qualified. (3) The will of Christopher Imhoff was duly probated and Henry Crew of Burke County qualified as Admr. with will annexed. (4) Gottlieb G. Ernst was appointed Guardian for Johanna Ernst, Christina and Richard Ernet, grandchildren of JONATHAN RAHN, dec'd. (5th) John Dugger was appointed Guardian of ALLEN CANNADY son of the late David Cannady. (6th) John Staley was summoned to show cause why the Court should not appoint a guardian for his son William Staley,"the Court not considering him a proper person".

(p.413) Last Will and Testament of JOHN KOGLER of Effingham Co., dated Feb. 27, 1818; probated July 5, 1819, with Codicil dated March 12, 1819. Bequeaths to Valentine Kesler 140 acres and cattle; to Margaret Becktley, 110 acres being his homeplace granted him,the dec'd., Jan. 13, 1786, also 200 acres granted Aug.8, 1792, to Martin Dasher Sr.; also certain household goods; to Gratiosa Weitman, daughter of Jedediah Weitman dec'd., the testator's two town lots in Ebenezer. Residue of estate including 600 acres to be sold and proceeds to be divided one-half to the children of John Hinely Sr., and one-half to Valentine Kesler, Elizabeth Fetzer wife of Gottlieb Fetzer, and Gratiosa Weitman. Executors: Friends, Gottlieb Ernst, Israel Weitman, John Neidlinger. Witnesses: David Helmly, Gottlieb Zitterauer, Benjamin Dasher. The Codicil directs that if he is a fortunate drawer in the Land Lottery the land so drawn to be sold and one-third of proceeds to go to Margaret Bechtley, and two-thirds to put out an interest for benefit of Lewis Hinely, youngest son of late John Hinely, and for John G. Kesler son of Valentine Kesler, until they become of age,then paid to them.

(END OF BOOK)
Note: The various bonds and returns of administrators, guardians and executors, with few exceptions, not abstracted.

******

DEED BOOK A--B
Effingham County

Editor's Note: Before publishing the next book, Book "C" of Miscellaneous Records in the Ordinary's office of Effingham County, GGM will publish the first deed book in the office of Clerk Superior Court. This first book is now designated as Book A-B; having been rebound in more recent years and laminated by the State Dept.of Archives & History, it would seem that original Books "A" and "B" have been re-bound together. Deed records in Effingham date from 1786 - about four years earlier than those in the Ordinary's office. This deed book is contemporary with the "Miscellaneous Records" book just concluded above.

(p.1) Commissioners of Confiscated Estates to WILLIAM CONE, Esq., of Effingham County. Deed dated Feb. 23, 1786, conveying as a gift from the State

said land lying on the Great Ogeechee River originally surveyed for Thomas Blacky
and confiscated as the property of William Powell, a person banished from the
State as an enemy to the State under the Act of Confiscation and Attainder.   It
is recited that the said Cone "has rendered the State some extraordinary services"
and that the General Assembly had by resolution adopted Feb.22, 1786, directed
the Commissioners to make him title to said property as a gift for his services.
Witnesses: -(blank)- Lanier and George Threadcraft, J.P.

       (p.3) RUDOLPH STROHAKER and wife Elizabeth of Savannah, to SAMUEL
RYALL of Effingham Co. Deed dated Jan. 19, 1786, for 250 acres lyingin two tracts.
Witnesses: J. Cuyler and Samuel Bowen.

       (p.11) JAMES COOK to WILLIAM PORTER, both of Eff.Co. Deed dated June
27, 1786, for 50 acres on south side Great Ogeechee River, being partof 200 acres
granted grantor in 1786. Witnesses: Benj.Lanier J.P., Wm.Holzendorf J.P.

       (p.12) JAMES COOK of Eff.Co., planter, to his childfen, Judea Bishop,
Lucia Braddock, the heirs ofJames Cook Jr., and Tabby Johnson and John Cook, Benjamin
Cook, Henry Cook,Polly Bennett and Lewis Cook. Bill of Sale (gift), dated Sept. 16,
1786, for his household goods, cattle, horses, hogs, sheep and one slave. Witnesses:
Thomas McCall Sr., John Rawls, George McCall Sr.

       (p.16) JESSE WILSON,planter, to WILLIAM THORNHILL,planter,both of
Eff.Co. Deed dated Nov.21, 1786, for 100 acres adj. Jacob Gnann, insaid county.
Witnesses: Thomas Lane, Bryant Lane. Probated Nov.23,1786,before J.G.Neidlinger CSC.

       (p.20) EMANUEL KIEFFER of Bethany district, Eff.Co.,planter, and
Anna Barbara his wife, to CHRISTRAIN SHUBTREIN, planter, of Eff.Co. Deed dated July
22, 1786, for 90 acres in Ebenezer District, granted Theobald Kieffer Dec.2,1757,
and inherited by said Emanuel. Witnesses: Samuel Kraus and David Steiner.

       (p.22) SARAH MIZELL, planter, to LUKE MIZELL, voth of Eff.Co. Deed
dated Nov. 10, 1786, for 200 acres on south side Ogeechee River. Witnesses: Francis Jones, James Williams.

       (p.23) BALTHASAR REISER of Bethany, planter, and Mary his wife, to
JOHN ADAM TRUETLIN of Ebenezer. Deed dated June 12, 1767, for 200 acres adjoining
Martin Dasher, and granted Dec.4, 1759. Wit: Samuel Turney?, Thomas Morris.

       (p.24) JOHN ADAM TRUETLIN and Ann Margaret his wife, of St.Matthews
Parish to DANIEL ZETTLER of same parish. Deed dated Dec.4, 1773, for 200 acres in
said parish adj. Martin Dasher, granted Belthasar Reiser Dec.4, 1759 and deeded
by him to grantor June 12, 1767.

       (p.28) JOSEPH WILLIAM SPENCER of Abercorn, Eff.Co., to his wife
DOROTHY SPENCER. Instrument dated July 7, 1786, empowering her to make her own will
as she sees fit, disposing of the property she received from her former husband
Henry Cuyler and of the inheritance she received by the death of her father,Peter
Miller. Witnesses: W. Lewden and Clement Martin Jr.

       (p.29) JONATHAN AHNSTORPH of Eff.Co. and his wife Christiana Eliza-
beth, to JACOB HOFFMAN, hatter, of Eff.Co. Deed conveying 50 acres adj. Leonard
Kraus, George Kogler, Carl Flerl. Witnesses: Thomas and Abial Schweighoffer.

       (p.33) Award of Arbitrators dated Feb.20, 1787, viz., James Moore,
John Postell, John Robert and Elias Robert, re: Settlement of estate of NATHANIEL
POLHILL, differences having arisen between Thomas Polhill, a son of dec'd., and
the late Hannah Scott, a daughter of dec'd and wife of Rev. Alexander Scott of Lincoln Co. S.C., relative to six slaves and a stock of cattle. The arbitrators find
that while the said Scott was not entitled to same by inheritance he should have
same for his trouble and expenses in looking after the estate. Witnesses: James
Greenhow, John Goldwire, William Porcher.

       (p.36) SIR PATRICK HOUSTOUN of St. AndrewsParish, baronet, to LEM-
UEL LANIER of St.George Parish,planter. Deed dated March 16, 1773, for 100 acres in
St. George Parish granted grantor Oct.6, 1772. Wit: Thos.Ross, Thos.Shruder J.P.

       (p.38) SHADRICK McGEE in his affidavit made Nov.17, 1798 in Bryan
Co., before Jesse McCall J.P., says that on Aug.3, 1793, he gave to his daughter

ANN McGEE now ANN DUKES, a certain slave named Ester about 6 years old. In a separate affidavit, JACOB IHLY of Eff'ngham Co., verifies same, Nov. 24, 1795.

(p.39) JAMES M. STEWART of Augusta, Gentleman, to LEMUEL LANIER of Burke Co. Deed dated July 20, 1786, for 200 acres in Eff.Co., granted Thomas Fleming and confiscated as his property by the State and sold to Francis Fannell and by him deeded to grantor. Wit: Benj.Lanier J.P., Israel Bird J.P.

(p.40) JOHN LAMAR, planter, of Eff. Co. to JOHN SLOAN of Eff.Co. Deed dated March 12, 1787, for 100 acres on n.e. side of Great Ogeechee River near Horse Creek, granted Wm. Coleson; also 50 acres granted grantor, adjoining above. Witnesses: Abraham Ravot, John Spencer, T. Lundy, J.P.

(41) ALEXANDER SCOTT of St. Matthews Parish, to NATHANIEL, THOMAS and MARY POLHILL of Eff.Co. Agreement dated March 1, 1781, respecting the debts of the estate of HANNAH SCOTT, dec'd., to which the parties are heirs.

(p.45) Quit-Claim deed dated March 1, 1781, from NATHANIEL,THOMAS and MARY POLHILL of St. Matthews Parish, to ALEXANDER SCOTT,conveying 8 slaves.

(p.46) ALEXANDER SCOTT of St. Matthews Parish to above THOMAS, NATHANIEL and MARY POLHILL. Quitclaim deed of same date for 30 slaves belonging to HANNAH SCOTT at her death.

(p.48) JAMES HARRIOT of Savannah, cooper, and Mary his wife, to OWEN OWENS of Savannah. Deed dated Dec.2, 1780, for 500 acres in St. Matthews Parish. Witnesses: John Kell, William Jones J.P.

(p.50) OWEN OWENS, of Savannah, merchant, to THOMAS WASHINGTON, Esq. Deed dated (blank), 1786, for the above 500 acres. Witness: John Penman.

(p.62) JOHN FORD of County of Norfolk, Virginia, blacksmith, and Mary his wife, to NATHANIEL HALL of Ga. Deed dated Aug. 17, 1770, for 40 acres in St. Matthews Parish bounded north by Richard Milledge, west by Thomas Bell, n.w. by James McClary, east by Robt.Humphreys. Witnesses: John Hull, Molvern Shelton.

(p.64) DANIEL DESAUSSURE, Gent., of Granville Co., Prince William Parish, S.C., to JOHN HALL of St. Matthews Parish. Deed dated Sept. 19, 1770, for 150 acres lying on the Savannah River in the District of Ebenezer, granted James McCrary June 7, 1757, and deeded by McCrary and his dau. Margaret, to grantor, Dec. 22, 1763. Witnesses: John Ford, Thomas Desaussure and James Fraser. Probated by Ford in Norfolk borough, Va., Nov. 10, 1772.

(p.66) NATHANIEL HALL of Effingham Co., to SAMUEL MANER of Lincoln Co. S.C. Deed dated June 15, 1787, for 150 acres on the Savannah River near Tuckesee King Creek, granted James McCrary June 7, 1757, and by McCrary and dau. Margaret to Daniel Desaussure and deeded by latter to John Hall, and then sold as the latter's property by Thomas Lane, Sheriff Effingham Co., to grantor. Also, 40 acres adjoining granted John Ford Jan.3, 1769. Wit: ThomasLane, J.G.Neidlinger.

(p.70) ISAAC FORD, Esq., of Eff. Co. to WILLIAM DUPUIS of (C.S.C. Beaufort Dist. S.C. Deed dated Oct. 16, 1786, for 100 acres in Eff.Co., bounded s.e. by Great Ogeechee River, s.e. by Boggy branch, and granted to grantor. Witnesses: William Holzendorf, Abraham Ravot J.P., and Abraham Mallette.

(p.74) WILLIAM COLSON and Martha his wife, of Eff. Co., to JOHN LANIER of Burke Co. Deed dated Sept.1, 1785, for 100 acres on Horse creek granted said Colson. Witnesses: Clement Lanier, Nathaniel Lunday, Garret Williams.

(p.78) JOHN MARTIN DASHER and Elizabeth his wife, to JOHN GOTTLIEB NEIDLINGER, Esq., all of Eff.Co. Deed dated July 30, 1785, for 200 acres in said county granted Martin Dasher Feb.5, 1765, and inherited by said John Martin Dasher as heir of said Martin Dasher. Witnesses: William Kennedy, Samuel Kraus.

(p.87) THOMAS LANE, Sheriff of Eff.Co., to HENRY JOICE of same. Sheriff's deed dated Sept.3, 1787, for 350 acres lyingon both sides of Brier Creek adjoining lands of grantee, John Conyers and Robert Hudson Sr., levied on and sold as property of Josiah Yawn (or Vaun? not plain). Witnesses: Caleb Howell, J.P., George McCall Jr., John McCook.

(p.88) WILLIAM ALLEN of Chatham Co. to HENRY JOICE of Eff.Co. Deed dated Feb.6, 1787, for 100 acres adj. Josiah Vawn andJohn Conyers. Wit: James Moore, James Thompson and Wm.Porcher. Probated before Wm.Holzendorf J.P.

(p.89) JOHN GODLIEB OTT of Eff.Co., planter, to CHRISTIAN
BIDDENBACH, shoemaker,of same county. Deed dated Aug.22, 1787, for two acres in
Ebenezer granted Charles Samuel Ott Apr. 5, 1757 and inherited by grantor from
his estate. Witnesses: John G. Neidlinger, Ebenezer Smith, David Delk. Probated
by Neidlinger before Jenkins Davis J.P.

EDITOR'S NOTE: It is the policy of the Editor in making these deed
abstracts for publication not to show or state that the land conveyed lies inEffingham County, but only if the land laid in another county. Readers will therefore
understand that the land in each case was in Effingham Co.,unless otherwise stated.

(p.90) THOMAS WASHINGTON of Savannah, to JACOB RUSSELL of E.Co.
Deed dated March 28, 1787, for 500 acres sold by James Harriot to Owen Owens and
by the latter to grantor. Witness: Return J. Meigs.   Executed in Savannah.
(p.91) Commissioners of Confiscated Estates to SAMUEL KRAUS of
Eff.Co. Deed dated Jan.7, 1784, for 100 acres adjoining grantee, confiscated as the
property of JOHN JOACHIM ZUBLY under the Act of Confiscation. Witnesses: Nehemiah
Wade, J. Morrison, William Glascock J.P.
(p.94) JEREMIAH DUCKWORTH and wife Christian, to CHARLES CRAW-
FORD of St. Paul's Parish, planter. Deed dated May 10, 1775, for 150 acres in St.
Phillips Parish lying near Ogeechee River, granted said Duckworth Aug.2, 1774.
Witnesses: George Roxborough, Nathaniel Barnett, William Barrett.
(p.96) WILLIAM HARRIS and Rebecca his wife ofGreene County, to
LEWIS McLEAN of Wilkes Co. Deed dated Oct. 13, 1787, for 300 acres formerly the
property of Thomas Fleming and confiscated as his property and sold to grantor by
the Comrs.of Confiscated Estates; land lying on Ogeechee River. Witnesses: Lawton
Smith, Anne Harris.
(p.97) DAVID REES of Chatham County to NATHANIEL LUNDAY of E.Co.
planter. Sale Contract or Bond for Title dated Dec. 8, 1787, agreeing to sell to
said Lunday 300 acres on Savannah River, lately the property of John Mulryne and
Josiah Tattnall and confiscated as their property. Witness: Theophilus Lunday.
(p.98) JOSEPH BURTON, hatter, of Camden County, 96 Dist., S.C.,
to CALEB HOWELL, planter, of Eff. Co. Deed dated Aug.9, 1784, for 1000 acres adj.
William Howell, Christopher Hudson. Witnesses: John Burton, Julius Nichols J.P.
Probated in 96 Dist. S.C., before William Moore J.P.
(p.106) JOHN LANIER, planter, of E.Co. to LUKE MEAZLE (MIZELL),
planter of same county. Deed dated March 11, 1788, for 100 acres on north side of
Great Ogeechee River adj. grantee. Witnesses: Caleb Howell J.P., Benj.Lanier J.P.
(p.107) TIMOTHY STALEY of Eff.Co. to WILLIAM LITTLEFIELD of Chatham Co. Deed to Secure Debt dated April 7, 1787, conveying slave and set of blacksmith tools. Witnesses: Peter Zipperer, John Postell, William Holzendorf J.P.
(p.109) Separation Agreement dated March 14, 1788, between JOS-
EPH HARRISON, carpenter, of the one part, and JOSHUA PEARCE and SARAH HARRISON nee
Pearce, wife of said Joseph Harrison, whereby said Joseph and Sarah renounce all
claims and demands they now or may hereafter have as against each other. Witnesses: Thomas Gibbons and J. Waldburger.
(p.111) Commissioners of Confiscated Estates to JOHN COBB and
RICHARD CALL of Richmond Co. Deed dated Jan. 1, 1786, for 2500 acres on Ebenezer
Creek, confiscated as property of John Mulryne and Josiah Tattnall under the Act
of Confiscation. Witnesses: William Harris, Thos. Washington.
(p.113) JOHN COBB and RICHARD CALL of Richmond Co., to JOHN
PENMAN of Savannah, merchant. Deed dated Aug.15, 1786, for the above land - 2500
acres. Witnesses: T. Washington, Thomas Carr.
(p.115) JAMES ALLEN of Glynn Co., to JAMES COLE of Glynn Co.
Bill of Sale dated Feb.20, 1788, conveying slave, sold by Allen as Atty.-in-fact
for Catherine Gottehorne. Witnesses: John Cole and B. Cole.

(p.116) STEPHEN MILLS, planter, to ROBERT IVEY, planter, both of Eff. Co. Deed dated April 29, 1786, for 100 acres near Great Ogeechee River. Witnesses: Theophilus Lunday J.P., Nathaniel Hudson J.P.

(p.117) JOHN PRICE of St. Matthews Parish, planter, to LEWIS PERRY of St.Phillips Parish, carpenter. Deed dated Apr.24, 1775, conveying 100 acres in St. Phillips Parish. Wit: William Blackmore, Robert Dickson.

(p.122) JAMES BELCHER of Chatham Co. merchant, to JOHN PENMAN of same county. Deed dated Jan. 1, 1787, for 800 acres granted to James Cochran July 4, 1769, and by him deeded Oliver Bowen Sept.18, 1877, and by Bowen deeded to grantor June 4th last. Witnesses: Robert Harvey, John Blair.

(p.124) OLIVER BOWEN of Savannah, to JAMES BELCHER of Savannah. Deed dated June 4, 1786, for the same land. Wit: Wm.C.Jameson, John Beatty.

(p.129) JOHN IHLY of Eff.Co., planter, and Catherine Margaret his wife, to JOHN GOTTLIEB NEIDLINGER of same. Deed dated Dec. 1, 1785, for 75 acres being half of 150 acre tract granted John Ulrick Neidlinger Dec.4, 1759,which 150-acre tract was afterwards deeded by John Ulrick Neidlinger to said Caterina Margaret McCoy (now Ihly). Wit: Thos.Lane, Christopher Cramer, John Waldhauer.

(p.134) JOHN GODLIEB NEIDLINGER,,Esq., and Hannah his wife, and JOHN IHLY and wife Catherina M., to JUSTUS HARTMAN SCHUBER, all of Eff. Co. Deed dated Jan. 26, 1786, for the above land. Wit: Christopher Cramer,JohnWaldhaue

(p.139) JOHN RENTZ of St. Matthews Parish, tavern-keeper, and Barbara his wife, to CHRISTOPHER PETERS of Savannah, carpenter. Deed dated Nov. 3, 1768, for two adjoining tracts,each of 100 acres.Witnesses: Asa Emanuel, Samuel Seeds (or Leeds?). Probated July 7,1788, by Emanuel before Henry Osborne, Chief Justice. The probate affidavit refers to Leeds as now being dec'd.

(p.141) FREDERICK HERB and Ursula his wife, WALTER COLEMAN and Elizabeth his wife, and ANN PETERS of Chatham Co., to JUSTUS HARTMAN SHUBER of Savannah, Gentleman. Deed dated Sept.26, 1785, for the above 200-acres of land, which it is stated,was owned by Christopher Peters at his death, and said property "being the property of grantors by virtue of a distribution as heirs of said Christopher Peters". Witnesses: Michael Wetzell, John Cline, John Smith.

(p.147) RICHARD SCRUGGS Sr., planter, to GROCE SCRUGGS,planter, both of Effingham Co. Deed dated Oct.15, 1784, for 100 acres. Witnesses: Paul Bevill and Thomas Lane.

(p.150) TIMOTHY STALY, vinter, to JOHN POSTELL, planter, both of Eff.Co. Deed dated Apr.27, 1785, for four 50-acre lots and one 47-acre lot all in the village of Goshen, known as Lots 8,11,12,13,16, the 50-acre lots granted to Gotlieb Stahly, and the 47-acre lot to Peter Zipperer. Witnesses: John Louiemour, Thomas Polhill, Phillip Ulmer.

(p.153) THOMAS NOBLE of Eff.Co., to his wife HANNAH NOBLE. Deed of Gift dated Aug.28, 1788, for 200 acres on Belcher's Mill Creek, together with his household goods, live-stock &c. Witnesses: Samuel Kraus and James Anderson. Probated by the latter before Jenkins Davis J.P.

(p.153) JAMES WILSON, planter, to his son JOHN WILSON, planter, both of Eff.Co. Deed of Gift dated Aug.26, 1788, for 100 acres where said John now lives. Witnesses: James Wilson Jr., John Wilson. Probated by the former before Jenkins Davis J.P.

(p.154) DAVID THORN, sadler, to PAUL BEVILL, Esq., both of Eff. Co. Deed dated July 1, 1788, for 44 acres on Reedy branch adj. Robert Hudson. Witnesses: Nathaniel Hudson, William Thorn, Matthew Rushing.

(p.157) JOHN MOORE of Currituck Co. N.C., blacksmith, to PAUL BEVILL of Eff.Co. Deed dated Oct.24, 1787, for 200 acres on Reedy branch adj. Abr Motte estate lands, Hillery Butts estate lands, bounded east by David Thorn and north by Robt. Hudson. Wit: Nathaniel Hudson, David Thorn, Wm. Thorn.

(p.159) SARAH BEVILL to ROBERT, PAUL and JAMES BEVILL, sons of ROBERT BEVILL. Deed of Gift dated March 8, 1774, for slaves; life estate reserve Witnesses: John Bonner, Thomas Lunday.

(p.163) JOHN MILLEDGE of Ga., to FANNY DUPUIS of S.C.,spinster.
Deed dated April 4, 1787 for 100 acres granted grantor, he being referred to in the
grant as John Milledge Jr. Witnesses: John Williams, Benjamin Porter.
(p.167) WILLIAM SHEPHERD, planter, to JOSEPH JACKSON, blacksmith,
both of Eff.Col. Deed dated Dec. 19, 1785, for 100 acres on Colson's branch, on the
north side of Great Ogeechee. Wit: Benj.Lanier J.P., Daniel Bonnell J.P.
(p.168) MARY STAFFORD of Eff.Co., widow, to her mother ANNE MARY
MAGDALINE GEIGER. Deed of Gift dated May 25, 1788, for 36 head of cattle. Witnesses:
John G. Neidlinger and Jacob Hoffman.
(p.170) GEORGE MINGERSTORPH of Lincoln Co. S.C., planter, and
wife Christiana Elizabeth, to GODLIEF ISRAEL SMITH. Bill of Sale for seven head of
cattle, five negroes. Witness: John G. Neidlinger.
(p.171) NATHANIEL OTT, planter, and wife Christiana Elizabeth,
SOLOMON GNANN, planter, and Salome his wife, to JOHN HANGLEITER, Sr., cordwinder,
all of Eff. Co. Deed dated Sept. 18, 1788, for 50 acres being 1/3rd part of 150-acre
tract granted to Urban Buntz Dec.4, 1759, lying on Savannah River, and deeded by
Buntz to Mathias Ashbocker Oct.16, 1760, and then by latter to Michael Weber on Oct.
16, 1762, and by the death of the latter's daughter Dorothy Weber "obtained" by the
grantors as her heirs-at-law on Aug.28, 1786. Witnesses: Jacob Mock, John Hangleiter Jr., and John G. Neidlinger.
(p.178) MAGDALENA HANGLEITER of Eff.Co., widow of John Hangleit-
er, Sr., to JOHN HANGLEITER Jr., cordwinter of Eff. Co. Agreement between them dated Feb.7, 1789, in which it is stated the said John Hanggleiter Sr., in his will
dated June 7, 1786, "ordained" that she should remain on their homeplace during
her lifetime. She now agrees with the said John, Jr., that should she marry again
to quit-claim the premises to said John Jr., and vacate same, provided she is not
during her widowhood molested by any of her husband's heirs. Witnesses: John G.
Neidlinger and Christopher Cramer.
(p.180) JOHN WADE of Burke Co., Gent., to MRS. BARBARA RICHARD,
wife of John Hart Richard of Savannah, Gent. Deed of Gift flor six slaves, dated
March 7, 1789. Witnesses: John G. Neidlinger, John Frickinger.
(p.181) SAMUEL KRAUS of Eff.Co., carpenter, to his niece,SALOME
SWEIGHOFFER, dau. of Abel Sweighoffer of Eff.Co. Deed of Gift dated Oct. 111,1788,
conveying 50 acres granted Paul Zitterauer and by the latter's son and heir deeded
to John Joachim Zubly who was later a person named in the Act of Attainder and Confiscation and the property confiscated as his property and sold to doncr by the
Com'rs of Confiscated Estates Dec. 8, 1783. Witnesses: Jenkin Davis, Jonathan Fetzer, JohnG. Neiglinger. Probated by the latter before Abraham Ravot J.P.
(p.182) ELIZABETH PRISON, widow, of Eff.Co., to her children
ELIZABETH PRISON and MARY NIX, minors. Deed of Gift dated 1788, for personal property. John Gnann, their godfather and guardian, to hold said property for said minors.
Witness: Thomas Wylly, J.P.
(p.183) FREDERICK RESTER, Sr., of Eff.Co. to his son FREDERICK
RESTER Jr. Deed of Gift dated Apr.15, 1759 "and in the 13th year of American Independence" (Editor's note: The recording clerk made an error in the year; it evidently was intended to read 1789). Conveys 400 acres on south side of Great Ogeechee
River about 5 miles on a straight line from the flat ford at a place called Big
Pond, granted grantor Dec.5, 1769 and part of it on Nov.3, 1772; also negro slave
named "August" about 10 years old. Witnesses: John G. Neidlinger, Godhelf Smith.
Probated July 8, 1789, by Smith before Israel Bird J.P.
(p.184) ABRAHAM MINCY to LEMUEL LANIER, both of Eff. Co. Deed
dated June 19, 1788, for 100 acres in Eff.Co., granted Wm.Colson Jan. 1, 1769, and
100 acres in Burke Co., granted grantor. Wit: Benj.Lanier J.P., Drury Jones J.P.

(p.185) MICHAEL DICKSON, planter, to JOHN MOORE, yeoman, both of Eff.Co. Deed dated May 15, 1788, for 100 acres granted Micajah Brumbly, March 4, 1785,and by him deeded grantor June 26, 1786, and lying on Jones Mill branch. Witnesses: Benjamin Lanier, J.P., Drury Jones J.P.

(p.187) DAVID HARRIS, planter, of Burke Co., and Sarah his wife, to WILL-IAM COLSON and PAUL BEVILL of Eff.Co., planters. Deed dated July 21, 1770 (which however is wrong year,it being followed by the phrase "in the second year of Amer-ican Independence.-Editor). Conveys 300 acres in Burke Co., bounded east by Brier Creek and on other sides by vacant land when surveyed. Witnesses: Theophilus Lun-dy, Rudolph Burgholder, Francis Lundy. Probated March 9, 1789, by Theophilus Lun-day before John Spencer J.P., Eff.Co.

(p.190) WILLIAM COLSON, planter, of Eff.Co. to THOMAS GARNETT of Eff.Co. Deed dated May 19, 1789, fôr 300 acres in said county bounded east by James Jones estate and land surveyed for Joseph Petit; South by Richard Scruggs,Jr., and Wm. Mannen, north and west by Benj. Daly, and being south part of 600 acres lying near Hudson's Mill branch. Witness: Theophilus Lundy, J.P.

(p.193) THOMAS GRAVES of Richmond Co., merchant, to THOMAS GARNETT of Eff.Co., planter. Deed dated Feb.13, 1788, for 100 acres being upper half of 200 acres onSavannah River adjoining grantee. Wit: Geo.Lundy,John Moore, T.Lundy J.P.

(p.194) LEMUEL TANNER, Esq., of Burke Co. to JOHN MOORE, Gentleman, of Eff.Co. Deed dated March 17, 1789, for 100 acres in Eff.Co. granted Sir Patrick Houstoun, adjoining William O'Bryan and Phillip Dell. Witnesses: Benjamin Lanier, J.P., and Drury Jones J.P.

(p.196) NATHANIEL HUDSON to JOHN MOORE. Deed dated Jan. 7, 1789. Conveys 200 acres on Black Creek2½ miles north? from Savannah River. Witnesses: David Thorn, William Mannen, Moses Horton.

(p.198) COMMISSIONERS OF CONFISCATED ESTATES to JAMES JACKSON, Esq.,Atty.at-Law, of Savannah. Deed dated May 24, 1785, for 315 acres bounded n.e. by Jon-athan Bryan, east by Great Ogeechee River, south by Mary Bryan; confiscated as property of William Knox, an enemy named in the Act of Confiscation. Witnesses: Benjamin Morel, John King, Samuel Stirk J.P.

(p.201) Same Commissioners as last above to CHRISTOPHER HILLERY. Deed dated Oct. 21, 1782, for 200 acres in Eff.Co. below Indian Bluff, bounded south by Great Ogeechee River, west by land granted to Gen. Thomas Lee Sr., East by lands granted Daxid Cutler Braddock; confiscated as property of Thomas Fleming, formerly of Eff.Co., a person named in the Act of Confiscation. Witnesses: Nathaniel Wade, J. Waldburg, David Rees J.P.

(p.204) CHRISTOPHER HILLERY, Esq., of Glynn Co., to JAMES JACKSON, Atty.-at-Law,of Savannah. Deed dated Dec.17, 1788,conveying above 200 acres. Witness: Samuel Stirk J.P., Chatham Co.

(p.210) PHILLIP DELL of Eff.Co., planter, and Dorothy his wife, to
SHEM BUTLER of Chatham Co., planter. Deed dated May 19, 1789, for 200 acres in
Eff. Co., bounded east by land granted Christopher Hudson; 150 acres adjoining
bounded south by Samuel Hudson, both tracts granted said Dell; and 400 acres gran-
ted Christopher Hudson and by him deeded grantor. Consideration ₤1000. Witnesses:
Caleb Howell J.P., Daniel Howell J.P.

(p.216) JOHN LOVE, late of Ga., now of Charleston, S.C., Practictioner
of Physic, to WILLIAM PORTER of Eff.Co., planter. Deed dated June 13, 1789, for
100 acres being part of 550 acres granted James Love, lying near Savannah River.
Witnesses: John A. Truetlin and Elias Roberts.

(p.219) ROBERT HUDSON to his daughter JANE LUNDAY, spouse of Nathaniel
Lunday. Deed of Gift dated June 1789 for slave "Peggy". Witnesses: John R. Cleary
and Isaac Hudson. Probated by Cleary before Paul Beville J.P.

(p.221) ROBERT HUDSON of Eff.Co., to his grandson JAMES BILBO. Deed of
Gift dated June 1789 for slave "Dennis" age 7 years, now in possession of Jane the
spouse of Nathaniel Lunday, "natural mother of said James Bilbo". Witnesses: John
R. Cleary and Isaac Hudson. Probated as above.

(p.222) ROBERT HUDSON of Eff.Co. to his grandson THEOPHILUS LUNDAY,son
of Nathaniel and Jane Linday. Deed of Gift dated June 1789 for slave child age 6
years.Same witnesses and probate as last above.

(p.223) ROBERT HUDSON of Eff.Co., to his grand-daughter MARY ESTHER
LUNDAY, infant daughter of Jane and Nathaniel Lunday. Deed of Gift dated June 1789
for mulatto girl named Phoebe about 4 years old now in said Jane's possession. Same
witnesses and probate.

(p.224) MICHAEL HADERER of St. Matthews Parish, planter, to EVA WEITMAN,
widow of same parish. Deed of Gift dated Feb.3, 1771, for 50 acres in said Parish
adjoining John Smith and lying on Ebenezer Creek, granted grantor Dec. 9, 1756.
Witnesses: Christopher Rothenberger, Jacob Meyer, Daniel Weitman, John Wertsch.
Attached is transfer of the said deed and property dated Dec.4, 1789, to Daniel
Weitman by Matthew and Solomon Weitman and Judia? Britmaln? (not plain).

(p.226) ABRAHAM RAVOT of Eff. Co., and wife Mary, to HENRY SHOOLBRED,
merchant, of Charleston, S.C., as Admr. of William Smith, merchant, of Charleston,
dec'd. Deed to Secure Debt dated July 26, 1789, securing debt of 2153₤, and conveying several tracts as follows: (1) 500 acres granted grantor; 600 acres granted
Samuel Hudson and by him deeded grantor; (3) 100 acres granted Thomas Wilson and
by him deeded Thomas Shruder now dec'd., and by J.E.Powell and Henry Young,Executor
of said Shruder's will, deeded Thomas Chisholm and by him and his wife Mary deeded
grantor· (4) 100 acres granted James Thomas and by him deeded James Harrison and by
him deeded grantor; (5) 200 acres granted Thomas Kesse? (6) 100 acres granted to
one Swan and by him deeded to Samuel Burren and by him to Adrian Loyer and by him
to James Pace;(6) 100 acres granted Michael Joyce and by him deeded to Nobles and
by him to James Pace: (7) 150 acres granted James N-- (not plain) and by him deeded
James Pace: (8) 25 acres granted John Blaton? and by him deeded John Wertsch and by
him deeded John Hall and Arthur Ryals and by them to said Pace. The last 4 tracts
composing 375 acres lying on Tuckasee King, and deeded grantor by Commissinners of
Confiscated Estates. Also conveys two slaves. Witnesses: J. Smith, Matthew
McAllister.

(p.231) NATHANIEL HALL of East Flarida, on the St. Marys River, formerly
of Eff. Co., planter, to JOHN KING of Chatham Co.,merchant. Deed dated Jan.25,1790,

conveying 58 acres on Tucksee King, and 150 acres granted John Hall, George Harnage and John Clayton, and sold to grantor by the Sheriff Thos.Lane, June 8, 1787, as John Hall's property. Witnesses: John G. and Hannah Neiglinger.

(p.233) JOHN RICHARDS and wife Barbara of Chatham Co., to ISRAEL BIRD of Eff. Co. Deed dated March 25, 1785, for 200 acres adjoining grantee's land, and granted grantor Richards March 10, 1769. Wit: Daniel McGaver?, Matthias Wisenbaker.

(p.235) JOHN BARBER, Sr., of Eff. Co., to his grandsons JAMES STUART and ALEXANDER STUART, all of Eff.Co. Gift of two cows and calves, dated Jan. 11, 1790. Witness: George Threadcraft J.P.

(p.236) JOHN BARBER, Sr., to his son JOHN BARBER Jr.,both of Eff. Co. Gift of 20 head of cattle, Jan.15, 1790. Witness: Geo. Threadcraft J.P.

(p.237) LEWIS McLANE and Rhodahis, wife of Wilkes Co., to RICHARD MOORE 6f Wilkes Co. deed dated Oct. 4, 1788, for 300 acres in Eff.Co., formerly owned by Thomas Fleming and confiscated as his property by the Commissioners of Confiscated Estates and deeded to Walton Harris, and bounded south by Justus Hartmann Scheuber, west by Ogeechee River, "formerly settled by Jeremiah Campfair". Witnesses: Buckner Harris, E. Harris, William Vardman, Robert North.

(p.238) JOHN HALL and Sarah his wife, late of Eff.Co., to WILLIAM KING, carpenter, of Eff.Co. Deed dated April 14, 1786, for 200 acres on Tuckaseeking branch, bounded north by John Claton· and granted grantor Oct.29, 1765. Witnesses: Nathaniel Hall, Simon Howard.

(p.242) JUSTUS GROVENSTEIN, chairmaker, to JOHN JUSTUS GROVENSTEIN. Bill of Sale for horse dated July 30, 1789. Witness: Thomas Wylly.

(p.242) HENRY WOOD of Liberty Co., and Rebecca his wife, to MATTHIAS ASH of Eff. Co. Deed dated Apr.12, 1785, for 100 acres in Eff.Co., bounded north by Bitt Lockner, east by Michael Weesea?; also 50 acres in the Dist. of Abercorn and Goshen,now Eff.Co., bounded north by Vite Lockner, south by Martin Lockner the Elder, and west by --- Nicholas. Witnesses: James Powell, James Whitefield. Said property having been deeded·grantor by Frederick Truetlin, Muly 31, 1777.

(p.247) JOHN SPENCER of Eff.Co., and ROSINA POSTELL, widow of John Postell. Marriage Contract dated May 20, 1790, whereby her estate is deeded in anticipation of marriage, to James Greenhow as her Trustee. Her estate consists of 250 acres in Dist. of Goshen now Eff.Co., and 100 acres adjoining: als0 330 acres adjoining Goshen lots· 14 slaves, 40 cattle, 20 sheep, household goods and silver plate. Witnesses: William Vander Locht, William Parker, Joseph William Spencer.

(p.250) JACOB GNANN and Catherine his wife, to MATTHIAS BEDDENBACH, all of Eff.Co. Deed dated Nov.30, 1787, for town lot #3 in Ebenezer, size 60x90'. Witnesses: John G. Neidlinger and Jacob Meyer.

(p.255) MATTHEW BIDDENBACH of Eff.Co., planter,and APOLINIA his wife, to CHRISTIAN BIDDENBACH. Deed dated June 13, 1789, for same lot #3 as last above.

(p.262) LUCY DASHER, widow, to her son BENJAMIN DASHER, son of Martin Dasher, Sr., dec'd, both of Eff.Co. Deed dated Sept.17, 1786, conveying all her household goods and chattels in her house in Ebenezer. Witnesses: John Wisenbaker, Samuel Zipperer, Christian Dasher. (Note: This instrument also recorded in Chatham Co. see p.1938 of this issue. Reason: Benj.Dasher probably resided in Chatham Co.)

(p.263) HENRY PUTNAM to DR. BENJAMIN PUTNAM. Bill of Sale for 9 slaves dated March 15, 1787. Executed in Savannah. Wit: Robert Montfort, Abraham Ravot J.P.

(p.263) JAMES JONES to FRANCIS JONES, both of Eff. Co. Deed dated Aug. 10, 1790. Conveys 100 acres being ½ of grant of 200 acres to Josiah Dickson,lying on north side of Great Ogeechee River, being the tract where said Francis Jones now resides. Witnesses: Henry Putnam J.P., Israel Bird J.P., Paul Bevill J.P.

(p.264) DAVID BROWNSON, planter, of Eff.Co. to his daughter ELIZABETH BROWNSON of Bryan Creek, Eff.Co. Gift of his household goods, plows, hoes, horse, 7 head of "neat cattle" and 12 hogs, on his plantation. Witnesses: Ann Howell and Caleb Howell J.P.

(p.265) WILLIAM RAY of Eff. Co., planter, to JOHN RAY of Chatham Co. Bill of Sale for 9 slaves dated Nov.5, 1790. Wit: John Waldhaeur, James Webb.

(p.266) Letters of Dismission issued by DavidMontaigut, Acting Registrar of Probates in and for Chatham Co., dated Aug.20, 1786, to WILLIAM RAY of Savannah, bricklayer, as Admr. of estate of Benjamin Ansley, tailor, late of Chatham Co., dec'd. It is stated Ray was appointed such Admr., June 5, 1783.

(p.267) JOHN LOWRMAN, planter, to PATRICK McKINTY,tutor,both of Eff.Co., and SAMUEL IHLY of Chatham Co., Trustees for grantor's children John Lowrman,James Lowrman and Mary Lowrman. Deed of Gift dated Sept.26, 1789, for four slaves. Witnesses: J.Cuyler and George Nowland.

(p.269) JOHN KOGLER of Eff.Co., cordwiner, and Christian Elizabeth his wife, to ABIAL SCHWEIGHOFFER of Eff.Co., wheelwright. Deed dated Nov.5, 1788, for 100 acres in Eff.Co. granted Christian Geiger Aug. 7, 1762, and by him "made over" to Sebila Geiger, the widow and relict of Christian Geiger by legacy and by her deeded to grantor. Wit: Jonathan Rahn, Andrew Seckinger, Abraham Mallett.

(p.274) WILLIAM CRAWFORD of Eff.Co., to his wife MARTHA and her children Thomas, Nelly, Patience, Leita? and Jesse. Gift of all his estate (undescribed) at his death. Dated March 9, 1796. Witnesses: William Stewart and John London J.P. Note: Neither the said Martha or her children are referred to as "Crawford", though she is referred to as William Crawford's wife.

(p.275) BENJAMIN WARREN of Eff.Co. planter, to JOHN ABBOT of Burke Co., schoolmaster. Deed to Secure Debt dated March 10, 1787, for 30 cattle, 40 hogs, 3 beds,all other household goods. Wit: Richard Rogers, Sinai Warren.

(p.276) JACOB MOHR, planter, of Eff. Co., and Sibella his wife, to JOHN KOGLER, of Eff.Co. Deed dated March 7, 1788, for 100 acres in Eff.Co. granted Christian Geiger Aug.3, 1762, and by him left to his wife Sibella (now Mohr) as his widow and sole heir. Witnesses: Thomas Lane, Jonathan Rahn, Lewis Buntz.

(p.281) ABIAL SCWEIGHOFFER of Eff.Co., wheelwright, and wife Margaret, to JOHN KOGLER of same. Deed dated Nov.5, 1788,for 50 acres in said County, granted Thomas Schweighoffer May 5, 1767 and by him devised to his son, the said Abial: also half of 100-acre tract in said county granted Thomas Schweighoffer Oct.2,1759 and "endorsed" by him to his son the said Abial, April 9, 1765. Witnesses: Jonathan Rahn and Andrew Sckinger.

(p.288) JOHN SHEROUSE Jr., and Anna Maria his wife, to JOHN MARTIN DASH-ER, planter, all of Eff.Co. Deed dated Dec. 1, 1777, for 150 acres in St.Matthews Parish now Eff.Co., granted John Sherouse Oct.3, 1762; also 100 acres being N½ of 200 acres granted Jacob Moore Sept.5, 1768; and by"legacy and heirship" passed to

36

the grantor John Sherouse. Witnesses: Daniel Zettler, Daniel Burgstiener, John
Rudolph Beninger?.

(p.291) COMMISSIONERS OF CONFISCATED ESTATES, Hugh Lawson, Hepworth
Carter and Abraham Ravot, to JOHN MARTIN DASHER of Eff. Co. Deed dated Aug. 1, 1789
for 50 acres in Eff.Co., confiscated as property of Christopher Frederick Triebner.
Public Sale. Witnesses: S. Stiles, Christopher Truetlin, Blasingame Harvey and
Asa Emanuel.

(p.297) DANIEL WEITMAN, shoemaker, and Salome his wife, to JOHN MAR-
TIN DASHER, all of Eff.Co. Deed dated Auf.9, 1785, for 50 acres granted Rev. Herman
Henry Lemke, Dec. 7, 1756. Witnesses: John Godlip Weidlinger, Matthew Weitman.

(p.303) APOLONIA LEIMBURGER, widow, to JOHN GEORGE ZETTROWER, both
of Eff.Co. Deed dated Dec.2, 1791, for stock of cattle and hogs. Witnesses: John
G. Neidlinger and Daniel Burgstiner.

(p.305) DANIEL BURGSTINER to JOHN MARTIN DASHER, both of Eff.Co. DBed
dated May 1, 1789, for 200 acres adjoining lands granted Martin Dasher and Christian Dasher; also 11 cattle, 32 hogs, household goods, 11 sheep, cart, ploughs etc.
Witnesses: Ann Davis, John G. Neidlinger and Hannah Neidlinger.

(p.308) THOMAS LANE,Sheriff Effingham Co., in his individual capacity
to DANIEL WEITMAN, both of Eff.Co. Deed dated Sept.16, 1791, for 90 acres on Ebenezer Creek. Witnesses: John Waldhaeur, John Moore. Plat of land attached.

(p.311) JENKIN DAVIS, Practictioner of Physic, of Lincoln Co.S.C.,
to his wife ANNE CATHERINE DAVIS. Gift of 4 slaves dated June 12, 1780. Witnesses:
Daniel Zettler and Matthew Zettler.

(p.321) JOHN KNIGHT to JOSEPH KNIGHT. Deed dated --- 1790, for 200
acres in Eff.Co. near Great Ogeechee. Witness: John London J.P.

(p.322) THOMAS LANE, Sheriff Eff.Co. to JAMES GREENHOW of Eff.Co.
Sheriff's deed dated Sept.27, 1786, for 650 acres in former St. Matthews Parish
now Eff.Co. granted Benjamin Stirk Jan. 6, 1767, also 100 acres in District of Abp
ercorn now Eff.Co. granted in 1755 to Hugh Ross; landslevied on and sold as the
property of Samuel Stirk, Admr. of Benj. Stirk's estate, under judgment and fifa
from Chatham Superior Court, March Term, 1784, in favor of Thomas Polhill.
Witnesses: John Polhill and John G. Neidlinger.

(p.325) JOHN EIGLE and JOHN RENTZ of Ga., to their friend, Jacob
Yakeley's children viz., Jacob and Sarah Yakeley. Deed of Gift dated June 20th,
1787, for 50 acres granted Michael Bornaman? Feb.27, 1786. Wit: John and Thos.Pol-
(hill.
(p.326) JOHN STIRK and Hannah his wife of St. Matthews Parish to
JOHN PATTEN "at present of said parish", planter. Deed dated July 23, 1776, conveying 200 acres on an island in the District of Ebenezer opposite Purysburgh,
S.C., bounded east by Savannah River, granted Nicholas Cronberger Sept.30, 1757,
ans deeded by him to grantor Dec.30, 1772. Wit: Edw. Jones, James Simpson.

(p.331) THOMAS LANE,Sheriff Eff.Co. to JOHN BEATTY, Pract.of Physic,
of Chatham Co. Sheriff's deed dated June 14, 1788, for the above island of 200 acres, levied on and sold as property of estate of John Patten, Elenor Patten and
John Irvine, Admrs., under fifa from Chatham Superior Court, favor of John Scott
et.al. Witnesses: Benjamin Lane, J. Whitefield J.P.

(p.332) JOSEPH KNIGHT to THOMAS JAMES KNIGHT. Deed dated Dec.4,1790, for tract of land (acreage not stated) on n.w. side of Williamson's Creek, surveyed for Mark Pridgen, lying near the Great Ogeechee River, the creek to be the line between the parties. Witness: John London J.P.

(p.333) JOSEPH DAVIS of Burke Co., planter, to LEMUEL LANIER of same. Bill of Sale for slave girl dated May 8, 1790. Wit: Joseph Tanner, William Sasser.

(p.334) JOSIAH TATTNALL Jr. of Chatham Co. and Harriet his wife, to NATHANIEL LUNDAY of Eff. Co. Deed dated June 2, 1790, for 350 acres in Eff. Co.,in two tracts, known as "Cool Springs", part being granted to Hillery Butt and part to Jacob Meyer, and sold as confiscated property Dec.25, 1789, to the grantor. Witnesses: George B. Spencer, William Pindar.

(p.336) LUKE MIZELL to JAMES JONES, both of Eff.Co. Deed dated Nov. 7, 1790, for stock of cattle and hogs, 2 mares, household goods, 5 sheep. Consideration L100. Witnesses: Robert Williams, Joseph Jackson J.P.

(p.337) Same parties as last above. Deed dated Dec.23, 1790, for 955 acres on south side of Great Ogeechee River, wounded west by John Nevill, south by Andrew Elton Wells. Also 95 acres bounded n.w. by said river, west by James Douglass, east by Robert Dickson. Also 200 acres on south side said river adjoining said Wells. AlsO 100 acres on north side said river, another tract of 200 acres on same side of the river. Total 955 acres. Witnesses: Michael Dickson, Jos.Jackson JP.

(p.340) ABRAHAM RAVOT, planter, and Mary his wife, to BENJAMIN MOODIE and WILLIAM WHITE of Charleston. Deed dated May 5, 1791. Consideration L1500. Conveys (1) 500 acres grantor grantor; (2) 600 acres granted Samuel Hudson and by him deeded to grantor; (3) 100 acres granted Thomas Wilson and by him deeded Thomas Shruder and by his executors deeeded to Thomas Chilsholm and by the latter and his wife Mary deeded to grantor; (4) 100 acres granted James Thomas and by him deeded James Harrison, then by latter to grantor; (5) 200 acres granted Thos. Kesee· (6) 100 acres granted --- Lucas and by him deeded to Samuel Burns and by him to Adrian Loyce and by him to James Pace. (7) 100 acres granted Michael Joyce,by him deeded to Nobles and by the latter to James Pace; (8) also 150 acres granted James Nix and by him deeded to Pace; (9) 75 acres granted John Blanton and by him to John Wertsch and by latter to John Hall and Arthur Ryalls and by them to said Pace; said last four tracts deeded grantor by the Commissioners of Confiscated Estates. Containing in all 1925 acres and known as Tuckaseeking in Eff.Co. Witnesses: Daniel Thorn, William Kennedy, Nathaniel Hudson J.P.

(p.345) ALEXANDER McQUEEN of Chatham Co. to GALEN BROWNSON. Deed dated Apr.29, 1791, for five tracts totalling 1428 acres, granted mostly to Nathan Brownson. Witnesses: E. B. Hopkins and William Mells.

(p.347) ROBERT BEVILL, planter, and wife Rebecca, to WILLIAM THORN, saddler, all of Eff.Co. Deed dated Nov. 10, 1789, for 180 acres lying at head of Three Runs in Eff.Co., being part of 200 acres adj. Paul Bevill, James Hudson and Wm. Colson. Witnesses: Wm. Webb, Nathaniel Hudson, Paul Bevill J.P.

(p.349) WILLIAM BLACKMON and Ann his wife, to JAMES SMITH, all of Eff. Co. Deed dated March 1, 1791, for 200 acres on Buck Creek on Savannah-Augusta Road Wm Eff. Co. Witnesses: William Pearce, Henry Joyce.

(p.350) JOHN BANDY, planter, to FREDERICK WOMACK,both of Eff.Co. Deed dated Mar.4, 1791, for 200 acres on Big Ogeechee River, granted grantor. Witnesses: Allen Womack, William Womack, Levi Thrower.

(p.352) ANN HOLLEMAN of Eff.Co. to her son-in-law JOHN PETERSON. Deed of Gift dated Aug.25, 1790, for 100 acres in Eff.Co. Wit: Nancy Holleman.

(p.354) JAMES MYERS of Savannah, bricklayer, and Mary his wife, to JOHN MARTIN DASHER, planter, of Eff.Co.. Deed dated Aug. 19, 1790, for 50 acres bounded s.w. by John Mikell's heirs, n.e. by John Igles, s.w. by John Grubbs,and n.w. by vacant land. Wit: Levi Abrahams, Coshman Polack.

(p.356) MARGARET MARRAN? widow, to JOHN MARTIN DASHER, both of Eff. Co. Deed dated March 19, 1791, for 50 acres in said Co., granted John Michael Hersly? April 5, 1757, and by his heirs John Christopher Huntz? Andrew Lebie and Mary Judith Lubie? (not plain) deeded grantor Sept.3, 1787. Witnesses: Henry McConky and John G. Neiglinger.

(p.358) GEORGE ARNSTORPH and Elizabeth his wife, and JONATHAN ARN- STORPH and Christian Elizabeth his wife, planters, to JONATHAN SECKINGER, black- smith, all of Eff.Col. Deed dated Oct.4, 1790, for 50 acres lying on Savannah Ri- ver: also lot 9 in 8th Tything in Ebenezer, and two-acre garden lot there all granted Peter Arnstorph Sept.20, 1757, said George and Jonathan being the only lawful heirs of said Peter. Witness: Andrew Seckinger, Godhelf Sherouse.

(p.363) GODHELF ISRAEL SMITH, planter, of Eff.Co., to EMANUEL KIEFFER of Savannah. Deed dated Oct. 11, 1790, for 200 acres granted grantor May 3, 1785, also 60 "neat cattle", mare and colt and gelding. Witnesses: Dennis Moriarty, David Metzger and Samuel Ihly.

(p.365) EMANUEL KIEFFER of Savannah, to CHRISTINA, DAVID, SALOME and SOLOMON SMITH "the natural children of Godhelf Israel Smith,of Eff.Co.,planter". Deed of Gift dated Oct. 12, 1790, for the above property in next deed above. Same witnesses.

(p.367) JOHN LOWRMAN to JOHN SPENCER, both of Eff.Co.. Deed dated Feb. 12, 1791, for 3 slaves. Witness: William Holzendorf, J.P.

(p.368) JOHN RUSHING of Ebenezer, laborer, to WILLIAM RUSHING of Eff. Co., laborer. Deed dated Apr.22, 1791, for 400 acres on Great Ogeechee River in Eff.Co., adjoining Nathaniel Lunday. Wit: Jos. Jackson J.P.,Thomas Wylly J.P.

(p.370) WILLIAM CRAWFORD to JAMES BREWER, Minister, both of Eff.Co. Deed dated Jan.12, 1790, for 100 acres surveyed for grantor. Witnesses: James Brewer Jr., John Crawford.

(p.371) JOHN CHRISTOPHER GUGEL of Chatham Co., cordwiner, as Executor of will of John Gugel, cordwainer,of same county, dec'd., to MATTHEW RAHN of Eff. Co. Deed dated Dec.29, 1790, for 50 acres being part of 200 acres granted dec'd July 1, 1768,deed being made in pursuance of verbal sale of the property by the dec'd in his lifetime to said Rahn, no deed having been made. It is recited that the will of dec'd was dated Jan.25, 1786, and named John C. Gugel and Sam- uel Gugel as Executors but said John C. is now the surviving executor. Witness- es: Christopher Cramer, Justus H. Scheuber,J.P., Chatham Co.

(p.378) SYLVANUS ROBESON of Eff.County to ISRAEL BIRD, Esq.,of Ga. Bill of Sale Nov.23, 1791, for 15 black cattle, sorrel mare, 6 horses, 2 feather- beds, household goods and plantation tools. Wit: Jesse McCall, Abraham Bird Jr.

(p.379) JOHN GEORGE ZETTROUR, planter, to JOHN KOGLER,cordwainer, both of Eff.Co. Deed dated March 3,1792,for lot #4 in Ebenezer. Witnesses: Dan- iel Burgsteiner and John G. Neidlinger J.P.

(p.381) SYLVANUS ROBERTSON (sic) to ISRAEL BIRD, Esq.,both of Eff.Co. Deed dated Nov.23, 1791, for 1387½ acres in St. JohnsParish now Liberty Co., in several grants made since 1767 (but otherwise undescribed---Editor). Considera- tion ₺100. Witnesses: Jesse McCall, Abraham Bird, Jr. Note: The usual receipt acknowledging receipt of the consideration money, recorded with the deed, is also signed by ANN ROBINSON; however she is not mentioned in or signed the deed.

(p.384) MATTHEW JONES, planter, to WILLIAM RUSHING, planter, both of Eff.Co. Deed dated Dec. 7, 1790, for 100 acres adjoining lands of grantee. Witness- es: Joseph Jackson J.P., Benjamin Lanier J.P.

(p.385) THOMAS LANE to GEORGE NOWLAN, both of Eff.Co. Deed dated Oct. 1, 1791, for 250 acres adjoining James Greenhow, Clement Martin dec'd., Matthias Ash and the Abercorn lots. Witnesses: J.Cuyler and John Moore.

(p.386) WILLIAM MARTIN, planter, to GEORGE GALPHIN NOWLAN, minor,both of Eff.Co. Deed dated Apr. 20, 1791, for 100 acres of river swamp bequeathed the grantor by his father (unnamed), also about 10 acres of Abercorn lots, also 50 ac- res in Goshen, in all 160 acres bounded n.e. by Abercorn Creek, south by Keebler and west by Moore, Walthour and village lots. Wit: J.Cuyler, George Nowlan.

(p.388) JOHN JACOB COPE and Elizabeth his wife, to JOHN and JOSHUA KEEBLER, allof Eff.Co. Deed dated April 16, 1792, for200 acres in said county,boun- ded north and east by Abercorn village, inherited by said Elizabeth Cope, nee Keeb- ler, from John Keebler, being devised by the willof said John Keebler to his wife the said Elizabeth (now Cope) for her lifetime then to pass to above grantees. Wit- nesses: Ep hriam Ihly, Patrick McKentz.

(p.391) Same parties and date as last above. Bill of Sale for three slaves, 15 cattle and household goods belonging to the John Keebler estate· con- veys all of said Elizabeth's interest. Witnesses: John Millen, Ephriam Ihly.

(p.394) JOHN RAWLS, planter, and Franky his wife, to JESSE BELL, Esq. all of Eff.Co. Deed dated Feb.20, 1792, for 200 acres surveyed for grantor Rawls June 18, 1787 lying on Great Ogeechee opposite the Flat-ford. Witnesses: Thomas Wylly J.P. and John Moore J.P.

(p.395) SARAH THORNTON (alias Freyermuth), ppinster, to JOHN PETER FREYERMUTH of Bethany in Eff.Co., planter. Quit-claim deed dated May 12, 1787 for her interest or equity in any and all his property by reason of her intermarriage with him. Witness: Jenkin Davis, J.P., Eff.Co.

(p.396) JUSTUS HARTMANN SCHEUBER of Savannah, Bentleman, and wife Pris- cilla, to GEORGE NEESE of Eff.Co., planter. Deed dated March 13, 1792, for 8 acres adjoining grantee and being part of grantor's land, being part of 200 acres grant- ed John Geogge Neise July 6, 1764 and of which he said John George deeded 125 acres Nov. 3, 1768 to Joseph Shuptrine: and the latter dying intestate same was claimed by the heirs of Christopher Gugel and Mary his wife and by Israel Ruper and Han- nah Margaret his wife,and was by them deeded to grantor Jan. 7, 1791. It is agreed that the grantee is not in anyway impede the flow of water from grantor's mill. Witnesses: Joseph Clay Jr. and J. Waldburger J.P., Chatham Co.

(p.402) JOHN HODGES and Tabby his wife to SAMUEL WALKER, planter, all of Eff.Co. Deed dated Nov. 6, 1790, for 150 acres on north side of Great Ogeechee. Witnesses: John R. Cleary and Joseph Burkett.

40

(p.404) COMMISSIONERS OF CONFISCATED ESTATES, Abr.Ravot, Hepworth Carter, Hugh Lawson, to JAMES HOUSTOUN, of Savannah, Pract. of Physic. Deed dated Jan. 31, 1780, for 500 acres in Chatham Co., on the Newington Road. Witnesses: William Barnard and John Barnard.

(p.406) HANNAH ELIZABETH WHITE of St. Matthews Parish, spinster, only heir of Christian Ernst White, dec'd., to HENRY LUDWICK BUNTZ, glazier, of same Parish. Deed dated Jan. 8, 1772 for lot #8 in Ebenezer, 2nd Tything. Witnesses: John Wertsch and Christopher Buntz.

(p.408) JACOB COOPER WALDHAEUR of Ebenezer, Executor of will of ANNA BARBARA BUNTZ, dec'd., to JOSEPH SHUBTRINE, JOHN REMSHART, SOLOMON SCHRIMP, DANIEL ZETTLER, JOHN GUGEL and CASPER GREINER, Elders of the Ebenezer Congregation. Deed dated Sept. 1, 1778, for Lot #8 in Ebenezer, 2nd Tything, size 60x90'. Witnesses: Nathaniel Reisser and John Rentz.

(p.410) WILLIAM WILKINS of Ga., planter, to MALBERRY MORRES, planter. Bill of Sale dated July 31, 1792 for cattle and 5 horses. Witnesses: Ann Bird, Jesse McCall J.P.

(p.411) JOHN BANDY to EMANUEL HARVEY, both planters. Bill of sale for slave dated July 4, 1792. Witness: Israel Bird J.P.

(p.413) JOHN RENTZ of St. Matthew Parish, Tavern-keeper, to DANIEL WEITMAN, shoemaker, of same parish. Deed dated Nov.20, 1774, for 50 acres in said parish. Witnesses: Charles McCoy and John Flerl.

(p.(p.415) MATTHIAS ASH of Eff.Co., planter, to JOHN G. and HANNAH NEIDLINGER as Trustees for their children John, Anna and Emelia Neidlinger. Deed in Trust dated June 29, 1792, being deed of gift for 10 cattle. Witnesses: Daniel Burgstiner and Gideon Zettler.

(p.417) JOHN RENTZ of St. Matthews Parish, Tavernkeeper, and wife Barbara, to DANIEL WEITMAN, shoemaker, of same parish. Deed dated Nov. 21, 1774, for 50 acres in said parish granted grantor April 7, 1772. Witnesses: Charles McCoy and John Flerl.

(p.419) DANIEL WEITMAN, planter, of Eff.Co. and Frederica his wife, to JUSTUS HARTMANN SCHEUBER, Gent., of Savannah. Deed dated March 19, 1792, for the 50 acres last above. Witnesses: John Freyermuth and Thomas Wylly J.P.

(p.422) CHRISTOPHER GUGELof Savannah, shoemaker, and Mary his wife, and ISRAEL REESSER of Eff. Co., and Hannah Margaret his wife, to J. H. SCHEUBER of Savannah. Deed dated Jan.7, 1791, for 250 acres in Eff.Co., granted Joseph Shubtrine Jan. 5, 1768, and 125 acres in same county being part of 200 acres granted March 6, 1764, to John George Neese and by him deeded Shubtrine Nov.3, 1768· and the latter dying intestate, same was inherited by the first parties or grantors above in this deed, they being sole heirs. Wit: Emanuel and Balthaser Kieffer.

(p.427) MARGARET STEINER of Eff. Co., widow, to her daughter LYDIA wife of ISRAEL KIEFFER of Eff.Co. Deed of Gift dated Sept.3, 1792, for slave. Witnesses: John Waldhauer and Thomas Wylly J.P.
(p.428) Bill of Sale (gift) from same grantor on same date to her daughter SALOME SEINER, Israel Kieffer Trustee, conveying slave. Same witnesses.
(p.429) Same donor on same date to her daughter MISS ELIZABETH STEINER Israel Kieffer Trustee, conveying slave; and on p.430) similar instrument of gift same donor to her daughter CATHERINE SEINER, same Trustee. Conveys slave.

(p.431) CHRISTIAN SHUBTRINE of E.Co. planter, to JONATHAN SECKINGER of same, blacksmith. Deed dated July 17, 1792. Conveys 150 acres granted Theobold Kieffer Dec.6, 1759, and inherited by Emanúel Kieffer, heir-at-law, and by him deeded grantor July 22, 1786. Witnesses: John Waldhaeur and J.G. Neidlinger J.P.

(p.434) SAMUEL MANER of Lincoln Co. S.C., planter, to JOHN AUDEBORT of same county. Deed dated March 5, 1789, for 290acres on Savannah River near Tuckaseeking Creek in Eff.Co. Witnesses: Elias Roberts, Wm. Gilleland. Probated by Roberts in Beaufort Dist.S.C., Srpt.3, 1792, before Joseph Lawton J.P.

(p. 437) JOHN AUDEBERT and wife Judith of St. Peters Parish, S.C., to THOMAS CAMPBELL of same. Deed dated July 14, 1792, for 190 acres on Savannah River in Eff.Co., 150 acres of which was granted James McClay June 7, 1757, and he with his daughter Margaret McClay gave Powerof Attorney to sell sameto Daniel DeSaussure and was later deeded by said Atty.-in-fact to John Hall, and sold by Thos. Lane, Sheriff, to Nathaniel Hall as John Hall's property, and by said Nathaniel deeded said Maner; the other tract of 40 acres adjoining,was granted John Ford Jan.3,1769 and by him deeded John Hall and was then added to said 150 acres.Witnesses: John Hutchinson, Martha Jaudon. Probated by Hutchinson in Beaufort Dist.S.C.

(p.440) JAMES GREENHOW of Eff.Co. planter, in right of his wife Hannah, Executrix of John Stirk's will, late of Eff.Co.,planter dec'd., to SAMUEL STIRK, Atty.-at-Law, of Savannah, also Executor of said John Stirk. Bill of Sale for 9 slaves bought by Greenhow with funds from the estate. Witnessed by Gideon Louis Pendleton and Thomas Gibbons in Savannah. On p.441, deed between same parties, same date, for 800 acres in Wilkes Co.Ga., deeded Greenhow by John Lowrman, 650 acres in Eff.Co., 100 acres in Dist.of Abercorn now Eff.Co., and 300 acres in Eff. Co., all bought with estate funds, in Greenhow's name. Same witnesses.

(p.447) CHRISTIAN SHUBTRINE, planter, and Lucia his wife, to JONATHAN SECK-INGER, blacksmith, all of Eff.Co. Deed dated July 18,1792, for 10 acres, being part of 150 acres granted Theobold Kieffer Dec.6,1759. Wit: J.Waldhaeur,J.G.Neidlinger
(J.P.

(p.450) JOHN MOORE to JOSHUA PEARCE, both of Eff.Co. Deed dated May 21, 1791, for 100 acres adj. Wm. O'Bryan and Phillip Dell. Wit: Allen Rawls,John Ful-
(sher.

(p.451) JOSEPH RODGERS to JOSEPH DAUGHTRY both of Eff.Co.,planters. Deed dated Feb.19, 1789, for 100 acres on Canoochee Creek. Wit: Robt.Laird,Michael Daugh-
(try.

(p.453) THEOPHILUS LUNDAY of Eff.Co.,surveyor, to JAMES BEVILL, planter,of Eff.Co. Deed dated Mar.16,1789, for 200 acres and 150 acres adjoining Caleb Howell. Witnesses: William Colson, Paul Bevill J.P.

(p.455) PRISCILLA MOLLIDAY,widow, to her dau. CHLOE HOWARD,both of Eff.Co. Gift of 16 cattle,horses,household goods,Apr.18,1792. Witness: Chas.McCall J.P.

(p.465) CHRISTIAN ELIZABETH MINGLEDORF to her brother GODHELP SMITH,both of Eff.Co. Power of Atty.dated July 13,1796,to settle her business as Admx. of the George Mingledorff estate. Witnesses: Jesse Bell and W. Gardner J.P.

(p.466) JOSEPH KNIGHT of Eff.Co. to GEORGE McCALL of Darlington Dist.S.C. planter. Deed dated Mar.28,1792, for 300 acres in former Craven Co.now Darlington Dist.S.C., granted John Knight Apr.21,1775,lying on south side Pedee River. Witnesses: John Moore J.P., William McCall, John McCall J.P.

(p.467) JAMES COPELAND and wife Dorcas of Eff.Co., to WILLIAM JOHNSTON, planter,of same. Deed dated July 20, 1791, for 100 acres granted grantor July 12, 1790,lying on Sculls Creek adj. Zachariah Coward. Wit.: Drury Jones,Jos.Hardyman.

42

(p.469) WILLIAM HOLZENDORF of Effingham Co., planter, to JAMES GREENHOW as Trustee for Rosina Postell now Rosina Spencer. Deed dated Aug. 10, 1790 for two slaves. Witnesses: Sarah Holzendorf, William Parker, John Reister.

(p.471) MRS. JULIANA MEYERS, widow, to GODHEIF SMITH, planter, both of Eff. Co. Deed dated March 6, 1792, for 40 acres in said county granted Jacob Meyers on Apr. 4, 1769; also two 5-acre lots in Ebenezer deeded said Jacob Meyer June 10, 177-, said grantor being the widow and only heir of said Jacob Meyer. Witnesses: Daniel Burksteiner and J. G. Neidlinger J.P.

(p.479) GODHELF SMITH and wife Christiana to MRS. JULIANA MEYERS, all of Eff.Co. Deed dated March 7, 1792 for 100 acres on Small's Creek granted grantor. Witnesses: D. Burgstiner and J.G. Neidlinger J.P.

(p.481) THOMAS LANE, Sheriff Eff. Co., to JOHN MARTIN DASHER of same Co. Sheriff's deed dated Oct.26, 1792, for 50 acres, levied on and sold as property of David and Christian Steiner, dec'd., under fifa in favor of Trustees Ebenezer Lutheran Congregation.

(End of Book)
DEED BOOK "C-D"

(p.3) JAMES JONES to FRANCIS JONES both of Eff. Co. Deed dated Dec. 29, 1792, for 250 acres on south side Ogeechee River in Liberty Co. Witnesses: Luke Mizell and Joseph Jackson, J.P.

(p.5) JOHN MIZELL to MATTHEW JONES both of Eff.Co. Deed dated Feb.11, 1793 for 200 acres on Fulsom's (Folsom's) branch in said county, adjoining Francis Jone and ----- Douglas. Witnesses: Benjamin Richardson JP.Joseph Jackson J.P.

(p.5) RICHARD ALBRITTON to WHARTON VAUGHTER, both of Eff. Co. Deed dated Dec.26, 1792, for 100 acres on east side of Horse Creek, being part of 200 acres granted grantor Jan.15, 1785. Witness: Benj. Richardson J.P.

(p.5) ANDREW TUCKER to JEMIMA TUCKER, Trustee for her children, unnamed. Gift instrument dated Sept.17, 1793, of live-stock, furniture, ½ of his corn and fodder, cotton and potatoes he to "have the liberty to eat of them while I stay on the place". He renounces all claim to same now and after his death, whether by matrimonial rights or otherwise. Witnesses: John Knight, Miles Hunter, John Cook.
EDITOR'S NOTE: This sounds like Andrew and Jemima may have been husband andd wife and that the instrument amounted to a separation agreement. The 1820 Census shows an Andrew Tucker in Camden Co., and the 1830 Census shows a Mrs.Jemima Tucker in Lowndes Co. Mrs.Jemima Tucker was in Camden Co., in March,1820,when she made a gift of property to her son Elijah Ross Tucker. The latter lived in Wayne Co. Two of the witnesses, John Knight and Miles Hunter, moved in the 1790s from Effingham, Knight to Wayne County and Hunter to McIntosh County.Sarah Tucker,sister to Elijah R.Tucker,married Abraham Knight of Wayne, son of said John.

(p.8) CALEB HOWELL to WILLIAM PEARCE, planter, both of Eff.Co. Deed dated Aug.9, 1792 for 200 acres adjoining J. Pearce and H. McDonald and Abr.Pavot. Witnesses: James Bevill and Daniel Howell.

(p.9) ROBERT IVEY and Mary his wife to JOSHUA STAFFORD, all of Eff. Co. Deed dated Jan. 29, 1788, for 200 acres bounded West by John McQueen, East by Bryce Creek and John Brinson; having been granted grantor June 24, 1785. Witnesses: William Harris, Louis D. Esanbleaux?.

(p.10) JESSE MIXON, ELIZABETH MIXON, SARAH COOK, all of Eff. Co.,heirs of John Cook, dec'd., in an instrument dated July 27, 1793, manumits or frees certain slave named George, theretofore the property of Rachel Shorter dec'd. Witnesses: Robert Scott and Mark Pridgen.

(p.11) JESSE MIXON, BENJAMIN COOK, WILLIAM COOK, ROBERT KELLY and MICHAEL PHILLIPS, all of Eff. Co., "joint-heirs of Rachel Shorter, dec'd", to HENRY WEBB of same county, oldest son of said Rachel Phillips. Deed of Gift dated March 15, 1793, conveying "all such goods and chattles as were laid off for his use by his grandmother, Rachel Shorter, dec'd., viz: Mare, saddle and bridle, horned cattle, feather-bed and furniture. Wit: Robert McCall, James Gill.

(p.13) MARY JONES, widow, to her children JAMES JONES and CIVILITY JONES, all of said Eff. Co. Deed of Gift dated Oct.30, 1793, for 12 head of black cattle to be James Jones', and 8 head of same to be Civility's; two featherbeds and other items to both of them jointly; also to them jointly, 50 acres of land granted to her where she resides in said county. Witnesses: Daniel Burgstiner and James Wilson. EDITOR'S NOTE: This Mary Jones was the widow of John Jones, a Revolutionary Soldier,and the 50 acres was granted her as a widow Dec. 10, 1788. The two children above named were the only issue of John and Mary Jones, and both moved to Liberty Co., by 1796, and from there to Glynn Co., in 1797, where she, Civility, married Isham Walker. James Jones lived and died in Wayne (now Brantley) county, and he and his wife Nancy Delk are the ancestors of the large Jones connection of Brantley and Ware counties. The Walker descendants lived and now live principally in Pierce and Brooks counties.

(p.18) HERMAN HERSON of Savannah, Gentleman, and Johanna his wife, and DANIEL WEITMAN, cordwainer, and Mary Frederica his wife, to JOHN MARTIN DASHER of Eff. Co. Deed dated June 24, 1793, for 25 acres in the Dist.of Ebenezer now Eff. Co., granted John Gruber Dec. 9, 1756, and by him was deeded Henry Lemke July 23, 1764; deed also conveys 50 acres adjoining to the above 50-acre tract, granted Henry Lemke Apr. 13, 1761; also 100 acres being part of 150-acre tract in Dist. of Ebenezer adjoining the said Gruber lands, granted Rev. Thomas Henry Lemke Dec. 9th, 1756; all of said lands having been inherited by grantors from estate of Herman Henry Lemke, deceased.

(p.18) JOHN GRUBER to HERMAN HENRY LEMKE. Deed dated Aug.23, 1764, for 50 acres in St. Matthews Parish, Dist.of Ebenezer, being a garden lot granted said Gruber Dec. 9, 1756. Witnesses: John Flerl, Sr., J.P., Jacob Gruber.

(p.19) JONATHAN NORTON, silversmith of Savannah, to ABRAHAM BIRD of Eff. Co. Deed dated Oct.3, 1793, for ¼ undivided interest in 400 acres on the River Ogeechee, bounded west by Elisha Butler, n.e. by said river, s.w. by Capt. John Milledge; lands having been granted to Lewis Smith Feb.3, 1762. Witnesses: Sheftall Sheftall and Justus H. Scheuber J.P. Deed executed in Savannah.

(p.20) DANIEL McGAVER of Savannah, tailor, and Dorcas his wife, to ABRAHAM BIRD, millwright, and JOHN GLASS, sadler "of the same place". Deed dated

June 14, 1790, conveying ½ undivided interest in the above 400-acre tract referred to in last deed above. It is recited that Lewis Smith who granted the lands,died intestate whereby said Daniel McGaver in right of his wife Dorcas, one of the daughters of said Lewis Smith,dec'd., became entitled to ¼ undivided part. Witnesses: Arnold Harvey and Andrew Bird.

(p.23) JOHN MARCUS of Washington Co., planter, to GIDEON DENNISON of Savannah, merchant. Deed dated Feb.28, 1794, consideration ₤1000, conveying 14,000 acres in Eff. Co., on Black Creek and Ash's branch, waters of Canoochee River, granted grantor Oct.25, 1793 in 14 grants of 1000 acres each. Also, 60,000 acres adjoining same, between the Canoochee and Ogeechee Rivers, granted grantor Feb. 20, 1794, in 60 grants of 1000 acres each. Witnesses: John Course J.I.C., and Samuel Jack.

(p.25) WILLIAM GARDNER, planter, of Richmond Co., to JOHN HOWELL, mariner, of Savannah. Deed dated Feb. 7, 1794, for 11,000 acres in Eff. Co., granted to grantor Oct.25, 1793, in 11 grants of 1000 acres each. Witnesses: G. Dennison and Samuel Jack J.P.

EDITOR'S NOTE: It is likely these two last deeds were part of famous (or infamous) land-grant frauds so common in Georgia in the middle 1790s. Deeds and grants for unusually large acreages especially where granted in so many grants of 1000 acres each, may well be charged off (so to speak) as being frauds, conveying non-existent lands. The late S.G.McLendon, Secty.of State, published a little book back in the 1920s while he was living (he died in office) entitled "History of the Public Domain in Georgia" which goes into much detail about the land-grant frauds of the 1790s. In one county, Washington, nearly a million acres more than the total acreage in the county, were granted by the State, all based on pretended surveys made by the County Surveyors. It was evidently planned by those acquiring such grants, to sell such supposed acreages to speculators in Pennsylvania, New York and other northern states. As a rule, the Editor does not abstract such conveyances having the earmarks of fraud, unless the deed contains some genealogical value.

(p.29) JOHN HOWELL, Capt. of the U.S. Revenue Cutter "Eagle", and Catherine his wife, to GIDEON DENNISON of Savannah, merchant. Deed dated March 15, 1794, conveying the same 11,000 acres above deeded him by John Marcus. Witnesses: Ananias Cooper and William Longstreet, J.P. (Editor's Note!' This Capt. John Howell later became a resident of St.Marys,Ga., and died there).

(p.34) JAMES GREENHOW, Trustee for ROSINA POSTELL "now Spencer", to JOHN KEEBLER, all of Eff.Co. Deed dated Nov.3, 1794, for 100 acres belong in two 50-acre tracts known as Garden lots 6 and 7 in the Township of Abercorn,Eff.Co. Witnesses: Joshua Keebler and Mary Rheny and John Spencer J.P.

(p.36) DAVID McCALL, planter, and Fanny his wife, to JAMES BREWER, planter, all of Eff.Co. Deed datedApril 14, 1798, for 50 acres on Wallowing branch. Witnesses: Francis Wells, William McCall J.P. (Editor's Note: Beginning with this deed, there is a four-year gap in the records in this book, jumping from 1794 to 1798. These records in Deed Books A,B,C and D., were all transcribed in the early 1800s from older books which were probably thrown away after being transcribed; and the officer doing the work, apparently did not copy the books in their order, and neither did the new books have the same numberof pages as the old books. Deeds recorded between 1794 and 1798 will be found further on.

(p.37) BENJAMIN STIRK of Eff.Co. and JAMES HOLDEN, also of Eff. Co. Deed of Division dated May 21, 1798, dividing between them the estate property left them by the will of JOHN STIRK of Effingham County, he having devised the same to his said son Benjamin Stirk and to testator's wife HANNAH, the said Hannah being now the wife of said Holden, and she being the mother of said Benjamin.   In the division amicably made between them, Benjamin the son received 29 slaves, a horse, ½ of the plantation tools and implements, and cattle; and the said Holden on behalf of said wife Hannah received 25 slaves, ½ of the plantation tools and implements, cattle and a horse. Witnesses: T. Cuyler J.P., George Nowlan.

(p.38) JOHN MOXHAM of Chatham Co., to JOHN MARTIN DASHER of Eff.Co. Deed dated May 2, 1798, for 50 acres in Eff.Co.,adjoining grantee's lands, and which were granted to --- (not stated who) Sept. 30, 1757. Witnesses: John Gindrat, Harman C. Fisher and John Glass.

(p.40) BENJAMIN HODGES and wife Letitia, to HENRY O'BERRY. Deed of division dated June 14, 1798. dividing 300 acres on Ogeechee River granted to said Hodges and O'Berry jointly Dec.14, 1797, whereby the E½ to be O'Berry's.   Witnesses: John Ellerbee and William Bishop.

(p.41) EDWARD LLOYD, Sheriff Chatham Co., to JOHN McKINNON of same Co. Sheriff's deed dated Apr. 20, 1795, conveying 5750 acres in Eff. Co., in 5 tracts of 1000 acres each and one of 750 acres, levied on and sold as property of Robert Montford, dec'd. It is recited that the property was first bid in by McKinnon on behalf of Mrs. Elizabeth Montford at 12¢ per acre, but she having failed to pay for same in full the property was again auctionedoff and bid in by McKinnon for himself at 8¢ per acre. Sold to satisfy fifa in favor of Samuel Stirk. Witnesses: Benjamin Butler and Francis McCall.

(p.44) JOHN McKINNON, Surveyor, and Ann his wife, of Chatham Co., to CORNELIUS SCHERMERHORN of New York. Deed dated May 7, 1795, conveying the above 5750 acres. Witnesses: John Robinson, J. Whitefield, Register of Probates Chatham Co. In an attached paper, MRS. ELIZABETH MONTFORD, widow of said Robert, on May 17,1795, waives all her dower and other rights in said lands and assents to the sale.

(p.46) ELEAZER BELL to JOSEPH HOLYDAY, both of Eff. Co. Deed dated Mar. 19, 1798, for 300 acres granted William Denmark June 2, 1791, lying opposite the flat ford on "the great Road on north side of Great Ogeechee River and including the plantation where said Denmark formerly lived"; also 200 acres granted Reading Denmark Jan.21, 1796; also 150 acres granted same man, same date, adjoining Wm. Denmark, Jesse Bell, and s.e. by Reading Denmark. AlsO 100 acres granted said Reading Denmark Jan. 21, 1796, lying on Great Ogeechee River; also 190 acres granted Wm. Denmark Jan.24, 1791 for 200 acres; being in all 947 acres lying in one body and deeded by Reading Denmark to above Bell Nov.24, 1796. Witnesses: John Moore and Stephen Denmark J.P.

(p.48) READING DENMARK to ELEAZER BELL, both ofEff. Co. Deed dated Nov.24, 1796, conveying the above lands. Wit: Wm. Denmark, Jesse Bell J.P.

(p.51) SOLOMON GNANN and Salomy his wife, to JONATHAN SCHNEEDER, all of Eff. Co. Deed dated Apr. 14, 1797, for 200 acres adj. Jacob Gnann, Wm.Wilson and Wm.Thornton; granted grantor Oct.29, 1795. Wit: John Godlieb Snider and John G. Neidlinger J.P.

(p.55) BENJAMIN STIRK to PATRICK McKINLY. Bill of sale for slave dated June 27, 1798. Witnesses: John Keebler and John M. Dasher.

(p.56) CHARLES SIGMUND OTT of Ebenezer, planter, and Magdalena his wife, to GABRIEL MAURER. Deed dated Jan. 30, 1763, for one-third part of 150 acres granted grantor Aug.7, 1759, lying in St. Matthews Parish.

(p.60) BENJAMIN STIRK to THOMAS POLHILL, Trustee, both of Eff.Co.
Bill of Sale (gift) dated July 13, 1798, conveying 29 slaves received by said
Stirk from the estate of John Stirk his father, conveyed to said Trustee for the
use and benefit of said Benjamin Stirk's wife Catherine. Executed in Savannah in
presence of T. Cuyler J.P. and Timothy Stahly.

(p.62) THOMAS WYLLY and Naomi his wife of Chatham Co., to CHRISTIANA
DASHER, widow, of Eff.Co. Deed dated March 7, 1798 for 50 acres in old District of
Goshen now Eff.Co., adjoining John Sheraus, granted Geirge Reisser May 1, 1759;
also 33 acres adjoining same, granted Dorothy Reisser, spinster, Nov.6, 1771.
Witnesses: Patrick Quinn and W. Gardner J.P.

(p.63) JACOB RUSSELL of Savannah, gunsmith, to WILLIAM NEELY of Eff.
Co. Deed dated Nov.15, 1796, for 350 acres lying on Great Ogeechee River. Witnesses: Jesse Dykes, Edmond Tyson.

(p.65) CHRISTIAN SHUBTREIN to GEORGE ZITTROUR and CHRISTIAN HEIDT as
Trustees for his children Godlieb Shubtrein and Hannah Shubtrein. Deed of Gift
dated June 13, 1798, for 90 acres granted Theobald Kieffer Dec. 6, 1757, and inherited by his son Emanuel Kieffer who deeded same to grantor July 22, 1786, said
property to be held in trust for said Godlieb Shubtrein;; also two acres on the
east side of Ebenezer, and town lot #6 in Ebenezer, size 60x90', granted Daniel
Shubtrein Dec. 8, 1756, and was inherited by his son the said Christian Shubtrein
he being the only son and heir, same to be held in trust for the said Hannah.
Witnesses: Jonathan Seckinger and John G. Neidlinger J.P.

(p.67) MATTHEW BIDDENBACK of Ebenezer, planter, and Appolina his wife
to EMANUEL KIEFFER all of Eff.Co. Deed dated Feb. 1, 1787, for 125 acres in Bethany district, St. Matthews Parish now Eff.Co., bounded north by John Christopher
Buntz, west and south by John Justus Grabenstein, and east by Andrew Biddenback.
Witnesses: Christian Biddenback and Andrew Biddenbach.

(p.68) WILLIAM DuPIUS, Sheriff, to JOHN BERRIE, both of Eff. Co. Sher-
iffss deed dated Feb.6, 1798, for 150 acres in said County adjoining John Christopher Buntz and John Justus Grabenstine, Geo. Gruber et.al., sold as property of
Emanuel Kieffer estate in the hands of Matthew Rahn, surviving Admr., under fifa
in favor of Trustees of German Luthern Congregation at Ebenezer. Witnesses: John
Kogler, Nathaniel Reisser, J.G. Neidlinger J.P.

(p.71) SAMUEL KRAUSE of Eff. Co., to JUDITH, wife of JOHN BOCK,planter,
of South Carolina. Deed dated June 7, 1798, for 100 acres in former St.Matthews Par
ish now Eff. Co., also two acres in township of Ebenezer; also town lot #9 in Ebenezer; all granted Leonard Krause Dec. 9, 1759, and was later inherited by grantor.
Also fifty acres being part of 100-acres granted Paul Zettrour and deeded by his
son and heir John George Zettrour to John J. Zubly and was later confiscated as
Zubly's property and sold by the Commissioners of Confiscated Estates to grantor
on January 7, 1784.

(p.73) JOHN G. NEIDLINGER and wife Hannah of Eff. Co., to JOSHUA LOPER
GODHELF SMITH, SAMUEL RYALS, DARIUS GARRISON and DAVID HALL, Commissioners for the
Courthouse and Jail of Eff. Co., appointed by the legislature. Deed dated Sept.8,
1798, conveying 100 acres being the s.w. part of moiety of 200 acres granted said
Neidlinger Dec. 25, 1793, lying on Jack's branch. Witnesses: Anna Neidlinger, P.
McKinty J.P. Consideration in deed $55.00. EDITOR's NOTE: This land was acquired
by said Commissioners for the county, on which to lay out a townsite and to locate
the court-house and jail; the town was named Springfield, and town lots were soon
afterwards sold off at public sale. This marked the beginning of the present town
of Springfield.

(p.75) WILLIAM STRINGER and wife Susannah of Screven Co., to DAVID
HALL of Eff. Co. Deed dated Aug.3, 1796, for 150 acres near the Great Ogeechee
River, adj. Richard Burford. Wit: James Rasen and Richard Dowdy.

(p.76) ROBERT H. HUGHES and Chloe his wife of Eff. Co., to JAMES BREWER
of Bulloch Co., minister. Deed dated Aug.28, 1798, for 100 acres on Wallowing branch, adjoining James Goldwire. Wit: John Williams, John London J.P. On page 77 is
another deed between same parties, same date and witnesses, for 400 acres adjoining James Goldwire and others.

(p.78) WILLIAM HURST and Mary his wife of Eff. Co., to JAMES BREWER,
minister, of Bulloch Co. Deed dated Sept.3, 1798, for 34 acres being the s.w. end
of 50-acre tract granted grantor Sept.7, 1797. Witnesses: R. H. Hughes, William
Hurst Jr., and David Jones.

(p.80) DAVID McCALL and wife Fanny to WILLIAM CRAWFORD, all of Eff.Co.
Deed dated May 10, 1790, ror 100 acres where Crawford lives, being part of tract
granted grantor in 1786, on Little Ogeechee. Wit: James Brewer, George McCall.

(p.82) JAMES SEAGROVE of Camden Co., and ANNE his wife, to REV. JOHN
BOCK. Deed dated June 25, 1798, for 600 acres being an island called Zubly's Ferry
bounded east by Savannah River, north and west by Kelly's Creek. Witnesses: Thomas
Howe? and Thomas King J.P., Camden Co.

(p.84) THOMAS TOWNSEND and WILLIAM TOWNSEND, heirs of William Townsend
dec'd., to ANN CHRISTINA DASHER, all of Eff. Co. Deed dated Jan. 16, 1799, for 200
acres of pine land granted said dec'd., and bounded west by Jacob Hensler, north
by John Stahly; Witnesses, John Wisenbaker and John Spencer J.P.

(p.85) JOHN BOYKIN and Sarah his wife of Screven Co., to PAUL TUSSING
of Eff. Co. Deed dated Sept.2, 1794, for 250 acres granted grantor May 28, 1788.
Witnesses: Geo. Williams, Joseph Casson, Asa Tanner. Probated by Casson before
D. Blackburn J.P., Screven Co.

(p.87) WILLIAM SHRIMPH of Eff. Co., planter, to CAMMEL TISON of Eff.Co.,
planter. Deed dated April 2, 1799, for 117 acres granted Hugh Kennedy March 3,1767,
and by him devised to Frederick Shrimph and obtained by grantor partly by heirship, he being the only son and heir of said Frederick. Witnesses: Gideon Zettler
and John G. Neidlinger, Clerk Superior Court.

(p.88) JAMES HOLTEN to THOMAS POLHILL, Trustee, both of Eff. Co. Bill
of Sale dated June 11, 1799, for 20 slaves to be held in trust for Holten's wife
Hannah, being the slaves he received in the right of said Hannah in a division of
estate of John Stirk, first husband of said Hannah. Wit: T. Cuyler J.P. and
Abial Schweighoffer J.P.

(p.89) Same parties as in instrument last above, same date. It is recited that "differences have arisen between Holten and his said wife Hannah by which
means they cannot live together, and it is only just that suitable provisions be
made for her support" etc. He by this deed of trust, conveys Polhill as Trustee
for said Hannah, 200 scres on Ebenezer Mill Creek, and 100 acres in Dist.of Abercorn
granted Hugh Ross and adj. said 200 acres; also 100 acres granted Abr. Cobb?, and
100 acres granted Frederick Helvenstein; also 650 acres granted Benj. Stirk; also
300 acres granted Godlieb Stahly; also 200 acres granted John Williams on Sawmill
Creek; also 500 acres granted John Stirk, on Great Ogeechee River; also 700 acres
in former St.George Parisho on said river; also 800 acres granted John Lourman and
adj. Thomas Glascock, all in Eff.Co. Same witnesses.

(p.92) JOHN RAY of Chatham County to JAMES KIRK of Savannah. Bill of Sale for slaves dated May 19, 1791. Witness: Israel Barber.

(p.94) JOHN POWERS to EPHRIAM DAVIS both of Eff. Co. Deed dated Feb. 8th, 1799, for 50 acres being part of grantor's homeplace near the Ditch bay. Witnesses: Robert H. Hughes and John Davis.

(p.95) COMMISSIONERS OF COURTHOUSE AND JAIL of Eff.Co., viz; David Hall, Joshua Loper, Godhelf Smith, to JOHN LONDON, planter, all of Eff.Co. Deed dated July 16, 1799, conveying one acre of land 210' square in town of Springfield in said county, known as Lot #2. Witness: John G. Neidlinger, Clerk S.C. (EDITOR'S NOTE: This appears as the first deed of record to a town lot in Springfield.)

(p.96) JOHN CHRISTOPHER MILLER, blacksmith, and Hannah his wife, to JOHN KOGLER, all of Eff. Co. Deed dated --- --, 1799, for 200 acres granted John Paul Miller Jr., April 2, 1771, and was later inherited by grantor as the only son and heir of said John Paul Miller, dec'd. Wit: Anna Zettrour, J.G. Neidlinger C.S.C.

(p.100) JOHN FRYERMUTH and SALOME his wife to JOHN KOGLER, all of Eff.Co. Deed dated June 17, 1799, for 100 acres granted John Maurer and by him deeded to John Gruber Feb.28, 1769, and by Gruber deeded Michael Henderson May 13, 1772, and by the latter deeded grantor Jan.2, 1797. Also 200 acres granted John Peter Fryermuth and by him deeded grantor Feb. 7, 1795. Witnesses: George Powledge, Andrew Seckinger and Samuel Snyder.

(p.102) JOHN CHRISTOPHER GUGEL of Chatham Co., shoemaker, and Mary his wife to JOHN KOGLER of Eff.Co., shoemaker. Deed dated May 21, 1799, for 37½ acres in Eff.Co., adj. Matthias Seckinger, Justus Hartman Schuber's mill land, and being part of 150 acres granted Matthias Brantner Aug.7, 1759, and inherited by Hannah wife of JohnFlerl, and by Israel Flerl, son and heir of said John and Hannah, was deeded grantor June 25, 1794. Witnesses: Jonathan Seckinger and Joseph Rahn.

(p.103) JONATHAN RAHN of Eff.Co., one of the Executors of will of JOHN MICKLER, dec'd., to JOHN KOGLER of Eff.Co., planter. Deed dated Aug.31, 1799, for town lot #3 in Ebenezer granted Robert Eyesperger Aug.30, 1757 amd deeded said John Mickler Nov.30, 1767 by John Martin Griner and Mary his wife, said Mary being the heir of said Eyesperger, dec'd. Also town lot #4 in Ebenezer, granted Paul Zetterour Nov. 7, 1755, and by his son and heir PaulZetterour, Jr., was deeded John Kogler March 3, 1792, and by Kogler and wife Elizabeth deeded John Mickler July 9, 1794. Witnesses: Jonathan Seckinger and Thomas Wylly.

(p.106) JAMES PORTER and Elizabeth his wife, to WILLIAM DUPIUS, planter,all of Eff. Co. Deed dated June 1, 1799, for 150 acres granted James Love Oct.4,1763, the other or south part of 100 acres of said tract having been deeded by said Love to William Porter, brother of said James Porter, in 1789. Witnesses: William Porter and Christian Truetlin J.P.

(p.108) JOHN LOVE, Practictioner of Physic, of Savannah, and Louisa his wif to JAMES PORTER of Eff.Co. Deed dated Sept.13, 1798, conveying same land as last above. Witness: Edward Cowan and Joseph Wilscher J.P., Chatham Co.

(p.109) WILLIAM SHRIMPH, planter, to HENRY O'BERRY, planter, both of Eff.Co. Deed dated Sept.21, 1799, for 100 acres said county adj. David Murray and granted John Frederick Shrimph Dec. 5, 1769, and was inherited by grantor as his son and only heir. Witness: Godhielf Smith J.I.C., and Gottlieb Ernst J.P.

(p.110) ELIZABETH BISHOP of Eff.Co. to her children MARY BISHOP, MARGARET BISHOP, ELIZABETH BISHOP, JOHN WILLIAM BISHOP, RACHAEL BISHOP, all of Eff. Co. Deed of Gift dated Oct.2, 1799, for slave "Hannah" and Flora her child, also all said Elizabeth's cattle, hogs and a black mare. Witnesses: William Bishop and John G. Neidlinger Clerk Superior Court.

(p.110) COMMISSIONERS OF COURTHOUSE & JAIL, Joshua Loper, Gottlieb Smith, David Hall, Darius Garrison, to SAMUEL KRAUSE of Eff.Co. Deed dated July 4, 1799, for lot #5 in town of Springfield, being 250' square, made under provisions of Act of General Assembly appointing said Comrs. Public Sale. Witnesses: William Kennedy and J. G. Neidlinger C.S.C.

(p.115) JOHN WILLIAMS, Sheriff, to GOGHEIF SMITH, both of Eff. Co. Sheriff's deed dated Oct.24, 1797, for 750 acres lying in fork of Ogeechee River and Black Oak, adjoining James Bullock, and granted Israel Kaeffer and sold as the letter's property underfifa in favor of JohnGreen Esq. Wit: Israel Flerl, William Kennedy, J.I.C., Eff.Co.

(p.115) JAMES PORTER to SOLOMON GRUBER both of Eff. Co. Deed dated Aug. 21, 1799, for slave "Santee" age about 6 years. Consideration$200. Witnesses: Henry Grovenstein and Jonathan Rahn.

(p.116) OLIVER BOWEN, United States Marshal for the Dist. of Georgia, to WILLIAM NORMENT of Chatham Co. Deed under levy and sale dated Apr.21, 1798, for 150 acres in Eff.Co., bounded n.e. by John Goldwire, and other sides vacant when surveyed; sold as property of Phillip Box, dec'd., under fifa in favor of Thomas Shubrick. Witnesses: Richard Wall and George Duke. Executed in Savannah. On page 117, is record of deed to same land from Norment and Elizabeth his wife to JAMES KING of Effingham Co., deed dated Oct. 14, 1799.

(p.118) ROBERT McBEE of St. Matthew Parish, yeoman, to JOHN GOLDWIRE, planter, of same parish. Deed dated May 13, 1772, for 100 acres in said parish on 3-Runs, adjoining grantee, granted grantor Sept.3, 1771. Witnesses: Thomas Chisholm and Benjamin Daly.

(p.123) JOHN KNIGHT, planter, and wife Rachael, to MOORE SPIER, all of Eff.Co. Deed dated Oct.22, 1799, for 250 acres granted said Knight Feb.13, 1799, bounded n.w. by Braddock's land, s.w. by Ogeechee River, s.e. by Hodges and O'Berry land, n.e. by Belcher and McCall. Witness: John London J.P.

(p.124) ANNE BRYAN at present of Savannah, to JESSE McCALL and ISRAEL BIRD of Eff.Co. Deed dated March 6, 1799, for 125 acres in Eff.Co., being the moiety or half part of 250 acres known as Bryan's Cowpens, bounded west by Ogeechee River; also 300 acres in Bryan Co., bounded west by said river, south by Jonathan Bryan's land, deeded by latter to James Bryan Sept.13, 1773. Witnesses: Allen M. Allen and J. Cuyler J.P.

(p.125) DR. JESSE WILSON to his son WILLIAM WILSON, carpenter, both of Eff. Co. Deed of Gift dated Dec.3, 1799, for 50 acres being ½ part of 100 acres adj. J.G. Neidlinger on Jack's branch and the road to Savannah. Witnesses: Peter Hawthorn and Henry W. Williams, Clerk Superior Court.

(p.126) Affidavit of CHRISTIANA ELIZABETH ARNSTORPH "late Shrimp", dated May 21, 1794 (or 1796,not clear) in which she says that sometime before the British took possession of "this country" (county?) her late husband SOLOMON SHRIMP told her he was going to sell his land on the Ogeechee River to Zettler; that he later went off and then returned home with the proceeds in money in a handerchief which he said was paid him for the land, and was soon after taken sick and died before he ever made titles to the land he had received payment for.

(p.127) CLEMENT LANIER, Sheriff Eff.Co., to CHRISTIAN DASHER: Sheriff's deed dated June 20, 1794, conveying 50 acres granted Solomon Shrimph, levied on and sold as property of John G. Neidlinger and wife as Executors of will of Daniel Zettler to satisfy fifa in favor of said Dasher. Witness: John Williams.

(p.128) JESSE HURST and wife Maddlin (sic), to WILLIAM HURST. Deed dated Aug.22, 1796, for 100 acres adjoining grantee, being part of 350 acre tract previously granted the grantor. Wit: Wm.Hurst Jr., James Oliver, Sealy Wylly.

(p.130) HENRY COOK and Lydia his wife to MARTHA HOLLINGER, all of Eff. Co. Deed dated May 28, 1798, for 150 acres on south side of Cowpens branch.Witnesses: Senate Powers, James Brewer.

(p.132) JOHN EPPINGER, bricklayer, of Chatham Co., and wife Hannah Elizabeth, to JOSHUA LOPER of Eff.Co., planter. Deed dated Nov.25, 1799, for 300 acres granted John Eppinger, dec'd., Nov.3, 1761, and left by his will tohis son, the grantor; land located on north side of Great Ogeechee adj. Jonathan Bryan and said Loper. Witnesses: Donald McCaskell, Balthazer Shaeffer, J.P.,Chatham Co.

(p.134) JOHN FITZGERALD of Savannah, in an instrument dated Dec. 17, 1799, says he has lately bought of Patrick McKendy of same county a certain negro girl Silvy and agrees that if she is taken for any debts of estate of John Stirk dec'd., he will not demand repayment of the consideration money $310.00. Witnesses: William Ulmer and Phillip Ulmer.

(p.134) Agreement dated Oct. 5, 1797, between MARTIN CRUGER and wife CATHERINE (nee Catherine Chisler),and WILLIAM and THOMAS TOWNSEND. It is recited: "Whereas, WilliamTownsend, mariner, of Ga., died intestate leaving real and personal property which be reason of the heirs being underage came into the hands of said Catherine Chisler (now Cruger); said Thomas and William being heirs of said deceased, now being of age" receipt in full the said Catherine for negro wench and 200 acres of land and town lot 16 in Ewensburgh, Chatham Co., and half part of 100 acres where Cruger lives; and said Cruger and wife acknowledges full satisfaction for the food, lodging, clothing, doctor bills &c., they expended on said Thomas and William Townsend "to this date". Witness: John Spencer, John Wisenbaker, Christian Dasher.

(p.135) JAMES HOLTON of Screven Co., to THOMAS POLHILL of Eff.Co. Deed dated March 20, 1800, for slave Isaac. Wit: Wm.L.Hall, Abiel Scheighoffer, J.P.

(p.142) THOMAS and WILLIAM TOWNSEND to MARTIN CRUGER, planter. Deed dated Oct.21, 1797, for 50 acres being ½ of 100-acre tract granted to --- Lockner adjoining George Reisser and John Staley. Witnesses: James Anderson, Thomas Spencer and John Spencer J.P.

(p.143) JOHN GEORGE ZETTROUER and CHRISTIAN HEIDT, Trustees for Godlieb and HannahShubtrine, having been appointed Trustees for saidminors by their father Christian Shubtrine, now dec'd., as per deed of trust (recorded on p.65 above abstracted) in an instrument dated March 4, 1800, relinquish their powers as such Trustees and turn over the trust property to Jonathan Seckinger, who has been appointed Guardian for said minors. Wit: Jno.C.Miller, J.G. Neidlinger C.S.C.

(p.144) JONATHAN SNYDER and Elizabeth his wife to JOHN WILLIAM BISHOP, a minor, all of Eff.Co. Deed dated March 3, 1800, for 200 acres granted Jonathan Snyder Nov.9, 1799,lying on Wilson's branch. Wit: Henry W. Williams and Godhelf Smith, J.I.C.

(p.146) Receipt dated July 14, 1783, from JOHN TISON to WILLIAM STAF-
FORD and DORCAS GINDRAT, Executors of SAMUEL STAFFORD, dec'd., for the share of
his wife Elizabeth, daughter of said Samuel Stafford. Also,Receipt dated Nov.
22, 1796, at Boggy Gut, S.C., from JOHN TISON to HENRY GINRAT for 1/5th part being
his wife's part or share of slave named Simon that did belong to Samuel Stafford
dec'd and left by the latter's will to his son RICHARD STAFFORD;now dec'd. Also,
Receipt of WILLIAM STAFFORD to HENRY GINDRAT dated Feb.24, 1798, for his share of
said slave Simon "left by my father to my brother Richard who died in his minor
age." Also, Receipt from MARY STAFFORD to H. GINDRAT dated Apr. 22, 1800, in
Eff. Co., for her share of said slave Simon "left to my brother Richard by my
father." Receipts all recorded at the same time.

(p.147) ISRAEL KIEFFER, FREDERICK NESLER "renounce" all their claim
and interest (on Oct. 9, 1795) in and to a negro slave "George" formerly belonging
to Christina Kieffer dec'd., and agree jointly with Joshua Zant as joint heirs of
the dec'd to pay their proportionate part of any debts due by said dec'd. Witnesses: David Ewing, Mary Ewing.

(p.147) HERGAN HERSON, husband of Hannah Herson nee Hannah Wertsch,
daughter and sole heir of John Casper Wertsch and Elizabeth his wife, gives a receipt in full for 25 guineas to CHRISTIAN DASHER for the legacy left by the will
saod Elizabeth Wertsch to Hannah Gugle wife of Christian Dasher of Goshen, planter.
Dated Aug. 6, 1791. Witnesses: John Wisenbaker and William H. Lang.

(p.149) ROBERT H. HUGHES and wife Chloe to JAMES BREWER, Minister, all
of Eff. Co. Deed dated Dec.28, 1799, to 400 acres adj. lands of grantee. Witnesses: Samuel Parrish and Richard Purvis.

(p.150) JOHN HOPKINS of Camden Co., cordwainer, toJOHN PALMER of Eff.
Co., planter. Deed dated Apr. 17, 1800, for 100 acres in Dist. of Ebenezer now
Eff.Co., lying on Savannah River, and granted grantor May 1, 1759. Witnesses:
William Kennedy and William Porter.

(p.161) THOMAS CAMPBELL, late of Eff.Co., having died intestate owning
real and personal property which has been divided among the five heirs, and they
being desirous that THOMAS CAMPBELL the only son of the dec'd.,should have a certain 340-acre tract, the other heirs relinquish same unto him by conveyance dated
March 15, 1800. Signed by JOSIAH DANIEL, SARAH DANIEL, ANN CAMPBELL, SAMUEL RYALL,
WILLIAM DUPIUS. Witnesses: William Daniel, Reubin Roberts, James Boston J.I.C.

(p.152) DAVID REISSER and wife Mary to JESSE BELL, all of Eff. Co.
Deed dated May 29, 1800, for 18 acres on south side of Exley's branch, being part
of 50 acres granted Christian Beddenbach, Oct. 2, 1759. Witnesses: Jonathan Rahn,
Henry W. Williams Clerk Superior Court.

(p.153) JESSE BELL and wife ANN, to DAVID REISSER, all of Eff.Co. Deed
dated May 29, 1800, for 80 acres being part of 150-acre tract granted John Grovenstein, Feb. 5, 1765. Same witnesses as last above.

(p.154) EMANUEL ZEIGLER and Abegail his wife, DAVID ZEIGLER and Mary
his wife, JOHN GLONER and Elizabeth his wife, JOHN HINELY and Margaret his wife,
and CATHERINE ZEIGLER, to DAVID REISSER, cordwainer, all of Eff.Co. Deed dated Oct
31, 1790, for 50 acres granted Elizabeth Renold (Hunold? dim)June 7, 1757, and the
heirs of said Elizabeth Hunold? being the grantors. Witnesses: Jonathan Rahn
and John G. Neidlinger Clerk S.C.

(p.156) ANNA MARGARET SEEINER,,widow, to JOHN MARTIN DASHER, both of Eff. Co. Deed dated March 1, 1794, for seven acres on Mill Creek near Ebenezer being part of a larger tract granted Dec. 9, 1756, to Rutrech Zimmerebner? and was inherited from his estate as sole heir by Anna Margaret, wife of David Seiner; and was later sold byThomas Lane, Sheriff, as David's property to said Anna Margaret. Witnesses: Patrick McKinly, Daniel Remshart, John Martin Dasher, Jr.

(p.163) CHRISTOPHER BAYLY to WILLIAM BEALE, both planters, of Eff. Co. Deed dated July 4, 1793, for 26 acres being part of 200 acres granted grantor on Nov. 17, 1791. Grantor's wife Grace signs deed also, both signing their names as "Baillee" but the name is spelled Bayly in body of deed. Witnesses: Robert Scott and Ann Crawford.

(p.165) MILBREE HARPER, spinster, formerly of S.C., now of Eff.Co. in an instrument dated 1793 binds herself as a servant unto JESSE WILSON of Eff. Co., laborer, for remainder of her natural life, agreeing "in all things to behave herself as a faithful servant ought to do".

(p.165) JESSE WILSON to JOHN MARTIN DASHER both of Eff.Co. Deed dated Jan. 13, 1794, for 100 acres adjoining grantee, and granted grantor Apr. 4, 1785. Witnesses: Daniel Burgsteiner, Gideon Mettler. In a memorandum attached signed by Solomon Staten, he receipts said Dasher for L25 for said land which had been sold him by Jesse Wilson "but the deed was not in proper form"; Staten assents to the sale and to the deed fromWilson to Dasher.

(p.170) WILLIAM COLSON of Eff.Co., planter, and MARTHA his wife, to JOSHUA STAFFORD of Eff.Co. Deed dated Nov. 17, 1792, for 100 acres known as Ford's Cowpens near Little Ogeechee River, granted to Isaac Ford Esq. Witnesses: Stephen Ford Sr., Abraham Colson, N. Hudson J.P.

(p.171) NATHANIEL OTT, laborer, to ERNST CHRISTIAN ZETTEROUR, both of Eff. Co. Deed dated Jan.5, 1784, for 50 acres in the Mill district of Ebenezer, granted Sept.30, 1757 to David Eeiberger? and by him deeded Charles Sigsmund Ott Aug. 24, 1759, and then by John Gottlieb Ott, son and heir of said Charles Sigmund, deeded grantor by deed of gift dated June 5, 1776. Wit: Jacob Cronberger, John Penrose.

(p.173) GODLIEB OTT of Eff. Co. to ERNST CHRISTIAN ZETTEROUR of Eff.Co. Deed dated Jan. 24, 1784, for 100 acres being the s.w. one-third of 150 acres granted Aug. 7, 1759, to Charles Sigmund Ott and inherited from his estate by grantor as son and heir. Witnesses: Jacob Cronberger, Jonathan Zetterour.

(p.179) JOHN JACOB YAKELY to JACOB IHLY, both of Eff. Co., planters. Deed dated May 30, 1791 for 50 acres granted Michael Bearman? Feb.27, 1756, and inherited from his estate by John Igle and John Rentz who deeded same to grantor. Witnesses: Pat. McKinty, Daniel Remshart.

(p.184) SAMUEL KRAUS, carpenter, and his wife JUDITH, to BENJAMIN DASHER, all of Eff.Co. Deed dated March 1, 1794, for 50 acres being part of a larger tract granted grantor Oct. 13, 1786. Wit: John M.Dasher, Dan'l Remshart, Jesse Bell J.P.

(p.187) MARGARET ANDERSON, widow, to WILLIAM HURST, both of Eff.Co. Deed dated Aug. 7, 1792, for 200 acres granted her April 8, 1791, lying on Wallowing branch. Witnesses: Thomas Lane, Thomas Hurst.

(p.188) JOHN FRYER, laborer, to MICAJAH BROMBLY, laborer. Deed dated Oct.31, 1792, for 100 acres granted Nov. 6, 1764, to William Odom and by him and his wife Sarah deeded Aaron Fryer Oct. 29, 1768. Wit: John Loney, Edward Lowther.

53

(p.189) ZACHARIAH HENDERSON to JOHN KNIGHT. Bill of Sale, undated, £ for three slaves, 60 head of cattle, two horses, four featherbeds and furniture, together with pots,pans and all other items of his furniture and household goods, given in payment of his bond (promissory note) to Knight dated March 10, 1770. No witnesses signed, however, David Hines signs affidavit Feb. 18, 1794, that he saw Zachariah Henderson sign the instrument.

(p.190) JOHN KNIGHT of Eff. Co. "out of his love and good will" gives the above personal property to MARY HENDERSON by Bill of Sale dated Mar. 11, 1793. Witnesses: David and Nancy Hines.

(p.191) THOMAS READING, schoolmaster, and Elizabeth his wife, nee Elizabeth Ratliff, of Eff.Co., to CAMEL TICE (probably meant to Tison) of Eff.Co. Deed dated Feb. 24, 1793, for 230 acres on Great Ogeechee River. Witnesses: Jesse Dikes, ElijahTiner.

(p.192) THOMAS LANE, SHERIFF Eff.Co. and STEPHEN FORD, ADMR. OF ISAAC FORD, to JOSEPH JACKSON. Deed dated Sept. 1, 1792, for 36 acres being part of a tract granted Isaac Ford lying on Colson's branch now known as Jackson's branch, and adjoining grantee. Witnesses: Michael Dickson, James Caswell, Josiah Jackson.

(p.194) JAMES COOK to WILLIAM RAWLS, both planters of Eff.Co. Deed dated Aug.13, 1793, for 200 acres surveyed March 18, 1786, for Patience Rawls and lying on Black creek, it being the place where Patience Cook, nee Patience Rawls mow lives. Witnesses: Israel Bird J.P., Joseph Jackson J.P., Jesse McCall J.P.

(p.196) THOMAS LANE, Commissioner appointed by the legislature for carrying into effect the law inflicting penalties and confiscating estates of persons declared guilty of treason against the State, to HOBERT MARLOW, planter of Eff. Co. Deed dated Oct. 9, 1789, for 100 acres on north side of Great Ogeechee and on east and west sides of Braddock's branch,"including the old fields", confiscated and sold as property of James Robinson, a person banished from the State. Witnesses: William Cone, Joseph Cone.

(p.197) THOMAS LANE, Sheriff Eff.Co. and STEPHEN FORD, ADMR. OF ISAAC FDBB, to MICHAEL DICKSON. Deed dated Sept.3, 1792, for 100 acres being part of 300 acres granted Isaac Ford, lying on Jackson's branch. Witnesses: Joseph Jackson J.P., James Caswell, Josiah Jackson.

(p.198) CALEB HOWELL, Esq., to WILLIAM PEARCE, planter, both of Eff. Co. Deed dated Aug. 9, 1792, for 200 acres on Little Ogeechee River. Witnesses: James Bevill and Daniel Howell.

(p.200) WILLIAM WILKINS and wife Charity, to WILLIAM RUSHING, all of Eff. Co. Deed dated June 6, 1792, for 200 acres on north side Great Ogeechee River, granted Wilkins Feb. 9, 1790. Witnesses: John Shuman, Fred'k Wommock,John Eigle.

(p.226) GEORGE KOGLER and Barbara his wife, to MARTIN DASHER, both of Ebenezer. Deed dated Sept.24, 1763, conveying lot #1 in town of Ebenezer. Witnesses: John Flerl, Rubrecht Zimmerburo?.

(p.228) GIDEON MALLETTE, cordwainer, and Elizabeth His wife, to JOHN Hangleiter, cordwainer, all of Eff.County. Deed dated Sept.14, 1793, for 50 acres in St.Matthews Parish now Eff.Co., adj. John Hangleiter and lying on Savannah River, granted John AdamTruetlin March 3,1767,and by him deeded Abr. deROCHE, Dec.19,1769, and by latter deeded grantor. Witnesses: Matthew Rahn, Michael Exley.

(p.230) JOHN MARTIN DASHER to LYDIA, wife of ISRAEL KIEFFER, SALOME STINER, CATHERINE STINER and ELIZABETH STINER, the daughters of David and Margaret Stiner, all of Effingham Co. Deed dated March 24, 1794, for 118 acres near Ebenezer Mill Creek and lying on both sides of Mill Creek, granted Dec. 9, 1756, to Rubrecht Zimmerbuer and inherited by his daughter, Anna Margaret the wife of said David Stiner (Stiener) and was sold as said David's property by Thomas Lane, Sheriff, to said Anna Margaret Stiner who deeded same to grantor March 20, 1794. Witnesses: G. Zettrouer and John G. Niedlinger J.P.

(232) JAMES GREENHOW, Trustee for Rosana Postel now Spencer, and Rosinda Speer, to JOHN KEEBLER, all of Eff. Co. Deed dated Nov.4, 1794. Conveys lots 6 and 7 being two 50-acre lots in the township of Abercorn, lying on Abercorn Creek. Wit. J. Cuyler J.P., Benjamin Stirk.

(p.234) SARAH CLYATT to THOMAS WILDER. Bill of Sale dated Feb.27, 1792, for all her rights and interest in six negro slaves belonging to the estate of Isaac Mills, dec'd., three beds and furnishings. Consid:$3000. Witness: Asa Loper.

(p.235) Same parties as last above. Deed dated Aug. 1, 1819, for 200 acres on Big Ogeechee near Bryan's Cowpens, adjoining Frederick Wiggins; also 300 acres on Saltehatchee in Colleton Dist. S.C., adjoining William Pickney. Wit: Asa Loper.

(p.236) JOHN RENTZ, baker, to HENRY LODWICK BUNTZ, both of Eff.Co., planter, both of Eff. Co. Deed dated Dec. 8, 1794, conveying lot 10 in Ebenezer, size 60x90 feet, granted grantor Aug. 2, 1774. Witnesses: Joseph Rahn, J.G.Niedlinger J.P.

(p.241) JOHN KOGLER and wife Elizabeth, to JOHN MICKLER, all of Effingham Co. Deed dated July 9, 1794, for lot #4 in Ebenezer granted Paul Zettrouer Nov.7,1755, and his son and heir John George Zettrouer deeded grantor March 3, 1792. Witnesses: Henry L. Buntz and T. Wylly J.P.

(p.243) WILLIAM LEWDEN, GEORGE NUNGAZER, JUSTUS H. SCHUBER, Executors of estate of JOHN RING late of Chatham Co. dec'd., and Guardians of Mary R., minor daughter of dec'd., to JOHN MOORE of Eff. Co. Executors' deed dated Jan.17, 1794, for 350 acres in Eff.Co., granted Aug.5, 1766, to Christopher Ring and later on May 21st, 1786 by deed of gift given to his son John Ring whose will dated Oct. 11, 1792,was duly probated. Witnesses: Benj. Butler, Balthazer Shaffer J.P. Chatham Co.

(p.245) THOMAS LANE, Sheriff, to THOMAS McCALL, Esq. Sheriff's deed dated Aug. 22, 1789, for 300 acres lying in two tracts in Eff. Co., one on Brier Creek and the other on Tyger Bay, levied on and sold as property of John Lynch. Witnesses: William Dupius and Jesse McCall.Public Sale.

(p.248) THOMAS LANE, Esq., Sheriff Eff. Co. to STEPHEN DENMARK of Eff.Co. Sheriff's deed dated Jan.4, 1792, for 100 acres on south side Great Ogeechee River above the flat ford, sold as property of John Casper Wertsch, merchant, dec'd. un - der execution in favor of William King and William Colson; land was granted Thomas Davis. Witnesses: Thomas Wylly J.P., Jesse Bell J.P.

(p.249) JOHN TRUETLIN, Gentleman, to STEPHEN DENMARK, planter, both of
Eff.Co. Deed dated Jan. 11, 1793, for 300 acres on north side Great Ogeechee River
about. two miles above the flat ford. Wit: William Denmark, William Cone J.P.

(p.250) JOHN ADAM TRUETLIN, yeoman, to STEPHEN DENMARK, both of Eff.Co.
Deed dated Oct.5, 1791, for 300 acres on south side of Great Ogeechee River and
lying on Ironmongers Creek, granted grantor Sept.2, 1766. Witnesses: George
Backley, Christian Truetlin J.P.

(p.252) CHRISTIAN BITTENBACH to JOHN BARREY, both planters of Eff.Co.
Deed dated Feb.1, 1794, for 150 acres granted July 6, 1774, to John Paulus and
inherited from him by his granddaughter Miss Mary Biddenbach as the only heir, and
inherited from her at her death by her half-brother the grantor. Witnesses: Godheif
Smith and Michael Exley.

(p.253) NATHANIEL ZETTLER of S.C., planter, to his niece, NAOMI ZETTLER
and his nephew GIDEON ZETTLER, both minors, of Eff. Co., John G. Niedlinger and
wife Hannah, Trustees for said minors. Gift of slaves dated April 5, 1794, slaves
formerly belong to estate of his brother Daniel Zettler, father of said minors,and
which had been bought in by him (the donor) at Sheriff's sale Jan. 1, 1794, at which
time they were sold as property of said dec'd (see p.254 for record of Sheriff's
sale); also conveys 300 acres consisting of a tract of 200 acres in said county granted Belthaser Reiser Dec.4, 1759, and by him deeded to John Adam Truetlin June 12,
1767, and by the latter deeded said Daniel Zettler Dec.4, 1770; and 100 acres being
a part of a 300-acre tract granted said Daniel Zettler. Said 300-acre tract having
been sold by Clement Lanier, Sheriff, to said Nathaniel, April 1794, as property of
Daniel Zettler dec'd. Witnesses: Matthew Rahn and Henry L. Buntz.

(p.257) GROSS SCRUGGS and wife Margaret of Scrven Co., to DANIEL/of Eff.
                                                              DAMPIER
Co. Deed dated July 3, 1794, for 100 acres on Three-Runs in Eff.Co. bounded on all
sides by lands granted Richard Scruggs Sr., July 24, 1783, and deeded Gross Scruggs
of then Eff.Co., Oct. 15, 1784. Witnesses: Daniel Daly, Christopher Hudson.

(p.260) DANIEL JOHNSON, planter, and Ann his wife, to HENRY COOK, all
of Eff. Co. Deed dated Apr.20, 1793, for 100 acres on Cowpens branch, adjoining the
grantee. Witnesses: Walton H. Griffin, Anthony Pitts.

(p.260) JOHN GEORGE ZEIGLER, planter, to HANNAH ELIZABETH SECKINGTON,
daughter of Andrew and Catherine Seckinger. all of Eff.Co. Gift of mare colt dated
Apr. 30, 1777. Witnesses: Samuel Kraus and Geo. Zettrouer. Probated by Kraus Jan.
8, 1795; before John G. Niedlinger C.S.C.

(p.262) JOHN KNIGHT of Eff. Co., to ANNA, MISEY, MARY and SARAK HENDERSON
children of Zachariah and Mary Henderson. Gift of three slaves Saturday, Flordda and
Sambo, 60 head of cattle, 2 horses, feather beds, furniture, pots, pans, farming
implements, dated Aug.30, 1794. Said Mary, mother of said children,to be Trustee.

(p.263) GODHEIF SMITH of Eff.Co. and wife Christiana, to JESSE BELL,
Practictioner of Physic, all of Eff.County, dated March 14, 1792. Deed conveys 50
acres lying on Ebenezer Creek in said county, granted Sept.30, 1757, to John
Smith and from him inherited by said grantor as his son and heir. Witnesses:
John Barry, J. G. Neidlinger J.P.

(p.266) WILLIAM HOLZENDORF of Eff.Co., toEDWARD TELFAIR of Savannah.
Mortgage on three slaves dated March 3, 1793. Executed in Savannah. Wit: Jos.Gibbons.

(p.268) JOHN GOTLIEB NEIDLINGER to BENJAMIN ST. MARK, Practictioner of

Physic. Bill of Sale dated May 21, 1790, for his dwelling-house and other adjacent buildings and fences at Ebenezer situated on the main road toAugusta, "at present occupied by Capt. Jacob Winckler". Witnesses: Jacob Mickler, Thomas Wylly. Transferred to Thomas Wylly Nov.4, 1791, and by Thomas and Naomi Wylly back to Dr. St. Mark June 11, 1792, and by him to Hergen Herson July 25, 1793.

(p.269) JOHN PETER FRYERMUTH, planter, to JOHN FRYERMUTH, cordwainer, both of Zffingham Co. Deed dated Feb. 7, 1795, for 50 acres lying on Savannah River and adjoining John George Gnann, and granted MatthiasGroll? Aug. 7, 1759, and afterwards was inherited by grantor in right of his wife Anna Catherine Fryermuth, one of the daughters and heirs of said Groll. Also 40 acres adjoining grantee, granted Nicholas Shubtrine Jan. 3, 1792, and by him andhis wife Anna Mary deeded grantor July 25, 1764; also 200 acres adjoining John Boykin, Jacob Russell et.al. and was granted Peter Fryermuth. Witnesses: James McCoy, J.G. Niedlinger J.P.

(p.271) JOHN FRYERMUTH to his wife ANNA CATHERINE FRYERMUTH. Deed of Gift dated Dec. 7, 1795, for the above described 50 acres. Same witnesses as last above.

(p.272) DAVID HINES, Sr. of Chatham Co., planter, to his grand-daughter SUSANNAH GRANT of Eff. Co., planter. Gift of slave dated Dec. 31, 1791. Witnesses: Abraham Bird Jr., Nathaniel Hawthorn.

(p.272) JOHN KEEBLER, Gentleman, to JOSHIA KEEBLER, planter, both of Eff. Co. Deed dared Feb. 1, 1795, for 50 acres in the village of Abercorn, being lot #7 granted Frederick Helvensteine and deeded to grantor by James Greenhow and Rosina Spencer. Witnesses: George Nowlan, Samuel Langley.

(p.275) JOSHUA KEEBLER and wife Elizabeth, of Abercorn, to GEORGE GALPHIN NOWLAN of Eff.Co. Deed dated May 18, 1795 for 50 acres in Goshen, being lot "C", also 50 acres granted Jacob Keebler. Witnesses: Geo. Nowlan, Benjamin Stirk.

(p.277) WILLIAM KENNEDY to WILLIAM DUPIUS of Eff.Co. Deed dated May 16, 1793, for 300 acres granted John A. Truetlin Dec.5, 1769 and by the latter's will devised to the grantor. Witnesses: John Kemp and John Largin.

(p.279) WILLIAM DENMARK, planter, of Eff.Co., to his wife ANNA DENMARK and her children Stephen Denmark, Susannah Jones, Jemima Denmark, LEVINA Rester, Clarisa Denmark, Martha Denmark, Reading (Redden) Denmark. Deed of Gift dated Jan. 21, 1795. Witnesses: Francis Covington, John Moore. Conveys to son Stephen 200 acres on the Great Ogeechee near Hickory Bluff, and to the other named children above named, certain items of personal property to each.

(p.279) JAMES BREWER Sr. of Eff.Co. to ROBERT H. HUGHES of Screven County. Deed dated Oct.3, 1794, for 100 acres on Wallowing branch, surveyed for William Crawford. Witness: John Lawton J.P. Wife Priscilla Brewer waives dower rights.

(p.282) SAMUEL KRAUSand wife Judith, to GEORGE ARNSTORPH, all of Eff.Co. Dedd dated March 29, 1795, for 100 acres granted Leonhard Kraus Sept. 5, 1758, and descneded to the grantor as his only son and heir. Witnesses: John Kogler, John M. Dasher, John G. Neidlinger J.P.

(p.283) JOHN CHRISTOPHER MILLER, blacksmith, of Eff. Co. to JOHN CHRIS- TOPHER GUGEL, cordwainer, of Savannah. Deed dated Dec.22, 1795, for 130 acres on Bear Creek,Eff.Co., granted to John Paul Miller Jr., Dec.3, 1760, and inherited by grantor as hks son and only heir. Witnesses: James McCoy, John G. Neidlinger Clerk Superior Court.

(p.295) JOHN FRYERMUTH, cordwainer, and Salomy his wife, and JOHN PETER
FRYERMUTH, planter, to JONATHAN BECHTLEY, all of Eff.Co. Deed dated Feb. 6, 1796,
conveying 40 acres granted Nicholas Shubtrine Feb. 3, 1782, and by him and his
wife Mary deeded to the said grantor. Witnesses: Andrew Gnann and John G.
Neidlinger Clerk Superior Court.

(p.281) ANNA CATHERINA FRYERMUTH, spinster, to ANDREW GNANN. Feb dated Feb.
6, 1796, for 50 acres lying on Savannah River and granted to the said Matthias
Gross Aug. 7, 1759, and obtained by John Peter Fryermuth in right of his wife the
said Anna Catherina, she being one of the daughters and heirs of said Gross.
Witnesses: Jonathan Backly, James McCoy, John G. Niedlinger C.S.C.

(p.289) Isom (Isham) Roberts and wife Polly to THOMAS HYLTON and wife Mary
(daughter of said Isham and Polly). Deed of Gift dated Aug. 10, 1793, conveying 150
acres on Scull's Creek. Witnesses: Wm. McCoy, Zachariah Coward, Francis Grimes.

(p.290) CHRISTIAN TRUETLIN and Mary his wife, to GIDEON MALLETTE, all of
Eff. Co. Deed dated Oct.26, 1795, for 80 acres on Turkey Creek, granted Aug. 27,
1795. Witnesses: James Porter, William Kennedy.

(p.292) ABIEL HUTTO and Lydia his wife to EMANUEL ZEIGLER, all of Eff. Co.
Deed dated Jan.25, 1793, for 75 acres being half of a tract granted George Hutto
May 1st, 1759. Witnesses: Solomon Gnann, John G. Neidlinger C.S.C.

(p.294) CIVILITY JONES of Liberty County, spinstress, to JOHN GODLIEB
NEIDLINGER, of Eff.Co., as Trustee for his minor sons John and Samuel. Trust deed
dated Feb.5, 1796, for 50 acres adjoining said Niedlinger, and granted to Mary
Jones, widow, Dec. 10, 1788, and deeded by her deed of gift dated Oct.30, 1793,
to James Jones and the said Civility Jones, and by said James Jones to the said
Civility by deed dated Oct.2, 1795, for his moiety. Witnesses: James McCoy and
Matthew Burgstiner.

(p.296) MATTHEW MEYER, shoemaker, to JOHN GEORGE GNANN, potter, both of St.
Matthews Parish. Deed dated Sept.23, 1773, for 50 acres in said parish bounded on
north by Matthew Gross and East by Savannah River. Granted grantor Aug.7, 1759.
Witnesses: Urben Buntz, Conrath Rahn, John Wertsch.

(p.297) CHRISTIPHER ROTTENBURGER of St. Matthews Parish, carpenter, to
ANDREW GNANN, shoemaker, and wife Anna, of same parish. Deed of Gift dated Oct.6,
1772, for seven acres in township of Ebenezer, said parish, granted grantor Jan.
3, 1769. (Note: This is an unfinished record, and names of witnesses not shown).

(p.302) JAMES WHITE to JOSHUA LOPER, both of Eff. Co. Deed dated June17,
1796. Conveys 350 acres granted Dec.4, 1764, to Cornelius McCarty and John Kelly
McCarty, Executor of will of said Cornelius McCarty, deeded Oct. 29, 1789, to Abraham Jones and by Jones to grantor Dec. 23, 1789. Witnesses: Lewis Bird and Justus H. Schueber.

(p.303) EMANUEL KIEFFER of Bethany, planter, and ANNA BARBARA his wife, to
HENRY GINDRAT. Deed dated July 19, 1788. Conveys 150 acres in said district and
parish, granted Daniel Shubtriene who deeded same to grantor. Witnesses: John
Boston, James Boston, Abraham Ravot J.P.

(p.307) EDWARD BOYKIN, planter, to HENRY GINDRAT of Eff.Co., late of S.C.
Deed dated Dec. 19, 1785, for 50 acres where grantor lives in Bethany District,
granted Dec. 6, 1757, to Nicholas Shubtriene and by him deeded grantor Oct.10,1767.
Also 50 acres being a part of grantor's homeplace, deeded by Joseph Shubtriene
Dec.23, 1768, to grantor. Also 50 acres adjoining deeded grantor Dec. 10, 1764,

by George Miller; and 200 acres adjoining the first two 50-acre tracts granted grantor Oct. 29, 1765. Witnesses: John Boykin, Natthew Myers.

(p.311) PETER GRANT, planter, and wife Susannah, to HOWELL HINES, planter, all of Eff. Co. Deed dated April 2, 1796, for 350 acres granted grantor Dec. 4, 1795, on re-survey found to be 231 acres, lying on Great Ogeechee River. Witnesses: Elijah Lewis, Stephen Woolf.

(p.313) JOHN KOGLER and Elizabeth his wife, to TIMOTHY STALEY, both planters and of Eff. Co. Deed Sept.13, 1796, conveying 100 acres granted Thomas Schweighoffer May 5, 1767, and inherited by his son Abiel and by the latter was deeded grantor Nov.5, 1788. Witnesses: Jonathan Rahn, Jonathan Seckinger and John G. Niedlinger, C.S.C.

(p. 314) JAMES HINES and wife Drusilla to their daughter SALLIE LEWIS, all of Eff. Co. Deed of Gáft dated (blank) for 303 acres on Great Ogeechee River. Witnesses: Peter Grant, Howell Hines.

(p.315) JAMES WILSON, planter, to his brother JESSE WILSON, planter, both of Eff.Co. Deed dated Nov.20, 1794, for 200 acres less 5 acres reserved for mill stream. Witnesses: Elijah Tyner, John Wilson, Millie Harper.

(p.316) JOHN WILEY of Eff.Co. to his wife ELIZABETH WILEY. Deed of Gift dated Oct. 11, 1784, for all his estate, real and personal (undescribed). Witnesses: Matthew Rahn, John G. Niedlinger,.J.P.

(p.317) FREDERICK CHRISTOPHER HECKLE, tailor, to NATHANIEL REYSER, shoemaker, both of Eff. Co. Deed dated Dec.30, 1796, for 150 acres granted Simon Reiter Sept.30, 1757, lying on Ebenezer Creek. Witnesses: John Gromet and Wm.Gardner J.P.

(p.321) GEORGE DAVIS of Bryan Co. to JOSHUA LOPER of Eff.Co. Deed dated Feb. 10, 1796, for 400 acres granted John Davis Nov. 19, 1791, and by him willed to grantor; land adjoins grantee. Wit: Hardy Lanier, Asa Loper.

(p.329) JAMES HINES and Drusilla his wife, to their son-in-law PETER GRANT, all of Eff.Co. Dedd of Gift dated April 2, 1796, for 231 acres on Great Ogeechee River being part of 800 acres granted grantor. Witnesses: Elijah Lewis and Howell Hines.

(p.330) JOHN EVERS Sr. to his daughter, ANNE GARRISON and her husband DARIUS GARRISON. Deed of Gift dated Aug.3, 1793, forthe upper half of tract he (grantor) bought from Matthew Bishop; made on condition grantees are not to sell same or settle anyone on the land so long as said Evers lives.Witnesses: Zachariah and Elizabeth White.

(p.331) JOHN HUSTON to JAMES TISON bothof Eff.Co. Deed dated Sept.5,1795, for 200 acres adjoining Daniel Zettler, being land granted Richard Bennett. Witnesses: John Cook, John London J.P.

(p.332) JAMES TISON, yeoman, to CAMMEL TISON, yeoman, both of Eff. Co. Deed dated Oct. 1, 1796, for 450 acres. Witnesses: Zachariah White,J.G.Niedlinger
(C.S.C.

(p.333) UNITY DYKES to her son JESSE DYKES both of Eff. Co. Deed of Gift dated Feb. 4, 1797, conveying 450 acres joining on the s.e. William Bishop and Jesse Dykes, n.e. by Matthew Bishop. Witnesses: Darius Garrison,Zachariah White.

(p.335) WILLIAM GILLELAND, schoolmaster, to HENRY GINDRAT, both of Eff.Co.

Mortgage on slave dated Nov.3, 1792. Witnesses: Wm. Porter, Simeon Reaves.

(p.338) JAMES COOK, Sr. to his friend ELEANOR GARNER. Gift dated 1796, for his bedstead,feather-bed,feather-bolster, two of his best spools, dutch blanket, green rug, pot hooks, pair smoothing irons, dated Dec.3, 1796. Witnesses: William Cone and Davis McCall, McKeen Green and Nelly Green and Mourning Shepherd. In a receipt attached signed by donor, he acknoqledges receipt of 1/16th of a dollar for all of his cattle branded "EC"; donee in this instrument referred to as Miss Nelly Garner.

(p.339) JOHN WISENBAKER to his son CHRISTIAN G. WISENBAKER. Deed of Gift dated Feb.20, 1797, for slave boy. Witnesses: Samuel Zipperer, James Anderson and Pat. McKenty, J.P.

(p.339) Same donor to his children JOHN, CHRISTIAN G. and ANN M. WISENBAKER. Deed of Gift dated Feb.20, 1797, for two slaves. Same witnesses.

(p.342) JOHN G. NIEDLINGER and wife Hannah to JOHN MARTIN DASHER, Gentleman, all of Eff. Co. Deed dated July 22, 1797, for200 acresgranted Martin Dasher Feb. 5, 1765, and inherited by John Martin Dasher as his son and heir, and by latter deeded said John G., July 30, 1785 (as per record in Book "B" page 95).Witnesses: Daniel Burgstiener and Gideon Zettler.

(p.344) JOHN KEEBLER to JAMES GREENHOW as Trustee for Rosanna Postell nee Spencer. Deed dated Oct. 9, 1794, for 50acres near Goshen, being half part of 100 acres granted Jacob Keebler Dec.23, 1756. Also 50 acres in Goshen village. Witnesses: Benjamin Stirk and J. Cuyler J.P.

(p.346) CURTIS LOPER of S.C. planter, to JAMES HUDSON of Eff.Co.,planter. Deed dated Dec.23, 1795, for one-third part of 200 acres granted John Bandy on Aug.5, 1788, lying on Great Ogeechee,. and by Bandy deeded to Frederick Womack Mar. 4, 1791, and by Womack to grantor Feb.14, 1793. Witnesses: James Webb and Noshua Loper J.P.

(p.348) ROBERT HUDSON of Eff.Co. to his son JAMES HUDSON of S.C. Gift of slaves dated Sept. 16, 1789. Witnesses: Nohn R. Cleary and Isaac Hudson.

(p.349) Same donor to his grand-daughter MARY HUDSON (daughter of his son James Hudson). Gift of slave dated Jan. 8, 1793. Witnesses: James Bilbo,Nathaniel Hudson J.P.

(p.349) MRS. JUDITH BISHOP to JONATHAN RAHN, both of Eff. Co. Bill of Sale dated 1797 for slave. Witnesses: Ann Rachel Mock and Thomas Wylly J.P.

(p.350) THOMAS SCHWEIGHOFFER and wife Susannah, of Savannah, shoemaker, to ABIEL SCHWEIGHOFFER of Eff. Co. Deed dated June 6, 1797, for 50 acres adj. grantor, bounded n.e. by David Unseld, and granted Thos. Schweighoffer Sr., Dec. 3, 1760, and inherited by grantor as one of his heirs as per Memorial entered in Clerk's office May 8, 1761 (in Book "C" pp.35-6). Witnesses: Israel Flerl and Thomas Polhill. Duly probated.

(p.352) JOSEPH MOCK, planter, to JAMES GUTHRIE, planter, both of Eff.Co. Deed of Gift (no relationship shown) dated Dec. 19, 1797, for 200 acres granted grantor Feb.25, 1795. Witnesses: William Bishop, Jonathan Seckinger, JohnG. Niedlinger J.P. Donor reserves life-estate in the property.

(p.354) WILLIAM PRAY, Sheriff Bryan Co. to THOMAS CATER, Esq. of Liberty County. Sheriff's deed dated Aug.29, 1796, for 300 acres in Eff. Co., bounded n.e. by Michael Muckingfuss, s.w. by John Eubbedge. Also 525 acres in former Christ Church Parish now Eff. Co., bounded east by Great Ogeechee, south by land ordered for Cubbedge; and levied on and sold as property of John Cubbedge estate, George Cubbedge Admr., under execution infavor of John Kell estate, issued by the Inferior Court of Bryan Co. Witnesses: Thomas Day, John Pray J.P.

(p.356) DANIEL BURGSTINER and wife Mary to JOHN MARTIN DASHER. Deed dated April 13, 1790, for 200 acres lying on Zettler's Crekk and adjoining grantee, and granted grantor Dec.4, 1787. Witnesses: Gideon Zettler, J.G. Niedlinger J.P.

(p.358) JOHN MARTIN DASHER and Elizabeth his wife, planter, to MATTHEW and SAMUEL BURGSTINER, planters, all of Eff.Co. Deed dated July 17, 1797, for 200 acres adjoining Zettler's land and grantor, and granted Daniel Burgstiner Dec. 4, 1787. Witnesses: Pat McKenly J.P., John M. Dasher J.P.

(p.359) CHARLES ODINGSELLS of ChathamCo., planter, to JOHN RENTZ, Sr. of same place. Deed dated Feb.20, 1787, for50 acres in Eff. Co., near Ebenezer, adjoining George Zeigler and MartinDasher, bought by grantor as confiscated property confiscated as property of Christopher Frederick Truetlin. Witnesses: Nicholas Miller and John Herb.

(p.361) JOHN RENTZ to JUSTUS H. SCHUBER, both of Chatham Co. Deed dated Feb.13, 1794, for same land as last above.Witnesses: Ichabod Higgins, Mordecai Sheftall, J.P.,Chatham County.

(p.362) GODLIEB SHEROUSE and Mary his wife, JOHN SHEROUSE, JONATHAN SECKINGER and Ann Mary Frederica his wife, GEORGE ARNSTORPH and Elizabeth his wife, ABIAL HEIDT and Elizabeth His wife (she signs as Lydia instead of Elizabeth), and DOROTHY SHEROUSE, all of Eff. Co. to JUSTUS HARTMAN SCHUBER. Deed dated June 17, 1794, for 100 acres bounded north by Michael Waters? and Geo. Neese, and on other sides vacant, being S½ of 200 acres granted Sept.5, 1758, to Jacob Maurer and at his decease was left to his daughter Johannah Sheely who dying without heirs the property was inherited by her sister Mary the wife of John Sherouse, dec'd., the mother of the grantors Godlieb, John, Anna Maria Frederica,Elizabeth, Lydia and Dorothy, the only surviving representatives of said Jacob Maurer. Witnesses: John Grovenstine and Jesse Bell J.P.

(p.364) CHRISTOPHER GUGEL of Savannah, shoemaker, and Mary his wife, ISRAEL KIEFER of Eff.Co., planter, and Hannah Margaret his wife, to JUSTUS HERTMAN SCHEUBER. Deed dated March 17, 1793, for 37½ acres adjoining grantee, being the N½ of 150 acres granted Mathias Brandner and at his death was divided between his three daughters, among them Hannah the wffe of John Flerl Jr., and Mary the wife of Joseph Shubtrine, who drew their shares together, and said Flerl and Shubtrien by deed of division between them on Feb. 5, 1767, whereby said N½ fell to said Mary. Said Joseph Shubtrien having since deceased said Mary wife of said Gugel and said Hannah Margaret wife of said Israel Reiser being the surviving heirs of said Shubtrien, became the owners. Witnesses: A. Mayer and Mordecai Sheftall J.P. Chatham Co.

(p.367) JAMES TALLER to JOSHUA LOPER. Bill of Sale for slave girl Beck, age two years. Dated Feb.28, 1794. Witnesses: Asa and Abel Loper.

(p.367) WILLIAM O'STEEN and wife Elizabeth to JOSHUA LOPER. Power of Attorney dated Dec. 7, 1793, to receive her share of estate of John Davis Sr. and wife Elizabeth,bothdec'd.,of Eff.Co. Witnesses: Abel Loper and Nancy Davis.

(p.369) JOHN MICKLER to ISRAEL KIEFFER. Quit-claim deed dated May 10, 1797, for all claims and demands he has by virtue of sale of slave belonging to estate of Solomon Zant of which estate said Kieffer is the Admr. and on which account the said Mickler has been sued. Witness: John G. Niedlinger C.S.C.

(p.369) JAMES TYSON to JOHN COOK, planter, both of Eff. Co. Deed dated Jan. 30, 1798, for 200 acres granted Richard Bennett May 19, 1789, and by him was deeded John Huston in 1791, and by the latter to grantor Sept. 5, 1795. Witness: John London J.P.

(p.371) WILLIAM BISHOP of Eff.Co. to his son STEPHEN BISHOP and daughter REBECCA BISHOP. Gift instrument dated Nov.25, 1797, for horses, cows, sheep, hogs, &c. Witnesses: Daniel Duffy and John London J.P. Wife Judith Bishop waives dower "except to what is reserved to her by the terms of the conveyance, viz., that she shall receive one-half of all the wool each year for her lifetime."

(p.372) Same donor to the same children, same date, Deed of Gift for 400 acres granted him April 12, 1791, and 200 acres granted him Jan. 19, 1797, made on condition that one-third of all produce raised on said lands to be given each year to their mother Judith Bishop. Same witnesses.

(p.374) JOHN MICHAEL HINDSMAN, planter, of Wilkes Co.,and Anna Ursula his wife, to JOHN FRYERMUTH of Eff.Co., cordwainer. Deed dated Jan. 2, 1797, for 100 acres adjoining Simon Reiter, Christian Steiner and George Kogler and Ulrich Niedlinger; granted John Maurer and by him deeded John Gruber Feb.28, 1769, and by Gruber deeded to grantor May 13, 1772. Also 50 acres adjoining Matthias Brandner and granted John Gruber July 2, 1765, and by Gruber deeded grantor May 13, 1772. Witness: J. Germein? J.P.

(p.376) JAMES PORTER and Elizabeth his wife, of Eff. Co. to JAMES DUPIUS of Lincoln Co. S.C. Deed dated March 29, 1798, for 12 acres being part of 93 acres purchased from Christian Truetlin in 1793. Wit: Wm.Dupius, Wm. Kennedy J.I.C.

(p.377) WILLIAM PORTER and wifeRachel his wife, of Eff.Co. to JAMES DUPIUS of Lincoln Co. S.C. Deed dated March 29, 1798, for six acres being part of 100 acres bought by grantor from Dr. John Love in 1788 and exchanged with James Porter. Same witnesses as last above.

(p.378) JAMES PORTER and Elizabeth his wife to WILLIAM PORTER, all of Eff.Co. Deed dated March 29, 1798, for 58acres being part of 93 acres deeded by said James to William Porter. Same witnesses as last above.

(p.380) CHRISTIAN TRUETLIN to JAMES PORTER both of Eff.Co. Deed dated May 16, 1792, for 93 acres granted Hugh Kennedy March 28, 1762. Witnesses: William Porter, Harmon Crum.

(p.381) ANN MARGARET STEINER and SAMUEL KRAUS, Admrs. of CHRISTIAN STEINER dec'd., to JOHN M. DASHER of Eff.Co. Bill of Sale for slave dated Dec. 3, 1792. Witness: Joel Kieffer.

(p.382) JOHN M. DASHER to ANNA MARGARET STEINER. Bill of Sale for slave dated Jan.24, 1795. Witness: Joel Kieffer.

(p.383) SAMUEL KRAUS and MARGARET STEINER, Admrs. of DAVID HINES estate to BENJAMIN DASHER. Bill of Sale dated Dec. 3, 1794, for slave. Same witness.

(p.384) BENJAMIN DASHER to SAMUEL KRAUS. Bill of Sale for slave dated Jan. 24, 1794. Witness: John G. Niedlinger J.P.

(p.84) RICHARD WALL, Sheriff Chatham Co. to JEREMIAH CUYLER of Eff. Co., Attorney-at-law. Sheriff's deed dated Dec. 8, 1798, for 100 acres in the District of Goshen, Eff.Co., about 15 miles from Savannah on the Augusta Road, adjoining John Spencer, George Nowlan, Jonathan Cline, Jacob Casper Waldhaeur. Levied on and sold as property of James Moore estate under execution in favor of Paul H. Wilkins. Witnesses: Richard H. Leake and Lewis Johnston J.P.,Chatham Co.

(p.385) JOHN CRAWFORD of Eff.Co. to MARTHA THOUCHSTON and her children THOMAS, NELLY, PATIENCE, SEALY and JESSE TOUCHTON. Deed dated Aug.23, 1799, for 300 acres adjoining Robert H. Hughes. Witnesses: J.Stewart, J. London J.P. Grantor's wife Priscilla Crawford waives dower rights.

(p.388) THOMAS READING of Charleston Dist. S.C. to WILLIAM BEALL ofEff. Co. Deed dated Dec. 18, 1798, for 200 acres. Witnesses: James Wilson, William Moggan, Elijah Tiner, J.G. Walsingham.

(p.389) Sales Account in re: Estate of Arthur Ryall, dec'd., dated May 15, 1800. Showing sales of slaves andother personal property, to whom sold and prices each item brought, etc.

(p.392) ISAAC CARTER toDR. JOHN McRORY both of Eff. Co. Deed dated Dec. 3, 1792, for 100 acres adjoining John Adam Truetlin, Christopher Bailey and Jonathan Cole. Witnesses: Robert Greer and N. Hudson J.P.

(p.393) JOHN BLANTON of Augusta to HON. ROBERT GOODLOE HARPER, member of Congress from S.C. Deed dated June 22, 1796, conveying 33,934 acres in Eff. Co. mostly in grants of 1000 acres each. Witnesses: James Chesnut, John Nelson and Abram Jones J.P. Deed executed in Pennsylvania. Editor's note: This is probably an attempted sale of lands granted on fraudulent grants.

(p.400) JOHN SPENCER frees a slave named William Russell, Aug. 30, 1800. Witness: Abial Schweighoffer J.P.

(p.403) HANNAH HUDSON of Eff.Co., widow, to her daughter EVELINE HUDSON. Gift instrument dated July 24, 1800, for three slaves. Wit: J.Cuyler J.P.,John
(Kiefer.
(p.404) WILLIAM HURST of Eff. Co., Last Will and Testament dated Oct. 19, 1800 - (Editor's note: This instrument may have been intended to be a deed to take effect at the donor's death,or may have been intended as a will. No probate in court seems to have taken place). Gives to wife Mary his home plantation with its tenements and "utensils" and all his live-stock and household goods, for her lifetime or widowhood, and afterwards the home plantation to go to his son William Hurst to include the mill and half of his livestock and household goods; and to his daughter Zilpha 100 acres bought of Jesse Hurst, and the other half of his livestock and household. Said Mary and William to be "Guardians of this deed". Witnesses: James Conner and Thomas Hurst. Conner on Dec. 1, 1800, pro-bates the deed and refers to William Hurst,the maker of the instrument,as being
(dead.
(p.405) CHRISTOPHER BAILLEY (BAILLIE) of Eff.Co. to SALLY MORGAN. Deed of Gift dated Oct.3, 1800, for 100 acres adjoining John A. Truetlin and William Boles. Also 200 acres adjoining. Witnesses: Senate Powers,James and Wm. Wilson.

(p.407) JOHN SPENCER, planter, to JONATHAN ZIPPERER both of Eff. Co. Deed dated May 24, 1800. Conveys 100 acres, and 100 adjoining known as the Cowper land, also adj. Wm. Holzendorf, and granted in two 50-acre tracts to John Stacy. Witnesses: John M.Dasher and Nathaniel Langley.

(p.408) JOHN CHRISTOPHER MILLER and wife Hannah of Eff. Co., on Jan.6,1801,

relinquishes to JOHN PAUL MILLER Jr. of Wilkes Co. all his rights, title, interest and claim in and to the estates of John Paul MillerSr. and the latter's son
Frederick Miller, both of Eff.Co.,dec'd. Wit: Wm. Shrimp and John Kogler J.P.

(p.409) JOHN WILLIAMS, Sheriff Eff.Co. to ROSINA CALDER of Eff.Co. Sheriff's deed dated Feb.16, 1801, for 75 acres in said county adj. John Stirk and
village of Abercorn, sold as property of John Keebler under a fifa issued in fav-
or of Jacob Ihly. Witnesses: John King, Thomas Polhill J.I.C.

(p.411) Same Sheriff as above to JOHN KING of Eff. Co. Sheriff's deed
same date, conveys 150 acres on Tuckaseeking branch, consisting of several small
tracts, sold as property of Samuel Bostick under fifa in favor of James Sims.
Witnesses: Matthew Rahn and Thomas Polhill J.I.C.

(p.413) DANIEL WHITEMAN of Eff.Co., shoemaker, to GOTTLIEB ERNST,teacher,
of Eff. Co. Deed dated Sept.27, 1798, for 14 acres in the edge of Ebenezer (town)
and 64 acres granted Rev. Herman Henry Lemke. Witnesses: Godheif Smith,John Kogler
(J.P.

(p.415) JOHN WILLIAMS, Sheriff Eff.Co. to THOMAS POLHILL. Sheriff's deed
dated - - - 1801, conveying slave, sold as property of JohnStirk estate underx
a fifa issued in favor of John Roberts. Witnesses: Thos.Campbell, J.Cuyler J.P.

(p.415) FREDERICK LOCKNER, wheelwright,and wife Hannah, to GOTTLIEB ER-
NST, tutor, of Eff.Co. Deed dated Aug.31, 1799, for 100 acres granted Frederick
Lockner Sr. Nov.5, 1764. Witnesses: Matthew Whiteman and John Fryermuth.

(p.418) H. HENRY LEMKE, Clerk, and LUCAS ZEIGLER, blacksmith, both of
Ebenezer. Agreement dated Oct. 6, 1798, to trade lots in Ebenezer. Witnesses:
Matthew Rahn and Solomon Witeman.

(p.419) WILLIAM KING and wife Mary, to JOHN KING. Deed dated Jan.1, 1798,
for 200 acres on Tuckaseeking Creek granted John Hall Oct.29, 1765, and deeded by
Hall to grantor Wm.King April 14, 1786. Witnesses: Herman Crum, William Dupuis
and James Boston J.I.C.

(p.420) GOTTLIEB ERNST and wife Catherine, to JOHN KING. Deed dated Aug.
7, 1800, for S½ of lot lying near Ebenezer, granted Christopher Rittenberger and
by him deeded to Andrew Gnann and Frances his wife and bythem deeded grantor.
Witness: Solomon Witeman.

(p.422) ANDREW GNANN, shoemaker, to GOTTLIEB ERNST,teacher,both of Eff.
Co. Deed dated Dec.24, 1800, for 7 acres granted Christopher Rittenberger Oct.6,
1770 and inherited from him by grantor. Witnesses: Johannis Gnann, David Gruber
and Andrew Gnann Jr. Deed also signed by Christopher Gnann, Jr.

(p.427) CHRISTOPHER F. HECKLE of Wilkes Co., tailor, to ANDREW GNANN,Jr.
of Eff.Co., laborer. Deed dated March 2, 1800, for 150 acres in the old District
of Ebenezer now Eff.Co. granted John Heckle Sept.3, 1765; also 50 acres on old
Ebenezer Creek granted George Heckle April 5, 1757, and by him deeded to John
Heckle and Hannah Margaret his wife, May 8, 1871. Witnesses: Jonathan Rahn and
John Kogler J.P.

(p.425) JOHN O'BERRY of McIntosh County, planter, and Elender his wife,
to ELIJAH TINER of Eff.Co. Deed dated Feb.26, 1801, for 200 acres in Eff.Co., add
bounded n.e. by Truetlin's and on other sides vacant. Witnesses: James Boston
and John King J.P.

(p.427) JAMES WILSON Jr. to ELIJAH TINER both of Eff.Co. Deed dated July

20, 1793, for 50 acres being ½ of 100-acre tract granted grantor May 28, 1788. Witnesses: Jesse Bell J.P., John McCall J.P.

(p.429) JOHN HARRIS, planter, and wife Patience, of Coosawhatchie Dist. S.C., to SAMUEL SNIDER of Eff.Co., wheelwright. Deed dated June 8, 1798, for 100 acres in Eff.Co., bounded east by John Hanglieter, William Thornhill; and west by John M. Dasher and Sarah Thornton; granted grantor Aug. 6, 1793. Witnesses: Jackel Erhart and John Kogler J.P.

(p.431) SAMUEL SNIDER, wheelwright, to DANIEL TURNER, planter, both of Eff.Co. Deed dated Jan.26, 1801, for same land as last above. Witnesses: John Gloner and J. Kogler J.P. Grantor's wife Catherine Snider waives her dowry rights.

(p.433) DAVID HALL, JOSHUA LOPER, GODHELF SMITH, SAMUEL RYALS, Commissioners for courthouse and gaol of Eff.Co., to JOHN LONDON, planter, of Eff. Co. Deed dated Sept.4, 1799, for lot #1 in village of Springfield, containing one acre. Witnesses: Matthew Rahn and J. Cuyler J.P.

(p.434) GEORGE NOWLAN and wife Elizabeth, of Abercorn, Eff.Co., to JOHN KEEBLER of same county. Deed dated Nov.14, 1797, for 75 acres being part of 100 acres granted Jacob Portz?,,bounded n.w. by public road and Riddlesperger, East by Savannah River and John Stirk estate, south by Abercorn lots. Also one acre "for a settlement" directly opposite the above 75-acre tract. Witnesses: Benjamin Stirk and P. McKenty J.P.

(Skip in page numbering from 436 to 486 - 10 pages)

(p.447) JOHN PALMER, shoemaker, and Elizabeth his wife, of Eff. Co. to JAMES DUPIUS Sr. of Lincoln Co. S.C. Deed dated March 6, 1801, for 100 acresgrantted John Hopkins May 11, 1759, bounded n.e. by Savannah River, and deeded by said Hopkins to the grantor in 1800. Wit: William Dupius and Christian Truetlin J.P.

(p.449) WILLIAM PORTER of Eff.Co. planter, and wife Rachel, to JAMES DUPIUS Jr. of Lincoln Co. S.C. Deed dated Feb.23, 1801, for 112 acres opposite the Sisters' Ferry on Savannah River, granted Hugh Kennedy in 1762 and deeded James Porter by Christopher Truetlin in 1790 and given grantor by said James Porter by way of exchange of lands; also 54 acres being part of 100 acres granted James Love and deeded grantor by Dr. John Love June 13, 1789. Witnesses: William Kennedy, John Palmer, Christian Truetlin J.P.

(p.451) THOMAS POLHILL to JOHN WILSON, both of Eff.Co. Deed dated May 20, 1801. Conveys 100 acres adjoining Gideon Mallette, John Berry; and granted grantor. Witnesses: Thomas Wylly and J.Cuyler J.P.

(p.452) JEDEKIAH WEIDMAN and wife Hannah, and NAOMI KIEFFER and LYDIA KIEFFER by an instrument dated April 27, 1801, relinquish to JOEL KIEFFER of Eff. Co., all their claim and interest by heirship in estate of Jacob Kieffer consisting of two tracts of land, one of 50 acres granted Simon Reiter April 5,1757, and 100 acres granted (blank) Aug. 7, 1759. Witness: J. Kogler J.P.

(p.453) Marriage Contract dated June 7, 180- (year-date not recorded in full) between ANNA BARBARA KIEFFER of Savannah, and ISRAEL REIPER (Reisser), whereby her estate consisting of three slaves is delivered to Jonathan Rahn as her Trustee to be held in trust for her use and benefit,free from husband's control and debts. Witnesses: John Frickinger and Thomas Wylly.

(p.456) JACOB C. WALDHAUERplanter to JEREMIAH CUYLER, Atty.-at-Law,both of Eff.Co. Deed dated July 18,1801,for 50 acres granted grantor Dec.6,1757, in the Dist. of Goshen. Wife Mary Waldhauer waives dower. Wit: David Gugel,Joshua Loper, J.I.C.

(p.458) MATTHIAS ASH of Eff.Co. planter, to DAVID GUGEL of Savannah. Deed dated Feb.4, 1801, for 150 acres in Eff.Co. granted Kel Lockner, adjoining Abercorn village. Also 100 acres adjoining, granted Michael Weaver. Also 50 acres granted said WEaver. All in Goshen district. Witnesses: Christian Gugel, James Shaffer and Godhelf Nease.

(p.460) JONATHAN BACKLY and wife Mary give receipt to JOHN KOGLER and JONATHAN RAHN as Executors of will of John Mickler, dec'd., June 13, 1801, for 6 slaves devised by John Mickler to his grand-daughter Mary Backly; also for her share in all funds on hand in the hands of said Executors derived from sale of estate property. Witnesses: Thomas Wylly and J.Cuyler J.P. Copy of Executors' Accounts attached, showing she had received half of the net estate, etc.

(p.463) JAMES GIBSON, planter, to PHILLIP MASSEY both of Eff.Co. Deed dated June 18, 1801, for 100 acres on Wills branch adjoining Christian Treutlin. Witnesses: Senate Powers, Names Wilson.

(p.465) WALTER DAVIS of Bryan Co. to JOSHUA LOPER, Esq. of Eff.County. Deed dated Oct.17, 1799, for 500 acres granted John Davis Nov. 19, 1791, and left by his will to said grantor; lands bounded south by Great Ogeechee, and adjoins lands of grantee. Witnesses: Abel G. Loper, Abby Loper.

(p.466) BENJAMIN GLONER, planter, and Hannah his wife, to EMANUEL ZEIG-LER all of Eff.Co. Deed dated May 6, 1801, for 100 acres adjoining John Sherouse, dec'd. Witnesses: John M. Dasher Sr., John M. Dasher Jr., P. McKenly J.P.

(p.468) JOHN HINELY and Ann Margaret his wife, to GEORGE POWLEDGE, all of Eff. County. Deed dated Sept.17, 1801, conveying 50 acres granted Geo.Kogler in 176-, and by hims deed of gift dated Oct.25, 1765, given to his daughter Maria Hinely; and then by her snly son and heir, the said grantor, was inherited. Witnesses: Christian Heidt, Israel Limeburger and John Kogler J.P.

(p.470) DORCAS GINDRAT of Eff. Co. to her three children ELIZABETH TISON, MARY TAYLOR and SETH STAFFORD. Deed of Gift dated Nov.3, 1801, for slave. Witnesses: Mary M. Stafford and William Porter.

(p.471) JOHN SPENCER to JEREMIAH CUYLER, Atty.aat-Law, both of Eff.Co. Deed dated May 18, 1801, for lot 13 containing 50 acres in village of Goshen. Witnesses: Joshua Keebler and Joel Kieffer and William H.Spencer.

(p.472) WILLIAM SHRIMPH to CAMMEL TISON, both planters of Eff.Co. Deed dated March 1, 1800, for 100 acres granted Frederick Shrimph July 5, 1774, and inherited by grantor as his only son and heir. Witnesses: J.G.Niedlinger, Christian (Heidt.

(p.474) GEORGE ARNSTORPH and Elizabeth his wife, to JOHN KOGLER, all of Eff.Co. Deed dated Nov. 17, 1801, for 100 acres granted Leonard Kraus Sept. 5, 1758, and by him and his wife deeded to grantor Mar.28, 1795. Witnesses: George Heidt and Henry W. Williams, Clerk Superior Court.

(p.479) Trustees of the German Luthern Congregation at Ebenezer,viz., JOHN KOGLER, JONATHAN RAHN, GODHEIF SMITH, JonathanSeckinger, Ernst Zettrouer,Solomon Gnann, Michael Exley, John Hinely, John Grovenstine, to JOHN MARTIN DASHER, Sr., Deed dated April 4, 1801, for 400 acres sold by U.S.Marshal to grantors Dec. 28,1793,by Wm.Thompson,Dept.Marshal,as property of Barbara Ravenhorst estate . Witnesses: J.M.Dasher Jr., Christopher Dasher,Jr., Gottlieb Ernst J.P.

Page 481: Rec. 21 Jan., 1802, deed dated 11 July, 1801, bet. ERNST CHRISTIAN ZITTROUER,
          planter of Effingham Co. and JOAN ZITTROUER his wife and JOHN MARTIN DASHER
of same place, in cons. of five hundred dollars, convey two tracts of land, one of which
cont. 50 acres in Mill District of Ebenezer bounded Southwest by GABRIEL MAURER, North
East by CHARLES SIGMUND (OTT?), said land orig. granted to DAVID ASHPERGER conveyed by
him to CHARLES SIGMUND OTT, from him to his son & heir at law, JOHN GOTLIEB OTT, then
conveyed by him to NATHANIEL OTT by deed of Gift, Sold by him to said ERNST CHRISTIAN
ZITTROUER. The other tract cont. 100 acres in Eff. Co. being the South westernmost 2/3
of one hundred and fifty acres bounded easterly by DAVID ASHPERGER and GABRIEL MAURER,
South by HERMAN LEMKE, Originally granted CHARLES SIGMUND OTT, conv. to JOHN GOTLIEB
OTT his only heir and sold by him to ERNST CHRISTIAN ZITTROUER. Signed: ERNSTZ ZITT____
JOAN (X) ZITTROUER. Wit: WILLIAM BIRD, CHRISTIAN DASHER, DANIEL BURGSTINER.

Page 484: Rec. 21 Jan. 1802, Indenture dated 11 July 1801, bet. ERNST C. ZITTROUER and
          JOHN MARTIN DASHER. INDEMNIFIED BOND., full sum of two hundred dollars. The
condition of this obligation is such that if the above bounden ERNST CHRISTIAN ZITTROUER,
his heirs, Executors, Administrators or assigns do well and truly and at all times forever defend and keep the above named JOHN MARTIN DASHER his heirs, Executors, Administrators, and assigns Indemnified that is to say from all damage or molestation of all
person or persons whatsoever that lays a claim down in any wise to a tract of land containing 50 acres which said tract is situated in the Mill District of Ebenezer in the
Co. of Eff. that is to say situated and bounded South West on Gabriel Maurer, Northeast
on Charles Sigmund Ott and also one other tract of land containing 100 acres situate in
the Co. of Eff. cont. adjoining the above said 50 bounded easterly on DAVID ASHPERGER
and GABRIEL MAURER, South by HERMAN LEMKE,....And the said land sold by said ERNST CHRIS-
TIAN ZITTROUER unto the said JOHN MARTIN DASHER then this obligation to be void and none
effect-otherwise to remain in full force and virtue. Signed: -------ZITTROUER. Wit:
WILLIAM BIRD, CHRISTIAN DASHER, JR.

Page 485: Rec. Jan. 22, 1802 - Deed dated 24 May 1800, bet. JONATHAN ZIPPERER and LUC-
          RETIA ZIPPERER his wife of Eff. Co. and JOHN MARTIN DASHER, planter, of same
cons. of sixty-six dollars and 67½ cents, tract of land cont. fifty acres in said Co.
bounded Southwesterly by CHARLES SIGMUND OTT and Northeasterly by MATTHIAS BURGSTINER,
orig. granted GEORGE SWIGER on April 5, 1757. Signed: JONATHAN ZIPPERER, LUCRETIA (X)
ZIPPERER. Wit: JOHN SPENCER, J.I.C., NATHANIEL (X) LANGLEY.

Page 486: Rec. Jan. 22, 1802 - Deed dated 24 May, 1800, bet. JONATHAN ZIPPERER AND LUC-
          RETIA ZIPPERER his wife of Eff. Co. and JOHN MARTIN DASHER of same, cons. of
sixty-six dollars and 67½ cents, tract of land cont. 50 acres bounded Southeasterly by

GEORGE SWIGER, CHARLES SIGMUND OTT, DAVID EISBURGER and GABRIEL MAURER, South by HERMAN
LEMKE, being the third part of 150 acres orig. granted CHARLES SIGMUND OTT, conveyed by
him to GEORGE SWIGER and DANIEL BURGSTINER, the half of which also conv. to GEORGE SWIGER.
SIGNED: JONATHAN ZIPPERER, LUCRETIA (X) ZIPPERER. Wit: JOHN SPENCER, J.I.C., NATHANIEL
(X) LANGLEY.

Page 487: Rec. Jan. 22, 1802 - Deed dated 24 May, 1800, bet. JONATHAN ZIPPERER and LUC-
RETIA ZIPPERER his wife of Eff. Co. and JOHN MARTIN DASHER, planter of same,
cons. of sixty-six dollars and 67½ cents, tract of 50 acres bounded Northerly by BOLZUIS
and Southerly by GEORGE SWIGER, orig. granted to DANIEL BURGSTINER on 5 April 1757.
Signed: JONATHAN ZIPPERER,LUCRETIA (X) ZIPPERER, Wit: JOHN SPENCER, J.I.C., NATHANIEL
(X) LANGLEY.

Page 488: Rec. Jan. 23, 1802 - Indeminfied Bond, dated 24 May, 1800, bet. JONATHAN ZIP-
PERER of Eff. Co. and JOHN MARTIN DASHER, sum of three hundred dollars, on
tract of land cont. 150 acres, bounded on South by CHARLES SIGMUND OTT and Northwardly
by BOLZERS. Signed: JONATHAN ZIPPERER. Wit: JOHN SPENCER.

Page 489: Rec. Jan. 23, 1802 - Bill of Sale from WILLIAM DUPUIS, Sheriff of Eff. Co. on
Dec. 1, 1797, for sale of Negro, JACOB, belonging to ABRAHAM LUNDAY, deceased,
to HANNAH HEERSON for five hundred dollars, dated 2 Jan. 1798. Signed: WILLIAM DUPUIS,
S.E.C. Wit: JOSHUA DASHER, CHRISTIAN DASHER, JR.

23 Jan. 1802 - CHRISTIAN DASHER Made oath that the within handwriting signed WILLIAM DU-
PUIS is signed by him and witnessed by JOSHUA DASHER. Signed: CHRISTIAN DASHER, HENRY
W. WILLIAMS, Clk.

Page 490: Rec. 4 Feb. 1802 - Deed dated 1 Dec. 1801, bet. JOHN MARKS of Eff. Co. and
JOHN COWARD of same, cons. of ninety dollars, tract of land cont. 100 acres
on waters of Cowpen Branch joining B-----ys land N.E., by WIDOW ROLLISON N.W., by vacant
land S.W. and by WORT_____ land, by ISAAC CARTER S. E. Signed: JOHN (X) MARKS, FANNY
(X) MARKS. Wit: SENATE POWERS, ANTHONY PILLS.

5 Jan. 1802 - SENATE POWERS made oath that the within handwriting signed JOHN MARKS and
FANNY MARKS is signed by them. Signed: SENATE POWERS, CHARLES TRUETLEN, J.P.

DEED BOOK E - F   1801 - 1811

Page 3: Rec. 26, Feb. 1802 - Bill of Sale of JOHN PALMER for five hundred dollars for
one Negro wench named FITT and her child BETTY to JOSHUA KEEBLER, dated 17
Feb. 1802. Signed: JOHN PALMER. Wit: ERNTZ ZITTROUR, JOEL KEIFFER

24 Feb. 1802 - ERNTZ ZITTROUR made oath that the within handwriting signed JOHN PALMER
is signed by him. Signed: ERNTZ ZITTROUR. JOHN KOGLER, J.P.

Page 4: Rec. 26 Feb. 1802 - Bill of Sale of JOSHUA KEEBLER of Eff. Co. for five hundred dollars for one Negro wench named FITT and her child BETTY to PATRICK Mc-
KENTY, dated 17 Feb. 1802. Signed: JOSHUA KEEBLER, Wit: ERNSTZ ZITTROUR, JOEL KEIFFER.

24 Feb. 1802 - ERNSTZ ZITTROUR made oath that the within handwriting signed by JOSHUA
KEEBLER is signed by him. Signed: ERNSTZ ZITTROUR. JOHN KOGLER, J.P.

Page 5: Rec. 6 March 1802 - Deed dated 27 April 1792, bet. WILLIAM MOORE of City of
Savannah gentlemen, acting and qualified executor of the last will and testament of AARON MOORE deceased and JESSE SCRUGGS of Effingham County, cons. of twenty-
two pounds sterling, two tracts of land in Eff. Co. one cont. 250 acres bounded South
Eastwardly by ELIZABETH MOORE, Northwestwardly and Northeastwardly by THOMAS FLYMING and

68

all the rest by vacant land. The other tract cont. 150 acres bounded North westwardly by lands of MOORE and on all other sides by land vacant adjoining each other, the one granted to GRACE MOORE THE other to ELIZABETH MOORE. Signed: WILLIAM MOORE. Wit: N. KING, J.P.

Page 6:   Rec. 6 March 1802 - Deed dated 26 April 1798, bet. GROSS SCRUGGS and MARGARET his wife and ANNE ABIGAIL GREENHOW, JAMES GOLDWIRE GREENHOW, and JACKSON MASON GREENHOW, cons. of one thousand dollars, several tracts of land to wit: All that tract or parcel lying and being in the Co. of Screven (formerly Eff.(cont. 107 acres granted to GROSS SCRUGGS in 1797, bounded southerly by DAVID THORN and PAUL BEVILE, Westwardly by ABRAHAM MOTTE, North by CHRISTOPHER HUDSON and East by ISAAC FORD. Also, tract or parcel in County of Screven (formerly Eff.) granted to RICHARD SCRUGGS and JOHN GOLDWIRE in 1785 cont. 50 acres bounded northwestwardly by ABRAHAM MOTTE, on the South by CHRIS-TOPHER HUDSON and on the North East by the Savannah River and on the S. West by ROBERT HUDSON. Also, tract of land in Co. of Eff. granted to THOMAS DAVIS in 1760 cont. 200 acres bounded westwardly by WM. MOORE and HUDSON, Eastwardly by Savannah River and on all other sides by vacant land. Signed: GROSS SCRIGGS, MARGARET SCRUGGS. Wit: JOHN KING, J.P.

Page 8:   Rec. 6 Mar. 1802 - Deed dated 26 April 1798, bet. GROSS SCRUGGS and MARGARET his wife and ABIGAIL GREENHOW, JAMES GOLDWIRE GREENHOW, and Jackson Mason Gree-hnow, cons. of two hundred and eighty-five dollars, three tracts of land lying and being in the Co. of Eff. and Screven, one cont. 250 acres in Eff. bounded South Eastwardly by ELIZABETH MOORE, Northwestwardly and Northeastwardly by lands of THOMAS FLYMING. Also, tract in Eff. Co. cont. 150 acres bounded Northwestwardly by lands of MOORE. Also, tract of land in Screven Co. formerly Eff. Co., granted RICHARD SCRIGGS cont. 100 acres bounded by JUDSON. Signed: GROSS SCRUGGS, MARGARET SCRUGGS, Wit: JAMES KING, JOHN KING, J.P.

Page 9:   Rec. 3 Jan. 1803 - Deed dated 3 April 1799, bet. HENRY WILDERS and MARY his wife and ABIGAIL GREENHOW, JAMES GOLDWIRE GREENHOW, and JACKSON MASON GREENHOW cons. of eighty dollars, tract of land in Eff. Co. cont. 150 acres granted DAVID HARRIS in 1787 bounded North by THOMAS DAVIS and Savannah River, east and west by Hilliary Butts, S. East by MARY------, S. West by unknown land. Signed: HARRY WILDERS, MARY WILDERS. Wit: GROSS SCRUGGS, JESSE SCRUGGS

4 Oct. 1802 - JESSE SCRUGGS made oath that the within handwriting signed HARRY WILDERS and MARY WILDERS and witnessed by GROSS SCRUGGS was signed by them. HENRY W. WILLIAM, Clk.

Page 11: Rec. 11 Mar. 1802 - Deed dated 25 Sept. 1801, bet. RICHARD SCRUGGS of the County of Screven planter and ANN his wife and JAMES GOLDWIRE GREENHOW and JACKSON MASON GREENHOW of same place, cons. six hundred and forty dollars, tract of land cont. 340 acres made up of 100 acres orig. granted to SAMUEL HUDSON and sold by his son to the said RICH-ARD SCRUGGS. 100 acres orig. granted to CHARLES HUDSON and by him sold to ROBERT COSHEN TANNER by R. C. TANNER sold to BENJAMIN DALY with 40 acres added to it granted to the said R. C. TANNER and sold by BEN. DALY to THOMAS GARNET and by THOMAS GARNET to WM. COL-SON, and by WM. COLSON sold to the said RICH SCRUGGS. 100 acres sold by the Commissioners of Confiscated Estates to THOMAS GRAVES and by said THOMAS GRAVES to THOMAS GARNETT and by TOOMAS GARNETT to WM. COLSON and by WM. COLSON to RICHARD SCRUGGS, which last 100 acres was sold as the property of JOSEPH FARLY the whole of which make up the tract of 340 acres bounded S. East and S. West by lands of ROBERT HUDSON, N.W. bylands held by ROBERT BEVILE at present. Also, that other tract of land granted said ROBERT SCRUGGS cont. 600 acres bounded North by WISEMAN and MUTERS land, South by lands of WM. THOMAS, East by lands of WIDOW JONES and HARDY and west by WISEMANS land together with 56 acres run up for the said RICHARD SCRUGGS and bounded on lands of Scruggs and WM.------the whole of which 2 tracts make up 996 acres. Signed: RICHARD SCRUGGS, ANN SCRUGGS, Wit: PAUL BEVILE, THOMAS POLHILL, J.I.C.

Page 13: Rec. 11 Mar. 1802 - Deed dated 2 Jan. 1801, bet. JOHN ROLLISON of Glenn County, planter, and JOHN DUGGER, planter of Eff. Co., cons. sum two hundred fifty dollars, tract of land orig. on 8 Jan. 1793 granted under the great seal of the said State to the said JOHN ROLLISON for 150 acres in Eff. Co. on Reedy Branch bounded on all sides by vacant land. Also, tract of land orig. on the 31 Jan. 1798 granted to the said JOHN ROLLISON for 150 acres bounded North west by JOSEPH CLAYS land, South east by said ROLLISON land which is the above ment. land and on all other sides by vacant land. The said tracts together cont. 300 acres. Signed: JOHN (X) ROLLISON, Wit: JOHN MOORE, MARCIA MOORE.

5 April 1801 - JOHN MOORE made oath that the within handwriting signed JOHN ROLLISON and witnessed by MARCIA MOORE is signed by them. Signed: JOHN MOORE, Wit: JOHN KING, J.P.

Page 14: Rec. 4 Aug. 1801 - Deed dated 15 Jan. 1801, bet. JOHN KNIGHT of Glenn County and MOORE SPIER of same, cons. of four hundred dollars tract of land cont. 200 acres of land in Eff. Co. orig. granted to the aforesaid JOHN KNIGHT on 19 May 1789, Registered in Secretarys office in Book S.S.S. for 168, bounding South west by Belchers and vacant land and on all other sides by vacant land. Signed: JOHN KNIGHT. Wit: WM. STEWART. MILLIS SPIER.

4 Aug. 1801 - WILLIAM STEWART made oath that the within handwriting signed JOHN KNIGHT is signed by him. Signed: WM. STEWART, Wit: MILNER HOLIDAY, J.P.

Page 16: Rec. 20 March 1802 - Deed dated 2 Sept. 1800, bet. WILLIAM PORTER, planter of Eff. Co. and RACHAEL his wife and JAMES PORTER, cons. of one dollar five shilling, tract of land cont. 300 acres bounded North by JAMES PORTER'S land, South and East by BLYTHS land, and on the other sides by land granted to WILLIAM DAVIS. Signed: WILLIAM PORTER, WIT: GINDRAT, J.P., SETH STAFFORD.

Page 17: Rec. 20 March 1802 - Deed dated 3 Sept. 1800, bet. WILLIAM PORTER and RACHAEL his wife and JAMES PORTER, cons. one hundred and fifty dollars, Doth grant, bargain and sell, alien, release and confirm unto the said JAMES PORTER in his actual possession now being by virtue of a bargain and Sale to him thereof made by the said WILLIAM PORTER for one whole year by Indenture of -------bearing date the day next before the day of the date of these presents and by force of the Statute for transforming uses into possession and to his heirs and assigns forever, tract of land cont. 300 acres bounded North by JAMES PORTER, South east by BLYTHS land, on other sides by land surveyed for WILLIAM DAVIS. Wit: H. GINDRAT, SETH STAFFORD Signed: WILLIAM PORTER

Page 20: Rec. 31 March 1802 - Bill of Sale from JOHN WILLIAMS, Sheriff of Effingham Co. on 19 Oct. 1801 for Judgement in favor of TIMOTHY STALY on estate of JOHN STIRK deceased, sale of 3 negroes, DIANNA and her two children, BETTY & AMY, to THOMAS POLHILL for four hundred and one dollar. Signed: JN. WILLIAMS, S.E.C. Wit: JOHN GOLDWIRE, SENR. ABIEL SCHWEIGHOFFER, J.P.

Page 21: Rec. 31 March 1802 - Receipt of JOHN WILLIAMS, Sheriff of Effingham County from THOMAS POLHILL for forty-three dollars for Negro, London the property of JOHN STIRK to satisfy balance of Judgement in favor of TIMOTHY STALY. Oct. 19, 1801. Signed: JON. WILLIAMS, S.E.C. Wit: ABIEL SCHWEIGHOFFER, J.P.

Page 21: Rec. 8 Nov. 1799 - Deed of Gift dated 21 March 1775, bet. MARTIN DASHER Innkeeper in Saint Matthews Parish to son-in-law DANIEL BURGSTINER, shoemaker of same, my daughter MARY BURGSTINER and granddaughter SALOME BURGSTINER, all that plantation in St. Matthews Parish bounded by vacant land, granted unto me by his present Majesty KING GEORGE the third on 6 Oct. 1772. Signed: MARTIN DASHER. Wit: JENKIN DAVIS, JACOB CRONBERGER

25 April 1775 - JACOB CRONBERGER made oath that the within handwriting signed by MARTIN DASHER is signed by him and witnessed by JENKIN DAVIS. Signed: JACOB CRONBERGER. Wit: JACOB C. WALDHAUER, Justice

Page 22: Rec. 2 April 1802 - Deed dated 15 Feb. 1802, bet. JONATHAN SECKINGER blacksmith and JOHN SHEARHOUSE, planter, cons. of one hundred dollars, tract of 200 acres orig. granted to JONATHAN SECKINGER on 18 Nov. 1801 by JOSIAH TATTNALL, Governor of Ga., bounding North west on said Seckinger's land on all other sides by vacant land. Signed: JONATHAN SECKINGER. Wit: GODHILF SHEAROUSE, HENRY W. WILLIAMS, C.S.C.E.C.

Page 24: Rec. 20 April 1802 - Bill of Sale dated 19 Nov. 1793 from SALLY STATON and SOL-OMON STATON to MARTHA BU--HOP, cons. of thirty pounds sterling for Negro girl, CLOW. Signed: SARAH STATON, SOLOMON STATON. Wit: JAMES HINES, TRYON PACE.

13 March 1802 - TRYON PACE made an oath taht the within handwriting signed SARAH STATON and SOLOMON STATON is signed by them. Signed: TRYON (X) PACE. Wit: CHRN. TREUTLEN.

Page 24: Bill of Sale dated 20 Jan. 1802 from THOMAS HENDERSON and SAM E. DUFF unto JOHN KING, for five Negroes, OBEY and her son, NELLY and her daughter, and NANCY, valued at thirteen hundred and ten dollars which has been paid by said JOHN KING. Signed: THOS. HENDERSON,SAM E. DUFF. Wit: B. MO_LL, WILLIAM KING Junr.

Page 25: Rec. 3 May 1802-Deed dated 20 Feb. 1802, bet CHARLES RYALL and JOHN KING, cons. one hundred and fifty dollars, tract of land cont. 350 acres granted to ARTHUR RYALL on 20 Feb. 1795 bounded N.W. and N.E. by land of JAMES JACKSON and NICKS, S.E. by JESSY BELL and S.W. by JAMES GOLDWIRE and THOMAS POLHILL. Signed: CHARLES RYALL. Wit: JAMES (J G) GIBSON, CHRN. TREUTLEN, J.P.

Page 26: Rec. 5 July 1902 - Deed dated 4 Jan. 1802, bet. JOSEPH RAHN of City of Sav-annah and AMY his wife and ROBERT BARTON, cons. of five hundred and twenty-five dollars, tract of land cont. 300 acres (more or less) bound by vacant land at time of survey, orig. granted to DANIEL MATTHIAS and NATHANIEL ZETTLER on 4 Dec. 1770 as will more fully appear in Secretaries Office of this State. Signed: JOSEPH RAHN, AMY RAHN. Wit: JOHN G. ALDERMAN, WILLIAM MATTHIES.

Page 28: Rec. 13 Sept. 1802 - Bill of Sale dated 19 Oct. 1801 from ROBERT HUDSON of Screven County unto JAMES HUDSON for three Negroes, ANTHONY, MONDAY, MILLY, valued at one thousand dollars which has been paid by said JAMES HUDSON. Signed: ROB-ERT HUDSON, Wit: ASA LOPER, ABEL LOPER.

20 July 1802 - ASA LOPER madeoath that the within handwriting signed ROBERT HUDSON is signed by him and witnessed by ABEL LOPER. Signed: ABEL LOPER. Wit: JOSHUA LOPER, J.I.C.

Page 29: Rec. 13 Sept. 1802 - Deed of Gift dated 10 July 1802 from ROBERT HUDSON to his son JAMES HUDSON, following Negroes: JACK and OLD SILVY, LITTLE JACK and LITTLE SILVY, PRINCE, CHARITY, MARY, JIM, BOB, DOLLY. Signed: ROBERT HUDSON. Wit: ASA LOPER, ABIGAIL M. CASKILL.

20 July 1802 - ASA LOPER made oath that the within handwriting signed ROBERT HUDSON is signed by him and witnessed by ABILGAIL M. CASKILL. Signed: ASA LOPER, Wit: JOSHUA LOPER, J.I.C.

Page 30: Rec. 13 Sept. 1802 - Deed of Gift dated 10 July 1802 from ROBERT HUDSON yeoman

of Screven County to his son JAMES HUDSON of Effingham County, fifteen hundred Spanish
or Federal dollars to be collected out of my estate after my death, and after the following Negroes shall be taken away: JACK and OLD SILVY, LITTLE JACK and LITTLE SILVY, PRIN-
CE, CHARITY, MARY, JIM, BOB, AND DOLLY, after my dear son JAMES HUDSON shall waive said
Negroes, then the above mentioned fifteen hundred Spanish or Federal dollars shall be
collected. Signed: ROBERT HUDSON. Wit: ASA LOPER, ABIGAIL M. CASKILL.

20 July 1802 -ASA LOPER made oath that the within handwriting signed ROBERT HUDSON is
signed by him and witnessed by ABIGAIL M.CASKILL. Signed: ASA LOPER. Wit: JOSHUA
LOPER, J.I.C.

Page 31: Rec. 17 Sept. 1802 - Affidavit dated 24 Aug. 1802, MARY ASBURY swore that in
       March 1800 being present at MATTHIAS ASH'S plantation the deponent saw MRS.
CALDRON late MRS. JOHN KEIBLER come there and in her presence requested MR. ASH to take
two heiffer than at TIMOTHY STALY'S pen for a debt due by her late husband JOHN KEIBLER
which heiffers was taken possession by said ASH. Signed: MARY (X) ASBURY. Wit: JOHN
SPENCER, J.P.

Page 32: Rec. 17 Sept. 1802 - Deed dated 2 Feb. 1802, bet. CHRISTIAN TREUTLEN, ESQUIRE
       and ELIJAH TYNER, cons. three hundred thirty seven and a half dollars, tract
of land cont. four hundred and fifty acres orig. granted to JACOB METZGER, 4 Oct. 1768,
on BAN--COWPEN Branch bounded on all sides by vacant land at time of survey, conv. to
JOHN A. TREUTLEN on 4 June 1773 and bequeathed by will to daughter MARY who married ED-
WARD DUDLEY, they then conv. tract to CHRISTIAN TREUTLEN on 13 Sept. 1795. Signed:
CHRISTIAN TREUTLEN. Wit: L. POWERS, M. KING, J.I.C.

Page 33: Rec. 16 Oct. 1802 - Deed dated 1 March 1802, bet. JOHN MARTIN DASHER, gentle-
       men, and ELIZABETH his wife and GEORGE NEISE, planter, cons. twenty one dollars
tract of land cont. seven acres in Effingham County on Birds Mill Creek bounded North
West by said GEORGE NEISES' land and on all other sides by land of said JOHN MARTIN DASH-
ER, said tract a parcel of land being a part of a larger tract orig. granted by KING GEO-
RGE the third, on or about the 3 Aug. 1762 unto JOHN SHEARHOUSE and by the said JOHN
SHEARHOUSE sold unto JOHN MARTIN DASHER. Signed: JOHN M. DASHER, ELIZABETH (CD) DASHER
Wit: JONATHAN RAHN, JOSHUA KEEBLER.

15 March 1802 - JONATHAN RAHN made oath that the within handwriting signed JOHN MARTIN
DASHER and ELIZABETH DASHER was signed by them and witnessed by JOSHUA KEEBLER. Signed:
JONATHAN RAHN. Wit: HENRY W. WILLIAMS, C.S.C.E.C.

Page 35: Rec. 18 Oct. 1802 - Deed dated 19 Oct. 1801, bet. JOHN WILLIAMS ESQUIRE, Sher-
       iff of Eff. Co. and THOMAS POLHILL, planter of same, cons. of one hundred and
ten dollars, sold and by virtue of the powers in him as Sheriff and by a Judgement issued by the Superior Court of Effingham County on a suit of THOMAS GIBBONS against JAMES
HOLTOH and HANNAH his wife and she is now Executrix of his last Will and testament of
JOHN STIRK, deceased, judgement for sum of one hundred dollars with lawful interest, doth
bargain and sell unto THOMAS POLHILL, being knocked off to him at public out-cry as highest bidder on 7 April 1801, tract of land cont. 700 acres on Ogeechee River in Parish of
Saint George from County of Jefferson and Bank, bounded South westwardly by great Ogee-
chee River, south easterly by land of PHILIP M__LKY, North westerly by land surveyed for
CHARLES WATSON and North easterly by vacant land. Signed: JN. WILLIAMS, S.E.C. Wit:
JOHN GOLDWIRE, SENR., ABIEL SCHWEIGHOFFER, J.P.

Page 37: Rec. 1 Nov. 1802 - Deed dated 6 March 1802, bet. JOHN KOGLER and ISRAEL FLERL,
       cons. on one hundred and thirty nine dollars, two tracts of land, one cont. 50
acres bounded North West on THEOBALD KEIFFER, South West on CHARLES FLERL, South East on

on JOHN FLERL and North East on THEOBALD KEIFFER, orig. granted unto JOHN PAUL MILLER, senior, by his Britannic Majesty George the second on 6 Dec. 1757, and by JOHN PAUL MIL-LER junr. son of JOHN PAUL MILLER senr. to JOHN KOGLER, and one tract cont. 50 acres, said 50 acres is half of 100 acres orig. granted to LEONARD-------by his Britannic Majesty George the second on 5 Sept. 1758 bounded South east on JOHN CRONBERGER and vacant land, North East on land of THEOBALD KEIFFER land, said 50 acres in the lower part of 100 acres. Signed: JOHN KOGLER. Wit: WILLIAM BIRD, GOTTLIEB ERNST, J.P.

Page 39: Rec. 1 Nov. 1802 - Bill of Sale dated 10 Aug. 1802, JOHN PALMER unto ISRAEL FLERL for one Negro Girl, WINNY, valued at two hundred and fifty dollars which ISRAEL FLERL has paid. Signed: JOHN PALMER. Wit: JOHN WALDAUER, J.P.

Page 39: 4 Nov. 1802 - Deed of Gift dated 20 Sept. 1802, WILLIAM BEAL for the love of his daughter ELIZABETH EDWARDS and son-in-law WILLIAM EDWARDS does grant her 200 acres orig. granted unto THOMAS READING by his EXCELLENCY JARED IRVIN, Governor and Commander in Chief of Georgia, on 14 Dec. 1797 and conv. by him on 18 Dec. 1798 to WIL-LIAM BEAL. Signed: WILLIAM BEAL, Wit: JN. WALSINGHAM, HENRY W. WILLIAMS, Clk.

Page 40: Rec. 31 Jan. 1803 - Deed dated 17 Feb. 1800, bet. JOHN WILLIAMS of City of Savannah in Chatham County and his wife FERIBY and JAMES HUDSON, planter of County of Scriven, cons. two hundred dollars, tract of 400 acres (more or Less) in Eff-ingham County on Bostons Branch, conv. to JAMES JONES by Indenture from FODERICK TANNER on 7 Jan. 1778, and conv. by JAMES JONES' death to his daughter FERIBEE WILLIAMS, wife of JOHN WILLIAMS. Signed: JOHN WILLIAMS, FERIBY WILLIAMS. Wit: ELIAS ROBERT, ABSOLOM DEMENT, JOSHUA ALLEN.

15 Dec. 1800 - ELIAS ROBERT made oath that the within handwriting signed by JOHN WILLIAMS and FERIBY WILLIAMS is signed by them and witnessed by ABSOLOM DEMENT and JOSHUA ALLEN. Signed: ELIA ROBERT. Wit: BALTHASER SHAFFER, J.P. in Chatham County.

Page 43: Rec. 31 Jan. 1803 - Deed dated 25 April 1800, bet. JAMES OVERSTREET and wife ELIZABETH and SAMUEL OVERSTREET, planter of South Carolina of one part and JAMES HUDSON, gentlemen, of City of Savannah, cons. of eight hundred dollars, western moiety of half lot of land known in the general plan of Yamacraw by the number eight, land once sold by PARSON ANDREW to MATTHEW MOTT, by MOTT to ROBERT STATHAM, by STATHAM to JAMES BEVILL, by BEVILL to THOMAS COLDING, by COLDING to JOHN GRANTHAM, by GRANTHAM to JAMES OVERSTREET and SAMUEL OVERSTREET. Signed: JAS. OVERSTREET, SAMUEL OVERSTREET. Wit: ELIAS ROBERT, BLANCHARD (B) COLDING

Jan. 1801 - ELIAS ROBERT made an oath that the within handwriting signed JAMES OVERSTREET and SAMUEL OVERSTREET is signed by them and witnessed by BLANCHARD COLDING. Signed: EL-IAS ROBERT. Wit: BALTHASER SHAFFER, J.P. Chatham Co.

Page 45: Rec. 3 Jan. 1803 - Bill of Sale dated 24 Jan. 1801 from SKELTON STANDIFER of Green County unto WILLIAM KING for a negro man named JACOB, valued at five hundred dollars which WILLIAM KING has paid. Signed: SKELTON STANDIFER. Wit: JOHN GOLDWIRE, Junr.

4 Oct. 1802 - JOHN GOLDWIRE made an oath that the within handwriting signed SKELTON STANDIFER is signed by him. Wit: HENRY W. WILLIAMS, Clk. S.C.E.C.

Page 46: Rec. 1 Feb. 1803 - Deed dated 3 Aug. 1802, bet. WILLIAM DUPUIS, Sheriff of Eff. Co. and JOHN MARTIN DASHER Junr. of same, cons. of seventy-seven dollars sold and by virtue of the powers in him as Sheriff at the suit of JOHN KOGLER against the Adm. of JOHN C. WERTSH being knocked off to him at public vendue, two tracts of land, one in Screvin Co. cont. 200 acres granted to JOHN C. WERTCH bounded _____eastwardly by land of THOMAS KEECE and POOR ROBBINS, North westwardly by land of SAML. HUDSON, and other sides vacant, the other tract in Scriven Co. cont. 100 acres granted to CHARLY NELL, bounded Eastwardly by SAVANNAH RIBER, North west by JAMES THOMAS, South easterly JOHN DAERS and sides vacant, the said 100 acres sold by NEEL to WERTCH on 1 Sept. 1763. Signed: WILLIAM DUPUIS, S.E.C. Wit: H. W. WILLIAMS, Clk., WILLIAM C. WYLLY.

Page 47:   Rec. 26 Feb. 1803 - Bond & Mortgage made 17 Feb. 1802, bet. JOSHUA KEEBLER,
           planter, and PATRICK McKENTY, planter. Whereas the said JOSHUA KEEBLER by
his bond oblication bearing even date with these presents stand held and firmly bound
unto the said PATRICK McKENTY in the penal sum of six hundred dollars conditioned for
the payment of the sum of three hundred dollars. Now be it known that for the better
securing the payment of the aforesaid sum of three hundred dollars and for in cons. of
the sum of one dollar, to me in hand paid before the sealing and delivery hereof the receipt whereof is hereby acknowledged the said JOSHUA KEEBLER, hath granted, bargained,
and sold and by these presents doth grant, bargain and sell unto the said PATRICK Mc-
KENTY, his heirs, Executors, Adm. and assigns. All that tract of land cont. 200 acres
made up of two tracts lying in Eff. Co. bounded by POLHILL and RABENHURST, J.M. DASHER
and vacant land near Mill Creek. To have and to hold the said 200 acres of land with
the appurtenances unto the said PATRICK McKENTY his heirs, Executors, Adm. or assigns
the aforesaid sum of three hundred dollars and interest agreeable to the aforesaid bond
then this deed to be void otherwise to remain in full force. Signed: JOSHUA KEEBLER.
Wit: ERNST ZITTROUER, JOEL KEIFFER.

10 July 1802 - ERNST ZITTROUER made oath that the within handwriting signed JOSHUA KEE-
BLER is signed by him and witnessed by JOEL KEIFFER. Signed: ERNST ZITTROUER. Wit:
JOHN KOGLER, J.P.

Page 49:   Rec. 26 Feb. 1803 - Deed dated 26 March 1802, bet. HENRY COOK, Minister of the
           Gospel, and LYDIA his wife and ANTHONY PITTS, planter - cons. thirty-five dol-
lars, tract of land cont. 80 acres being part of 300 acres orig. granted on 19 Nov. 1791
by his EXCELLENCY EDWARD TELFAIR, ESQ. Governor of Ga. unto DANIEL JOHNSTON, conv. by
him to said HENRY COOK. Signed: HENRY COOK. Wit: JAS. GADDY, ROBERT COOK.

12 April 1802 - JAMES GADDY made oath that the within handwriting signed HENRY COOK is
signed by him and witnessed by ROBERT COOK. Signed: JAS. GADDY, Wit: CHRN. TREUTLEN,
J.P.

Page 51:   Rec. 30 March 1803 - Bill of Sale and dated 26 Aug. 1799, from WILLIAM DUPUIS
           Sheriff of Eff. Co. and bet. WILLIAM KING, cons. twenty-five dollars, knocked off
to WILLIAM KING at public outcry on 26 Aug. tract of land on Savannah River cont. 100
acres which was for HENRY KING on 11 March 1786 bounded N.E. by Savannah River, SE. by
WILLIAM KENNEDY land, S. West by vacant land, N. West by JOHN ADAM TREUTLEN land, sold
by virtue of powers in him as Sheriff and by petition of Justices of Inferior Court on
land on HENRY KING deceased. Signed: WILLIAM DUPUIS, S.E.C. Wit: HERMAN_____, JAS.
BOSTON, J.I.C.

Page 52:   Rec. 5 April 1803 - Deed dated 23 Nov. 1795, bet. JOHN MARTIN of Bryan Co.,
           planter, and ELIZABETH his wife and GIDEON MALLET of Eff. Co., cons. six dol-
lors specie, tract of land cont. 200 acres in Eff. Co. bounded Southwestwardly on lanes
and vacant land, North westwardly on vacant and __ulters on other sides vacant land,
orig. granted on 7 Aug. 1795 unto JOHN MARTIN by his EXCELLENCY GEORGE MATTHIAS, Gov.
of Ga. Signed: JOHN MARTIN. Wit:_____ _____, DAVIS (X) LASH_____, JOHN RAWLS,
J.P.

Page 54:   Deed dated 18 May 1801, bet JOHN WILLIAMS, Sheriff of Eff. Co. and JOHN KOGLER,
           ESQ. of same, for cons. of one hundred dollars, sold by virtue of the power in
him as Sheriff and of a Writ of fieri Facias issued out of the Inferior Court of Eff. Co.,

for Judgement obtained by the Administrators of JOHN WERTSCH plaintiff, deceased, against
the administrators of JOHN SHEEROUSE, late of Co., namely GODHILF SHEEROUSE, being knocked
off to JOHN KOGLER, ESQ. at public outcry tract of land cont. 350 acres bounded by GOD-
HIELF SHEEROUSE and GEORGE ARNSTORFF. Signed: JNO. WILLIAMS, S.E.C. Wit: JOHN McCALL,
HENRY W. WILLIAMS, C.S.C.E.C.

Page 55: Deed dated 17 Nov. 1801, bet. JOHN KOGLER and ELIZABETH his wife, and GEORGE
ANRSTORFF, cons. one hundred dollars, tract of land cont. 350 acres bounded by
GODHILF SHEEROUSE and GEORGE ARNSTORPH orig. granted unto JOHN SHEEROUSE, said tract of
land sold by JOHN WILLIAMS, Sheriff of Eff. Co. at Sheriffs Sale on the 18 May 1801 as
the property of the above said JOHN SHEEROUSE and was knocked off unto aforesaid JOHN
KOGLER. Signd: JOHN KOGLER, ELIZABETH (X) KOGLER. Wit: HENRY W. WILLIAMS, GEORGE
(OT) HEITH.

Page 58: Rec. 5 June 1803 - Deed dated 2 Feb. 1803, bet. JAMES (LOURMAN?) and JAMES
HENDLY and MARY his wife of Chatham Co. and DAVID GUGEL of said Co. cons. two
hundred dollars, all those undivided 2/3 parts of all that tract of land cont. 240 acres
in Eff. Co. bounded South by lands of Matthias Ash, West by JAMES GREENHOW, East by CLE-
MENT MARTIN, deceased, commonly called the Abercorn Estate, North by SAMUEL POLTON.
Signed: JAS. LO___MAN, GEO HENLEY, MARY HENLEY. Wit: C. GUGEL, JAMES LAVENDER, ___F.
BRITTON

5 Feb. 1803 - CHRISTIAN GUGEL made oath that the within handwriting signed by JAS. LO__
_MAN, GEO. HENLEY, and MARY HENLEY is signed by them. Signed: C. GUGEL. Wit: HENRY
W. WILLIAMS, Clk., S.C.E.C.

Page 60: Rec. 5 June 1803 - Whereas the underwritten together with JOHN (LOHVMAN?) are
entitled to a certain tract of land in Eff. Co., two-thirds of which we have
this day sold to DAVID GUGEL and whereas the aforesaid JOHN (LOHVMAN?) has been missing
four years past as is supposed to be dead and we in that case will be lawful heirs of
the said JOHN ___ _ _ _ and consequently entitled to the remaining third of the aforesaid
land, now this Instrument of writing Witnesseth that we have for the cons. of fifty dollars which we acknowledge to have received, bargained, and sold by these presents do bargain and sell all our claim to the third of said land which would have been the said JOHN
(LOH_MAN?) if he was in life and we do bind ourselves our heirs and administrators, to
make titles to the said third of the said tract of land whenever it is ascertained that
the said JOHN (LOH_MAN?) is dead, should we be the heirs thereto. Signed: JAS.(LOH_MAN?)
GEO. HENLY, MARY HENLY. Wit: C. GUGEL, JAMES LAVENDER, _F. BRITTON.

Page 61: Rec. 8 June 1803 - Indenture dated____of_____in 1780, bet. ARTHUR RYALL and
MARY ANN CONNAWAY of South Carolina, Beauford district, widow, cons. thirty-
two pounds ten shillings....confirm unto MARY ANN CONAWAY in her actual possession now
being by virtue of a bargain and sale to her - thereof made by the said ARTHUR RYALL
for one whole year for the cons. of five shillings by an Indenture of Lease - all that
part of a tract of land cont. 33 acres in Parish of St. Matthews it being part of a tract of land laid off for JOHN CLAYTON the 3 Dec. 1760, bounded on N. East by JEREMIAH
SWANN and on other sides by land vacant which said land cont. 100 acres, sold by CLAY-
TON to JOHN CASPER WERTSCH by Indenture on 2 July 1760, by WERTSCH to JOHN HALE by Indenture in 1769, by HALE to ARTHUR RYALL by Indenture on 12 Sept. 1772 - all that part
of said tract being between the branch called little Tuckaseeking and the Country road
cont. 33 acres. Signed: ARTHUR RYAL, ANN RYAL.

Page 65: Rec. 8 June 1803 - Indenture dated 22 Sept. 1787, bet. MARY ANN CONNAWAY and
SAMUEL BOSTICK, planter, cons. one hundred pounds sterling, confirm unto SAM-
UEL BOSTICK in his actual possession being by virtue of a bargain and sale to him there-
of made, by MARY ANN CONNAWAY for one whole year for cons. of five shillings by an In-

denture of Lease, all that part of tract of land cont. 33 acres in Parish of St. Matthew,
it being a part of a tract of land laid off for JOHN CLAYTON on 3 Dec. 1760, bounded N.E.
by JEREMIAH SWAN and on other sides by vacant land which said land cont. 100 acres made
out to JOHN CASPER WERTSCH by Indenture on 12 July 1760, by WERTSCH to JOHN HALE by Indenture in 1769, and by HALE to ARTHUR RYALL by Indenture 10 Sept. 1772, by RYALL to
MARY ANN CONNAWAY by Indenture - All that part of said tract being between the branch
called little Tuckaseeking and the County road   Signed: MARY ANN CONNAWAY. Wit: SIM-
EON RIVES, THOMAS RIVES, ABN. RA_OT, J.P.

Page 68: Rec. 9 June 1803 - Deed dated 7 May 1803, bet. CHARLES RYALL and MARY his wife
        and JOHN KING - cons. of one hundred dollars - tract of land cont. 105 acres
bounded by Savannah River formerly the property of ABRAHAM RAVOT and land granted to
SAMUEL BOSTICK. Signed: CHARLES RYALL, MARY X RYALL. Wit: CHRISTIAN TREUTLEN, J.P.,
JOHN GARNETT.

Page 70: Rec. 9 June 1803 - Deed dated 4 June 1803 - bet. SAMUEL BOSTICK and JOHN KING,
        cons. one hundred dollars for two tracts of land, one tract on waters of Tuck-
aseeking cont. 100 acres bounded N. E. by JOHN AUDIBERT and land of BOSTICK, N. West by
THOMAS CAMPBELL, West by surveyed land, South by vacant land and S. E. by BOSTICK--tract
granted to BOSTICK on 13 May 1795 - also, tract on big Tuckaseeking Branch cont. 50 acres
bounded N. E. by Ravot, S. E. by_____, S. W. by King, and West by Bostick, said tract
granted to Bostick on 13 May 1795. Signed: SAMUEL BOSTICK. Wit: H. W. WILLIAMS, Clk,
S. C. E. C.

Page 71: Rec. 10 June 1803 - Deed dated 4 June 1803, bet. SAMUEL BOSTICK of South Car-
        olina and JOHN KING - cons. two hundred dollars - tract cont. 38 acres bounded
east by Tuckaseeking Creek and land of Ravots, S. W. by Bostick, West by Milledge, N.E.
by Audipert and land unknown - land granted to SAMUEL BOSTICK on 12 April 1791 - Also
tract cont. 2 acres on Tuckaseeking Creek bounded S. E. by said Creek, North and West by
Connaways, which tract was granted to MARY ANN CONNAWAY on 28 May 1798 - Also tract cont.
38 acres being part of tract granted to JOHN CLAYTON on 3 Dec. 1760 bounded North east
by land granted to JEREMIAH SWAN, on other sides by vacant land, which said tract cont.
in the whole 100 acres was conv. by CLAYTON to JOHN CASPER WERTSCH on 12 July 1760, by
WERTSCH to JOHN HALE in 1769, by HALE to ARTHUR RYALL on 12 Sept. 1772, from RYALL to
MARY ANN CONNAWAY in 1784, from MARY ANN CONNAWAY to SAMUEL BOSTICK on 22 Sept. 1787,
tract on lower side of little Tuckaseeking and the upper side of Big Tuckaseeking. Signed: SAMUEL BOSTICK. Wit: HENRY W. WILLIAMS, Clk. S. C. E. C.

Page 72: Rec. 10 June 1803 - Deed dated 11 April 1800, bet. WILLIAM NORMENT and ELIZA-
        BETH his wife of Chatham Co. and JAMES GOLDWIRE, cons. one hundred and sixty
dollars - tract of land cont. 450 acres bound South Easterly by JOHN GOLDWIRE and on
other sides by vacant land. Signed: W. NORMENT. Wit: _ _ BOX, GRO. ENOE

Page 74: Rec. 10 June 1803 - Deed dated 11 Mar. 1802, bet. JOHN KING and SARAH his wife
        and JAMES GOLDWIRE, cons. one thousand dollars - tract of land adjoining lands
of Goldwire, Savannah River and lands orig. belonging to THOMAS FLYMING cont. 300 acres.
Signed: JN. KING, SARAH KING. Wit: RODGER (R) HODGES, Chrn. TREUTLEN, J.P.

Page 75: Rec. 10 June 1803 - Deed dated 18 April 1803, bet. DAVID METZGER, planter and
        WILLIAM DUPUIS, planter, cons. of three hundred and thirty-three dollars -
tract cont. 100 acres _____to WILLIAM BRUSTON and bounded Northwestwardly by JAMES___
and vacant, N. Eastwardly by vacant land, S. Eastwardly by TIMOTHY O'BRYAN and S. Westwardly by DAVID O'BRYAN. Also, tract cont. 200 acres granted to DAVID METZGER bounded
S. East by BRUNSTON, S. West by BRYAN, N. West by _MILLEN. Also, tract of land cont.
33 acres the same being part of 400 acres granted to TIMOTHY O'BRYAN by KING GEORGE the

third, which said 33 acres the said DAVID METZGER obtained by heirship, said tracts of land make up in whole 333 acres. Signed: DAVID METZGER. Wit: MATTHIAS RAHN, J.P., HENRY WILLIAMS

Page 77: Rec. 10 June 1803 - Bill of Sale dated 19 Mar. 1803 from JAMES MAUGH of Virginia, Co. of Fairfax, unto JOHN KING for 5 Negroes, CLARY and her daughter, DINAH and her son and daughter valued at one thousand and fifty dollars which said JOHN KING has paid. Signed: JAMES MAUGH. Wit: JAS (JC) GIBSON

31 Mar. 1803 - JAMES GIBSON made oath that the within handwriting signed JAMES MAUGH is signed by him. Signed: JAMES (JC) GIBSON. Wit: Chr. TREUTLEN, J.P.

Page 77: Rec. 19 July 1803 - Deed of Gift dated 23 Dec. 1793 from JACOB C. WALDHAUER of City of Savannah in Chatham County, shopkeeper, to his son JOHN WALDHAUER tract of land in Eff. Co. cont. 250 acres bounded North Easterly by HENSLER and SWITZER, S. West by WILLIAM EWING, S. East by _____ STIRK and the said Hensler and North West by vacant land, the same having been heretofore ordered and surveyed for GEORGE STROBARDT, deceased , the said tract having been sized for debt of said GEORGE STROBARDT against MATTHEW ASH and FREDERICK ROSEBUNGE executors of said deceased and sold by PROVOST MARSHALL, LEWIS JOHNSTON, on 31 Oct. 1775 at public outcry to JACOB C. WALDHAUER. Signed: JACOB C. WALDHAUER. Wit: DAVID GUGEL, DANIEL GUGEL

30 June 1803 - DAVID GUGEL made an oath that the within handwriting signed JACOB C. WALDHAUER is signed by him and witnessed by DANIEL GUGEL. Signed: DAVID GUGEL. Wit: JOHN KOGLER, J.P.

Page 79: Rec. 19 July 1803 - Bill of Sale dated 27 June 1803 from CHRISTOPHER GUGEL of Savannah unto JOHN WALDHAUER, ESQ, for a negro man, DAVID, valued at five hundred dollars which JOHN WALDHAUER has paid. Signed: CHRISTOPHER GUGEL, Wit: DAVID GUGEL, JOHN KIGLER, J.P.

Page 79: Rec. 28 July 1803 - Marriage Settle dated 25 June 1802, bet. WILLIAM DUPUIS of first part and DORCAS GINDRAT, widow, of second part and CHRISTIAN TREUTLEN and JOHN KING, Trustees nominated and appointed by WILLIAM DUPUIS and DORCAS GINDRAT of the third part - Whereas a marriage is to be solemized between WILLIAM DUPUIS and DORCAS GINDRAT and that DORCAS GINDRAT has in her possession in her own right, Negroes, Household, lands, etc, and in cons. of intended marriage and further cons. of trust in CHRISTIAN TREUTLEN and JOHN KING and of ten shillings a piece to CHR. TREUTLEN and JOHN KING, WILLIAM DUPUIS and DORCAS GINDRAT have sold and set over all and singular of Estate of DORCAS GINDRAT unto CHRISTIAN TREUTLEN and JOHN KING. In trust for DORCAS GINDRAT and they shall and do permit and suffer the said DORCAS GINDRAT to have the sole use and control of all and every part of her said Estate. Signed: DORCAS GINDRAT, WILLIAM DUPUIS. Wit: SARAH KING, JOEL WAISTCOAT.

23 Mar. 1803 - JOEL WAISTCOAT made an oath that the within handwriting signed DORCAS GINDRAT and WILLIAM DUPUIS is signed by them and witnessed by SARAH KING. Signed: JOEL WAISTCOAT. Wit: ELEAZER BELL, J.P.

Page 81: Rec. 14 Sept. 1803 - Deed dated 9 June 1803, bet. THOMAS NORTON, Sheriff of Chatham County To DAVID GUGEL of Co. aforesaid, cons. of one hundred and five dollars - Whereas ARTHUR BRYAN did obtain out of Superior Court of Chatham County a Judgement against MORDECAI SHEFTALE deceased in hands of (MOUS?) SHEFTALE, Executor, Whereupon a Writ of Fieri Facias issued from said Court directed to Sheriff that lands, goods, etc. of MORDECAI SHEFTALE should cause to be made three hundred and eighty-nine dollars and fifty-six cents and the sum of eighteen dollars which ARTHUR BRYAN was advanced -

THOMAS NORTON, Sheriff by virtue of said Writ of Fieri Facias did seize and expose to
sale at public outcry on 7 June all lot of land cont. 50 acres in district of Abercorn
bounded on South by land granted to Gasper _ate, West by Vest Lackner--said DAVID GUGEL
being highest bidder was knocked off to him. Signed: T. NORTON, S. C. C. Wit: BEN
WEBLEY, C. GUGEL.

Page 83: Rec. 20 Sept. 1803 - Deed dated 29 Jan. 1803, bet. WILLIAM DUPUIS, planter,
and DAVID METZGER, planter, cons. five hundred and thirty-three dollars, two
tracts of land cont. 300 acres adjoining each other, bounded on North by Stone, S. W.
by LOVE and on all other sides vacant, orig. granted to JOHN ADAM TREUTLEN the 5 Dec.
and Nov. 1769 and 1771 by last Will and testament of TREUTLEN to WILLIAM KENNEDY and by
WILLIAM KENNEDY conv. to WILLIAM DUPUIS by Indenture dated 16 May 1793. And other tract
of land cont. 200 acres bounded N. W. by Estate of WERTSCH and BELL's land, N. E. by
DAVIS'S land, S. E. by said DUPUIS, on other sides by vacant land, orig. granted to his
Excellency GEORGE MATTHEWS, then Governor on 27 August 1795 to the said WILLIAM DUPUIS
and also other tract of land cont. 100 acres granted to said DUPUIS as next above ad-
joining GINDRAT'S land and said DUPUIS, which several tracts make up in whole 600 acres.
Signed: WILLIAM DUPUIS. Wit: B._____, MATHEW RAHN, J.P.

Page 85: Rec. 20 Sept. 1803 - Deed dated 6 Jan. 1803, bet. ELIJAH TYNER and BENJAMIN
ALEXANDER, cons. one hundred and sixty-eight and three-quarter dollars - one
half of tract of land which ELIJAH TYNER bought CHRISTIAN TREUTLEN cont. 223 acres on
Cowpen Branch orig. granted to JACOB METZGER on 4 Oct. 1768, later conv. to JOHN ADAM
TREUTLEN on 4 June 1773, bequeather by him by last Will and testament to daughter MARY
who intermarried EDWARD DUDLY, who conv. tract to CHRISTIAN TREUTLEN on 13 Sept. 1795.
Signed: ELIJAH (E) TYNER. Wit: SENATE POWERS, WM. (X) THORNTON.

16 July 1803 - SENATE POWERS made oath that the within handwriting signed by ELIJAH TY-
NER is signed by him and witnessed by WILLIAM THORNTON. Signed: SENATE POWERS. Wit:
HENRY W. WILLIAMS C. S. C. E. C.

Page 87: Rec. 20 Sept. 1803 - Deed dated 16 Dec. 1802, bet. CHRISTIAN DASHER and ANN
ELIZABETH DASHER his wife and ROBERT BURTON, cons. of two hundred and sixty
dollars - tract of land cont. 100 acres bounded by JACOB KEIFFERS land and on other
sides by vacant land, orig. granted to SOLOMON SHRIMPH about two miles from Ogeechee
River, cont. 100 acres. Signed: (in German) ANN ELIZABETH (X) DASHER. Wit: JOHN
SPENCER, J.P., WILLIA SPIER.

Page 88: Rec. 29 Nov. 1823 - Deed dated 7 Aug. 1795, bet. JOSIAH TATTNALL, NICHOLAS
LONG, and PHILIP CLAYTON, Commissioners, appointed to carry into effect "An
act to amend pointing out the mode under which property reverting to the State shall be
disposed of" passed on 20 Dec. 1793 and JAMES POWELL of Liberty Co. By virtue of act
passed 4 May 1782 entitled "An Act for inflicting penalties on and confiscating the estates of such persons as are therein declared guilty of Treason and for other purposes
mentioned," said Commissioners did sell unto DAVID REES in fee simple for a valuable
cons. tract of 300 acres of land of late JOHN MULRYNE and JOSIAH TATTNALL in two surveys each other bounded North by Savannah River which said tract had been found the property of JOHN MULRYNE and JOSIAH TATTNALL, confiscated and vested in the State of Georgia.
DAVID REES for securing to State payment of money stipulated took use of mortgage upon
said tract. At a Superior Court held in Eff. Co. a suit was instituted by the Governor
for foreclosing the equity of Redemption of mortgage, the said Court adjudged and de-
creed that the said DAVID REES should be foreclosed of and from all equity of redemption of said mortgaged premises, and in pursuance of a resolution of the General Assembly
bearing date 1 Dec. 1794, the Commissioners were to execute title to said JAMES POWELL
for desired said land - cons. of seven hundred pounds in public securities, the said

Commissioners sold to JAMES POWELL said tract of 300 acres. Signed: JOSIAH TATTNALL, JUNR., PH CLAYTON. Wit: THOS. LETTELTON, JN. MILTON, ABN. CLANDLESH, CLAND THOMPSON.

Page 91: Rec. Jan. 11, 1804 - Deed dated 21 Sept. 1796, bet. JAMES POWELL of Liberty County, Esq. and JOSIAH TATTNALL of Chatham County, Esq. - cons. of two hundred pounds - tract of land cont. 300 acres of land JOHN MULRYNE and JOSIAH TATTNALL in Eff. Co. being 2 surveys adjoining each other bounded North by Savannah River. Wit: _____ H.WOOD.

Page 92: Rec. 26 Jan. 1804 - Deed dated 7 Mar. 1824, bet. JOSIAH TATTNALL JUNR. and GROSS SCROGGS - cons. one thousand and thirty-six dollars - tract of land about forty-five miles from Savannah known as the Cool Spring tract of land, cont. 420 acres, orig. the property of JOHN M. TATTNALL and JOSIAH TATTNALL JUNR. and purchased at the sales of reverted Estates by JAMES POWELL of Liberty Co., conv. by him to said JOSIAH TATTNALL, tract bounded on North by Savannah River, West by land surveyed for DAVID HARRIS. Signed: JOSIAH TATTNALL JUNR. Wit: BALTHAZER SHAFFER, J.P., GEO. THROOP.

Page 94: Rec. 27 Jan. 1804 - Deed dated 10 June 1796, bet. JOHN KING of Savannah and JAMES GOLDWIRE and JOHN GOLDWIRE, cons. six hundred dollars - tract of land bounded at Savannah River, cont. 600 acres. Signed: JOHN KING. Wit: THOS. B_GGS, WILLIAM KING, JUNR.

19 Dec. 1803 - WILLIAM KING made oath that the within handwriting signed by JOHN KING is signed by him and witnessed by THOMAS B_GGS. Signed: WILLIAM KING. Wit: W. WILL- IAMS, Clk., S. C. E. C.

Page 96: Rec. 27 Jan. 1804 - Deed dated 13 Jan. 1780, bet. JOHN BAKER, JOHN M. LANE, CHARLES ODINGSELLS, HUGH LAWSON, CADEL HOWELL, and ABRAHAM ROVOT, Esquires, the majority of the Commissioners appointed by House of Assembly at Augusta on May 4, 1782 for carrying into execution "An act for inflicing penalties on and confiscating the Estates of such persons as are therein declared guilty of treason and for other purposes therein mentioned" and ABRAHAM RAVOT, ESQ. Commissioners found that on 19 April 1775, JAMES PACE was banished from State forever - possessions be confiscated for use of the state - the land to be sold on the following terms and conditions to wit: seven years credit to be given to purchaser of land and other real estates and four years credit to purchaser of personal estates, and said sales to be public and held between hours of ten o'clock in forenoon and three o'clock in afternoon - on 2 Jan. in Savannah in Chatham County said land cont. 100 acres orig. granted to _____SWAN, by SWAN to SAMUEL CURREN, by CURREN to ADRION (L?)OYER, by (L?)OYER to JAMES PACE, also tract cont. 100 acres orig. granted MICHAEL (L?)OYER, by (L?)OYER to NOBLES, by NOBLES to JAMES PACE; tract cont. 150 acres to JAMES NIX, by NIX to JAMES PACE; and tract of 25 acres orig. granted to JOHN CLAYTON, by CLAYTON to JOHN WERTSCH, by WERTSCH to JOHN HALL and ARTHUR RYALLS, by them to JAMES PACE, said tracts compose tracts of land known as Tuckaseeking cont. in whole 375 acres, was sold to ABRAHAM RAVOT the highest bidder for six hundred and eighteen pounds fifteen shillings specie. Signed: JOHN BAKER, JOHN M. LEAN, CHARLES ODINGSELLS, HUGH LAWSON, CA_ _ HOWELL, THOS. LEWIS, ABN. RAVOT. Wit: BEN. LLOYD, J.P., SAML. STIRK.

Page 99: Indenture dated 1 July 1803 , bet. BENJAMIN MOODIE and WILLIAM WHITE of City of Charleston and state of South Carolina and JOHN KING of Effingham County in Georgia - cons. five shillings - tract of land cont. 100 acres in Eff. Co. granted to SWAN, by SWAN to CURREN, by CURREN to ADRION (L?)OYER, by (L?)OYER to JAMES PACE. Also, tract cont. 100 acres orig. granted MICHAEL (L?)OYER, by (L?)OYER to NOBLES, by NOBLES to JAMES PACE; tract cont. 150 acres orig. granted to JAMES NIX, by NIX to JAMES PACE; tract of 25 acres granted to JOHN CLATON, by CLATON to JOHN WERTSCH, by WERTSCH to JOHN HALL and ARTHUR RYALL, by them to JAMES PACE, tracts compose tracts known as

Tuckaseeking cont. in whole 375 acres - for his use for one year. Signed: BENJAMIN MO-
ODIE, WILL WHITE. Wit: G. REED, WM. WILKIE, JUNR.

Charleston, S. C. - 1 July 1803 - WILLIAM WILKIE made oath that the within handwriting
signed BENJAMIN MOODIE and WILLIAM WHITE was signed by them and witnessed by GEORGE REED.
Signed: WM. WILKIE, JUNR. Wit: ISAAC MOTTE DART.

Page 101: Indenture dated 1 July 1803, bet. BENJAMIN MOODIE and CAROLINE his wife and
           WILLIAM WHITE of City of Charleston in South Carolina and JOHN KING of Eff-
ingham County - cons. seventeen hundred and fourteen dollars and twenty-eight cts. tract
of 100 acres granted to SWAN, by SWAN to CURREN, by CURREN to ADRION (L?)OYER by (L?)
OYER to JAMES PACE; also tract cont. 100 acres orig. granted MICHAEL (L?)OYER, by (L?)
OYER to NOBLES, by NOBLES to JAMES PACE; tract cont. 150 acres orig. granted to JAMES
NIX, by NIX to JAMES PACE; tract of 25 acres granted JOHN CLATON, by CLATON to JOHN WER-
TSCH, by WERTSCH to JOHN HALL and ARTHUR RYALL, by THEM to JAMES PACE, tracts compose
tracts known as Tuckaseeking cont. in whole 375 acres. Signed: BENJAMIN MOODIE, CARO-
LINE MOODIE, WILL WHITE. Wit: G. REED, WM. WILKIE, JUNR.

Charleston, S. C. - 1 July 1803 - WILLIAM WILKIE made oath that the within handwriting
signed BENJAMIN MOODIE, CAROLINE MOODIE, and WILLIAM WHITE is signed by them and wit.
by GEORGE REED. Signed: WM. WILKIE, JUNR. Wit: ISAAC MOTTE DART

Page 103: Rec. 30 Jan. 1804 - Dated 1 July 1803-Know all men by these presents that
           whereas the several tracts or parcels of land within mentioned were conv. to
the said BENJ. MOODIE and WILLIAM WHITE, by ABRAHAM RAVOT and MARY his wife of State of
Georgia in payment of a debt due to MR. JOHN SHOLBRED late of London dec., who was in
his life time and whose estate since his death and at the time of the within conveyance
was interested in the said land, and the purchase money therefore on the present sale,
is to go to the use and behalf of the said Estate by reason whereof the said BENJAMIN
MOODIE and WILLIAM WHITE the within granted not having bound themselves to warrant it,
it hath become requisite that some person interested for and in the Estate of JOHN SHO-
LBRED Should grant the used clauses and covenants that attend deeds conveyancing lands
in fee simple to the end and therefore to supply the several clauses and covenants aforesaid. Know ye that I JAMES SHOOLBRED of the City of Charleston for the cons. aforesaid
and for the further cons. of one dollar to me in hand paid by the said JOHN KING the receipt whereof I do hereby acknowledge have for myself, my heirs, Executors and Administrators covenanted and agreed to and with the said JOHN KING, his heirs and assigns in
manner following, that is to say that he the said JOHN KING, his heirs and assigns shall
and may from time to time and at all times hereafter peaceably and quietly have, hold,
occupy, possess, and enjoy all singular the aforesaid tracts or parcels of land heredit-
aments, and premises within granted and conveyed and realeased without the lawful suit,
trouble, hindrance, molestation, interruption, eviction, or disturbance of them the said
BENJAMIN MOODIE and WILLIAM WHITE, their heirs or assigns or of any other person or persons lawfully claiming or to claim by from or under them or any of them and further that
I the said JAMES SHOOLBRED and my heirs the aforesaid tracts or parcels of land and all
and singular other the premises within mentioned or_____to be thereby granted, bargained,
sold, released, and confirmed and every part and parcel thereof with the appurtenances
unto the said JOHN KING, his heirs and assigns against them the said BENJAMIN MOODIE and
WILLIAM WHITE their heirs and against all other persons whomsoever and any Estate having
a lawfully claiming of, in to or out, of the said premises or, of in and to any part or
parcel thereof with the appurtenances shall and will warrant and for ever Defend by these
presents.
       In witness wherof I have hereunto set my hand and affixed my seal at Charleston the
first day of July in the year of our Lord one thousand eight hundred and three and in the
twenty-seventh year of the Sovereignty and Independence of the United States of America.
Signed: JAMES SHOOLBRED. Wit: G. REED, WM. WILKIE, JUNR.

Page 105:   Rec. 1 July 1804 - Deed of Gift dated 21 April 1775, SIMON REITER of Parish
            of St. Matthew to his daughter, JOHANNE, Negroes DAVID, MARY, JOHN, CATHARINE,
MARTHA. Signed: SIMON REUTERS. Wit: SIGMUND OTT, _____ _____

3 Oct. 1803 - JOHN KOGLER made oath that the handwriting of SIGMUND OTT and JOHN HINELY
on Indenture is actually their handwriting. Signed: JOHN KOGLER. Wit: HENRY W. WILL-
IAMS, Clk.

 Page 106: Rec. 2 Feb. 1804 - Deed dated 16 Nov. 1803, bet. JOHN IVEY and MARY his wife
            and ROBERT BURTON, cons. one hundred and twenty dollars, tract of land cont.
100 acres bounded on North by NATHANIEL HAWTHORNE, South by WALDHAUER, West by NATHANIEL
ZETTLER, orig. granted to JOHN IVEY on 3 Oct. 1801. Signed: JOHN IVEY, MARY IVEY. Wit:
WM. HAWTHORNE, BENJ. BURTON.

22Dec. 1803 - WILLIAM HAWTHORNE made oath that the within handwriting signed JOHN IVEY
and MARY IVEY is signed by them and witnessed by BENJAMIN BURTON. Signed: WM. HAWTHORNE
Wit: HENRY W. WILLIAMS, Clk.

Page 107: Rec. 13 Feb. 1804 - Dated 6 Feb. 1804 - WM. KENNEDY stated that he had re-
            ceived from CHRISTIAN TREUTLEN Executor of Last Will and testament of JOHN
ADAM TREUTLEN satisfaction for share of the estate of JOHN ADAM TREUTLEN to which said
KENNEDY was entitled by right of his wife ELIZABETH, daughter of JOHN ADAM TREUTLEN.
Signed: WM. KENNEDY. Wit: JOHN KING, THOMAS POLHILL, J.I.C.

Page 108: Rec. 2 March 1804 - Deed dated 23 Feb. 1804, bet. WILLIAM ROPER and JEREMIAH
            CUYLER, said WM. ROPER is bound unto JEREMIAH for sum of two hundred and ten
dollars, for better securing of said sum, said ROPER puts up for sale tract of land cont.
50 acres adj. lands of JOHN SPENCER, JEREMIAH CUYLER, and the Church lands, orig. granted
JOHN STALY and bought at Sheriff's sale as property of EDWARD DAVIS, said land to be sold
to CUYLER if sum of one hundred and five dollars is not paid by 1st Oct. next - if said
sum be paid, then this deed of bargain to be void, if default should occur and land is
sold, all excess is to be paid to WILLIAM ROPER. Signed: WM. ROPER. Wit: MORRIS MIL-
LER.

24 Feb. 1804 - MORRIS MILLER, ESQ. swore that he was a subscribing witness to deed and
saw same regularly executed. Signed: MORRIS MILLER. Wit: JOHN G. WILLIAMSON, J.I.C.

Page 109: Rec. 3 Sept. 1804 - Deed dated 25 Mar. 1803, bet. JOHN KING, planter, and
            JAMES SHOOLBRED of City of Charleston, State of South Carolina - JOHN KING
is bound unto JAMES SHOOLBRED in sum of three thousand four hundred and twenty-eight
dollars for the better securing of eight hundred and fifty-seven dollars and fourteen
cents at or before 1 Jan. 1804 and eight hundred and fifty-seven dollars and fourteen
cents on or before 1 Jan. 1805, said JOHN KING has released unto JAMES SHOOLBRED for
fee of one dollar tract of land cont. 100 acres orig. granted to SWAN, sold by SWAN to
SAMUEL CURREN, by CURREN to ADRION (L?)OYER, by (L?)OYER to JAMES PACE; tract of 100
acres of land granted MICHAEL (L?)OYER, from (L?)OYER to NOBLES,by NOBLES to JAMES PACE;
tract of 150 acres granted to JAMES NIX, from NIX to JAMES PACE; and tract cont. twenty-
five acres granted to JOHN CLATON, by CLATON to JOHN WETSCH, by WERTSCH to JOHN HALL and
ARTHUR RYALL, by them to JAMES PACE,which said tracts compose tract known as Tuckaseeking
cont. in whole 375 acres-if said sums are paid to JAMES SHOOLBRED, then deed to be void.
Signed: JOHN KING. Wit: JOHN CAIG, PETER MITCHELL.

11 April 1804 - JOHN CAIG sworn he saw JOHN KING sign deed and witnessed by PETER MIT-
CHELL. Signed: JOHN KING.Wit: _TOBLER, J.P.

Page 111: Rec. 7 Mar. 1810 - Indenture dated 9 Mar. 1804 - Know all ment by these presents that I PATRICK McKENTY of Chatham Co. have this day assigned and transferred unto CHRISTIAN DASHER SENR. the balance due on the within being one hundred and
fifty dollars. Signed: P. McKENTY. Wit: CHRISTIAN DASHER JUNR., JOHN WISENBAKER.

28 June 1804 - JOHN WISENBAKER made oath that the within Indenture was signed by PATRICK
McKENTY and witnessed by CHRISTIAN DASHER JUNR. Signed: JOHN WISENBAKER. Wit: JOHN
WISENBAKER, J.P.

Page 112: Rec. 5 Sept. 1804 - Deed dated 19 Mar. 1804 - WILLIAM ROPER being indebted
to DANIEL HOLMES, planter of South Carolina, Colleton District, St. Barthol-
emeus Parish, Jacksonborough for four hundred pounds sterling by note dated 4 May 1794
said note transferred to ANN McLAUGHLIN, for better securing of said note does sell unto
ANN McLAUGHLIN 3 Negroes, SID, RACHAEL, and HARRY toghether with 50 acres of land in
GOSHEN District Effingham Co. joining lands of JEREMIAH CUYLER, ESQ., JOHN SPENCER of
Estate of MR. CRUGER the said land formerly granted JOHN STALY; also 2 parcels of land
of Estate of JACOB METZGER, one tract in Eff. Co. joining estate of HENRY GINDRAT, ESQ.
other in Scriven Co. on waters of Boyer Creek, the other near Savannah river.- if WM.
ROPER shall pay or cause to be paid said note before 4 May 1804, obligation to be void.
Signed: WILLIAM ROPER. Wit: JAMES BEARFIELD.

5 July 1804 - JAMES BEARFIELD made oath that he was a subscribing witness and that he
saw WILLIAM ROPER sign same. Signed: JAMES BEARFIELD. Wit: MALL. DRISCOLL.

Page 114: Rec. 7 Sept. 1804 - Deed dated 1 May 1804 - Bet. JOHN DUPUIS of South Carolina and County of Lincoln and CHRISTIAN TREUTLEN ESQ. - cons. of one hundred and forty dollars - tract of land cont. 100 acres - orig. granted JOHN HOPKINS on
1 Mar. 1759 by his EXCELLENCY HENRY ELLIS, Governor of the Province now St. of Georgia,
bounded North East by Savannah river joining lands of WM. KENNEDY and CHRISTIAN TREUTLEN
and sold by JOHN HOPKINS to JOHN PALMER in 1800, and conv. to JAMES DUPUIS SENR. by
PALMER on 6 March 1801 and willed by JAMES DUPUIS, SENR., to JOHN DUPUIS and by him
conv. to CHRISTIAN TREUTLEN, ESQ. Signed: JOHN (X) DUPUIS, MARY DUPUIS. Wit: WILL-
IAM DUPUIS, BENJAMIN KENNEDY, MATTHEW RAHN, J.P.

Page 115: Rec. 20 Nov. 1804 - Indenture dated 23 Aug. 1804 - STEPHEN BRITTON and SARAH
his wife of Chatham County are firmly bound and oblinged to JOHN LILLIBRIDGE
for sum of two hundred and eighty-four dollars - sum of one hundred and forty-two dollars be paid before 23 Aug. 1805, obligation then to be void. Signd: STEPHEN BRITTON,
SARAH BRITTON. Wit: GEORGE SHICK, OLIVER M. LILLIBRIDGE.

14 Sept. 1804 - OLIVER M. LILLIBRIDGE made oath that the within handwriting signed STE-
PHEN BRITTON and SARAH is signed by them and witnessed by GEORGE SHICK. Signed: OLIVER
M. LILLIBRIDGE. Wit: HENRY W. WILLIAMS, Clk.

Page 116: Rec. 20 Sept. 1804 - Mort. dated 23 Aug. 1804, bet. STEPHEN BRITTON and SAR-
AH his wife of County of Chatham and JOHN LILLIBRIDGE-BRITTON bound unto LIL-
LIBRIDGE for sum of two hundred and eighty-four dollars and that payment of one hundred
and forty-four dollars be paid on or before 23 Aug. 1805, for better securing of said
money, BRITTON sells unto LILLIBRIDGE plantation or tract of land in village of ABER-
CORN, County of Effingham - cont. 48 1/2 acres, bounded on South and West by estate of
LEO. NOWLAN, East by JEREMIAH CUYLER, ESQ., North by lot no. 8 - in case of payment of
money, bargain to be void. Signed: STEPHEN BRITTON, SARAH BRITTON. Wit: GEORGE SH-
ICK, OLIVER M. LILLIBRIDGE.

14 Sept. 1804 - OLIVER M. LILLIBRIDGE made oath that the within handwriting signed STE-
PHEN BRITTON and SARAH BRITTON is signed by them and witnessed by GEORGE SHICK. Signed:

82

OLIVER M. LILLIBRIDGE. Wit:

Page 118: Rec. 29 Sept. 1804 - Dated 22 June 1802, bet. DORCAS GINDRAT to her children
           to stepson JOHN GINDRAT a Negro woman named PHEBE, to D. GINDRAT her daughter
PHEBE'S child, LUCH; to children ELIZABETH TISON, MARY TAYLOR and SETH PAFFORD three Negroes, SIMON, NELL and NELL'S child ELIZA; to daughter ELIZABETH, ELEANOR; to HENRIETTA
her daughter a sorrel mare; to granddaughter VIRGINIA D. TAYLOR, NELL'S child NELLY but
she must remain in daughter MARY TAYLOR'S possession till VIRGINIA comes of age or marries; and furniture to be divided among them. Signed: DORCAS GINDRAT. Wit: PAUL (X)
T_____, HANNAH (X) TREBLE.

27 Aug. 1804 - HANNAH TREBLE made oath that the within handwriting signed by DORCAS GIN-
DREAT is signed by her and witnessed by PAUL TOOSING. Signed: HANNAH (X) TRIBLE, Wit:
CHRN. TREUTLEN, J.P.

Page 119: Rec. 29 Sept. 1804 - Deed dated 1 Sept. 1800, bet. JOSEPH HOLLIDAY, planter
           and MILNER HOLLIDAY, cons. of three hundreddollars - tract of land cont. 400
acres on North side of great Ogeechee River, being the northerly or upper part of several tracts conv. on 24 Nov. 1796 by REDDING DENMARK to ELEAZER BELL, and on 19 Mar.
1798 conv. by BELL to JOSEPH HOLLIDAY. Signed: JOSEPH HOLLIDAY. Wit: JOHN MOORE,
FERNEY HOLLIDAY.

5 Dec. 1803 - JOHN MOORE, ESQ. made oath that he and FURNEY HOLLIDAY did sign as witnesses the Indenture signed by JOSEPH HOLLIDAY and MILNER HOLLIDAY. Signed: JOHN MOORE
Wit: CHR. TREUTLEN, J.P.

Page 121: Rec. 29 Sept. 1804 - Bill of sale dated 9 April 1804, bet. BENJAMIN OGLESBY
           of Goshen District and GEORGE ELLIOTT, school master, of same - cons. four
hundred dollars - for one Negro fellow, CESAR. Signed: BENJN. (X) OGLESBY. Wit:
WILLIAM ROPER.

4 Sept. 1804 - WILLIAM ROPER made oath that he saw BENJAMIN OGLESBY make his mark on
within writing. Signed: WILLIAM ROPER. Wit: HENRY W. WILLIAMS, Clk.

Page 122: 29 Sept. 1804 - Deed dated 19 Oct. 1801, bet. JOHN WILLIAMS, Sheriff of Eff.
           Co. and CHRISTIAN DASHER, cons. one hundred and one dollars - tract of land
cont. 50 acres bounded by JACOB KEIFFER, orig. granted SOLOMON SHRIMP about 2 miles from
Ogeechee river, CHRN. DASHER by Writ of fieri facias issued by Superior Court against
JNO. G. NEIDLINGER and wife, Executrix of DANIEL ZETTLER for one hundred and eighty dollars and forty-four cents with interest and twenty-four dollars costs, had said 50 acres
of land of estate of DANIEL ZETTLER conf. by sheriff and sold at public auction where
said land was knocked off to CHRISTIAN DASHER. Signed: JNO. WILLIAMS, S. E. C. Wit:
GEO. ELLIOTT, JOHN WISENBAKER.

2 July 1804 - GEORGE ELLIOTT made oath that he saw JOHN WILLIAMS sign within Indenture
and that it was witnessed by JOHN WISENBAKER. Signed: GEO. ELLIOTT. Wit: HENRY W.
WILLIAMS, Clk., S.C.E. C.

Page 124: Rec. 29 Sept. 1804 - Deed dated 2 July 1804, bet. CHRISTIAN DASHER and ANN
           ELIZ. his wife and ROBERT BURTON, cons. of two hundred and sixty dollars,
tract or parcel of land cont. 100 acres bounded by JACOB KEIFFER, orig. granted SOLOMON
SHRIMP, about 2 miles from Ogeechee river, said land seized and sold by virtue of Exe-
cution against estate of DANIEL ZETTLER at which time CHRN. DASHER became purchaser.
Signed: (in German), ANN ELIZABETH (X) DASHER. Wit: ANN ELIZABETH (X) DASHER,
HENRY W. WILLIAMS, Clk, S.C.E.C.

83

Page 125: Rec. 9 Nov. 1804 - Deed dated 5 May 1804, bet. JESSEE SCRUGGS and ALETHIA his wife and JOHN KING and WILLIAM KING, JUNIOR, cons. sum of thirteen hundred dollars, two tracts of land, oen cont. 250 acres in Parish of St. Matthew granted NATHANIEL LANGLEY on 7 May 1771; also tract granted NATHANIAL LANGLEY cont. 250 acres bounded westwardly by JOHN GOLDWIRE, northeastwardly by TONDEE and LANGLEY granted on 1 Sept. 1772, which said tracts on stream called three Runs which tracts were conv. to said SCRUGGS. Signed: JESSEE SCRIGGS, ALLETHIA SCRUGGS. Wit: WILLIAM BEACH, CHRN. TREUTLEN, J.P.

Page 127: 21 Sept. 1804 - NATHANIEL LUNDAY made oath that he possessed a bond or obligation signed by JOHN KING and JOHN MOORE bearing date about 12 July 1790 conditioned that JOHN KING should make deponent titles to three tracts of land, each 50 acres, which bond the deponent says is lost so that he can't get it. Signed: N. LUNDAY. WIT: CHRN. TREUTLEN, J.P.

9 Nov. 1804 - NATHANIEL LUNDAY acknowledged that he received of JOHN KING full satisfaction for bond by having made titles to MR. GROSS SCRUGGS. Signed: N. LUNDAY. Wit: CHRN. TREUTLEN, J.P.

Page 127: Rec. 12 Nov. 1804 - Deed dated 8 Sept. 1803 - Bill of Sale from LEWIS G. CUTHBERT, planter, of Chatham County to THOMAS POLHILL, planter - sum of three hundred dollars for Negro mulatto, SAM. Signed: LEWIS G. CUTHBERT. Wit: JOHN ROBINSON.

10 Nov. 1804 - JOHN ROBINSON swore that he saw LEWIS G. CUTHBERT sign within Indenture. Signed: JOHN ROBINSON. Wit: JOHN KING, J.I.C.E.C.

Page 128: Rec. 29 Nov. 1804 - Dated 11 Jan. 1802 - EDWARD DUPREE, Attorney for SHAROD HINES, has sold to HOWELL HINES a Negro wench, HANNAH, for two hundred and fifty dollars. Signed: EDMUND DUPRESS, Attorney for SHAROD HINES. Wit: MILNER HOLIDAY, J.P., SHAR_ _D McCALL.

Page 129: Rec. 29 Nov. 1804 - Dated 13 April 1803 - Articles of Agreement bet. HOWELL HINES and MARTHA WEST, HOWELL HINES acknowledges to endow her with all her worldly goods in presence of STEPHEN WOOLF and MILNER HOLIDAY. Signed: HOWELL HINES Wit: MILNER HOLIDAY, J.P., STEPHEN WOOLF.

Page 129: Rec. 29 Nov. 1804 - Dated 29 May 1786, bet. OLIVER BOWEN of Savannah, ESQ. and JAMES BELCHER, merchant - cons. sum of five shillings sterling - tract cont. 400 acres in Saint Matthews Parish now Eff. Co. bound South easterly by WILLIAM BELCHER, South West by Ogeechee river; also, one tract cont. 700 acres adj. westerly to above mentioned tract, South West by Great Ogeechee river and easterly by BERNARD ROMAN; and those other 2 tracts of land cont. 900 acres adj. each other on Great Ogechee river - released for one year. Signed: OLIVER BOWEN. Wit: PETER DEVEAUX, JOHN BEATTY.

Page 130: Rec. 29 Nov. 1804 - Dated 13 May 1786, bet. OLIVER BOWEN of Town of Savannah Esq. and JAMES BELCHER, merchant - NATHANIEL HUDSON, Sheriff of Eff. Co. by deed of bargain and sale bearing date 17 May 1784 did expose at public outcry on 6 Nov. 1784 when OLIVER BOWEN purchased it - OLIVER BOWEN received of JAMES BELCHER five hundred pounds sterling - tract cont. 400 acres in St. Matthews Parish now Eff. Co. bound South easterly by WILLIAM BELCHER, South West by Ogechee river; also tract cont. 700 acres adj. westerly above mentioned tract, South West by great Ogechee river, easterly by BARNARD ROMANS; two other tracts cont. 900 acres adj. each other on Great Ogechee

84

river. Signed: OLIVER BOWEN. Wit: PETER DEVEAUX, JOHN BEATTY.

6June 1786 - JOHN BEATTY of Savannah, Practitioner in Physick made oath that he saw
OLIVER BOWEN sign within Indenture. Signed: JOHN BEATTY. Wit: SAM STIRK, J.P.

Page 133: Rec. 29 Nov. 1804 - Dated 22 Nov. 1804 - bet. JAMES BELCHER and ANN his wife
          of City of Savannah and JOSEPH BEVAN of Wilkes County, planter - cons. seven
hundred and seventy-eight dollars and seventy-five cents - tract of land in St. Matthews Parish now Eff. Co. bounded South West by Great Ogechee river, South East by DAVID
MURRAY - cont. 707 1/2 acres. Signed: JAS. BELCHER, ANN BELCHER. Wit: JOHN POOLER,
J.P., J. LAWSON.

Page 135: Rec. 30 Nov. 1804 - Deed dated 18 Feb. 1803 - Bet. BENJAMIN TENNILLE of Wash-
          ington Co. and JESSEE DYKES of Eff. Co. - cons. of ten dollars, parcel of
land cont. 250 acres in Tattnall Co. on waters of Ohoopie being part of a survey of
1,000 acres bounded by part of tract belonging to GRANTHAM, on South West and North
East by F. FENNELL and on North West by part of survey. Signed: BENJAMIN TENNILLE, Wit:
WILLIAM HANCOCK, JOHN BRIDGES.

19 Feb. 1803 - JOHN BRIDGES made oath that he saw BENJAMIN TENNILLE sign within Indenture and that WILLIAM HANCOCK witnessed. Signed: JOHN BRIDGES. Wit: N. ROBERTSON, J.P.

Page 136: Rec. 30 Nov. 1804 - Deed dated 19 May 1803, bet. CANNUEL TISON, planter and
          JESSEE DYKES, planter, cons. fifty dollars, tract cont. 300 acres bound N.
East by BISHOP and DYKE, S. East by DYKES and O'BERRY, S. West by JAMES TISON, N. West
by vacant land, granted CAMMUEL TISON on 3 Oct. 1798 by his EXCELLENCY JAMES JACKSON,
Gov. Signed: CAMMUEL TISON. Wit: MILNER HOLIDAY, J.P. JOHN (M) MERCHANT.

Page 137: Rec. 1 Dec. 1804 - Deed of Gift dated 2 Aug. 1802 - JOSEPH DUSSEIGN of South
          Carolina for friendship of LEWIS GROVENSTEIN grants unto GROVENSTEIN tract of
land in Eff. Co. willed to DUSSEIGN by his father granted 10 Mar. 1759 and certified 14
Mar. 1759, cont. 150 acres to which he is entitled to one third part - joining North
East by lands formerly MICHAEL SWINCOFFS in _____of GEORGE TEIKENS. Signed: JESSEE BELL,
PAUL (P) TOOSING, ELEAZER BELL, J.P.

Page 138: Rec. 17 Dec. 1804 - Deed dated 10 May 1772, bet. JOHN GRUBER of Parish of
          Saint Matthew, planter, and MARY MAGDALENA his wife, and MICHAEL HEINTZMAN
of same, tanner, cons. of seventy pounds, tract, the 1st cont. 100 acres bounded North
East by land of SIMON REUTER, South East by CHRISTIAN STEINER, and GEORGE KOGLER, North
West by ULRICK NEIDLINGER and South West by vacant land, orig. granted JOHN MAURER, pur-
chased by JOHN GRUBER on 28 Feb. 1769; other tract cont. 50 acres bound North West on
MATTHEW BRANDNOU, South East on JOHN BLETTER, said tract gntd. on 2 July 1765 to JOHN
GRUBER. Signed: (written in German) Wit: JOHN (L) LASTINGER, GEORGE (ND) MINGER-
STORF, JACOB CRONBERGER.

11 May 1804 - JONATHAN SECKINGER made oath that he was well acquainted with the handwriting of JOHN GRUBER and JACOB CRONBERGER and that the handwriting is theirs. Signed:
JONATHAN SECKINGER. Wit: HENRY W. WILLIAMS, Clk. S.C.E.C.

Page 142: Deed dated 19 Sept. 1787, bet. JOHN LOURMAN, planter, and _____LOURMAN his
          wife and JAMES GREENHOW, cons. one hundred pounds sterling, tract of land
cont. 800 acres in Fishing Creek in Wilks Co. bounded southerly by land formerly WILL-
IAM JONES and westerly by ____M. CLENDALS land, orig. granted to JOHN LOURMAN. Signed:
JOHN LOURMAN. Wit: EDW. JONES, THOMAS POLHILL.

31 Jan. 1805 - THOMAS POLHILL made oath that he saw JOHN LOURMAN sign within Indenture
and that EDWARD JONES was a witness. Signed: THOMAS POLHILL. Wit: HEN. W. WILLIAM,
Clk.

Page 144: Rec. 20 March 1805 - Deed dated 22 Dec. 1804, bet. AUGUSTUS EASTER, planter
and MARY EASTER his wife and JOHN STRAHAN, planter, cons. of thirty dollars,
tract cont. 200 acres on North East side of Smalls Creek bounded Westerly by JOHN STRA-
HAN, surveyed in name of AUGUSTUS EASTER on 30 Jan. 1801. Signed: AUSUSTUS (X) EASTER,
MARY (X) EASTER. Wit: DARIUS GARRASON.

12 Jan. 1805 - DARIUS GARRASON made oath that he saw within persons sign Indenture.
Signed: DARIUS GARRASON. Wit: HEN. W. WILLIAM, Clk.

Page 146: Rec. 1805 - Deed dated 8 Dec. 1804, bet. JOHN WALDHAUER ESQ. and MARY his
wife and ROBERT BURTON, planter, cons. of three hundred and fifty dollars,
tract of land cont. 200 acres in Parish of St. Matthew bounded North by MATTHIAS ZET-
TLER, Easterly by SOLOMON SHRIMPH, orig. granted JOHN JACOB KEIFFER by MAJESTY GEORGE
the third on 2 Aug. 1768, by KEIFFER conv. JACOB WALDHAUER bylease and release dated
16 and 17 June 1775, obtained by JOHN WALDHAUER from JACOB WALDHAUER by heirship. Sig:
JOHN WALDHAUER, MARY (MW) WALDHAUER. Wit: J. G. NEIDLINGER, C.C.O.E.C., GODHILF NEASE.

Page 148: Rec. 20 March 1805 - Deed dated 17 April 1804, bet. DAVID KENNEDY, planter
and RUTH his wife and DARIUS GARRASON, cons. thirty dollars, tract of land
cont. 150 acres on south side of Shrimps Creek, bounded southerly by DARIUS GARRASON,
JOSEPH_____, south westerly by JOHN EPPINGER and surveyed in name of DAVID KENNEDY
on 21 Feb. 1804. Signed: DAVID (X) KENNEDY, RUTH (X) KENNEDY. Wit: JOHN STRAHAN.

12 Jan. 1805 - JOHN STRAHAM made oath he saw within parties sign Indenture. Signed:
JOHN STRAHAN. Wit: HEN. W. WILLIAMS, Clk.

Page 149: Rec. 20 Mar. 1805 - Deed dated 14 July 1803 - Bet. MICHAEL EXLEY, planter
and ELIZABETH his wife and DAVID LOVETT, cons. of three dollars, tract of
land cont. 200 acres bound N. East by LOVETT, S. West by RUSSELL, orig granted 18 Nov.
1801 by His Excellency JOSIAH TATTNALL JUNR. ESQ. Gov. Signed: MICHAEL EXLEY, ELIZA-
BETH EXLEY. Wit: MATTHEW RAHN, J.P., JONATHAN RAHN, WILLIAM KENNEDY.

Page 151: Rec. 28 March 1805 - Deed dated 23 Mar. 1805, bet. JONATHAN SECKINGER, black-
smith, and MARY his wife and DAVID LOVETT, planter, cons. three dollars, tract
of land cont. 200 acres bound N. eastwardly by JOHN METZGER, N. Westerly by DAVID MET-
ZGER, S. westwardly by DAVID LOVELL, orig. granted 3 Dec. 1801 by His Excellency JOS-
IAH TATTNALL, JUNR. GOV. ESQ. to JONATHAN SECKINGER. Signed: JONATHAN SECKINGER, M.
FREDERICA (M) SECKINGER. Wit: JOHN KOGLER, TIMOTHY STALY, JOHN WALDHAUER.

Page 152: Rec. 10 April 1805 - Deed dated 1 Dec. 1805, bet. SAMUEL WADE, planter and
THOMAS HURST, planter, cons. one hundred dollars, tract of land cont. 250
acres, orig granted JESSE HURST on 5 Sept. 1793 and conv. by HURST to SAMUEL WADE adjoining HURST and vacant land. Signed: SAML. (S) WADE, HANNAH (X) WADE. Wit: CLE-
MENT LANIER, J.I.C., WILLIAM HURST.

Page 153: Rec. 10 April 1805 - Deed dated 21 July 1804, bet. WILLIAM HOLZENDORF of
Darien, County of McIntosh and RICHARD M. WILLIAM of Savannah, Co. of Chatham
cons. of two hundred dollars, tract of land in Goshen, Effingham County, on or near
Black Creek and known by name of Pine Hill plantation, cont. 436 acres. Signed: WILL-
IAM HOLZENDORF. Wit: GARDNER TUFTS, JOHN L. K. HOLZENDORF.

21 July 1804 - JOHN L. K. HOLZENDORF made oath that he saw WILLIAM HOLZENDORF sign Indenture and that GARDNER TUFTS witnessed. Signed: JOHN L. K. HOLZENDORF. Wit: W. A. DUNHAUR, J.P.

Page 155: Rec. 16 April 1805 - Deed dated 6 Jan. 1784, bet. HUGH LAWSON, ABRAHAM RAVOT, HEPWORTH CARTER, Commissioners appointed by Honorable House of Assembly at Augusta on 4 May 1782 for carrying into execution an act for inflicting penalties on and confiscation the estates of such persons are therein declared guilty of Treason, on 19 April 1775, JOHN____TUBBY was sold tract cont. 100 acres bounded North East by MATTHIAS SECKINGER, East and West by MATTHIAS BRANTNER, orig. granted by His Magesty KING GEORGE the second on 1 May 1759 unto JOHN GEORGE ZITTROUR, by ZITTROUR to JOHN____TUBBY, sold by Commissioners to NICHOLAS SHUBTRINE for five pounds eight shillings and four pence. Signed: H. LAWSON, AM. RAVOT, HEPWORTH CARTER. Wit: ____WADE, J. MORRISON.

Page 159: Rec. 30 April 1805 - Deed dated 12 Sept. 1803 - bet. NICHOLAS SHUBTRINE of Wilks County, planter and JOHN CHRISTOPHER GUGEL of Savannah, cons. one hundred dollars, tract cont. 100 acres bounded North East by MATTHEW SECKINGER, East and West by MATTHIAS BRANDNER, orig. granted by His Britannic Majesty KING GEORGE the second on 1 May 1759 to JOHN GEORGE ZITTROUR, conv. by him to JOHN____TUBBY, taken from him by Act of Confiscation and Banishment and sold to NICHOLAS SHUBTRINE. Signed: NICHOLAS SHUBTRINE. Wit: SAMUEL KRAUSE, JOHN G. NEIDLINGER, ANNA NEIDLINGER.

1 Oct. 1804 - JOHN G. NEIDLINGER made oath that he saw NICHOLAS SHUBTRINE sign within Indenture. Signed: J. G. NEIDLINGER. Wit: HENRY W. WILLIAMS, Clk.

Page 159: Rec. 30 April 1805 - Bill of Sale dated 2 April 1805, WILLIAM WILSON, Sheriff of Eff. Co. for cons. of one thousand nine hundred and eighty-three dollars by THOMAS POLHILL, SENR. planter, eleven Negroes, HAMPTON and F____, BEN, BENALEA and child PHILES, ___ORTEN amt. to three hundred and eighty-two dollars, also LUCY and her children named JOHN, BECK, CUPID and MARY ANN amt. to one thousand six hundred and one dollars, the whole amt. to one thousand nine hundred and eighty-three dollars sold under and by virtue of two Writs of Fieri facias of suit of Adms. ofWILLIAM WYLLY on Judgement obt. in Superior Court of Chatham Co. against the Adms. of JOHN STIRK and QUINTON KOOLER, dec. Signed: WILLIAM WILSON, S.E.C. Wit: JONATHAN LOPER, HENRY W. WILLIAMS, Clk. S.C.E.C.

Page 160: Rec. 1 May 1805 - Deed dated 12 Feb. 1805 - bet. FREDERICK DONSLER of Savannah, chairmaker and CHARLES TONDEE of same place, shopkeeper - cons. four hundred and fifty dollars, tract in Eff. Co. formerly Saint Matthews Parish cont. 350 acres orig. granted HENRY DONSLER bounded South by Ogeechee River, North West by lands ordered JOSEPH BARNER, eastwardly by HENRY MONRO which said land F. DONSLER drew as his part of his father, HENRY DONSLER'S real estate. Signed: FREDERICK DONSLER. Wit: WM. MITCHELL, ___(written in German), J. P.

Page 162: Rec. 1 May 1805 - Deed dated 27 May 1804, bet. ANTHONY PITTS and NANCY his wife and WILLIAM COWARD of South Carolina, Beauford District, cons. sum of one hundred dollars, tract of land cont. 200 acres on waters of Turkey Branch joining lands of Ryal. Signed: ANTHONY PITTS, NANCY (X) PITTS. Wit: JOHN COWARD, BENJAMIN ALEXANDER.

3 Dec. 1804 - JOHN COWARD made oath that he saw within parties sign Indenture and it was witnessed by BENJAMIN ALEXANDER. Signed: JOHN COWARD. Wit: HEN. W. WILLIAMS, Clk. S.C.E.C.

Page 164: Rec. 4 May 1805 - Deed of gift dated 21 Feb. 1801 - JOSHUA LOPER to grandson
JOSHUA HUDSON son JAMES HUDSON and SARAH his wife, 300 acres of land being
part of 750 acres granted JOSHUA LOPER on 7 Nov. 1792 by His Excellency EDWARD TELFAIR,
Gov. Signed: JOSHUA LOPER. Wit: ABEL G. LOPER, ARA. LOPER.

30 Jan. 1805 - ABEL G. LOPER and ARA LOPER made oath that they saw JOSHUA LOPER sign
within Indenture. Signed: ABEL G. LOPER, ARA. LOPER. Wit: CURTIS LOPER, J.P.

Rec. 4 May 1805 - Indenture dated 21 April 1802 - MARY LEMLY of Savannah sold to HOWELL
HINES a negro wench, JENNY, for five hundred dollars. Signed: MARY LEMLY, MANUS LEMLY
Wit: ALEX. YOUNG.

29 Mar. 1804 - SAMUEL BURKSTINER Made oath that he saw MARY LEMLY sign within Indenture
and did see HOWELL HINES pay LEMLY balance of three hundred and fifty dollars which was
in full for wench. Signed: SAMUEL BURKSTINER. Wit: U. TOBLER, J.P.

Page 166: Rec. 22 May 1805 - Deed dated 2 April 1805, bet. WILLIAM WILSON, Sheriff and
ROBERT WATKINS of City of Augusta, Attorney at Law, whereas EMANUEL WANB____
in Superior Court, dec. for two hundred and thirty-nine dollars and seventy-one cents
and also thirteen dollars and ten cents costs and whereas a Writ of fieri facias directed to Sheriff that should be made said sum of money out of HERGEN HENSON; Sheriff
seized tract of land con sides of EBENEZER CREEK orig. granted MULRYNE and TATTNALL
cont. by orig. survey 2500 acres, but commonly estimated at 5,000 acres which said land
was conf. as property of British subjects and sold at public outcry by Commissioners to
JAMES THOMPSON who mortgaged said tract to Governor and because JAMES THOMPSON failed
to make payment of said money, land was foreclosed and again sold to HERGEN HENSON and
OWEN OWENS and since death of HENSEN said undivided land was claimed by OWEN OWENS-Un-
divided moiety was sold by Sheriff to ROBERT WATKINS for four hundred and sixty dollars.
Signed: WILLIAM WILSON, S.E.C. Wit: JAMES BRYAN, HENRY W. WILLIAMS, Clk., S.C.E.C.

Page 168: Rec. 23 May 1805 - Deed dated 15 May 1805, bet. OWEN OWENS of Island of Saint
Catharines in Liberty Co., Esq. and ROBERT WATKINS of _____in Richmond Co-
ounty, Esq. cons. five hundred dollars - one undivided moiety or half of tract cont.
2500 acres in Eff. Co. on both sides of Ebenezer Creek, orig. granted JOHN MULRYNE,
CLAUDIA MULRYNE, and JOSEPH TATTNALL which said tract was conf. as property of British
subjects and sold at public outcry to JAMES THOMPSON who took out mortgage to Gov. and
having failed to pay off mortgage, mortgage was foreclosed, and land was sold to HERGEN
HENSEN and OWEN OWENS on 26 July 1794. Signed: OWEN OWENS. Wit: JAS. WALLACE, RICH-
ARD M. STILES, NOT. PUB.

Page 170: Rec. 23 May 1805 - Indenture dated 1 Oct. 1801, bet. PHILIP DELL, planter
and JOHN M. DASHER JUNR., of Scriven Co. - cons. fifteen dollars, tract of
land cont. 32 acres in Scriven Co. bounded north by JOHN M. DASHER, JUNR, south by Mc-
KENNY, east by JOHN M. DASHER JUNR. Signed: PHILIP DELL. Wit: WM. PEARCE, DANIEL
DALY.

25 Jan. 1804 - DANIEL DALY made oath that he saw PHILIP DELL sign within Indenture and
that WM. PEARCE was a witness. Signed: DANIEL DALY. Wit: SHEFTALL SHEFTALL, J.P.

Page 171: Rec. 26 Aug. 1805 - Deed dated 2 July 1805, bet. WILLIAM WILSON, Sheriff
and ROBERT WATKINS of Richmond Co., by a Writ of fieri facias from Superior
Court at suit of JOHN HINELY against Adm. of JOHN G. WERTSCH, dec., the said Sheriff
did seize tract of land of JOHN WERTSCH and it was sold to ROBERT WATKINS at public
outcry for twenty-six dollars - tract of land on Ebenezer Creek. Signed: WILLIAM WIL-
SON, S.E.C. Wit: GOTTLIEB ERNST, JN. KING, J.I.C.

Page 172: Rec. 26 Aug. 1805 - Deed dated 23 Aug. 1804, bet. JOHN LILLIBRIDGE and SARAH
             his wife and OLIVER M. LILLIBRIDGE, his son, and SARAH BRITTON of Chatham Co.
planter, cons. of eight hundred dollars, plantation or tract of land in village of Abercorn cont. 48 1/2 acres bounded on South and West by GEORGE NOWLAN, East by JEREMIAH
CUYLER, Esq. Signed: JNO. LILLIBRIDGE, SARAH (X) LILLIBRIDGE, OLIVER M. LILLIBRIDGE.
Wit: GEORGE SHICK, JOHN SHICK.

11 July 1805 - JOHN SHICK made oath that he saw within parties sign Indenture. Signed:
JOHN SHICK. Wit: HEN. W. WILLIAMS, Clk., S.C.E.C.

Page 174: Rec. 7 Sept. 1805 - Deed dated 15 March 1805 - bet. GUNNING C. BEDFORD of
             Savannah; THOMAS POLHILL SENR. of Eff. Co., gentlemen; and ELIZABETH ANN
BURCH. Whereas a marriage is about to be between GUNNING C. BEDFORD and ELIZABETH ANN
BURCH and whereas E. A. BURCH has one plantation cont. 250 acres in district of Ebenezer;
one unimproved lot of 5 acres in suburbs of Savannah; and eight Negro slaves, DICK, BAC-
CHUS, FLORA, LUCY, NELLY, MARY, BECK, GRACE; household furniture, and because of impend-
ing marriage, ELIZABETH ANN BURCH will sell all of her personal and real estate to THO-
MAS POLHILL for five dollars to be held in Trust. Signed: E. A. BURCH, G. C. BEDFORD,
THOMAS POLHILL. Wit: THOS. POLHILL, JUNR., JOHN W. WILLIAMS, Clk.

Page 176: Rec. 24 Sept. 1805 - Articles of Agreement dated 20 June 1805, bet. WILLIAM
             DUPUIS, and HANNAH TRIBBLE, widow of JOSEPH TRIBBLE - HANNAH TRIBBLE is now
possessed of the following Negroes, BECK and PHILLIS, also tract of land cont. 130 acres
adj. WILLIAM KENNEDY, JAS. PORTER, and YOUNG - Whereas a marriage is to be between WILL-
IAM DUPUIS and HANNAH TRIBBLE - that above mentioned property will be solely HANNAH TRI-
BBLE'S. Signed: WILLIAM DUPUIS, HANNAH (X) TRIBBLE. Wit: WM. KENNEDY, CHR. TREUTLEN,
J.P.

Page 177: Rec. 29 Sept. 1805 - Deed dated 2 July 1803, bet. CAMEL TISON, planter and
             UNITY TISON his wife and NOAH DYKES - cons. of thirty dollars - tract cont.
239 acres on West side of Shrimps creek including part of Teals Island bounded North
Easterly by FREDERICK FARM and SNYDER, South Easterly by JOHN EPPINGER and JAMES HINES,
South Westerly by JAMES HINES and PORTER GRANT, North Westerly by HOWELL HINES, orig.
granted on 23 Nov. 1801 under the great seal of said State unto CAMEL TISON.Signed:
CAMMEL TISON, UNITY (X) TISON. Wit: MILNER HOLIDAY, JOHN (M) MERCHANT.

Page 179: Rec. 2 Dec. 1805 - Deed dated 4 Nov. 1804 - bet. HENRY EDWARDS and JOHN FOR-
             SYTH cont. of fifty dollars - tract of land cont. 200 acres on waters of Sav-
annah river bounded westwardly by POLHILL. Signed: HENRY (H) EDWARDS. Wit: WILLIAM
BEAIL, GRACY (X) BEAIL.

4 May 1805 - WILLIAM BEAL made oath that he saw HENRY EDWARDS sign within Indenture and
that MISS GRACY BEAL was a witness. Signed: WILLIAM BEAIL. Wit: CHRN.TREUTLEN, J.P.

Page 180: Rec. 2 Dec. 1805- This is to certify HENRY EDWARDS and SALETA FORSYTHE agrees
             before the under written witnesses makes a final separation of their property
and encrease of their property to each of them and their heirs June 5th, 1797, I JAMES
GIBSON bought one cow and calf of ANTHONY PITTS and sold the same to SILETA FORSYTHE as
I received full satisfaction of her. Signed: JAMES GIBSON. Wit: HENRY (H) EDWARDS.

Page 180: Rec. 2 Dec. 1805 - One three year old heiffer, two two year old heiffer, one
             three year old heiffer marked and branded thus; figure three in the end of
one ear and under bit swallow fork in one ear and under bit, in same branded thus S E.

The above cattle and their increase is for my three children SALLY, CATY and HENRY to be equally divided among them. Signed: SIRLETER FORSYTHE.

HENRY EDWARDS binds himself before us not sell or destroy any of the above cattle. Signed: HENRY (X) EDWARDS. Wit: SENATE POWERS, HENRY CRAWFORD, WM. BEAL.

Dated 2 Mar. 1804 - A final settlement bet. HENRY EDWARDS and SIRLETER FORSYTHE in every circumstance from the beginning of the world until this present time. Signed: HENRY ( ) EDWARDS. Wit: HENEY CRAWFORD, SENATE POWERS.

7 Oct. 1805 - WM. BEAL made oath that he saw within parties sign Indenture and SENATE POWERS and HENRY CRAWFORD were witnesses. Wit: HEN. W. WILLIAMS, Clk.

Page 181: Rec. 31 Dec. 1805 - Deed dated 1 May 1805, bet. DANIEL DAMPIER, planter, and his wife and WILLIAM DAMPIER - cons. seventy-five dollars - tract of land cont. 150 acres bounded S. Eastwardly by GROSS SCRUGGS and CECIL.Signed: DANIEL DAMPIER, ELIZABETH (X) DAMPIER. Wit: HUGH GRAHAM, GROSS SCRUGGS.

4 May 1805 - HUGH GRAHAM made oath that he saw DANIEL DAMPIER and ELIZABETH DAMPIER sign within Indenture. Signed: HUGH GRAHAM. Wit: CHRN. TREUTLEN, J.P.

Page 182: Rec. 31 Dec. 1805 - Deed dated 2 March 1805, bet. JAMES GADDY, Scriven Co., Brick layer and HENRY COOK, Eff. Co., Preacher of GOSPEL - cons. of twenty dollars - tract of 20 acres a part of 100 acres orig. granted JAMES GADDY. Signed: JAS. GADDY. Wit: JORDAIN CLARK, CLEMENT LANIER, J.I.C.

Page 183: Rec. 31 Dec. 1805 - Deed dated 2 March 1805, bet. MARTHA HOLLINGER, Scriven Co., and REVEREND HENRY COOK, Eff. Co. - cons. one hundred dollars, 80 acres of land being part of 150 acres formerly conv. from HENRY COOK to MARTHA HOLLINGER. Signed: MARTHA HOLLINGER. Wit: JORDAIN CLARK, CLEMENT LANIER, J.I.C.

Page 184: Rec. 31 Dec. 1805 - Bill of Sale dated 2 Dec. 1805 - JOHN DASHER sold to JOHN MARTIN DASHER, SENR., two Negro slaves, a fellow and wench, SAM and HANNAH; one Sorrel mare colt; one sorrel horse - cons. nine hundred and seventy-two dollars. Signed: JOSHUA DASHER. Wit: CHRISTIAN COPE, HEN. W. WILLIAMS, Clk.

Page 185: Rec. 31 Dec. 1805 - Deed dated 5 Dec. 1805, bet. CATHARINE SECKINGER, Widow and ADM. of ANDREW SECKINGER, dec. and SOLOMON HEINTY - cons. one hundred and six dollars - tract of land cont. 200 acres on Alligator branch bound North East by DANIEL BURGSTINER, South West by JONATHAN SECKINGER, orig. granted ANDREW SECKINGER, dec, by His Excellency JARED IRVIN, Gov. on 14 Dec. 1797. Signed: CATHARINAH (X) SECK-INGER. Wit: JONATHAN RAHN, MICHAEL EXLEY, MATTHEW WHITEMAN.

16 Dec. 1805 - MATTHEW WHITEMEN made oath that he saw CATHARINE SECKINGER sign within Indenture and that JONATHAN RAHN and MICHAEL EXLEY were witnesses. Signed: MATTHEW WHITEMAN. Wit: JOHN KOGLER, J.I.

Page 187: Rec. 20 May 1801 - Deed dated 16 May 1801, bet. DAVID FISHER, Chatham, Co. and JAMES COOK, planter - cons. three hundred dollars - tract of land cont. 500 acres, granted DAVID FISHER by His Excellency JAMES WRIGHT Gov. in 1766 adj. Great Ogeechee River. Signed: DAVID (F) FISHER. Wit: U. TOBLER, J.P.

Page 188: Rec. 20 May 1806 - Deed dated 13 March 1806, bet. JAMES COOK, planter, and MARGARET his wife and ROBERT BURTON, planter, cons. of five hundred dollars tract of land cont. 500 acres orig. granted on 5 Aug. 1766 by GEORGE the third, King

of Great Brittain to DAVID FISHER, conv. by FISHER to JAMES COOK on 16 May 1801 - situated on North side of Great Ogeechee river, bound North West by DAVID MURRAY, North
East by HESSE BELL and JOHN RAWLS, South East by JOHN STEVENS, South West by great Ogee-
che River. Signed: JAMES COOK, MARGARET (X) COOK. Wit: MILNER HOLIDAY, J.P. BENJ-
AMIN (X) GROOMS.

Page 190: Rec. 21 May 1806 - Deed dated 2 March 1806, bet. CHRISTOPHER FREDERIC BUNTZ,
          planter, and JONATHAN RAHN. cons. of two hundred dollars, tract of land cont.
350 acres bound North East by JOHN KUGEL and CONRAD ROAN, orig. granted MATTHIAS KUGEL
by His Britannic Majesty George the third on 3 Dec. 1761, sold by MATTHIAS ROACHE, act-
ing provost marshall by virtue of fieri facias on Judgement obt. by MORDECCAI and Le_y
Shefftall against MATTHIAS GUGEL unto URBAN BUNTZ on 28 Oct. 1766, bequeather by URBAN
BUNTZ on 24 Mar. 1774 to JOHN CHRISTOPHER BUNTZ, and bequeathed by JOHN CHRISTOPHER
BUNTZ to CHRISTOPHER FREDERICK BUNTZ on 26 Dec. 1785. Signed: CHRISTOPHER F. BUNTZ.
Wit: GOTTLIEB ERNEST, JOHN KOGLER, J.P.

Page 192: Rec. 25 May 1806 - Deed dated 26 Feb. 1805 - Bet. WILLIAM WILSON, ESQ. Sher-
          iff and HANNAH DASHER - Whereas JOHN HEINLEY did in Superior Court obt. Jud-
gement against HANNAH DASHER and JOHN M. DASHER, JUNR. Adm. of Casper Wertsch, dec. and
whereas a Writ of fieri facias on Judgement directed the estate of WERTSCH be made the
amount of Judgement, WILLIAM WILSON, sold tract of land cont. 50 acres on Savannah river
bound East by M. REESER, South of Cronberger, West by CHARLES FLERL, for forty-two dollars and fifty cents to HANNAH DASHER. Signed: WILLIAM WILSON, S.E.C. Wit: DANIEL
REMSHART, GOTTLIEB ERNST.

Page 193: Rec. 23 May 1806 - Deed dated 26 Feb. 1806, bet. WILLIAM WILSON, Sheriff and
          HANNAH DASHER - Whereas JOHN HEINTY obt. Judgement against HANNAH DASHER and
JOHN DASHER, JUNR. Adm. of CASPER WERTSCH, dec., and a Writ of fieri facias-Sheriff
seized and sold tract of land cont. 70 acres, East joining Creeks heading Savannah river,
North by CHARLES FLERL, to HANNAH DASHER for thirty-five dollars and fifty cents. Sig:
WILLIAM WILSON, S.E.C. Wit: DANIEL REMSHART, GOTTLIEB ERNST.

7 May 1806 - GOTTLIEB ERNST made oath that he saw WILLIAM WILSON sign within Indenture
and that DANIEL REMSHART was a witness. Signed: GOTTLIEB ERNST. Wit: J. G. NEIDLINGER,
C.C.O.E.C.

Page 195: Rec. 23 May 1806 - Deed dated 26 Feb. 1806 - bet. WILLIAM WILSON, Esq. Sher-
          iff and HANNAH DASHER - Whereas JOHN HEINLY obt. a Judgement against HANNAH
DASHER and JOHN DASHER, JUNR., Adm. of CASPER WERTSCH, dec. and A Writ of fieri facias
on Judgement, WILLIAM WILSON did seize and sell at public outcry tract of land being a
lot in Ebenezer - said lot was property of MERCHANT GRAFT conv. by him to CASPER WERT-
SCH by REVEREND RABENHORST Adm. of GRAFTS Estate and now bought by HANNAH DASHER for
thirty dollars. Signed: WILLIAM WILSON, S.E.C. Wit: DANL. REMSHART, GOTTLIEB ERNST.

7 May 1806 - GOTTLIEB ERNST made oath that he saw WILLIAM WILSON sign within Indenture
and witness by DANIEL REMSHART. Signed: GOTTLIEB ERNST. Wit: J. G. NEIDLINGER, C.C.
O.E.C.

Page 197: Rec. 7 June 1806 - Deed dated 8 Dec. 1804 - bet. MICHAEL EXLY, JOHN KOGLER,
          JONATHAN RAHA, GOTHIELF SMITH, JOHN FRYERMUTH, SOLOMON GNANN, JOHN GROVEN-
STEINE, and JOHN HEINLY, Trustees of German Congregation at Ebenezer and JOHN SPENCER,
ESQ. - Trustees authorized by special Act of Assembly passed at Louisville on 26 Nov.
1802 authorizing sale of the Glebe granted JOHN MARTIN BOLZUIS - for eight hundred and
seven dollars paid by JOHN SPENCER - tract of land cont. 300 acres bound north by MAR-
TIN LOCKNER and BALTHAZER BACKLER, East by schoolhouse lands of GOSHEN and lands of

NICHOLAS LITLOE, South by DUNCAN McGILLI _ _ _ _ and CHRISTIAN DASHER West by JOHN REU-
TER. Signed: MICHAEL EXLY, JOHN KOGLER, JONATHAN RAHN, GODHILF SMITH, JOHN FRYERMUTH,
SOLOMON GNANN, JOHN HEINLY. Wit: JONATHAN SECKINGER, ISRAEL FLERL, GOTTLIEB ERNST.

Page 199: Rec. 7 June 1806 - Deed dated 22 July 1805 - WILLIAM WILSON, ESQ. Sheriff and
           ELIJAH TYNER - Whereas a Writ grounded on a Judgement from the Comptroller
General against JOHN WILLIAMS formerly tax collector, directed to Sheriff, Sheriff did
seize land of JOHN WILLIAMS and sold at public outcry cont. 200 acres to ELIJAH TYNER
for thirty dollars. Signed: WILLIAM WILSON, S.E.C. Wit: WM. KENNEDY, LUKE WILSON.

7 June 1806 - LUKE WILSON made oath that he saw WILLIAM WILSON sign within Indenture
and WILLIAM KENNEDY was a witness. Signed: LUKE WILSON. Wit: J. G. NEIDLINGER, C.
S.C.E.C.

Page 201: Rec. 7 June 1806 - Deed dated 1 Jan. 1806 - bet. JOHN GRYERMUTH, JUNR. and
           SETH G. THREADCRAFT of Chatham Co., planter - cons. of sixty dollars (Spanish)
tract of land cont. 50 acres bound East and West by land granted JOHN HORNBERGER, North
by JOHN KOGLER, South by SAMUEL KRAUSE, orig. granted PAUL ZITTROUER, conv. by him to
JOHN _____ TUBBY a person named in Act of Attainder and confiscation - sold to said SAM-
UEL KRAUS on 8 Dec. 1783, given by SAMUEL KRAUSE in deed to MISS SALLY SCHWEIGHOFFER
who is consort of SETH G. THREADCRAFT and who renounces all claim to said tract. Signed:
SETH G. THREADCRAFT, SARAH THREADCRAFT. Wit: J. SALMON, JOHN SPENCER, J.P.

Page 202: Rec. 7 June 1806 - WILLIAM BIRD, GEORGE PAUL _ _ _ _, ISRAEL KEIFFER and
           JOEL KEIFFER are firmly bound unto SAMUEL KRAUSE ADM. of Estates of DAVID
STEINER, dec., for sum of three thousand dollars, dated 8 April 1806 - The condition of
the above obligations is such that of the above bounded WM. BIRD, GEORGE PAUL _ _ _ _,
ISRAEL KEIFFER and JOEL KEIFFER do and shall from time to time at all times hereafter
save, defend, keep harmless and Indemnified the said SAMUEL KRAUS---from and against
all former and other gifts, titles, bills of sale, mortgages, or other incumbrances
whatsoever also any time heretofore had made, committed, or done by any person or persons whatsoever whereby or by means a certain Negro Negro woman slave named HANNAH with
her increase and issue the property of the Estate of the said DAVID STEINER or either
of them may be charges, seized, recovered, or in anywise incumbered, and also of, from
and against all actions, suits, complaints, damages, losses, costs and charges whatsoever which shall or may at anytime or times hereafter be brought, sued commenced, prosecuted, or awarded against the said SAMUEL KRAUS, or which he or any or either of them
shall or may sustain or be put unto for or by reason or means of any defect or imperfection of or in the title of the said Estate to the said Negro slave named HANNAH or
any or either of the increase or issue of the said Negro wench slave named HANNAH then
this obligation to be void and of none effect otherwise to remain and continue in full
force and virtue. Signed: WILLIAM BIRD, GEORGE POWLIGE, ISRAEL KEIFFER, JOEL KEIFFER.
Wit: ISRAEL FLERL, C. DASHER, J.P.

Page 203: Rec. 7 June 1806 - NOAH PARRAMORE of Scriven County and WILLIAM BIRD of Eff.
           Co. are bound unto SAMUEL KRAUS of Eff. Co. Adm. of DAVID STEINER, dec., in
penal sum of three thousand dollars, dated 8 April 1806 - The condition of the above
obligation is such that if the above bound NOAH PARRAMORE and WILLIAM BIRD do and shall
from time to time and at all times hereafter, save, defend, keep harmless and indemnified the said SAMUEL KRAUS from and against all former and other gifts, grants, titles,
bills of sale, mortgages, or any other incumbrances whatsoever at any time heretofore
had, made, committed, or done by any person or persons whatever whereby or by means
whereof a certain Negro woman slave named HANNAH with her increase and issue the property of the Estate of the Estate of the aforesaid DAVID STEINER or either of them may

be charges, seized, recovered, taken in or anywise incumbered and also from and against all actions, suits, complaints, damages, losses, costs, and charges whatsoever which shall or may at any time or times hereafter be brought, sued, commenced, prosecuted, or awarded against the said SAMUEL KRAUS or either of them shall or may sustain or be ____ for or by reason or means of any defect or imperfection of in or to the title of the said Estate to the said Negro slave named HANNAH or any or either of the increase and issue of the said Negro woman slave named HANNAH then this obligation to be void and of none effect, otherwise to be, remain, and continue in full force and virtue. Signed: N. PARRAMORE, WILLIAM BIRD. Wit: ISRAEL FLERL, C. DASHER, J.P.

Page 204: Rec. 7 June 1806 - Bill of sale dated 28 Jan. 1806 - MARTHA BISHOP and JAMES CRUSE sell to JONATHAN LOPER a Negro woman named FILIS for two hundred dollars.. Signed: MARTHA (X) BISHOP, JAMES CRUSE. Wit: MILNER HOLIDAY, J.P.

Page 205: Rec. 12 June 1806 - Bill of sale dated 25 Jan. 1806 - EMANUEL ZIPPERER for four hundred dollars sold unto JOHN GEORGE ZITTROUR a Negro woman named PHO-EBE. Signed: EMANUEL ZIPPERER. Wit: JONATHAN ZIPPERER.

2 June 1806 - JONATHAN ZIPPERER Made oath that he saw EMANUEL ZIPPERER sign within Indenture. Signed: JONATHAN ZIPPERER. Wit:

Page 206: Rec. 17 June 1806 - Deed of Gift dated 10 June 1801 - JOSHUA LOPER, planter, granted to CURTIS, ASA, ABEL, and ARA LOPER the exclusive right and privilege of building and erecting a saw and g_ _ _mill on his lands on Senates Creek at the place where there is now a Dam and race made for that purpose the said mill to be built by an equal expense by such of them and to be kept in repair by them as also the profits shall be equally divided as joint copartners - to have sole privilege of cutting any timber needed to build said mills and keep in repair, also to cut any timber to saw at mills for market so that there shall be no wanton waste made by same. Signed: JOSHUA LOPER. Wit: ABILGAIN M. CASKILL, JOHN POWERS, J.I.C.

Page 207: Rec. 4 July 1806 - Deed dated 1 Jan. 1806 - bet. JOSEPH BEVAN, planter and CHARLES ODINGSELLS of Chatham Co., planter, - cons. of one thousand five hundred dollars - tract of land cont. 707 1/2 acres in Eff. Co. bound South West by Great Ogeechee river, South East by DAVID MURRAY. Signed: JOSEPH BEVAN. Wit: JOHN G. WILLIAMSON, J.I.C., THOS. BOURKE.

Page 208: Rec. 22 July 1806 - Indenture dated 18 July 1806 - CHRISTIAN ISRAEL HEIDT and JOHANNAH M. LOCKNER do relinquish, annul, and discharge all charges, claim and demands whatsoever that either of us may have against each other and we further agree by this present that we will not make any charge or demand against each other in any wise, manner, or form whatsoever nor shall any of our heirs,---do same from the date of this present and for ever. And it is further agreed on that case the said JO-HANNAH M. LOCKNER should live or stay in the family of the said CHRISTAIN I. HEIDT shall not charge her boarding or any other charges and the said JOHANNAH M. LOCKNER shall likewise make no charge against the said CHRISTIAN I. HEIDT excepting such three notes that were given to the said JOHANNAH M. LOCKNER for the full payment of sixty dollars payable in three different payments and dated with date of this present and we further declare this present as lawful to all intents and purposes as if drawn by an attorney. Signed: CHRISTIAN I (H) HEIDTE, JOHANNAH M. (F) LOCKNER.

Page 208: Rec. 5 Sept. 1806 - Deed dated 16 Oct. 1802 - bet. JAMES BREWER, Minister and JOSEPH BREWER, planter, - cons. of one hundred dollars - tract of land cont. 100 acres on Wallowing branch bound by MAZONG and JAMES GOLDWIRE, orig. surveyed for WILLIAM CRAWFORD. Signed: JAMES BREWER, PRISCILLA ( ) BREWER. Wit: RICHARD

TOUCHSTONE,   THOMAS CRAWFORD, CLEMENT LANIER, J.I.C.

Page 209: Rec. 5 Sept. 1806 - Deed dated 16 Oct. 1802 - bet. JAMES BREWER, Minister
           and JOSEPH BREWER - cons. thirty-four dollars - tract of 34 acres of South
West end of a 50 acre tract which was orig. granted to and surveyed for WILLIAM HURST,
senr. on 2 Aug. 1797 by WILLIAM GARDNER, Co. Surveyer. Signed: JAMES BREWER, PRIS-
CILLA ( ) BREWER. Wit: RICHARD TOUCHSTONE, THOMAS CRAWFORD, CLEMENT LANIER, J.I.C.

Page 211: Rec. 5 Sept. 1806 - Deed dated 16 Oct. 1802 - bet. JAMES BREWER, Minister
           and JOSEPH BREWER, cons. fifty dollars - tract of land cont. 50 acres on
Wallowing branch bound S. westwardly by CRAWFORD. Signed: JAMES BREWER, PRISCILLA
( ) BREWER. Wit: RICHARD TOUCHSTONE, THOMAS CRAWFORD, CLEMENT LANIER, J.I.C.

Page 212: Deed dated 31 Jan. 1804 - Bet. JAMES BREWER, Minister and PRISCILLA BREWER
           and JOSEPH BREWER, - cons. of four hundred and fifty dollars - tract cont.
400 acres on Wallowing branch bound by GOLDWIRE, CRAWFORD, MCCALL. Signed: JAMES BREW-
ER, PRISCILLA ( ) BREWER. Wit: JAMES BREWER, JR., NATHAN BREWER, JAMES (X) CRAWFORD.

14 Aug. 1806 NATHAN BREWER made oath that he saw JAMES BREWER sign within Indenture and
witnesses were JAMES BREWER, JUNR. and JAMES CRAWFORD. Signed: NATHAN BREWER. Wit:
J. G. NEIDLINGER, C.C.O.E.C.

Page 213: Rec. 8 Sept. 1806 - Deed dated 5 Aug. 1806, bet. LUKE WILSON, Sheriff and
           HANNAH DASHER, widow- Whereas STEPHEN DENMARK obt. Judgement against JOHN
CASPER WERTSCH and a Writ of fieri facias directed to Sheriff demanding of them to be
made of goods of JOHN CASPER WERTSCH the amt. of Judgement - LUKE WILSON, Sheriff, did
seize and sell at public outcry all that town lot in Ebenezer cont. 60 feet in front
and 90 feet in depth bet. THEOBALD KEIFFER and CHRISTIAN BIRK - sold to HANNAH DASHER
for five dollars. Signed: LUKE WILSON, S.E.C. Wit: J. G. NEIDLINGER, C.S.C.E.C.,
JOHN WILSON.

Page 214: Rec. 8 Sept. 1806 - Deed dated 5 Aug. 1806 - bet. LUKE WILSON, Sheriff and
           HANNAH DASHER - STEPHEN DENMARK obt. Judgement against JOHN CASPER WERTSCH
and a Writ of fieri facias directed to Sheriff ordering amt. of Judgement be paid out
of goods of JOHN CASPER WERTSCH - Sheriff did seize and sell at public outcry lot of
land cont. 2 acres in town of Ebenezer, which was bought by HANNAH DASHER for three
dollars and fifty cents. Signed: LUKE WILSON, S.E.C. Wit: J. G. NEIDLINGER, C.S.C.
E.C., JOHN WILSON.

Page 216: Rec. 8 Sept. 1806 - Deed dated 5 Aug. 1806 - bet. LUKE WILSON, Sheriff and
           HANNAH DASHER - STEPHEN DENMARK obtained a Judgement against JOHN CASPER
WERTSCH and a Writ of fieri facias directed to Sheriff commanding that amount of Judgement be made of the goods of JOHN CASPER WERTSCH - Sheriff did seize and sell at public
outcry to HANNAH DASHER for four dollars all that lot cont. 2 acres. Signed: LUKE WIL-
SON, S.E.C. Wit: J. G. NEIDLINGER, C.S.C.E.C., JOHN WILSON.

Page 217: Rec. 8 Sept. 1806 - Deed dated 5 Aug. 1806 - bet. LUKE WILSON, Sheriff and
           JONATHAN RAHN - STEPHEN DENMARK obtained a Judgement against JOHN CASPER
WERTSCH and a Writ of fieri facias directed to Sheriff commanding that amount of Judgement be made of goods of JOHN CASPER WERTSCH - Sheriff did seize and sell at public outcry lot of land in Town of Ebenezer cont. 60 feet in front and 98 feet in depth bound
westwardly by SIMON REUTER to JONATHAN RAHN for four dollars. Signed: LUKE WILSON,
S.E.C. Wit: J. G. NEIDLINGER, C.S.C.S.E., CHRISTOPHER BAILLIE.

Page 218:   Rec. 8 Sept. 1806 - Deed dated 5 Aug. 1806 - bet. LUKE WILSON, Sheriff and
JONATHAN RAHN - STEPHEN DENMARK obtained a Judgement against JOHN CASPER WERTSCH and a
Writ of fieri facias directed to Sheriff commanding the amount of Judgement to be made
of goods of JOHN CASPER WERTSCH - Sheriff did seize and sell at public outcry lot in
town of Ebenezer cont. 60 feet in front and 90 feet in depth to JONATHAN RAHN for three
dollars. Signed: LUKE WILSON, S.E.C. Wit: J. G. NEIDLINGER, C.S.C.E.C., CHRISTOPHER
BAILLEE.

Page 219:   Rec. 8 Sept. 1806 - Deed dated 30 Aug. 1806 - bet. HANNAH DASHER, widow of
            late JOHN DASHER, dec., of EBENEZER and GOTTLIEB ERNST - cons. twenty-five
dollars - tract of land cont. 6 acres adjoining Savannah river easterly and Ebenezer,
South East, and all other sides by lands of GOTTLIEB ERNST, orig. granted REV. M. BOL-
ZIUS, conv. by him to REV. GRONAU, from thence becoming property of REV. C. F. TRIEBNER
by marriage, said TRIEBNER Being a Loyalist his property being conf. and sold to HERGON
HENSON, who dying it became subject to Execution and JOHN CAIG obt. Judgement against
HERGON HENSON and Writ of fieri facias, Sheriff seized and take in Execution at risk
off JEREMIAH CUYLER, ESQ. made default in payment as purchaser and land cont. 6 acres
was sold to HANNAH DASHER. Signed: H. DASHER. Wit: CHRISTOPHER FREDERICK BUNCE, JOHN
KOGLER, J.I.C.

Page 221:   Rec. 8 Sept. 1806 - Deed dated 5 Aug. 1806 - bet. LUKE WILSON, Sheriff, and
            JOHN BERRY - STEPHEN DENMARK obt. a Judgement against JOHN CASPER WERTSCH
and a Writ of fieri facias directed Sheriff to get amount of Judgement of goods of JOHN
CASPER WERTSCH - Sheriff did seize and sell at public outcry tract of land cont. 100
acres bound north eastwardly by ANDREW GNANN, orig. granted MICHAEL GNANN - cons. six
dollars. Signed: LUKE WILSON, S.E.C. Wit: J. G. NEIDLINGER, CHRISTOPHER BAILLEE.

Page 222:   Rec. 8 Sept. 1806 - Deed dated 29 April 1806 - bet. NATHANIEL LUNDAY, planter
            of Scriven County and JOHN G. KING, ESQ. - cons. two hundred and ten dollars,
tract cont. 297 acres in Eff. Co. on the south side of the runs swamp adj. land surveyed
for LANGLY and JOHN GOLDWIRE, MOUTFORD, and CECIL, DANIEL DAMPIER and EDWARD TELFAIR.
Signed: N. LUNDAY. Wit: THS. BRANNEN, J.I.C., WINIFORD LANEY LOUTHER.

Page 224:   Rec. 8 Sept. 1806 - Deed dated 5 Aug. 1806 - bet. LUKE WILSON, Sheriff and
            FREDERIC BUNTZ - STEPHEN DENMARK obtained Judgement against JOHN CASPER WERT-
SCH and Writ of fieri facias directed to Sheriff commanding the amount of Judgement be
made out of goods of JOHN CASPER WERTSCH - Sheriff seized and sold at public outcry
tract cont. 100 acres bound by DAVID UNSELD on Bassets pen branch for one hundred dollars. Signed: LUKE WILSON, S.E.C. Wit: J. G. NEIDLINGER, C.S.C.E.C., STEPHEN DENMARK.

Page 225:   Rec. 8 Sept. 1806 - Deed dated 5 Aug. 1806 - bet. LUKE WILSON, Sheriff and
            FREDERIC BUNTZ - STEPHEN DENMARK obtained a Judgement against JOHN CASPER
WERTSCH and a Writ of fieri facias directed Sheriff to get amount of Judgement from
goods of JOHN CASPER WERTSCH - Sheriff seized and sold at public outcry tract of land
cont. 250 acres on Bassets pen branch - cons. one hundred and ten dollars. Signed:
LUKE WILSON, S. E.C. Wit: J. G. NEIDLINGER, C.S.C.E.C., STEPHEN DENMARK.

Page 227:   Rec. 9 Sept. 1806 - Deed dated 5 Aug. 1806 - bet. LUKE WILSON, Sheriff and
            FREDERIC BUNTZ - STEPHEN DENMARK obtained a Judgement against JOHN CASPER
WERTSCH and a Writ of fieri facias directed Sheriff to get amount of Judgement from
goods of JOHN CASPER WERTSCH - Sheriff seized and sold at public outcry tract cont.
150 acres on Bassets pen branch - cons. forty-five dollars Signed: LUKE WILSON, S.E.C.
Wit: J. G. NEIDLINGER, C.S.C.E.C., STEPHEN DENMARK.

Page 228:   Rec. 9 Sept. 1806 - Deed dated 4 Jan. 1806 - bet. ROBERT IVEY and RICHARD
            WELSH of Bryan County - cons. one hundred dollars - half that tract of land

cont. 200 acres bound west by Great Ogeechee river, North by SHEWMAN; also 100 acres of pine land bound South East by SHEWMAN, North West by SHEWMAN, and South West by W. RUSHING, granted W. WILKINS on 9 Feb. 1790 and W. RUSHING on 2 Oct. 1794. Signed: ROBERT IVEY, MARY (X) IVEY. Wit: BRYANT WELCH, STEPHEN BAXTER.

11 Aug. 1806 - BRYANT WELCH made oath that he saw ROBERT IVEY sign within Invoice and that STEPHEN BAXTER was a witness. Signed: BRYANT WELCH. Wit: CURTIS LOPER, J.P.

Page 229: Rec. 9 Sept. 1806 - Deed dated 20 Jan. 1800 - bet. ELIAS HODGES, planter, and MARY his wife and ZACHARIAH HENDERSON, planter, cons. of one hundred dollars tract of land granted on 17 Oct. 1798 to ELIAS HODGES - 100 acres bound Southeast by DAVIS, southwest by HERB, Northwest by HUNT. Signed: ELIAS HODGES, MARY (X) HODGES. Wit: JOHN MOORE, ABEL G. LOPER.

19 Mar. 1806 - ABEL G. LOPER made oath that he saw ELIAS HODGES sign within Indenture and that JOHN MOORE was a witness. Signed: ABEL G. LOPER. Wit: CURTIS LOPER, J.P.

Page 231: Rec. 9 Sept. 1806 - Deed dated 23 Nov. 1802 - bet. ZACHARIAH HENDERSON, planter and ELIZABETH his wife and WILLIAM RUSHING - cons. of one hundred dollars, tract of land orig. granted on 17 Oct. 1798 to ELIAS HODGES cont. 100 acres conv. on 20 Jan. 1800 to ZACHARIAH HENDERSON bound south east by DAVIS, southwest by HERB, north west by HUNT. Signed: ZACHARIAH (H) HENDERSON, ELIZABETH (X) HENDERSON. Wit: SAMUEL (X) THORNTON, JOSHUA LOPER, J.I.C.

Page 233: Rec. 9 Sept. 1806 - Deed dated 21 Jan. 1804 - bet. WILLIAM RUSHING, planter and JONATHAN LOPER, planter - cons. one hundred dollars - tract of land cont. 100 acres orig. granted ELIAS HODGES on 17 Oct. 1798 and conv. by him on 20 Jan. 1800 to ZACHARIAH HENDERSON, and conv. by him to WILLIAM RUSHING. Signed: WILLIAM RUSHING. Wit: ASA LOPER, MATTHEW RUSHING.

19 March 1806-ASA LOPER made oath that he saw WILLIAM RUSHING sign within Indenture and that MATTHEW RUSHING was a witness. Signed: ASA LOPER. Wit: CURTIS LOPER, J.P.

Page 235: Rec. 22 Sept. 1806 - Deed dated 15 Aug. 1806 - bet. LUKE WILSON, Sheriff and GODHILF SMITH - STEPHEN DENMARK obtained a Judgement against JOHN CASPER WERTSCH and a Writ of fieri facias to Sheriff to get amount of Judgement from goods and estate of JOHN CASPER WERTSCH - Sheriff did seize and sell at public outcry tract cont. 100 acres on Turkey Branch, granted JOHN CASPER WERTSCH, bound south east by DAVID UNSELD - cons. sixteen dollars six and a quarter cents. Signed: LUKE WILSON, S.E.C. Wit: CHRISTIAN J. ZIPPERER, JAMES BIRD.

22 Sept. 1806 - JAMES BIRD made oath that he saw LUKE WILSON, Sheriff sign within Indenture and that CHRISTIAN I. ZIPPERER was a witness. Signed: JAMES BIRD. Wit: J. G. NEIDLINGER, C.S.C.E.C.

Page 236: Rec. 22 Sept. 1806 - Deed dated 30 June 1797 - bet. JOHN MARTIN DASHER, gentleman, and ELIZABETH his wife and GEORGE FREDERICK GUYER, shoemaker - cons. twelve pounds sterling dollars and four shillings and eight pence, tract of land cont. 50 acres bound southwardly by GEORGE KOGLER, Northwardly by DANIEL REMSHART, sold by Writ of fieri facias on estate of CHRISTIAN STEINER by Sheriff, THOMAS LANE, on 6 Oct. 1792 to JOHN MARTIN DASHER. Signed: JOHN M. DASHER, ELIZABETH (E) DASHER. Wit: JNO. NEIDLINGER, ISRL. FLERL

Page 238: Indenture dated 28 Mar. 1806 - JOHN EXLY stated that he received of JONATHAN RAHN and JOHN KOGLER, ESQ. Executors of Estate of JOHN MICKLER, dec., his full share of Estate left him by his grandfather JOHN MICKLER. Signed: JOHN EXLY.

Wit: THOMAS WYLLY, JONATHAN BACKLY.

Page 238: Rec. 30 Sept. 1806 - Deed dated 24 Sept. 1806 - bet. WILLIAM HURST, planter
           and ROSY his wife and WILLIAM BREWER of Edgefield district of South Carolina,
cons. of one hundred dollars - tract of land cont. 50 acres on Wallowing branch where
Old Mill stood bound north by JOSEPH BREWER, JAMES BREWER, SENR. and THOMAS HURST.Sig:
WILLIAM HURST, ROSY ( ) HURST. Wit: JAS. GADDY, J.P., JAS. BREWER.

Page 240: Rec. 8 Oct. 1806 - Deed dated 5 April 1805 - bet. NATHANIEL RUSSELL, ESQ.,
           of Charleston in South Carolina and CHARLES TROT, ESQ. of Chatham County -
cons. five shillings sterling - tract in Eff. Co. cont. 1,000 acres commonly called
Knoxborough. Signed: ADAM GILCHRIST, JOHN CAIG.

8 Oct. 1806 - JOHN CAIG made oath that he saw NATHANIEL RUSSELL sign within Indenture
and that ADAM GILCHRIST was a witness. Signed: JOHN CAIG. Wit: RICHD. N. STILES.

Page 241: Rec. 8 Oct. 1806 - Indenture dated 6 April 1805 - bet. NATHANIEL RUSSELL of
           Charleston, South Carolina and SARAH his wife and CHARLES TROT of Chatham
County - cons. seven thousand dollars - releasing unto CHARLES TROT in his actual possession now being by virtue of a bargain and sale to him by indenture of lease - tract
of land in Eff. Co. cont. 1,000 acres commonly called Knoxborough which was former property of WILLIAM KNOX, whose Estate was confiscated on 13 Jan. 1783 and sold to JOHN
WARD of St. Bartholemews Parish in South Carolina, planter, conv. by deeds of lease and
release after his death on 3 and 4 April 1784 to JOHN PETER WARD the eldest son and WIL-
LIAM S_IRVING, and ROGER PARKER SAUNDERS, Executors of JOHN WARD, dec., and sold to
JOHN McQUEEN of Charleston, South Carolina, gentleman, who conv. to THOMAS WASHINGTON
who mortaged tract for purchase money to JOHN McQUEEN on 1 and 2 Jan. 1805 for 3 bonds
dated 2 and 3 Jan. amounting to ten thousand pounds - said mort. was on 7 Jan. 1791 as-
signed by JOHN McQUEEN to THOMAS SH_ONICH of South Carolina, ESQ., who transferred same
to NATHANIEL RUSSELL who was Executor of ABRAHAM LIVINGSTON, ESQ., HENRY ALEXANDER LIV-
INGSTON heir of ABRAHAM LIVINGSTON, dec., and ELIZABETH his wife sold to NATHANIEL RUS-
SELL said mort. and upon default of payment of mort. by THOMAS WASHINGTON, NATHANIEL
RUSSELL became owner. Signed: NATHL. RUSSELL, SARAH RUSSELL. Wit: ADAM GILCHRIST,
JOHN CAIG.

13 Aug. 1806 - JOHN CAIG made oath that he saw NATHANIEL RUSSELL and SARAH RUSSELL sign
within Indenture and that ADAM GILCHRIST was a witness. Signed: JOHN CAIG. Wit: RICHD.
STILES, Not. Pub.

Page 245: Rec. 23 Oct. 1806 - Deed of Gift dated 8 Sept. 1806 - JOHN MARTIN DASHER,
           , SENR. to daughter-in-law, DOLLY DASHER - two Negro slaves, SAM and HANNAH;
one sorrel mare colt; one sorrel horse with flax mane and tail; branded on both should-
ers and on mounting buttoc D2,; two sows, all household and kitchen furniture; two ploughs; one cart and geers; one cow and calf; and crops of corn, peas, potatoes, fodder
and oats. Signed: JOHN M. DASHER. Wit: MATTHEW (B) BURGSTINER, TASSET ( ) DUGLESS

23 Oct. 1806 - MATTHEW BURGSTINER made oath that he saw JOHN MARTIN DASHER sign within
Indenture and that TASSET DUGLESS was a witness. Signed: MATTHEW (B) BURGSTINER. Wit:
CHRISTIAN DASHER, J.P.

Page 247: Rec. 12 Nov. 1806 - Deed dated 7 May 18 - bet. GOTTHILF SMITH of Bryan County
           planter and CHRISTIAN his wife, and MATTHEW BURKSTINER and SAMUEL BURKSTINER,
planter - cons. of five dollars - tract of land cont. 437 1/2 acres being north west half
of a tract cont. 875 acres orig. granted GOTTHIELF SMITH on 1 Jan. 1800, bound N. E. by
CHRISTIAN DASHER, Junr. Sig: GODHILF SMITH, CHRISTIANA (C) SMITH. Wit: JAMES BIRD, DAN-
IEL BURKSTINER.

12 Nov. 1806 - DANIEL BURGSTINER made oath that he saw GODHILF SMITH and CHRISTIANA SMITH sign within Indenture and it was witnessed by JAMES BIRD. Sig: DANIEL BURGSTINER. Wit: J. G. NEIDLINGER, C.S.C.E.C.

Page 249: Rec. 12 Nov. 1806 - Deed dated 1 Nov. 1806 - bet. GEORGE HEITH and SALLOMED his wife and GEORGE ZITTROUER - cons. of one hundred and six dollars - parcel of land cont. 200 acres of pine land bound N. East by April Heith, North West by GODHILF SHERROUSE, South East by JOHN SHERRAUSS, granted by His Excellency JOHN MILLEDGE, Gov., to GEORGE HEITH on 15 Nov. 1802. Sig: GEORGE ( ) HEITH, SALOMEA ( ) HEITH.

Page 251: Rec. 23 Nov. 1806 - Deed dated 4 June 1806 - bet. JOHN BEDDENBACK and HERMAN CRUM - cons. one hundred and thirty-one dollars - all that half of land being a tract or two tracts of a tract of land left between him and MATTHEW BEDDENBACK both bodily heirs of ANDREW BEDDENBACK, dec. by their father BIDDENBACK, dec., which half JOHN BEDDENBACK claims as an heir (half is 57 1/2 acres), tract orig. granted JACOB MIERS by His Excellency JAMES WRIGHT, Gov., on 29 Oct. 1765, conv. by him to JOHN ROTTENBERGERS on 12 June 1773, from ROTTENBERGER to son-in-law, ANDREW BEDDENBACK, tract bound southerly by EBENEZER CREEK, northerly by MATTHEW ZETTLER, northwesterly by CHRISTOPHER ROBBENBERGER, and North east by ROTTENBERGER. Sig: JOHN BEDDENBACK. Wit: SAMUEL MANER, GOTTLIEB ERNST.

17 Nov. 1806 - GOTTLIEB ERNST made oath that he saw JOHN BEDDENBACK sign within Indenture and SAMUEL MANER was a witness. Sig: GOTTLIEB ERNST. Wit: J. G. NEIDLINGER, C.S.C.E.C.

Page 253: Rec. 27 Nov. 1806 - Deed dated 24 Oct. 1805 - bet. JAMES PORTER and ELIZABETH his wife and HERMAN CRUM - cons. of thirty-five dollars - tract of land cont. 50 acres at blue bluff, orig. granted FREDERICK EPPINGER on 5 Aug. 1766 bounded N. E. by Savannah river, N. W. by FREDERICK SHRIMP, S. W. by GEORGE BOLLINGER, and S. E. by URBAN BUNTZ. Sig: JAMES PORTER, ELIZABETH (E) PORTER. Wit: JOHN PORTER, THOMAS (X) PORTER, SUSANNAH PORTER

17 Nov. 1806 - SUSANNAH PORTER made oath that she saw JAMES PORTER and ELIZABETH PORTER sign within Indenture and that it was witnessed by JOHN PORTER and THOMAS PORTER. Sig: SUSANNAH PORTER. Wit: J. G. NEIDLINGER, C.S.C.E.C.

(p.1) JOHN M. LUCAS was suly qualified administrator of the Est. of WM. Mc-
GAHAGIN. July 2, 1827.

(p.1) Accounts of JOHN GARHAM, Executor of the Est. of WILLIAM McGAHAGIN were
produced and there appeared a balance in his hands of $521.96.

(p.1) Granted dismission of JOHN GARHAM from his Executorship of the Est. of
WILLIAM McGAHAGIN. July 2, 1827.

(p.1)

(p.1) JONATHAN SECKINGER applied for dismission from adm. on the Est. of WIL-
LIAM SHRIMP. July 2, 1827. Granted Mar. 3, 1828.

(p.2) DAVID ZITTROUR applies for adm. on the Est. of MARY CATHERINE ZITTROUR.
Aug. 1827. Granted Oct. 15, 1827.

(p.2) Granted marriage license to WILLIAM W. WILSON with MARY SHEEROUSE. Sept.
1, 1827.

(p.2) Granted Administratrix of the Est. of WILLIAM H. WOMACK, dec'd. leave to
sell two Negroes named JACOB and CERAS. Sept. 3, 1827.

(p.3) Accounts of GEORGE H. SHUMAN, Executor of the Est. of JAMES SHUMAN, dec'd,
were produced and appeared a balance in the hands of the Executor of $1,411.29. Sept.
3, 1827.

(p.3) MATTHEW RESIER appeared and offered security to the court to become administrator on the Est. of JAMES PORTER, dec'd. Sept. 3, 1827. Refused.

(p.3) Ordered that Clerk pay to CHRISTOPHER H. $10.00 for his support. Sept.
3, 1827.

(p.3) JOSHUA GNANN applies for adm. with Will annexed on the Est. of SOLOMON
GNANN, dec'd. Sept. 27, 1827. Granted Nov. 5, 1827.

(p.4) EMANUEL ZIPPERER and SOLOMON ZIPPERER applies for administration on the
Est. of GIDEON ZIPPERER, dec'd. Oct. 27, 1827. Granted Dec. 3, 1827.

(p.4) Granted marriage license to JOHN T. MILLER with ANGELINE HOLIDAY. Nov.
1, 1827.

(p.4) Ordered that JOHN CHARLTON, Administrator on the Est. of JAMES PORTER
appointed by the Court, have leave to sell 4 Negroes for benefit of heirs and creditors.
Nov. 1, 1827.

(p.4) Ordered that WILLIAM WILLIAMS and JESSE WHEELER receive from Clerk $5.00
for their support. Nov. 5, 1827.

(p.5) ROBERT BARTON applies for dismission from the Est. of BENJAMIN BARTON.
Nov. 5, 1827. Granted May 8, 1828.

(p.5) Granted Letters of Collection to JOHN WOOLF on the Est. of GEORGE WOOLF,
dec'd. Who applies for administration on said Est. Nov. 19, 1827.

(p.5) Granted marriage license to JAMES KEEBLER with ELIZABETH ISHLY. Nov.
22, 1827.

(p.5) Granted marriage license to BENJAMIN GNANN with SALOMI RAHN. Dec. 5,
1827.

(p.6) Granted marriage license to BENJAMIN RHINOWER with HANNAH POWLEDGE. Dec.
5, 1827.

(p.6) Granted marriage license to JAMES HURST with ANN WILSON. Dec. 31, 1827.

(p.6) LEVI DLYON, administrator of the Est. of CHRISTIAN TRUETLEN, applies for
dismission from his adm. on said Est. Jan. 3, 1828.

(p.6) JOHN CHARLTON applies for adm. on the Est. of JOSEPH C. TREUTLEN, dec'd.
Jan. 3, 1828.

(p.6) JOHN CHARLTON applies to have leave to sell the real Est. of JAMES PORTER.
Jan. 7, 1828.

(p.7) Ordered that a writ of partition be issued to divide the whole Est. of
JAMES PORTER, dec'd, agreeable to a partition presented by heirs. Jan. 7, 1828.

(p.7) Ordered that Clerk pay to JAMES JENKINS $5.00, CHRISTOPHER HEIDT, $10.00,
and WILLIAM WALSINGHAM $5.00, each for their support. Jan. 7, 1828.

(p.7) LEWIS WEITMAN and DAVID ZEIGLER applied to have leave to sell the real
estate of EMANUEL ZEIGLER, dec'd. Jan. 7, 1828.

(p.7) Will of CATHERINE SNYDER was ordered to be recorded and LEWIS WEITMAN was qualified Executor of said CATHERINE SNYDER. Jan. 7, 1828.

(p.7) JOHN WOOLF applies for administration on the Est. of GEORGE WOOLF. Jan. 7, 1828.

(p.7) Ordered that Clerk pay to CHRISTOPHER HORNING and his wife $5.00 each for their support. Jan. 7, 1828.

(p.7) Ordered that JOHN WOOLF, adm., have leave to sell the perishable property of the Est. of GEORGE WOOLF. Jan. 7, 1828.

(p.8) IRVIN WOOLF, a minor son of GEORGE WOOLF made choice of JOHN WOOLF as his guardian whereupon he was appointed guardian of IRVIN WOOLF. Jan. 7, 1828.

(p.8) Granted marriage license to DAVID ZEIGLER, JR., with EVELINE CRAMER. Jan. 8, 1828.

(p.8) Granted marriage license to JOHN HINELY with ELIZABETH HELMLY. Jan. 14, 1828.

(p.8) HENRY GROVENSTEIN, Executor of the Est. of JOHN P. TOOSING, applies for dismission from Executorship on said Est. Jan. 28, 1828.

(p.8) Granted marriage license to GEORGE NEASE, JR. with CHRISTIAN ELIZABETH SHRIMP. Feb. 6, 1828.

(p.8) Inventory of rents and hiring of the Negroes of the Est. of WILLIAM McGAHAGIN. Jan. 2, 1828.

(p.9) Granted marriage license to MR. VALENTINE KESLER with CATHERINE SECKINGER. Feb. 18, 1828.

(p.9) Granted marriage license to DR. FRANCIS HEAGOOD with MARY G. MOREL. Feb. 18, 1828.

(p.9) Accounts of MARY A. PORTER were produced and appeared a balance due administratrix of $394.90. Mar. 3, 1828.

(p.10) Accounts of JOHN B. BERRY, Guardian of OBADIAH BERRY, were produced and appeared a balance in the hands of the guardian of $1246.89. Mar. 3, 1828.

(p.10) Accounts of JOHN M. LUCAS, Adm. of the Est. of WILLIAM McGAHAGIN were produced and there appeared a balance in the hands of the adm. of $360.05. Mar. 3,1828.

(p.10) Accounts of JOHN RAHN, Executor of the Est. of MATTHEW RAHN were produced and there appeared a balance due to Est. of $140.42. Mar. 3, 1828.

(p.10) Accounts of CHRISTIAN WISENBAKER, Administrator of the Est. of JOHN WISENBAKER, dec'd, were produced and thereappeared a balance due the adm. of $149.59. Mar. 3, 1828.

(p.10) Accounts of JOSHUA LINEBURGER, Executor of the Est. of DAVID LINEBURGER, dec'd, were produced and there appeared a balance in the hands of the Executor of $32.29. Mar. 3, 1828.

(p.10) Accounts of LEVI DLYON, adm. of the Est. of CHRISTIAN TREUTLEN, were produced and there appeared a balance in the hands of the adm. of $4.25. Mar. 3, 1828.

(p.10) Accounts of LEWIS WEITMAN, adm. of the Est. of EMANUEL ZEIGLER, were produced and there appeared a balance in the hands of the adm. of $1,839.41. Mar. 3, 1828.

(p.10) Accounts of LEWIS WEITMAN and SARAH WEITMAN, Executrix of the Est. of ISRAEL FLERL were produced and appeared a balance due LEWIS WEITMAN and SARAH WEITMAN of $1624.60. Mar. 3, 1828.

(p.11) Accounts of LEWIS WEITMAN, Guardian of SARAH ANN GRALINE FLERL, were produced and there appeared a balance in the hands of the guardian of $13.81. Mar. 3, 1828.

(p.11) Accounts of LEWIS WEITMAN, Guardian of MARY C. FLERL, were produced and there appeared a balance due the said guardian of $20.21. Mar. 3, 1828.

(p.11) JOHN CHARLTON was qualified adm. of the Est. of JOSEPH C. TREUTLEN. Mar. 3, 1828.

(p.11) Ordered that Clerk pay to GEORGE ARNSDORFF and WILLIAM WILLIAMS and JESSE WHEELER $5.00 each for their support. Mar. 3, 1827.

(p.11) M. SUNDAY applies for dismission from his Executorship on the Est. of GROLL SCRUGGS. Mar. 3, 1828.

(p.11) Granted marriage license to JOHN ROBERT SECKINGER with ELIZA NEMSBART. Mar. 7, 1828.

(p.12) Granted marriage license to GIDEON DASHER with REBECCA ZITTROUR. Apr. 9, 1828.

(p.12) Ordered that the securities of JOHN B. BERRY as Guardian of OBADIAH BERRY be exonnerated any discharge from his securityorship and JOHN B. BERRY do enter into a new Bond in the amount of $2,000.00. May 5, 1828.

(p.12) ANN BECK, adm. of the Est. of JOHN BECK, dec'd, petitions that Court ratify the proceedings of a Division of all the property which has taken place in the State of South Carolina. May 5, 1828.

(p.12) Ordered that Court approve proceedings. May 5, 1828.

(p.12) Ordered that JOSHUA GNANN have leave to sell the real est. of SOLOMON GNANN, JR., dec'd. May 5, 1828.

(p.13) DAVID GUGEL, Executor of the Est. of GEORGE C. NOWLAN, granted leave to sell so much property as will discharge the debts of said Estate. May 5, 1828.

(p.13) Ordered that Clerk pay JAMES JENKINS $5.00 for support. May 5, 1828.

(p.13) Granted marriage license to THOMAS FRAZIER with MARTHA LANCASTER. June 28, 1828.

(p.13) Ordered that Clerk issue citation according to law on the petition of JACOB GNANN, adm. of the Est. of EMANUEL RAHN asking for leave to be discharged from his administration. July 7, 1828.

(p.14) Accounts of JOSHUA GNANN, adm. of the Est. of SOLOMON GNANN, SR. were produced and appeared a balance in his hands of $172.24. July 7, 1828.

(p.14) Accounts of JOSHUA GNANN, adm. of the Est. of SOLOMON GNANN, JR. were produced and appeared a balance in his hands of $132.87. July 7, 1828.

(p.14) Accounts of JACOB GNANN, adm. of the Est. of EMANUEL RAHN, dec'd, were produced and there appeared a balance in his hands of $960.27. July 7, 1828.

(p.14) Accounts of JOHN CHARLTON, adm. of the Est. of BENJAMIN KENNEDY were produced and appeared a balance in his hands of $196.70. July 7, 1828.

(p.14) MARIA CHRISTIAN, one of the orphans of EMANUEL RAHN, appeared and made choice of JACOB GNANN, JR. as her guardian. He was so appointed. July 7, 1828.

(p.15) Ordered that JACOB GNANN, JR. be appointed guardian of ANN EVELINE, WILLIAM OBADIAH, CHARLOTTE CAROLINE and SUSANNAH, SALOMI RAHN, orphans of EMANUEL RAHN. July 7, 1828.

(p.15) Ordered that Clerk pay to MRS. WALSINGHAM $5.00 for her support and also to WILLIAM WILLIAMS $5.00 for his support. July 7, 1828.

(p.15) Granted marriage license to PHILIP ULMER with ELIZA FOX. July 15, 1828.

(p.16) Accounts of HENRY GROVENSTEIN, Executor of the Est. of JOHN P. TOOSING were produced and there appeared a balance due to the Executor of $10.00. Sept. 1, 1828.

(p.16) HENRY S. GROVENSTEIN was granted dismission from his Executorship of the Est. of JOHN P. TOOSING. Sept. 1, 1828.

(p.16) Accounts of GEORGE H. SHUMAN, Executor of the Est. of JAMES SHUMAN, were produced and found correct. Sept. 1, 1828.

(p.16) Accounts of DAVID GUGEL, Executor of the Est. of GEORGE G. NOWLAN were produced and appeared a balance due to the Executor of $1,448.86. Sept. 1, 1828.

(p.16) JOHN C. BLANCE was granted leave to sell Negroe named CELIA for the purpose of discharging the debts of Est. of ELIZA GRIFFIN. Sept. 1, 1828.

(p.17) Accounts of HANNAH E. CREWS, Executrix of the Est. of JAMES CREWS, were produced and appeared a balance due the Executrix of $62.94. Sept. 1, 1828.

(p.17) VALERIE WOMACK, minor and one of the heirs of WILLIAM H. WOMACK, dec'd, appeared and made choice of CHARLES TONDEE as her Guardian. Sept. 1, 1828. Granted Oct. 6, 1828.

(p.17) Ordered that JACOB GNANN, JR., adm. of the Est. of EMANUEL RAHN, have leave to sell the real estate belonging to EMANUEL RAHN. Sept. 1, 1828.

(p.17) Ordered that JACOB GNANN, JR., have leave to sell the Negroes belonging to EMANUEL GNANN for the purpose of making a division with the heirs. Sept. 1, 1828.

(p.17) Ordered Clerk to pay ABIAL HEIDT $5.00 for the support of his son.

101

Sept. 1, 1828.
    (p.17) Granted marriage license to WILLIAM ROWNSHEND with ANN MARGARET HINELY.
Sept. 16, 1828.
    (p.17) Issued citation on the application of WILLIAM KING for administration
on the Est. of WILLIAM G. PORTER which has not been already administered. Sept. 1, 1828
Granted administration Oct. 6, 1828.
    (p.18) JOSHUA GNANN applies to be discharged from his administratorship on the
Est. of SOLOMON GNANN, SR., dec'd. Nov. 3, 1828.
    (p.18) Accounts of BENJAMIN PORTER, guardian of the orphans of T. PORTER were
produced and appeared a balance in his hands of $8.23. Nov. 3, 1828.
    (p.18) Accounts of JOHN WOOLF, adm. of the Est. of GEO. WOOLF were produced and
there appeared a balance in his hands of $53.00. Nov. 3, 1828.
    (p.19) Granted marriage license to CHARLES ZITTROUR with ANN RYLINDER. Nov.
3, 1828.
    (p.19) Granted marriage license to JOSEPH T. HELVENSTON with ROSANNAH COPE.
Nov. 8, 1828.
    (p.19) Granted marriage license to JAMES RAHN with JANE ELIZA NEASE. Nov. 16,
1828.
    (p.19) ANDREW GRINER applies for adm. on the Est. of SARAH GNANN, widow of the
late SOLOMON GNANN. Nov. 1828.
    (p.19) Granted marriage license to ROBERT H. DWHEBELL with ELIZABETH AMBROSE.
Dec. 2, 1828.
    (p.19) Granted marriage license to FRANCIS CHAMPION with ELIZA ANN DISCOMBE.
Dec. 3, 1828.
    (p.19) Granted marriage license to JAMES M. DICKINEAN with DOROTHY AMBROSE.
Dec. 5, 1828.
    (p.20) MARIA PATTERSON applies for dismission on the Est. of WILLIAM PATTERSON,
dec'd. Jan. 5, 1829.
    (p.20) Accounts of CHRISTIAN H. DASHER, Executor of the Est. of PHILIP DANSLER
were produced and there appeared a balance due the Est. of $122.25. Jan. 5, 1829.
    (p.20) CHRISTIAN H. DASHER applies for dismission on the Est. of PHILIP DANSLER,
dec'd. Jan. 5, 1829.
    (p.21) Accounts of LEWIS MYERS, guardian of his children, were produced and
appeared a balance in his hands of $520.50. Jan. 5, 1829.
    (p.21) ANDREW GRINER was duly qualified adm. on the Est. of SARAH GNANN, widow.
Jan. 5, 1829.
    (p.21) Ordered that Clerk pay to MRS. WALSINGHAM $5.00 for her support. Jan.
5, 1829.
    (p.21) Granted marriage license to GODLIFE ARNSDORFF with ANN MARGARET FREYER-
MUTH. Jan. 9, 1829.
    (p.21) Granted marriage license to JOHN EXLEY with SARAH RAHN. Jan.13, 1829.
    (p.21) Granted marriage license to JOHN R. MORGAN with ANN RYALS. Jan. 20,
1829.
    (p.21) Granted marriage licesne to JESSE DAVIS with MARGARET METZGER. Jan. 24,
1829.
    (p.21) THOMAS ELKINS applies for adm. on the Est. of JOHN DUNY. Also letters
of collection were granted to take charge of the said property until regular adm. takes
place. Jan. 28, 1829.
    (p.22) Granted marriage license to JOHN DASHER with MARY MILLER. Feb. 25,1829.
    (p.22) Appeared DAVID GUGEL, Executor of the Est. of GEORGE NOWLAN, dec'd, and
guardian of the orphans of the said GEORGE NOWLAN, partitions for leave to sell a certain
tract of land drawn in the land lotter by said orphans. Mar. 2, 1829.
    (p.22) Accounts of JACOB GNANN, JR., adm. of the Est. of EMANUEL RAHN, dec'd,
were produced and there appeared a balance in the hands of the Exec. of $1,512.15. Mar.
2, 1829.
    (p.22) Granted JACOB GNANN dismission from adm. on the Est. of EMANUEL RAHN.
Mar. 2, 1829.

(p.23) Accounts of JOSHUA GNANN, adm. of the Est. of SOLOMON GNANN, SR. were produced and there appeared a balance in his hands of $330.30. Mar. 2, 1829.

(p.23) Petition of the heirs of SOLOMON GNANN, SR. was produced and wishes Court to grant leave to divide the property of said deceased. Mar. 2, 1829.

(p.23) Accounts of JOHN C. RAHN, Exec. of the Est. of MATTHEW RAHN, dec'd were examined and there appeared a balance due to Est. of $183.29. Mar. 2, 1829.

(p.23) Accounts of CHRISTIAN WISENBAKER, adm. of the Est. of JOHN WISENBAKER, dec'd, were examined and there appeared a balance due the adm. of $1.56. Mar. 2, 1829.

(p.23) Accounts of JOHN M. LUCAS, adm. of the Est. of WILLIAM McGAHAGIN were examined there appearing a balance due Est. of $586.70. Mar. 2, 1829.

(p.23) Accounts of JOHN B. BERRY as guardian of OBADIAH BERRY were examined there appearing a balance due OBADIAH BERRY of $1,175.50. Mar. 2, 1829.

(p.23) Accounts of JOSHUA LINEBURGER, Exec. of the Est. of DAVID LINEBURGER, dec'd, were examined there appearing a balance due Est. of $3.14. Mar. 2, 1829.

(p.23) Accounts of ELISHU WILSON, guardian of the orphans of GABRIEL WILSON were examined there appearing a balance due the orphans of $402.10. Mar. 2, 1829.

(p.24) THOMAS ELKINS applies for adm. on the Est. of JOHN DENNY, dec'd. Mar. 2, 1829.

(p.24) Ordered that THOMAS ELKINS, adm. on the Est. of JOHN DENNY, have leave to sell the perishable property. Mar. 2, 1829.

(p.24) CHRISTOPHER LINEBURGER was qualified Exec. of the Est. of DAVID LINE-BURGER. Mar. 2, 1829.

(p.24) Accounts of WILLIAM SPEIR, adm. of the Est. of TEMPLE TULLOS and PATIENCE TULLOS were examined there appearing a balance due to Est. of $444.36. Mar. 2, 1829.

(p.24) LEWIS WEITMAN and DAVID ZEIGLER applies for dismission on the Est. of EMANUEL ZEIGLER, dec'd. Mar. 2, 1829.

(p.25) Granted marriage license to THELPHILUS ZIPPERER with MARY PROPER. Mar. 3, 1829.

(p.25) Granted marriage license to JOSHUA GROUVER with SARAH SNIDER. Mar. 7, 1829.

(p.25) Granted marriage license to HEZEKIAH AMBROSE with KEZIAH LEE of Screven County. Mar. 17, 1829.

(p.25) Accounts of WILLIAM KING, adm. of the Est. of WM. PORTER, dec'd, were produced and examined there appearing a balance in his hands of $2,661.60. Mar. 2, 1829.

(p.25) Accounts of JACOB GNANN, JR. guardian of the orphans of EMANUEL RAHN, dec'd, were produced and examined there appearing a balance in his hands of $1,237.10.

(p.25) Accounts of EMANUEL and SOLOMON ZIPPERER, adms. of the Est. of GIDEON ZIPPERER were produced and examined there appearing a balance in his hands of $174.24.

(p.26) Accounts of HANNAH E. CREWS, Exec. of the Est. of JAMES CREWS, were produced and examined there appearing a balance due the Exec. of $62.84. May 4, 1829.

(p.26) JACOB GNANN, JR. was appointed guardian for the minor heirs of MATTHEW RAHN, dec'd; ELIZA RAHN, ALEXANDER RAHN, JOSHUA RAHN, and ISRAEL RAHN. May 4, 1829.

(p.26) Granted heirs of MATTHEW RAHN, dec'd division of said Est. May 4,1829.

(p.26) Ordered that JOHN C. RAHN, Exec. of the Est. of M. RAHN have leave to sell Negroes belonging to the Est. of MATTHEW RAHN for the purpose of making a division with the heirs. May 4, 1829. Also have leave to sell real estate.

(p.27) JOSHUA HELVENSTON appointed guardian of the minor heirs of CHRISTIAN COPE, dec'd, named JOHN COPE, SR., and MARIA COPE. May 4, 1829.

(p.27) JOHN C. RAHN, applies to be dismissed from his executorship of the Est. of MATTHEW RAHN, dec'd, May 4, 1829.

(p.27) Granted ANDREW GRINER leave to sell the real est. of SARAH GNANN. May 4, 1829.

(p.27) Ordered that clerk pay to A. WHEELER and WILLIAM WILLIAMS $5.00 for their support. May 4, 1829.

(p.27) Ordered that Clerk of Court take possession of the property of J. Seckinger, dec'd, and that he act as adm. receive what may be due him and pay his debts. May 4, 1829.

(p.28) Granted marriage license to ELIAS GROUVER with SUSANNAH REISER. May 11, 1829.

(p.28) Rules to be observed for the regulation of the Superior Court and Court of Ordinary.

(p.29) Accts. of JOHN CHARLTON, Adm. of the Est. of JONATHAN BACKLEY, dec'd, were produced and examined there appearing a balance due him of $12.18. July 6, 1829.

(p.29) Accts. of JOHN CHARLTON, Adm. of the Est. of BENJAMIN KENNEDY were produced and examined there appearing a balance in his hands of $762.92. July 6, 1829.

(p.30) EPHRAIM KEIFFER applies for adm. on the Est. of GOTTLIEB ERNST, dec'd. July 6, 1829.

(p.30) Accts of CHRISTIAN H. DASHER, Exec. of the Est. of PHILIP DENSLER, were produced and examined and found correct. July 6, 1829.

(p.30) BENJAMIN C. PORTER was made guardian of DOROTHY KENNEDY, one of the heirs of BENJAMIN KENNEDY. July 6, 1829.

(p.30) Ordered that SOLOMON METZGER be appointed of BENJAMIN KENNEDY and ANN KENNEDY, minor heirs of BENJAMIN KENNEDY, dec'd. July 6, 1829.

(p.30) Granted division of the personal property of EMANUEL ZEIGLER, July 6, 1829.

(p.31) Ordered that SOLOMON ZIPPERER Be appointed guardian of WILLIAM PROPER, ANN MATILDA PROPER, and CAROLINE PROPER, orphans of I.H. PROPER, dec'd. July 6, 1829.

(p.31) MARY ANN ISHLY and JOHN CHARLTON applies for adm. on the Est. of JOHN JACOB ISHLY, dec'd. Granted Sept. 7, 1829.

(p.31) CHRISTIAN I. HEIDT and CHRISTINE, his wife, caveats the application of LEWIS WEITMAN and DAVID ZEIGLER for dismission from adm. on Est. of EMANUEL ZEIGLER. July 17, 1829.

(p.31) GEORGE POWLEDGE applies for adm. on the Est. of DAVID POWLEDGE, dec'd. Aug. 1, 1829.

(p.32) Granted division of the property of Est. of BENJAMIN KENNEDY. Sept. 7, 1829.

(p.32) Granted JOHN CHARLTON leave to sell est. of BENJAMIN KENNEDY. Sept. 7, 1829.

(p.32) Accts. of BENJAMIN C. PORTER, guardian of the heirs of THOMAS D. PORTER were produced and examined and ordered to be recorded. Sept. 7, 1829.

(p.33) GEO. POWLEDGE applies for adm. on the Est. of DAVID POWLEDGE, dec'd. Sept. 7, 1829.

(p.33) GEO. POWLEDGE applies to be appointed guardian of the orphans of GIDEON ZIPPERER, dec. SOPHIA, JACOB, and SOLOMON. Sept. 7, 1829.

(p.33) Granted leave to WILLIAM A. PREVATT, adm. and SARAH REVATT, adm. on the Est. of WM. WOMACK, to have leave to sell several tracts of land on the Louisville Road in this Co. Sept. 7, 1829.

(p.33) MARY BACKLEY applies to be appointed guardian of the person and property of LUKEY BACKLEY, a minor and orphan of JONATHAN BACKLEY. Sept. 7, 1829.

(p.33) Ordered that a Writ of Division be issued to divide the personal property of JONATHAN BACKLEY, dec'd. Sept. 7, 1829.

(p.33) JOHN CHARLTON, adm. of the Est. of JONATHAN BACKLEY, have leave to sell the Negroes belonging to said est. Sept. 7, 1829.

(p.34) Granted marriage license to GEORGE ZITTROUR and LOUISA NEASE. Sept. 14, 1829.

(p.34) Granted marriage license to DR. JOACHIM B. SAUPY of South Carolina with MARGARET G. NOWLAN. Nov. 19, 1829.

(p.35) Granted marriage license to MATTHEW WEITMAN with LAONIA STANTON. Nov. 29, 1829.

(p.35) Granted marriage license to JOHN METZGER with DOROTHY KENNEDY. Dec. 4, 1829.

(p.35) Granted marriage license to GEO. D. DUKES with MARY ROSANNAH HURST. Dec. 22, 1829.

(p.35) Accts. of DAVID GUGEL, Exec. of the Est. of GEO. G. NOWLAN, were produced and examined and found correct. Jan. 4, 1830.

(p.36) Granted division of the personal property of the Est. of DAVID POWLEDGE.
Jan. 4, 1830. Also granted leave to sell Negroes of said est. Jan. 4, 1830.

(p.36) Accts. of LEWIS WEITMAN, adm. of the Est. of EMANUEL ZEIGLER, dec'd,
were produced and examined and found correct. Jan. 4, 1830.

(p.36) Granted WILLIAM KING, adm. of the Est. of WILLIAM G. PORTER, dec'd.
leave to sell undivided half of 137 acres of land in Effingham Co. Jan. 4, 1830.

(p.36) CLEM POWERS appointed guardian of DR. HENRY SHUMAN, a minor of JAMES
SHUMAN. Jan. 4, 1830.

(p.37) Granted marriage license to SOLOMON ZITTROUR with ESTHER GNANN. Jan.
23, 1830.

(p.37) JOHN CHARLTON, adm. of the Est. of BENJAMIN KENNEDY, dec'd, applies for
dismission from his adm. Mar. 1, 1830. Also applies for dismission from adm. on the Est.
of JONATHAN BACKLEY. Mar. 1, 1830.

(p.38) MARY ANN ISHLY made choice of child's part of Est. of JOHN JACOB ISHLY,
dec'd. Mar. 1, 1830.

(p.38) All accounts that were produced were found correct.

(p.39) JEREMIAH MULLETT applies for adm. on the est. of DAVID MULLETT, dec'd.
Mar. 6, 1830. Granted May 3, 1830.

(p.39) All accounts that were produced were found correct.

(p.40) MARIA PATTERSON was discharged from adm. of the Est. of WM. PATTERSON.
May 3, 1830.

(p.40) MARIA PATTERSON granted guardianship of her daughter HARRIET ELIZABETH
PATTERSON. Mar. 3, 1830.

(p.40) Ordered that EPHRAIM KEIFFER have leave to sell real est. of GOTTLIEB
ERNEST. May 3, 1830.

(p.41) ISRAEL T. WALDHOUR applies for adm. on the Est. of JOHN WALDHOUR, dec'd.
May 6, 1830. Granted July 5, 1830.

(p.41) SELINA ELKINS applies for adm. on the Est. of SOLOMON ELKINS, May 6,
1830. Granted July 5, 1830.

(p.42) Last Will and Testament of JOSEPH HELVENSTON was admitted to record.
July 5, 1830.

(p.42) Granted marriage license to JAMES BLITCH with MAHAL TYSON. July 23,
1830.

(p.43) All accts. produced and examined and found correct. Sept. 6, 1830.

(p.43) Granted division of personal property of WM. P. PATTERSON. Sept. 6,
1830.

(p.44) Granted EPHRIAM KEIFFER leave to sell 2 Negroes belonging to the Est.
of GOTTLIEB ERNEST. Sept. 6, 1830.

(p.44) FURNEY WILLIS has resigned as JUSTICE of Superior Court and an election
will be held first Monday in Oct. to fill vacancy. Sept. 6, 1830.

(p.44) Granted marriage license to JAMES PACE with MARY ANN ISHLY. Sept. 11,
1830.

(p.44) BENJ. DASHER applies for adm. on the Est. of CHRISTOPHER LINEBURGER.
Sept. 1830.

(p.45) ELISHU WILSON applies for adm. on the Est. of JOSHUA GROUVER. Sept.
28, 1830.

(p.45) Granted marriage license to THOMAS ELKINS with MARIA P. PATTERSON. Oct.
5, 1830.

(p.45) Accts. produced were found correct.

(p.45) JOHN WISENBAKER appointed guardian of minor heirs of JOHN WISENBAKER,
dec'd. Nov. 1, 1830.

(p.46) Granted division of Est. of JOHN WISENBAKER, also granted CHRISTIAN
WISENBAKER leave to sell as many Negroes as will make a division of said est. Nov. 1,
1830.

(p.46) Accts. of J. F. HELVENSTON were produced and found correct. Nov. 1, 1830

(p.46) Granted division of Est. of CHRISTIAN COPE. Nov. 1, 1830.

(p.46) Granted ELISHU WILSON, adm. of the Est. of JOSHUA GROUVER, leave to sell perishable property. Nov. 1, 1830.

(p.46) Ordered that clerk pay to WALDEN GRIFFIN for support at attending on a transcient person named SHERLOCK CASE who died at his house. Nov. 1, 1830.

(p.46) Ordered that Clerk pay to JOHN C. RAHN for making a coffin for JOHN FRASER who died in Ebenezer. Nov. 1, 1830.

(p.46) Granted guardianship of JOHN C. RAHN of ROBERT ISHLY, minor of JOHN C. ISHLY, dec'd. Nov. 1, 1830.

(p.47) Granted guardianship to JAMES PACE of minor children of JOHN J. ISHLY. Nov. 1, 1830.

(p.47) Granted marriage license to JOHN PALMER with MARY HELVENSTON. Nov. 9, 1830.

(p.48) SARAH BARTON and ROBERT BARTON applies for adm. on the Est. of HENRY A. BARTON, dec'd. Nov. 1830.

(p.48) FREDERICK WOMACK applies for adm. on the Est. of WILLIAM WOMACK, dec'd. Nov. 15, 1830.

(p.48) AMOS COOK applies for adm. on the Est. of MARGARET COOK, dec'd. Nov. 18, 1830. Granted Jan. 3, 1831.

(p.48) Granted marriage license to ALEXANDER H. McDONALD, with ANN ELIZABETH NOWLAN. Nov. 24, 1830.

(p.48) Granted marriage license to JESSE D. DYKES with FANNY ANN BLITCH. Nov. 22, 1830.

(p.48) JOHN DUGGER be granted adm. on the Est. of EMANUEL D. DUGGER at expiration of citation. Jan. 3, 1831.

(p.50) PETER FREYERMUTH applies for dismission on the Est. of JOHN FREYERMUTH, dec'd. Jan. 3, 1831.

(p.51) J.M. LUCAS acts. were produced and found correct. Mar. 7, 1831.

(p.51) JOHN B. BERRY accts. were produced and found correct. Mar. 7, 1831.

(p.51) CHRISTIAN WISENBAKER accts. were produced and found correct. Mar. 7, 1831.

(p.51) WILLIAM SPEIR accts. produced and found correct. Mar. 7, 1831.

(p.51) CLEM POWERS accts. produced and found correct. Mar. 7, 1831.

(p.51) JOSHUA LINEBURGER accts. produced and found correct. Mar. 7, 1831.

(p.52) JOSHUA LINEBURGER, adm. of the Est. of MARY C. LINEBURGER, asks for a division of said Est. Mar. 7, 1831.

(p.52) Granted division of the Est. of WILLIAM SPEIR, dec'd. Mar. 7, 1831.

(p.52) Granted ELIZABETH JONES, adm. of the Est. of PHILIP JONES, dec'd, leave to sell real est. of said dec'd. Mar. 7, 1831.

(p.52) WILLIAM A. PREVATT was chosen as guardian of ALFRED JACKSON WOMACK. Mar. 7, 1831.

(p.52) Granted marriage license to SOLOMON ARNSDORFF with ANN EVE WEITMAN, Mar. 22, 1831.

(p.53) Granted marriage license to MR. WILLIAM A. BLACK with JANE RAWLS. Mar. 25, 1831.

(p.53) Granted marriage license to LEABORN ROOKS with SOPHIA HOLIDAY. Mar. 26, 1831.

(p.53) REUBEN KEIFFER applies for adm. on the Est. of JOEL KEIFFER, dec'd. Apr. 23, 1831.

(p.53) Last Will and Testament of JAMES KEEBLER was admitted to record. May 2, 1831.

(p.53) Ordered that WILLIAM A. PREVATT be appointed guardian of WILLIAM C. WOMACK. May 2, 1831.

(p.54) Accts. of BENJ. C. PORTER were produced and found correct. May 2, 1831.

(p.54) Accts. of WM. KING were produced and found correct. May 2, 1831.

(p.54) Ordered that lot known as No. 12 in town of Springfield be reserved for county purposes and the upper 1/2 of fractional lot known as No. 37 in said plat be granted to the Methodist Episcopal Church for purpose of building a place of worship there. May 2, 1831.

(p.54) JOSHUA KEEBLER, JR. appointed Exec. of the Last Will and Testament of JAMES KEEBLER, dec'd. May 9, 1831.

(p.54) Granted marriage license to LEWIS MULLETT with ELIZA GRACY ANN WILSON. May 9, 1831.

(p.54) JAMES MOBLEY applies for adm. on the Est. of LEVI E. MOBLEY. May 30, 1831.

(p.54) Granted marriage license to JOSHUA LOVETT with ANN ELIZABETH KEEBLER. June 16, 1831.

(p.56) Accts. of EPHRAIM KEIFFER were produced and found correct. July 11, 1831.

(p.56) Accts. of CHARLES TONDEE were produced and found correct. July 11, 1831.

(p.56) Accts. of ISRAEL T. WALDHOUR were produced and found correct. July 11, 1831.

(p.57) JESSE DAVIS applies for adm. on the Est. of MARY HUNKS. Aug. 16, 1831. Granted Sept. 17, 1831.

(p.57) HEZEKIAH EVANS, adm. of the Est. of JOHN and MARCEY MOORE applies to be dismissed from his adm. Sept. 5, 1831.

(p.57) Accts. of JEREMIAH MULLETT were produced and found correct. Sept. 5, 1831.

(p.57) Accts. of JOHN CHARLTON were produced and found correct. Sept. 5, 1831.

(p.57) Accts. of LEWIS MYERS were produced and found correct. Sept. 5, 1831.

(p.58) Last Will and Testament of ELIZABETH COPE was admitted to record. Sept. 5, 1831.

(p.58) Granted marriage license to EDWARD BOURQUIN with AWSELLE ELKINS. Oct. 3, 1831.

(p.58) Granted marriage license to JOHN G. PITTS with JANE SCHRODER. Oct. 11, 1831.

(p.59) Granted marriage license to WILLIAM EDWARDS with ELEANOR SOUTHWELL. Oct. 21, 1831.

(p.59) EPHRAIM KEIFFER applies to be dismissed from the adm. on the Est. of GOTTLIEB ERNST. Nov. 7, 1831.

(p.59) Accts. of SOLOMON METZGER were produced and found correct. Nov. 7, 1831.

(p.60) Accts. of BENJ. C. PORTER were produced and found correct. Nov. 1, 1831.

(p.60) Accts. of JACOB GNANN, JR. were proudced and found correct. Nov. 1, 1831.

(p.60) Accts. of ELISHU WILSON were produced and found correct. Nov. 1, 1831.

(p.60) Accts. of THOMAS ELKINS were produced and found correct. Nov. 1, 1831.

(p.61) Granted marriage license to WILLIAM BLITCH with ELIZA TULLUS. Dec. 13, 1831.

(p.61) Granted marriage license to THOMAS A. WILSON with ELIZA BACKLEY. Dec. 12, 1831.

(p.61) Granted marriage license to JESSE HURST with MARY ANN LEE. Dec. 12, 1831.

(p.61) Granted marriage license to JOHN WISENBAKER with MARGARET WALDHOUR. Dec. 12, 1831.

(p.61) Granted marriage license to JEREMIAH MULLETT with ELIZA METZGER. Dec. 12, 1831.

(p.61) Granted marriage license to CLETUS RAHN with ELIZA H. RAHN. Dec. 24, 1831.

(p.61) WILLIAM B. DOPSON applies for adm. on the Est. of ELVIRA ANN DOPSON. Dec. 23, 1831.

(p.62) Accts. of DAVID GUGEL were produced and found correct. Jan. 2, 1832.

(p.62) Granted division of the Est. of GEO. G. NOWLAN. Jan. 1, 1832.

(p.62) CHARLES A. BARTON, ROBERT BARTON, BENJAMIN BARTON, CLEM POWERS, and ZAZA POWERS were appointed Trustees of the person and property of SIMEON BARTON. Jan. 2, 1832.

(p.62) GOTTLIEB SECKINGER was chosen guardian of EBELINE FREYERMUTH. Jan. 2, 1832. Granted Mar. 5, 1832.

(p.63) Accts. of CHARLES TONDEE were produced and found correct. Jan. 2, 1832.

(p.62) Granted division of the Est. of JOHN FREYERMUTH. Jan. 2, 1831.

(p.63) JOHN M. LUCAS applies for adm. on the Est. of ELIZA McGAHAGIN. Jan.5, 1832.

(p.63) Granted marriage license to BENJAMIN BLITCH with HARRIET WILSON. Jan. 9, 1832.

(p.63) Granted marriage license to ROBERT MINGLEDORFF with LEVINE ZITTROUR. Jan. 11, 1832.

(p.63) Granted marriage license to POTER W. KETTLER with REBECCA WILSON. Jan. 21, 1832.

(p.63) Granted marriage license to ELIAS WILSON with SARA SHUTTRINE. Feb. 11, 1832.

(p.63) MILLY ANN WILSON applies for adm. on the Est. of ELIAS WILSON, dec'd. Mar. 2, 1832.

(p.64) Accts. of JOHN M. LUCAS were produced and found correct. Mar. 5, 1832.

(p.64) Accts. of SARAH E. CREWS were produced and found correct. Mar. 5, 1832.

(p.64) Accts. of H. CREWS were produced and found correct. Mar. 5, 1832.

(p.64) Accts. of John DUGGER were produced and found correct. Mar. 5, 1832.

(p.64) Accts. of JOHN BERRY were produced and found correct. Mar. 5, 1832.

(p.65) Accts. of WILLIAM PREVATT were produced and found correct. Mar. 5, 1832.

(p.65) Granted division of the Est. of JOHN FREYERMUTH, dec'd. Mar. 5, 1832.

(p.66) GRACY AMBROSE and HENRY T. MORGAN applies for adm. on the Est. of DAVID AMBROSE. Nov. 12, 1832.

(p.66) JOHN ISRAEL REISER applies for adm. on the Est. of DAVID REISER, dec'd. Mar. 12, 1832.

(p.67) MISS ANN WILSON qualified adm. of the Est. of ELIAS WILSON, dec'd. May 7, 1832.

(p.67) GRACY AMBROSE and HENRY T. MORGAN qualified adm. of the Est. of DAVID AMBROSE. May 7, 1832.

(p.67) Ordered that Clerk qualify JOHN ISRAEL RESIER adm. on the Est. of DAVID REISER. May 7, 1832.

(p.67) Accts. of PETER FREYERMUTH were produced and found correct. May 7, 1832.

(p.67) Accts. of REUBEN KEIFFER were produced and passed. May 7, 1832.

(p.68) Accts. of WILLIAM KING were produced and found correct. July 2, 1832.

(p.68) FRANCIS GOLDWIRE and JAMES O. GOLDWIRE applies for adm. on the Est. of JOHN GOLDWIRE. July 12, 1832.

(p.68) Granted marriage license to HARDY PITTS with ELIZABETH HUDSON. July 21, 1832.

(p.68) WILLIAM WILSON applies for adm. on the Est. of JESSE WILSON. July 28, 1832.

(p.69) HOWELL HINES applies for adm. on the Est. of ELIZABETH WILSON, dec'd. July 31, 1832.

(p.69) Accts. of EPHRAIM KEIFFER were produced and passed. Sept. 3, 1832.

(p.69) EPHRAIM KEIFFER was dismissed from adm. on the Est. of GOTTLIEB ERNST. Sept. 3, 1832.

(p.69) FRANCES GOLDWIRE qualified adm. on the Est. of JOHN GOLDWIRE, dec'd. Sept. 3, 1832.

(p.69) HOWELL HINES qualified adm. on the Est. of ELIZABETH WILSON, dec'd. Sept. 3, 1832.

(p.69) ELIZABETH SALTERS, widow of JACOB SALTERS, appears and says that he has been dead about two years and 9 months and that she is entitled to the pension due her late husband agreeable to an Act. of Congress passed in 1829. Sept. 3, 1832.

(p.70) JOHN HODGES applies for adm. on the Est. of DANIEL HENDERSON. Sept. 6, 1832.

(p.70) MARY C. BERGMAN and LEWIS WEITMAN applies for adm. on the Est. of REV. C.F. BERGMAN. Sept. 7, 1832.

(p.70) Granted marriage license to CHARLES R. TONDEE with VALEIRA WOMACK. Sept. 7, 1832.

(p.71) BENJ. METZGER applies for adm. on the Est. of SOLOMON METZGER. Sept. 29, 1832.

(p.71) Granted marriage license to JACOB HINELY with MARY MAGDALANE GUYER. Oct. 13, 1832.

(p.71) Accts. of ELISHU WILSON were produced and passed. Nov. 5, 1832.

(p.72) Accts. of LEWIS MYERS were produced and passed. Nov. 5, 1832.

(p.72) Accts. of JEREMIAH MULLETT were produced and passed. Nov. 5, 1832.

(p.72) Accts. of JOSEPH HELVENSTON were produced and passed. Nov. 5, 1832.

(p.72) BENJ. J. METZGER qualified adm. of the Est. of SOLOMON METZGER. Nov. 5, 1832.

(p.72) WILLIAM HURST appointed guardian of _____WILSON and gtd. Div. of Est. of ELIAS WILSON. Nov. 5, 1832.

(p.73) WILLIAM H. WILSON qualified adm. of the Est. of JESSE WILSON. Nov. 5, 1832.

(p.73) Granted division of Est. of ELIZA McGAHAGIN. Nov. 5, 1832.

(p.73) Last Will and Testament of JOHN POWERS was admitted to record. Nov. 5, 1832.

(p.73) Accts. of JACOB GNANN, JR. were produced and passed. Nov. 5, 1832.

(p.74) Accts. of JOSEPH HELVENSTON were produced and found correct. Nov. 5, 1832.

(p.74) Granted dismission to PETER FREYERMUTH. Nov. 5, 1832.

(p.74) Granted marriage license to SOLOMON EXLEY with MARIA CHRISTIANA RAHN. Nov. 22, 1832.

(p.75) Granted marriage license to THOMAS HURST with ELIZABETH LEE. Nov. 24, 1832.

(p.75) Granted marriage license to JACKSON TYNER with SARAH PACE. Dec. 1, 1832.

(p.75) Granted marriage license to HENRY WILSON with HANNAH MINGLEDORFF. Dec. 18, 1832.

(p.75) Granted marriage license to GIDEON EMANUEL ZIPPERER with ANN HESTER. Dec. 21, 1832.

(p.75) Granted marriage license to HENRY T. MORGAN with MARY PACE. Dec. 21, 1832.

(p.76) Ordered that Clerk qualify JAMES O. GOLDWIRE, adm. of the Est. of JOHN GOLDWIRE. Jan. 7, 1833.

(p.76) Accts. of MILLY ANN WILSON were produced and found correct. Jan. 7, 1832

(p.76) Accts. of JESSE DAVIS were produced and found correct. Jan. 7, 1832.

(p.76) JOHN M. LUCAS was chosen guardian of WILLIAM L. McGAHAGIN and JOSHUA L. McGAHAGIN. Jan. 7, 1833.

(p.76) FRANCIS GOLDWIRE appeared and made choice of child's part of the Est. of JOHN GOLDWIRE. Jan. 7, 1833.

(p.77) HANNAH GROVENSTEIN applies for adm. on the Est. of HENRY L. GROVENSTEIN, dec'd. Jan. 12, 1833.

(p.77) Granted marriage license to JAMES A. LEE with CYNTHIA RICHARDSON. Jan. 12, 1833.

(p.77) Granted marriage license to BENJ. GNANN with HANNAH CHRISTIE. Jan. 14, 1833.

(p.77) Granted marriage license to THOMAS H. BREWER with ANN TULLUS. Jan. 26, 1832.

(p.77) Granted marriage license to EDWIN DASHER with SUSANNAH WISENBAKER. Feb. 6, 1833.

(p.77) Granted marriage license to JOSEPH C. EDWARDS with FRANCES CONE. Feb. 11, 1833.

(p.77) Granted marriage license to EDWARD ZITTROUR with JOHANNAH ZEIGLER. Feb. 19, 1833.

(p.78) Granted marriage license to ISAAC LANIER with SARAH HURST. Mar. 4, 1833.

(p.78) Granted marriage license to WM. McDONELL with AGNES MELROSE. Mar. 4, 1833.

(p.78) EMANUEL SHEEROUSE was qualified Exec. of the Last Will and Testament of GODHIEFF SHEEROUSE. Apr. 1833.

(p.79) Granted marriage license to WM. PARISH with EVELINE FRYERMUTH. Apr. 4, 1833.

(p.79) Granted marriage license to WM. HODGES with MARTHA COLSON. Apr. 4, 1833.

(p.79) Granted marriage license to ELBERT WILSON with LAVINA GRAHAM. Apr. 4, 1833.

(p.79) Benj. Jos. Morrel applies for adm. on the Est. of BENJ. MORREL, dec'd. May, 1833.

(p.79) SIMON BUNTZ applies for adm. on the Est. of HENRY L. BUNTZ, dec'd. May 2, 1833.

(p.80) Granted marriage license to JAMES O. GOLDWIRE with MARIA GOLDWIRE. May 6, 1833.

(p.80) Granted marriage license to WINTON JONES with SARAH FLINCY. June 10, 1833.

(p.80) JAMES O. GOLDWIRE duly qualified adm. of the Est. of JOHN GOLDWIRE. June 10, 1833.

(p.80) Last Will and Testament of JAMES BRYAN was produced and admitted to record. July 1, 1833.

(p.80) CATHERINE BRYAN was named executrix of the Last Will and Testament of JAMES BRYAN. July 1, 1833.

(p.80) Accts. of W.A. PREVATT were produced and found correct. July 1, 1833.

(p.80) Accts. of JOHN M. LUCAS were produced and found correct. July 1, 1833.

(p.81) Accts. of CLEM POWERS were produced and passed. July 1, 1833.

(p.81) Accts. of WM. SPEIR were produced and passed. July 1, 1833.

(p.81) Accts. of ELISHU WILSON were produced and found correct. July 1, 1833.

(p.81) Accts. of FRANCES GOLDWIRE were produced and found correct. July 1, 1833.

(p.81) MARY C. BERGMAN made choice of child's part of the Est. of HENRY BUNTZ. July 1, 1833.

(p.81) SIMON BUNTZ qualifed adm. of the Est. of HENRY BUNTZ. July 1, 1833.

(p.82) Granted SELINA ELKINS leave to sell 2 negroes and proceeds of sale be place in such a way by the purchase of other property for the benefit of Est. July 1, 1833.

(p.82) Accts. of ELISHU WILSON were produced and passed. July 1, 1833.

(p.82) Accts. of JOHN B. BERRY were produced and passed. July 1, 1833.

(p.82) Accts. of JOSHUA GNANN were produced and passed. July 1, 1833.

(p.82) Granted HEZEKIAH EVANS dismission from adm. on the Est. of JOHN and MARCEY MOORE, dec'd. July 1, 1833.

(p.82) CLETUS RAHN applies for adm. on the Est. of FREDERICK RAHN, dec'd. July 30, 1833. Granted Sept. 2, 1833.

(p.83) ISRAEL J. WALDHOUR, adm. of the Est. of JOHN WALDHOUR, dec'd, applies to be dismissed from his trust. Aug. 23, 1833.

(p.83) Accts. of HANNAH E. CREWS were produced and found correct. Sept. 2, 1833.

(p.83) Accts. of HANNAH GROVENSTEIN were produced and found correct. Sept. 2, 1833.

110

(p.83)   Accts. of B.J. METZGER were produced and found correct. Sept. 2, 1833.
(p.84)   Ordered that Clerk, at the expiration of 30 days, grant adm. to JESSE
D. DYKES and WILLIAM CURRY on the Est. of Furney Willis. Further ordered upon there
obtaining adm., they have leave to sell perishable property belonging to said est. Sept.
3, 1833.
(p.84)   WILLIAM CURRY and JESSE DYKES applies for adm. on the Est. of FURNEY
WILLIS, dec'd. Sept. 4, 1833. Granted Oct. 19, 1833.
(p.84)   JOHN CHARLTON applies for adm. on the Est. of HANNAH NOWLAN, dec'd. Sept.
20, 1833. Granted Nov. 4, 1833.
(p.84)   Granted marriage license to GEORGE PACE and JOHANNAH GNANN. Oct. 7,
1833.
(p.84)   Granted marriage license to JAMES A. DASHER with MARY A. WISENBAKER.
Oct. 7, 1833.
(p.85)   Last Will and Testament of JAMES WILSON was admitted to record. Nov.
4, 1833.
(p.85)   Accts. of LEWIS MYERS were produced and found correct. Nov. 4, 1833.
(p.85)   Accts. of W.C. TISON were produced and found correct. Nov. 4, 1833.
(p.85)   Accts. of JOS. F. HELVENSTON were produced and found correct. Nov. 4,
1833.
(p.85)   JOHN WILSON was chosen as guardian of KESIAH E. WILSON. Nov. 4, 1833.
(p.85)   Granted JOHN ISRAEL REISER leave to sell the real est. of DAVID REISER,
dec'd. Nov. 4, 1833.
(p.86)   Last Will and Testament of WILLIAM EDWARDS, dec'd, was admitted to record. Nov. 4, 1833.
(p.86)   Granted ELISHU WILSON leave to sell real est. of ANN WILSON, dec'd. Nov.
4, 1833.
(p.86)   Ordered that four months notice be published for leave to sell a Negro
belonging to the est. of FREDERICK RAHN. Nov. 4, 1833.
(p.86)   Ordered that four months notice be published for leave to sell real est.
of JAMES WILSON, dec'd. Nov. 4, 1833.
(p.86)   Ordered that four months notice be published for leave to sell the
Negroes and real estate of JOEL KEIFFER, dec'd. Nov. 4, 1833.
(p.87)   Granted marriage license to CHARLES C. PLATT with LUCRETIA G. DAVIS.
Nov. 27, 1833.
(p.87)   Granted marriage license to EDWARD PARISH with ELIZABETH BRYAN. Dec.
4, 1833.
(p.87)   Granted marriage license to DAVID HINELY with SALOMI ARNSDORFF. Dec.
9, 1833.
(p.87)   Granted marriage license to FELIX HURST with ORFY COLE. Dec. 9, 1833.
(p.88)   Granted marriage license to DAVID A. MORGAN with ANN C. CHRISTEE. Feb.
10, 1834.
(p.88)   Granted marriage license to ARCHIBALD WILKINS with AMANDA M. PORTER.
Feb. 22, 1834.
(p.88)   Accts. of JOHN CHARLTON were produced and passed. Mar. 3, 1834.
(p.88)   Accts. of JOHN B. BERRY were produced and passed. Mar. 3, 1834.
(p.88)   Accts. of WM. A. PREVATT were produced and passed. Mar. 3, 1834.
(p.89)   Accts. of JESSE DAVIS were produced and passed. Mar. 3, 1834.
(p.89)   Granted JOHN CHARLTON leave to sell all Negroes belonging to the est. of
HANNAH NOWLAN, dec'd. Mar 4, 1834.
(p.89)   Last Will and Testament of PAUL BEVILL admitted to record. Mar. 4, 1834.
(p.89)   Granted JOHN WILSON and JOHN G. MINGLEDORFF leave to sell all the Negroes belonging to the Est. of JAMES WILSON. Mar. 4, 1834.
(p.89)   Granted CLETUS RAHN leave to sell a Negro belonging to the est. of
FREDERICK RAHN. Mar. 4, 1834.
(p.89)   Granted REUBEN KEIFFER leave to sell all Negroes belonging to the est.
of JOEL KEIFFER. Mar. 4, 1834.

(p.89)   Last Will and Testament of WILLIAM DOURY was admitted to record. Mar. 4, 1834.

(p.90)   Granted JOHN CHARLTON leave to sell property of the est. of BENJ. MOR-RELL, dec'd. Mar. 4, 1834.

(p.90)   Accts. of JOHN M. LUCAS were produced and passed. Mar. 4, 1834.

(p.90)   Accts. of C. POWERS were produced and passed. Mar. 4, 1834.

(p.90)   W.H. SCRUGGS granted leave to sell perishable property of est. of PAUL BEVILL. Mar. 4, 1834.

(p.91)   EMANUEL ZIPPERER applies for adm. on the Est. of JONATHAN ZIPPERER. Mar. 4, 1834. Granted May 5, 1834.

(p.91)   Granted marriage license to JOHN ISRAEL REISER with ESTHER EXLEY. Mar. 4, 1834.

(p.91)   Granted marriage license to WILLIAM TOWNSEND with CYNTHIA AMBROSE. Mar. 25, 1834.

(p.91)   Granted marriage license to DANIEL HEIDT with MARY BODDENBECK. Mar. 27, 1834.

(p.91)   Granted marriage license to BRINSON WHEELER with GRACY AMBROSE. Mar. 31, 1834.

(p.91)   Granted marriage license to ZACCHEUS EXLEY with SUSANNAH GROVENSTEIN. Apr. 8, 1834.

(p.91)   Granted marriage license to ISRAEL HINELY with JOHANNAH E. SECKINGER. Apr. 26, 1834.

(p.91)   Granted marriage license to JOHN J. MOREL with ELIZABETH DUDLEY. Apr. 28, 1834.

(p.92)   Accts. of EMANUEL SHEEROUSE were produced and passed. May 5, 1834.

(p.92)   Accts. of MARY BACKLEY were produced and passed. May 5, 1834.

(p.92)   Ordered that JAMES O. GOLDWIRE be appointed guardian of FRANCIS GOLD-WIRE, REBECCA GOLDWIRE, and SARAH JANE GOLDWIRE. Also guardian of OBEDIENCE A., WILL-IAM JOSEPH J., and MARY ANN GOLDWIRE., MINOR ORPHANS OF JOHN GOLDWIRE, dec'd. May 5, 1834.

(p.93)   Granted marriage license to HENRY BACKLEY with HANNAH E. CREWS. May 7, 1834.

(p.93)   Granted marriage license to DANIEL ZETTLER with CHRISTIANNA GNANN. June 13, 1834.

(p.93)   W.W. BLACK applies for adm. on the Est. of WM. WOMACK. June 1, 1834. Granted Nov. 3, 1834.

(p.93)   Accts. of the Executrix of JAMES M. CREWS, dec'd were produced and found correct. July 7, 1834.

(p.93)   Accts. of B.C. PORTER were produced and found correct. July 7, 1834.

(p.94)   Accts. of MR. GROVENSTEIN were produced and found correct. July 7, 1834.

• (p.94)   Accts. of WILLIAM KING were produced and passed. July 7, 1834.

(p.94)   Accts. of CLETUS RAHN were produced and passed. July 7, 1834.

(p.94)   Accts. of JOSHUA RAHN and ISRAEL RAHN, minor heirs of MARTHA RAHN,dec'd who made choice of JACOB GNANN, JR. as their guardian, was so appointed. July 7, 1834.

(p.94)   Appointed C.H. DASHER guardian for JOHN THOMAS RAHN, minor son of JOHN C. RAHN. July 1, 1834.

(p.95)   Granted marriage license to THOMAS KEEBLER with LOUISA A. MOREL. Sept. 29, 1834.

(p.95)   GEORGE W. BOSTON and JAMES O. GOLDWIRE applies for adm. on the Est. of WILLIAM KING, dec'd. Oct. 23, 1834. Granted Nov. 3, 1834.

(p.95)   Granted marriage license to PAUL ZIPPERER. Oct. 25, 1834.

(p.96)   Accts. of ZAZA POWERS were produced and found correct. Nov. 3, 1834.

(p.96)   Accts. of BENJ. METZGER were produced and found correct. Nov. 3, 1834.

(p.96)   Accts. of JOSHUA WILSON were produced and found correct. Nov. 3, 1834.

(p.96)   Accts. of REUBEN KEIFFER were produced and found correct. Nov. 3, 1834.

(p.97)   MISS GEORGIANNA MOREL and H.W. MOREL made choice of JOHN G. MOREL as guardian. Nov. 3, 1834.

(p.97)   JOHN CHARLTON was granted leave to sell all real and personal est. of BENJ. MORELL. Nov. 3, 1834.

(p.97)   EMANUEL ZIPPERER was granted leave to sell the real est. Nov. 3, 1834.

(p.98)   ARCHIBALD WILKINS, JR. applies for adm. on the est. of WILLIAM G. PORTER. Nov. 1834. Granted Jan. 5, 1835.

(p.98)   Ordered that administrator of the Est. of BENJ. MOREL have leave to sell Negroes belonging to said est. Jan. 5, 1835.

(p.99)   Accts. of WILLIAM CURRY were produced and found correct. Jan. 5, 1835.

(p.99)   Accts. of W.H. SCRUGGS were produced and found correct. Jan. 5, 1835.

(p.99)   Will of WILLIAM KING, dec'd. was admitted to record. Jan. 5, 1835.

(p.99)   Granted WILLIAM CURRY leave to sell real property of the est. of FURNEY WILLIS, dec'd. Jan. 5, 1835.

(p.99)   Accts. of SARAH BARTON were produced and found correct. Jan. 5, 1835.

(p.99)   Ordered that ARCHIBALD WILKINS be appointed guardian of MARY ANN PORTER. Jan. 5, 1835.

(p.99)   Ordered that CHRISTIAN TREUTLEN be appointed guardian of ALBERT S. PORTER. Jan. 5, 1835.

(p.99)   GEORGE W. BOSTON applies for adm. on the Est. of JOHN TISON, dec'd. Jan. 13, 1835. Granted Mar. 2, 1835.

(p.100) Granted marriage license to THOMAS TISON with ELVIRA SOUTHWELL. Jan. 14, 1835.

(p.100) Granted marriage license to JOHN W. GRAHAM with ANN BREWER. Jan. 28, 1835.

(p.100) Granted division of the Est. of WILLIAM G. PORTER. Feb. 9, 1835.

(p.101) Last Will and Testament of FREDERICK WOMACK was admitted to record. Mar. 2, 1835.

(p.101) Accts. of JAMES O. GOLDWIRE were produced and found correct. Mar. 2, 1835.

(p.102) Accts. of JACOB GNANN were produced and passed. Mar. 2, 1835.

(p.102) Accts. of C. POWERS were produced and passed. Mar. 2, 1835.

(p.103) Accts. of JOHN B. BERRY were produced and passed. Mar. 2, 1835.

(p.103) Accts. of LEWIS MYERS were produced and passed. Mar. 2, 1835.

(p.103) Accts. of W. A. PREVATT were produced and passed. Mar. 2, 1835.

(p.103) Accts. of LEWIS WEITMAN were produced and passed. Mar. 2, 1835.

(p.103) Granted LEWIS WEITMAN dismission from adm. on the Est. of EMANUEL ZEIGLER. Mar. 2, 1835.

(p.104) Granted marriage license to GEORGE BREWER with PENELOPE ELKINS. Mar. 2, 1835.

(p.104) Granted marriage license to WILLIAM W. WILSON with HENRIETTA CLARK. Apr. 19, 1835.

(p.104) JAMES GRIFFIN and JOHN GRIFFIN applies for adm. on the Est. of HENRY GRIFFIN, dec'd. Mar. 10, 1835. Granted May 4, 1835.

(p.104) MOSES METZGER applies for adm. on the Est. of BENJ. J. METZGER. Arp. 30, 1835.

(p.104) THOMAS WOMACK, brother of FREDERICK WOMACK, objects to the probate of Last Will and Testament of Frederick Womack. Mar. 23, 1835.

(p.105) Accts. of J.M. LUCAS were produced and found correct. May 4, 1835.

(p.105) Accts. of ELISHU WILSON were produced and passed. May 4, 1835.

(p.105) Accts. of JESSE DAVIS were produced and passed. May 4, 1835.

(p.105) Accts. of JEREMIAH MULLETT were produced and passed. May 4, 1835.

(p.106) BENJ. C. PORTER appointed guardian of the orphans of BENJ. KENNEDY. May 4, 1835.

(p.106) Ordered that MOSES METZGER be qualified adm. on the est. of BENJ. METZGER at the expiration of the citation. Granted June 13, 1835, and also ordered that he have leave to sell perishable property. May 4, 1835.

(p.106) Caveat of THOMAS WOMACK dismissed.

(p.106) ELISHU WILSON applies to be dismissed from his adm. of the Est. of ANN WILSON, dec'd. May 4, 1835. Granted May 7, 1836.

(p.107) JOHN METZGER applies for adm. on the Est. of SOLOMON METZGER. May 6, 1835. Granted Mar. 7, 1836.

(p.107) Granted marriage license to GEORGE BRIDGES with SARAH O. BOWMAN. May 11, 1835.

(p.107) Granted marriage license to JAMES CRANE with KESIAH TAYLOR. May 26, 1835.

(p.108) Accts. of EMANUEL SHEEROUSE were examined and passed. July 6, 1835.

(p.108) Accts. of HANNAH GROVENSTEIN were examined and passed. July 6, 1835.

(p.108) Granted GEORGE BOSTON leave to sell tract of land containing 640 acres lying on the Runs in Effingham County. July 6, 1835.

(p.108) JAMES CRANE applies for adm. on the Est. of JAMES TAYLOR, dec'd. JULY 17, 1835. Granted Oct. 5, 1835.

(p.109) Granted marriage license to JOSIAH CROSBY with CATHARINE HINELY. July 27, 1835.

(p.109) Granted marriage license to MOSES METZGER with JANE MINGLEDORFF. Sept. 8, 1835.

(p.109) Granted marriage license to CHRISTOPHER GNANN with ELIZABETH MARY FETZER. Sept. 25, 1835.

(p.110) Granted marriage license to JAMES BLITCH with MARTHA ANN MILLIS. Oct. 11, 1835.

(p.110) Accts. of WILLIAM EDWARDS were produced and passed. Nov. 2, 1835.

(p.110) Accts. of WILLIAM CURRY were produced and passed. Nov. 2, 1835.

(p.110) Accts. of EMANUEL ZIPPERER were produced and passed. Nov. 2, 1835.

(p.110) Accts. of WILLIAM SPEIR were produced and passed. Nov. 2, 1835.

(p.110) Last Will and Testament of JESSE DYKES was admitted to record. Nov. 2, 1835.

(p.111) Accts. of JEREMIAH MULLET were produced and passed. Nov. 2, 1835.

(p.111) MARY S. METZGER applies for guardianship of orphas of SOLOMON METZGER, DEC"D. Granted Nov. 2, 1835.

(p.111) Granted heirs of the Est. of BENJ. J. METZGER, dec'd, leave to sell the real and personal property of said est. Nov. 2, 1835.

(p.111) Granted heirs of the Est. of MARY HUNCK, dec'd, leave to sell real estate and a write of partition be issued for the division of Negroes of said est. Nov. 2, 1835.

(p.111) Last Will and Testament of NICHOLAS MYERS, dec'd, admitted to record. Nov. 2, 1835.

(p.112) LUKE WILSON enters a caveat against ELISHU WILSON'S obtaining dismission on the Est. of ANN WILSON, dec'd. Nov. 20, 1835.

(p.112) Granted marriage license to JOHN R. NEASE WITH MARY E. SHEEROUSE. Dec. 8, 1835.

(p.112) Granted marriage license to ARCHIBALD GUYTON with SELINA ELKINS. Dec. 14, 1835.

(p.113) JOHN C. GRIFFIN was chosen as guardian of FRANKLIN GRIFFIN. Jan. 4, 1836.

(p.113) Granted heirs of HENRY GRIFFIN, dec'd, leave to sell real est. of said deceased. Jan. 4, 1836.

(p.113) Last Will & Testament of JOHN GRAHAM was admitted to record. Jan. 4, 1836.

(p.113) Granted HENRY BACKLY adm. on the Est. of JAMES W. CREWS. Jan. 4, 1836.

(p.114) ANDREW BIRD and CLEM POWERS applies for adm. on the Est. of HENRY W. CREWS. Jan. 8, 1836. Granted Mar. 7, 1836.

(p.114) ARCHIBALD GUYTON applies for adm. on the Est. of HERMAN ELKINS, dec'd. Feb. 3, 1836. Granted Mar. 7, 1836.

114

(p.114) Granted marriage license to MILLENTOW SMITH with SARAH G. NEWTON. Feb. 8, 1836.

(p.114) Granted marriage license to JOHN J. HINELY with CAROLINE WILSON. Feb. 8, 1836.

(p.114) Granted marriage license to JEFFERSON ZIPPERER with

(p.114) JOHN ROGERS applies for adm. on the Est. of JAMES W. CREWS. Mar. 12, 1836.

(p.115) FRANKLIN B. COX chose JESSE DAVIS as his guardian. Mar. 7, 1836.

(p.115) Granted division of the Est. of MARY HUNCK. Mar. 7, 1836.

(p.116) Accts. of W.A. PREVATT were produced and passed. Mar. 7, 1836.

(p.116) Accts. of JESSE DAVIS were produced and passed. Mar. 7, 1836.

(p.116) Accts. of LEWIS MYERS were produced and passed. Mar. 7, 1836.

(p.116) Accts. of JOHN B. BERRY were produced and passed. Mar. 7, 1836.

(p.116) Accts. of JOHN M. LUCAS were produced and passed. Mar. 7, 1836.

(p.116) Accts. of WM. H. SCRUGGS were produced and passed. Mar. 7, 1836.

(p.117) CLEM POWERS was granted adm. on the Est. of PAUL BEVILL. Mar. 7, 1836.

(p.117) Granted marriage license to REV. JOHN L. SOUTHWELL with MARY ARCHER. Apr. 5, 1836.

(p.117) Granted marriage license to SIMON ZITTROUR with ANN HINELY. Apr. 6, 1836.

(p.118) JAMES O. GOLDWIRE applies for adm. on the Est. of FRANCES GOLDWIRE. May 4, 1836. Granted Sept. 5, 1836.

(p.118) JAMES TUTTE applies for adm. on the Est. of CAROLINE AMANDA TUTTE. May 16, 1836.

(p.118) MARGARET ANN GRAHAM objects to JAMES TUTTE becoming guardian of CAROLINE AMANDA GRAHAM or TUTTE because she is the mother of the said CAROLINE AMANDA GRAHAM or TUTTE. June 1, 1836.

(p.118) Granted marriage license to SAMUEL ELKINS with MARRIET PATTERSON. June 18, 1836.

(p.119) Granted marriage license to MR. FRANKLIN GRIFFIN with PRUDENCE WILLIS. July 4, 1836.

(p.119) No. Date for the following

(p.119) Accts. of JAMES O. GOLDWIRE were examined and found correct.

(p.120) Accts. of SARAH BARTON were examined and found correct.

(p.120) Accts. of REUBEN KEIFFER were examined and found correct.

(p.120) Accts. of MOSES METZGER were examined and found correct.

(p.120) Accts. of JOHN METZGER were examined and found correct.

(p.120) Accts. of STEPHEN HESLER were examined and found correct.

(p.120) Granted marriage license to EBENEZER JENCKS with JULIA ELKINS. July 18, 1836.

(p.120) Granted marriage license to JOHN BURCKSTEINER with ELIZABETH HELMLY. July 18, 1836.

(p.120) Granted marriage license to AMOS RAHN with ANN ELIZABETH DASHER. July 30, 1836.

(p.121) Granted marriage license to JESSE DASHER with CATHARINE HEISLER. Sept. 20, 1836.

(p.121) Accts. of JAMES O. GOLDWIRE were examined and found correct. Sept. 5, 1836.

(p.122) Accts. of SARAH BARTON were examined and found correct. Sept. 5, 1836.

(p.122) Accts. of REUBEN KEIFFER were examined and found correct. Sept. 5, 1836.

(p.122) Accts. of MOSES METZGER were examined and found correct. Sept. 5, 1836.

(p.122) Accts. of JOHN METZGER were examined and found correct. Sept. 5, 1836.

(p.122) Accts. of STEPHEN HESLER were examined and found correct. Sept. 5, 1836.

(p.122) Accts. of CLEM POWERS were examined and found correct. Sept. 5, 1836.

(p.123) Accts. of ARCH. WILKINS were examined and found correct. Sept. 5, 1836.

(p.123) Ordered that JOHN CHARLTON, Clerk of Court of Ordinary do take charge of Est. of JAMES M. CREWS.

(p.123) Ordered that JAMES CRANE have leave to sell real est. of Est. of JAMES TAYLOR.

(p.124) Ordered that clerk grant adm. to THOMAS H. BREWER on the Est. of JOHN GRAHAM, dec'd, at the expiration of citation. Granted adm. Oct. 10, 1836.

(p.124) Ordered that THOMAS ELKINS be appointed guardian of LAWRENCE T. ELKINS & GEORGIANNA ELKINS.

(p.124) Accts. of GEORGE W. BOSTON were examined and found correct.

(p.124) Granted marriage license to JEREMIAH ZIPPERER with LAVITHA KELLER. Sept. 5, 1836.

(p.124) Issued following citations: THOMAS H. BREWER applies for adm. on the Est. of JOHN GRAHAM, dec'd. and CHRISTIANNA RYALS and JOHN R. MORGAN on Est. of CHARLES RYALS, dec'd. Sept. 9, 1836.

(p.124) Granted marriage license to JOHN PORTER with HANNAH C. GROVENSTEIN. Sept. 17, 1836.

(p.125) Granted marriage license to THOMAS ULMER with LETILU ANN PARRISH. Sept. 28, 1836.

(p.125) BENJ. DASHER, JR. applies for adm. on the est. of APPOLONIA LINEBURGER. Oct. 4, 1836.

(p.125) Granted marriage license to DAVID RENSHART with AMANDA GEORGIANNA NOWLAN. Oct. 5, 1836.

(p.126) Last Will and Testament of JOHN EXLEY was admitted to record. Nov. 7, 1836.

(p.126) Accts. of MRS. GROVENSTEIN, Exec. of the Est. of HENRY L. GROVENSTEIN, dec'd, were examined and found correct. Nov. 6, 1836.

(p.126) SELETA GRAHAM appeared and made choice of child's part on the Est. of her husband, JOHN GRAHAM, dec'd. Nov. 7, 1836. Accts. of B. C. PORTER examined.

(p.126) CHRISTIANA RYALS and JOHN R. MORGAN were granted mad. on est. of CHARLES RYALS. Nov. 7, 1836.

(p.127) Granted division of the est. of HERMAN ELKINS. Nov. 7, 1836.

(p.127) JAMES ERNST applies for adm. on the Est. of CATHARINE ERNST, dec'd. Dec. 15, 1836. Granted Jan. 2, 1837.

(p.127) Granted marriage license to REV. GEORGE R. WRIGHT with MARGARET ELIZABETH CHARLTON. Dec. 27, 1836.

(p.127) Granted marriage license to follow persons to wit: EMANUEL CRAWFORD with JOHANNA ELIZABETH HEIDT, WILLIAM HESTON with JANE ZIPPERER and JAMES CONNOR with ELEANOR MARLOW. Dec. 27, 1836.

(p.128) Last Will and Testament of LYDIA COOK was admitted to record. Jan. 2, 1837.

(p.128) Accts. of LEWIS MYERS were examined and passed. Jan. 2, 1837.

(p.128) CHRISTIANA RYALS appointed guardian of MARY MERCY RYALS. Jan. 2, 1837.

(p.128) REBECCA KETTLES was granted adm. on the est. of PETER M. KETTLES at the expiration of citation. Jan. 2, 1837.

(p.129) Granted marriage license to MOORE BLITCH with VASTY FUTRELL. Jan. 30, 1837.

(p.129) Granted marriage license to HENRY G. BOWMAN with ISRALINE HEIDT. Feb. 11, 1837.

(p.129) Granted marriage license to DAVID B. NEWTON with MARY ANN TULLIS. Feb. 12, 1837.

(p.129) Granted marriage license to JOHN FETZER with MISS CHRISTIANNA BEDENBACK. Feb. 25, 1837.

(p.129) Last Will and Testament of JOHN DUGGAR declared null and void. Mar. 6, 1837.

(p.130) Accts. of SARAH BARTON were produced. Mar. 6, 1837.

(p.130) Accts. of THOMAS BREWER were produced and passed. Mar 6, 1837.

(p.130) Accts. of SELETA GRAHAM were produced and passed. Mar. 6, 1837.

(p.130) Accts. of JOHN B. BERRY were produced and passed. Mar. 6, 1837.

(p.130) Accts. of B. C. PORTER were produced and passed. Mar. 6, 1837.

(p.130) Accts. of H. SCRUGGS were produced and passed. Mar. 6, 1837.

(p.131) JOHN CHARLTON was granted adm. on the Est. of PETER L. Mar. 6, 1837.

(p.131) PAUL MARLOW and B. EDWARDS were qualified Exec. of the Last Will and Testament of JOHN DUGGAR, JR., dec'd. Mar. 6, 1837.

(p.131) LYDIA PARRISH applies for adm. on the est. of EDWARD PARRISH. Mar. 13, 1837.

(p.132) ELIZABETH JONES and NATHANIEL ZETTLER applies for dismission on the Est. of PHILIP JONES, dec'd. May 17, 1837.

(p.132) Granted marriage license to CHARLES CONAWAY with SARAH HESTOR. May 19, 1837.

(p.132) Granted marriage license to JOHN COPE with SELINA CREWS. May 30, 1837.

(p.133) Accts of JAMES O. GOLDWIRE were examined and passed. July 2, 1837.

(p.133) Accts. of STEPHEN HESTOR were examined and passed. July 2, 1837.

(p.134) Accts. of WILLIAM CURRY were examined and passed. July 2, 1837.

(p.134) Accts of JOHN M. LUCAS were examined and passed. July 2, 1837.

(p.134) Accts of C. H. Dasher were examined and passed. July 2, 1837.

(p.134) Accts of W. A. PREVATT were examined and passed. July 2, 1837.

(p.134) Accts. of HANNAH GROVENSTEIN were examined and passed. July 2, 1837.

(p.134) Accts. of CLEM POWERS were examined and passed. July 2, 1837.

(p.135) Accts. of JOSHUA C. were examined and passed. July 2, 1837.

(p.135) Accts. of WILLIAM SPEIR were examined and passed. July 2, 1837.

(p.135) Ordered that HENRY T. MORGAN, adm. of the Est. of DAVID AMBROSE, have leave to sell real est. of the same. July 2, 1837.

(p.135) Ordered that LETITIA GRAHAM, Exec. of the Est. of JOHN GRAHAM, dec'd. have leave to sell the real est. of the same. July 2, 1837.

(p.135) Accts. of JOHN M. LUCAS upon re-examination are laid over to the next court. July2, 1837.

(p.135) Ordered that clerk give notice by publishing in one of the Gazettes to grant dismission on the est. of James WILSON, dec'd. July 2, 1837.

(p.135) CALEB GRINER was granted adm. on the est. of ANDREW GRINER. July 2, 1837.

(p.136) Accts of GEORGE W. BOSTON were examined and found co-rect. Sept. 4, 1837.

(p.136) Accts of JOHN M. LUCAS were examined and passed. Sept. 4, 1837.

(p.136) Accts. of EST. of JAMES W. CREWS were examined and passed. Sept. 4, 1837.

(p.136) Last Will and Testament of LYDIA POWERS was produced and proved by Robert BOURQUIN. Sept. 4, 1837.

(p.136) Ordered that JOHN ISHLY be appointed guardian of _____ISLY minor heir of JACOB ISHLY, dec'd. Sept. 4, 1837.

(p.136) LYDIA CREWS appeared and made choice of CHRISTIANNA WISENBAKER as her guardian. Sept. 4, 1837.

(p.136) Granted adm. on the Est. of JAMES W. CREWS and sell Negroes and land agreeable to the Will of said JAMES W. Crews. Sept. 4, 1837.

(p.137) JAMES RAHN applies for adm. on the Est. of SOLOMON WEITMAN. Sept. 15, 1837. Granted Nov. 6, 1837.

(p.137) Granted marriage license to JAMES WISENBAKER with SARAH A. DASHER. Oct. 16, 1837.

(p.137) ANN CATHARINE BURGSTEINER and JAMES RAHN applies for adm. on the est. of SAMUEL BURGSTEINER. Oct. 25, 1837.

(p.138) THOMAS PURSE, .Esq., President of the Union Society in Savannah, made application desiring that the following boys be bound to the said Society: MAYHEW JOHN WILLIAMS, HARRIS, WILLIAM HERRINGTON AND JOHN CAMPBELL. Nov. 6, 1837.

(p.138) Ordered that LYDIA PARRISH have leave to sell all the real estate of EDWARD PARRISH. Nov. 6, 1837.

(p.139) Ordered that NAOMI WEITMAN have leave to sell the real estate of MATTHEW WEITMAN. Nov. 6, 1837.

(p.139) Ordered that CALEB GRINER have leave to sell the real estate of ANDREW GRINER. Nov. 6, 1837.

(p.139) Accts. of HENRY T. MORGAN were produced and found correct. Nov. 6, 1837.

(p.139) Ordered that ARCHIBALD GUYTON have leave to sell 200 acres lying in Effingham County. Also one lot of land in Carroll County and one lot in Muscogee County. Nov. 6, 1837.

(p.139) Accts. of ANDREW BIRD and CLEM POWERS were produced and found correct. Nov. 6, 1837.

(p.139) Ordered that clerk grant administration to JAMES RAHN and ANN CATHARINE BURCKSTEINER at the expiration of the citation. Nov. 6, 1837.

(p.140) Ordered that a writ of partition be issued to the following persons to divide personal property of PAUL BEVILL dec'd::GRANVILLE BEVILL, JOHN S. REISER, PAUL COLSON, HENRY PILLS, GEORGE BOSTON and JOHN SCRUGGS. Nov. 6, 1837.

(p.140) ELIZABETH JONES appeared and made choice of BRADFORD JONES as her guardian. Nov. 6, 1837.

(p.140) Ordered that a writ ofpartition be issued to WILLIAM BIRD, JOHN G. MINGLE-DORFF, JOHN CHARLTON, EMANUEL SHEEROUSE, AND CHRISTIAN DASHER to divide the personal property of PHILIP JONES, dec'd. Nov. 6, 1837.

(p.140) Granted marriage license to JAMES ZITTROUR with BELINDA HEIDT. Dec. 5, 1837.

(p.140) JOHANNAH ZITTROUR applies for adm. on the Est. of EDWARD ZITTROUR. Dec. 19, 1837. Granted Mar. 1838.

(p.141) Granted marriage license to BENJAMIN JENNINGS with REBECCA KETTLES. Jan. 1, 1838.

(p.141) Granted marriage license to ALBERT G. PORTER with EVALINE HUMBART. Jan. 4, 1838.

(P.141) Granted marriage license to John Richard SHEEROUSE with EVELINE NEASE. Feb. 3, 1838.

(p.141) Granted marriage license to JOHN S. SECKINGER with MARY GROVENSTEIN. Feb. 5, 1838.

(p.141 Granted marriage license to MATTHEW M. MORGAN with MARY C. CARTER. Feb. 7, 1838.

(p.141 Granted marriage license to JOHN D. HUGHES with KESIAH WILSON. Feb. 12, 1838.

(p.141) Granted marriage license to _____REISSER with CHARLOTTE RAHN. Feb.12, 1838.

(p.141) JOHN SUBTRINE applies for administration on the Est. of ISRAEL SHUBTRINE. Feb. 15, 1838. Granted May 7, 1838.

(p.142) Ordered that administrator of the Est. of SOLOMON METZGER, dec'd, do make good and sufficient titles to JOHN GEORGE MINGLEDORFF agreeable to the bond of the deceased. Mar. 1838.

(p.142) JOHN CHARLTON applies for administration on the Est. of ZACHARIAH WHITE, dec'd. Mar. 12, 1838. Granted May 7, 1838.

(p.142) Granted marriage license to JOSHUA MARTIN DASHER with HANNAH ELIZABETH GROVENSTEIN. Mar. 19, 1838

(p.142) Granted marriage license to WILLIAM BOUTWELL with REBECCA DUGGER. Apr. 14, 1838.

(p.143) Accts.: From here on, I will discontinue writing down accounts that are produced and examined, unless a new name comes up.

(p.144) Accounts

(p.145) Ordered that Clerk qualify HENRY WILSON, Adm. of the Est. of Peter KETTLES at the expiration of the citation. May 7, 1838.

(p.145) Ordered that JOHN B. BERRY have leave to sell a Negroe named ADAM belonging to OBADIAH BERRY. May 7, 1838.

(p.145) ALEXANDER H. McDONALD applies for adm. on the Est. of BENJAMIN SMITH. May 10, 1838. Granted July 2, 1838.

(p.146) HENRY WILSON applies for the adm. on the Est. of PETER KETTLES. May 11, 1838. Granted June 16, 1838.

(p.146) Granted marriage license to E. M. GARDNER with REBECCA KETTLES. May 14, 1838.

(p.146) MARY C. HARRISON applies for adm. on the Est. of EDWARD L. HARRISON. June 22, 1838.

(p.147) Last Will and Testament of JOHN CHRISTOPHER GNANN was admitted to record. July 2, 1838.

(p.147) Last Will and Testament of SOLOMON GNANN was admitted to record. July 2, 1838.

(p.147) ANN C. BURCKSTEINER made choice of child's part in the est. of her husband, SAMUEL BURCKSTEINER. July 2, 1838.

(p.147) MARGARET WEITMAN makes choice of child's part in the est. of her husband, SOLOMON WEITMAN. July 2, 1838.

(p.147) Ordered that NATHANIEL ZETTLER and ELIZABETH JONES be dismissed from the administration of the est. of PHILIP JONES. July 2, 1838.

(p.148) Granted marriage license to THOMAS HANNAH with MARTHA GRAHAM. Aug. 25, 1838.

(p.148) AMY BLAKE was appointed guardian of SARAH and AMANDA KETTLES. Sept. 3, 1838.

(p.149) SELITA DUNCAN GRAHAM, JESSE GRAHAM and ALEXANDER GRAHAM appeared and chose SELITA GRAHAM, their mother as guardian. Sept. 3, 1838.

(p.149) Ordered that John CHARLTON have leave to sell real est. of ZACH. WHITE and also 2 Negroes named ESTHER and JANE. Sept. 3, 1838.

(p.149) Ordered that NAOMI WEITMAN have leave to sell the real est. of MATTHEW WEITMAN, dec'd. and also the following Negroes, BILL RILER and her daughter. Sept. 3, 1838.

(p.149) Granted marriage license to ALEXANDER M. RAHN with JANE CAROLINE DASHER Sept. 15, 1838.

(p.150) Granted marriage license to TRION PACE. Sept. 18, 1838.

(p.150) Granted marriage license to RICHARD J. FETZER with SALOMI C. KEIFFER. Oct. 1, 1838.

(p.150) ALBERT PORTER applies for adm. on the Est. of DAVID HUMBART. OCT. 5, 1838. Granted Jan. 7, 1839.

(p.150) Granted marriage license to DAVID METZGER with SARAH GROUVER. Oct. 9, 1838.

(p.150) Granted marriage license to JOSHUA ZEIGLER with SUSANNAH DASHER. Oct. 31, 1838.

(p.150) Granted marriage license to OBADIAH EDWARDS with LYDIA WOMACK. Nov.2, 1838.

(p.150) Granted marriage license to JONATHAN SNYDER with ESTHER CAROLINE ARNSTORFF. Nov. 12, 1838.

(p.151) Granted marriage license to JOHN J. HINELY with SOLOMI GRINER. Nov. 15, 1838.

(p.151) Granted marriage license to JOHN SHUBTRINE with CHRISTIANNA GNANN. Nov. 17, 1838.

(p.151) Granted marriage license to JOSEPH A. EVERITT with GRACY ANN BLITCH. Nov. 29, 1838.

(p.151) MATTHEW HEIDT applies for adm. on the Est. of ABIAIL HEIDT, dec'd. of Chatham County. Nov. 28, 1838.

(p.151) Granted marriage license to HARMON E. WILLIAMS with SARAH HODGE. Dec. 6, 1838.

(p.151) Granted marriage license to THOMAS BLITCH with ANN JANE BROGDEN. Dec. 19, 1838.

(p.151) Granted marriage license to M. G. JOHNSON with PAMELIA ROOKS. Dec. 29, 1838.

(p.152) JAMES CRANE applies for dismission from his adm. on the est. of JOSEPH TAYLOR, dec'd. Jan. 7, 1839.

(p.152) Ordered that HEZEKIAH EVANS have leave to sell a part of the real est. of JOHN and MARY MOORE. Jan. 7, 1839.

(P.153) Accounts

(p.154) Ordered that THOMAS BREWER have leave to sell all real est. of JOHN M. GRAHAM, dec'd. Jan. 7, 1839.

(p.154) Ordered that HENRY A. WILSON have leave to sell the ferry and land attached to it known as the Sister Ferry for the benefit of heirs of PETER KETTLES, dec'd. Jan. 7, 1839.

(p.154) ALBERT G. PORTER appointed guardian of HARRIET HUMBART. Jan. 7, 1839.

(p.154) Granted marriage license to JOHN M. CLARK with ELIZABETH JONES. Jan. 9, 1839.

(p.154) Granted marriage license to JOHN WALDHOUR with CHRISTIANNA GNANN. Jan. 28, 1839.

(p.155) Granted marriage license to WILLIAM SHEEROUSE with ROSANNAH H. NEICE. Feb. 16, 1839.

(p.155) LEWIS WEITMAN applies for adm. on the est. of ISRAEL ARNSTORFF. Feb. 23, 1839. Granted Mar. 25, 1839.

(p.156) Granted marriage license to ALLEN WILSON with ANNIAH GRINER. Mar. 30, 1839.

(p.156) HARDY G. PITTS applies for adm. on the est. of ANN M. ZIPPERER. Mar. 30, 1839. Granted June 10, 1839.

(p.157) Granted marriage license to ISRAEL N. HINELY with ANN ABIGAIL SCRUGGS. Apr. 15, 1839.

(p.157) Granted marriage license to EDWARD A. MINGLEDORFF with JULIANN A. DASHER. Apr. 29, 1839.

(p.157) Granted marriage license to SAMUEL B. WHITE with MARY G. HARRISON. May 21, 1839.

(p.158) NAOMI WEITMAN, administrator of the est. of MATTHEW WEITMAN, applies for dismission on the est. of said MATTHEW WEITMAN. July 1, 1839.

(p.159) THOMAS H. BREWER applies for adm. on the est. of JOHN W. GRAHAM, dec'd. July 1, 1839.

(p.159) Granted marriage license to CHARLES HINELY with TABITHA HEIDT. July 8, 1839.

(p.159) Granted marriage license to GILBERT GILL with MARY PAGET. July 10, 1839.

(p.159) Granted marriage license to ELI KENNEDY with MARGARET ECHOLS. Aug. 20, 1839.

(p.159) JOHN McROY applies for adm. on the est. of RACHAEL McROY. Aug. 26, 1839.

(p.159) JESSE GRAHAM applies for adm. on the est. of JOHN GRAHAM with the Will annexed. Aug. 30, 1839. Granted Nov. 4, 1839.

(p.159) Granted marriage license to FREDERICK J. NEASE with ROSANNAH A. BURCK-STEINER. Aug. 31, 1839.

(p.160) JOHN M. LUCAS applies for dismission from his adm. on the Est. of WILLIAM McGAHAGIN and ELIZA McGAHAGIN. Sept. 2, 1839.

(p.160) Last Will and Testament of SOLOMON CRAMER was produced and proved by DAVID ZEIGLER. Sept. 2, 1839.

(p.160) Last Will and Testament of SEBLER GRAHAM was produced and proved by SAMUEL HODGES. Sept. 2, 1839.

(p.161) Appeared SELITA DUNCAN GRAHAM, ALEXANDER GRAHAM AND JANE ELIZABETH GRAHAM, who made choice of JESSE GRAHAM their guardian. Sept. 2, 1839.

(p.161) JACOB HINELY applies for adm. on the est. of ERNST M. GUYER. Sept. 6, 1839.

(p.161) Granted marriage license to JOHN L. MORGAN with ANN DOROTHY GNANN. Sept. 21, 1839.

(p.162) Appeared JEREMIAH BURCKSTEINER and made choice of FREDERICK I. NEASE as his guardian. Nov. 4, 1839.

120

(p.162) Granted division of the personal property of SAMUEL BURCKSTEINER, dec'd. Nov. 4, 1839.
(p.162) Last Will and Testament of ROBERT BURTON, dec'd. was produced and proved by CLEM POWERS. Nov. 4, 1839.
(p.162) Ordered that OBADIAH EDWARDS be appointed guardian of FREDERICK WOMACK. Nov. 4, 1839.
(p.162) Ordered that STEPHEN HESTON be appointed guardian of the property of FREDERICK WOMACK. Nov. 4, 1839.
(p.1630 Ordered that the Clerk take possession of the Est. of JOHN SAMUEL SECKINGER. November 4, 1839.
(p.163) Granted division of the Est. of WILLIAM McGAHAGIN. Nov. 4, 1839.
(p.163) Ordered that JENNY WOOLF be appointed guardian of minor heirs of JOHN WOOLF. Nov. 4, 1839.
(p.163) Granted marriage license to WILLIAM A. JENKINS with ELIZABETH WILLIAMS. Nov. 9, 1839.
(p.163) Granted marriage license to ZARA POWERS with ELVIRA ELKINS. Nov. 16, 1839.
(p.162) Granted marriage license to WILLIAM BOUTWELL with CLARA DAVIS. Nov. 28, 1839.
(p.164) ELIZA BURTON was qualified Executrix of the Last Will and Testament of ROBERT BURTON, Sr. dec'd. Dec. 11, 1839.
(p.164) CHARLES BURTON was qualified guardian of SIMEON BURTON. Dec. 11, 1839.
(p.164) CHARLES BURTON applies for adm. on the est. of JAMES BURTON, dec'd. Dec. 16, 1839.
(p.165) Last Will and Testament of William RYALS was produced and proved by JAMES MORGAN. Jan 6, 1840.
(p.165) STEPHEN HESTER appeared and was qualified guardian over the property of FREDERICK WOMACK. Jan. 6, 1840.
(p.165) SARAH BURTON was qualified guardian of MARSHA ELIZA and MARY ELVIRA BURTON. Jan. 6. 1840.
(p.166) JIMMY WOOLF was qualified guardian of CLEM and MARY, MILLY, MARCIA, JOHN, REBECCA, and ROBERT THOMAS WOOLF. Jan. 6, 1840.
(p.166.)Ordered that Clerk qualify CHARLES A. BURTON as Adm. of the Est. of JAMES BURTON at the expiration of the citation. Jan. 6, 1840.
(p.166) MATTHEW HEIDT, adm. of the est. of ABIAL HEIDT, applies for dismission. Jan. 6, 1840.
(p.166) Granted marriage license to JAMES W. MORGAN with SARAH D. RYALS. Jan. 18,1840.
(p.166) Granted marriage license to JOHN BENJ. GNANN with ANN ELIZABETH METZER. Feb. 1, 1840.
(p.168) Granted division of the est. of FREDERICK WOMACK, dec'd. Mar. 2, 1840.
(p.168) MARY S. METZGER, applies for guardianship of JAMES T.,WILLIAM W., and CAROLINE G. METZGER. Mar. 2, 1840.
(p.168) Granted marriage license to JOHN W. FETZER with LOUISA STROBHART. Apr. 6, 1840.
(p.169) Granted marriage license to JAMES CONNER with FRANCES ELVIRA JANE WOOD. May 12, 1840.
(p.169) Granted marriage license to GEORGE NEASE with MARGARET GNANN. May 27, 1840.
(p.170) JOHN CHARLTON, adm. of the est. of JOHN S. SECKINGER, dec'd. applies for leave to sell the real est. of said dec'd. Granted same day. July 6, 1840.
(p.170) JACOB HINELY, adm. of the est. of ERNST W. GUYER, applies for leave to sell the real est. of said dec'd. Granted same day. July 6, 1840.
(p.170) Jesse Graham, adm. of the est. of SELITA GRAHAM, applies for leave to sell the real est. of said dec'd. Granted same day. July 6,1840.
(p.171) Ordered that NAOMI WEITMAN be appointed guardian of JOHN LEWIS WEITMAN, July 6, 1840.

(p.171) Ordered that JOHN METZGER, adm. of the est. of SOLOMON METZGER, dec'd.
give up 3/4 of tract of land being the proportion that would fall to 3 minor children
and the same proportion of a Negro woman belonging to said est. unto Mrs. MARY A.
METZGER who is guardian of minor children. July 6, 1840.
   (p.171) JOHN METZGER applies for dismission on est. of SOLOMON METZGER. July 6,
1840. Granted May 4, 1841.
   (p.172) DAVID METZGER is appointed guardian of the minor child of GROUVER, dec'd.
July 6, 1840.
   (p.172) Granted marriage license to WILLIAM BOUTWELL with SABRINE DAVIS. July 22,
1840.
   (p.172) Granted marriage license to EDWARD W. BARNWELL with SARAH ANN LEE. Aug. 5,
1840.
   (p.172) Granted marriage license to SAMUEL HODGES with MARGARET ANN GRAHAM. Aug. 6,
1840.
   (p.172) JOHN METZGER applies for adm. on the est. of DAVID METZGER, dec'd. in behalf of kindred and creditors. Aug. 17, 1840. Granted Sept. 28, 1840.
   (p.173) JOHN CHARLTON applies for adm. on the est. of DAVID . Aug. 17, 1840.
   (p.173) MATTHEW HEIDT applies for adm. on the est. of HENRY G. BOWMAN, Aug. 24,
1840. Granted Sept. 26, 1840.
   (p.173) JOHN M. LUCAS applies for dismission on the est. of WILLIAM McGAHAGIN.
Sept. 2, 1840.
   (p.174) Ordered that Clerk have leave to grant adm. to JOHN METZGER on the Est.
of DAVID METZGER at the expiration of the citation. Sept. 2, 1840.
   Also that the same leave be granted to grant the adm. to MATTHEW HEIDT on the est.
of HENRY G. DOWMAN. Sept. 2, 1840.
   Last Will and Testament of JONATHAN RAHN was admitted to record. Sept. 2, 1840.
   Ordered that STEPHEN HESTER have leave to sell one horse and stock of cattle for
benefit of FREDERICK WOMACK. Sept. 2, 1840.
   (p.175) Granted marriage license to JOHN CLEARY with IALES BLACK. Sept. 25,1840.
   Granted marriage license to WM. ARNSTOFF with ELIZABETH MOORE. Oct. 19, 1840.
   (p.176) ROBERT BARTON was qualified Exec. of the Last Will and Testament of
ROBERT BURTON, Sr., dec'd. Nov. 2, 1840.
   Granted marriage license to SOLOMON EXLEY with HANNAH ELIZABETH REISER. Nov. 11,
1840.
   Granted marriage license to JAMES ARMSTRONG COURNOISE with MARY ANN OLCOTT CHARLTON.
Nov. 12, 1840.
   (p.177) Granted marriage license to GODHIEF I. NEASE with MARY SHUPTRINE. Nov. 26,
1840.
   THOMAS R. HINES applies for adm. on the est. of MARTHA HINES, dec'd. Nov. 26, 1840.
Granted Jan. 4, 1841.
   FREDERICK GNANN and CLETUS GNANN applies for adm. on the est. of JACOB GNANN, Sr.
dec'd. Dec. 3, 1840. Granted Jan. 4, 1841.
   Granted Marriage license to ISAAC HODGES with FLORA GNANN. Dec. 11, 1840.
   Granted marriage license to MOORE BLITCH with MARY ANN COCHRAN. Dec. 26, 1840.
   (p.178) JINNY WOOLF applies for leave to sell 2 lots of land to wit. No. 523.17
and No. 274.2 in the Cherokee County. Jan. 4, 1841.
   (p.179) Ordered that Clerk qualify MARH HUST and JOHN HURST admix. and adm. on the
est. of WM. HURST, dec'd. at expiration of citation. Jan. 4, 1841.
   HENRY M. WILSON applies for dismission from acting as adm. on the est. of PETER
KETTLES. Jan. 4, 1841.
   ARCHIBALD WILKINS was relieved of all further liabilities concerning the guardianship of MARY PORTER by GUILDFORD DUDLY. Jan 4, 1841.
   Ordered that after the qualification of the admix. and adm. of WM. HURST dec'd,
that they have leave to sell the perishable property of said est. Jan. 4, 1841.
   (p.180) MARY HUST, widow and JOHN HURST applies for adm. on the Est. of WM. HURST.
Jan. 7, 1841.

(p.180) Granted marriage license to NATHANIEL SHEEROUSE with SARAH ELIZ. ARNSDORFF.
Jan. 21, 1841.
    Granted marriage license to JOHN J. HINELY with HANNAH GUYER. Feb. 8, 1841.
    Granted marriage license to JOSHUA GRINER with ELEANOR WILSON. Feb. 13, 1841.
    WILLIAM RAHN and JOHN WILSON applies for dismission on est. of JOHNATHAN RAHN.
Mar. 1, 1841.
    (p.180a) Granted marriage license to ZACHARIAH W. BOWMAN to ELIZABETH ANN LEWIS.
Mar. 1, 1841.
    Granted marriage license to BENJ. GROVENSTEIN with MARY ELIZA ASH. Mary. 16. 1841.
    Granted marriage license to PETER ROGERS and GRACE WHEELER. April 8, 1841
    Granted marriage license to STEPHEN HESTOR with SALOMI HEIDT. Apr. 22, 1841.
    (p.181) Executors of the est. of ROBERT BURTON, dec'd. have leave to sell the real
est. of said est. May 3, 1841.
    (p.182) SUSAN S. RAHN made choice of CHRISTOPHER R. REISER as her guardian. May 3,
1841.
    ELBERT GNANN, GEORGE BERGAMN GNANN, and JANE ELIZA GNANN made choice of their
mother, CHRISTIANNA GNANN, as their guardian. May 4, 1841.
    Ordered that SARAH METZGER be appointed guardian of her child, VALETIA B. Also
that she be appointed guardian of JOHN DAVID GROUVER. May 4, 1841.
    Court appointed Clerk guardian of the children of SOLOMON METZGER. May 4, 1841.
    Granted division of the est. of DAVID METZGER. May 4, 1841
    Granted marriage license to THOMAS BLITCH with ANN MARLOW. June 9, 1841.
    (p.184) Granted division of the est. of JACOB GNANN. July 5, 1841.
    Last Will and Testament of STEPHEN TOLLOS was admitted to record. July 5, 1841.
    Ordered that JOHN McROY have leave to sell a tract of land lying in Henry County
belonging to the est. of RACHEL McROY, July 5, 1841.
    (p.185) JOHN J. PITTS applies for adm. on the est. of HARDY G. PITTS. Granted
same day. July 5, 1841.
    Last Will and Testament of JOHN DUGGER was admitted to record. July 5, 1841.
    MARY HURST made choice of child's support of the est. of her husband. July 5, 1841.
    MARY HURST appointed guardian of her children MARTHA ANN and FELIX HURST. July 5,
1841.
    Granted marriage license to JOHN B. WILSON with JANE A. EDWARDS, July 6, 1841.
    Granted marriage license to JOHN CRAWFORD with MINNY NEWMANS, July 22, 1841.
    (p.186) Granted marriage license to LUKE WILSON with ANN CATHARINE GRINER. Aug. 10,
1841.
    Granted marriage license to JOHN T. TULLY with ELIZA ANN GRAHAM. Aug. 24, 1841.
    Granted marriage license to CUYLER W. YOUNG with SARAH McDONALD. Aug. 31, 1841
    (p.187) Granted JOHANNAH ZITTROUR Leave to sell a Negroe boy named AARON 16 years
old. Sept. 6, 1841.
    (p.188) JAMES RAHN, adm. on the est. of SAMUEL BURCKSTEINER, applies to be dismissed
from said est. Sept. 6, 1841. Granted
    JOHN METZGER applies for dismission from the adm. on the est. of SOLOMON METZGER.
Granted. Sept. 6, 1841.
    Granted MARY HURST and JOHN HURST leave to sell 17 negores and lands belonging to
the est. of WM. HURST, dec'd. Sept. 6, 1841.
    WM. H. DUDLEY made choice of his mother as his guardian. Sept. 6, 1841.
    (p. 189) Granted marriage license to WM. BLITCH with ANN SPEIR. Sept. 20, 1841.
    SOLOMON EXLEY applies for adm. on the est. of LUKE EXLEY. Sept. 22, 1841. Granted
Nov. 1, 1841.
    Granted marriage license to DAVID ____ with   P.ABIALIS.Sept. 25,1841
    HARRY DUGGER applies for adm. on the est. of HUGH DUGGER, dec'd. Sept. 27, 1841.
Granted Nov. 1, 1841.
    Granted marriage license to JOHN KESLER with SARAH ANN ZIPPERER. Sept. 27, 1841.
    Granted marriage license to EDWARD MURRAY with SELINA WALLS, Nov. 1, 1841.
    (p.190) SHADROCK GROVENSTEIN made choice of BENJ. GROVENSTEIN as her guardian.
Nov. 1, 1841.

(p. 190) H. FURNY was qualified guardian of   WILSON orp. of ELIAS WILSON. Nov. 1, 1841.

Granted marriage license to EDWIN McROY with MARTHA JANE EDWARDS. Nov. 1, 1841.

Granted marriage license to JOSEPH MILLIS with MARTH PERIGREE. Nov. 29, 1841.

(p.191) Granted marriage license to GEORGE ARNSTOFF with JINNY WOOLF. Dec. 4, 1841.

Granted marriage license to EPHRAIM SECKINGER with LYDIA C. SECKINGER. Dec. 9, 1841.

Granted marriage license to WM. TORRESTORS with MARY T. HARRISON. Dec. 23, 1841.

(p.191) Granted marriage license to Mr. GEORGE ARNSTORFF with Miss JINNY WOOLF. Dec. 4, 1841.

Granted marriage license to Mr. EPHRAIM SECKINGER with Miss LYDIA C. SECKINGER. Dec. 9, 1841.

(p.191a) JOHN METZGER, adm. of the Est. of DAVID METZGER dec'd, applied for Letters Dismissory on said estate. Jan. 3, 1842. Granted July 4, 1842.

Letters Dismissory granted WILLIAM RAHN and JOHN WILSON. Jan. 3, 1842.

FREDERICK GNANN and CLETUS GNANN applied for Letters Dismissory on the Est. of JACOB GNANN, dec'd. Jan. 3, 1842. Granted July 4, 1842.

Ordered that the Commissioners of the Academy of Effingham County, to wit: C. POWERS, W. BIRD, JOHN BERRY, W. SPEIR, and C. E. TREUTLEN be appointed Commissioners of the Poor School fund for the County of Effingham. Jan. 3, 1842.

MARY DUGGER made choice of ROBERT J. MINGLEDORFF as her guardian. Jan. 3, 1842.

(p.192) JOHN HURST and MARY HURST, admin. and adminix. of the Est. of WILLIAM HURST, dec'd, applied for Letters Dismissory on said estate. Jan. 3, 1842. Granted Mar. 2, 1842.

Granted marriage license to Mr. DAVID GRINER with Miss CAROLINE GRIFFEN. Feb. 26, 1842.

Granted marriage license to Mr. JOHN CRAWFORD with Miss MINNEY NEWMAN. Mar. 2, 1842.

Granted marriage license to MILTON POWERS with Miss WILSON. Mar. 29, 1842.

(p.193) last Will and Testament of DAVID GUGEL was produced and proved. Mar. 2, 1842.

(p.194) Last Will and Testament of HENRY WILSON was produced and proved. Mar. 2, 1842.

HANNAH GROVENSTEIN asked to be dismissed from Executrix of the Est. of HENRY GROVENSTEIN, dec'd. Mar. 2, 1842. Granted Jan. 2, 1843.

Ordered that Clerk have leave to grant administration to FRANKLIN GRIFFIN on the Est. of JAMES GRIFFIN. Mar. 2, 1842. Granted May 15, 1842

(p.195) JOHN CHARLTON granted administration on the Est. of DANIEL SHULTZ, dec'd. Mar. 2, 1842.

Granted marriage license to Mr. WALDON GRIFFEN, Jr. to Miss JUNE MICKORY. May 1, 1842.

Granted marriage license to JAMES DOOIS with Miss BARNARD DENNY. June 18, 1842.

(p.196) Granted marriage license to Mr. WILLIAM RAHN with Miss HENRIETTA B. MYERS. Aug. 5, 1842.

(p.198) Ordered that the interest of the money belonging to the minor heirs of SOLOMON METZER and also the hire of the following Negroes to wit: EVELINE, MARY, ISRAEL and HANNAH be paid to MARY METZGER, widow of SOLOMON METZGER for the school and maintenance of her three children JAMES, WILLIAM, and CAROLINE. Sept. 5, 1842

Ordered that DAVID GRIFFIN be appointed adm. of the Est. of JAMES GRIFFIN, dec'd. Sept. 5, 1842, Granted Sept. 12, 1842.

(p.199) Granted marriage license to Mr. ELBERT GNANN with Miss SALOMI ARNSTORFF. Sept. 22, 1842.

Last Will and Testament of CHRISTIAN DASHER, dec'd, was produced and proved. Nov. 14, 1842.

ELIZABETH S. DASHER made choice of WILLIAM B. DASHER as her guardian. Nov. 14, 1842.

(p.200) CAROLINE M. HEIDT, widow, applied for adm. on the Est. of SOLOMON HEIDT, dec'd. Nov. 9, 1842.

(p.200) Granted marriage license to WALLACE BEBEE with Miss MARY SECKINGER. Nov. 20, 1842.
Gtd. marriage license to____ BLITCH with Miss FRANCIS CAROLINE EDWARDS. Nov. 1842.
(p.201) Ordered that Clerk qualify GEORGIA A. ASH adm. of the Est. of HENRY A. BURTON. Jan. 2, 1842. Granted May 24, 1843.
Ordered that Clerk qualify CAROLINE M. HEIDT, adminx. of the Est. of COLOMON HEIDT. Jan. 2, 1843. Granted Jan. 9, 1843.
(p.202) Granted marriage license to Mr. JOHN THEOPHILUS ZIPPERER with Miss LOUISA M. KESLER. Jan 9, 1843.
Granted marriage license to ISBY DANIELS with LYDIA ANN BOWMAN. Feb. 2, 1843.
ZACHARIAH ZIPPERER applied for adm. on the Est. of JAMES ZIPPERER, dec'd. Feb. 4, 1843. Granted Sept. 20, 1843.
Granted marriage license to DAVID SMITH with ELIZABETH EDWARDS. Feb. 8, 1843.
Granted marriage license to ELIHU WILSON with ANN WARREN. Feb. 16, 1843.
Granted marriage license to JOHN BURCKSTEINER with ANN. W. WEITMAN. Feb. 28, 1843.
(p.203) ALBERT S. PORTER applied for adm. on the Est. of L. ANN REISER. Mar. 6, 1843.
Granted marriage license to JOSEPH MORRELL with ___RAHN. Mar. 24,1843
Granted marriage license to S. GROVENSTEIN with SUSANNAH KEIFFER. Mary 24, 1843.
Granted marriage license to STEPHEN F. KEEBLER with ELIZA ROGERS. April 17, 1843.
(p.204) AMY BLAKE objects to ALBERT G. PORTER on his applying for adm. on the estate of LUNEXER ANN REISSER. May 1, 1843.
(p.206) Granted MARY HURST leave to purchase two Negroes amounting to $979.00. May 1, 1843.
Last Will and Testament of CHRISTIAN RYALS was admitted to record. May 1, 1843.
JOHN R. MORGAN was appointed guardian of MARY M. RYALS. May 1, 1843.
CHESLEY DUGGER was appointed guardian of RICHARD HINELY, VIRGINIA HINELY, and SARAH HINELY. May 1, 1843.
HENRY J. WILSON applied for adm. on the est. of JOHN B. WILSON. Aug. 21, 1843.
(p.207) Granted division of the Est. of HENRY A. BURTON, dec'd. Sept. 2, 1843.
(p.208) Granted marriage license to SAMULE J. SECKINGER with ELEANOR C. GUYER. Sept. 26, 1843.
Granted marriage license to HENRY J. TULLIS with REBECCA FUTRELL. October 14, 1843.
Granted marriage license to GEORGE HALL with GRACE CRAWFORD. Nov. 3, 1843.
(p.209) Granted marriage license to HENRY J. STROBBAR with HENRIETTA J. BEVILL. November 18, 1843.
(p.210) HENRY J. STROBBAR applied for adm. on the Est. of JOHN D. STROBBAR. Jan. 23 1844. Granted April 20, 1844.
Granted marriage license to DAVID SNOOKS with REBECCA RYALS. Jan. 31, 1844.
Granted marriage license to JOSHUA HINELY with MARTHA BRYAN. Feb. 5, 1844.
Granted marriage license to JOHN C. MINGLEDORFF with ELIZABETH S. DASHER. Feb. 6, 1844.
Granted marriage license to WILLIAM DUGGER with SARAH ANN SHEEROUSE. March 11, 1844.
Granted marriage license to KELAND S. BLITCH with MARICE A. HURST. Mar. 18,1844.
Granted marriage license to RICHARD J. EXLEY with MARY ANN REISSER. Mar. 25, 1844.
(p.212) Granted marriage license to WILLIAM AMBROSE with KIZIAH AMBROSE. Mar. 28, 1844.
Dr. J. R. SAUSSY applied for adm. on the Est. of DAVID GUGEL. Apr. 2, 1844. Granted May 6, 1844, and an appeal entered by Executor.
Granted marriage license to HENRY HURST with NANCY BOGREE. Apr. 22, 1844.
JOHN CHARLTON caveats the application of J. R. SAUSSY for adm. on the Est. of DAVID GUGEL. Apr. 22, 1844.
(p.213) Granted JOHN R. MORGAN dismission on the Est. of MARY M. RIALS. May 6, 1844.
LAURINA STROBBAR and ALEXANDER STROBBAR made choice of HENRY J. STROBBAR as their guardian. May 6, 1844.

(p.214) Granted marriage license to WILLIAM B. KESLER with CATHERIN ZIPPERER. June 7, 1844.

Granted marriage license to SHEPPARD DAVIS with DELIA WILSON. June 11, 1844.

Granted marriage license to WHERRY COUSETE to ANN PITTS. June 20, 1844.

SAMUEL WHITE applied for adm. on the est. of JAMES WHITE and applied for Letters of Collection on said estate. Granted adm. Sept. 2, 1844.

(p.215) Granted marriage license to J. W. OLIVER with MARY DUDLEY. Aug. 21, 1844.

Granted marriage license to W. B. STROBBAR with JANE C. GNANN. Aug. 22, 1844.

Granted marriage license to RODERICK H. WALLS with MARGARET D. PITTS. Aug. 28, 1844.

(p.216) Last Will and Testament was produced and proved. Sept. 2, 1844.

GEORGE A. ASH was appointed guardian of MARY BURTON, minor heir of HENRY A. BURTON, dec'd. Sept. 2, 1844.

Granted marriage license to ALEXANDER CRAMER with MARGARET WALDHAUER. Sept. 9, 1844.

Granted marriage license to WILLIAM BIRD with ELLEN G. ZETTLER. Sept. 24, 1844.

Granted marriage license to SAMUEL HEIDT with MARY DUGGER. October 15, 1844.

Granted marriage license to JOHN KING with JULIE HARPER. October 14, 1844.

Granted marriage license to JOHN I. REISSER with EMILY DASHER. October 22, 1844.

(p.217) Granted marriage license to GEORGE I. BRIDGES with ELIZA OWEN. Nov. 23, 1844.

WILLIAM HESTER applied for adm. on the Est. of JOSEPH HESTER, dec'd Dec. 3, 1844.

Granted marriage license to STEPHEN DOUGLASS with KEIFIA AMBROSE. Dec. 11, 1844.

Granted marriage license to JESSE A. LEE with ANN EDWARDS. January 6, 1844.

Granted marriage license to RICHARD B. BORES with MARGARET BURGESS. Jan. 11, 1845.

(p.219) Last Will and Testament of JOSEPH HESTER was rec'd. . Jan. 13, 1845.

Granted the division of the Est. of JAMES GRIFFEN. Jan. 13, 1845.

WALDON GRIFFEN was appointed guardian of the minor children of JAMES GRIFFEN. Jan. 13, 1845.

MARY METZGER was appointed guardian of the minor heirs of SOLOMON METZGER, dec'd. Jan. 13, 1845.

JEREMIAH MULLET appointed guardian of VALETA B. METZGER minor of DAVID METZGER, dec'd. Jan. 13, 1845.

DAVID HELMLY was appointed to take the census of Effingham County. Jan. 13, 1845.

(p.220) Granted marriage license to FREDERICK HINELY with ELIZABETH WISENBAKER. January 18, 1845.

Granted marriage license to JAMES HAYS with ESTHER GRIFFEN. January 20, 1845.

Issued Letters guardianship to JAMES EDWARDS as guardian of ANTHONY P. EDWARDS... Also to WALDRUM C. GRIFFEN as guardian of MARTHA GRIFFEN and to WALDRUM GRIFFEN as guardian of MARIA GRIFFEN, JAMES GRIFFEN, and MARGARET GRIFFEN.

Granted marriage license to WILLIAM G. MORGAN with ABIGAIL F. GNANN. Feb. 20, 1845.

Granted marriage license to GEORGE W. SMITH with MARIA A. WOOLF. March 8, 1845.

Granted marriage license to PHILIP HORNING with DEBORAH CARTER. March 27, 1845.

(p.221) Granted marriage license to JAMES I. HEIDT with ANN R. HORNING. Apr. 9, 1845.

Granted marriage license to JOHN I. HINELY with DOROTHY GUYER. Apr. 22, 1845.

DAVID A. METZGER and FREDERICK BACKLY applied for adm. on the Est. of JOHN JACOB METZGER, dec'd. Apr. 23, 1845.

Granted marriage license to OBADIAH EDWARDS, JR. with LUCRETIA G. PLATT. Apr. 29, 1845.

Granted marriage license to GORDON BEBEE with MARGARET M. WEITMAN. May 3, 1845.

(p.222) The Last Will and Testament of GOTTHIEF I. ZITTROUR was ordered to be recorded. May 5, 1845.

(p.223) W. W. WILSON appointed as guardian of the orphan child of ISHU SECKINGER. May 5, 1845.

Granted adm. on the est. of JOHN JACOB METZGER, dec'd, to DAVID A. METZGER and FREDERICK BACKLEY. May 27, 1845.

(p.223) JESSE LEE applied for adm. on the est. of JESSE LEE, dec'd. July 5, 1845. Granted July 7, 1845.

THOMAS HURST and JESSE HURST applied for adm. on the est. of JESSE LEE, SR., dec'd. June 10, 1845.

Granted marriage license to WILLIAM HALLMAN with SARAH P. HARRIS. June 20, 1845.

(p.224) Last Will and Testament of SPIER BLITCH was produced and ordered to be recorded. July 7, 1845.

(p.225) Last Will and Testament of VALENTINE KESLER was produced and proven. July 7, 1845.

GEORGE BOSTON applied for guardianship for his two children MARGARET K. BOSTON and WILLIAM K. BOSTON. July 7, 1845.

Last Will and Testament of MARY GOUNDERS was produced and proven. July 7, 1845.

Granted marriage license to W. V. N. JOHNSON with FRANCIS A. McROY. July 19, 1845.

Granted marriage license to W. WILLIAMS with DICY ANN NEWTON. July 29, 1845.

Granted marriage license to RICHARD H. CLARK with HARRIET G. CHARLTON. Aug. 7, 1845.

Granted marriage license to JOHN M. CAINS with HARRIET R. SMITH. Aug. 15, 1845.

(p.226) ELIZABETH SNIDER, widow of JONATHAN SNIDER, a Revolutionary Soldier, proved before the Court that her husband died on the 7th day of Sept. 1835.

Last Will and Testament of THOMAS H. BREWER was produced and proven. Sept. 1, 1845.

Granted marriage license to GEORGE MOTTLEDER (?) with MARY ANN WEITMAN. Nov. 19, 1845.

(p.227) JAMES LOVE applies for adm. on the est. of JAMES HUDSON, dec'd. Dec. 7, 1845. Granted Jan. 13, 1846.

GEORGE ASH, Adm. on the est. of HENRY A. BURTON, dec'd, applied for dismission on said est. Jan. 12, 1846. Granted Sept. 8, 1846.

(p.228) Ordered that EDWIN ZITTROUR and RICHARD ZITTROUR have leave to sell real est. of GOTTHIEF ZITTROUR. Jan. 12, 1846.

Ordered that JESSE LEE, JR. sell 2 tracts of land in Effingham County and one in Bulloch County and one Negroe man named MONDAY, he having complied with the law. Jan. 12, 1846.

(p.229) Last Will and Testament of WILLIAM BIRD, SR. was admitted to record. Jan. 12, 1846.

BRADFORD JONES applied for adm. on the Est. of GUILDFORD DUDLEY, dec'd. Jan. 13, 1846. Court decided he was not entitled to adm. having considered the reasons stated in the Caveat.

Granted marriage license to Dr. T. SMITH with MARIA VIVY. Jan. 22, 1846.

JAMES W. OLIVER cateats the application of BRADFOR JONES on the Est. of GUILDFORD DUDLEY, dec'd. Feb. 6, 1846. Granted.

(p.230) Granted marriage license to WILLIAM B. HARMS with UNITY E. WOOLFE. Feb. 7, 1846.

(p.232) Granted marriage license to JAMES A. ERNST with Miss GNANN. Feb. 26, 1846.

(p.233) Granted marriage license to M. G. L. GNANN with Miss GNANN. March 23, 1846.

Granted marriage license to JOEL BARRET with GEORGIA ANN ELKINS.

JACKSON L. SMITH of Sumter County appointed CHARLES A. BURTON OF Burk County as his attorney for his benefit to ask, demand, sue, GEORGE A. ASH for whatever is due him from the est. of HENRY A. BURTON, dec'd. Dec. 9, 1845.

(p.234) SAVANNAH, Jan. 21, 1846. Receipt from GEORGE A. ASH to CHARLES A. BURTON, attorney for J. L. SMITH for the sum of $317.05.

SAVANNAH, Jan. 6, 1846. Receipt from GEORGE A. ASH to A. S. C. HORNE for $277.21.

EDWIN McROY applies for adm. on the Est. of JOHN P. McROY and JACKSON McROY. May 6, 1846. Granted July 4, 1846.

Granted marriage license to PAUL A. TULLIS with MARTHA P. BLITCH. April 25, 1846.

Granted marriage license to CHRISTIAN EDWARD ZIPPERER with SALOMI SECKINGER. April 27, 1846.

Granted marriage license to W. B. DASHER with ANN ELIZA GNANN. June 12, 1846.

(p.234) Granted marriage license to SIMEON KEEN with CAROLINE McROY. June 27, 1846.

(p.235) JOHN CHARLTON, Executor of the Est. of DAVID GUGEL, dec'd, applied for dismission on said est. July 4, 1846.

Last Will and Testament of THOMAS WYLLY, SR., dec'd, was admitted to record. July 4, 1846.

Last Will and Testament of BENJ. BLITCH was admitted to record. July 4, 1846.

Last Will and Testament of HANNAH WEITMAN was admitted to record. July 4, 1846.

Last Will and Testament of CATHARINE BURCKSTEINER was admitted to record. July 4, 1846.

G. W. BOSTON appointed as guardian of CAROLINE G. KING and ELIZABETH G. KING. July 4, 1846.

(p.237) Granted division of the personal property of W. KING. July 4, 1846.

Granted marriage license to WILLIAM JACOB MILLER with MARY ANN HINELY. July 27, 1846.

Granted marriage license to JOHN COONEY with SARAH ANN McROY. July 29, 1846.

GIDEON C. BEVILL and CLEM POWERS applied for adm. on the Est. of PETER SCHERMER-HORN, dec'd. Aug. 6, 1846. Granted Sept. 7, 1846.

(p.239) CHRISTOPHER GNANN applied for adm. on the est. of ANDREW GNANN. dec'd. Sept. 10, 1846. Granted Oct. 19, 1846.

Mrs. LOUISA M. K. BACKLEY, widow, applied for adm. on the est. of FREDERICK BACKLEY. Sept. 10, 1846. Granted Nov. 7, 1846.

CLETUS RAHN applied for adm. on the est. of GOTTHIEF SECKINGER, dec'd. Sept. 24, 1846. Granted Nov. 7, 1846.

CLETUS RAHN applied for adm. on the est. of GOTTHIEF ARNSDORFF, dec'd. Sept. 24, 1846. Granted Nov. 7, 1846.

THOMAS ELKINS applied for adm. on the est. of P. N. ELKINS, dec'd. Oct. 1846. Granted Nov. 7, 1846.

(p.240) GEORGE NEASE applied for guardianship of BENJAMIN NEASE. Oct. 5, 1846. Granted same day.

Granted division of the personal property of HERMAN ELKINS, Oct. 5, 1846.

Granted marriage license to ELIAS GROUVER with SUSANAH SNIDER. Oct. 17, 1846.

Rec'd Jan. 10, 1846 of CHARLES A. BURTON, adm. of the est. of JAMES BURTON, dec'd. $373.04 to A. S. C. HORN.

Rec'd of CHARLES A. BURTON, adm. of the est. of JAMES BURTON $350.00 to J. L. SMITH.

(p.241) Granted marriage license to JOSIAH W. HEIDT with JULIA ELIZA MILLER. November 2, 1846.

LENORA CAROLINE METZGER made choice of JAMES RAHN as her guardian. Nov. 7, 1846.

REBECCA ELIZABETH METZGER choice JOHN B. BERRY as her guardian. Nov. 7, 1846.

Court appointed JOHN B. BERRY guardian of AMELIA METZGER. Nov. 7, 1846.

(p.242) Last Will and Testament of EMANUEL SHEEROUSE was produced and proven. November 7, 1846.

Granted marriage license to DANIEL C. SHUPTRINE with CAROLINE NEWTON. Nov. 16, 1846.

Granted marriage license to CALVIN WOOLF with SABRINE HODGE. Jan. 4, 1847.

Granted marriage license to GEORGE W. BOSTON with LAURA L. STROBBAR. Nov. 25, 1846.

(p.243) Granted division of the personal property of JOHN D. STROBBAR. Jan. 11, 1847.

Last Will and Testament of JOHN C. MILLER was produced and proven. Jan. 11, 1847.

Last Will and Testament of SOLOMON HINELY was produced and proven. Jan. 11, 1847.

(p.244) ALEXANDER STROBBAR, orphan of J. D. STROBBAR, made choice of HENRY J. STROBBAR as his guardian. Jan. 11, 1847.

LOUISA EVELINE GNANN, orphan of SOLOMON GNANN, made choice of JOHN GEORGE NEACE as her guardian. Jan. 11, 1847.

Court appointed JOHN GEORGE NEACE guardian of JOHN ANDREW and GEORGE BENJAMIN GNANN. Jan. 11, 1847.

SAMUEL G. BOWMAN was appointed guardian of JUNE ELIZABETH BOWMAN and HENRIETTA BOWMAN, minors of HENRY G. BOWMAN. Jan. 11, 1847.

128

(p.244) Granted marriage license to WILJANETTE (?) SECKINGER to SYDIA R. SHEEROUSE. Feb. 8, 1847.

(p.245) Rec'd Jan. 21, 1847 from BENJ. GNANN, exec. of the Est. of SOLOMON GNANN, dec'd, the sum of $698.94 in full amount what is due minor heirs of SOLOMON GNANN, to wit: LOUISA EVELINE, JOHN ANDREW and BENJ. GNANN.   GEO. NEACE, Guardian.

BENJ. GNANN, Exec. of the Est. of SOLOMON GNANN, dec'd. applied for dismission on said Est. Mar. 1, 1847.

THOMAS WALDHAUER applied for adm. on the Est. of ALEXANDER CRAMER. March 1, 1847. Granted April 17, 1847.

Granted marriage license to JOSHUA KESLER with LOUISA E. GNANN. Mar. 9, 1847.

(p.246) FREDERICK HINELY applied for adm. on the Est. of DAVID HELMLY. Mar. 25, 1847. Granted May 4, 1847.

GEORGE W. BOSTON applied for adm. on the Est. of CAROLINE KINE. Mar. 25, 1847. Granted May 4, 1847.

LEWIS HINELY applied for adm. on the Est. of SOLOMON HEIDT. Mar. 25, 1847. Granted May 4, 1847.

Granted license to JAMES DEULOU with LOUISA McCALL. March 29, 1847.

Granted marriage license to WILLIAM TAWCETT with MARTHA A. FARMER. May 1, 1847.

(p.247) EDWIN ZITTROUR and RICHARD E. ZITTROUR, Exec. of the Est. of GODHIEFF ZITTROUR applied for dismission on said est. May 4, 1847.

JOHN G. KESLER with granted guardianship of ISRAEL KESLER, orphan of VALENTINE KESLER. May 4, 1847.

WILLIAM KESLER was appointed guardian of ELBERT KESLER, orphan of VALENTINE KESLER. May 4, 1847.

JOHN T. ZIPPERER granted guardianship of FREDERICK KESLER, orphan of VALENTINE KESLER. May 4, 1847.

(p.248) RICHARD ZITTROUR was granted guardianship of EPHRAIM KESLER, orphan of VALENTINE KESLER. May 4, 1847.

JAMES RAHN was granted guardianship of JOSEPH KESLER, orphan of VALENTINE KESLER. May 4, 1847.

PHILIP HORNING granted guardianship of JUNE BOWMAN and HENRIETTA BOWMAN, orphans of HENRY G. BOWMAN, dec'd. May 4, 1847.

Granted marriage license to JEREMIAH MULLETT with MARY ANN PORTER. May 11, 1847.

CLETUS RAHN, adm, of the Est. of GOTHIEF ARNSTORFF applied for dismission on said est. July 5, 1847.

CLETUS RAHN adm. of the Est. of GOTTHIEF SECKINGER applied for dismission on said est. July 5, 1847.

(p.249) Last Will and Testament of DANIEL DAMPUR was produced and proven. July 5, 1847.

Last Will and Testament of DAVID P. SNOOKS was admitted to record. July 5, 1847.

JAMES OSGOOD A. CLARK, minor of JOSIAH H. CLARK chose Rev. GEORGE R. WRIGHT as his guardian. Also, guardian of JOSIAH H. CLARK, minor of JOSIAH CLARK, dec'd. July 5, 1847.

ROBERT SCHLEY applied for adm. on the est. of ROBERT BOWMAN, dec'd. July 8, 1847. Granted Sept. 6, 1847.

OBADIAH EDWARDS applied for adm. on the est. of WILLIAM WOMACK, dec'd. July 27, 1847. Granted Sept. 6, 1847.

MOSELLE BOURQUOIS, widow, applied for adm. on the est. of ROBERT H. BOURQUOIS, dec'd. July 31, 1847. Granted Sept. 6, 1847.

(p.250) Rec'd June 25, 1847 from CHRISTIAN WISENBAKER, Exec. of the est. of HANNAH WEITMAN, dec'd, the sum of $8.00 being 1/3 share of the amount of said est. R. E. ZITTROUR.

Rec'd June 23, 1847 from CHRISTIAN WISENBAKER, Exec. of the est. of HANNAH WEITMAN, dec'd, the sum of $8.00 being 1/3 share of the amount of said est. JAMES RAHN.

Rec'd June 23, 1847 from CHRISTIAN WISENBAKER, Exec. of the est. of HANNAH WEITMAN, dec'd, the sum of $8.00 being 1/3 share of the amount of said est.

(p.250) JOSIAH H. CLARK chose GEORGE R. WRIGHT as his guardian. July 24, 1847. GEORGE R. WRIGHT was qualified guardian Sept. 4, 1847.

(p.251) BENJ. GNANN, SR., Exec. of the est. of SOLOMON GNANN, dec'd, applied for dismission from said est. Sept. 6, 1847. Granted same day.

(p.252) JOHN DASHER applied for adm. on the est. of EPHRAIM MILLER, dec'd. Sept. 9, 1847. Granted Nov. 20, 1847.

(p.253) Granted marriage license to HENRY S. HAWLEY with ELLEN M. KELLOGG. Sept. 25, 1847.

DANIEL REINSHART applied for adm. on the est. of JAMES S. OLCOTT, dec'd. Oct. 8, 1847.

Granted marriage license to JONATHAN SHEEROUSE with ELIZABETH FREYERMUTH. Nov. 8, 1847.

DAVID A. METZGER, adm. of the est. of JOHN JACOB METZGER, applied for dismission from said est. Nov. 20, 1847.

CHARLES A. BURTON, adm. of the est. of JAMES BURTON, dec'd, applied for dismission from said est. Nov. 20, 1847.

(p.254) JOSHUA DASHER made application to be appointed guardian of AMELIA METZGER, minor of JOHN J. METZGER, dec'd, Nov. 20, 1847.

Granted marriage license to PAUL R. DUGGER with MARTHA ANN HURST. Nov. 22, 1847.

Granted marriage license to GEORGE B. GNANN with REBECCA DASHER. Dec. 11, 1847.

(p.255) Granted marriage license to SAMUEL A. BLOUNT with ANN D. COLSON. Dec. 11, 1847.

T. R. WYLLY, applied for adm. on the est. of NAOMI WYLLY. Dec. 28, 1847. Granted Mar. 6, 1848.

Rec'd of ARCHIBALD GUYTON, adm. of the est. of HERMAN ELKINS, dec'd, the sum of $2839.92 being the full amount of LAWRENCE T. ELKINS and GEORGIA ANN ELKINS part of the personal property of said est. Nov. 26. 1836.

(p.256) L. N. K. BACKLEY, adm. of the est. of FREDERICK BACKLEY, dec'd, applied for dismission on the said est. Jan. 10, 1848.

Last Will and Testament of CATHARINE PAVERY, dec'd, was admitted to record. Jan. 10, 1848.

Granted marriage license to HENRY O. MORTON with BELINDIE CAROLINE MORGAN. Jan. 20, 1848.

Granted marriage license to Rev. WILLIAM   with VALVIRA POWERS. Jan. 25, 1848.

Granted marriage license to JOSHUA SECKINGER with LAVINIA COHORN. Feb. 14, 1848.

Granted marriage license to JAMES EVERITH with HARRIETT F. TROY. Mar. 3, 1848.

(p.257) Rec'd from DAVID A. METZGER, adm. of the est. of JOHN J. METZGER, dec'd.. $626.18 in full of my portion of said est. Nov. 27, 1847... LOUISA N. K. BACKLEY.

Rec'd from DAVID A. METZGER, adm. of the est. of JOHN J. METZGER, dec'd. . . $626.18 in full of my portion of said est. Nov. 27, 1847... JONATHAN GNANN.

Rec'd from DAVID A. METZGER, adm. of JOHN J. METZGER, dec'd...$995.18. . .my share of said est. as guardian of LEONORA METZGER. Dec. 11, 1847... JAMES RAHN

Rec'd from DAVID A. METZGER. . .$587.10. . .share of AMELIA METZGER. . . Nov. 27, 1847. . . JOSHUA M. DASHER.

(p.258) Rec'd from DAVID A. METZGER. . .$587.18. . .Nov. 27, 1847...JOHN B. BERRY Guardian of REBECCA METZGER.

Rec'd from DAVID A. METZGER. . . $626.18. . .Nov. 27, 1847. . . GEORGE S. METZGER.

Rec'd from DAVID A. METZGER. . . $626.18. . .Nov. 27. 1847. . . LYDIA METZGER.

(p.260) Last Will and Testament of MARY C. BERGMAN was admitted to record. Mar. 6, 1848.

DAVID ZITTROUR, minor of WILLIAM ZITTROUR, who made choice of his father, WILLIAM ZITTROUR, as his guardian. Mar. 6, 1848.

Granted marriage license to FREDERICK R. SECKINGER with ELIZA ZIPPERER. Mar. 13, 1848.

Granted marriage license to JOSHUA GNANN with SUSANNAH M. HINELY. Mar. 21, 1848.

(p.260) Granted marriage license to WILLIAM OSCAR CHARLTON with MARY THERESA FULTON. March 29, 1848.

EPHRAIM KEIFFER applied for adm. on the est. of SOLOMON CARMER, dec'd. Mar. 29, 1848. Granted May 1, 1848.

Granted marriage license to FURNEY WILLIS with Miss SPIER. Mar. 30, 1848.

(p.262) EDWIN McROY, adm. of the est. of JOHN P. McROY, applied for dismission from said est. May 1, 1848.

Granted marriage license to SIMEON BLITCH with HENRIETTA WARREN. May 1, 1848.

Rec'd Nov. 1, 1845 of CHRISTINIA GNANN, guardian for me in my part of the est. of JACOB GNANN, JR., . . .$855.22. . . GEORGE B. GNANN.

(p.263) Rec'd Apr. 12, 1848 of CHRISTINIA GNANN, guardian for me in my part of the est. of JACOB GNANN, JR.,. . .$586.15. . . JANE C. GNANN.

Granted marriage license to F. T. BROGDON with MARY C. SHUPTRINE. June 9, 1848.

Rec'd from RICHARD ZITTROUR and EDWIN ZITTROUR, Exec. of the est. of GODHIEF ZITTROUR. . .$572.00 for our part of said est. May 2, 1847. . . I. F. CORDEL, HANNAH M. CORDEL, W. R. SECKINGER, SARAH A. SECKINGER, JOHN B. BARNWELL, LOUISA A. BARNWELL.

(p.264) Rec'd from RICHARD ZITTROUR and EDWIN ZITTROUR, Exec. of the est. of GODHIEF ZITTROUR. . .$572.00 for our part of said est. May 2, 1847. . . CHARLES ZITTROUR, WILLIAM ZITTROUR.

(p.265) EDWIN ZITTROUR and RICHARD ZITTROUR, Exec. of the est. of GODHIEF ZITTROUR, applied for dismission from said est. July 10, 1848.

JOHN R. IHLEY, adm. of the est. of ROBERT BOWMAN, dec'd, applied for dismission from said est. July 10, 1848.

DANIEL REINSHART, adm. of the est. of JAMES OLCOTT, dec'd, applied for dismission on said est. July 10, 1848.

(p.266) CLETUS RAHN, adm. of the est. of GODHIEF SECKINGER, dec'd, applied for dismission from said est. July 10, 1848.

CLETUS RAHN, adm. of the est. of GODHIEF ARNSTORFF, dec'd, applied for dismission from said est. July 10, 1848.

FREDERICK R. WYLLY applied for dismission on the est. of NAOMI WYLLY, dec'd. July 10, 1848.

ISRAEL HINELY applied for adm. on the est. of JOHN HINELY. Sept. 12, 1848. Granted Oct. 9, 1848.

(p.270) Qualified ELIZABETH HURST as the adm.of THOMAS HURST, dec'd. Oct. 16, 1848.

Granted marriage license to THOMAS LUTHER WINSLOW with Miss R. R. WOOLF. Oct. 23, 1848.

(p.271) JOHN CHARLTON, Exec. of the est. of DAVID GUGEL, dec'd, applied for dismission on said est. Nov. 6, 1848.

EDWIN McROY, adm. of the est. of JOHN P. McROY, dec'd, applied for dismission on said est. Nov. 6, 1848.

Last Will and Testament of ESTHER DUGGER, dec'd, was admitted to record. Nov. 6, 1848.

Last Will and Testament of CLEM POWERS was admitted to record. Nov. 6, 1848.

EDWIN McROY, applied for dismission from the Est. of JACKSON McROY, dec'd, Nov. 6, 1848.

(p.272) Granted marriage license to ISRAEL HINELY with ELLEN CONAWAY. Nov. 13, 1848.

Granted marriage license to EDWIN ABBOT with ELIZA ANN WOOLFE. Nov. 14, 1848.

A. A. SONETS applied for Letters Collection to secure the property of Mr. T. C. SOLOMONS and also was granted adm. on said est. Nov. 22, 1848.

Granted marriage license to JOHN D. GROUVER with ELVIRA C. DAVIS. Dec. 20, 1848.

Rec'd from JESSE LEE, JR., adm. of the est. of JESSE LEE, SR., $179.00 to THOMAS HURST in full of his portion of said est. Jan. 13, 1849.

(p.274) Acknowledgement of receipt of two Negro women and part of est. of JESSE LEE, SR. entitled to SARAH H. BARNWELL. Jan. 13, 1849.

131

(p.275) Rec'd from JESSE LEE, JR., adm. of the est. of JESSE LEE, SR., $179.00 in full of demands on said est. to E. W. BARNWELL. Jan. 13, 1849.
Acknowledgement of settlement of est. of JESSE LEE, SR. to MARY A. HURST and JESSE HURST. Jan. 10, 1848.
(p.276) Rec'd from JESSE LEE, JR., adm. of the est. of JESSE LEE, SR., $179.00 in full of demands on said est. to JESSE HURST. Jan. 13, 1849.
Rec'd Nov. 28, 1848 of JOHN B. BERRY my guardian the sum of $534.97 share of the whole of est. of JOHN METZGER. . . REBECCA METZGER.
(p.277) DANIEL RESINHART, adm. of the est. of JAMES S. OLCOTT, applied for dismission from said est. Jan. 8, 1849.
FREDERICK R. WYLLY, adm. on the est. of NAOMY WYLLY, dec'd, applied for dismission from said est. Jan. 8, 1849.
JAMES RAHN was appointed Clerk of the Court of Ordinary for two years. Jan. 8, 1849.
A. A. SMITH applied for adm. on the est. of FRANCES C. SOLOMONS. Jan. 8, 1849.
(p.278) ELBERT G. WEITMAN, applied for adm. on the est. of ISRAEL WEITMAN, dec'd. Jan. 18, 1849. Granted Mar. 17, 1849.
Granted marriage license to JARED LLOYD with MARTHA NEWTON. Jan. 20, 1849.
Rec'd Sept. 13, 1838 of JESSE LEE, adm. of the est. of JESSE LEE, SR., dec'd, $179.00 in full of demands on said est. . . CHARLES LEE.
Rec'd from JESSE LEE, adm. of the est. of JESSE LEE, SR., dec'd, $179.00 in full of demands on said est. Jan. 31, 1849. . . HENRY J. TULLIS, guardian of JOHN A. TULLIS.
(p.279) Rec'd of JESSE LEE, adm. of the est. of JESSE LEE, SR., dec'd, $179.00 in full of demands on said est. Jan. 29, 1849.
(p.280) MILTON H. POWERS applied for adm. on the est. of JAMES S. CRUM, dec'd, April 25, 1849. Granted May 7, 1849.
(p.281) Rec'd Nov. 20, 1848 from GEORGE NEASE, guardian for the heirs of SOLOMON GNANN, dec'd, $231.53. . . JOSHUA KESLER and LOUISA C. KESLER.
Rec'd Nov. 20, 1848 from GEORGE NEASE, guardian of heirs of SOLOMON GNANN, dec'd, $21.00 for part in full of est. of ANDREW GNANN, dec'd. . . JOSHUA KESLER and LOUISA C. KESLER.
PHILIP A. STROBBAR caveats further execution of a certain instrument of writing purporting to be the Last Will and Testament of MARY C. BERGMAN. (No date) Court refused and overruled on May 7, 1849.
(p.284) Granted marriage license to JESSE GRAHAM to MARGARET A. WALKER. July 3, 1849.
(p.284) ELBERT KESLER made choice of JOSHUA KESLER for his guardian. Granted same day. July 9, 1849.
JOHN G. KESLER applied for dismission from the est. of VALENTINE KESLER. July 9, 1849. Granted Nov. 5, 1849.
(p.286) Granted marriage license to SIMON SMITH with CAROLINE E. EDWARDS. July 13, 1849.
Granted marriage license to THOMAS ELKINS with LAVINIA BLACKMAN. Sept. 1, 1849.
(p.287) Granted marriage license to WILLIAM H. ARNSDORFF with SARAH METZGER. September 12, 1849.
Granted marriage license to WILLIAM CANUET with SARAH FUTRELL. Sept. 26, 1849.
Granted marriage license to JOHN EDWARDS to SUSANNAH E. DASHER. Oct. 2, 1849.
ANN E. MORGAN and JAMES W. MORGAN applied for adm. on the est. of JOHN R. MORGAN, dec'd. Oct. 11, 1849. Granted Nov. 5, 1849.
Granted marriage license to BENJAMIN J. DASHER and SOPHIA GNANN. Oct. 15, 1849.
(p.288) Granted marriage license to H. K. Harrison of Chatham County and SARAH E. ELKINS. Oct. 30, 1849.
MARY ANN HURST applied for adm. on the est. of JESSE HURST. Nov. 1, 1849. Granted Jan. 14, 1850.
(p.289) Will of PAUL MARLOW, dec'd, was admitted to record. Nov. 5, 1849.
(p.290) Last Will and Testament of JOHN CHARLTON was admitted to record. Nov. 17, 1849.

(p.291) Granted marriage license to REDDICK FUTRELL and ELIZA JANE GIEGERS. Nov. 17, 1849.

Granted marriage license to JAMES NEASE and SUSAN E. DASHER. Nov. 21, 1849.

Granted marriage license to THOMAS FLOOD and MARTHA SMITH. Nov. 30, 1849.

Granted marriage license to WILLIAM O. RAHN and HANNAH WILSON. Dec. 18, 1849.

Granted marriage license to RICHARD G. DAWSON and MARTHA M. MORGAN. Dec. 18, 1849.

Granted marriage license to WILLIAM B. MINGLEDORFF and MARY B. BERRY. Jan. 1, 1850.

Granted marriage license to JAMES S. NEIDLINGER with ANN C. KEEBLER. Jan. 3, 1850.

(p.293) Will of CHRISTIAN DASHER was admitted to record. Jan. 14, 1850.

(p.295) Granted adm. on the est. of HORACE MALLORY, dec'd, to Clerk of this Court. Jan. 14, 1850.

FREDERICK KESLER was appointed guardian of ISRAEL KESLER. Jan. 14, 1850.

(p.296) Rec'd Jan. 1, 1849 of JAMES RAHN my guardian $108.00 in full from the est. of my father. . . JOSHUA KESLER.

Rec'd of JOHN S. ZIPPERER $80.00 being the sum in full due me of my father's est. Dec. 22, 1849. . . FREDERICK KESLER.

January, 1850. LEIR G. DLYON applied for adm. on the est. of NAOMI WYLLY, dec'd.

February 4, 1850. Granted marriage license to ROBERT J. CHRISTIE and JULIA M. WEITMAN.

Rec'd July 4, 1850 of FREDERICK I.NEASE and JOHN A. NEASE $179.00 in full of all demands of the est. of GODHIEF I. NEASE.

(p.297) Granted marriage license to GEORGE W. GROVENSTEIN and CAMELIA K. METZGER. February 6, 1850.

Granted marriage license to MIDDLETON SMITH and CAROLINE BEST. Feb. 19, 1850.

Granted marriage license to CHARLES H. THIOT and ANN CHARLTON. Feb. 21, 1850

Granted marriage license to FREDERICK SECKINGER and CHRISTIANA M. ZIPPERER. Mar. 1, 1850.

Rec'd Mar. 14, 1850 of FREDERICK GNANN and CLETUS GNANN, Exec. Last Will and Testament of CHRISTIANA GNANN, dec'd, $50.00 in full of all demands on said est. . . GEORGE B. GNANN.

Rec'd Mar. 14, 1850 of FREDERICK GNANN and CLETUS GNANN, Exec. Last Will and Testament of CHRISTIANA GNANN, dec'd, $70.00 in full of all demands on said est. . . JANE E. GNANN.

Rec'd Mar. 14, 1850 of FREDERICK GNANN and CLETUS GNANN, Exec. Last Will and Testament of CHRISTIANA GNANN, dec'd, $50.00 in full of all demands on said est. . . ELBERT GNANN.

(p.1) Inventory of Estate of JOHN KOGEL dated July 15, 1819. Total estated valued at $611.50.

(p.1) Inventory of Estate of JOHN KOGEL sold July 16, 1819.

(p.10) JOHN WOMACH granted Letters of Collection of WILLIAM WOMACK, dec'd., July 27, 1819.

(p.10) ANN CATHERINE SHRIMP appeared in Court and made choice of Child's share of the Estate of WILLIAM SHRIMP. July 27, 1819.

(p.10) JOHN CHARLTON appointed guardian of children of JOHN HALEY. July 27, 1819.

(p.10) SARAH WOMACK appeared in court and made choice of a child's share of the Estate of WILLIAM WOMACK, dec'd., July 27, 1819.

(p.11) JOHN JONES of Screven applies for administration on the Estate of JAMES JONES, October 11, 1819.

(p.11) Bond dated September 6, 1819 of JOHN WOMACK & SARAH WOMACK, administrator and administratrix of WILLIAM WOMACK, dec'd.

(p.12) Granted marriage license to Mr. AARON LOVETT with Miss ESTHER RAHN, September 22, 1819.

(p.12) Granted marriage license to GEORGE ARNSDORFF with Miss PHOEBE WHEELER. September 23, 1819.

(p.12) MARY WISENBAKER & CHRISTIAN WISENBAKER applies for administration on the Estate of JOHN WISENBAKER, dec'd., October 21, 1819. Granted November 1, 1819.

(p.12) Granted marriage license to Mr. DRURY MAPPER with Miss NIECE JONES, October 4, 1819.

(p.12) Court of Ordinary present their honors - DAVID GUGEL, FURNEY WILLIS & JOHN WALDHOUR, November 1, 1819.

(p.12) MARY WISENBAKER appeared in court and made choice of a child's share in the Estate of JOHN WISENBAKER, dec'd., November 1, 1819.

(p.12) Granted marriage license to JOHNATHAN JONES with ANN HARRIS, November 5, 1819.

(p.12) CATHERINE WALSINGHAM applies for administration on Estate of JOHN S. WALSINGHAM, dec'd., November 5, 1819. Granted December 6, 1819.

(p.13) ESTHER RICKER applied for administration on the Estate of SHAPLEIGH RICKER, dec'd., November 5, 1819. Granted Dec. 28, 1819.

(p.13) Bond dated November 1, 1819 of JOHN JONES, minor heirs of JAMES JONES, dec'd.

(p.14) Bond dated Nov. 1, 1819, of MARY WISENBAKER and CHRISTIAN WISENBAKER, administrators of JOHN WISENBAKER, dec'd.

(p.14) WILLIAM B. SHUTTS granted temporary administration on the Estate of DANIEL SHUTTS, dec'd., Nov. 23, 1819. Granted full administration Jan. 3, 1820.

(p.15) Bond dated Nov. 23, 1819 of WILLIAM B. SHUTTS of Savannah and Benjamin MORELL of Effingham, heirs executors and administrators of DANIEL SHUTTS, dec'd.

(p.16) Granted marriage license to BURRIS BREWER with LYDIA MOBLEY, Nov. 25, 1819.

(p.16) VALENTINE KESLER applies for administration on the Estate of MARGARET BECKLEY, Nov. 25, 1819. Granted Jan. 3, 1820.

(p.16) Inventory of WILLIAM WOMACK dated Oct. 9, 1819 valued at $3,619.37 1/2.

(p.18) Sold part of personal Estate of WILLIAM WOMACK Oct. 9, 1819 valued at $2,699.18.

(p.19) Granted marriage license to LEY DAVIS and SUSANNAH BRAGG, Dec. 4, 1819.

(p.19) Bond dated December 6, 1819 of CATHERINE WALSINGHAM and JOHNATHAN SECKINGER, heirs and executors and administrators of JOHN B. WALSINGHAM, dec'd.

(p.20) Granted marriage license to Mr. MARION LAWTON with Miss MARY ANN KING, Dec, 13, 1819.

(p.21) Inventory dated Nov. 17, 1819 of JOHNATHAN FETREA, dec'd., valued at $38.50.

(p.21) Granted marriage license to JOHN EDWARDS with Miss HANNAH SHEAROUSE, Dec. 19, 1819.

(p.21) Granted marriage license to JOHN HARMES with MARGARET BIRD, Dec. 28, 1819.

(p.22) GOOP SCRUGGS appointed administrator and will on Estate of JAMES SCRUGGS.

(p.22) Accounts of C. F. TRIEBNER was produced by G. ERNST and ordered to be examined by clerk of next term. Jan. 3, 1820.

(p.22) Accounts of Estate of JOHN KING was produced by LARCK KING and ordered to be examined by clerk of next term. Jan. 3, 1820.

(p.22) Accounts of Estate JOHN WALDHOUR WILSON was examined by the court and ordered by the court and FURNEY WILBER, IIC admitted to record. Jan. 3, 1820.

(p.22) Accounts of Estate of JOHN MOORE, dec'd., was examined by the court and admitted to record. Jan. 3, 1820.

(p.23) ISRAEL WHITEMAN applies for administration on the Estate of DANIEL WHITE-MAN, dec'd. January 6, 1820. Granted March 6, 1820.

(p.23) SAMUEL NEIDLINGER applies for administration on the Estate of JOHN NEID-LINGER, dec'd., Jan. 6, 1820. Granted Mar. 6, 1820.

(p.23) Business transaction by the subscribers relative to the Estate of JOHN MOORE, dec'd., for the year 1819. At death, balance on hand, $136.75. Jan. 12, 1820.

(p.23) Minister authorized to marry LEY DAVIS and SUSANNAH BRAGG, Jan. 12, 1820.

(p.24) Last Will and Testament of JAMES HAMILTON SCRUGGS, dated May 17, 1819. He directs all debts be paid. Give to JOSEPH PERRY, his uncle, one-half of his estate. Gives to GROLL (?) SCRUGGS, his cousin, one-half of his estate. He appointed GROLL (?) SCRUGGS, SR., JOSEPH PERRY, GROLL (?) SCRUGGS, Jr. executors. Wit. WILLIAM LOWRY, SARAH WHITE, and HENRY WHITE.

(p.25) Appraisal of Negroes to be hired out belonging to the Estate of JOHN MARTIN DASHER, Jan. 1, 1820.

(p.26) Last Will and Testament of JAMES KING, dated March 29, 1819. To brother, WILLIAM KING, who estate consisting of plantation. Containing 1285 acres with buildings, fences, gardens, orchards, timber and timber trees, water courses, commodities. Also seven Negroes with their increase (three other Negroes emancipated immediately after his death), household furn. and bedding, all stock of cattle, homes, sheep and hogs, library books and carpenters and farming tools. Appointed JOHN GOLDWIRE and WILLIAM KING executors. Wit: JAMES H. SCRUGGS, WILLIAM E. OFFALT (?), JOHN GOLDWIRE.

(p.27) LEVY STEPHENS applies for administration on the Estate of JOHN CREEL, Jan. 22, 1820. Granted March 11, 1820.

(p.27) Inventory of Estate of JOHN WISENBAKER dated Feb. 18, 1820.

(p.27) Granted marriage license to HENRY CHAMBERS with MILLY PARRISH, Feb. 24, 1820.

(p.27) Inventory of the Estate of MARGARET BECKLY dated Feb. 18, 1820 valued at $67.00.

(p.29) Granted Marriage license to RICHARD DAVIS & LIBRA PORTER, Mar. 1, 1820.

(p.29) SAMUEL NEIDLINGER appeared in court and said he believes property belonging to the Estate of JOHN NEIDLINGER is in perishable situation and can sell agreeable to his advertisement. March 6, 1820.

(p.29) LEWIS LANIER applies for guardianship for orphan children of EDWARD MOBLEY. March 6, 1820. Granted April 20, 1820. Requested leave as guardian and the rent or personal property so that distribution may be made among children. Granted July 3, 1820.

(p.29) DANIEL GUGEL, executor of GEORGE G. NOWCAR Estate, produced his accounts. There appeared a balance due him of $1,333.00. March 6, 1820.

(p.29) GOTTACH ERNST appeared, administrator on the Estate of C. F. TRIEBNER, produced accounts, there appeared a balance due him of $78.33.

(p.29) Mr. LEWIS WIETMAN was appointed to take down names of persons who are intitled to draw in the present land lottery. March 6, 1820.

(p.30) Granted marriage license to CHRISTIAN I. HEIDT and ELIZABETH MARTIN. March 30, 1820.

(p.30) Granted temporty administration to SEVY PARKER on the Estate of WILLIAM WEST, April 20, 1820. Granted full administration July 3, 1820.

(p.30) Granted marriage license to JOHN RAHN and MARGARET ZIPPERER, Apr. 25, 1820.

(p.30) Capt. WM. I. DUDLEY was qualified Justice of Superior Court.

(p.30) Mr. ARTHUR SCRUGGS solemnly swears he is the Heir at Law of the late WM. LESON (?) and produced satisfactory papers to that effect.

(p.31) CHRISTIAN WISENBAKER appeared. Balance due of $248.61 on the Estate of JOHN WISENBAKER.

(p.31) TURNEY WILLIS appointed administrator on the Estate of DANIEL MOORE, dec'd. May 11, 1820.

(p.31) Inventory on Estate of HP. SCRUGGS. dec'd., valued at $2,162.12. June 21, 1820.

(p.32) JACOB GNANN and BERY GNANN appointed administrators of Estate of JOHN GNANN, dec'd., July 3, 1820.

(p.32) JAMES PORTER appeared at Court of Ordinary and produced accounts of Estate of BEN PORTER. Balance due him $337.30. July 3, 1820.

(p.33) Inventory of goods and cattle of JOHN NEIDLINGER valued $2,254.81.

(p.34) Inventory of Estate of the dec'd. BENJAMIN PORTER valued at $1,617.53. July 3, 1820.

(p.38) Granted marriage license to Mr. JOHN WILSON and Miss SUSANNAH RAHN. Aug. 17, 1820.

(p.38) JOHN MITCHELL applies for allownace be made him for the expense and funeral charges of WILLIAM BARRETT, dec'd., court order that clerk should pay him $8.00.

(p.38) JOHN MITCHELL came forward stated to court that he had $35.83 belong to JOHN BENNETT who was confined to the penetentiary for theft. Sept. 4, 1820.

(p.39) Granted marriage license to JORDON TYNES and MARY STOKES. Sept. 16, 1820.

(p.39) Last Will and Testament of ERNST ZITTROUR. . .Give to bel. wife ANNA CATHERINE ZITTROUR 2 Negroes, DANIEL and NANCY, dur. life and widowhood. Shall keep seat on plantation dur. life and widowhood. Also give her 5 cows and calfs dur. life and widowhood. 3 sows and pigs. A barrow and cow for beef. My home with cart. Ploughs and such plantation tools· and at her death or marriage all the above property shall be equally divided among children, GODLEIGH ZITTROUR no Share. DAU. SALOME SECKINGER 1 share. Grandchildren, WILLIAM and DAVID ZITTROUR 1 share. Wife shall have share of crop on plan. standing share and share alike with son, dau., & grandchildren.

Son. GODLEIGH ZITTROUR, Plan. after death of wife or marriage, with all lands adjoining say 1 tract 250 acres Schweiger tract, also 1 tract 200 in my own name. Also the tract of Mr. DIOTTS made to me by Deed of conveyance. Also 5 Negroes names JOHN, MARY, MORIAH, LUCY and JACK and an equal share of property not herein named or willed to him and his heirs forever.

Dau. SALOME SECKINGER - 4 acres of swamp inc. ground where she now plants rice also 20 acres of land adjoining him, where I was entitled to see unto BENJAMIN SECKINGER, also the half part of tract of land con. 300 acres in the whole, adjoining lands of DASHER WALSHOUR JONA ZIPPERER. 5 Negroes, BETSEY, SARAH, ANDREWS, STEVEN, SAM with an equal share of my other property not herein named or willed to her and her heirs forever.

Grandchil. WILLIAM and DAVID ZITTROUR, sons of my son DAVID ZITTROUR, dec'd, the other half of part of abstract of land con. 300 acres adjoining as aforesaid. 4 Negroes, LUKEY, RACHAEL, ELICK and JAMES. An equal part out of my other property herein not willed to them and their heirs.

Give to JOHN SCHALFER and American Quarter Dollar. My old Negroe man BUDY shall stay on the plan. as long as wife shall live or be unmarried, and then shall be divided equally among my heirs. Directred that all debts be paid and funeral charges be paid by Executors - GODLEIGH ZITTROUR, JOHN KOGLER, JOHN NEIDLINGER Executors. Aug. 28, 1817. Wit: JOSHUA HELMLY, ISRAEL HINELY, JOHN HELMLY.

(p.41) Granted marriage license to THOMAS DASHER and REBECCA ZITTROUR. Nov. 6, 1820.

(p.41) Ordered administration on Estate of TEMPLE TULLOS to WILLIAM SPEIR. Nov. 6, 1820.

(p.41) JOHN DUGGER, Jr., appeared and produced accounts on the Estate of DAVID CANNADY, dec'd., there appeared balance due him $119.12. Nov. 6, 1820.

(p.41) Order that TIMOTHY GNANN, administrator on the Estate of JOHN BECK, dec'd., have leave to sell real estate of said Estate on producing a regular notification according to laws from printer to clerk.Nov. 6, 1820.

(p.41) Ordered that DAVID GUGEL, Executor on Estate of GEO. G. NOROLAN have leave to sell part of real estate of said estate producing certificate of the printer according to the law to clerk. Nov. 6, 1820.

(p.41) Ordered that clerk grant letters temporary to WILLIAM BIRD, Executor of Estate of M. BIRD. Nov. 6, 1820.

(p.41) NATHANIEL ZETHER and E. JONES applies for administration on the Estate of PHILIP JONES, dec'd. Nov. 6, 1820.

(p.42) Granted marriage license to HENRY STRICKLAND and SARAH LANIER. Nov. 6, 1820.

(p.42) Last Will and Testament of WILLIAM BIRD. Dated Sept. 16, 1820. Do Certify that 1 property be disposed of according to the laws of this state. Appointed WILLIAM BIRD, my son, as executor. Wit: DAVID WOOD, JOHN NARMES, LEWIS BIRD.

(p.42) Granted letters Testamentary to WILLIAM BIRD, Executor of the Estate of WILLIAM BIRD, dec'd., agreeable to order or last court. Nov. 11, 1820.

(p.43) List of sales of the personal property of DAVID CANNADY, dec'd. Nov. 18, 1820.

(p.43) Granted marriage license to FREDERICK FELL with HARRIET NESLER. Nov. 18, 1820.

(p.44) Inventory of Estate of DANIEL MOORE Valued at $420.25.

(p.44) Granted Administration to WILLIAM FRIER on the Estate of PATIENCE TULLOS. November 22, 1820.

(p.46) Granted marriage license to JOHN CURRY and RODY TYNE, Dec. 18, 1815.

(p.47) Granted marriage license to STEPHEN H. MARTIN with MARIA C. HELVESTON, Nov. 25, 1820.

(p.47) EMANUEL RAHN produced Will of MARIA BERRY, dec'd, and was granted him to sell perishable property of said Estate and the remaining part of personal property of MARIA BERRY, giving 20 days notice. Dec. 4, 1825.

(p.47) Proceedings and amount of Administrators Jobs of the personal property of JOHN NEIDLINGER. Dec. 4, 1825.

(p.51) Inventory of the Estate of JOHN GNANN, dec'd, dated Aug. 24, 1820. No value listed. Sold Aug. 25, 1820 for $826.30.

(p.62) JOHN CHARLTON reappointed Clerk of Court of Ordinary. Jan. 1, 1821.

(p.62) ELIZABETH GUYER appeared in court and made choice of a child's share of the Estate of her late husband, GEORGE FREDERICK GUYER.

(p.62) ERNST WILLIAM GUYER appeared in Court and was qualified Executor to the Last Will and Testament of GEORGIA FREDERICK GUYER, dec'd. Jan. 1, 1821.

(p.62) BENJAMIN GNANN was appointed guardian of the person and property of BENN GNANN. Jan. 1, 1821.

(p.62) On petition of JACOB GNANN, Jr., BENN GNANN, Jr., JOHNATHAN GNANN and BENN GNANN, Sr., as guardian of BENJAMIN GNANN, Jr., was granted to divide personal property of JOHN GNANN, dec'd. JONATHAN RAHN, THOMAS WYLLY and GOTTIEB ERNST was appointed to divide said Estate. Jan. 1, 1821.

(p.62) It was ordered that the court notify LEWIS LANIER, guardian of minors of EDWARD MOBLEY, to come forward and give sufficient security otherwise they will proceed according to laws. Jan. 1, 1821.

(p.62) Granted administration on the Estate of MARY CATHERN LYNBURGER to SAMUEL SNYDER. Jan. 1, 1821.

(p.63) Granted marriage license to SAMUEL DASHER with JANE MARIA ZITTROUR, Jan. 6, 1821.

(p.63) Granted marriage license to NATH. ZETTLER with MARY JONES, Dec. 27, 1820.

(p.69) Inventory of the Est. of JOHN CREEL, Mar. 17, 1820. Value $408.56.

(p.71) Inventory of the Estate of JAMES JONES, dec'd, Dec. 29, 1819. Value $650.25.

(p.75) Will of MARIA BERRY OF Effingham County. Dated April 19, 1820 . . ."being very sick and weak of body. . .to my bel. dau. SALOME, riding chair and harness. . . unto HANNAH E. RAHN $20.00. . .Grandchildren, MARIA, LOUISA and JOHN B. METŹGER $20.00. . Son, JOHN B. BERRY my bay horse and the other half to OBADIAH. . .Son, OBADIAH, 4 head of sheep and 1/2 already mentioned. . .All my lawful debts to be paid. Constitute EMANUEL RAHN and JOHN B. BERRY, Executors. Wit: THOMAS MOCK, SAMUEL GROVER, DAVID REIFER.

(p.76) Will of GEORGE FREDERICK GUYER of Savannah, Dated April 8, 1818. . .To Son, WILLIAM GUYER, my tract of land in County of Effingham con. 50 acres - where he now resides. . .I charge my sons portion with $30.00 to be paid to ANN WINTER, my granddau. at the age of 21 or day of marriage. All remainder of estate devise to son, WILLIAM and granddau. ANN, to be equally divided between them. Appoint Son, WILLIAM GUYER, Executor. Wit: R. R. CUYLER, Public Notary, I. ROBERTS, Tm. STONE.

(p.77) Granted marriage license to GEORGE KING with CAROLINE GOLDWIRE, Feb. 12, 1821.

(p.88) Will of ANN ZITTROUR produced in court and proved by JOSHUA SECKINGER, one of the Executors. March 5, 1820.

(p.88) Will of MATTHEW BODDENBECK was probated March 5, 1820.

(p.88) It is ordered by the court that no charge will be allowed an Executor administrator for a Negro that is over 7 years of age. March 5, 1820.

(p.88) JAMES PORTER was granted leave of personal property of Estate of BENN PORTER and that BENN KENNEDY, WM. PORTER, BENN MORRELL, JAMES WILSON divide the property and report proceedings to court. March 5, 1820.

(p.89) Will of MATTHEW BODDENBECK of Effingham County dated Jan. 20, 1821. All Lawful debts to be paid by selling all my real and personal property that I now hold and should there be any over. . . .to be and belong to my bel. brother, JOHN BODDENBECK. Lot I live on, I leased to GOTTIEB ERNST for 6 years with the rent of $10.00 per yr. as long as I acknowledge said lot. I recommend to my Executor the leasing out of lot to the highest bidder yearly or length of lease or for him to sell the improvements and give unto said GOTTLIEB ERNEST again as Executor sees fit, Appoint JOHN BODDENBECK Executor. Wit: GOTTLIEB ERNST, JOHN RAHN, GEORGE TOY.

(p.90) Will of ANN ZITTROUR of Effingham County dated July 13, 1813. To Stepson, JOHN GOTTLIEB one cow and calf. . . stepson, SOLOMON, 1 cow and calf, Brother, JONATHAN, 1 cow and calf. . .JANNAH THRUBLREN, 3 head breeding cattle. . .Son, JOHN C. MILLER, the Negro and remainder of cattle together with the rest of my property. . .Appoint my son, JOHN CHRISTOPHER MILLER, Executor. Wit: JOSHUA SECKINGER, JONATHAN SECKINGER.

(p.97) Inventory of Estate of MARY C. SECKINGER, dec'd, Feb. 23, 1821, Valued at $172.25. Sold Feb. 24, 1821.

(p.110) Granted marriage license to SAMUEL DASHER and JANE MARIA ZITTROUR, Jan. 6, 1821.

(p.110) Estate of JOHN GNANN, dec'd, divided into 4 parts: 1 share to JACOB GNANN, Sr., 1 share to BENJAMIN GNANN, Sr., 1 share JONATHAN GNANN, 1 share to BENJAMIN GNANN. Jan. 1, 1821.

(p.112) Granted marriage license to WILLIAM SPEIR and HENRIETTE MULLETT. Apr. 4, 1821.

(p.119) Granted marriage license to WILLIAM SPENCER and MARGARET BACKLEY, Nov. 23, 1820.

(p.120) Mr. LEWIS LANIER appeared in court May 7, 1821 and entered into bond with HENRY STRICKLAND as his security as guardian of minor children of EDWARD MOBLEY.

(p.123) Granted marriage license to WILLIAM McCORDELL with MARGARET McGAHAGIN, May 29, 1820.

(p.123) Granted marriage license to WILLIAM HURST with MARY BLITCH, June 2, 1820.

(p.123) Granted marriage license to WILLIAM WILLIAMS with ELIZABETH WOOD, June 3, 1820.

(p.124) EMANUEL RAHN Made application to court to be appointed guardian of the person and property of OBADIAH BERRY who is an idiot. Granted.

(p.124) THOMAS MOCK applies for administration on Estate of HENRY GROVENSTEIN. July 17, 1821. Granted Sept. 3, 1821

(p.125) Granted marriage license to JOHN CRAWFORD with GRACE BEALL, July 10, 1821.

(p.125) RICHARD RICHARDSON, administrator of Estate of JOSEPH BREVAN, applies order to sell Negro slaves. July 9, 1821. Granted same day.

(p.127) Will of HENRY GROVENSTEIN, Jr., of Effingham County Dated Nov. 17, 1819. To THOMAS MOCK, Estate real and personal the property of my Father, JOHN JESTES GROVEN-STEIN. Wit: SAMUEL GROVENSTEIN, EMANUEL RAHN.

(p.127) MARY BACKLEY applies for administration on Estate of JONATHAN BACKLEY, July 17, 1821.

(p.128) Granted marriage license to REUBEN ROBERTS with AMY WYLLY, July 26, 1821.

(p.128) Granted marriage license to ALEXANDER ELKINS with ANN KNIGHT, July 31, 1821.

(p.137) Granted marriage license to JOHN MACCOOL with LUCY HIGHSMITH, Nov. 9, 1821.

(p.137) Granted marriage license to JOHN W. STROBLAN with RACHAEL KETTLES, Nov. 15, 1821.

(p.137) Granted marriage license to HENRY GREENE with ELIZABETH KING, Nov. 16, 1821.

(p.137) Receipt to SOLOMON ZITTROUR by Stepmother, ANN ZITTROUR, for cow and calf, April 21, 1821.

(p.137) Receipt to JONATHAN SECKINGER by ANN ZITTROUR, Sister, for cow and calf, June 11, 1821.

(p.137) Receipt to HARLING PARKER by JOHN C. MILLER for part of Estate of ANN ZITTROUR, Aug. 14, 1821.

(p.138) Granted marriage license to ALLEN WILSON with MARY HURST, Nov. 29, 1821.

(p.138) Granted marriage license to JOHN HINELY with DOROTHY WEITMAN, Dec. 3, 1821.

(p.138) Granted marriage license to WILLIAM PEARSON with HANNAH GILCHRIST, Dec. 5, 1821.

(p.138) Granted marriage license to B. THOMAS with LYDIA RAHN, Dec. 19, 1821.

(p.138) Granted marriage license to JOHN HELVENSTON with ESTHER FLERL, Jan. 2, 1822.

(p.139) WILLIAM SPEIR applies for administration on Estate of TEMPLE TULLOS, Dec. 19, 1821.

(p.140) Bond dated Nov. 6, 1817 of MARY CATHERINE ZITTROUR, widow of ERNST ZITT-ROUR, dec'd.

(p.140) Receipt by MARY CATHERINE ZITTROUR to Executors of Estate of ERNST ZIT-TROUR, dec'd. Nov. 6, 1817.

(p.140) ALTHEA SCRUGGS applies for guardianship of two orphan children, JOHN J. SCRUGGS and RICHARD T. SCRUGGS, of J. SCRUGGS. Granted Jan. 7, 1822.

(p.140) JOHN METZGER applies for guardianship of his three children; MARIA ELIZA FRANCES, LOUISA NAOMI KALISTA, and JOHN BENAJAH WASHINGTON METZGER. Jan. 7, 1822. Granted same day.

(p.140) Will of JOHN FREYERMUTH probated Jan. 7, 1822.

(p.142) Granted marriage license to JOHN WILLIAM EXLEY with ELIZA MARGARET MULLETT, Jan. 8, 1822.

(p.142) Granted marriage license to WILLIAM T. MORGAN with CHRISTIANA ELIZ. HEIDT, Feb. 5, 1822.

(p.142) Granted marriage license to CALVIN TYSON with MARY JOHNSON, Feb. 11, 1822.

(p.142) Granted marriage license to SAMUEL BUCKSTEINER with ANN CATHERINE SHRIMP, Feb, 12, 1822.

(p.143) Will of JOHN FREYERMUTH, of Effingham County dated Nov. 18, 1821. My Will that all debts be paid out of my personal property. The Negroes are to be hired out and the hire to be applied in payment of debts. Any remaining property to be divided among children and wife. Appointed PETER FREYERMUTH and GOTTLIEB ERNST, Executors, Wit: MARTIN DASHER, THOMAS SCHWEIGHOFFER, JOHN METZGER, Jr.

(p.148) Inventory of Estate of ERNST ZITTROUR valued at $5,760.20.

(p.149) Bond dated Nov. 5, 1817 of MARY CATHERINE ZITTROUR, GOTTLIEB ZITTROUR, BENAJMIN SECKINGER, WILLIAM ZITTROUR and DAVID ZITTROUR, heirs of the late ERNST ZITTROUR.

(p.150) THOMAS B. MITCHELL of Telfair County appointed attorney for CIVLLY MOORE, JANE MOORE, and ELIZABETH MOORE of IRWIN County, Jan. 9, 1822.

(p.151) Receipt to TURNEY WILLIS by T. G. MITCHELL between him and the Estate of DANIEL MOORE, Feb. 14, 1822.

(p.151) Granted marriage license to WILLIAM BLAKE with AMY KETTLES, Mar. 27, 1822.

(p.151) Granted Administration to HEZIKIAH EVANS on the Estate of JOHN MOORE and MARRY MOORE, dec'd. Apr. 22, 1822.

(p.153) BENJAMIN KENNEDY applied to be made guardian for a free man of colour by the name of SAM which was granted. May 6, 1822.

(p.153) It was ordered that EMANUEL RAHN, guardian of OBADIAH BERRY, be allowed $6.00 per month for board and lodging. May 6, 1822.

(p.154) Receipt to EMANUEL RAHN by JOHN B. BERRY for $707.13 3/4 in full for my share of whole Estate of JOHN BERRY. Mar. 8, 1822.

(p.154) Receipt to EMANUEL RAHN by JOHN B. BERRY for $360.00 in full my share of the whole of the estate of MARIA BERRY, Mar. 8, 1822.

(p.155) BENJAMIN GNANN and JACOB GNANN, Sr. applied for Letters dismissing on Estate of JOHN GNANN, dec'd. on May 8, 1822.

(p.156) Will of JAMES SHUMAN probated July 1, 1822.

(p.159) Will of JAMES SHUMAN of Effingham County dated May 3, 1822. To oldest Son, JOHN SHUMAN, Negro girl named PHYLLIS,2 years old. . .Second Son, WILLIAM HENRY SHUMAN, Negro boy called SIMBRECK, 4 years old. . .DAU. REBECCA SHUMAN, Negro girl LYDIA, 6 years old. . .Third Son, JAMES SHUMAN, Negro girl SETT,3 years old. . .Son, Dr. HENRY SHUMAN, Negro girl, DINE, 10 years old. . .All my prop. both real and personal be equally divided among my 5 children. My will that my wife, MARTHA SHUMAN, who is insane shall remain with my children in possession of my plantation until Division is made and before division is made my Executors shall make choice for her of 1 of my Negroes SAM or BETTY, a bed and its furniture and 5 cows and their calves to be employed by them so they think best, or the court direct her support and she shall have a home on the land, during her natural life and at her death or if she should be taken from state then the property shall be equally divided among 5 children. Appoint GEORGE HENRY SHUMAN and CLEM POWERS, Executors. Wit: C. LOPER, BENJ. HARVEY, MARY HARVEY.

(p.160-169) Inventories

(p.170) Receipt to EMANUEL RAHN by JOHN J. METZGER $20.00 in full for the share of my three children, heirs of MARIA BERRY, dec'd. Mar. 8, 1822.

(p.170) Receipt to EMANUEL RAHN by JOHN J. METZGER $862.13 3/4 for the share belonging to three children, heirs of JOHN BERRY, dec'd. Mar. 8, 1822.

(p.174) Receipt to JOHN GRINDRAT by B. GILLELAND $340.00 full amount of distributing share of my Father's, H. GRINDRAT's Estate. July 1, 1814.

(p.174) Receipt to JOHN GRINDRAT by GEORGE A. CURRY $253.00 full amount of the distributing share of my wife, DORCASE, dau. of H. GRINDRAT. Aug. 26, 1815.

(p.174) Receipt of JOHN GRINDRAT by B. MORILA for $340.00 in full amount of distributing share of wife, SUSAN, dau. of HENRY GRINDRAT. June 5, 1818.

(p.175) Receipt to JOHN GRINDRAT by HENRIETTA GRINDRAT for $2,061.25 in full amount of distributing share of father, H. GRINDRAT's Estate. Apr. 24, 1818.

(p.175) JOSHUA GNANN applies for administration on the Estate of SOLOMON GNANN. August 13, 1822. Granted Sept. 2, 1822.

(p.179) JOHN CHARLTON applies for administration on the Estate of JONATHAN BACKLEY. Sept. 19, 1822. Granted Oct. 20, 1822.

(p.179) EMANUEL COX and BENJAMIN COX applies for administration on the Estate of ARTHUR RYALL, dec'd. Sept. 19, 1822.

(p.179) JACOB GNANN, Jr. applies for administration on the Estate of EMANUEL RAHN, dec'd. Oct. 10, 1822. Granted Nov. 11, 1822.

(p.180) Granted marriage license to JAMES OLCOTT with ESTHER MILLER. Oct. 19, 1822.

(p.180) DANIEL MULLETT applies for administration on the Estate of GIDEON MULLETT, dec'd. Oct. 19, 1822. Granted Nov. 20, 1822.

(p.184) Granted marriage license to DAVID GARRASON with MARY GILBERT. Oct. 23, 1822.

(p.184) Inventory of the Estate of JAMES SHUMAN valued at $3,522.68 3/4. July 1, 1822.

(p.186) Granted marriage license to ISRAEL ARNSDORFF with KRATZ GNANN. Nov. 4, 1822.

(p.186) Granted guardianship to MATHEW SCRUGGS for the two orphans of JESSE SCRUGGS, NOV. 7, 1822.

(p.186) MARIA PATTERSON applies for administration on the Estate of WILLIAM PATTERSON, Nov. 7, 1822. Granted Dec. 10, 1822.

(p.186) Granted Letters of Collection to WILLIAM G. PORTER on the Estate of JAMES PORTER, Nov. 7, 1822.

(p.191) MURRY REED applies for administration on the Estate of ELIZABETH RYLINDER, Nov. 23, 1822.

(p.192) Granted marriage license to JAMES EDWARDS with NANCY PITTS, Nov. 25, 1822.

(p.192) Receipt of JOEL KEIFFER by S. GANT for $371.00 as full amount of demand against him of part in Estate of JOSHUA GANT, Nov. 25, 1822.

(p.192) BENJAMIN DASHER applies for Letters Dismissory of the Estate of JOHN M. DASHER from the Executorship of said Estate, Dec. 6, 1822.

(p.193) A writ of Partition be issued to the heirs of JESSE SCRUGGS, dec'd, to divide property of said dec'd. Dec. 2, 1822.

(p.193) Last Will and Testament of MATTHEW RAHN probated Dec. 2, 1822.

(p.193) Granted administration to WILLIAM PORTER on the Estate of JAMES PORTER, Dec. 9, 1822.

(p.193) Granted Letters Testamentary to JOHN B. and CHRISTOPHER SECKINGER on the Estate of MATTHEW RAHN, dec'd. Dec. 18, 1822.

(p.194) Granted marriage license to SAMUEL P. MILLER with ELIZA HANNAH ZIPPERER, Dec. 25, 1822.

(p.195) Will of MATTHEW RHAN of Effingham County dated Sept. 30, 1822. Will that all debts be paid from real and personal property. My wife keep seat for residence where we now live with stock and provision during widowhood. All Negroes be hired out except old Negro woman. Out of hire place is to be repaired and as much as required for the necessary want of supplying the children at home then balance equally divided with each child. Children of both wives. Division cannot be made while my wife liveth. Appointed Son, JOHN RAHN, wife and son-in-law, CHRISTOPHER SECKINGER, Executors. Wit: EPHRAIM KEIFFER, CLETUS RAHN, GOTTIEB ERNST.

(p.197) Will of GROLL (?) SCRUGSS, Sr. of Effingham County dated Nov. 18, 1822. "Being of weak mind and body. . .All debts should be paid out of money arising from the sale of the following property: All stock, 1/3 of remaining crop, 5 tracts of land in County of Wilkinson, known by No. 234, 103, 6, 173, 215. Also a tract, formerly Casons, sold as property of WILLIAM SAUNDERS. Also the amount of notes of hand on sundry persons. . .Give and bequeath to GROLL SCRUGGS, Jr., son, 1 dollar, before having his share of Estate. . .Also 1/2 of 1200 acres made up of 4 tracts and part of fifth. . . 2 feather beds and furniture - 2 bolsters, 4 pillows, 4 sheets and 4 blankets. . . LOUISA HUDSON, FANNY HUDSON, ABIGAIL HUDSON, and INFANT WHOSE MOTHER IS ELIZABETH HUDSON. . . 3 Negroes. Also the . . .of the Estate of JAMES H. SCRUGGS, dec'd. . .Also 1/2 of the tract of land on which I am now settled. . .All and every household goods not given to son, JOSIAH, and farming utencils. . .1 horse named FOX and 1 gig. . .ELIZABETH HUDSON shall have lease of Negroes and property given to children during natural life. . That all property remain in hands of Executors until debts are paid. . .appoint MACKLIN SUNDAY, JOHN SCRUGGS, WILLIAM SCRUGGS, and ROBERT SCRUGGS, Executors. . .Wit: M. HELE, J. MATTHEWS, C. G. WHITE.

(p.203) Granted marriage license to GIDEON ZIPPERER with SARA POWLEDGE, Jan. 28, 1823.

(p.207) Granted Letters Dismissory to JACOB GNANN, Sr. and BENJ. GNANN on Estate of JOHN GNANN.

(p.208) Will of WILLIAM McGAHAGIN admitted to record Mar. 3, 1823.

(p.208) Will of JOHN McCALL admitted to record, Mar. 3, 1823.

(p.208) Granted administration to TIMOTHY GNANN on the Estate of APOLINA LINBURGER, Mar. 3, 1823.

(p.208) ELIZABETH McCALL applies for administration on the Estate of JOHN McCALL, Mar. 3, 1823.

(p.209) Will of JOHN McCALL of Effingham County dated February 5, 1823. To dau. ELIZABETH McCALL 5 Negroes, HANNAH, ISAAC, MINDER, VIRGINIA, SAM. . .1 bay horse, 1 cow and calf. . .1 set of plated Castors, 7 bed quilts, 2 bed spreads, 1 set bed curtains, 2 beds and bedsteads, 1 pr. of sheets to each bed, 1 riding gig and harness, with in- crease of Negroes, 2 looking glasses, 1 water, 1 bread pan, 1 tea chest, 6 wine glasses, 6 tumblers, 2 small pine tables, 6 small silver tea spoons, 1 pr. sugar tongs. . .Son, JAMES McCALL. . .1 Negroe-CYRUS. . .1 sorrel horse, 2 feather beds, 2 bedsteads, 2 pr. sheets for each bed and other furn. belong to them. . .1 tract of land by Ledge pond. . Son, GEORGE McCALL. . .2 Negroes-SIMBRICK and NANCY. . .3 tracts of land con. land where I now live, 2 beds and bedsteads with 2 pr. sheets to each bed and all other furn. belong- ing to them. . .2 horses and all my wearing apparal, 3 shot guns and 1 rifle, All planta- tion tools and all stock. . .Appointed JOHN HODGES and LEWIS LANIER, Executors. Wit: JOHN CHARLTON.

(p.213) Granted ELIZABETH McCALL guardianship of person and property of GEORGE C. McCALL, May 5, 1823.

(p.213) Inventory of Estate of WILLIAM McGAHAGIN valued at $6,670.21, Apr. 17, 1823.

(p.216) Inventory of the Estate of JOHN McCALL valued at $3,659.63, Apr. 26, 1823.

(p.224) Will of HANNAH HINES admitted to record July 7, 1823.

(p.224) Will of SOLOMON GNANN admitted to record July 7, 1823.

(p.224) JACOB GNANN makes application for SALOMI RAHN, widow of EMANUEL RAHN, for administration and makes choice for her a child's proportion of said Estate. Granted July 7, 1823.

(p.224) JOSHUA GNANN, administrator for the Estate of SOLOMON GNANN, Jr., appeared and made application in behalf of the widow of SOLOMON GNANN and made choice for her a child's proportion of said Estate. July 7, 1823.

(p.225) Will of HANNAH HINES of Effingham County dated August 7, 1820. To my son, SHERROD HINES' 2 sons, 2 heiffers, 1 Negroe woman given them by my Executors...my sons, HOWELL HINES, 1 Negroe woman, 2 cows and calves. . .THOMAS R. HINES, 1 young heiffer... Dau. TEMPLE WOLFE, 1 cow and calf. . .DAVID WOLFE, 1 heiffer. . .Dau. MARY LEMBER, my horse and 1 cow and calf with stock of hogs and 1 feather bed. . .Dau. NANCY LOMACIAH, 1 cow and calf to be given her by my Executors. . .Dau. CYNTHIA GARRASON, 1 cow and calf. 1 chest, 1 large table and 1 mattress with 2 blankets. . .RICHARD GARRASON, 1 heiffer. . .Dau. WINNEY TISON, 1 cow and calf, 1 Negroe woman all her life and then be- come property of her oldest daughter ANTONETTA TISON. . .All rest of property be divided equally between my children. . .Appoint HOWELL HINES, Executor. . .Wit: AN GARRASON, LEASON CAPPS, HOWELL HINES.

(p.226) Will of SOLOMON GNANN of Effingham County dated September 20, 1807. To my bel. wife SARAH GNANN, all property so long as she lives and at her death, $200.00 to be collected out of Estate for use and benefit of the Lutheran Church at Ebenezer. Appoint wife, SARAH GNANN and EMANUEL ZEIGLER, Executors. Wit: F. WALSINGHAM and JOHN SCHNYDER.

(p.227) Granted marriage license to SOLOMON ARNSDORFF with ELIZABETH STALEY, July 7, 1823.

(p.227) Granted marriage license to JAMES T. CRAWFORD with ANN WHEELER, Aug. 20, 1823.

(p.228) Granted marriage license to DANIEL EDWARDS with MARIA TYNER, Oct. 6, 1823.

(p.228) Receipt of JACOB GNANN by HANNAH RAHN for $20.00 in full amount for share of whole Estate of MARIA BERRY.

(p.229) Granted marriage license to THOMAS NESLER with ELORIA NIESE, Oct. 20, 1823.

(p.229) Granted marriage license to JOHN C. GRIFFIN with FRANCIS ANN BALL, Oct. 31, 1823.

(p.233) Granted marriage license to GUILDFORD DUDLEY with SUSAN GILLELAND, Dec. 3, 1823.

(p.235) Granted marriage license to JAMES STRICKLAND with SARAH MILLS, Dec. 16, 1823.

(p.235) Granted marriage license to CHRISTOPHER L. MORGAN with CHRISTIANA HEIDT, Dec. 13, 1823.

(p.235) MARGARET SPENCER, widow, applies for administration on the Estate of · WILLIAM SPENCER, Dec. 19, 1823.

(p.236) Inventory of the Estate of MATTHEW RAHN valued at $3,168.75 dated Dec. 19, 1823.

(p.241) Appointed WILLIAM KING, PAUL BEVILL, WILLIAM DUDLY, JOHN GOLDWIRE and DANIEL DAMPIER or any three to divide property of JESSE SCRUGGS, dec'd, in four equal parts, Dec. 2, 1822.

(p.246) Granted marriage license to SAMUEL SHUMAN with SARAH JONES, Jan. 24, 1824.

(p.246) Granted marriage license to SIMEON TYNER with ANN HIGHSMITH, Feb. 11, 1824.

(p.246) Will of SAMUEL SNIDER of Effingham County dated September 23, 1823. Advise that all lawful debts be paid by any Executors. . .Rest of Estate be kept in wife's possession during natural life. After death Estate shall belong to Neice SUSANNAH SNIDER, daughter of JONATHAN SNIDER. Appoint LEWIS WEITMAN and WILLIAM GUYER Executors. Wit: LEWIS WEITMAN, JOHN WALDHOUR, JOHN C. GROVENSTEIN.

(p.247) Will of SAMUEL SNYDER admitted to record Feb. 9, 1824.

(p.248) Order by Court that JOHN DUGGER, administrator on Estate of DAVID CANNADY, make titles to WILLIAM DAVID CANNADY as a bounty for servitude in U. S. Army.

(p.248) HEZEKIAH EVANS appointed guardian of JAMES MOORE and WILLIAM MOORE, heirs of JOHN MOORE. Mar. 1, 1824.

(p.248) JOHN B. BERRY appointed guardian of his brother, OBADIAH BERRY. Mar. 1, 1824.

(p.248) Granted marriage license to BENJAMIN KENNEDY and ANN MARY MASON, Mar. 17, 1824.

(p.249) ELIAS REED applied for administration on the Estate of WILLIAM SPENCER, Mar. 16, 1824. Granted Apr. 24, 1824.

(p.249) Bond dated Mar. 18, 1824 to JOHN B. BERRY.

(p.250) JAMES BLITCH appointed guardian of the person and property of THOMAS BLITCH. May 3, 1824.

(p.251) Granted marriage license to HERMAN ELKINS with SALINA TONDEE, June 19, 1824.

(p.257) CHARLES TONDEE, HERMAN ELKINS, FURNEY TULLIS, THOMAS ELKINS, & LUTHER TESON are required to divide property of JOHN & MARY MOORE into four equal parts. Given to HEZEKIAH EVANS, JOHN MOORE, HEZEKIAH EVANS, the guardian of JAMES MOORE & WILLIAM MOORE. Mar. 1, 1824.

(p.258) Granted marriage license to JOHN GRONOBLY with JULIA HINELY, July 28, 1824.

(p.263) Receipt to Justices of Superior Court of Effingham County by ABRAHAM MALLETT for LEWIS MATTETT's part and legacy in full of the Estate of GIDEON MALLETT, dec'd. Feb. 9, 1824.

(p.263) Receipt to Justices of Superior Court of Effingham County by HANNAH MALLETT for part and legacy in full of the Estate of GIDEON MALLETT, dec'd, her husband. Feb. 9, 1824.

(p.263) Receipt to Justices of Superior Court of Effingham County by JOHN W. EXLEY for part and legacy in full of the Estate of GIDEON MALLETT. Feb. 9, 1824.

(p.264) Receipt to Justices of Superior Court of Effingham County by JEREMIAH MALLETT for part and legacy in full of the Estate of my father, GIDEON MALLETT, dec'd. Feb. 9, 1824.

(p.264) Receipt to Justices of Superior Court by ABRAHAM MALLETT for part and legacy in full of the Estate of my father, GIDEON MALLETT, dec'd. Feb. 9, 1824

(p.265) Executor of the Estate of PHILLIP DENSLER was ordered to return all property of said Estate until the widow of PHILIP DENSLER comply with the laws giving bond and security. Sept. 6, 1824.

(p.266) LEWIS WEITMAN was appointed guardian of the Estate of THOMAS FLERL and MARY FLERL, orphans of ISRAEL FLERL. Sept. 6, 1824

(p.266) SARAH WEITMAN was appointed guardian of ISRALINE FLERL, orphan of ISRAEL FLERL, Sept. 6, 1824.

(p.266) DAVID GUGEL and JOSHUA HELVENSTEIN appointed to divide Estate of ISRAEL FLERL. Sept. 6, 1824.

(p.   ) Ordered that DANIEL MALLETT, administrator of GIDEON MALLETT, be dismissed from the administration of said Estate. Sept. 6, 1824.

(p.   ) LEWIS WEITMAN appointed guardian of ISRALINE FLERL: SARAH WEITMAN'S name taken off. Oct. 6, 1824.

(p.   ) ELIAS REED, Administrator of the Estate of WILLIAM SPENCER stated that proceeds of sale of the personal property together with hire of Negroes is insufficient to pay the debts due by Estate. Ordered administrator to have leave to sell four Negroes.

(p.268) Will of JAMES CREWS of Effingham County dated August 2, 1824. "being of sound and disposing mind and memory. . .desire and bequeath to my wife, HANNAH ELIZABETH CREWS all tract of land on plantation con. 2 tracts of 50 acres. . .during her natural life and after death to go to my children. . .I further give to my wife and children, MARTHA ELIZA, ANN CEMANTHA, CELINA, MARY ANN AND LYDIA A., and any other children born: tract of land in Effingham County con. 500 acres which I bought from WILLIAM BIRD. Also 12 Negroes. . .Also household furniture, stock of cattle, hogs, horses and all rest of residue of estate real and personal together with the future issue of the female slaves and all other property. If any daughter should die before age 21, go to wife. If any should marry, at their death, property will go to my wife. That yearly proceeds of above mentioned be applied to maintenance and education of my children. Executors have full power to cultivate and cut wood on all lands which income shall be applied for the support of children for 13 years. Estate be kept together 13 years and no division take place until that time. Can sell any Negroes or stock or exchange any provided they replace it all so estate will not sustain any loss. Appoint HANNAH CREWS Executrix, HENRY S. GROVENSTEIN, JAMES WILSON, JR., JONATHAN RAHN AND JOHN WILSON, Executors. Wit: MARY OGLESBY, JEFFERSON ZIPPERER, SAMUEL CREWS.

(p.270) B. BERRY, guardian of OBADIAH BERRY, asks for leave to sell the old buildings and rails on a plantation on the Augusta Road. Nov. 1, 1824.

(p.270) Granted marriage license to HENRY CHAMPION with ISABELLA GIDEON of Savannah. Nov. 9, 1824.

Granted marriage license to THOMAS PURSE with ELIZA GUGEL of Savannah, Nov. 13, 1824.

Granted marriage license to JOSHUA GNANN with MARY ELIZABETH ZEIGLER. Nov. 27, 1824.

Granted marriage license to JONATHAN OATS with SARAH GNANN. Dec. 16, 1824.

(p.274-275) Granted division of personal property of Estate of ISRAEL FLERL. Sept. 6, 1824.

(p.283) Will of JAMES WILSON admitted to record March 7, 1825.

(p.284) Receipt of L. WEITMAN by tax collector for $385.00 in part for tax of 1835.

(p.284) Ordered that clerk appropriate $100.00 for the entertainment of General LaFayette who is passing through Effingham County, March 1, 1825.

(p.285) Will of JAMES WILSON of Effingham County dated September 25, 1819. "being sick and weak in body. . .desire that all lawful debts be paid. . .Three eldest sons, JOHN WILSON, JAMES WILSON, and JESSE WILSON Have already received proportion of property . . .gave each of them $1.00 as legacy. . .All other sons has had property of certain value at division of property each heir to receive an equal part after LUKE WILSON, the heirs of GABRIEL WILSON, JEREMIAH WILSON and ALLEN WILSON has had an equal part with ELISHU WILSON. . .And bel. wife, ANN WILSON, to have a child's part. . .SARAH FRANCES WILSON $10.00 as her legacy in full. Appoint HOWELL HINES and BENJAMIN BLITCH, Executors. Wit: WILLIAM B. HURST, THOMAS NEPELS, L. WILSON, JR.

(p.286) Granted marriage license to GEORGE SPENCER with CAROLINE ESTHER THREAD-CRAFT. Mar. 21, 1825.

(p.286) Granted marriage license to SOLOMON HINELY with HANNAH ELIZABETH ARNS-
DORFF. Mar. 21, 1825.

(p.287) Ordered that the Court take bond agreeable and issue letters of guardianship to JOHN WINTER, the natural guardian of ANN WINTER, for the purpose of receiving
her proportion of property from the Estate of her grandfather, T. GUYER. May 2, 1825.

(p.287) Receipt to ELIZA McCALL by GEORGE McCALL for part in full of JOHN McCALL
Estate of Effingham. May 2, 1825.

(p.287) HOWELL HINES applies for Letters Dismissory on the Estate of HANNAH HINES,
dec'd. May 3, 1825. Granted Mar. 6, 1826.

(p.287) THOMAS HURST applies for Letters Dismissory from the Executorship of the
Estate of WILLIAM McGAHAGIN, dec'd. May 3, 1825. Issued Nov. 7, 1825.

(p.287) Granted marriage license to PHILIP HORNING with GRACY WEITMAN. June 1,
1825.

(p.288) Receipt to ERNEST WILLIAM GUYER by JOHN WINTER for $65.00 in full the
proportion of the Estate of GEO. T. GUYER belonging to ANN WINTER. May 19, 1825.

(p.288) ROBERT P. BARTON applies for administration on the Estate of BENJAMIN
BARTON. June 17, 1825.

(p.288) Inventory of the Estate of JAMES WILSON valued at $3,565.25. Apr. 22,
1825.

(p.293) Granted marriage license to JAMES STRICKLAND with SENITH EVERS. June 23,
1825.

(p.293) Granted marriage license to DAVID ZITTROUR with THURSA FITZPATRICK,
June 27, 1825.

(p.294) ELIAS REED applies for Letters Dismissory from the Estate of WILLIAM
SPENCER as administrator. June 27, 1825.

(p.294) JOHN CHARLTON, guardian of EDMUND LAVENDER, MARTHA LAVENDER, and BENJAMIN
LAVENDER, minor heirs of JAMES LAVENDER. July 17, 1825.

(p.295) Granted marriage license to WILLIAM SPEIR with ELIZABETH FUTRESS. July
11, 1825.

(p.295) ELEANOR V. BARTON, widow of BENJAMIN BARTON, caveats the grant of administration on the Estate of BENJAMIN BARTON to ROBERT P. BARTON. July 17, 1825.

(p.295) Granted marriage license to SAMUEL F. ISAACKS with SARAH E. QUINN of
South Carolina. July 14, 1825.

(p.299) MATTHEW RESIER applies for administration on the Estate of JAMES PORTER.
Aug. 27, 1825. Granted Nov. 7, 1825.

(p.299) Granted ROBERT P. BARTON, administrator, to have Estate of BENJAMIN BARTON
divided. Sept. 5, 1825.

(p.299) JONATHAN SECKINGER appointed guardian of the orphans of WILLIAM SHRIMP,
dec'd. Sept. 5, 1825.

(p.300) Heirs of Estate of WILLIAM SHRIMP applies for property to be divided.
Sept. 5, 1825.

(p.301) MARY ANN PORTER applies for administration on the Estate of WILLIAM
PORTER, dec'd. Sept. 22, 1825.

(p.301) Inventory of the Estate of BENJAMIN BARTON, dec'd, valued at $5,119.62.
Sept. 6, 1825.

(p.304) Granted marriage license to HENRY BARTON with SARAH EVANS, Oct. 15, 1825.

(p.304) Granted marriage license to ALEXANDER WALT of Chatham Co. with HANNAH
ANN HINES. Oct. 30, 1825.

(p.304) Will of CATHERINE HORROCKS of Effingham County dated August 23, 1825.
"being weak in body...desire all debts be paid...SOPHIA DENSLER 2 tenements and out
buildings situated on a half lot belonging to the Estate of late W. JOHN ROBERTS which
ground is on lease situated in Washington in the City of Savannah together with all
household and kitchen furniture and 1 Negro...SUSANNAH WATSON that house and kitchen
together with all out buildings and the half lot which said house and building stands on
situated in Carpenters Row in Savannah, not subject to her husband, JAMES WATSON or any
future husband and in case of her having no children disposal at her death by will deed
of gift or otherwise. Also, a note of hand drawn by JAMES WATSON for $50.00...Appoint
JOHN CHARLTON, Executor. Wit: DAVID GUYER, JOSHUA KUBLER, ELIZA CHASTON.

Addition to will. . .SUSANNAH WATSON, in case I should draw a tract of land in the present comtemplated land lottery.

(p.304) ELEANOR BARTON and ROBERT BARTON made petition for dividing the property of BENJAMIN BARTON, dec'd. Sept. 6, 1825. Granted Sept. 7, 1825.

(p.308) Receipt to ROBERT P. BARTON by ELEANOR BARTON for $2,220.62 1/2 in full for proportion of all personal property belonging to the Estate of BENJ. BARTON. Sept. 8, 1825.

(p.310) Granted marriage license to WILLIAM W. BLACK with ELEANOR BARTON.

(p.312) Following orphan children of JOHN G. WALSINGHAM ordered to be bound out as apprentices according to law: CHARLES to FLERNIAN ELKINS: CLARISSA MARIA to JOHN W. EXLEY.

(p.312) Receipt to THOMAS HURST by JOHN GRAHAM for all the property papers of every kind, together with the money and has come to settlement of Estate of WILLIAM McGAHAGIN. Oct. 25, 1825.

(p.312) Granted marriage license to DANIEL JAMES MCKENZIE with ELIZABETH GNANN, Nov. 12, 1825.

(p.312) Granted marriage license to CHARLES TONDEE with GINA GADDY. Dec. 5, 1825.

(p.312) Granted marriage license to JOSHUA MILLER with LOUISA HOLLIDAY. Dec. 5, 1825.

(p.312) G. ERNST objects to ELIAS REED, adm. of the Estate of WILLIAM SPENCER, dec'd, from being dismissed as adm. Dec. 5, 1825. Granted dismissal to ELIAS REED May 1, 1826.

(p.312) MARY ANN PORTER, administratrix of the Estate of WILLIAM PORTER, come forward and give further and more significant security. May 1, 1826.

(p.312) BENJAMIN BLITCH, executor of the Estate of JAMES WILSON applies for dismissal from his adm. Jan. 2, 1826. Granted July 3, 1826.

(p.312) SAMUEL NEIDLINGER, Adm. of the Estate of JOHN NEIDLINGER applies to be dismissed from his adm. Jan. 2, 1826. Granted July 15, 1826.

(p.315) Granted marriage license to THOMAS SCHWEIGHOFFER with SARAH ANN TODD. Feb. 10, 1826.

(p.315) Granted marriage license to GEORGE GLONER with MARGARET SPENCER. Feb. 20, 1826.

(p.315) Inventory of the Est. of WILLIAM PORTER. Nov. 25, 1825. Valued at $11,561.25.

(p.319) JOSEPH C. TREUTLEN applies for administration on the Estate of CHRISTIAN TREUTLEN, dec'd. Mar. 3, 1826. Granted May 1, 1826.

(p.321) WILLIAM BANDY applies to be appointed guardian on the Estate of HAVENS LOPER, a minor orphan of ARA LOPER. Granted same day. Mar. 6, 1826.

(p.322) Granted marriage license to JOHN B. BERRY with MARY A. METZGER. Apr. 21, 1826.

(p.322) Granted marriage license to SOLOMON WEITMAN with MARGARET RAHN. Apr. 26, 1826.

(p.323) Will of BENJAMIN SECKINGER order void and not admitted to record. May 1, 1826.

(p.324) DAVID ZEIGLER and LEWIS WEITMAN applies for administration on the Estate of EMANUEL ZEIGLER, dec'd. May 25, 1826. Granted July 3, 1826.

(p.324) Issued Letters of Collection to DAVID ZEIGLER and LEWIS WEITMAN to charge of the Estate of EMANUEL ZEIGLER. May 30, 1826.

(p.325) LEVI DLYON applies for administration on the Estate of CHRISTIAN TREUTLEN. June 9, 1826. Granted Aug. 15, 1826.

(p.326) Court orders that LYDIA COOK be discharged from said role in payment of courts and executors named in will apply to court to establish said will as ...

(p.326) MARY ANN PORTER, widow and administratrix of the Estate of WILLIAM PORTER, dec'd, appears and makes choice of a child's share of the said estate.

(p.327) WILLIAM KING, adm. of the Estate of WILLIAM KING, dec'd, was granted Letters Dismissory July 3, 1826.

(p.327) BENJAMIN PORTER was chosen guardian of CATHERINE ANN PORTER and ELVIA ANN PORTER. July 3, 1826.

(p.328) JOHN GRAHAM applies for dismission on the Estate of WILLIAM McGAHAGIN, July ?, 1826.

(p.328) MARY ANN KENNEDY, widow, and GOTTIEB ERNST applies for administration on the Estate of BENJAMIN KENNEDY. July 20, 1826. Granted Oct. 2, 1826.

(p.329) LYDIA COOK, widow, applies for adm. on the Estate of HENRY COOK. July 15, 1826.

(p.329) Granted marriage license to EDWARD SHEAROUSE with ELIZABETH MILLER, July 10, 1826.

(p.329) LEVI DLYON makes caveat against LYDIA COOK on the Estate of HENRY COOK. July 17, 1826.

(p.332-336) Inventory of Estate of EMANUEL ZEIGLER dated Aug. 18, 1826 and valued at $2,615.12.

(p.341) Granted marriage license to JAMES ALEXANDER BURCKSTEINER with ELIZABETH CATHERINE KEEBLER Sept. 13, 1826.

(p.342) Last Will and Testament of ELIZABETH DASHER was admitted to record. Oct. 2, 1826.

(p.342) Last Will and Testament of DAVID AMBROSE, dec'd, was admitted to record. Oct. 2, 1826.

(p.343) Granted marriage license to Rev. C. F. BERGMAN with MARY C. FLERL. Oct. 4, 1826.

(p.343) Granted marriage license to THOMAS TONDEE with JULIANN WOMACK. Oct. 12, 1826.

(p.343) Will of DAVID AMBROSE of Effingham County dated October 24, 1826. "being low in health...Will that my dear wife ELIZABETH should keep in possession and enjoy my estate real and personal during nature life to support my children. I request my property be taken care of by my wife for benefit of children after her death. After death of wife my property be equally divided among children, except son DAVID, have had share by deed of gift. Appoint WILLIAM KING and JOHN GOLDWIRE, Executors. Wit: CHRISTIAN TREUTLEN and BENJAMIN KENNEDY.

(p.344) Will of ELIZABETH DASHER dated February 29, 1822..."being of sound mind... bequeath to CHRISTIAN WISENBAKER $1,000.00...he shall keep for sole use of my daughter ELIZABETH SCHEURMAN, wife of JOHN SCHEURMAN, but if said daughter desire payment, he should do so, but only for use not husband's...Give rest of estate to be divided among children; CHRISTIAN DASHER, GOTTIEB DASHER, ROSANNAH COPE. Appoint CHRISTIAN WISENBAKER, Executor. Wit: E. JACKSON, JR., T. DOYLE, R. R. CUYLER.

(p.345) JOHN M. LUCAS do hereby caveat JOHN GRAHAM, Executor of the Estate of WILLIAM McGAHAGIN from obtaining Letters Dismissory from said Estate. Nov. 15, 1826.

(p.345) Granted marriage license to NOAH PACE with SARAH ZITTROUR. Nov. 15, 1826.

(p.350) Ordered that ELISHU WILSON be appointed guardian for the heirs of GABRIEL WILSON, dec'd. Jan. 1, 1827.

(p.350) CHRISTIAN DASHER applies for Letter Dismissory on the Estate of JAS. BIRD. Jan. 1, 1827.

(p.350) MARY BREWER applies for guardianship for the heirs of JOSEPH BREWER. Jan. 1, 1827.

(p.351) JOHN CHARLTON applies for adm. on the Estate of BENJAMIN KENNEDY, dec'd. in behalf of the heirs and creditors. Jan. 9, 1827. Granted Feb. 12, 1827.

(p.351) Will of PAUL TOOSY of Effingham County dated August 14, 1826. "being of perfect mind. . .My will that and order that funeral charges be paid. Rev. LEW MYERS's children to children $100.00. MR. HENRY GROVENSTEIN'S two children-each child $100.00.. The remainder of money to H. L. GROVENSTEIN. . .SAMUEL BODDENBACK receive all my clothing, saddle and bridle and saddle bags. . .Funeral expenses be paid from money remaining after Mr. MYER'S and Mr. GROVENSTEIN's children receive their legacy. Appoint HENRY GROVENSTEIN and EPHRAIM KEIFFER, Executors. . .Wit: L. C. PEARCE, LUKE EXLEY.

(p.353) Granted marriage license to WILLIAM D. PHILIPS with SUSANNAH THROWER. Jan. 15, 1827.

(p.352) Will of DAVID LEINBURGER of Effingham County dated September 6, 1826.
"being very weak in body. . .desire all debts be paid by Executors. . .All property
both real and personal belong to well bel. wife NAOMI LEINBURGER during natural life.
My bel. son, CHRISTOPHER LEINBURGER, shall maintain his mother dur. natural life. . .
After death of wife, all real estate belonging to me shall belong to son, CHRISTOPHER.
To son, JOHN LEINBURGER, $50.00 as share out of sd· land and personal property be divided
equally between my three children CHRISTOPHER LEINBURGER, JOHN LEINBURGER and ELIZABETH
DASHER. Appoint CHRISTOPHER LEINBURGER and JOSHUA LEINBURGER, Executors. . .Wit: JOHN
LEINBURGER, CHRISTIAN LEINBURGER, LEWIS WEITMAN.
(p.353) Granted Letter of Collection to JOHN C. BLANCE on Estate of ELIZA GRIFFEN.
Jan. 12, 1827.
(p.354) Granted marriage license to W. SOLOMON GNANN with MARGARET FETZER. Jan.
26, 1827.
(p.354) Granted marriage license to THOMAS BLITCH with LYDIA WILSON. Feb. 2,
1827.
(p.355) Granted marriage license to DAVID HELMEY with MARY ANN HINELY. Feb. 19,
1827.
(p.356) Receipt to HENRY GROVENSTEIN by SAM BODDENBACK for 1 saddle, saddle bags
and clothing which was legacy left by JOHN P. TOOSING. Jan. 11, 1827.
(p.357) LEWIS MYERS granted guardianship for his five children. Mar. 5, 1827.
(p.357) GEORGE H. SHUMAN appointed guardian for REBECKAH SHUMAN, JAMES SHUMAN,
and HENRY SHUMAN. Mar. 5, 1827.
(p.357) ISAAC GARRASON appointed guardian for ANGELINEOR HOLIDAY, orphan of
JOSEPH HOLIDAY, JR. Mar. 5, 1827.
(p.358) Granted adm. to JOHN C. BLANCE on the Estate of ELIZA GRIFFEN. Mar. 5,
1827.
(p.358) WILLIAM GADDY appointed guardian of minor heirs of WILLIAM WOMACK, dec'd.
Mar. 5, 1827.
(p.360) Granted marriage license to ELIAS WILSON with AMELIA ANN HURST. Mar. 10,
1827.
(p.360) Granted marriage license to BENJAMIN C. PORTER with SARAH KENNEDY.
Mar. 17, 1827.
(p.360) JOHN M. LUCAS applies for adm. with the will Annexed in behalf of the
heirs and creditors of the Estate of WILLIAM McGAHAGIN. Mar. 25, 1827.
(p.360) JESSE HITTS Makes caveat against the application of LYDIA COOK for adm. on
the Estate of HENRY COOK. July 17, 1820.
(p.362) Will of HENRY COOK dated August 15, 1825. "being weak in body. . .my bel.
wife, LYDIA COOK, all my estate real and personal during natural life. . .and after her
death to JESSE L. PITTS, grandson of wife. . .In case of death of JESSE PITTS then to
my brothers LEWIS COOK AND BENJAMIN COOK. . .MARY MERCER, my Negro man, HARRY. . .to my
nephew, GEORGE COOK after death of bel. wife, my Negro girl, LEAK. Appoint bel. wife
LYDIA COOK, Executrix and LEVI DLYON, Executor. Wit: LEVI DLYON, R. DLYON, CALDEN
GRIFFIN.
(p.362-366) Inventory of Estate of BENJAMIN KENNEDY, dec'd.
(p.368) Granted marriage license to SAMUEL COWARD of Chatham Co. with ESTHER
SNAPWELL. April 16, 1827.
(p.368) Granted marriage license to SAMUEL HEIDT with ELIZABETH ELKINS. Apr. 16,
1827.
(p.368) Granted guardianship to WILLIAM GADDY for the orphans of WM. H. WOMACK.
April 19, 1827.
(p.368) Granted marriage license to SIMEON TYNER with ESTHER ANN SOUTHWELL.
April 20, 1827.
(p.377) Granted leave to divide Estate of WM. H. WOMACK. May 7, 1827.
(p.378) Granted leave to sell personal property of the Estate of DAVID LEINBURGER,
dec'd. to JOSHUA LEINBURGER. May 7, 1827.
(p.379) Granted marriage license to JOSHUA HINELY with ANN ELIZA BURCKSTEINER.
March 28, 1827.

(p.383) Granted division of Estate of JOSEPH HOLIDAY. Mar. 5, 1827.
(p.384) Granted division of Estate of JAMES SHUMAN. Mar. 5, 1827.
(p.385-386) Division of Estate of JAMES SHUMAN.
(p.387-388) Granted division of the Estate of WILLIAM SHRIMP. Sept. 5, 1825.
(p.388-389) Division of Estate of WM. SHRIMP.
(p.389-392) Copy of marriage licenses already granted.
(p.392-393) Division of Estate of JOHN BECK, May 3, 1828.
(p.394) All heirs of WILLIAM H. WOMACK apply for division of personal property of WILLIAM WOMACK. Jan. 1, 1827. Granted May 7, 1827.
(p.395) Division of personal property of WILLIAM WOMACK.
(p.395) All heirs of EMANUEL RAHN, dec'd, apply for division of said Estate. June 26, 1828.
(p.397-398) Division of Estate of EMANUEL RAHN. July 7, 1828.
(p.399-404) Copy of marriage license already granted.
(p.404) Heirs of JONATHAN BECKLY desire Estate be divided. Granted Apr. 17, 1830.
(p.405-407) Copy of marriage license already granted.
(p.408) Heirs of JOHN WISENBAKER desire Estate to be divided. Nov. 1, 1830. Granted Jan. 5, 1831.
(p.409) Division of Estate of JON WISENBAKER.
(p.410) Heirs of DAVID POWLEDGE desire that the said Estate be divided between them. Jan. 4, 1830. Granted division Feb. 10, 1830.
(p.411-412) Petition shows that EMANUEL ZEIGLER, dec'd, died leaving a considerable personal estate and which is undivided. Petitioner would like court to grant an order to dividing estate. July 4, 1829. Granted July 6, 1829.
(p.413-414) Petition of the heirs of THOMAS D. PORTER, dec'd, of Savannah shows that he died leaving a considerable personal Estate undivided. Petitioners would like court to grant an order for dividing personal estate. Feb. 1, 1831. Granted Mar. 7, 1831.
(p.415-416-417) Copy of marriage license already granted.
(p.417) Petition of the heirs of JOHN FREYERMUTH, dec'd, shows that he died leaving a considerable personal estate and would like for court to grant an order for dividing said estate. Feb. 9, 1832. Granted Apr. 21, 1832.
(p.419) Petition of heirs of ELIAS WILLIAMS shows that he died leaving a considerable personal estate undivided and would like court to grant an order for division. Nov. 12, 1832. Granted same day.
(p.420-421) Copy of marriage license already granted.
(p.421-422) The heirs of ELIZABETH McGAHAGIN, dec'd, desire personal estate be divided. Jan. 7, 1833. Granted Feb. 16, 1833.
(p.421-425) Copy of marriage license already granted.

NOTE: Various inventories not abstracted. Seemed to be of no great importance.

(p.1) Granted adm. on the estate of NAOMI WEITMAN to L. L. DELYON. Mar. 4, 1850.

(p.2) Petition of WILLIAM T. HAM for revocation of probate of the alledged Will of T. L. CRUM and adm. to MILTON H. POWERS and HUGH E. CASSIDY be discontinued. Mar. 4, 1850.

Ordered that MILTON H. POWERS and HUGH E. CASSIDY to show case at next term of Court why the prayers of the Petition should not be granted. Mar. 4, 1850.

(p.3) Granted marriage license to Mr. STEPHEN HESTER and HANNAH HEIDT. Apr. 2, 1850.

HUGH E. CASSIDY applied for temporary adm. on the estate of HUGH CASSIDY and obtained by giving bond and also applied for permanent adm. on said estate. Apr. 5, 1850. Granted May 6, 1850.

Granted marriage license to THOMAS WHEELER and MATILDA WILSON. Mar. 22, 1850.

Issued 6 subpoenas to wit: WRIGHT LOFLEY, ELIZA CASSIDY,   WILSON, JAMES LOVE and MARY ANN GORDON (?) and CYNIS BIRD of Bryan County in the suit of JAMES N. SIMMONS, adm. with Will annexed of JAMES CRUM, Dec'd. April 18, 1850.

(p.4) Granted marriage license to P. H. STANTON and JANE E. GNANN. Apr. 22, 1850.

Granted marriage license to ISRAEL HEINDLEY and MARY ANN MORGAN. Apr. 23, 1850.

Granted marriage license to THOMAS B. HENDRICKS and ELIZABETH DICKSON of Scriven County. April 27, 1850.

(p.5) A receipt in full from GEO. W. GROVENSTEIN to BENJAMIN GROVENSTEIN, his guardian giving him full discharge. May 6, 1850

HUGH CASSIDY, dec'd, died without any will as far as I know. . .and applied for adm. on said estate. Granted same day. May 6, 1850. HUGH E. CASSIDY.

(p.6) Will of JAMES S. CRUM, dec'd, was produced and admitted to record is the will of JAMES S. CRUM and that the same is proved and that probate of the same be and is confirmed. May 7, 1850.

(p.7) MILTON H. POWERS applied for adm. on the est. of PETER SCHERMERHORN, late of the State of New York. May 7, 1850. Granted Sept. 6. 1850.

Granted marriage license to EDWARD BIRD and ANN E. WILSON. May 18, 1850.

JAMES J. NEASE and LEWIS B. DASHER applied for adm. on the estate of GIDEON DASHER, dec'd. June 6, 1850. Granted July 8, 1850.

Granted marriage license to WILLIAM BEST and FRANCES EDWARDS. June 27, 1850.

(p.9) We do solemnly swear that GIDEON DASHER died without any will, as far as we know and believe that we will well and truly administer on all and singular the estate.. LEWIS B. DASHER, J. J. NEASE.

(p.10) JOSHUA KESLER petitioned to court to be discharged from guardianship of ELBERT KESLER. July 8, 1850.

JOHN G. MOREL applied for adm. on the estate of HOMER V. MOREL. July 31, 1850. Granted Nov. 4, 1850.

ALLEN WILSON and ANNA HURST applied for adm. on the estate of JAMES HURST. Aug. 10, 1850. Granted temporary adm. Sept. 13, 1850.

LEWIS J. MORGAN and SARAH D. MORGAN applied for adm. on the estate of JAMES W. MORGAN. Aug. 23, 1850. Granted Sept. 27, 1850.

(p.11) LEWIS MORGAN applied for adm. on the estate of THOMAS MORGAN. Aug. 23, 1850. Granted Sept. 27, 1850.

Granted marriage license to JOHN SNIDER and JANE AMANDA ARNSDORFF. Aug. 24, 1850.

I MILTON H. POWERS do solemnly swear that PETER SCHERMERHORN died without any will as far as I now or believe; and that I will well and truly administer all and singular the estate . .Sept. 2, 1850.

(p.14) Granted marriage license to DAVID A. FRIERS and SARAH A. T. EDWARDS. Sept. 5, 1850.

Granted marriage license to LAWRENCE T. ELKINS and MARGARET FRANCIS WILSON. September 27, 1850.

We LEWIS J. MORGAN and SARAH D. MORGAN do solemnly swear that JAMES W. MORGAN died without any will as far as we know and believe and that we will well and truly administer on all and singular the estate. . .Sept. 27, 1850.

(p.15) I LEWIS MORGAN do solemnly swear that THOMAS MORGAN died without any Will as far as I know and believe that I will well and truly administer on all and singular the estate. . .Sept. 27, 1850.

Granted marriage license to JOHN D. BERRY and MARGARET L. MINGLEDORFF. Sept. 28, 1850.

Granted marriage license to JAMES D. LEE and ELVIRA A. EDWARDS. Oct. 15, 1850.

(p.16) BENJAMIN J. DASHER applied for adm. on the estate of JOSHUA GNANN. Oct. 24, 1850. Granted Dec. 26, 1850.

Granted marriage license to CHARLES E. WALDHAUER and SUSAN E. JOYNER. Oct. 29, 1850.

Granted marriage license to JOSHUA HINELY and JANE HARRISON. Nov. 4, 1850.

Will of FELIX HURST, dec'd, was proven and admitted to record. Nov. 4, 1850.

ORPHA HURST appeared and took the following oath. I do solemnly swear that this writing containing the true Last Will and Testament of FELIX HURST, dec'd, as far as I know and believe; and I will well and truly execute the same...Nov. 4, 1850.

(p.17) Letters Testamentary were granted ORPHA HURST on the Estate of FELIX HURST, dec'd. Nov. 4, 1850.

Minor Heirs of JAMES GRIFFIN chose JAMES RAHN as their guardian. Nov. 4, 1850.

Granted division of the estate of THOMAS MORGAN. Nov. 4, 1850.

(p.18) Granted marriage license to J. R. BREWER and JANE E. GRAHAM. Nov. 16, 1850.

Granted marriage license to ALEXANDER W. DALEY and ELIZABETH BRINSON of Scriven County. Nov. 27, 1850.

Granted marriage license to WILLIAM A. PORTER and AMANDA KETTLES. Dec. 1850.

(p.19) Granted marriage license to JOHN W. WILSON and MARY M. RYALL. Dec. 13, 1850.

Granted JAMES RAHN guardianship of the minor heirs of JAMES GRIFFIN, dec'd. Dec. 16, 1850.

I BENJAMIN J. DASHER do solemnly swear that JOSHUA GNANN died without any Will as far as I know and believe and that I will well and truly administer on all and singular the estate. . .Dec. 26,1850.

Granted marriage license to HUGH E. CASSIDY and SARAH ANN ELIZA BOURQUIN. Dec. 30, 1850.

(p.20) Granted marriage license to ISAIAH HEIDT and SARAH M. Speir. Dec. 30, 1850.

I do solemnly swear that HOMER V. MOREL died without any will as far as I know and believe; and that I will well and truly administer on all and singular the estate. . .Jan. 6, 1851...JOHN G. MOREL.

(p.22) JAMES RAHN was appointed adm. of the estate of JAMES HURST. Jan. 13, 1851.

(p.23) LUCRETIA MORGAN was given child's share of the estate of THOMAS MORGAN, dec'd. Jan. 13, 1851.

Will of EPHRAIM KIEFFER, dec'd, was admitted to record. Jan 13, 1851.

We do solemnly swear that this writing contains the true Last Will and Testament of EPHRAIM KIEFFER, dec'd, as far as we know; and that we will well and truly execute the same. . .Jan. 13, 1851...ALLEN KIEFFER, SHADROCK GROVENSTEIN.

Letters Testamentary were granted ALLEN NEWTON KIEFFER and SHADROCK GROVEN- STEIN. JAN. 13, 1851.

EMILIA E. WILSON, orphan of HENRY M. WILSON, made choice of WILLIAM O. RAHN as her guardian. Jan. 13, 1851.

MARION M. WILSON, orphan of HENRY M. WILSON, made choice of EDWARD A. MINGLE- DORFF as his guardian. Jan. 13, 1851.

(p.24) SARAH KETTLES, a minor, made choice of WILLIAM A. PORTER as her guardian. Jan. 13, 1851. Granted guardianship Jan. 13, 1851.

Granted marriage license to EDWARD L. NEASE and ELIZA T. EDWARDS. Jan. 20, 1851.

151

(p.25) Granted marriage license to DAVID DASHER and PERMILIA HEIDT. Jan. 21, 1851.
Granted marriage license to JAMES FRANKLIN BERRY and EMILIA E. WILSON. Feb. 3, 1851.
Granted marriage license to LEWIS J. MORGAN and FRANCES M. MALLETTE. Mar. 1, 1851.

LEWIS WEITMAN applied for dismission as Executor of the Last Will and Testament of MARY C. BERGMAN. Mar. 3, 1851. Granted Sept. 1, 1851.

JAMES RAHN, adm. of the estate of SARAH P. WYLLY, dec'd, applied for dismission from said estate. Mar. 3, 1851.

(p.27) BUNYAN KIEFFER, orphan of EPHRAIM KIEFFER, made choice of ALLEN KIEFFER as his guardian. Mar. 3, 1851.

Granted guardianship to ELIZA L. CASSIDY on the person and property of MARY JANE CASSIDY. MAr. 3, 1851.

I, ROBERT J. MINGLEDORFF, do solemnly swear that I will do and perform the duties of me as guardian for MARION WILSON. Mar. 3, 1851.

(p.28) Granted marriage license to FREDERICK GNANN, JR. and MARY A. WILSON. Mar. 10, 1851.

(p.29) Rec'd Mar. 22, 1850 of FREDERICK I. NEASE and JOHN R. NEASE, Exec. of the Last Will and Testament of GODHIEF NEASE, dec'd, $179.00 in full upon the said estate.. E. L. NEASE.

Rec'd Mar. 22, 1850 of FREDERICK I. NEASE and JOHN R. NEASE, Exec. of the Last Will and Testament of GOFHIEF I. NEASE, dec'd, $179.00 in full satisfaction of all demands on said estate...JOHN R. SHEROUSE.

(p.30) Rec'd Mar. 22, 1850 of FREDERICK I. NEASE and JOHN R. NEASE, Exec. of the Last Will and Testament of GODHIEF I. NEASE, dec'd, $179.00 in full of all demands on said estate...J. J. NEASE.

(p.29) Rec'd Mar. 22, 1850 of FREDERICK I. NEASE and JOHN R. NEASE, Exec. of the Last Will and Testament of GODHIEF I. NEASE, dec'd, $179.00 in full of all demands on said estate...WM. H. SHEROUSE.

(p.30) Rec'd of BENJAMIN GNANN, Exec. of the estate of SOLOMON GNANN, for the heirs of said estate $698.96...GEORGE NEASE, Guardian.

(p.31) Granted marriage license to WILLIAM CARUTHERS of the City of Savannah and CAROLINE S. METZGER. April 9, 1851.

Granted marriage license to SAMUEL MERCER and FRANCES EDWARDS. April 5, 1851.

Granted marriage license to STEPHEN TULLIS and SARAH JANE FURNIS. April 12, 1851.

Granted marriage license to ISAIAH E. SECKINGER and MALVINA L. H. .NEWTON. April 29, 1851.

(p.32) ELISHA WYLLY, Exec. of the Last Will and Testament of THOMAS WYLLY, dec'd, applied for dismission. May 6, 1851.

(p.34) CARMEL TYSON and GEORGE TYSON, orphan Children of CALVIN TYSON, dec'd, made choice of THOMAS R. HINES, esq., as their guardian. May 6, 1851.

(p.35) Granted marriage license to JOSHUA EDWARDS and ELIZABETH E. AMBROSE of Scriven County. May 17, 1851.

Granted marriage license to ALBERT V. McROY and MARY ANN JENKINS. June 4, 1851.

Granted marriage license to SAMUEL A. JENKINS and FRANCES S. JOHNSON. July 4, 1851.

Granted marriage license to JAMES A.MOCK and SARAH FLAKE both of Scriven County. July 4, 1851.

(p.38) WILLIAM RAHN was appointed guardian of LEWIS MYERS, SR. July 7, 1851.

(p.39) Ordered that JOHN McROY, ALBERT O. McROY, and SIMON R. are appointed to act as a committee to examine THOMAS WHEELER and see if he has the smallpox and if he does they are to act as nurse and guard. July 7, 1851. (He did have the small pox.)

(p.40) DAVID A. METZGER applied for adm. on the estate of JOHN B. METZGER July 7, 1851. Granted Sept. 1, 1851.

152

(p.40) JOSEPH C. EDWARDS applied for adm. on the estate of CHARLES G. EDWARDS. July 7, 1851. Granted Sept. 1, 1851.
Granted swap of land belonging to the children of GEORGE T. BRIDGES for the benefit of his children. July 14, 1851.
(p.41) Granted marriage license to JAMES W. HINELY and ANN KESLER. July 14, 1851.
Granted marriage license to WILLIAM SEVANGEN of Nausau County Florida and MARY BLITCH. Aug. 13, 1851.
(p.42) Mrs. AMY BLAKE, guardian of AMANDA KETTLES, applied for dismission. Sept. 1, 1851.
Mrs. AMY BLAKE, guardian of SARAH KETTLES, applied for dismission. Sept. 1, 1851.
I, DAVID A. METZGER, do solemnly swear that JOHN B. METZGER died without any Will as far as I know and believe; and that I will well and truly administer on all and singular the estate. . .Sept. 1, 1851.
(p.43) Will of MICAJAH FUTRELL was produced and admitted to record. Sept. 1, 1851.
We do solemnly swear that this writing contains the true Last Will and Testament of MICAJAH FUTRELL, dec'd, as far as we know and believe; and that we will well and truly execute the same. . .Sept. 1, 1851. WM. SPEIR, REDDICK FUTRELL.
Granted WILLIAM SPEIR and REDDICK FUTRELL Letters Testamentary on the estate of MICAJAH FUTRELL, Sept. 1, 1851.
Granted ELIZABETH HINELY guardianship of EDWIN HINELY, orphan child of JOHN HEINLY, dec'd. Sept. 1, 1851.
(p.44) HUGH E. CASSIDY, refused to give security on the estate of JAMES S. CRUM, dec'd, so he was dismissed giving full adm. to MILTON H. POWERS. Sept. 1, 1851.
(p.45) I, JOSEPH C. EDWARDS, do solemnly swear that CHARLES G. EDWARDS died without any Will as far as I know and believe; and that I will well and truly administer on all and singular the estate. . .Sept. 1, 1851.
Granted marriage license to JAMES R. RAHN and SALOMI FRYERMUTH. Oct. 1, 1851.
Granted marriage license to THOMAS E. SECKINGER and LAVINIA ARNSDORFF. Oct. 4, 1851.
(p.46) Granted marriage license to EPHRAIM HELMLY and SARAH FERGUSON. Oct. 18, 1851.
Granted marriage license to JOHN SOWELL, JR. and MIRRIAM BOROUGHS. Oct. 18, 1851.
Granted marriage license to MORGAN RAWLS of Bulloch County and SALIVA V. ELKINS. Oct. 18, 1851.
Granted marriage license to GEORGE MATTIOCELLER and MARGARET HINELY. Oct. 25, 1851.
CHARLES HINELY applied for adm. on the estate of CHRISTIAN T. HEIDT, dec'd, Nov. 10, 1851.
(p.47) Granted marriage license to WILLIAM SPIER and JULIA A. WARREN. Dec. 20, 1851.
Granted marriage license to JOHN R. HEIDT and ANN F. GNANN. Jan. 2, 1851.
(p.48) WILLIAM RAHN, guardian of LEWIS MYERS, SR., applied for dismission. Jan. 12, 1851.
(p.52) Will of JONATHAN GNANN was produced and recorded. Jan. 12, 1852.
Will of LYDIA METZGER was produced and recorded. Jan. 12, 1852.
Letters Testamentary were granted D. A. METZGER, Exec. of the Last Will and Testament of LYDIA METZGER, dec'd. Jan. 12, 1852.
(p.53) Granted dismission to AMY BLAKE, guardian of AMANDA KETTLES. Jan. 12, 1852.
(p.54) Granted marriage license to WILLIAM A. ORMOND and FRANCES H. BEVILL. Jan. 12, 1852.
(p.55) Granted marriage license to STEPHEN A. WILSON and JANE L. DASHER. Jan. 30, 1852.
Rev'd Feb. 4, 1850 of FREDERICK I. NEASE and JOHN R. NEASE, Exec. of the Last Will and Testament of GODHIEF I. NEASE, dec'd, $179.00...HANNAH E. NESLER.
(p.56) JAMES RAHN was qualified Ordinary for Effingham County. Feb. 9, 1852.

(p.56) Granted marriage license to HENRY F. ZETTLER and MOSELLE BOURQUIN. Feb. 11, 1852.

Granted marriage license to JOSIAH J. WALDHAUER and JANE L. HINELY. Feb. 11, 1852.

Issued subpeonias for JOSHUA HINELY, JOHN T. RAHN, JESSE T. WILSON, and GEORGE R. WRIGHT. Feb. 15, 1852.

JAMES GRIFFIN applied for adm. on the estate of WILLIAM M. CRAIG. FEB. 25, 1852. Granted May 3, 1852.

(p.57) Will of TRYON PACE was ordered to be recorded. Mar. 1, 1852.

I so solemnly swear that this writing contains the true Last Will and Testament of TRYON PACE, dec'd, as far as I know and believe; and that I will well and truly execute the same. . .Mar. 1, 1852...GEORGE PACE.

Letters Testamentary were granted GEORGE PACE. Mar. 1, 1852.

Will of LEWIS MYERS, dec'd, was admitted to record. Mar. 1, 1852.

(p.58) We do solemnly swear that this writing contains the true Last Will and Testament of LEWIS MYERS, dec'd, as far as we know or believe; and that we will well and truly execute the same. . .Mar. 1, 1852. . .F. M. STONE, WM. RAHN.

Letters Testamentary were granted FELL STONE and WM. RAHN. Mar. 1, 1852.

WM. RAH, guardian of LEWIS MYERS, an insane person now dec'd, applied for dismission. Mar. 1, 1852.

(p.59) Granted marriage license to JOHN W. WHITNEY and ANNA HURST. Mar. 5, 1852.

Granted marriage license to ARCHIBALD W. GILL and CAROLINE HANGRAVES. Mar. 13, 1852.

(p.60) Granted marriage license to JOHN BIRD and LOUISA C. WILSON. Apr. 14, 1852.

Granted marriage license to ERNST W. GUYER and MARIA CORNELIA HUNCAS. Apr. 28, 1852.

(p.61) I do solemnly swear that WILLIAM M. CRAIG died without any Will as far as I know and believe and that I will well and truly administer on all and singular the estate. . .May 3, 1852.

(p.62) EDMUND A. MINGLEDORFF was appointed guardian of the minor heirs of JAMES GRIFFIN. May 3, 1852.

On the petition of ZARA POWERS and MILTON H. POWERS stating that HUGH E. CASSIDY, adm. of HUGH CASSIDY, dec'd. was wasting and mismanaging said estate. Ordered that he give other security on his bond as adm. if he failed to do so, the prayers of the petitioners be granted. May 3, 1852.

(p.63) JAMES R. RAHN took an oath and will truly perform his duties as Receiver of the Estate of HORACE MALLORY, dec'd, and power and authority was granted him. May 5, 1852.

Guardianship of MARIA P. and MARGARET A. B. GRIFFIN, orphans of JAMES GRIFFIN, was granted E. A. MINGLEDORFF. May 5, 1852.

Granted marriage license to BENJAMIN J. FARMER and MARY ANN STEWART. May 8, 1852.

Granted marriage license to HENRY PERY and ELIZABETH HINELY. May 19, 1852.

(p.65) Granted marriage license to THOMAS ALFRID DAVIS and REBECCA SARAH A. ELKINS. June 28, 1852.

(p.66) HENRY T. ZETTLER applied for adm. on the estate of ROBT. H. BOURQUIN, he being the husband of MONILLE BOURQUIN. July 5, 1852. Granted July 5, 1852.

ELIZABETH HINELY, mother of EDWIN J. HINELY, orphan of JOHN HINELY, dec'd, petitioned to be appointed guardian of said orphan. July 5, 1852. Granted same day.

(p.67) I ELIZABETH HINELY do consent and agree that my security GEORGE MOTTIWEILER shall take charge of all the moneys that shall come to or belong to EDWIN J. HINELY, July 5, 1852.

I do solemnly swear that ROBT. H. BOURQUIN died without a Will as far as I know or believe, and that I will well and truly administer on all and singular the estate. July 5, 1852.

(p.68) Granted marriage license to SIMON SMITH and CAROLINE E. MORGAN. July 12, 1852.

(p.68) Granted marriage license to JOHN W. EDWARDS and MARIA H. MORGAN. July 24, 1852.

Granted marriage license to CLETUS GNANN and MARY G. WEITMAN. July 29, 1852.

EDMUND A. MINGLEDORFF applied for adm. on the estate of ROBERT J. MINGLEDORFF. July 29, 1852. Granted Sept. 6, 1852.

(p.69) Dismission was granted JAMES RAHN, adm. of the estate of SOLOMON WEITMAN. Aug. 2, 1852.

The granting of dismission to MARY ANN HURST, admix. of the estate of JESSE HURST, is postponed until said objections are withdrawn on the grounds of said objection regularly dispursed of. Aug. 2, 1852.

NATHANIEL ZETTLER applied for and obtained temporary adm. on the estate of HENRY T. ZETTLER. Aug. 14, 1852.

NATHANIEL ZETTLER applied for adm. on the estate of HENRY T. ZETTLER. Aug. 14, 1852.

(p.71) Granted marriage license to DAVID A. AMBROSE and CATHARINE E. WALLS. Aug. 21, 1852.

Granted marriage license to Dr. O. P. BEALER and REBECCA L. MYERS. Aug. 31, 1852.

I do solemnly swear that ROBT. J. MINGLEDORFF died without a Will, as far as I know or believe, and that I will well and truly administer on all and singular the estate. . .Sept. 6, 1852...E. A. MINGLEDORFF.

(p.72) MARY ANN HURST was granted dismission as admix. of the estate of JESSE HURST. Sept. 6, 1852.

(p.73) MOSELLE ZETTLER applied for adm. on the estate of ROBT. H. BOURQUIN. Sept. 6, 1852. Granted Nov. 1, 1852.

Granted marriage license to JOHN M. HARRISON and LOUISY R. COLSON. Sept. 15, 1852.

(p.74) Granted marriage license to JAMES J. EXLEY and SUSANNAH A. EXLEY. Sept. 25, 1852.

ISRAEL HINELY, adm. of the estate of JOHN HINELY, dec'd, applied for dismission. Oct. 4, 1852. Granted May 2, 1853.

(p.75) I do solemnly swear that HENRY F. ZETTLER died without any Will, as far as I know and believe, and that I will well and truly administer on all and singular the estate. . .Oct. 4, 1852. . . NATHANIEL ZETTLER.

Granted NATHANIEL ZETTLER adm. on the estate of HENRY F. ZETTLER. Oct. 4, 1852.

MARION M. WILSON, orphan of HENRY M. WILSON, dec'd, made choice of JAMES F. BERRY as his guardian. Oct. 4, 1852.

(p.76) Ordered that Will of C. BEVILL, dec'd, be recorded. Oct. 4, 1852.

I do solemnly swear that this writing contains the true last Will and Testament of C. BEVILL, as far as I know and believe, and that I will well and truly execute the same. . .Oct. 4, 1852...E. M. SOLOMON.

Letters Testamentary were granted E. M. SOLOMON. Oct. 4, 1852.

(p.77) BENJAMIN BLITCH applied for guardianship to GEORGE, ALLEN, and ADELINE HURST, minors of JAMES HURST, dec'd. Oct. 4, 1852. Granted Dec. 6, 1852.

JAMES RAHN, adm. of the Estate of SARAH G. WYLLY, dec'd, was dismissed. Nov. 1, 1852.

(p.78) JAMES J. HINES applied for guardianship to HANNAH A. WATT, a Lunatic. Nov. 1, 1852.

Granted marriage license to THOMAS H. BEASLEY and MARTHA A. GRIFFIN. Nov. 12, 1852.

Granted marriage license to EDMOND T. MORTON and MARIA TISON. Nov. 14, 1852.

Granted marriage license to LEWIS B. DASHER and LAURA A. NEASE. Nov. 17, 1852.

(p.79) CAMELL TYSON applied for adm. on the estate of CALVIN TYSON. Nov. 24, 1852. Granted Jan. 10, 1853.

155

(p.80) MARY HURST and JANE HURST, minors of JAMES HURST, dec'd, made choice of Dr. PETER M. STOTESBURY as their guardian. Dec. 6, 1852.
Granted REDDICK FUTRELL adm. on the estate of CHRISTOPHER T. FUTRELL dec'd. Dec. 6, 1852.
(p.81) I do solemnly swear that CHRISTOPHER T. FUTRELL, died without any Will, as far as I know or believe, and that I will well and truly administer on all and singular the estate. . .Dec. 6, 1852. . .REDDICK FUTRELL.
Granted marriage license to CARMUND TYSON and AMANDA E. CANUET. Dec. 20, 1852.
Granted marriage license to KEELAND S. BLITCH and MARY A. HUNT. Jan. 3, 1853.
(p.82) JOHN T. ZIPPERER applied for adm. on the estate of JOSHUA GLOUVER. Jan. 3, 1853. Granted Mar. 3, 1853.
Jan. 10, 1853 - D. H. SHUMAN applied for adm. on the estate of JAMES SHUMAN, with Will annexed. Granted Mar. 7, 1853.
I do solemnly swear that CALVIN TYSON died without any Will, as far as I know or believe, and that I will well and truly administer on all and singular the estate. . .Jan. 10, 1853. . .CAMMEL TYSON.
(p.83) THOMAS HURST, minor of JAMES HURST, made choice of KEELAND S. BLITCH as his guardian. Jan. 10, 1853.
GEORGE TYSON, minor of CALVIN TYSON, dec'd, made choice of ARCHIBALD GUYTON as his guardian. Jan. 10, 1853.
(p.84) Granted marriage license to JAMES L. HILTON of Darien, Georgia and AMANDA C. BIRD. Jan. 15, 1853.
Granted marriage license to MATTHEW BURGSTEINER and JANE FRYERMUTH. Jan. 20, 1853.
Dr. P. M. STOTESBURY applied for guardianship to ROBERT M. RIEVES and HANNAH RIEVES, minors of JOHN G. RIEVES. Feb. 1, 1853. Granted May 4, 1853.
(p.85) ALEXANDER A. SMETS, adm. of the estate of FRANCES C. SOLOMONS, was granted dismission. Feb. 7, 1853.
(p.86) Granted guardianship to SARAH D. MORGAN to her four children, to wit: RYALL, LUCRETIA, VIOLA, and REBECCA. Feb. 7, 1853.
(p.87) GEORGE ANN FUTRELL, minor of CHRISTOPHER T. FUTRELL, made choice of REDDICK FUTRELL as her guardian. Feb. 7, 1853.
(p.88) REDDICK FUTRELL applied for guardianship to the orphans of CHRISTOPHER T. FUTRELL, dec'd. Feb. 11, 1853.
Granted marriage license to EPHRAIM R. WALDHAUER and JULIA C. ZEIGLER. Feb. 21, 1853.
JOHN BEATTICE WATT applied for adm. on the estate of ALEXANDER WATT, dec'd. Feb. 1853. Granted Apr. 4, 1853.
SOLOMON ZEIGLER applied for guardianship to the orphans of JOSHUA GNANN, dec'd. Mar. 1, 1853.
Granted marriage license to HENRY TULLIS and REBECCA T. FUMES of Scriven County. Feb. 26, 1853.
Granted marriage license to NORMAN MINGLEDORFF and GEORGIA A. DASHER. Mar. 3, 1853.
(p.89) GEORGE PACE, Exec. of the Last Will and Testament of TRYON PACE, applied for dismission. Mar. 7, 1853.
I do solemnly swear that JOSHUA GNANN died without any Will as far as I know or believe, and that I will well and truly administer on all and singular the estate. Mar. 7, 1853. . .JOHN T. ZIPPERER
(p.90) I GEORGE KELLER do solemnly swear that SARAH KELLER died without any Will as far as I know or believe and that I will well and truly administer on all and singular the estate. . .Mar. 7, 1853.
Adm. on the estate of SARAH KELLER was granted GEORGE KELLER. Mar. 7, 1853.
(p.91) Granted marriage license to JACOB L. FREYERMUTH and AMANDA L. WEITMAN. Mar. 8, 1853.

(p.90) I do solemnly swear that this writing contains the true last Will and Testament of JAMES SHUMAN, dec'd, so far as I know or believe; and that I will well and truly execute the same. . .Mar. 7, 1853. . .D. H. SHUMAN.

(p.91) Granted marriage license to GEORGE L. METZGER and ANN C. ARNSDORFF. Mar. 10, 1853.

(p.92) ARCHIBALD GUYTON applied for temporary adm. on the estate of ZARA POWERS. Mar. 24, 1853. Granted Mar. 24, 1853.

I do solemnly swear that ZARA POWERS died without any Will as far as I know or believe, and that I will carefully collect and preserve from waste or loss all the goods and effects of said deceased. . .Mar. 24, 1853. . .ARCHIBALD GUYTON.

ARCHIBALD GUYTON, ELVIRA POWERS and MILTON H. POWERS applied for adm. on the estate of ZARA POWERS, dec'd. Mar. 24, 1853. Granted ELVIRA POWERS adm. on May 2, 1853. ARCHIBALD GUYTON and MILTON H. POWERS declined.

(p.93) Will of ALEXANDER WATT was produced and admitted to record. Apr. 4, 1853.

(p.94) I do solemnly swear that this writing contains the true last Will and Testament of ALEXANDER WATT as far as I know or believe; and that I will well and truly execute the same. . .Apr. 4, 1853. . .JOHN BEATTICE WATT.

(p.95) BRADIE M. WATT was granted adm. on the estate of HANNAH A. WATT. Apr. 4, 1853.

I do solemnly swear that HANNAH A. WATT died without any Will as far as I know or believe, and that I will well and truly administer on all and singular the estate. . .Apr. 4, 1853. . .BRADIE M. WATT.

(p.96) MILTON H. POWERS, adm. with the Will annexed of JAMES S. CRUM, dec'd, applied for dismission. Apr. 4, 1853.

Granted marriage license to SAMUEL BIDDENBACK and ELIZABETH DASHER. Apr. 16, 1853.

Granted marriage license to LEWIS GROVENSTEIN and THURZA A. MOREL. Apr. 20, 1853.

(p.98) I do solemnly swear that ZARA POWERS died without any Will as far as I know or believe, and that I will well and truly administer on all and singular the estate. . May 6, 1853. . .ELVIRA POWERS.

(p.100) Granted marriage license to JOHN R. PACE of Chatham County and MARY I. DASHER. May 12, 1853.

Granted marriage license to MILTON HESTER and SUSAN BOWMAN. May 18, 1853.

(p.101) Ordered that an insturment of writing purporting to be a will of MARIA S. MALLORY be recorded. June 6, 1853.

ALBERT G. PORTER applied for adm. with Will annexed of MARIA S.MALLORY. June 28, 1853. Granted Aug. 1, 1853.

(p.102) Guardianship was granted SOLOMON ZEIGLER to JOSEPH H., VIRGINIA I., EURSELIA and MARIA I. GNANN, minors of JOSHUA GNANN, dec'd. July 4, 1853.

(p.103) Granted marriage license to DANIEL ZETTLER and ELIZABETH FINKLEY both of Chatham County. July 18, 1853.

(p.105) I do solemnly swear that these writings (not yet proved) contains the true last Will and Testament of MARIA S. MALLORY. . . A. G. PORTER.

(p.106) ANN ROBBINS applied for temporary adm. on the estate of DANIEL J. ROBBINS, dec'd. Aug. 17, 1853.

I do solemnly swear that DAVID J. ROBBINS died without any Will as far as I know or believe, and that I will collect and preserve from waste or loss all and singular the estate. . .Aug. 17, 1853. . .ANN X ROBBINS.

Letters Testamentary were granted ANN ROBBINS. Aug. 17, 1853.

ANN ROBBINS applied for adm. on the estate of DAVID J. ROBBINS, dec'd. Aug. 17, 1853. Granted Oct. 3, 1853.

WILLIAM J. MANNER applied for adm. on the estate of FRANCES C. SOLOMON. Aug. 23, 1853. Granted October 3, 1853.

Granted marriage license to JOHN WOLF and JANE HURST. Sept. 3, 1853.

(p.107) Ordered that a Commission examin WILLIAM MORGAN as to his alleged insanity and incapacity to manage his affairs and to make a return of their proceedings to this Court next term. Sept. 5, 1853.

(p.108) Granted GEORGE PACE, Exec. of the estate of TRYON PACE, dismission. Sept. 5, 1853.

(p.109) I do solemnly swear that DANIEL J. ROBBINS died without any Will as far as I know and believe; and that I will well and truly administer on all and singular the estate. . .Oct. 3, 1853. . .ANN X ROBBINS.

(p.110) I do solemnly swear that FRANCES C. SOLOMONS died without any Will as far as I know or believe, and that I will well and truly administer on all and singular the estate. . .Oct. 3, 1853. . .WILLIAM J. MANER.

JOHN B. WATT applied for guardianship to the minor children of ALEXANDER WATT, dec'd. October 18, 1843. Granted Jan. 2, 1854.

WILLIAM B. DASHER applied for adm. on the estate of WILLIAM THOMAS, dec'd. Oct. 27, 1853. Granted Dec. 5, 1853.

(p.111) JAMES BIRD, WASHINGTON BIRD, and FRANKLIN BIRD, minors of WILLIAM BIRD, dec'd, made choice of EDWARD BIRD as their guardian. Nov. 7, 1853. Granted Dec. 15, 1853.

(p.112) We the commissioners appointed by the Court of Ordinary of Effingham County to examine WILLIAM MORGAN as to his alleged insanity of mind this 5th day of Nov. 1853, return as our decision that in our belief he is of sane mind. O. P. BEALER, M. C. FOREMAN, JEREMIAH MALLETTE, M. METZGER, A. G. PORTER, JOHN TROWELL, W. D. BUSSY, E.A. MINGLEDORFF, JAMES EDWARDS, J. G. MINGLEDORFF, WM. O. RAHN, G. D. MINGLEDORFF.

Ordered that application be dismissed. Nov. 7, 1853.

JOHN ROBERT NEASE was appointed guardian of JAMES B. SHEAROUSE, JANE LOUISA SHEAROUSE, JOSHUA C. SHEAROUSE, WASHINGTON E. SHEAROUSE, and FRANCES M. SHEAROUSE, Minors of EMANUEL SHEAROUSE, dec'd. Nov. 7, 1853.

(p.113) Granted MILTON H. POWERS, adm. with Will annex of JAMES S. CRUM, dec'd, dismission. Nov. 7, 1853.

Granted marriage license to WILLIAM NUNGEZER of Chatham County and MARY E. EXLEY. Nov. 28, 1853.

No Pages 114 and 115

(p.116) Granted ELIZABETH HURST guardianship of JESSE HURST and JOHANNA HURST, minors of THOMAS HURST, dec'd, Dec. 5, 1853.

(p.117) WILLIAM S. HURST and MARY J. HURST, minors of THOMAS HURST, dec'd, made choice of ARCHIBALD GUYTON as their guardian. Dec. 5, 1853.

I do solemnly swear that WILLIAM DASHER, died without any Will as far as I know or believe, and that I will well and truly administer on all and singular the estate. Dec. 5, 1853. . .WM. B. DASHER.

(p.118) WALLACE W. WATT, and ACTANIUS G. WATT, minors of ALEXANDER WATT made choice of JOHN B. WATT as their guardian. Dec. 5, 1853.

(p.119) Ordered that the probate of the Will of EMANUEL SHEAROUSE be revoked, and it is further ordered that the said EMANUEL SHEAROUSE under the act of 1834 died interstate and that his estate be distributed under the laws of this state regulating the distribution of interestates estates.....Dec. 5, 1853.

(p.120) Granted marriage license to G. W. ABBOTT, JR., and MARY A. ELKINS. Dec. 9, 1853.

Granted marriage license to JAMES SPEIR and MARY J. HURST. Dec. 21, 1853.

Granted marriage license to BENJAMIN J. DAVIS and CAROLINE ZIPPERER. Dec. 23, 1853.

Granted marriage license to HUGH E. BENTON and SARAH COUSEY. Dec. 24, 1853.

Granted marriage license to JOHN L. ARNSDORFF and JANE L. SHEAROUSE, Dec. 26,.1853.

(p.121) Granted marriage license to FELIX M. HURST and JANE P. MORTON. Jan. 3, 1854.

Granted JAMES R. RAHN, Receiver of the estate of HORACE MALLORY, dec'd, dismission. Jan. 9, 1854.

(p.122) Granted division of the estate of THOMAS HURST, dec'd. Jan. 9, 1854.

(p.123) Granted marriage license to JAMES B. SHEAROUSE to SOLOMIE DASHER, Jan. 11, 1854.

158

(p.123) SAMUEL E. MILLER applied for adm. on the estate of WILLIAM J. MILLER.
Jan. 13, 1854.

Dr. T. E. DeFORD applied for temporary adm. on the estate of Dr. WILLIAM
B. DEWES. Jan. 16, 1854. Granted Jan. 16, 1854.

I do solemnly swear that Dr. WILLIAM B. DEWES died without any Will as far
as I know or believe, and that I will carefully collect and preserve from waste or loss
all the goods and effects of said deceased. Jan. 16, 1854. . .JOHN D. DEFORD.

(p.124) Granted marriage license to STEPHEN A. WILSON and LAURA DAVIS. Jan. 24,
1854.

REDDICK FUTRELL, adm. of the estate of CHRISTOPHER F. FUTRELL, dec'd
applied for dismission. Jan. 24, 1854.

GEORGIA COURT-HOUSE RECORDS

EFFINGHAM COUNTY

MARRIAGES

Editor's Note: As previously explained in publishing marriage records in
GGM., there was no law in Georgia requiring the return of marriage-licenses to the
issuing officer after a marriage was performed, until 1806. In some of the counties that were in existence at that time, the clerks of the Court of Ordinary had
kept a list of licenses they had issued together with the date of issuance, but as
the licenses were never returned such list or record carried no date of marriage;
and after the new law went into effect, a good many ministers and Justices of the
Peace were either in ignorance of the law or didn't attach any importance to it,
and failed to return the license with an entry thereon showing the marriage.

Effingham County was one of those counties where the Clerk kept a list
of the licenses he issued, and as a result we of to-day have a record of licenses
issued dating back to 1791 in Effingham County, which antedates the creation of
counties later made out of partly out of Effingham. While it is true that the issuance of a marriage license did not necessarily mean a couple were married, it is
safe to assume that fully 98% or 99% of the licenses were duly executed (that is,
the marriages were performed). In Effingham County this list as well as (after
1806) a verbatim copy of the license with the return thereon of the officiating
Justice or minister, was mixed in with administrations and wills &c., in two rather
large volumes entitled "Miscellaneous Records" down as late as about 1827-28, after
which the record of licenses was kept in a separate book.

The historic old Salzburger church named Ebenezer in Effingham County
was organized long before the Revolutionary War, and the church pastors kept a list
of the marriages they performed which with other early church records has been published in book form. No effort has been made here to incorporate that list in with
those found in the court-house, as was done by the Editor in publishing Liberty Coun
ty marriages and including those shown in Midway Church records.

In the following list of marriages the dates are those of the marriages
except those marked with (*) and in those instances the dates are of when the marriage license was issued. Names of officiating ministers or Justices are omitted
as having no genealogical significance. Most of the licenses showed the county
of residence of the groom and bride after about 1810, but few before then did.
The omission of the name of a county of course denotes no county was named. The
abbreviation of "E.C." or "Eff.Co." in the following list, means "Effingham County"
Only a few of the marriage licenses fail to show "Miss" or "Mrs."

Date	Groom:	Bride:
Oct. 7, 1791*	Solomon Groover	Miss Hannah Elizabeth Powledge
- - 1792*	Jarvis Jackson	Catherine Hodges
Mar. 26, 1792*	Daniel Clifton	Siney Warren
Apr. 16, 1792*	David Rieser	Mary Grovenstein
June 6, 1792*	Joseph Helvenstine	Miss Sarah Frazier
June 14, 1792*	John Moore	Mersie (Mercy) McCall
Mar. 31, 1793*	Daniel O'Neil	Ann Clyatt
Apr. 30, 1793*	John Grovenstine	Sarah Seigler (Zeigler?)
Dec. 7, 1793*	Isaac Mott	Miss Polly Colson
Dec. 11, 1793*	Matthew Cantey	Mrs. Lydia Ford
Dec. 13, 1793*	Abraham Colson	Miss Elizabeth Mott
Dec. 22, 1793*	Bird Lanier	Miss Elizabeth Dixson
Jan. 5, 1794*	David Snook	Miss Elizabeth Porter
Feb. 22, 1794*	John Michael (Mikell?)	Miss Elizabeth Groover

Mar. 12, 1794*	James Greenhow, Jr.	Miss Abegail Scruggs
Mar. 24, 1794*	John Williams	Miss Rhettee London
Apr. 21, 1794*	Joshua Stafford	Mrs.Mary Lane,relict of Thos.Lane
Apr. 22, 1794*	Henry W. Williams	Miss Sarah McCall
Apr. 25, 1794*	Joseph Rahn	Miss Naomi Setter
May 24, 1794*	Anthony Pitts	Miss Ann Rawleson (Raulerson?)
June 27, 1794*	Christian Shubtrine	Mrs. Ann Catherine Dimnam
July 8, 1794*	Daniel Weitman	Mrs. Ann Catherine Kramer
July 26, 1794*	William Crawford	Miss Betsy Bailey
July 30, 1794*	John Garnet	Miss Mary Bostick
Aug. 4, 1794*	John Staton (Staten)	Miss Penelope Sellers
Aug. 14, 1794*	Jonathan Snider	Miss Elizabeth Gnann
Nov. 1, 1794*	David Metzger	Mrs. Mary Reasor (Reisser?)
Nov. 13, 1794*	James Boston	Miss Elizabeth Briggs
Dec. 20, 1794*	John Lucas	Miss Claricy Denmark
Dec. 30, 1794*	David Ewing	Miss Mary Conway
Jan. 14, 1795*	William Brterwith (sic)	Mrs. Rachel Garnet
Jan. 16, 1795*	John Porter	Miss Henrietta Ravot
	(This license carries a notation "Marriedthe same day".)	
Feb. 9, 1795*	Charles Gachet	Miss Mary Gobert
Feb. 18, 1795*	Josiah Daniel	Mfs. Sarah Campbell
Feb. 21, 1795*	Jonathan Beckley	Miss Mary Reaser
Feb. 5, 1795*	Spence Cox	Miss Mary Ryell (sic)
Mar. 11, 1795*	Jacob Kittles	Miss Amy Garnet
June 20, 1795*	Walden Griffin	Miss Esther Rawleson (Raulerson?)
May 4, 1795*	William Morgan	Miss Sarah Bailie
May 5, 1795*	John Folk	Mrs. Mary Sheely
July 2, 1795*	George Heite (Heidt?)	Miss Sally Remshart
Aug. 4, 1795*	John Ivy	Miss Naomi Woodlif
Aug. 29, 1795*	John Heck	Miss Agnes Powledge
Sept.17, 1795*	George Powledge	Miss Sarah Stiner
Sept.18, 1795*	Thomas Roberts	Miss Elizabeth Pinninger

(Editor's Note: It seems likely that not all the marriage licenses
issued were listed by the clerks in the early years, as for instance,
the fact that there is no record of licenses issued from the last one
above,Sept. 1795, until May,1796, and only four shown for that year.)

May 9, 1796*	Joshua Zant	Miss Catherine Steiner
June 9, 1796*	Martin Busche	Mrs. Judith Buntz
Nov. 18, 1796*	John Grabenstine (sic)	Mrs. Catherine Hangleiter
Dec. 27, 1796*	James Goldwire	Miss Sarah King
Jan. 24, 1797*	David Zitterauer	Miss Elizabeth Ihly
Feb. 4, 1797*	Noah Dikes	Miss Sally Staton (Staten?)
May 9, 1797*	John Keebler	Mrs. Rosanna Stockman
June 10, 1797*	Thomas Schweighoffer	Miss Salome Zant
July 26, 1797*	James Sharbrough	Mrs. Mary Lewis
July 29, 1797*	David Porter	Miss Sally Bostick
Oct. 19, 1797*	Henry Lewis Grabenstine	Mrs. Judith Bush
March 6, 1798*	Christopher Hudson	Mrs. Hannah Heersen
Mar. 21, 1798*	James Holten (sic)	Mrs. Hannah Greenhow
Apr. 27, 1798*	William Bird	Miss Elizabeth Stiner
Apr. 25, 1798*	Christian Biddenbach	Mrs. Mary Frederica Foy
June 20, 1798*	Samuel Snider	Miss Catherina Zeigler
July 3, 1798*	Richard Touchstone	Mrs. Martha Crawford
Aug. 16, 1798*	Tryon Pace	Miss Mary Dykes
Sept.18, 1798*	Gottlieb Ernst	Miss Catherine Fields

Oct. 24, 1798*	John Stewart	Mrs. Mary Hunter
Nov. 13, 1798*	David Groover	Miss Hannah Shearousé
Dec. 28, 1798*	Benjamin Morel	Miss Susannah Gindrat
Jan. 16, 1799*	Jacob Hinely	Miss Elizabeth Mick (sic)
March 7, 1799*	Rev. James Sweat	Miss Susannah Anderson
Mar. 30, 1799*	John F. Lockner	Miss Hannah Heisler
Apr. 16, 1799*	Gideon Zettler	Miss Martha Wilson
Apr. 24, 1799*	Israel Leimberger	Miss Mary Catherine Snider
July 24, 1799*	Gross (or Grass?) Scruggs	Miss Ann Lunday
Aug. 3, 1799*	John Palmer	Miss Elizabeth Mikell
Aug. 10, 1799*	Jesse Wilson	Miss Elizabeth Cook
Oct. 16, 1799*	Christian Bechtly	Miss Elizabeth Reisser
May 28, 1799*	Minis Lamley (sic)	Miss Pollie Hines
July 4, 1799*	James Garrison	Miss Martha Dykes
Oct. 2, 1799*	Green Hill of Screven Co.	Miss Chrissy Bridger
Nov. 6, 1799*	Timothy Gnann	Miss Catherine Leimberger
Jan. 18, 1800*	John Coward	Miss Lydia Rollison (Raulerson?)
Apr. 18, 1800*	John Grovenstine	Miss Mary Reiser, dau.of Israel
June 2, 1800*	Israel Reiser	Mrs. Anna Barbara Kieffer, widow
		of Emanuel Kieffer,late of Chatham Co.
June 21, 1800*	Frederick William Kahnden	Mrs. Rosina Keebler,relict of John
June 27, 1800*	John Snyder,tailor,Chatham Co.	Miss Salome Gnann
June 28, 1800*	Anthony Oglesbee	Mrs.Salome Metzger,relict of Jacob
July 31, 1800*	John Martin Dasher, Jr.	Mrs.Hannah Hudson,widow of Christo-
Oct. 29, 1800*	David Helmly	Miss Dorothy Shearouse (pher
Nov. 5, 1800*	Israel Flerl	Miss Salome Waldhauer
Dec. 18, 1800*	Reubin Grant Taylor	Miss Mary Stafford
Jan. 31, 1801*	Christian Dasher Jr. of Sav.	Miss Anne Bird
Feb. 22, 1801*	Christian Zipperer	Miss Susannah Wilson
Apr. 30, 1801*	Christopher Hechel	Mrs. Ann Hornsbee of Wilkes Co.
May 14, 1801*	Thomas Waugh	Miss Mary Lewis
June 15, 1801*	William Shuman	Miss Mary Bridges
Aug. 17, 1801*	William Hurst	Miss Rosannah Bleachington (Blitch?)
Sept.19, 1801*	James Shuman	Miss Martha Key
Sept.19, 1801*	Seth G. Threadcraft of Chat-	Miss Salome Schweighoffer of E.Co.
Oct. 5, 1801*	John Dampier (hamCo.	Miss Esenure Hodge (Hodges?)
Jan. 14, 1802*	William Wylly of Chatham Co.	Miss Naomi Dasher
Jan. 29, 1802*	Andrew Gnann	Miss Agatha Cramer
Feb. 1, 1802*	Joel Waistcoat	Miss Cynthia Millnor
Feb. 2, 1802*	Matthew Rahn	Miss Hannah Elizabeth Dolwich
Apr. 12, 1802*	Charles Zyall	Miss Mary Boston
April 2, 1802*	John Leimberger	Miss Christian Elizabeth Seckinger
Apr. 10, 1802*	John Michael Mock, Jr.	Miss Catherina Sherraus
Apr. 15, 1802*	Christopher Gnann	Miss Catherina Freyermuth
July 2, 1802*	William Dupuise	Mrs.Dorcas Gindrat, relict of Henry
July 5, 1802*	Gottlieb Ernest, Esq.	Miss Margaret Rahn, dau.of Matthew
Aug. 9, 1802*	James Gibson	Mrs.Sarah Parker of Chatham Co.
Oct. 30, 1802*	William Wright	Miss Sarah Jenkins
Sept.20, 1802*	Jesse Hurst	Miss Mary Hodges
Dec. 3, 1802*	Jonathan Ernst	Mrs.Catherine Birch,relict of Benj.
Dec. 7, 1802*	William Roper	Miss Sarah Mitzger
Dec. 15, 1802*	Lewis Bird	Miss Hannah Nessler
July 26, 1802*	James Guttery (Guthrie?)	Miss Elizabeth Jenkins
Aug. 3, 1802*	James Thomica? of Chatham Co.	Miss Anne Hines
	(Practicbioner of Physic)	
Dec. 27, 1802*	David Leimberger	Miss Naomi Kieffer
Feb. 17, 1803*	Asa Loper	Miss Ester (Esther?) Lanier
Apr. 13, 1803*	Howell Hines	Miss Margaret West

May 23, 1803*	John Wisenbaker	Miss Mary Densler
Sept. 5, 1803*	Thomas Morgan	Miss Creacy (Lucretia?) Crawford
Sept.24, 1803*	Benjamin Blitch	Miss Sarah Spears (Spiers?)
Sept.22, 1803*	Emanuel Zipperer	Mrs.Martha Zettler,relict of Gideon
Sept.22, 1803*	William Townsend	Miss Mary Ernst
Oct. 17, 1803*	Spier Blitch	Miss Zilpha Hurst
Nov. 15, 1803*	Jacob Peterson	Miss Mary Holliday
Dec. 3, 1803*	Edward Cook of Bulloch Co.	Miss Sarah Bird
Dec. 13, 1803*	Benjamin Oglesbee	Mrs.Mary Wisenbaker,widow of John
Jan. 23, 1804*	Joseph Helvenstine	Miss Sarah Read
Feb. 25, 1804*	William Loper of S.C.,	Miss Hannah Burgsteiner
Feb. 23, 1804*	Joel Kieffer	Mrs. Catherine Zant
March 9, 1804*	Charles Goolsby	Mrs. Abigail Goolsby
Mar. 10, 1804*	Joshua Dasher	Miss Dolly (Dorothy?) Moore
Nov. 24, 1804*	Benjamin Jones of Bryan Co.	Miss Rebecca Bishop
Dec. 25, 1804*	Edmond Tison	Miss Nancy Cook
Jan. 2, 1805*	Ansel Walker of Glynn Co.	Miss Alley Tison
Jan. 27, 1805*	Eleazer Bell, Esq.	Miss Mary Causey
Mar. 15, 1805*	Gunning C. Bedford	Mrs.Eliza Ann Burch
June 2, 1805*	William Hawthorn	Miss Elizabeth Canada (Cannady?)
Sept. 2, 1805*	Joseph Holliday	Miss Cynthia Hines
Nov. 20, 1805*	Eliakim Tison	Miss Anne Hearn
March 8, 1806*	Luke Wilson	Miss Patience Crawford
May 30, 1806*	Nathaniel Hall	Miss Mary Pace
May 30, 1806*	Hugh Smith	Miss Catherine Elkins
June 12, 1806*	Whitson Pugh of Burke Co.	Mrs. Susannah Grant
July 22, 1806	Christian Heidt	Miss Elizabeth Pepper
July 29, 1806	William Shrimph	Miss Anne Catherine Seckinger
Sept. 9, 1806*	Edmond Hester	Idy Lanier
Sept.30, 1806*	David Wilson of Bulloch Co.	Miss Polly Temples
Oct. 6, 1806*	Peter Hawthorn	Margaret Cook
Nov. 7, 1806*	James Gibson	Elizabeth Denny
Nov. 18, 1806*	Joshua Lee,Barnwell Co.S.C.,	Sarah Elkins
May 5, 1807	John Gottlieb Fetzer	Miss Elizabeth Erhardt
Nov. 2, 1807$	John Christopher Reinlander	Mrs.Elizabeth Beckley,widow of Chris-
Nov. 24, 1807	Israel Hinely	Miss Hannah Hensler (sic) (tian
Nov. 16, 1807*	John Adam Metzger	Miss Christina Rahn
Nov. 26, 1807	John George Mingledorff	Miss Emelia Neidlinger
Oct. 1, 1807*	Andrew Grinier (Griner?)	Miss Anne Gnann
Dec. 29, 1807	Gabriel Wilson	Miss Sarah Oglesbie
Dec. 28, 1807*	George Nowlan	Miss Hannah Gugel
Feb. 11, 1808	Benjamin Alexander	Miss Elenor Crawford
Feb. 12, 1808	Benjamin Burton	Miss Elenor Rowell
Feb. 24, 1807	John Waldhauer, Jr.	Miss Margaret Weidman
Dec. 5, 1807	John Christopher Seckinger	Miss Agneta Rahn
Jan. 28, 1808	John Hurst of Burke Co.	Miss Elizabeth Blitch
June 30, 1808	Ernst William Geyer	Miss Elizabeth Helmly
Aug. 2, 1808	John Slaser (Staser?)	Miss Gratiosa Zetterauer
Oct. 20, 1808	Thomas Porter	Miss Salome Gruber
Mar. 12, 1807	Seth Daniel of Effingham Co.	Miss Mary Kennedy of Eff.Co.
March 9, 1809	John Goldwire, Jr. of Eff.Co.	Miss Frances Offutt of Eff.Co.
Mar. 16, 1809	Temple Tullis	Miss Patience Spear of Eff.Co.
Mar. 23, 1809	William Stevens of Eff.Co.	Miss Anne Marks of Eff.Co.
March 7, 1808*	John McLin	Chloe Day
Apr. 6, 1808*	John T. Pearce	Rosanna Calder
Oct. 17, 1808*	Samuel Fitzpatrick	Vinia (Lavinia?) Buy (sic)
Nov. 1, 1808*	Evans James	Louisa Cook

Mar. 22, 1809* James Anderson Hannah Glaner
Mar. 12, 1809* James Cruse (Crews?) Anna Cruse (Crews?)
Nov. 13, 1809* James Lovett Catherina Zitterauer
Jan. 31, 1810* John Exley Anna Porter
Feb. 23, 1810* Stephen Tullis Sinai London
June 7, 1810 Thomas Stuart of Savannah Mrs. Hannah Dahher of Ebenezer
July 12, 1810 William King of Effingham Co. Miss Margaret Mary Ravot of E.Co.
May 10, 1810 Benj. Seckinger of Eff.Co. Miss Salome Zitterauer of Eff.Co.
Mar. 13, 1810 John Christopher Cramer of EC. Miss Mary Weidman of Eff.Co.
Aug. 2, 1810 John Barnard Staley of EC. Mrs.ElizaAnn Bedford of E.Co.
Jan. 23, 1811 Abel G.Loper of Eff.Co. Miss Phoeby O'Neal of Eff.Co.
Apr. 23, 1811 John Gottlieb Seckinger,E.C. Miss Mary Weidman of Eff. Co.
Jan. 4, 1811 Gottlieb Zitterauer Miss Margaret Gugel of E. Co.
May 21, 1811 JohnWinter of Savannah Miss Dorothy Geiger of Eff.Co.
Sept. 5, 1811 John Elkins of Eff. Co. Mrs. Mary --- (blank) of Eff.Co.
Aug. --, 1811 Thomas Elkins of Eff.Co. Sarah Rivers of Eff. Co.
Aug. 10, 1811 Robert Burton of Eff.Co. Eliza Denmark of Bulloch Co.
Nov. 22, 1811* John J. Metzger of Eff.Co. Miss Nadine Berry of Effingham Co.
Apr. 23, 1811 Joshua Helmly of Eff. Co. Miss Salome Seckinger of Eff. Co.
Oct. 3, 1811 Stephen Dampier of Eff.Co. Miss Anne Graham of Effingham Co.
Nov. 26, 1811 Emanuel Rahn of Effingham Co. Miss Sarah Berry of Effingham Co.
Jan. 18, 1812 Waitstill C.Orvis of Savannah Miss Susannah J.Gromet of Ebenezer
Jan. 17, 1812* Solomon Hinely of Eff. Co. Miss Elizabeth Beichenbach of E.Co.
Jan. 27, 1812* Gottlieb Ernst of Eff. Co. Miss Catherina Kieffer of Eff. Co.
June 9, 1812 John Freyermuth, Sr.of E.Co. Miss Hannah Elizabeth Weidman of E.Co
June 17, 1812 John Bittenbach of Eff.Co. Miss Naomi Seckinger of Eff.Co.
Dec. 7, 1812* Solomon Gnann,Jr. of E.Co. Miss Sarah Heidt of Effingham Co.
Dec. 7, 1812* Jacob Gnann of Eff. Co. Mrs. Christina Metzger,relict of Adam
Dec. 7, 1812* Ernest Zetior (sic) Mrs. Catherine Cruger. (of EC.
Dec. 15, 1812 Solomon Gnann of Eff.Co. Miss Sarah Weidman of Eff.Co.
April 2, 1812 John Neidlinger of Savannah Miss Catherine Dasher of Eff.Co.
Jan. 19, 1813 Emanuel Sherraus Miss Lydia Heidt of Eff. Co.
Feb. 9, 1813 Solomon Dasher Miss Mariah Wylly
Feb. 15, 1813* Allen Box of South Carolina Miss Moriah Newton
April 6, 1813 William G. Porter Miss Mary Truetlin
May 19, 1813* Silas Morton Miss Mary Huntdr of Screven Co.
May 20, 1813 John Alexander Snowden Miss Ann Margaret Wisenbaker of E.Co.
Dec. 23, 1813 Daniel Toomer Miss Martha Hodges
Oct. 14, 1813 Martin Dasher of Eff.Co. Miss Lydia Witeman of Eff.Co.
July 11, 1813 John Rigedale Miss Mary Wheeler
March 1, 1813* Thomas Teleton (sic) Mrs. Elcy Coleman
Jan. 5, 1813 Richard Touchton Miss Martha Penrow
Jan. 5, 1814 J. J. Helvenston Miss Margaret Tiner of Eff.Co.
Jan. 22, 1814* John Lessler Miss Mary Tison,dau.of Cammel Tison
Jan. 13, 1814 Murry Reed Miss Lydia Rieser (of EC
June 26, 1814* William Carlton of U.S.Troops)Miss Sarah McRory "from up-country".
              stationed at or near Court House
Sept. 3, 1814* Luther Tison of Eff. Co. Miss Winnifred Hines of Eff.Co.
Sept. 8, 1814 John Neidlinger Miss Catherine Bergman of Ebenezer
Sept.12, 1814* Benjamin Dowdy Miss Elizabeth Brock
Sept.22, 1814* Joshua Seckinger Miss Salome Niess
Apr. 17, 1815* John McRory of Eff. Co. Miss Jane Pitts of Eff.Co.
Nov. 6, 1815* EEihu Wilson of Eff.Co. Miss Catherine Tullis of Eff.Co.
Nov. 13, 1815 Israel Heidt of Eff.Co. Miss Catherine Nettles of Eff.Co.
Nov. 28, 1815 Matthew Heidt of Eff.Co. Miss Hannah Weitman of Eff. Co.
Dec. 21, 1815 John Curry Miss Rhody Tyner
Dec. 28, 1815 John G. Tyner Miss Mary Curry

164

Apr. 2, 1815	Solomon Arnsdorff of E.Co.	Miss Sarah Weitman of E.Co.
Apr. 2, 1815*	Richard Pellam	Mrs. Sarah Wilson
Apr. 29, 1816*	James Reisser	Miss Dysi (sic) Dykes
(no date) *	Elijah Walsingham	Miss Mary Shuffel (Sheffield?)
Nov. 7, 1816	Abel Hill of Effingham Co.	Mrs. Agnes Atler of Eff. Co.
July 3, 1817	Valentine Kisler of Eff. Co.	Miss Christiana Seckinger of Eff.Co.
Sept.11, 1817	John Knight of Eff. Co.	Miss Ann M. Barrs of Eff. Co.
Oct. 30, 1817	John Jacob Metzger of Eff.Co.	Miss Lidia Dasher of Effingham Co.
Jan. 29, 1818	Godlip Sherraus of Eff. Co.	Miss Salome Freyermuth of Eff. Co.
Feb. 4, 1818	John Alexander Mason of Va.	Mrs. Ann Mary Triebner of Eff. Co.
June 25, 1818*	Solomon Exley of Eff. Co.	Miss Sarah Backley of Eff. Co.
July 2, 1818	Lewis Weitman of Eff. Co.	Mrs. Sarah Flerl of Effingham Co.
Jan. 8, 1819*	Christian E. Trueline of S.C.	Miss Ann M. Fruelandof Effingham Co.
Jan. 25, 1819*	John Arnsdorff of Eff. Co.	Miss Sarah Morgan of Eff. Co.
March 4, 1819	Willis Bleach (Blitch?)	Miss Amy Tyner
March 5, 1819	Willey Wright	Ann M. Wisenbaker of Effingham Co.

(End of Marriages in Book "B" of Miscellaneous Records)

****

Page 1:   L. W. & T. of CATHARINE SNYDER, Dec. 26, 1826. First - desire that all
          lawful debts be paid. Second - all the Estate coming from brother, EMANUEL
ZEIGLER, shall be divided into three equal parts or shares and 1/3 to SUSANNAH SNYER,
1/3 to DAVID HINELY, 1/3 be equally divided between DAVID MALLET and ROBERT LEWIS
MALLET, sons of niece, SUSANNAH MALLET. Third - if draw lot of land in the present
contemplated land lottery be sold to best advantage by Executor, and profit be
divided among same persons as heretofore in second clause. Appoint LEWIS WEITMAN as
sole Executor. Wit: ISREAL WALDHAUER, JOHN WALDHAUER, THOMAS FLERL.

Page 2:   L. W. & T. of CHRISTOPHER BAILEY, (no date). After all just debts and bills
          are paid that wife, GRACY BAILY, shall keep and have all real and personal
Estate for her to live on and support during her natural life and after her
death go to daughter, SARAH MORGAN. Also, desire Executor and Excutrix sell some
part of property and raise money to clear a certain tract of land drawed in land
lottery known by number 76 in 14th District of Carrol County. Appoint wife, GRACY
BAILEY, and WILLIAM MORGAN, SR., son-in-law, as Executrix and Executor. WIT:
JOHN SOUTHWELL, JOSHUA BEDDENBACK.

Page 4:   L. W. & T. of MARY KENNEDY, Jan. 1, 1827. Give and bequeath to son,
          RICHARD ALEXANDER THADEUM (THADEUS?) MASON, son of GERRARD ALEXANDER MASON
dec'd of N.C. two beds left him by his grandmother, HANNAH DAPRES, also silver spoon
and such as will come to me from the estate of BENJAMIN KENNEDY. Appoint friend,
GOTTLIEB ERNST, as Executor. Will him to take child into his care and receive
compensation for his schooling until age he can be put out to learn trade. WIT:
B. MORREL, CHRISTINA RYALL.

Page 5:   L. W. & T. of HENRY COOK, Aug. 15, 1825. First give to wife, LYDIA COOK,
          all estate real and personal during natural life and after decease give
one half real and personal estate to brother, LEWIS COOK, to his heirs Executor of
Administrator forever; and the other half real and personal estate after death of
wife to JESSE L. PILLS. Give unto MARY MERCER negro man, HARRY. Unto my nephew,
GEORGE COOK, after death of wife, my Negro girl, LEAH. Appoint wife, LYDIA COOK,
Executrix and LEVI LYON, EXECUTOR. WIT: LEVI LYON, R. LYON, WALDEN GRIFFIN.

Page 8:   L. W. & T. of JOSEPH HELVENTON, Mar. 26, 1829. 1st - desire all lawful
          debts be paid. 2nd - give unto son, JOHN JOSHUA HELVENSTON, a Negro named
JACK, a Negro man named BILLY, and a Negro girl, FANNY & her increase. Also four
hundred acres of land. 3rd - give unto son, JOHN CHARLES HELVENSTON a Negro woman,
SALLY, Negro boy, TOBY and a Negro girl named CHARLOTTE & their increase. 4th -
give unto my son, JOSEPH T. HELVENSTON a Negro boy named LONON and a Negro boy named
JIM and four hundred acres of land. 5th - give unto daughter, MARY M. HELVENSTON, a
Negro woman named BETSY, a Negro girl LYDIA, a Negro boy GLASCOW, and a Negro girl
HETTY and their increase. 6th - give unto my grandson, WILLIAM WALLACE MARTIN, one
dollar. 7th - desire that my horse and stock be sold by Executors and money be
equally divided between sons and daughter. Appointed sons, JOHN JOSHUA HELVENSTON
and JOHN CHARLES HELVENSTON, to be Executors. WIT: JOS. GROMET, J. WALDHAUER,
ISRAEL HINELY.

Page 10: L. W. & T. of JOSHUA LINEBURGER, Oct. 4, 1830. 1st - wish to be buried
          in decent manner and debts occuring during sickness be paid. 2nd - give
unto son, E. WILLIAM GIER, a feather bed, two blankets, two sheets, two pillows,
a mattress to be sold or appraised at sons discretion and him to have one half of
money from sale. 3rd - give unto grand child, ANNA WINTER, daughter of my late
daughter, DOROTHY GIER married unto JOHN WINTER (now deceased) a bed, two blankets,
two pillows, two sheets and other half of money arising from sale of mattress,
provided for security of said property of grandchild, ANNA WINTER. Appointed son,
ERNST WILLIAM GEIR, as Executor. WIT: JOSHUA LINEBURGER, GOTTLIEB ERNST.

Page 11: L. W. & T. of DAVID REISER, Nov. 5, 1830. 1st - will that debts and
          funeral charges be paid. 2nd - desire that eldest son, JEREMIAH, take
possession of my residence and that he order a sale and dispose of as much of my
personal effects as will satisfy my debts. 3rd - daughter, CATHARINE, equal part.
Appoint son, JEREMIAH, Executor. WIT: J. B. BERRY, LUKE EXLEY, EPHR. KEIFFER.

Page 13: L. W. & T. of JAMES KEEBLER, Nov. 13, 1830. 1st - give unto my brethren
          JOSHUA KEEBLER, JR., THOMAS KEEBLER, WILLIAM KEEBLER all my right, title,
interest or share I may have in the Estate of John Thly, dec'd, to them and their
heirs. 2nd - give unto aforesaid brethren and my sister, CATHARINE E. BURCKSTEINER,
my right, title, or share to the tract of land on which my father, JOSHUA KEEBLER, SR.
now resides containing 200 acres more or less to them and their heirs. 3rd - give
and bequeath unto my wife, ANN ELIZABETH KEEBLER, one dollar to be paid to her by my
Executor. Appoint brother, JOSHUA KEEBLER, Executor. WIT: JOSEPH GROMET,
JOSHUA KEEBLER, SR., JOHN COPE.

Page 16: L. W. & T. of ELIZABETH COPE, Nov. 8, 1825. Give to daughter-in-law, wife
          of JOSHUA KEEBLER, not subject to any contract or debts of her present or
any future husband to grand children JOSHUA KEEBLER, JR., THOMAS KEEBLER, CATHARINE
ELIZABETH KEEBLER, JAMES KEEBLER, and WILLIAM KEEBLER. Appoint son, JOSHUA KEEBLER,
Executor.

Page 16: L. W. & T. of HENRY GROVENSTEINE, Feb. 19, 1826. 1st - give unto my
          wife whole and sole benefit of all my real and personal property during
the minority of children, and after youngest child comes of age, an equal division to
be made among children. 2nd - desire children receive decent education and be
brought up and instructed in the true religion of the Saviour of the world. 3rd -
if wife not willing to keep Negroes, them be hired out to such people as would do
them justice and hire of them to support her and children. 4th - if wife should
marry after my death, wish she should live comfortable during her life, property
be distributed among children after her death. Appoint wife, HANNAH, as first
manager and secondly nominate EPHRAIM KEIFFER to act with her in the management of
my Estate agreeable to her wish. WIT: LUKE EXLEY, PAUL TOOSING, JEREMIAH REISER.

Page 17: Will of CAMMEL TISON, Jan 3, 1828. 1st - to my wife, UNITY TISON, house
          and plantation during her life or widowhood. Also bay mare saddle and
bridle and an equal share in stock of cattle with three youngest sons, and household
furniture. 2nd - to my elder son, LUTHER TISON, one dollar and a quarter American
money. 3rd - to son, CALVIN TISON, one dollar and a quarter American money. 4th -
to daughter, TIMNY WOOLF, one spinning wheel. 5th - to MAHATA TISON, one good
feather bed with furniture, two cows and calves, two setting chairs, two ewes and
lambs. 6th - to daughter, UNITY, one spinning wheel. 7th - three youngest sons:
WILLIAM C. TISON, JONATHAN TISON, and THOMAS TISON, all real estate be equally
divided between them. Also plantation tools with household furniture. Also, my
stock of cattle, hogs and sheep with all horses. Appointed sons, CALVIN TISON and
WILLIAM C. TISON, Executors. WIT: MICAJAH FUTRELL, TISON, J. CARRASON.

Page 19: Will of JOHN C. RAHN, Aug. 12, 1832. 1st - desire crop and horses be
          sold to satisfy creditors, only reserving sufficient for maintenance of
family and negroes be hired out for benefit of my heirs and creditors. 2nd - remainder of estate be equally divided between wife, MARGARET RAHN, and son JOHN THOMAS
RAHN and share and share alike. Appointed CHRISTIAN H. DASHER as Executor. WIT:
CLETUS RAHN, JOHN FETZER, L. WEITMAN.

Page 20: Will of JOHN POWERS, July 21, 1832. 1st - my wife, LYDIA, four negro
          slaves and give her use of my lands and plantation together with the
buildings and improvements thereon and my stock of cattle, horses and hogs, plantation
tools and household and kitchen furniture which is not hereafter bequeathed. 2nd -
to my son-in-law, THOMAS ELKINS, husband of my late daughter, SARAH, who left several
children, eight slaves, one feather bed and its furniture and a tract of land in
Bulloch County. 3rd - son-in-law, HENRY CRUM, husband of late daughter, ABIGAIL, a
tract of land in Bryan County, a small stock of cattle, feather bed and its furniture.
4th - to sons, ZARA and CLEM, ten slaves and after death of my wife to be equally
divided as aforesaid all the property above bequeathed to wife. Appointed ZARA
POWERS and CLEM POWERS Executors. WIT: JOHN SOUTHWELL, STEPHEN HESTER, SR.,
JAMES CRUM.

Page 23: Will of GODHIEF SHEEROUSE, April 13, 1832. 1st - desire all lawful debts
          be paid. 2nd - unto my wife, MARY, her bed and bed clothes and a cow and
calf to be chosen by her out of my stock and a sow and pigs and all the poultry in
the yead. 3rd - unto grandson, WILLIAM HENRY SHEROUSE, one heiffer now chosen.
4th - desire all estate be sold by executor excepting that already bequeathed and to

be equally divided between my wife, MARY SHEEROUSE, EMANUEL SHEEROUSE, GODLIEB
SHEEROUSE, my sons, and HANNAH EDWARDS, AGUATA FRYERMUTH, MARY WILSON, my daughters,
and WILLIAM HENRY SHEEROUSE, my grandson. 5th - appoint EMANUEL SHEEROUSE, my son,
as executor. WIT: JOHN ARNSDORFF, WILLIAM ARNSDROFF, JOSEHUA GNANN.

Page 25: Will of JAMES BRYAN, Dec. 17, 1831. Give to wife, KATHARINE, my tract of
land on which I now live containing 320 acres, together with all household goods and my stock of all kinds, horses included and at her death be divided
between my two sons, JAMES and JOSEPH. Give to daughters, SARAH and ELIZABETH, one
hundred dollars to be paid one year after the death of my wife. Also give to
daughter, ANN, tract of land which Mr. ISAAC BRYAN now lives on after my death and
after her death be divided equally among the lawful heirs of her body. Daughters,
MARY, JANE, RACHAEL and stepdaughter, ELIZABETH, have received their portion of
estate in several tracts of land. Appoint RALPH BOWMAN and KATHARINE BRYAN as
Executor and Excutrix. WIT: WILLIAM HARRISON, BENJAMIN GENOBLY, ROBERT BOWMAN.

Page 27: Will of James Wilson, April 6, 1825. Give unto wife, ELIZABETH, a child's
part of my personal property which will be her part out of whole estate
and who ever takes care of her during her natural life. Give unto sons, JOHN &
HENRY, and also unto daughters, REBECCA & KESIAH all remaining property real and
personal to be equally divided among them, with the following exception that the
share of son, JOHN, be eighty dollars less in value than the regular shares. Also
enjoin on my excutors to appropriate adequate sum previous to division given unto
my son, HENRY, and my daughter, KISIAH, a liberal education and a reserve kept out of
estate for support of HENRY & KESIAH until they are of age. Appoint son, JOHN,
and JOHN GOLDWIRE, I. G. MINGELDORFF, Executors. WIT: JOHN B. BERRY, CLETUS RAHN,
SOLOMON EXLEY.

Page 28: Will of William Edwards, Sr., Sept. 30, 1833. Already given to two sons,
BEAL and OBADIAH, by deed the real estate and given to daughter, CHLOE
DOWNS, and her eldest child, ANN ELIZA, a bed and furniture and such stock of cattle
as intended them to have, I exclude them all from any portion of the balance, except
plantation tools which wish divided equally between said sons. Give to two other
grandchildren, CATHARINE CAROLINE and GEORGIA ANN and VALERIA GRACY, each one cow
and calf. The balance be given to five daughters: GLADY, ELIZABETH, ANN, DORCAS,
& RUTH be equally divided. Appoint BEAL and OBADIAN, Executors. WIT: JOHN DUGGER,
SR., C. POWERS.

Page 30: Will of PAUL BEVILL. 1st - all my just debts be paid. 2nd - give to wife
SARAH BEVILL, estate real and personal with exception of which has been
disposed of to daughter, SARAH FORD MATHEWS, in deed of true. 3rd - give unto
grandson, PAUL BEVIL, one negro boy, one tract of land containing five hundred acres,
one other tract containing four hundred and fifty acres. 4th - give to following
grandsons: PAUL B. GARNELL, STEPHEN T. BEVILL, JAMES BEVILL, CLAIBORNE BEVILL,
JOHN G. BEVILL, PAUL R. BEVILL and WILLIAM COLSON, residue of my property when
STEPHEN P. BEVILL comes to years of maturity, also five negroes. Appoint JOHN
GOLDWIRE MATTHERS and WILLIAM H. SCRUGGS, Executors. WIT: HENRY WHITE, JOHN PITTS.

Page 32: Will of William Downs, Nov. 20, 1830. Unto wife, Elsy, all real and
personal property. Unto children of late daughter, LUCY CONAWAY, two
dows and calves or ten dollars. Also balance of estate give to seven surviving
children, their heirs and assigns, to be divided equally between them. Appoint
son, BARRET DOWNS, Executor. WIT: WILLIAM HOLLINGWORTH, SARAH COX, C. POWERS.

Page 34: Will of WILLIAM KING, Oct. 7, 1834. 1st - lawful debts be paid.
2nd - give to wife, MARGARET M. KING, dwelling house and buildings and
plantations after her death give to son, JAMES. 3rd - when children attain maturity
they may require and have a division which shall be equally divided. Appointed
JAMES GOLDWIRE and GEORGE W. BOSTON, Executors. WIT: JOHN G. MATHERS, JAMES O.
GOLDWIRE.

Page 36: Will of JESSE DYKES, Nov. 29, 1830. 1st - to wife, MARY DYKES, old
plantation and timber and one third of all stock or horses, cows and hogs
and all household and kitchen and household furniture of all kinds and after her
death to go to two sons, JESSE D. DYKES and GEORGE D. DYKES. 2nd - give to JESSE D.
DYKES and GEORGE D. DYKES all land, one third of horses, cattle, hogs, and kitchen
and household furniture. Give to daughter, PANSEY, wife of TURNEY WILLIS, five

dollars she having had her portion before. Appoint sons, JESSE D. DYKES and GEORGE D. DYKES, Executors. WIT: DANIEL EDWARDS, WILLIAM CURRY, JOHN CRAWFORD.

Page 38:   Will of NICHOLAS MYERS, Aug. 10, 1835. 1 - funeral expense and just debts be paid. 2 - unto BENJ. C. PORTER all estate consisting of one negro man, a stock of cattle and hogs. 3 - Appoint BENJ. C. PORTER, sole Executor. WIT: WILLIAM H. KENNEDY, I. R. MORGAN.

Page 39:   Will of JOHN GRAHAM, Oct. 24, 1835. 1 - unto wife, SELITA GRAHAM and children: JESSE SELETA DUNCAN, ALEXANDER, JANE ELIZABETH, SUSAN MATILDA, and WILLIAM DUGAL GRAHAM, all tract of land on which I now reside containing 200 acres with dwelling house, kitchen and all out houses, household and kitchen furniture with provisions and plantation tolls with all horses, cattle, except such as shall dispose in will, and hogs. Also plantation on which formerly resided, two negro slaves. 2 - daughter, MARGARET ANN, five cows and calves and one feather bed and furniture. 3 - daughter, MARTHA, five cows and calves and one feather bed and furniture. 4 - daughter, FLORA, five cows and calves and one feather bed and furniture. 5 - as first six named children arrive to age of maturity shall receive five cows and calves and one feather bed each and furniture. 6 - son, JOHN W. GRAHAM, one half dollar, already received the same amount as is given to three daughters. 7 - daughter LAVINI WILSON, wife of JAMES ELBERT WILSON, one half dollar, having received same amount as son JOHN GRAHAM. 8 - when youngest child shall arrive year to maturity, balance of property shall be sold and equally divided. 9 - Appoint wife, SELITA GRAHAM, Executrix and son, JOHN W. GRAHAM, Executor. WIT: M. G. MATHERS, FLORA GRAHAM, WILLIAM HODGES.

Page 41:   Will of JOHN EXLEY, Aug. 13, 1836. 1 - wife to raise daughter, GEORGI- ANNA & MATILDA, my negro man with a 50 area lot of land also the right and title to use of 300 acres for the raising and educating two daughters until they become of age and then an equal division to take place. 2 - give to son, RICHARD, 50 acres. 3 - 50 acres be sold until all debts is fully discharged. Appoint JOHN B. BERRY and EPHRAIM KEIFFER, Executors. WIT: JACOB GNANN, LUCAS EXLEY, LYDIA EXLEY.

Page 43:   Will of LYDIA COOK, Apr. 17, 1833. 1 - give unto WM. H. TUCKER five negroes with my plantation and plantation tools with my stock of cattle, sheep and hogs and four head of horses with my household and kitchen furniture. 2 - give unto MARY MERCER, one dollar. 3 - GEMEMA TUCKER, one dollar. 4 - WM. GADDY, SARAH PRESATT and MARIAH KNIGHT, one dollar each. 5 - JOHN TUCKER, ELIJAH TUCKER & ELIZABETH KNIGHT, one dollar each. 6 - SAMUEL ANDERS, ELIZABETH TAILOR & JOURDAN ANDERSON, one dollar each. Appoint WM. H. TUCKER & WM. SPIER, Executors. WIT: WILLIAM WILSON, BENJAMIN BLITCH, GARY WHEELER

Page 45:   Will of SOLOMON GNANN, Jan. 13, 1838. 1 - real estate and personal effects be sold. 2 - $50.00 to wife and bedding. 3 - children be educated with remaining money. 4 - after boys reach proper age be bound to learn trade. Appointed UNGLE BENJAMIN GNANN, Executor. WIT: ANDREW GNANN, RICHARD FETZER, EPHRAIM KEIFFER.

Page 46: Will of CHRISTOPHER GNANN, Nov. 23, 1837. Bequeath $10.00 to GRACIE ARNS- DORFF, widow, $10.00 to CATHERINE GNANN, daughter of TIMOTHY GNANN, my brother, and $10.00 to ANN MARGARET ARNSDORFF, widow. Bequeath to each brother and sister $15.00. Appoint brother, BENJAMIN, Executor. WIT: WM. RAHN, EPHRAIM KEIFFER.

Page 48:   Will of JOHN DUGGER, (no date). Desire my Negro woman, ANTONINETTE, and her two children, together with my Negro man, JACK, be set free. I direct my Executors to sell all real estate and remaining Negroes and all cattle, horses, etc., and proceeds given to my Father and Mother and brothers, and sisters equally. Appoint BEAL EDWARDS and PAUL MARLOW, Executors. WIT: RAYMOND HARRIS and WM. LORN.

Page 49:   Will of SOLOMON CRAMER, Oct. 2, 1838. Give to wife, MARY CRAMER, bedding, bedstead, bed clothes after payment of all lawful debts. Give to wife and children living with her all provisions for their support. Give wife estate both real and personal and after her death be given to son, ALEXANDER. Tract of land on Ebenezer Creek be sold to pay children: SOPHIA, SARAH, ELIZABETH and ALEXANDER

money due them which was bequeathed to them by their Grandmother being $100.00. Two
lots in Ebenezer be sold and overpluss be divided equally. Give to son, ALEXANDER,
blacksmiths tools. Appoint wife, MARY CRAMER, and EPHRAIM KEIFFER, Executors.
WIT: DAVID ZEIGLER, CHRISTOPHER GNANN, ISRAEL WEITMAN.

Page 51:   Will of SELITE GRAHAM, July 22, 1839. Give unto three sons: JESSE
            GRAHAM, ALEXANDER GRAHAM and WILLIAM DUGAL GRAHAM; 400 acres of land,
including all plantations and premises to be equally divided. Give to son, JESSE
and ALEXANDER GRAHAM, trustee for five daughters: MARGARET ANN GRAHAM, FLORAH
GRAHAM, SELITE DUNCAN GRAHAM, JANE ELIZABETH GRAHAM, SUSAN MATILDA GRAHAM, 500 acres
of land to be equally divided. Give to daughter, MARTHA HANNAH, $30.00. Give to
daughter, LAVINA WILSON, $1.00. Leave all the rest of estate to be equally divided
among eight children. Appoint two sons, JESSE and ALEXANDER GRAHAM, Executors.
WIT: WILLIAM HODGES, SAMUEL HODGES, MARGARET ANN GRAHAM.

Page 53:   Will of ROBERT BURTON, May 21, 1835. Give to son, CHARLES A. BURTON, 17
            slaves. Give to grandchildren, MARTHA BURTON and MARY BURTON, daughters
of late son, HENRY A. BURTON, four slaves. Give to daughter-in-law, SARAH BURTON,
widow of said dec'd son, $25.00. Give to son, SIMON BURTON, one slave. After pay-
ment of all just debts give to wife, ELIZA BURTON and sons: ROBERT BURTON and
BENJAMIN BURTON, the balance of estate consisting of lands, negroes, stock, furniture
and other property be equally divided. Appoint wife, ELIZA BURTON, Executrix and
sons: CHARLES A. BURTON, ROBERT BURTON, and BENJAMIN BURTON, Executors. WIT:
C. POWER, B. WATERS, MILTON H. POWERS.

Page 55:   Will of WILLIAM RYALLS, Oct. 13, 1839. Give negro man, JACK, be sold and
            debts be paid. Give unto mother sorrel horse with a white face called the
brandy horse. Give to brother, ISAIAH, negro woman PEG and her children. Remainder
of property real and personal be sold and amount be shared equally between mother,
brother, and sisters. Wish that articles that belonged to dec'd wife be sent to her
Father and Mother. I leave my mother my Executrix and JOHN MORGAN, Executor. WIT:
THOMAS MAYS, SR., I. M. MORGAN, J. R. MORGAN.

Page 56:   Will of JONATHAN RAHN, Jan. 9, 1839. Desire that pine lands in survey
            map beginning at number four and ending at number ten, also Bollinger
Tract, Sheerouse tract, Hanleiters tract and Rushes tract be divided between WILLIAM
RAHN, CLETUS RAHN, JACOB GNANN, JOHN WILSON and BENJAMIN GNANN amount to $2,201.50.
Give to grandchildren of dec'd son, EMANUEL, $314.50 and to grandchildren of dec'd
daughter, MARGARET, $314.50. Desire negro property be disposed of in following
manner - son, CLETUS RAHN to have JULY for $500.00. JACOB GNANN and my daughter,
CHRISTINA, to have JACOB for $500.00. JOHN WILSON and my daughter, SUSANNAH, to have
BEN for $500.00. BENJAMIN GNANN and my daughter HANNAH to have ADAM for $500.00.
My grandchildren of dec'd son EMANUEL to have BILLY for $350.00. To grandchildren of
dec'd daughter, MARGARETTA, in lieu of negro I give $407.14. Give to SARAH EXLEY 50
acres of land being part of a tract no. four on survey map with improvements. Balance of estate be equally divided. Appoint son, WILLIAM RAHN, JACOB GNANN, and JOHN
WILSON Executors. WIT: JONATHAN GNANN, JOHN I. REISER, EPHRAIM KEIFFER.

Page 58:   Will of STEPHEN TULLIS, Jan. 3, 1841. Give to wife, LINEY TULLIS, tract
            of land containing 300 acres known as McCall tract with all buildings and
improvements. Give to wife, one negro woman and her two children. Desire that all
estate be kept together while wife lives. Children: HENRY I. TULLIS, MARY ANN TULLIS,
PAUL F. TULLIS, WILLIAM I. TULLIS, SARAH M. TULLIS, ELYHEM TULLIS, have equal part of
estate if wife departs this life or marries. Appoint wife, LINEY TULLIS, and JENRY
TULLIS, Executors. WIT: HENRY I. TULLIS, PAUL A. TULLIS.

Page 60:   Will of JOHN DUGGER, Dec. 16, 1836. Give to wife, ESTHER DUGGER, my
            plantation and six cows and calfs or yearlings, two bunches of hogs, in one
bunch eighteen or twenty head in other about three sows and pigs about thirteen or
fourteen head and one horse, all ready money, three beds and furniture, my provision
crop consisting of corn, potatoes, and bacon, kitchen furniture and plantation tools.
Give unto daughter, TABILBU MARLOW, one tract of land containing 250 acres. Give unto
son, JOHN, and daughter, MARY, all lands which I have not already disposed of to be
equally divided between them. Also, plantation which I live on be equally divided
between them at death of my wife. Balance of stock of cattle and hogs, three head
of horses and one tract of land in Early County containing 250 acres be sold at public
sale and money be equally divided among children. Appoint PAUL MARLOW & JOHN DUGGER,
Executors. WIT: JOHN M. HINES, JOHN MULLIS, DAVID DUGGER.

Page 61:   Will of DAVID GUGEL, Dec. 25, 1841. Give to daughter, ELIZA CHARLTON,
            wife of JOHN CHARLTON, and her children all that tract of land known as my
plantation called Ashville where I now live containing 750 acres, together with all
buildings and appurtenances thereon, together with mill. Also a part of 100 acres of
land on mill and Racoon Creek. Also 11 slaves and my stock, all the silver plate,
one cart. Second, give to granddaughter, ANN E MCDOWELL, wife of ALEXANDER MCDOWELL,
and her children one half of my lot and buildings thereone, one fourth of personal
property not herein bequeathed. Third, give to grandaughter, MARGARET G. SAUSY, wife
of Dr. J. R. SAUSY, to her and her children one half of my lot with buildings. Also
one fourth of personal property not herein bequeathed. Fourth, give to grandaughter,
GEORGIANNA A. REINHART, wife of DAVID REINHART, other half of lot. Also 250 acres
of land. Also one fourth of personal property not herein bequeathed. Fifth, give to
grandson, JAMES OLCOTT, son of late daughter, MARY ANN OLCOTT, other half of lot.
Also 490 acres of land. Also, one fourth of personal property not herein bequeathed.
Sixth, give to grandson, JOHN DAVID CHARLTON, my silver watch. Seventh, my clock
remain with the family in the house. Eighth, all personal property to daughter,
ELIZA CHARLTON, and her children, be sold by Executors to pay off lawful debts and to
make the division amongst the four above named grandchildren. Ninth, Appoint JOHN
CHARLTON and RICHARD CUYLER, Executors. WIT: LEWIS MYERS, I. A. COURVORSIE, JOSHUA
HINELY.

Page 66:   Will of HENRY M. WILSON, Dec. 29, 1841. Desire estate be kept together
            until youngest child comes to year of maturity unless wife should marry,
then be divided among heirs. Appoint JOHN C. MINGLEDORFF, Executor. WIT:
CHRISTOPHER REISSER, SOLOMON EXLEY, ELIAS MANN.

Page 67: Will of CHRISTIAN DASHER, Sept. 27. 1842. Give unto wife, ANN DASHER, my
            negro girl, MARCIA, ten cows and calves, or cows & year., her choice, one
feather bed, one mattress, two pillows, and a bolster and bed cloaths to suit one
bedsted. Give to here with $50.00 per annum be paid by executors. Give to son,
JOHN DASHER, and W. B. DASHER, my negro boy, JOHN, my negro boy, FRIDAY, my negro girl
CHARLOTTEE, in trust for daughter, JANE ELIZA DASHER. Give her an equal share of
other property with other children. Give to son-in-law, GEORGE TROY, $.50.
Daughter-in-law, MARY DASHER, $.50, and daughter-in-law, SUSAN C. DASHER, $.50, and
daughter-in-law, MARY ANN DASHER, $.50, daughter-in-law, HANNAH E. DASHER, $.50,
son-in-law, EDMUND A. MINGLEDORFF, $.50, daughter-in-law, WINNEFRED ANN DASHER, $.50.
Give to son, JOHN DASHER, $36.00. Give to daughter,JULIANNA A. MINGLEDORFF, $50.00
less than the other children they having received that amount the balance of property.
Give to children share and share alike except JESSE E. DASHER, who is not to have
any more negro property but is to have equal share of other property with other
children names: REBECCA FOY, JOHN DASHER, JAMES A. DASHER, EDWIN DASHER, WM. B.
DASHER, JOSHUA M. DASHER, ANDREW I. DASHER, JANE E. DASHER, JULIANNA A. MINGELDORFF,
ELIZABETH DASHER. Appoint JOHN and WM. B. DASHER, Executors. WIT: NATHANIL
SHEAROUSE, ALEXANDER W. RAHN, E. THUROWH.

Page 70:   Will of CHRISTINA RYALL, Dec. 24, 1842. Give to daughter, ANN E MORGAN,
            negroe girl, CATY. To daughter, SARAH D. MORGAN, my boy MALLORY, cattle
and hogs. To son, ISAIAH B. RYALS, negro man, JACK, the horse, Brandy, my cart and
plantation tools. To daughter, REBECCA RYALS, my negro man, GEORGE, but she must pay
to her sister, MARY M. RYALS, $100.00. To daughter, MARY M. RYALS, my negro boy,
TONEY. My mare and colt be divided between daughters, REBECCA and MARY. To son-in-
law, DAVID P. SNOOKS, husband to daughter, EDNEY P., dec'd. $1.00. Appoint JOHN R.
MORGAN, Executor. WIT: JOSEPH T. SMITH, MATTHEW M. MORGAN, M. R. MORGAN.

Page 72:   Will of GODHIEF I. NEASE, June 24, 1844. Give to son, JAMES JEREMIAH NEASE,
            plantation on which I now live, also 200 acres joining East side of
plantation, a negro boy, one clock and ten head of cattle which he is to make choice
of out of stock of cattle. Give to son, EDWARD LEONARD NEASE, two tracts of land in
Effingham County; one tract containing 75 acres and other containing 100 acres, a
negro boy, a red cherry table, and ten head of cattle which he is to make choice of
out of stock of cattle. Give to two named sons one mattress each and the bed cloath-
ing that belongs to each mattress. Give to daughter, HARRIET SHEEROUSE, wife of
WILLIAM SHEEROUSE, a negro girl. Give to son, FREDERICK NEASE, a negro boy. Give to
daughter, EVELINE, wife of RICHARD SHEEROUSE, a negro girl. Give to daughter,
ELVIRCE KESLER, negro girl, RACHAEL, my two negroes, BEUTON and L, together with the
plantation tools and provisions, together with other household furniture not herein

bequeathed. All cattle, hogs, sheep be sold occasionally, as it may be required for payment of debts. Two shotguns to two sons, JAMES and EDWARD. 200 acres of land in county of Bryan be sold. Appoint FREDERICK I. NEASE and JOHN ROBERT NEASE, my two sons, Executors. WIT: J. G. MINGLEDORFF, J. MOREL, JAMES CHARLTON.

Page 75:   Will of G. T. ZITTROUR, Jan. 11, 1845. Give to wife, MARGARET, a negro man named JACK. Desire that balance of estate be sold at public sale after my death and proceeds be equally divided between my children and wife, eight shares, one share be given to my wife, one share to son, CHARLES I. ZITTROUR, one share to EDWIN I. ZITTROUR, one share to HANNAH M. CAUDELL, one share to RICHARD E. ZITTROUR, one share to WILLIAM I. ZITTROUR, one share to SARAH ANN ZITTROUR, one share to LOUISA AMANDA BARNWELL. Appoint two sons, EDWIN I. ZITTROUR and RICHARD E. ZITTROUR, Executors. WIT: FRED HINELY, JACOB HINELY, BENJ. SECKINGER, JR.

Page 77:   Will of VALENTINE KESLER, Dec. 20, 1843. Give to wife, CATHARINE, plantation with all lands which I claim in County, except tract which lies below called Helmly bay. If children do not want to keep place, it be sold and money be equally divided between wife and all children, except JOHN and WILLIAM. Desire that son, JOHN, have all land lying below called Helmly bay, a bay horse with a blaze face. Give to son, WILLIAM, 150 acres of land known as Heidts place, a black mare. Will that land lying in Irwin County be sold for benefit of family. Desire that as many of my children to whom I did not give any cattle during my life shall have two cows and calves. Wife keep together remainder to personal property for benefit of family. Appoint son, JOHN, Executor. WIT: JOHN WALDHAUER, JOSHUA HELMLY, SR.

Page 80:   Will of SPEIR BLITCH, Mar. 22, 1845. Give to wife, HANNAH BLITCH, all lands in Effingham County, including plantation I now live on, all plantation tools, household & kitchen furniture, six negroes, ten cows and calves, three Beeves and fifteen head of sheep, eighteen head of good meat hogs, four sows, and twenty head of shoates and two good work horses. Wish remaining part of stock be sold and money be put out on interest until youngest child comes of age and then an equal division be made. Appoint WILLIAM BLITCH and HENRY BLITCH, Executors. WIT: WILLIAM SPEIR, REDDICK FUTRELL.

Page 82:   Will of THOMAS H. BREWER, June 3, 1845. Give to wife, ANN BREWER, six cows and calves, one three year old steer and one four year old steer, two work horses, twelve head of good meat hogs, and all home hogs with one sow and give shoats, one cart and plantation tools, three feather beds and furniture, three bedsteds, two tables, one clock, one side saddle, twelve chairs, one lot of books. Remaining property be sold to pay just debts. Appoint ANN BREWER, Executrix and GEORGE W. BREWER, brother, Executor. WIT: STEPHEN TULLIS, WM. SPEIR, WILLIAM BLITCH.

Page 84:   Will of WILLIAM BIRD, SR., Nov. 14, 1845. Will that real and personal property be sold and divided equally between wife, MARIA BIRD, and all children herein named: WILLIAM, EDWARD, JOHN, AMANDA, JAMES, WASHINGTON, FRANKLIN, and LAURA LOUISA. Appoint sons, WILLIAM and EDWARD, Executors. WIT: G. R. WRIGHT, N. FETZER, JOHN CHARLTON.

Page 85: Will of HANNAH WEITMAN, Sept. 1, 1845. Give to daughter, MARY ANN, two tenement houses with three quarters of a lot and small office in City of Savannah. All other property: lot of land known by no. 132 in 13 district, household and kitchen furniture, together with few head of cattle, give to daughter, MARGARET ZITTROUR, and to heirs of daughter, SARAH COURVORSIE, and heirs of son, SOLOMON WEITMAN, be equally divided between them. Appoint daughter, MARY ANN, Executrix and CHRISTIAN WISENBAKER, Executor. WIT: JOHN C. WALDHAUER, FREDERICK HINELY, T. S. MILLER.

Page 87:   Will of BENJAMIN BLITCH, Oct. 27, 1845. Give to son, HENRY BLITCH, 445 acres of land whereon I now live, one mare named Pin, six cows and calves, two good Beaves, three negroes, one horse waggon with all plantation tools, household and kitchen furniture except two beds and furniture, one cart and one waggon. Give unto under named heirs: THOMAS BLITCH, MOORE BLITCH, BENJAMIN BLITCH, and CHRISTOPHER FUTRELL, all remaining undivided real and personal property, with two beds and furniture, cart and wagon to be divided equally. Appoint THOMAS BLITCH and MOORE BLITCH, sons, Executors. WIT: WM. SPEIR, REDDICK FUTRELL, JAMES SPEIR.

Page 88:   Will of ANN C. BURCKSTINER, Sept. 14, 1844. Give to son, JEREMIAH
           BURCKSTINER, my slave named JAKE. Give to grandson, BENJAMIN ROBERT
NEASE, my plantation which I now reside and 100 acres of land on which it is situated,
my mare and cart, all cattle, hogs, and sheep, all household and kitchen furniture,
plantation tools, family clock, my bedding and bed cloathes and bedsted. Give to
sister, DOROTHY SECKINGER, all above premises in trust for grandson, BENJAMIN ROBERT
NEASE. Give money owing to me when collected and all estate expense paid to my
daughter, ROSANNA AMANDA, wife of FREDERICK I. NEASE, $50.00 and my side saddle.
The balance of money owing me I give to my grandchildren, the children of daughter,
CHRISTINA ELIZABETH, former wife of GEORGE NEASE, my daughter, SALOME, wife of
JOSHUA LINEBURGER and sister, DOROTHY SECKINGER, be equally divided among them. taking
notice the children of my daughter, CHRISTINA ELIZABETH, are to have mothers share.
All estate I have in my possession marked with the mark of GEORGE NEASE, give to
granddaughter, FELICIA AMANDA, daughter of GEORGE NEASE. Appoint, JAMES RAHN,
Executor. WIT: R. ELKINS, A. RAHN, HENRY SECKINGER.

Page 90:   Will of THOMAS SYLLY, SR., Apr. 7, 1841. Give to wife, SARAH GRACE WYLLY
           and her childredn, be equally divided between JAMES and HENRY TISON,
JAMES GOLDWIRE's children, and GEORGE BURTON's two children. Give to son, WILLIAM C.
WYLLY, $5.00, but to his children a full share of estate. Give to son, ELISHA, $5.00,
but to his children a full share of estate. Give to son, LEONIDAS, one full share of
Estate. Give to son, FREDERICK ROSEBURG, a full share of State. Give to son,
THOMAS, a half share of Estate. Give to daughter, NAOMI SEALY, $5.00. Give to
daughter, ELIZABETH WILLIAM, $5.00. Give to daughter, SARAH ANN WEEKS, one full share
of Estate. Give to dec'd daughter MARIA's children a half share of Estate. Give to
wife, SARAH, old savery during natural life. Appoint ELISHA WYLLY, LEONIDAS WYLLY,
and SARAH GRACE my Executors and Executrix. WIT: MATTHEW M. MORGAN, ISAIAH RYALL,
M. R. MORGAN.

Page 91:   Will of EMANUEL SHEEROUSE, Aug. 9, 1846. Give to wife, ELIZABETH, a
           tract of land containing 200 acres called the Beddenback tract, also 50
acres of the tract I bought of Spann. Give to son, JONATHAN, 150 acreas of land, and
to son, JAMES BRADFORD, 150 acres. After death of my wife, give to two sons, JOSHUA
CHRISTOPHER and WASHINGTON EDWARDS, my plantation lands with 150 acres known as Bear
Bay tract to be divided equally between them. The balance of estate consisting of
lands, negroes, horses, cattle, hogs, and sheep be left in possession of wife until
youngest child arrives at age of 21, then divided equally among wife and children:
JOHNATHAN, JAMES BRADFORD, JOSHUA CHRISTOPHER, WASHINGTON EDWARD, MARY ELIZABETH
(wife of JOHN R. NEASE), SARAH ANN (wife of WILLIAM DUGGER), REBECCA, JANE LOUISA, and
FRACES MILESSE. Appoint sons, WILLIAM HENRY and JONATHAN SHEEROUSE, Executors.
WIT: PETER FRYERMUTH, ALEXANDER W. RAHN, GORDON WALLACE BESBEE.

Page 93:   Will of SOLOMON HINELY, Oct. 28, 1846. Wish that wife, HANNAH ELIZABETH,
           and children should keep together possessions. Give daughter, SALOME,
three heiffers, one to daughter, CHATARINA, and one to daughter, ANN. Should wife
marry or depart this life or after youngest child arrives at age of 21, all estate
remaining give to following children: SOLOMON, ISRAEL, JOHN, ELIZABETH AMANDA, and
FRANCES to be equally divided among them. Appoint son, SOLOMON HINELY, JR.,
Executor. WIT: PETER FRYERMUTH, JOHN ARNSDORFF, DAVID HINELY.

Page 95:   Will of JOHN C. MILLER, Nov. 9, 1846. Give to daughter, REBECCA, my
           homestead and plantation and the two tracts of land upon which the same
is seated containing two hundred and inety odd acres. Also give to said daughter
during the time she remains unmarried, my negro man slave. If she marries he is to
be divided among heirs hereafter named. The crop made this year not to be sold.
Hogs not to be sold but remain for family use. Balance of estate - land, horses,
cattle - give to my children to wit: ANN HEIDT, wife of JOHN HEIDT, JOSHUA MILLER;
JONATHAN MILLER, ELIZABETH SHEEROUSE, widow of EMANUEL SHEEROUSE, EMPHRAIM MILLER,
FREDERICK MILLER, MARY DASHER, wife of JOHN DASHER, to be equally divided among them
with the provision my son, FREDERICK, has received from me property to the amount of
$125.00 and my daughter, ANN HEIDT, property to amount of $55.00. If daughter,
REBECCA, marries, she is to have an equal share. Appoint son, EPHRAIM MILLER, and
son-in-law, JOHN DASHER, Executors. WIT: SAMUEL RAHN, ISRAEL HINELY, JHEIN HUNDLEY.

Page 97:   Will of DAVID DAMPIER, Nov. 9, 1844. Give to MARTHA PITTS, wife of
            JOHN PITTS, all stock of cattle, hogs and whatever personal property I
may possess at time of death. Desire that a portion of property be sold for purpose
of paying doctors bill, funeral expenses. Appoint JOHN PITTS and JOHN K. MORGAN,
Executors and MARTHA PITTS, Executrix. WIT: MARGARET D. MILLS, J. R. MORGAN,
JOHN CHARLTON.

Page 100:   Will of CATHARINE PAVERY, July 13, 1847. Give to granddaughter, HARRIET
            ADAMS, two head of cattle and one third of hogs, and the bed which I gave
here heretofore and small lot of crockery which is called hers. Give to grandson,
DAVID ZITTROUR, one third of hogs, four head of cattle and a colt and the land which
I now live on, my bed and bested and bed clothes and some quilts which are not yet
quilted. (HARRIET is also to have some quilts. Give to son-in-law, WILLIAM ZITTROUR,
my young mare but not to sell or trade her away, my cart, and one third of hogs, the
bed and bedding. Also desire that he take care of DAVID's stock and he can live on
the place but not cut any wood for market. Desire that remaining part of estate be
sold and money equally divided between grandchildren, HARRIET ADAMS and DAVID
ZITTROUR. Appoint RICHARD ZITTROUR, Executor. WIT: SARAH WEITMAN, JULIA M. WEITMAN,
I. WEITMAN.

Page 102:   Will of MARY C. BERGMAN, Feb. 15, 1848. Give to sister, SARAH STROBEL,
            four negroes and appoint MR. CHRISTIAN WISENBAKER and I WEITMAN as
Trustees to act for her and her children and should she die all property will to them
to returned to other heirs named by one in this will. Give to mother, SARAH WEITMAN,
two negroes and one hundred acres of land. After her death go to SARAH STROBEL.
Also give to mother my buggy, corn and fodder. The balance of property be sold.
Appoint CHRISTIAN WISENBAKER and I. WEITMAN, Executors. WIT: J. C. WALDHAUER,
JONATHAN TOOLE, M. C. WISENBAKER.

Page 103:   Will of WILLIAM G. BROGDEN, July 22, 1845. Give to wife the remainder of
            natural life or widow, all property for the support of herself and such
children as shall remain with her. At her death or inter-marriage property be equally
divided between children, to wit: MARY ANN JANE BLEACH, LOUIZA ANN MARY BROGDEN,
and WILLIAM F. JONES BROGDEN. Appoint MARY BROGDEN, Executrix. WIT: WM. SPEIR,
TAS, WILSON, C. G. FUTRELL.

Page 104:   Will of ESTHER DUGGER, July 22, 1846. Give to daughter, TABITHA MARLOW,
            wife of PAUL MARLOW, all stock in Effingham County consisting of those
given to me by my late son, JOHN DUGGER, JR. Also a cow and calf which I bought from
BEAL EDWARDS. Also one large Mahogany dining table, all my beds, bedding and
bed clothing and all my wearing apparel and all other personal estate. Appoint
grandson, ROBERT A. MARLOW, Executor. WIT: LEVI S. DLYON.

Page 105:   Will of CLEM POWERS, Sept. 22, 1848. Give to wife, ANN ELIZABETH, five
            negro men and one negro woman and such part of household and kitchen
furniture not to exceed $100 worth, one horse and buggy. Give to daughter,
INDIANNA, $600 in addition to a share hereinafter provided for purpose of keeping
her at school at least 3 years longer. Balance of estate be equally divided among my
six children as follows: to my son, MILTON H. and VIRGIL, and WM. COOPER, as
trustees I give trust for the use and benefit of each of my daughters, VIRGINIA and
INDIANNA, one equal part of estate. Oee equal and undivided sixth part to son, VIRGIL,
one sixth to son, HORACE, one sixth part to daughter, VATIRIA. Appoint sons, MILTON
H., and VIRGIL POWERS & WM. COOPER, Executors. WIT: JAS. E. CRUM, I. B. MURROW,
JAMES H. CASSIDY.

Page 108:   Will of PAUL MARLOW, Oct. 24, 1845. Give unto wife, TABITHA MARLOW, all
            estate, from which is my Will, that my three children, JAMES E. MARLOW,
JOHN D. MARLOW and MARY JANE MARLOW, minors, shall be raised and educated. Give to
each of children when reach age of 21, one horse in value of $60., 4 cows and calves,
one bed, bedstead and furniture, corresponding with what I have already given to my
son, ROBERT A. MARLOW, and TABITHA ANN EDWARDS, my daughter. Give to wife a mullato
woman. Give to my two daughters, viz, TABITHA ANN EDWARDS, wife of I. A. EDWARDS,
and MARY JANE MARLOW, to be bested in PETER CONE, ROBERT A. MARLOW, and JAMES E.
MARLOW, as trustees, each, one equal portion of personal estate and $200 to each of
said daughters. Give to sons, ROBERT A. MARLOW, JAMES E. MARLOW and JOHN D. MARLOW,
share and share alike, all land in Effingham County, having in lieu of giving my

daughters a portion. Give to daughter, MARY JANE MARLOW, two feather beds and the balance of beds, bedding and household and kitchen furniture. Give to said three sons & daughter, MARY JANE, to be equally divided. Appoint wife, TABITHA MARLOW, & son, ROBERT A. MARLOW, Executrix and Executor. WIT: P. C. PENDLETON, R. J. MINGLEDORFF, G. W. BOSTON.

Page 112:   Will of CHRISTINA GNANN, May 13, 1849. Direct that all pine lands con-
            sisting of 250 acres, the dwelling and improvements thereon where I now
reside with two negro boys, all cattle, hogs, poultry, household and kitchen furniture and everything connected with the place to go to and belong to my two sons,
FREDERICK & CLETUS, provided they pay to my son, ELBERT, $50. to my son, GEORGE C.,
$50., to daughter, EVELINE SHEROUSE, $50., to daughter JANE ELIZA, $70. Appoint
two sons, FREDERICK & CLETUS GNANN, Executors. WIT: WM. RAHN, JOHN WILSON, JAMES
WILSON.

Page 114:   Will of FELIX HURST, Sept. 24, 1850. Give to wife, ORPHA, all my tract
            of land which I now living containing 228 acres, farming utensils, my
bay mare, Wag, all stock of cattle and hogs, together with all the crop, all household and kitchen furniture, my negro woman, FLORA. Give to son, EMANUEL, all my
tract of land aforesaid at said wife's decease or if she should marry. Also my
negro boy, BOB. Also my horse, Jack. Give to granddaughter, NARCISSUS PERRY, daughter of JOSEPH PERRY, my negro boy, JOE. Appoint wife Executrix. WIT: JESSE BREWER,
HELAND BLITCH, FELIX HUNT, HENRY TULLUS.

Page 116   Will of EPHRAIM KIEFFER, Dec. 9, 1850. Give to wife, CATHARINE KIEFFER,
            place I now reside, 280 acres, together with all privileges and appur-
tenances thereunto belonging, consisting of Horses, hogs, cattle, household and
kitchen furniture, plantation tools and also my tract of land containing about 25
acres, also my tract containing 63 acres, the place of my former residence, together
with five negroes. Give to son ALLEN NEWTON, two negroes. Give to son, JOHN BUNYON
two negroes, to be delivered to him when he becomes of age. Desire that the woman
called FANNY and her two children be disposed of as children may see proper and proceeds be equally divided among them. Desire and the two negro men, DANIEL and SAM,
be hired out and proceeds go to wife. Desire that a tract of land near Ebenezer
Causeway, containing 200 acres and a tract of pine land containing 275 acres be divided
into four equal parts and divided among my four children. Desire that five shares of
Central Rail Road stock be divided among my wife and four children equally. Appoint
wife, CATHARINE KIEFFER, son, ALLEN NEWTON KIEFFER, and son-in-law, SHADRACH
GROVENSTINE, Executors. WIT: BENJ. GROVENSTEINE, CLETUS RAHN, DAVID A METZGER.

Page 119:   Will of MICAJAH FUTRELL, Sept. 1, 1849. Give to wife, CATHARINE FUTRELL,
            during her life time or widowhood, all estate. After her death or widow-
hood, give to son, JOHN FUTRELL of Crawford County, ELIZABETH SPIER, daughter, wife
of WILLIAM SPIER, daughter, ANNY ROBBINS, wife of DAVID ROBBINS, daughter, PAMELIA
FUTRELL, grandchildren, the childred of dec'd son, CHRISTOPHER FUTRELL, daughter,
REBECCA TILLIS, wife of HENRY TILLIS, and son, REDDICK FUTRELL. Give to son, WILLIAM
FUTRELL every provisory note and notes I now have. Appoint son, REDDICK FUTRELL,
and friend and son-in-law, WILLIAM SPIER, Executors. WIT: ARCH. GUYTON, ELIZABETH
WILLIS, WILEY FANNY WILLIS.

Page 122:   Will of LYDIA METZGER, Oct. 1, 1851. Give to son, DAVID A. METZGER, a
            tract of land upon which I now reside, known as Resier tract, containing
86 acres. Also a tract containing 50 acres, known as the Haque tract. Give to son,
GEORGE L. METZGER, $100. Desire that negro man slave, Bill, be taken by son, GEORGE.
If he refuses, desire he be sold and that proceeds together with proceeds of the
sale of the balance of estate be equally divided among my children but instead of
giving ROSANNAH PHILIPS, my daughter's share, it is my wish that her share be given
to her children, share and share alike. Appoint son, DAVID A. METZGER, and nephew,
BENJAMIN GROVENSTEIN, Executors. WIT: JOSHUA M. DASHER, ELBERT GNANN, ALLEN N.
KIEFFER.

Page 125:   Will of JONATHAN GNANN, Feb. 1, 1848. Give to wife, MARIA E. F., during
            her natural life and widowhood, 150 acres of land upon which I now reside,
my negro girl named FANNY, all stock of cattle, hogs, all horses, household and
kitchen furniture, plantation tools. At the death or intermarriage of wife, desire
that aforesaid be placed in possession of children. When children reach age of 21

desire estate be equally divided between my children and wife. Appoint son, DAVID E. GNANN, Executor. WIT: JAMES E. RHAN, AMOS F. RAHN, JOSEPH F. WEITMAN, JAMES RAHN.

Page 128: Will of LEWIS MYERS, Jan. 13, 1849. Give to friend, JOHN CHARLTON, esquire, my secretary. Give silver headed cane to F. M. STONE, Esquire of Savannah, given to me by sister MARY BECU, the first Methodist powerfully converted to God in Savannah. My watch I give to Bishop JAMES C. ANDREW. Give two shares of stock in the Central Raid Road and Baking Company of Georgis to my niece, HARRIET F. WHEELER. Give eight shares of stock in the Central Rail Road and Baking Co. of Georgia to the Georgia Conference of the Methodist Episcopal Church South in trust that they apply the dividend on yearly income to missionary purposes, the principal to remain untouched. My books I desire shall be divided among my five children equally. My manuscripts and papers not of a private character give to Georgia Conference. To SARAH C. COMBS and to EMMA G. COMBS give $10.00 to each of them. To my daughter, MARY L. COOMBS give my lot of land in Savannah on the West side of Farm Street, number 29, my negro man, SAM, and a negro girl named JUNES. To my daughter, HENRIETTA B. RAHN, wife of WILLIAM RAHN, give one half of my lot of land in Savannah, no. 4,including a double tenement house. Also my negro men named JESS and BOB. Also my negro woman named SUSANNAH and her son POMPEY. Give to son, LEWIS MYERS, 200 acres of land in Effingham County adjoining the lands of Mullette known as the Russell tract. Also a lot in the Town of Springfield having a small cabin joining the lot of Mr. SORREL and others, four share of stock in the Central Raid Road and Banking Company of the State of Georgia. He is not permitted to sell any property herein named. To daughter, REBECCA L. give the aforesaid lot of land, my negro boy named CHARLES and a negro woman named BELLER and her son MORRIS. To my daughter, HANNAH NOWLAN, give my lot of land in Savannah, no. 15, my negro men named SMART and ISAAC and a girl named SARAH. Desire that negro boy, RICHARD, be hired out by Executors and income be appropriated toward the education of grandson, GASSAWAY L. COOMBS. Also the tract of land whereon I now live containing 300 acres and the land I purchased from CHRISTIAN ZIPPERER containing 110 acres. All property not herein before disposed of I desire be sold at public auction and be divided in as many shares as there will be daughters living at the time of my death. Desire a copy of will be given to the Georgia Conference of the Methodist Episcopal Church South. Appoint F. M. STONE, JOHN CHARLTON, and WM. RAHN, Executors. WIT: G. R. WRIGHT, W. H. WILNN, T. WILSON.

Page 135: Will of TRYON PACE, Nov. 11, 1845. Previous to my death, have given to my several children herein named, monies and property each one varying in amount, to my son, GEORGE, the property he has had from me, amounts to $465, and it is my desire that they should all receive equal to this amount arising from sale of my property hereinafter named. Son, JAMES, having already received $300, direct Executors to pay him further sum of $165. Son, NOAH, now dead, having received $200, direct that Executors pay unto his four children share and share alike $265. Daughter UNITY, having received $100, direct Executors pay her $365. Daughter, MARY, wife of HENRY THOMAS MORGAN, having received $300, direct that Executors pay her $165. Daughter, SARAH ANN, wife of JACKSON TYNER, having received $100, direct Executors pay her $365. Desire all property I possess be sold for purpose of paying several sums of money above mentioned and balance be equally divided between children and grandchildren named to wit: one share to JAMES, one share to be divided among four children of son, NOAH, one share to UNIT, one share to MARY, one share to GEORGE, one share to SARAH ANN. Give to wife, SARAH, one American dollar had Conduct to me being such as I could approve of she should have had a full share of my worldly possessions as I did love her as a wife and respected her as such. Appoint son, GEORGE PACE, JACKSON TYNER, and HENRY T. MORGAN, Executors. WIT: JAMES RAHN, G. R. WRIGHT, JOHN CHARLTON.

Page 139: Will of CLAIBORNE BEVILL, Mar. 10, 1852. Give to daughter, ANN REBECCA SOLOMONS, and daughter, HENRIETTA ELIZABETH STROBHAR, and grandson, FRANCIS B. BEVILL, all real estate be equally divided. Give to said grandson 4 negro slaves. Give remainder slaves to daughters above named, be equally divided between them. Remainder of property be equally divided between daughters and grandson above named. Appoint sons, EDWARD W. SOLOMONS and HENTRY STROBHAR, and friend, FRANCIS BARTON, Executors. WIT: L. WEITMAN, ROBERT CHRISTIE, JOSHUA KESSLER.

Page 141:   Will of ALEXANDER WATT, Mar. 2, 1851. Five to two eldest sons, BEATTIE
            and BRADIE, each a silver watch. Give unto sons: ALEXANDER, HABERSHAM,
WALLACE, GUSTAVUS and CARROLL, my place of residence known as the Mackinfuss tract
containing 500 acres, also one bay horse and one gray mare. My wife HANNAH ANN
WATT, she can remain on said place. Appoint son, BEATTIE, Executor. WIT:
R. A. MARLOW, W. H. SHEAROURSE, A. C. N. LINDS.

Page 144:   Will of Mrs. MARCIA MALLORY, July 28, 1848. Give to nephew, ALBERT G.
            PORTER, a negro man named DICK. Give unto WILLIAM R. PORTER that tract
of land known as the Henritta Tract containing 400 acres. Give unto FERDINAN M.
PORTER, negro boy named OSGAR. Give unto MICHOL A. PORTER a negro boy named ABSALOM.
Also give unto nephew ALBERT G. PORTER one fourth part of my household and kitchen
furniture, plantation tools, provisions, horses, cattle, sheep, hogs, carriages,
waggons and everything else that may be in possession at my death. WIT: AMANDA
KITTLES, JOSEPH PORTER, J. R. MORGAN.

Page 147:   Will of Mrs. MARCIA MALLORY No. 2, July, 1848. Give unti ISABELLA
            TREUTLEN, sister, a negro man named FRANK, MARY a woman & JUDY a woman.
Also one fourth part of all stock of horses, cattle sheep, and hogs and one fourth
part of all household and kitchen furniture. WIT: AMANDA KITTLES, JOSEPH PORTER,
J. R. MORGAN.

Page 149:   Will of THOMAS ELKINS, Jan. 20, 1844. Give unto my six following named
            daughters to wit: MOSELLE ZETTLER, JULIA ZEUCKS, LYDIA ELKINS, SARAH
HARRISON, CAROLINE ELKINS and SELICIA RAWLS, the following tracts of land - one
tract containing 513 acres known as the Tondee Old Place, one tract known as number
279, one tract in Pike County known as number 241, one tract in Baker County known as
number ___, one tract in Dooly County, one tract in Effingham County containing 200
acres known as the tract upon which GRODIVER W. ABBOT, SR. now resides, the above
tracts of land to be sold and proceeds be equally divided among six daughters. Give
to son, THOMAS P. ELKINS the following lands: the place known as Whitesville, Also
200 acres joining Whitesville on the West Side. Also 700 acres lying between
Springfield and Whitesville. Also 200 acres granted to JOSHUA SECKINGER. Also 200
acres granted to JOHN C. MILLER. Also 290 acres granted to JOHN EXLEY. Also seven
negroes. Give unto daughter, MOSELLE ZETTLER, seven negroes. Give to daughter,
JULIA ZEUCKS, nine negroes. Give to daughter, LYDIA ELKINS, 8 negroes and also two
lots in Village of Whitesville, number 61 and 62. Give to daughter, SARAH HARRISON,
9 negroes. Give to stepdaughter, HARRIET ELKINS, late wife of SAMUEL ELKINS, lot of
land in Village of Whitesville known as Lot Number 63. Give to two sons, CHARLES &
LEANDER, the balance of lands with exception of a life estate in a tract of land
containing 200 acres known as the land on which my present residence is located which
I give unto wife, MARIA P. ELKINS. Balance of negro property is to remain together
in possession of wife until youngest child becomes of age of 21, then be equally
divided among four youngest children - CAROLINE ELKINS, SELINA RAWLS, CHARLES ELKINS
and LEANDER ELKINS and wife. Appoint wife, MARIA P. WLKINS, Executrix and sons,
THOMAS P. ELKINS, MORGAN RAWLS, CHARLES C. ELKINS & LEANDER L. ELKINS, Executors.
WIT: ARCHIBALD GUYTON, AMOS RAHN, JAMES RAHN.

Page 155:   Will of JOHN ELKINS, June 23, 1852. To wife, MARY ELKINS, give whole of
            property both real and personal and it is for her to dispose of same at
her death in equal distributive pacts to all heirs of her body. Declare wife,
MARY ELKINS, Executrix. WIT: HENRY LOVE, STEPHEN HESTER, SR., WM. COOPER.

Page 157:   Will of STEPHEN HESTER, June 23, 1852. Give to wife, EDITH HESTER, all
            lands and mill plantation, horses, cattle, hogs, plantation tools, house-
hold furniture, etc. Be disposed of at her death to whom she pleases. Also give
wife five negroes. Appoint wife, EDITH HESTER, Executrix. WIT: HENRY LOVE, SUSAN
E. ELKINS, WM. COOPER.

Page 159:   Will of MILTON H. POWERS, Feb. 13, 1855. Direct that all property be
            kept together for joint use of wife and children until youngest child
arrives at age of 18 years, then same shall be divided between wife and children
equally. Direct that all stock of horses, cattle and hogs be sold. Direct that all
slaves be hired out. Direct that Rivers Plantation called Hickory Hill be sold.
Direct executors dispose of any timber on hand and discharge note held by Misses
COOPER and GILLILAND. Appoint LAWRENCE T. ELKINS and ARCHIBALD GUYTON, Executors.
WIT: E. T. JENKINS, STEPHEN F. KELLER, WM. MOREL.

Page 162: Will of JOHN W. EXLEY, Nov. 9, 1855. Desire that executors sell and dispose of all real and personal estate which he may think best and apply the proceeds first to payment of debts and then all balance to pay into hands of wife, ELIZA M. EXLEY. At time of wife's death, remaining proceeds be equally divided among my children. Appoint son, WILLIAM L. EXLEY, executor. WIT: JAMES RAHN, SAMUEL E. MILLER, FREDERICK KESSLER, EPHRAIM E. KESSLER.

Page 164: Will of CLETUS RHAN, Nov. 26, 1855. Give to wife, ELIZA HANNAH, the tract of land I now live on, 160 acres, and at her death be equally divided among my children. Give residue of property to wife and children to share and share alike. Appoint son, JOSEPH A. RAHN, and friend, JOHN B. BERRY, Executors. WIT: WM. RAHN, CHRISTOPHER F. REISSER, ALLEN N. KIEFFER.

Page 166: Will of ELIHU WILSON, Nov. 22, 1853. Desire that all possession of lands and negroes remain together until son, ANDREW, comes to age of 21, then whole estate be equally divided among my heirs and perishable property be sold and balance of estate be divided equally among heirs. Will that wife, Ann, shall share and share alike with children but at her death or intermarriage her part of estate shall revert back and be equally divided among heirs. If daughter, CAROLINA ZIPPERER, dies without a child her part revert back and be equally divided among heirs. Appoint sons, HENRY J. WILSON and STEPHEN A. WILSON, Executors. WIT: LIDDY SMITH, SIMON BLITCH, BARNETT NEWTON.

Page 168: Will of EDITH HESTER, Sept. 22, 1855. Give to EMANUEL CRAWFORD all that lot of land on plantation containing 384 acres being resident of late husband and myself, together with the mill, dwelling house, out buildings and improvements thereon. Give unto heirs of FREDERICK WOMACK, dec'd, the foster son of late husband, STEPHEN HESTER, six negroe slaves. Give the remainder of estate unto ANN WILLIAMS, my sister, with the exception of bed and bedding which I give to T. DAVIS. Appoint STEPHEN KELLER Executor. WIT: M. BLITCH, HENRY LOVE, JOSHUA ZEIGLER.

Page 171: Will of CHRISTIAN ARNSDORFF, Apr. 18, 1853. Give to wife, ELIZABETH, all tract of land on which I now reside containing 200 acres, together with all cattle, hogs, household and kitchen furniture, in fact, all property. After her death, give the aforesaid 200 acres of land to my son, JOHN ELBERT ARNSDORFF, and all the balance of my property at the death of my wife, give to following children JOHNATHAN, JOSHUA & MARY ANN ARNSDORFF to be equally divided among them. Appoint son, *___ , Executor. WIT: JONATHAN LUDER, JOHN LUDER, JOHN ARNSDORFF.

Page 173: Will of LUCRETIA MORGAN, Nov. 25, 1856. Give all property I may have to my son, LEWIA J. MORGAN. Appoint son, LEWIA J. MORGAN, executor. WIT: JAMES M. MORGAN, CHRISTIAN MORGAN, CHRISTOPHER L. MORGAN.

Page 175: Will of SAMUEL DASHER, 1845. Give to son-in-law, STEPHEN A. WILSON, $1.00. Give to wife, JANE M. DASHER, one half of the tract of land on which I now reside, containing 800 acres, together with such horses, hogs, and cattle and sheep as shall be necessary to her comfort and convenience. Also such of my negroes as shall be necessary to her comfort and support. Give to son, WILLIAM B., one half of the tract of land on which I now reside. Desire that interest being half of the land on which son, ROBERT, now resides be sold as soon as practible after my death provided son, ROBERT, is not willing to buy it. Desire Executors to sell all such stock or property as shall seem to them unnecessary to the comfort and happiness of my family and money be put at interest until son, WILLIAM B. arrives at age of 21. Then desire property not herein bequeathed be equally divided among children, with one exception, my son, GEORGE S., is to have no share in none of lands. Desire property left to wife, JANE M., during her widowhood or life time be equally divided after her death among my children. Appoint my two sons, ROBERT DASHER and BENJAMIN J. DASHER, Executors. WIT: JAMES DASHER, DANIEL C. SHUPTRINE, BARNETT NEWTON.

Page 180: Will of MATTHEW BURGSTINER, Aug. 11, 1855. Give to wife, JANE BURGSTINER, one feather bed, two pillows and furniture for said bed, a large looking glass, & $50. in cash. During her natural life or widowhood, my mulatto man slave, HAMPSHIRE, after her death or marriage to revert back to estate. Appoint Dr. W. M. WILSON trustee for wife, JANE BURGSTINER. Direct that residue of estate be sold to highest bidder. Give to each of the children of my daughter,

178

ELIZA HINELY, one hundred dollars. Give to JANE ABBOTT, wife of EDWIN ABBOTT, $100.
Give to granddaughter, CAROLINE IHLY, $100. Give to son, JOHN R. BURGSTINER, $300.
Balance of proceeds of estate give to sons, JAMES A. BURGSTINER and JOHN R. BURGSTINER,
be divided between them equally, and proceeds of the sale of mulatto man slave,
HAMPSHIRE, after wife's estateis over. Appoint son, JOHN R. BURGSTINER, Executor.
WIT: E. W. RAHN, D. F. RAHN, JAMES RAHN, W. H. WILSON.

Page 185:   Will of OBEDIAH EDWARDS, Apr. 2, 1857. Give to wife, TABITHA, one negro
            girl named NANCY, one horse and buggy, all my stock of cattle consisting
of 13 head marked with swallow fork in our ear and figure three in other. All
house and furniture and following notes: give promissory notes on son, JOSEPH C.
EDWARDS, amounting to $200. besides interest. Two notes on DANIEL A. SMITH amounting
to $100 besides interest. One note on B. NEWTON for $150. interest on which is paid.
One note on JAMES M. SHEPPERD calling for $60 exclusive of interest. One note on
WILLIAM A. PORTER calling for $38. 12½ dollars besides interest. The negro girl,
NANCY, cattle, horse and buggy and so much of the money as may be due on said notes
desire at the death of wife be equally divided among following daughters: JANE A.
NEWTON, wife of BARNETT NEWTON; MARYAN E. SHEPPERD, wife of JAMES M. SHEPPERD;
SARAH ANN T. FRIAR, wife of DAVID FRIAR: FRANCIS ANN WILSON, wife of HENRY WILSON,
and children of late daughter, ELIZABETH D. SMITH, late wife of DAVID SMITH. Such
portion as may be alloted to children of late daughter I desire paid over to son,
JOSEPH O. EDWARDS. Desire 500 acres of land which I hold a warrant of survey over be
sold and proceeds be equally divided among all children, excluding son, WILLIAM P.
EDWARDS, he having had his share of estate. Appoint son, JOSEPH C. EDWARDS, and
son-in-law, BARNETT NEWTON, Executors. WIT: WILLIAMS BEST, BENJAMIN GRINER, ALEXAN-
DER W. DALEY.

Page 189:   Will of SARAH WEITMAN, Apr. 14, 1857. Give to my adopted daughter,
            SALOME GNANN, wife of ELBERT GNANN, my negro boy, MITCHELL. Give to my
nephew, JOHN C. WALDHAUER, one lot of land containing 48 acres known as the Weitman
Lot. Give to daughter, JULIA N. CHRISTIE and her children, my negro girl, MARTHA.
Desire Executors to expose to public outcry a lot of land if not sold before I die
and other property belonging to me and shall collect notes that I may hold at my
death as soon as it can lawfully be done and as soon as they can get the money for
property and notes. I bequeath it to all my grandchildren to be equally distributed
among them. My grandson, JOHN FLERL STROBLE, by my daughter, SARAH A. STROBLE, and
my grandchildren by my daughter, ESTHER HELVINSTON, and my grandchildren by my
daughter, JULIA M. CHRISTIE. Appoint grandson, JOSEPH C. HELVENSTON, and friend,
JAMES RAHN, executors. WIT: W. R. SECKINGER, E. R. WALDHAUR, E R. WALDHAUR, JOHN
WALDHAUR.

Page 196:   Will of THOMAS BLITCH, SR., Dec. 13, 1858. Give to wife, ANN BLITCH,
            during ten years or widowhood, or so long as she shall stay on the place (but if
she shall leave the place then the lands to be all sold), 159 acres of land containing
plantation and improvements, the other 200 acres of land to lye unmolested, and
after ten years shall expire then all lands shall be sold and an equal division be
made between all my children. Give wife, five hoes, one plow and gear, one horse,
one sow and six shoats, and six cows and calves, one chart and all house and kitchen
furniture, except one feather bed. to my daughter, ELIZABETH, two pillows to go with
bed. Balance of property be sold and an equal division be made between all my
children, to wit: HENRY JAMES BLITCH, THOMAS LUKE BLITCH, ELIZABETH BLITCH, ELENOR
JANE BLITCH, GEORGIA ANN BLITCH, WILLIS STEPHEN BLITCH, WILLIAM MILTON BLITCH,
SUSANNAH TABITHA BLITCH, CANARA ANGELICA BLITCH. Appoint son, HENRY JAMES BLITCH
and THOMAS LUKE BLITCH, Executors. WIT: JAMES E. WILSON, A. WILSON, DAVID WILSON.

Page 199:   Will of OBADIAH EDWARDS, No. 2, Feb. 16, 1848. To two oldest sons,
            WILLIAM BEAL and OBADIAH WINFIELD EDWARDS, the lands and appurtenances
situated thereone known and described as my resident now, containing about 600 acres,
a tract of land containing 200 acres known as the Montmullier land. Desire that
wife, SARAH ELENOR EDWARDS, shall reside upon my place of residence now, bequeathed
as above, until youngest son, OBADIAH WINIFIELD, becomes of age. All other lands
be sold and proceeds be equally divided between wife and daughter, CAROLINE UGENIA,
and all other future heirs of my body. To my son, WILLIAM BEAL, a negro girl slave
named JENNY. To son, OBADIAH WINIFIELD, a negro girl slave named ANN. To daughter,
CAROLINE EUGENIA, a negro girl named BINAH. Also give to wife and all children four
negro slaves. Devise remainder of estate to wife and children to be divided equally
between them. Appoint JAMES E. MARLOW and S. F. KELLER, Executors. WIT: JOHN W.
EDWARDS, W. D. OSTEEN, HENRY LOVE.

Page 203:   Will of HENRY T. MORGAN, July 26, 1855. Give to wife, MARY MORGAN,
            all property. After her death or upon her marrying again, I give all
estate to all my children to be equally divided among them. Wish it to be remembered
at final division of estate that some children are married and have received some
bedding, and one some cattle. Appoint wife, MARY MORGAN, Executrix and brother,
DAVID A. MORGAN, and brother-in-law, GEORGE PACE, Executors. WIT: E. W. RAHN,
MARGARET BIDDENBACK, JAMES RAHN.

Page 206:   Will of WILLIAM MORGAN, Oct. 2, 1854. Give to sons, WILLIAM I MORGAN,
            HENRY T. MORGAN & DAVID A. MORGAN, $100 each. To pay legacies, funeral
expense and debts, direct that some portion of property be sold immediately after
death. Given to son, CHRISTOPHER L. MORGAN, by deed a certain tract of land containing 146 acres. Also did give to daughter, GRACY WHEELER, by deed the same as
foregoing. Give unto daughter, MARIA MORGAN, 100 acres of land in front and adjoining
the tract on which I now reside. Balance of estate I give to following five children,
to wit: JOHN L. MORGAN, GRACY WHEELER (wife of BRINSON WHEELER), SARAH ARNSDORFF
(wife of JOHN ARNSDORFF), ELIZA GNANN (wife of CHRISTOPHER L. GNANN) and MARIA
MORGAN to be equally divided among them. Appoint son, JOHN L. MORGAN, and son-in-law,
JOHN ARNSDORFF, Executors. WIT: WILLIAM G. MORGAN, M. DOUGHTEY, I. B. KIEFFER,
JAMES RAHN.

1805 LAND LOTTERY - EFFINGHAM COUNTY

BB Albritton, Richard	BB Gruver, Solomon
PB Ambrose, David	" Gnann, Andrew
BB Alston, Joshua	B Gibson, James
	BB Garrison, James
PB Bell, Jesse	BB Grovenstine, Henry L.
B Bell, Eleazer	" Grovenstine, John J.
BB Beckley, Jonathan	B Gladish, Gillium
" Burgstiner, Matthew	BB Garrison, Darius
B Burgstiner, Samuel	" Gruver, David
BB Berry, John	" Gnann, Mary, widow
P Beatenbach, Christian	" Gnann, Jacob
B Beatenbach, Matthew and John, orphs.	" Gnann, Solomon
PB Bird, Lewis	B Gnann, Catherine and Benj. orphs.
BB Bird, Sarah	BB Goldwire, James
" Beall, William	
" Bozeman, Howell	B Hagins, Malachi
PP Bandy, John	BB Hines, David
BB Burgstiner, Daniel	" Hines, Drusilla, widow
" Bird, William	" Hineley, John
" Burton, Robert	" Helmly, David
B Bleech (Blitch?), Benjamin	B Hinely, Israel
BB Bailey, Christopher	BB Heidt, George
" Bleech (Blitch?), Ann	" Hayne, John
B Boston, John, Jr.	" Hodges, Roger
BB Boston, James	B Howard, Joshua, orphan
BP Brewer, James, Jr.	" Hawthorn, William
BB Brewer, James, Sr.	BB Hinely, Jacob
	PB Hawthorn, Peter
BB Crum, Harmon	BB Hurst, Felix
" Collins, Bridget	" Hurst, William
" Cook, James, Sr.	" Hurst, Jesse
" Crosby, Aaron	BP Hurst, Thomas
	BB Hurst, Mary, widow
BB Dasher, Benjamin	" Holliday, Miller
B Davis, John	" Holliday, Joseph
BB Dasher, Christian	" Hollingsworth, William
B Davis, Samuel	B Hangleiter, Jacob, orphan
BB Dasher, John M. Sr.	BB Hines, Howell
" Dasher, John M. Jr.	" Hines, Hannah, widow
B Dasher, Joshua	
BB Downs, William	BB Ivey, John
" Dykes, Jesse	" Ivey, Robert
" Dykes, Noah	
	P King, James
BB Exley, Michael	B Kieffer, Joel
" Edwards, William	BB Kogler, John
" Edwards, Obediah	BB King, William, Sr.
" Edwards, Henry	B King, William, Jr.
" Easter, Augustus	PB Kieffer, Israel
" Ernst, Godlieb	BB Keebler, Joshua
	" King, John
BB Flerl, Israel	B Kittles, Peter
" Freckinger, John	BB Kittles, Jacob
B Foy, Hannah and George, orphans	PB Kennedy, William
BB Fryarmouth, John	BB Kennedy, Benjamin
BB Forsyth, Leety, widow	" Krouse, Samuel
" Fryermouth, John A.	B Kirksey, Isaac
BB Goldwire, John, Sr.	BB Lovett, David
B Goldwire, John, Jr.	PB Loper, Joshua
BB Guire, George F.	B Loper, Ara (sic)
B Guire, William	BB Loper, Curtis
" Gnann, Timothy	PB Loper, Asa
BB Gnann, Jonathan	B Loper, Abel G.
" Gnann, John	BP London, John
" Gnann, Christopher John	

BB	Morgan, Lewis		BB	Tullos, Temple
"	Miller, John C.		"	Tucing, Paul
"	Mallette, Gideon		"	Tison, Camel
BP	Merchant, John		PB	Taylor, Reubin G.
PB	Moore, John		BB	Treble, Hannah, widow
BB	Metzger, John		"	Tison, James
PB	Metzger, David		B	Tison, William
B	Metzger, John Jacob		"	Tison, Edmond
PB	Marks, John		"	Tison, Eliakim
BB	Mott, Zephaniah		BB	Touchstone, Richard
P	Mills, Shadrack			
BB	Morgan, William		BB	Ulmer, Charles
"	Mock, John M.			
P	Marchment, John		BB	Williams, Henry W.
			B	Wallace, John
BB	McCall, John		BB	Wilson, Elizabeth, widow
"	McGahagan, Lewis		BP	Wilson, James, Sr.
B	McGahagan, William		BB	Wilson, Jesse
BB	McCardel, John		"	Woolf, Stephen
			PB	Woolf, George
BB	Neiss, George		BB	Whiteman, Daniel
"	Neidlinger, John G.		PB	Whiteman, Jedediah
B	Nessler, Samuel, orphan		BP	Whiteman, Mathew
BB	Nichols, Henry		BB	Wilson, John
			"	Wilson, James, Jr.
BB	O'Berry, Henry		"	Waldhauer, John
			"	Wylly, William
BB	Polhill, Thomas		"	Wylly, Thomas
"	Powledge, George		"	Whiteman, Hannah, widow
"	Powledge, Gideon		B	Wisenbaker, Christian and John, orphs
"	Powers, John		B	Wilson, William
"	Powers, Senate		BB	Wisenbaker, Mary
"	Pitts, Anthony		"	Wade, Joseph
"	Porter, James		B	Wilson, David
"	Porter, John		PB	Wheeler, James
BP	Porter, Rachel, widow		BB	White, Zachariah
BB	Porter, Benjamin		"	Williamson, Aquilla
BP	Pace, Trion		B	Wilson, John, orphan
BB	Rahn, Matthew		BP	Yarborough, John
B	Robertson, John			
BB	Reiser, David		BB	Zittrouer, George
PB	Rahn, Jonathan		"	Zittrouer, Ernst
B	Reiser, James and John, nat. orphans		"	Zittrouer, Gotlieb
BB	Rusheon, Matthew		B	Zittrouer, Godhief
"	Ryall, Charles		BB	Zittrouer, Solomon
"	Rushion, William		"	Zeigler, David
			"	Zant, Catherine, widow
BB	Scruggs, Gross		"	Zipperer, Samuel
"	Seckinger, Jonathan			
PB	Snider, Jonathan			
BB	Shearhouse, Godheif			
"	Shearhouse, John			
"	Schwighoffer, Saloma, widow			
"	Sibley, Reddick			
"	Staley, Timothy			
B	Sheubtrine, Hannah and Godleip, orphs.			
BB	Spier, Willis			
B	Speir, Willis and Patience, orphs of James			
PB	Strahan, John			
B	Speir, James			
BB	Stewart, William			
"	Scruggs, Jesse			
B	Turner, Daniel			
BB	Tiner, Elijah			
"	Treutlin, Christian			

EFFINGHAM COUNTY
1807 LAND LOTTERY

Following are the names of persons who resided in Effingham County and were fortunate drawers of land in the 1807 land lottery. Only the county in which they drew land is listed here; "B" for Baldwin County and "W" for Wilkinson County. The book The 1807 Land Lottery may be consulted for the lot and district numbers. Fortunate drawers were not required to live on the land - they could sell it if they so desired.

Alston, John	B		Holliday, Joseph Junr.	B
Alston, John*	W		Heinley, John	W
*Granted to Joshua Alston			Hull, Nathaniel	W
See Ex. Journal 5 Apr 1810			Hensler, Jacob	W
Beall, William	W		Jones, David	W
Backley, Elizabeth	B		Kieffer, Christiana D. &	
Blitch, Spear	W		Ephraim (orphans of)	W
Buntz, Semon (orphan)	B		Kent, Laban	W
Britton, Stephen	W		King, John	W
Brewer, Joseph	W		Loper, Curtis	W
Boston, James	W		Loper, Asa	B
Blitch, Benjamin	W		Loper, Curtis	W
Berry, John	B		Loper, Abel G.	W
Burton, Robert	B		London, Elizabeth (widow)	W
Bird, James	W		Marks, Anna (single woman)	W
Boston, John Junr.	W		Metzger, John	W
Bergman, John Ernst.	W		Morgan, William	W
Brewer, Joseph	B		Martin, Lewis	B
Blitch, Benjamin	B		Mallett, Gideon	W
Burgsteiner, Samuel	W		Mannen, Lucy (single woman)	B
Cruse, James	W		Morgan, Lewis	W
Cook James Junr.	W		Miller, John C.	B
Crum, Herman	W		Morgan, Thomas	W
Cope, Christian	B		Nicolls, Henry	W
Crawford, James	W		Nicolls, Henry	W
Cook Henry	B		Neidlinger, John G.	W
Dampier, Daniel	W		Neidlinger, John G.	B
Dampier, William	B		Nees, Gotthelf Israel	W
Dasher, Christian L.	W		Oglesbie, Benjamin	W
Dasher, Christiana Ann(wid)	B		Oberry, Henry	W
Dasher, Thomas (orphan)	B		Porter, Annie (orphan)	B
Davis, Samuel	W		Pitts, Anthony	B
Davis, Hezekiah	B		Pitts, Anthony	B
Downs, William	W		Polhill, Thomas Junr.	W
Evers, Mary (widow)	W		Pitts, Hardy (orphan)	W
Elkins, John Junr.	W		Shrimph, Wm.	W
Edwards, William	B		Scruggs, Gross	W
Freyermuth, John Senr.	B		Shubtrain, Gottlieb & Han (orphs)	B
Freyermuth, John Senr.	B		Seckinger, John G., Salome,	
Freyermuth, Sarah (wid)	W		Caty & Christ'r. (orphs)	B
Foresythe, Serlester (wid)	W		Scherraus, Gotthelf	W
Flerl, Israel	W		Schweighoffer, Thomas (orph)	W
Gill, Thomas	B		Shuman, James	B
Gruber, Solomon	B		Scherraus, John	W
Gravenstien, John	B		Scruggs, Mary (widow)	W
Gnann, Jacob	W		Schneider, Gottlieb	B
Coolesby, Charles M.	W		Townsend, William	W
Gromet, John J. Judy S.,			Toomer, Daniel	B
Margaret M. & John C. (orp)	B		Tullos, John	B
Gnann, Solomon	W		Tullos, Temple (son of John)	B
Gruber, Solomon	W		Tison, Edmond	B
Gaffney, James	W		Tondee, Charles	W
Goldwire, James	B		Tucker, Gabriel	W
Gnann, John	W		Tison, Camel	W
Gill, Jeremiah	B		Tiner, Elijah	B
Heinley, Israel	B		Tison, Eliakim	W
Hughes, Robert H.	W		Taylor, Joseph (orphan)	W
Howard, Abigail (orph)	W		Ulmer, Charles	W
Hill, Charles	B		White, Zachariah	W
Hensler, Hannah			Wylly, Wm. C.	W
(single woman)	W		Wilson, Jesse	W
Helmley, Elizabeth (single)	W		Wilson, Jesse	W

Wilson, Elizabeth (widow	W	Zitterauer, Solomon	B
Walsingham, John George	B	Zipperer, Christian, Hann,	
Wilder, William	W	Jonathan & Sam'l. (orphs)	W
Wright, William	B	Zipperer, Samuel	W
Wilson, Luke	W	Zitterauer, Solomon	W
Wright, William	W	Zitterauer, John Geo.	B
Wilson, William Junr.	W	Zipperer, Anne Mary (widow)	W
Zipperer, Christiana (widow)	W	Zipperer, Christian J.	W

THE 1820 LAND LOTTERY

Listed below are the fortunate drawers who were registered in Effingham County, and the county in which they drew land. Consult the book, The 1820 Land Lottery, for Militia District, Lot Number and Section. Abbreviations: App - Appling; Ear - Early; Gwi - Gwinnett; Hab - Habersham; Hal - Hall; Irw - Irwin; Rab - Rabun; Wal - Walton.

Armstroff, Israel	Hab	Dykes, Jesse	Irw
Arnstoff, Gothiel	Irw	Davis, Levi Senr	Ear
Arstoff, Christian	App	Denny, John	Irw
Anderson, James	Irw	Davis, Benjamin	Irw
Akins, Alexander	Rab	Dasher, Christian	App
Ammonds, William	Ear	Dykes, Jesse	App
Anderson, James	Irw	Dasher, Elizabeth Wid.	App
Arnstorff, George, Junr.	Irw	Edwards, William	Ear
Baas, Rebecca (wid)	Rab	Exley, Elizabeth (wid)	Ear
Bass, Daniel A.	Ear	Evers, John	App
Bettenbock, John	App	Exley, Jacob	Irw
Blitch, Ann (wid)	Irw	Edwards, Obediah	Ear
Burckstiner, Matthew	Ear	Elkins, Alexander	
Bird, William	Ear	(See Exec. Order 29 Nov 1830)	Rab
Brewer, Mary (wid)	Irw	Fitzpatrick, Saml	Ear
Bassett, John	Irw	Flerl's, Isarel orphans	Irw
Berry, Benajah	Irw	Fitzee, Gottiel	App
Bettenbock, Matthew	Ear	Fetzer, Jonathan	Ear
Brock, Benjamin	Irw	Futrall, Micajah	Hab
Bowman, Robert	App	Griner, Andrew	Ear
Bettenbock, John	Ear	Garrison, Michael	Ear
Boston, Pharis	Irw	Gilchrist, Thomas (orphs)	Ear
Burton, Charles	App	Grayham, John	Ear
Brown, Thomas	Ear	Gilchrist, Hannah (wid)	Irw
Blitch, Willis	App	Gaddy, Mariah & Sine (orphs)	App
Bowlin, Christopher	Wal	Garrason, David	Ear
Bailey, Christopher	Ear	Grinor, Andrew	Irw
Bergman, Frederick C.	App	Garnett, Thomas	Hab
Baas, Rosannah & Sarah	Ear	Gnann, Solomon	Wal
Crawford, John	Ear	Gnann, Jonathan Sr.	Ear
Crosley, Thomas	Hab	Grouver, Elias	Hab
Carelish, Tressa	Ear	Gugle, David	App
Cook, Sarah	Ear	Gnann, Christinea (orphs)	Irw
Charleton, Jno	Ear	Grey, Benjamin	Ear
Cramer, Solomon	Hab	Gnann, Benjn.	App
Clary, Samuel (orph)	Wal	Gnann, Jonathan Jr. (son of John)	Irw
Cochran, George L.	Irw	Garrason, Daviss	App
Cochran, Hugh Rev. Sol.	App	Gnann, Solomon Sr.	Gwi
Curry, William	Gwi	Goldwire, Mariah & Caroline(orph)	Hab
Cochran, Hugh R.S.	App	Gnann, Jacob Sr.	App
Crews, Asa	App	Grayham, Archibald	App
Dasher, Herman C.	App	Gnann, Jacob Jr.	Irw
Denny, John	Irw	Goldwire, John	Irw
Denslers, Phillip (orphs)	App	Gnann, Christopher	Ear
Davis, Hezekiah	Hab	Greyer, William E.	App
Dugger, John Jr.	Ear	Gnann, Jonathan Sr.	Ear
Dasher, Gottiel	Rab	Gugel, David	Irw
Dampier, Stephen	Irw	Gnann, Johnathan Junr.	
Davis, Levi Senr	Irw	(son of Jonathan Gnann Junr.)	App

Heidt, Christian J.R.S.	Ear	Riesser, David	Irw
Harris, William	Ear	Rahn, Mathew R.S.	Ear
Hinely, Soloman	Hab	Ridgedell, John	Ear
Helvenstien, Joseph Sr.	Ear	Rahn, Mathew Rev. Sol.	Irw
Hurst, James	App	Rahn, Cletus	Irw
Hinley, Margarett Ann	Gwi	Reisser, Mathew	Irw
Hawthorn, Josiah & Mahala(orph)	Ear	Rahn, Mathew R.S.	Ear
Hinley, John (orphs)	Hab	Rhan, Jonathan S.	App
Heit, Abial	Irw	Rdgeden, Samuel R.S.	App
Holiday, Lonezer & Angalina		Ryals, Charles	Ear
(orphans)	Ear	Rhan, John	Wal
Hanning, Christopher	Ear	Spier, Milley (wid)	App
Hinely, David	Ear	Stewart, Charles	App
Helvenstien, Joseph Sr.	App	Scruggs, Aliotha	App
Hester, Joseph	Ear	Snider, Samuel	App
Hinely, John	App	Seckinger, Catharine (wid)	App
Heit, Mathew	Ear	Seckinger, John C.	Ear
Heidt, Christian J. Rev.Sol.	Ear	Salters, Jacob	App
Heit, George	Ear	Shults, Christian	Irw
Helveston, Joshua	App	Stanly, Benjamin	App
Jones, Philip	Ear	Shecrouse, Gottel	Ear
Jackson, John Junr.	Ear	Shecrouse, Gottiel	Ear
Jackson, John Junr.	Ear	Seckinger, John C.	Ear
Ihley, John J.	Irw	Seckenger, Joshua	App
Irwin, John R.	Ear	Stewart, Walter	Ear
King, William	Irw	Stewart, Charles	Ear
Koyler, John	Ear	Tiner, Gideon	App
Kesler, Volantine	Irw	Tuterall, Micager*	Hab
Keiffer, Ephraim	App	*Sept 6th Micajah Tutrall	
Kennedy, Benjamin	Hab	altered & entered under letter "F"	
King, George	Ear	Micajah Futrall	
Lemley, Mary (wid)	Ear	Tison, Luther	Irw
Lyneburger, Abeloni	Ear	Threadcraft, Seth G.	Ear
Lovett, David	Ear	Tiner, Gideon	App
Lyneburger, Joshua	Irw	Tinor, Ephraim	App
Lyneburger, David	Ear	Tullis, Patience (wid)	App
London, Jane John G.H.	Irw	Tumbling, Rebecca	App
Lovett, Aron	Irw	Tippron, Emanuel	Hal
Lyneburger, John	Hab	Tison, James R.S.	Irw
Molborn, John	Irw	Vining, Cader	Rab
McCall, John R.S.	Ear	Wilsons, Gabriel (orphs)	Irw
Masey, Tabith (wid)	Ear	Walsinghams, John (orphs)	Hab
Mobley, Lydia (wid)	Irw	Woods, Robert	Ear
Mock, Thomas	Ear	Wilson, James	Ear
Magahagan, William	Hal	Weitmans, Solomon (orphs)	Rab
Metzger, John J.	Ear	Waldhaner, William	Ear
Morgan, Christopher L.	Ear	Wilson, Jeremiah	Irw
McDormon, Jane Orph.	Irw	Wilson, James	Wal
Morgan, William	App	Williams, William	App
Mingledorf, John G.	Rab	Walder, John	Gwi
Mock, John M.	Ear	Woolf, Stephen	Ear
Moore, Daniel	Gwi	Weitman, Lewis	Rab
McCall, John R.S.	Ear	Womock, Frederick	App
Mullett, Abraham	Irw	Wilson, William	Ear
Mingledorf, John G.	Ear	White, Henry	Ear
Mock, John M.	Ear	Womack, William Sr.	App
Masse, Moore	Irw	Willis, Ferry	Rab
McCordell, William	Ear	White, Zachariah	App
Metzgar, Solomon	App	Willet, Henry R.S.	Hab
Neise, George Junr.	App	Willis, Joseph Senr. R.S.	Ear
Neidlinger, Hannah (Wid)	Irw	Weitman, Mathew	Irw
Parker, Eli	Irw	Wylly, Thomas	Irw
Porters, Benjamin (orphs)	Irw	Weitmans, Jediah (orphs)	Ear
Ponledge, Ephraim	Irw	Womack, James	Ear
Parrish, Samuel	Hal	Weitman, Hannah (wid)	Irw
Phillips, Onesimus	Irw	Wisenbaker, Christian	Ear
Pitts, Daniel	App	Walsingham, Catharine	Hab
Powers, Clem	App	Waldhaner, John Senr.	Irw
Royler, John	Ear	Willis, Joseph Senr. R.S.	Ear
Rodoh, Victory (orphs)	App	Zeigler, David Jr.	Irw
Ryals, Charles	App	Zeigler, Emanuel	Ear

Zitrouer, Godhelf J.	App	Zitrouer, William	App
Zants, Joshua (orphs)	Ear	Zitrouer, David	Irw
Zant, Joshua	Ear	Zipprow, Emanuel	Hal
Zitrouer, Godhelf J.	Irw		

THE 1821 LAND LOTTERY

Listed below are the fortunate drawers who were registered in Effingham County, and the county in which they drew land. Consult the book, The 1821 Land Lottery, for Militia District, Lot Number and Section. Abbreviations: Doo - Dooly; Fay - Fayette; Hen - Henry; Hou - Houston; Mon - Monroe.

Abbott, John Junr.	Mon	Glover, George	Hou
Arnstorph, George Junr.	Doo	Genobly, John	Hen
Arnstorff, Jonathan	Mon	Grovenstien, Mary (wid)	Hen
Arnstoff, John	Mon	Grouver, Saml.	Hen
Blitch, Thomas Jr.	Hen	Groversteirns, Jno. Justus,orp	Hou
Blitch, James	Hou	Glover, John	Doo
Benton, Louis	Doo	Grouver, Joshua	Doo
Beddenboch, Samuel (orph)	Hen	Garrason, Levi, orph.	Hen
Bayn, Robert	Hou	Gnann, Solomon, son of Andrew	Hen
Bevan, Joseph V.	Mon	Gieger, Jeremiah	Mon
Burton, Henry A.	Hen	Gnann, Timothy	Hen
Blake, Wm.	Mon	Guiton, Archibald	Hou
Burckstiner, Jas. Alex'r.	Hou	Garrason, James	Mon
Bird's, Wm. (orphs)	Hou	Garrason, Isaac	Doo
Backley, Henry	Doo	Gnann, Joshua	Mon
Beddenbock, Mary (wid)	Mon	Garrason, Isaac	Hen
Bryant, Isaac	Mon	Gorham, Thomas	Mon
Brewer's, Joseph (orphs)	Mon	Helmley, David Senr.	Hou
Bennett, Mary (wid)	Mon	Hines, Howell	Doo
Brown, Mary (wid)	Mon	Heidt, Christian, Junr.	Hen
Conner, Cretia (wid)	Doo	Hines, Wm.	Hou
Crum, Henry W.	Hen	Helmley, David	Mon
Crum, Herman	Doo	Hineley, Barbara (wid)	Hen
Cockran, Hugh	Hen	Hines, Howell	Hen
Creal's, John (orphs)	Hou	Hurst, Wm., Senr	Hou
Commeline, Robt. C.	Hou	Havens, Andrew	Mon
Crawsby, Edward	Doo	Hinely, Jacob	Ear
Chadbourn, Jacob	Hen	Heck, John	Doo
Capps, Lurany (wid)	Mon	Heck, James	Hen
Crews, Ann (wid)	Mon	Heck, John Reuben	Doo
Downs, Barrot	Hen	Helmley, Joshua	Hen
Daily, John	Mon	Heidt, John G.	Hou
Dasher, Benj. Senr	Hen	Hines, Wm.	Hen
Dasher, Samuel	Doo	Knight, Ann (wid)	Hou
Dugger, David	Hen	Keiffer, Joel	Doo
Dasher, Solomon	Hou	Kenida, Allen (orph)	Mon
Dasher, Solomon	Hou	Lineberger, John E.	Hen
Dasher, Benjn. Senr.	Hen	Lofley, Wright	Doo
Dasher, Samuel	Hou	Love, James	Hen
Dasher, Thomas	Hen	Lucas, John M.	Hen
Elkins, Mary (wid)	Hen	Love, James	Hen
Edwards, James	Hou	Lymburger's, Israel (orphs)	Hou
Elkins, Saml. (orphs)	Hou	Loper's, Asa (orphs)	Mon
Exley, John	Hen	Metzger, John J. Senr	Hen
Elkins, Thomas	Mon	Mason, Ann Mary (widow)	Hou
Ernst, Gottliet	Mon	Morrell, Benjamin	Hen
Exley, John	Hou	McRory, Rachael (wid) * Altered	Hen
Exley, Luke	Mon	by E. order 18 Dec 1839	
Exley, Solomon	Hen	Moore, James & William (orphs)	Hou
Elkins, Thomas	Doo	Masons, Alexander (orphs)	Hen
Foy, George	Mon	Martin, Stephen H.	Hou
Ferguson, Wm.	Mon	Mallett, Jeremiah	Hen
Fitzer, Magdelena (wid)	Hen	Moore, John	Hen

Morrell, Benjamin	Doo	Tetchstone, Christopher	Mon
Metzger, John J. Senr	Doo	Troutland, Joseph	Mon
Metzger, John	Hen	Thomas, Nicholas (orph)	Mon
Napper, Drewry	Mon	Tiner, Gorden	Ear
Napper, Drewry	Hen	Womack, Sarah (widow)	Hen
Neise, George, Senr.	Doo	Wilson, Allen	Hou
Neidlinger, Samuel	Doo	Wheeler, Wm.	Doo
Pouledge, Ephraim	Mon	Wisenbaker, Mary (wid)	Hou
Pickels, Jacob	Hou	Wall, Samuel	Doo
Poacher, Josiah	Doo	Wyley, Martha (wid)	Doo
Pace, James	Hen	Waldhauer, Israel F.	Mon
Poacher, Josiah	Hen	Williams, James	Doo
Porter, James	Doo	Welch, Jane (orph)	Doo
Phillips, Wm.	Doo	Webber, John (orph)	Mon
Porter, James	Mon	Willson, Wm.	Hou
Powledge, Gideon	Hou	Weitman, Solomon	Doo
Rowell, Rebecca (wid)	Doo	Wisenbakers, John (orphs)	Mon
Rahn, Samuel	Hen	Wheeler, Jesse	Doo
Rahn, Emanuel	Hen	Wolf, David	Hen
Rylinder, John C.	Doo	Willis, John	Doo
Shearouse, Emanuel	Hen	Williams, Ann E. (orphan)	Doo
Shuman, John	Hen	Wilson, William	Doo
Shearouse, Emanuel	Mon	Young, Isaac	Mon
Swelly, Abel	Hou	Zittrour, John	Doo
Snyder, Samuel	Doo	Zittrour, George	Mon
Saunders, Fredrick, (orphs)	Mon	Zipperer, Jonathan	Doo
Shuptrine, Israel	Fay	Zipperer, Christian	Hou
Seckinger, Benjamin	Hen	Zipperer, Theophilus	Hen
Spencer, Wm. I.	Hou	Zipperer, Johnathan	Hou
Scruggs, Gross, Jr.	Hou	Zipperer, Solomon	Hou
Tison, Calvin	Hen	Zittrour, John R.	Mon
Tetchstone, Christopher	Hen		
Tullir's, Temple (orph)	Mon		

Cook, Eliz. 161
Cook, George 147, 165
Cook, Henry 9, 14, 27, 50, 55, 73, 89, 146, 147, 165, 182
Cook, James 27, 53, 89, 90
Cook, James Jr. 27, 182
Cook, James Sr. 59, 180
Cook, John 21, 27, 42, 43, 58, 61
Cook, Lewis 27, 147, 165
Cook, Louisa 162
Cook, Lydia 50, 73, 115, 145, 146, 147, 165, 168
Cook, Margaret 89, 90
Cook, Margaret 105, 162
Cook, Nancy 162
Cook, Patience 53
Cook, Robert 73
Cook, Sarah 43, 183
Cook, William 4, 43
Coombs, Gassaway L. 175
Coombs, Mary L. 175
Cooney, John 127
Cooper, Ananias 44
Cooper, Wm. 173, 176
Cope, Charles 7
Cope, Christian 89, 102, 105, 182
Cope, Elizabeth 39, 106, 166
Cope, John 116, 166
Cope, John Sr. 102
Cope, John Jacob 39
Cope, Maria 102
Cope, Rosannah 101, 146
Copeland, Dorcas 41
Copeland, James 41
Cournoise, James Armstrong 121
Course, John 44
Courvorsie, I. A. 170
Courvorsie, Sarah 171
Cousete, Wherry 125
Cousey, Sarah 157
Covington, Francis 56
Cowan, Edward 48
Coward, John 67, 86
Coward, Samuel 147
Coward, William 86
Coward, Zachariah 41, 57
Cowper 62
Cox, Benjamin 139
Cox, Emanuel 139
Cox, Franklin B. 114
Cox, Jasper 7
Cox, Sarah 167
Cox, Spence 7, 16, 18
Cox, Spence 160
Craig, Wm. M. 153
Cramer, Agatha 161
Cramer, Alexander 125, 128, 168
Cramer, Ann Catherina 4
Cramer, Catherine 14
Cramer, Christopher 2, 4, 30, 31, 38
Cramer, Eveline 99
Cramer, J. C. 14

Cramer, John 14
Cramer, John C. 18
Cramer, John Christopher 14, 163
Cramer, Mary 168, 169
Cramer, Sarah Eliz. 168
Cramer, Solomon 119, 168, 183
Cramer, Sophia 168
Crane, James 113, 136, 115, 119
Crawford, 93
Crawford, Alexander 4
Crawford, Ann 53
Crawford, Charles 29
Crawford, Creasy 162
Crawford, David 21
Crawford, Elenor 162
Crawford, Emanuel 115, 177
Crawford, Frances 21
Crawford, Grace 124
Crawford, Henry 89
Crawford, James 93, 182
Crawford, James T. 141
Crawford, Jesse 35
Crawford, Joel 23
Crawford, John 14, 21, 38, 62, 122, 123, 138, 168, 183
Crawford, Leita 35
Crawford, Marsy 21
Crawford, Martha 21, 35
Crawford, Martha 160
Crawford, Mary 3, 4, 20
Crawford, Nancy 20
Crawford, Nellie 21, 35
Crawford, Patience 35, 162
Crawford, Pollie 21
Crawford, Priscilla 62
Crawford, Thomas 21, 35, 93
Crawford, William 35, 38, 47, 56, 92, 160
Crawsly, Edward 185
Creal, John 185
Creel, John 134
Crew, Eliza 24
Crew, Henry 26
Crews--also Cruse
Crews, Ann 185
Crews, Ann Cemantha 143
Crews, Asa 183
Crews, Celina 143
Crews, H. 107
Crews, Hannah E. 100, 102, 109, 111
Crews, Hannah Elizabeth 143
Crews, Henry W. 113
Crews, James 100, 102, 143
Crews, James M. 111, 114
Crews, James W. 113, 114, 116
Crews, Lydia 116
Crews, Lydia A. 143
Crews, Martha Eliza 143
Crews, Mary Ann 143
Crews, Sara E. 107
Crews, Selina 116
Croft, David 2
Cronberger 90
Cronberger, Jacob 2, 52, 69,

70, 84
Cronberger, John 72
Cronberger, Nicholas 36
Crosby, Aaron 3, 180
Crosby, Elizabeth 3
Crosby, Henry 3
Crowder, John C. 18
Crosby, Josiah 113
Crosley, Thomas 183
Cruger, Mr. 81
Cruger, Catherina 12, 13, 50
Cruger, Catherine 163
Cruger, Martin 12, 13, 50
Crum, Harmon 5, 15, 17, 19, 24, 61, 63, 97, 180
Crum, Henry 166
Cru, Henry W. 185
Crum, Herman 163, 182, 185
Crum, James 149
Crum, Jas. E. 173
Crum, James Herman 24
Crum, James S. 131, 149, 152, 156, 157
Cruse, Arena 163
Cruse, James 14, 92
Cruse, James 163, 182
Cubbedge, George 60
Cubbedge, John 60
Curren, SAmuel 78, 79, 80
Curry, George A. 139
Curry, John 136
Curry, Dorcase Grindat 139
Curry, John 163
Curry, Mary 163
Curry, William 110, 112, 113, 116, 168, 183
Cuthbert, Lewis G. 83
Cuyler, Henry 27
Cuyler, J. 27, 35, 39, 49, 54, 59, 62, 63, 64, 65
Cuyler, Jeremiah 13, 62, 64, 65, 80, 81, 88, 94
Cuyler, R. R. 137, 146
Cuyler, Richard 170
Cuyler, T. 45, 46, 47

Daers, John 73
Daley, Alexander W. 150, 178
Daley, Benj. 32, 49, 68
Daly, Daniel 55, 87
Daily, John 185
Dampier, David 173
Dampier, Daniel 55, 89, 94, 142, 182
Dampier, Elizabeth 89
Dampier, John 161
Dampier, Stephen 163, 183
Dampier, William 89, 182
Campur, Daniel 128
Daniel, Enoch 3
Daniels, Isby 124
Daniel, Josiah 51, 160
Daniel, Sarah 3, 51
Daniel, Seth 162
Daniels, Thomas 10
Daniel, William 51
Danslyer, Philip 101
Dapres, Hannah 165

Index prepared by Brent H. Holcomb, G. R. S. and John C. Dennis.

www.ingramcontent.com/pod-product-compliance
Lightning Source LLC
Chambersburg PA
CBHW021844020426
42334CB00013B/181

9 780893 080198